Hitler, Jews, and Hate

JOE GRANGER

> Nothing is so firmly believed as what we least know
> —Lord Michel Eyquem de Montaigne

The opinions expressed in this manuscript are solely the opinions of the author and do not represent the opinions or thoughts of the publisher. The author has represented and warranted full ownership and/or legal right to publish all the materials in this book.

Hitler, Jews, and Hate
All Rights Reserved.
Copyright © 2015 Joe Granger
V3.0

Cover Photo © 2015 thinkstockphotos.com. All rights reserved - used with permission.

This book may not be reproduced, transmitted, or stored in whole or in part by any means, including graphic, electronic, or mechanical without the express written consent of the publisher except in the case of brief quotations embodied in critical articles and reviews.

Granger Publishing

Paperback ISBN: 978-0-578-16226-3
Hardback ISBN: 978-0-578-16227-0

PRINTED IN THE UNITED STATES OF AMERICA

DEDICATION

To the Germans, a people unjustly maligned
by establishment historians. And especially
to the people of Soden, nearby Aschaffenburg.

Contents

PREFACE i
CHAPTER 1: About Hitler 1
   Hitler as Seen by His Best Friend 15
   Types of Hitler 20
   Fiendish Qualities 27
   The Real Hitler 30
   Romanticism, Volksgeist, and Modernity 60
   Enlightenment, Reason, Rationality 62
   The Frankfurt School 63
   Darwin 74
   Hitler, Man of His Age 77
   Hitler's Heroes 80
   Jews of Germany 83
   Power from Small Numbers 86
   Engines of Change 89
   A Pickpocket in the Market of Ideas 91
   Hitler's Aesthetics 95
   Architecture 104
   Demeaning Hitler, Trite Claims 106
   Jewish-Bolshevik Equivalency 118
CHAPTER 2: About Hitler's Vienna 128
   Fin de siècle Vienna 136
   Jewish Immigration to Austria 138
   Vienna and the Revolution of 1848 156
   Creation of the Dual Empire 163
   Hitler's Hate of the Austro-Hungarian Empire 164
   Character of Austria-Hungary, 1907–1913 166
   France 167
   Protocols of Learned Elders of Zion 168
   Dreyfus Affair 175

    Jacob Schiff—Russia 180
    Hitler's Political Heroes in Vienna 180
CHAPTER 3: World War I, The Opening Salvo
of World War II 193
    National Humiliations 200
    Hitler's War 209
    The Jew Count 223
    Balfour Declaration 259
    Beginning of the End 266
    Treaty of Brest-Litovsk 269
    Kiel Mutiny 276
    Propaganda Lessons 287
CHAPTER 4: Treaty of Versailles 292
    Treaty Provisions and Problems 302
    Wilson's Mistakes 307
    Humiliation and Loss 309
CHAPTER 5: The Weimar Republic 327
    Time line, Late 1918 through November 1923 327
    Creation of the Republic—the German Revolution 329
    Prelude to the Spartacist Uprising 332
    Revolution Everywhere 338
    The Weimar Republic 343
    Prelude to Defeat of Revolutionary and
        Insurrectionist Movements 345
    The Christmas Crisis 347
    Prelude to the Spartacist Revolution 350
    The Spartacist Uprising 351
    The Constitution and Early Weimar Republic 353
    Russia's Need for Germany's Fall 359
    The Bavarian Revolution 362
    The Hoffmann Government 375
    The Hungarian Revolution and Its German Impact 376

The Toller Government—Bavaria	381
The Leviné Government—Bavaria	383
Noske to the Rescue of Bavaria	387
Aftermath of the Bavarian Revolution	388
Kapp Putsch	396
March Action	398
Inflationary Period: 1921–1924	401
Jewish Prominence in Politics and Society	407
CHAPTER 6: Weimar Culture	411
Germany: the Culture Nation	423
Prussian Militarism	427
Hitler, His Nazis, and Regard for German Culture	428
Cultural Counterrevolution	442
Jews and German Culture	453
Architecture	492
Berlin, a Cesspool	504
Anita Berber—A Personification of Berlin	507
Die Weltbühne	515
Education, Judiciary, and the Economy	525
Purging German Culture	534
CHAPTER 7: Success of Hitler—Ascension to Power	536
Setting the Stage for Hitler's Success	536
Jewish Criminality	548
Contentious Books	554
Threat of Bolshevism	555
Communist and Nazi Clashes	559
Anti-Semitic Rhetoric	560
Zionism Joins the Nazis in Spirit	564
Events in Russia and Elsewhere	565
Death of Stresemann	567
U.S. Recalls Loans	568
Reichstag Elections, 1930	571

Success at Last 580
Composition of the Nazi Vote 584
Fall of the Weimar Republic 587
The Boycott 590
Zionism to Hitler's Rescue 595
The Transfer Agreement: Its Origins and Players 598
Hitler's Successes 603
Why Did Hitler Hate the Jews? 606
Appendix: POLITICAL PARTIES 614

PREFACE

"[T]he history of the Jews in Germany from 1870 to 1933 is probably the most glorious rise that has ever been achieved by any branch of the Jewish people."
—*Mein Leben als Deutscher Jude* (Goldman)

As the title makes clear, this is a book about Adolf Hitler, Jews, and the hate they had for each other, but particularly Hitler's hatred of Jews. This text seeks to answer the oft-posed but never adequately answered question, "Why did Hitler hate Jews?" The text also seeks to provide certain correctives with respect to our understanding of Hitler as a man and politician, an understanding that for the vast majority of Americans is based entirely upon what is consumed by way of various Hollywood productions concerning Hitler and his people. To meet these objectives it is essential that popular historical orthodoxy be challenged.

People are largely perplexed by the fact that Hitler ultimately enjoyed the enthusiastic support of virtually all Germans. Establishment historians often blithely explain that phenomenon as attributable to some deep-seated anti-Semitic flaw in the character of the German being. This text utterly rejects that contention. Before the rise of Hitler the German people admirably resisted anti-Semitism, a fact that serves as a subtext to this narrative. After coming to power prior to World War II, the German people adored Hitler, and they did so with good reason—in the early years of his regime he had performed veritable miracles on their behalf.

Hitler was bad, and so too were many of his various henchmen—the German people as a whole acted honorably both before and after Hitler achieved power.

A highly problematic subset of actual Jews doing actual things that were justifiably perceived as inimical to German interests were at the root of Hitler's hate. This subset of Jews were informed by the likes of Marx, Freud, and others of their ilk. They were a small minority of Jews in Europe but managed to exert a stupendous influence. Therein lies the thrust of this narrative. I assign to them the fundamental source of Hitler's demonic loathing: I reject a variety of competing but popular contentions and conjectures as to the source of his loathing.

I have no interest in defending the horrific acts of Adolf Hitler, and this narrative does not do that; nor, however, do I provide much in the way of ritual scolding of him and his henchmen so that my presentation may be deemed "balanced." I offer no apologies for the despicable conduct of Hitler—nor do I offer justifications or apologies for the acts of inimical Jews who were so detested by him.

Like the distinguished British historian Hugh Trevor-Roper, "I do not believe that men are born sour and inhuman: if they are so, it is because they have been made so; and what I look for in Hitler's . . . character is evidence not so much of the result as of the process of its formation."[1] I flatter myself in believing that I am more faithful to Roper's contention than he himself was.

A significant part of the formation of Hitler's character was founded on his perception of things that Jews had done throughout history and on similar things that they were doing during his era. It is those things that are the focus of this narrative.

Classicist historian Theodor Mommsen (1817–1903) is quoted by historian Albert Lindemann in *Esau's Tears* as having said that "Even in the ancient world Judaism was an effective leaven of cosmopolitan national decomposition."[2] Ancient Egyptian hatred of Jews was not formulated in the absence of real Jews or imaginary aspects of Judaism, "Real Jews and real problems, economic, social, political, and religious, were involved," he says. He goes on to tell us that so powerful and privileged were the Jews of Egypt, the Egyptian populace of Alexandria was to the Jews what the serfs were to European nobility[3]—they were people being oppressed, not by all Jews of course, but by enough of them to engender hate for Jews en masse.

Hitler's intense personal studies of ancient history and the Jews included the Jewish experience in Egypt. There, said Hitler to

Dietrich Eckart,* Jews had been expelled (around 1,450 years before Christ and therefore Christianity) because they had tried to incite revolution by propagandizing the people with humanitarian phraseology in much the same way as modern Marxists. Moses, claimed Hitler, was the first leader of Bolshevism.[4] These real, palpable factors provided the context, the appeal, the driving force for the "fantastic" beliefs of Egyptians about Jews.[5] The same could be said of the anti-Semitism of Germans. But Germany, unlike the other countries, also suffered, as we shall see, a unique set of blows and a unique Jewish influence that ultimately fostered unique hate in a minority there. It was a clash of minorities: a minority of Jews, who were themselves a fairly small minority of the entire population, clashed with a minority of anti-Semitic Germans. Adolf Hitler was among the German minority.

Professor Kevin MacDonald, a professor of psychology at California State University, is a man who writes with both great courage and scholarship on the subject of Jew-Gentile relations. He observes that "discussion of the role of Jews either in contemporary Russia or even in the theoretically more open United States is prohibited in principle."[6] He goes on to assert that there has been an overwhelmingly consistent similarity in complaints about Jews in different places and times, giving credence to the idea that prominent themes of anti-Semitism have had a firm basis in reality. In particular, he says:

> These themes, including the "alienness" of Jews, Jewish economic, political, or cultural domination, the idea that Jews possess negative personality traits making them willing to engage in unscrupulous economic exploitation of gentiles, and Jewish disloyalty, continue to figure prominently in anti-Semitism around the world.7

---

* Eckart was a poet, journalist, and a successful playwright. He was one of the founders of the early Nazi Party (German Worker's Party). He was also a rabid anti-Semite who was very close to Hitler and exercised influence over him.

Jewish racism, often euphemistically described as Jewish "particularism," which is defined as that "exclusive commitment to one group, especially when detrimental to the interest or well-being of a larger group,"[8] exists and is practiced by Jews on a daily basis as they show favoritism to their own in matters of personnel placements, business advantage, charity, marriage, and social, political, and national loyalty. That is, particularism has to do with in-group concern, in-group aggrandizement, and not the least, racism. Particularism and concomitant ethnocentrism and endogamy have to do with racism by politically correct names.

Particularism was a special characteristic—a stereotype—of eighteenth- and nineteenth-century Jewry to sanction individuals who violated group norms by intermarrying with Gentiles, socializing with them, patronizing businesses owned by them, or bidding against other Jews who owned franchises obtained from Gentiles.[9]

Author Anthony Kauders, in *German Politics and the Jews*, says, "We all know [but we nevertheless deny] that charges against the Jews would not be 'nearly as persuasive if they did not bear some relation to ascertainable fact and to a hard core of genuine evidence.'"[10] Historian Albert Lindemann says, "That Jewish conduct is the main cause of hatred of Jews, has been described by Edward Alexander . . . as 'an argument of wide and enduring popularity.'"[11] Lindemann also makes the point that:

> The disproportionate numbers, visibility, and volubility of Jews in modern art roughly corresponded to the disproportionate numbers of Jews in journalism, medicine, law, banking, and revolutionary parties. In Weimar Germany, these were all arenas that saw attacks on the traditional status quo, that were restlessly innovative and often destructively dissatisfied with the past.[12]

And the foregoing were all areas of particular sensitivity to Adolf Hitler.

Hitler studied Jews and their history assiduously. On the basis of his observations while living in Vienna between 1907 and 1913, he arrived at a conclusion that the terms "Jew" and "Marxist" went hand in hand; where there was the one the other was also prominent.[13] During World War I he correctly discerned that Jews were at the forefront of the radically anti-German "pacifist" movement throughout the country. At the conclusion of the war he assessed Jewish participation in the creation and implementation of the despised Treaty of Versailles, their influence in the German government, and in the upheavals that followed the war. Throughout the 1920s he was enraged by the precipitous decline in German culture and saw Jews at the focal point of that decline. And, finally, he had cause to oppose Jews as heartily as they opposed him when he finally attained power—and then in their quite understandable opposition to him and his exercise of power. The actions and events just broadly described, I conclude, represent the foundations for Hitler's hate and each is discussed in some detail within this narrative.

I am, of course, acutely aware that this book is highly critical of Jews; I provide little in the way of positive imagery for them. I say nothing of the good that they have done, nothing of the Jewish contribution to cures for awful diseases or all the many other things that humanity knows very well would plague our daily lives were it not for all those great humanitarian Jews who have made the being of all people everywhere, better. Bookstores and libraries have goodly numbers of shelves dedicated to the praise of Jews, their victimhood, and their accomplishments—this book, admittedly, ignores them because they are not germane to Hitler and his hate.

The time is long past due for acknowledging that Hitler's hate had a legitimate object: it was the real, palpable acts of Jews, many of whom were newly arrived in Germany as they fled oppression in the East. That is, much like Voltaire's assessment of Jews, his hate was founded on an entirely plausible relationship to their actual conduct[14]—again, not all Jews, but enough to be highly problematic.

I have presented some views of Adolf Hitler in this text that are at odds with depictions of him in the so-called balanced popular press, theater, and some history books. In particular, I have highlighted some of his humanizing qualities that are so sorely lacking in popular depictions of him but are acknowledged here and there in scholarly works. Both my criticism of Jews and my relatively soft treatment of Hitler are justified by the actual historical record, skewed versions made popular by the mass media and the mainstream press notwithstanding.

Historian Alan Bullock claims in the preface to his book, *Hitler, A Study in Tyranny*, that he does not seek to indict Adolf Hitler, but then goes on, even in his title, to do just that.[15] My reader will find my descriptions of Hitler to be less of an indictment than other authors. I want to be quick to emphasize, however, that Hitler was a despicable man. No man could implement anything as horrific as the Holocaust and not be deemed despicable: and make no mistake about it, the Holocaust happened and it happened at Hitler's direction. That said, he also had humanizing qualities that endeared him to both his entourage and the German nation. I highlight some of Hitler's positive qualities herein because it was just such endearing qualities that caused both his entourage and the German people as a whole to embrace him—he was not the insane, expectorating madman of popular Hollywood depiction. As we scour the world looking for our next potential dictator we should not look for the popular depiction of Hitler; we should, instead, look for someone with great charm and charisma, a John F. Kennedy gone awry, as it were.

It is now manifest to all that any criticism of Jews by a Gentile is to be taken as anti-Semitism. My reader will believe of me what he will. Charges of sexism, racism, and anti-Semitism are now bandied about with such intemperance and abandon that the whole of it numbs me. I have no interest in even trying to argue in opposition to such charges. I have documented my thesis by way of copious citations. A fair reading of my text and reference to other works that I cite should speak for themselves.

* * * *

We readily accept all manner of falsehood, ludicrous speculation, and misrepresentation about Hitler and the German people as veritable gospel, but we are simultaneously so acutely sensitized to Jewish sensibilities that we are touchy about even the use of the term "Jew." When he was young, the Austrian-born philosopher Martin Buber (1878–1965) avoided the use of the term in public, for, as he had it, it was then considered something of an obscenity in cultured circles,[16] and in many circles it remains so today. The term is certainly taken to be a slight when mentioned in a context that is in any way critical. Some authors use alternative terms to avoid this apparently troublesome word. Jews might be represented as Jacob while Esau designates Gentiles, or one might use the term Hebrew or Semite in place of the term Jew. One author has Jews as Mercurians and Gentiles as Apollonians. Jewish historian Peter Gay seemed to like the use of the terms "insider" and "outsider" to distinguish between Jews and Gentiles. I use the term "Jew" throughout this text in what I hope is a neutral sense; I use it to identify a discernable segment of the world's population. On the whole, I use the term to refer to Jews in general, to the Jewish race, the Jewish nation, and the Jewish religion. Hopefully, the context makes clear which reference is meant, for just who or what is a Jew is, by itself, something of a troubling concept. Since the founding of Israel in 1948, the issue of just who is a Jew has been the subject of multiple Israeli court cases, but several issues nevertheless remain in dispute.

Daniel Goldhagen, the author of *Hitler's Willing Executioners*, which was published in 1996, makes the point that "obfuscating labels" like "Nazis" and "SS men" should be discarded when assigning blame for the Holocaust—for him, only the term "Germans" should be used. While I disagree with Goldhagen on that point and almost all others of consequence, I at the same time wish to avail myself of his thought process. Certain nefarious Jews of history (Marx, et al.), claim Jewish apologists, had abandoned Jewry and therefore should not be referred to as Jews. I hold that all such people should indeed be referred to as Jews and not some other "obfuscating label."

Some linguistic puritans contend that the use of the definite article "the" in referring to Jews should be used with caution; "the Jews" represents all Jews and can imply that they act conspiratorially while the term "Jew," by itself, may refer to a subset acting independently. An article in the Israeli *Haaretz* newspaper illustrates this point as it complains about Jewish-German political theorist Hanna Arendt's use of the term "the Jews":

> As Arendt would have it [in her widely acclaimed book, *The Origins of Totalitarianism*], "the Jews" were all bankers, financiers, court Jews and privileged, or in her generalizing language: "The Jews had been purveyors in wars and the servants of kings." Not some individual Jews, but "the Jews."[17]

As I am neither a linguist nor wordsmith, I use the article "the" where it seems appropriate without any regard whatever for the Talmudic niggling that it has for rigorous wordsmiths.

*   *   *   *

John Abbott (University of Illinois at Chicago) claimed it as a truth that throughout European history, and for that matter, world history, *"what passed for plausible in the anti-Semitic imagination was privileged by exceptionally low standards of proof..."*[18] (Italics are in the original.) His claim is succinct and true enough as far as it goes but is unfairly restrictive in applicability. We need not be too concerned with Abbott's important actual fact, for it is every bit as true with respect to Jewish criticism of Western Gentile precepts, culture, people, religions, and conduct. It is most certainly true with respect to Jewish criticism of Germans and Germany. Goldhagen serves as one exemplar among many who accuses on the basis of "exceptionally low standards of proof" — his text is full of illustrations of this phenomena (we need to acknowledge here that many Jewish scholars objected to Goldhagen's thesis—but he sold over 500,000 books with it; it is described as a "publishing phenomenon").

It is also true that Jewish suffering at the hands of Gentiles has been massively overstated by Jewish apologists and remains so today. Anyone who closely follows the Israeli-Arab conflict in the Middle East, for example, knows full well that the Israelis own the vast majority of blame for the despicable atrocities there, not the Arabs and not the Palestinians, yet the American public has been largely convinced and conditioned by the popular media to hold those entities at fault. We have been led to believe by our various news media outlets that Jewish suffering there is comparable to or even exceeds that of the Arabs (the overall Arab-Jewish death ratio in that conflict is on the order of about 10 to 1, and in some particular engagements it has been over 100 to 1 and more). Israeli leaders such as Menachem Begin, Ariel Sharon, and now Benjamin Netanyahu have continuously brutalized their neighbors. The Jewish claim to victimhood in the Middle East was illustrated by an assertion of Golda Meir, the former Israeli prime minister, who said in 1972 that she would never forgive the Arabs for forcing Israel to hurt their children—victimhood and apologia at its worst.[19*] All manner of despicable acts by Israelis are shielded by the guise of Jewish victimhood and national security claims.[20]

It has been historically true that Jews have offered up plentiful portions of tripe about Gentiles that did not require much imagination or exceptionally high standards of proof. It is a truth supported by the record that Jews applied the same *privilege* of low standards of proof to Gentiles; and a too large subset of them applied that privilege with particular vehemence to German Gentiles and German sensibilities before, during, and after Hitler's rise to power. On the whole, it is that too large subset of Jews about whom I write, for it was they who torched the pyre of Hitler's demonic hate.

---

*The complete quotation is "We can forgive the Arabs for killing our children. We cannot forgive them for forcing us to kill their children."

I do not grant to Jews the claims of their apologists: I do not subscribe to contentions that depict Jews as forever good and Gentiles forever bad. Nor do I grant that Jews have suffered without cause from Gentiles. Gentiles have suffered mightily from the actions of actual Jews acting in concert with other actual Jews as religious, racial, national, and international bodies. I will argue that Jews have never been the passive objects depicted by their apologists but have instead been active subjects. During Hitler's formative years they were much too often the actors, the doers, the verbs of terrorism. I will argue as well that actual Jews doing actual things inimical to Germany and others were the taproots of Hitler's hate. I will argue too that Hitler had reason, if not "good" or "sufficient" reason, for his hate.

Germans have long been excoriated by historians as the source of anti-Semitism that led to the horrors inflicted by Hitler's Nazis while almost entirely sidestepping the acts of organized Jewry and those of individual Jews that all but demanded a defensive, anti-Semitic response. Goldhagen's 1996 book is but one of the more recent outrageous literary attacks on the German people, and by extension, all Gentiles, and more particularly, West European culture and its associated Christianity. Goldhagen has it that "The underlying need to think ill of Jews, to hate them, to derive meaning from this emotional stance, [is] woven into the fabric of Christianity itself."[21] Similarly, he claims that "European anti-Semitism is a corollary of Christianity."[22] He, like so many other Jewish apologists, employs whopping helpings of exaggeration and misrepresentation to support his contentions: veritably every slight to Jews is represented by him as genocidal—his text is full of such drivel as the "psychic equivalent of genocide,"[23] "a form of bloodless genocide,"[24] and "functional . . . equivalent of genocide."[25] He also vastly broadens the scope of complicity for the Nazi genocide: the oft-repeated claim of "no Hitler, no Holocaust" is broadened by Goldhagen to "no Germans, no Holocaust."[26] And he, like too many others, also claims that Germans have always been rabid anti-Semites, that there is something in the very being of Germans that makes them so; but it seems to him and his too many others that there is nothing whatever in the Jewish character to warrant any criticism whatever.

In actual fact, German Jews were treated with great deference prior to the rise of Hitler. This point was illustrated by Otto Brahm, the famous Jewish theater owner and cultural critic in Berlin who was in 1912 the manager of the Lessing Theater there: he refused to perform Arthur Schnitzler's *Professor Bernhardi*, a drama about Catholic anti-Semitism in Vienna's medical circles because the subject matter would be too foreign to Berliners—not only because the Prussian capital lacked a Catholic majority, but also because as he said, "Berlin's Jewish doctors are not persecuted, they are predominant,"[27] as indeed they were.

Jewish apologist John Willett, referring to the atrocities committed by the Jewish regime in Hungary in 1919, says that "A policy of Red Terror was adopted as a defensive measure, but its effects were certainly later exaggerated."[28] A defensive measure, was it? The murderous vengeance extracted by the leadership clique in Hungary was composed entirely of Jews. The terror, the rank atrocities that they committed, is deftly sidestepped; the Willett claim is that it was simply a defensive measure and it really wasn't all that bad to boot. Our history books are replete with such apologia. Here is a fact: Jews were the principal organizers and actors for deeds of terrorism in Europe throughout the nineteenth and twentieth centuries—and Hitler knew that. Worse still, they were often brutal players in the subjugation and oppression of European peoples—and I will support that claim later in this narrative.

*   *   *   *

Amos Elon comments on the genealogical-historical origins of the term "nation" as follows:

> In Prussian and other German records [from the Middle Ages] Jews were often referred to as a nation, a term that had as yet no political connotation. Derived from the

Latin *natio*, it was originally a genealogical-historical term loosely used by Saint Jerome in his Latin translation of the New Testament to denote non-Christians—that is, "others." Its politicization (as in the French "*la nation*") came only during the French Revolution. In Berlin, "nation" and "colony" were used interchangeably in speaking of the local Jewish or Huguenot community.[29]

Jews of Germany, as elsewhere, were regarded by local citizens as a nation within the nation. And the Jewish nation was consistently disruptive to its host nation, but always and forever with the aid of members of the host nation to advance its causes.

That Jews were joined in their terrorism by Gentiles does no more than underscore, as MacDonald points out, "the importance of philosemitism and other alliances Jews typically must make in Diaspora situations in order to advance their perceived interests."[30] Think of the Pentagon, that Stop and Shop of the Israeli military. Think, too, of the undue influence of Jews over the U.S. Senate and their overwhelming influence in matters of U.S. law, social thought, and foreign policy. Jews need not govern directly so long as they can, as formulated by Lord Cromer, "govern the governors."[31] That formulation is very close to Hitler's view of Jews as the "wirepuller of the destinies of mankind."[32] Israeli journalist Akiva Eldar tells a joke that is all too close to the truth. The joke has it that the president of the United States is conversing with the Israeli prime minister thusly:

> "Mr. Prime Minister, would you like Israel to become our 51st state?"
>
> "Thanks but no thanks, Mr. President."
>
> "Why not?"
>
> "Because, as a U.S. state, we would have only two senators."[33]

German Jews, as they have everywhere, organized and operated as a nation within the nation of Germany. They were not simply organized into individual nodes but rather as a highly coordinated collection of nodes, a mosaic that could only be recognized by standing back from it and examining it work as a coordinated whole. Within Germany and in various other countries they acted as an exceptionally powerful force on the world stage. Their organization and influence were remarkable. "The Jew," said the anti-Semite F. Roderich-Stoltheim (aka Theodor Fritsch, 1852–1933) in *The Riddle of the Jew's Success*, "never identifies himself with the interests of the country in which he lives. He has his own peculiar nationality, and constitutes, with those of his kind, an international nation as it were; and the interests of this nation are supreme with him; they form, literally, the base of his religious faith."[34] He went on to say that they "resemble drops of quicksilver, which disperse themselves and run about in all directions, but which, on the slightest shock, reunite themselves into one mass."[35] Anyone familiar with current-day Jewish community support for the atrocities committed by Israel in the Middle East (e.g., treatment of the Palestinians, destruction of homes, uprooting ancient olive groves, the several incursions into the Gaza Strip and Lebanon, etc.) and worldwide Jewish reaction to criticism of those atrocities will know of what Stoltheim spoke. So too did Adolf Hitler.

As an international entity, Jews became so powerful and their oligarchical influence so pervasive and damaging to Germany that corrective action was essential. But what could be done? In the early days after World War I Hitler held the view that anti-Semitism should not be based on emotion; it should, instead, said he, be based on facts. An emotional stance, thought Hitler, would result in pogroms while a fact-based anti-Semitism would lean toward reason and the systematic removal of the privileges of Jews.[36] At that time, he envisioned the removal of Jews from all centers of power, and then expelling them from the country; ultimately, of course, both of those actions were, in fact, implemented (albeit only partially in the case of expulsion). And, of course, concentration camps were also employed, and finally, death camps—the Holocaust.

It is certainly reasonable to assert that no action, however hurtful, could even remotely justify the Holocaust. It is equally reasonable to proffer a contention that actions of corporate Jews were primary sources of Hitler's anti-Semitism, of his hate. The first point is trumpeted and the second is denied in the popular media. We must challenge those who deny the underlying "justification" for Hitler's hate—the inimical, malefic acts of Jews; Jews as individuals and as a highly organized and supremely effective national and international entity.

Goldhagen provides a good example of how too many historians describe events in Germany during the early decades of the twentieth century: he claims that Jews throughout Weimar (the term used to refer to Germany and the German government during the period 1919–1933) were attacked beginning already in 1918 in Munich and Berlin and still again in the period of 1923–1924.[37] Yet, before the war, "Munich," as historian John Williams informs us, "was widely regarded as the most liberal and progressive of German cities and the Reich's most important centre of early twentieth-century modernist culture."[38] So what happened that altered Munich's previous noteworthy tolerance and progressiveness? If Goldhagen had any interest whatever in informing us of the truth he would have mentioned that the attacks during those periods were directed at Bolshevistic Marxists, not Jews per se—that Jews were indeed the objects of many of these attacks serves only to illustrate that they were so many and prominent in Marxist ranks of the time. He might also have pointed out that the periods of which he speaks were just after the revolution in which Jews played a dominant role—it was the period after the German revolution when Marxists took control of the government, after the Spartacus Uprising in Berlin, after the Bavarian Revolution, after the March Action, and after the debilitating inflationary period during which unsavory Jews managed to acquire vast riches while the general populace lost its savings, jobs, and properties (we will discuss each of the foregoing in some detail later in this text). He might also have wanted to mention that political violence occurred on both the Left and the Right of the political spectrum during those periods and that right-wing forces were by far the more seriously impacted objects and victims of such violence. If he had any interest whatever in the truth he would have also mentioned that the violence in Bavaria by right-wing forces in 1919 and 1920 was preceded in that city by Jewish atrocities in early 1919 (the Bavarian Revolution). He mentions none of the foregoing because such mention would place his claim in proper historical perspective and thereby badly damage his balderdash claims.

*   *   *   *

Pop rationale has it that historians examining the Hitler era must restrict themselves to what Hitler did, not to what Jews of history and of his time did. Goldhagen's manner of argument is illustrative of such rationale. Refreshingly, historian R. H. S. Stolfi refers to Hitler's anti-Semitism as "a kind of historical physics operating: for every action there is an opposite and equal reaction."[39] That is, what Hitler did was largely a reactionary response to what Jews did, yet that aspect of history remains all but absolutely prohibited from consideration and publication. MacDonald quotes a 1989 publication by Igor Shafarevich, a mathematician and member of the U.S. National Academy of Sciences, as saying that "any possibility that Jewish interests conflict with the interests of others cannot even be proposed as an hypothesis."[40] And that is precisely why it must be left to the likes of people like me to challenge orthodoxy; establishment historians are denied the ability to do so without risk to their livelihood.

It happens, though, that some few modern historians are increasingly willing to challenge orthodox versions of history. The 2013 book by historian Richard Tedor, *Hitler's Revolution*, is illustrative of a trend that may be in the offing: Tedor factually and unemotionally challenges the popular depiction of Hitler, his objectives, and his accomplishments. Historians of Tedor's kind are seemingly willing to challenge the tripe that is so common in the popular media and also in far too many history books by establishment historians. R. H. S. Stolfi's book, *Hitler: Beyond Evil and Tyranny*, is yet another that demonstrates a good deal of literary courage and what one may hope is a developing trend. Professor Kevin MacDonald is still another historian of note who is willing to challenge many of the myths that we call history. For about the last twenty to thirty years, historians have also been increasingly willing to challenge the charge that Germans have some deep-seated flaw in their makeup that caused them to have forever been anti-Semites. Some fewer still, men such as Stolfi, are even willing to grant that Hitler had positive qualities, rationality and objectivity being among them, that endeared him to his people.

Mainstream establishment historians are understandably reticent to address in detail the subject of Jewish culpability out of fear of a Jewish backlash, so the subject is suppressed under the protective rubric of the Holocaust. Such a backlash would be of little concern if, say, it was a religious denomination (and Jews are not simply a religious denomination) or a powerless minority group making the fuss; they could easily be discounted for any number of reasons. The Armenian Genocide of 1915 is illustrative of this point. Jews vociferously object to the use of the term "Holocaust" in describing that genocide because the term "Holocaust," capital H, is a term reserved unto themselves. When a day of remembrance for the Armenian genocide was proposed in the U.S. Congress, Jewish lobbyists blocked it[41] lest people confuse it with *the* Holocaust, the Jewish one—never mind that millions of other people suffered the same fate as did Jews.[*] And never mind as well that many of those millions were horrifically killed at Jewish direction, as, for example, was the case in Russia and Ukraine under the egis of such people as Grigory Zinoviev and Lazar Kaganovich.

---

[*] Israel continues to object to recognition of the Armenian genocide, ostensibly to avoid souring relations between Israel and Turkey, which are by now so atrocious that they could hardly be worse.

The Holocaust is an expression of Jewish uniqueness, of their privileged place in the annals of suffering. It is not to be shared with other peoples, not Russians nor Ukrainians nor current-day Palestinians—those many peoples who have suffered holocaust-like atrocities under Jewish auspices. To acknowledge the genocide against the Armenians or the Romani, or, for that matter, the citizens of Dresden, Germany, or any other group, is to dilute the purity of connection between Jews and the Holocaust and thereby also dilute the value of the moral and financial capital it provides for them.[42] To provide a contemporary example, some Israelis assert that the atrocities committed by Israeli Defense Forces (IDF) during its January 2009 incursion into the Gaza Strip should not be held to standards of international laws of war: what the Israelis did, they hold, stems from their unique historical experiences,[43] the Holocaust. Such assertions are apologia of the poppycock kind, and all too many of that kind exist. Stated more bluntly, Ari Shavit commented on Israel's 1996 brutal incursion into Lebanon by saying, disapprovingly, that "Israel could act with impunity because 'we have the Anti-Defamation League . . . and Yad Vashem and the Holocaust Museum.'"[44]

Thus it has been that, as Michael Berkowitz points out,

> . . . the [faults] of Jews . . . has a long and complex history that is not often recalled, in large part because many scholars would not think to ask. This historical blind spot is also a result of reticence or censorship on the part of historians who believe it impertinent to even deal with the subject, especially in the wake of the Holocaust.[45]

The Holocaust framework, says Norman Finkelstein,

> . . . apprehended anti-Semitism as a strictly irrational Gentile loathing of Jews. It precluded the possibility that animus toward Jews might be grounded in a real conflict of interests. . . . Invoking The Holocaust was therefore a ploy to delegitimize all criticism of Jews: such criticism

[it followed] could only spring from pathological hatred.[46]

As a good many prominent men of good faith and sterling character have learned, to tell tales of truth about Zionism, Israel, or Jews, in general, is to invite social, political, and financial ruin.

Israel, because of Jewish power, enjoys the privilege of exemption from criticism in the vast array of Western journalistic sources. Journalists do not report the truth about Israeli actions because they understandably fear blacklisting and other forms of retaliation. Israel Shahak is entirely correct in making the claim that "political, cultural, and intellectual figures, especially in Europe and the United States, go out of their way to praise Israel and shower it with the greatest largesse of any nation on earth, even though many of them are aware of the injustices of the country."[47] What he said in making that charge, if one may be permitted some leeway in interpretation, is that our political, cultural, and intellectual figures are cowards. They praise the despicable—and their kind existed in Germany between the wars in very much the same ratio as they exist today in the United States.

Jewish critic William Zukerman states the issue of criticism of Jews as follows:

> Criticism and self-criticism which were the basis of inspiration of the Enlightenment period, have been discredited as almost the equivalent of treason. By a kind of perverted chauvinistic reasoning, criticism of anything pertaining to Jews, whether it is of Israel, of the dominant nationalist party, its institutions, or of its ideology, has been defined as anti-Semitism.[48] Neoconservative Irving Kristol says that his people have a "propensity to gloss over their own shortcomings and blame the always available anti-Semite for their misfortunes."[49]

We can agree with Zukerman without much fear of reprisal because he is Jewish. Only Jews are permitted to criticize Jews, but there are too few of them who choose to do so, and those who do are only rarely published in the popular press of America.

* * * *

Historian Douglas Reed,* in *The Controversy of Zion*, highlights the issue and use of the term "pilpulism." The term "pilpul" in Hebrew means "sharp analysis" and is derived from the verb "pilpel," "to spice," "to season," and metaphorically, "to dispute violently" or "cleverly."[50] Pilpulism is rife with logomachy. The pilpul method originated as far back as the 1400s. The Cracow rabbi Jacob Pollak (1460–1541) was among the early adherents of the method, and he was instrumental in its establishment as a formal process.[51] It was later widely disseminated by the Kabbalist Nathan Gaza (1655–1680),[52] and is still used today in yeshiva learning centers, from grade school to college. The originators of the pilpul method, and especially in the Shabtaian (Shabtai Tsevi) Movement, thought of their leaders as messiahs, but strange ones; the Messiah was said to "surrender to evil" and was able to do what is forbidden; nay, even glorified for that surrender.

Today's political correctness is a diluted form of pilpulism; it calls things by alternative names to dampen controversy. Under pilpulism, God was to be found through heightened ecstasy and sexual ecstasy, in particular. The "halls of holiness," as historian Heiko Haumann recounts, were to be entered through the "gate of licentiousness." Humanity was thoroughly degraded in the many orgiastic celebrations of the Frankists (a Jewish sect named after its founder Jacob Frank, 1726–1791, born Jacob Leibowicz) who believed in "purification through transgression."[53] The Frankists

---

* Reed was a widely read author and historian of substance, known especially for the thoroughness of his research. He published a great many books that were well received. And then he published criticisms of Zionism. He was thereafter roundly attacked and diminished. Similar attacks were made against former President Jimmy Carter after he published his book, *Palestine: Peace Not Apartheid*.

influenced the establishment of the Hasidic sect—a sect that is part of the much larger Ashkenazi branch of Judaism. Hasidic Jews are now those who comprise the Haredim, a sect that remains highly problematic even in today's Israel.

Reed says the following about pilpulism:

> This practice . . . [of making any desired outcome legal under Talmudic law and therefore pilpul argumentation] gives the key to a mystery which often baffles Gentiles: the agility with which Zionists are often able to justify, in themselves, precisely what they reproach in others. A polemist trained in pilpulism would have no difficulty in showing the Judaic law ordaining the enslavement of household Gentiles to be righteous and the Roman ban on the enslavement of Christians by Jewish masters to be "persecution"; the Judaic ban on intermarriage to be "voluntary separation" and any Gentile counter-ban to be "discrimination based in prejudice" (Dr. Kastein's terms); a massacre of Arabs and others [witness current-day Palestine] to be rightful under The Law and a massacre of Jews to be wrongful under any law.[54]

A Wikipedia entry concerning pilpulism says in part that "A frequently heard accusation is that those who used this method were often motivated by the prospect of impressing others with the sophistication of their analysis, rather than by a disinterested love of truth."[55] Lenni Brenner, in his book *51 Documents, Zionist Collaboration with the Nazis*, defines "pilpul" pretty simply: it is, says he, "Talmudic nitpicking."[56]

Pilpulism is central to the argumentation of a great many Jewish apologists, including Goldhagen and his ilk. It provides a means by which the moral and immoral can be produced according to wish. It is by way of pilpulism that Jewish dominance in various illegal and immoral activities such as pornography, prostitution, white slavery, stock fraud, treason, and the like are invariably excused in one way or another as having been forced upon Jews or Jewish individuals by powerful, nefarious Gentiles, and especially

Christian ones. Even Jewish participation in massacre and genocide is glossed over, rationalized, pilpulized. Russian author Arkady Vaksberg claims, for example, that Stalin conspired to appoint Jews as commanders of eleven of twelve major Russian concentration camps because he wanted to diminish Jews, to make them culprits. To highlight Jews with respect to such camps and activities, then, is to "blame the victim," the demonic murderous Jews who were in charge of the camps. On the other hand, to assign blame for the Holocaust to all Germans or all Christians, is to be taken, according to Goldhagen and his all too many supporters, as actuality, as truth— it is pilpulized history.

Dr. MacDonald is highly skeptical of Jewish disavowals:

> "Surface declarations of a lack of Jewish identity may be highly misleading." He notes that Jewish publications write about the power and influence of American Jews in language Jews would immediately denounce as "anti-Semitic" if used by gentiles. He agrees with [*National Review*[*] writer] Joseph Sobran, who has said "they want to be Jews among themselves but resent being seen as Jews by Gentiles. They want to pursue their own distinct interests while pretending that they have no such interests."[57]

Pilpulist logic can be seen in claims that nefarious Jews were not actually Jews, that they had abandoned their Jewishness. Such a claim was made with respect to Karl Marx and the notorious Jewish-American atomic weapon spies, Ethel and Julius Rosenberg;[58] it is "logic" that is frequently employed toward iniquitous characters of Jewish origin.

S. Friedlander discusses the nefarious Jews of Hitler's era as follows:

---

[*] Sobran, an exceedingly popular and insightful commentator, was fired from the National Review in 1993 after being accused of anti-Semitism by Norman Podhoretz.

> There was no mystery in the fact that Jews joined the revolutionary left in large numbers. These men and women belonged to the generation of newly emancipated Jews who had abandoned the framework of religious tradition for the ideas and ideals of rationalism and, more often than not, of socialism (or Zionism). Their political choices derived both from the discrimination to which they had been subjected, mainly in Russia but also in Central Europe, and from the appeal of the socialist message of equality. In the new socialist world, all of suffering humanity would be redeemed, and with that, the Jewish stigma would disappear. It was, for at least some of these "non-Jewish Jews," a vision of a secularised messianism, which may have sounded like a distant echo of the message of the Prophets they no longer recognised. In fact, almost all of them were actually hostile, in the name of revolutionary universalism, to anything Jewish. . . . Much of this was ignored by the non-Jewish public. Particularly in Germany the nationalist camp's accumulated hatred needed a pretext and a target for its outpourings. And so it pounced on the revolutionary Jews.[59]

But they *were* Jews. To claim, for example, that the Zionists were anything other than Jews is to want for sanity—they were not "non-Jewish Jews," they were, instead, fervent, nationalistic, racialist, and too often terroristic Jews. The Jews who joined the various revolutionary movements were ideologically—canonically and racially—Jewish. Nowhere was the foregoing claim more evident than it was with respect to the vast majority of Communist Jews in Russia and throughout the West. Many of the radicals of the early twentieth century, if not most, were raised in Jewish households, studied the Talmud, and fantasized about revenge against Gentiles. Indeed, according to Jewish author Yuri Slezkine, Talmudic-like revenge was a predominant motivation for Communist Jews. And those who abandoned the Jewish religion nevertheless remained Jews on a racial level, or at the very least their penchant for ethnocentrism, and were operating in accordance with their purported racial tendencies. That they later claimed their divorce from Judaism has no merit. The famous Jewish author Franz Kafka stated the situation thusly:

> Most wanted to [leave their Jewishness behind them] and started to write in German; that's what they wanted, but with their hind legs they clung on to the Judaism of their fathers and with their forelegs they were unable to find new footing.[60]

Pilpulized apologia aside, for Soviet Jews it was Jewish blood that mattered most. And so it was for German Jews as well. Moreover, a great many Jews who claimed to have abandoned Judaism later found their way back—they became born-again Jews.

Some distinguished Jews have an unfortunate propensity to blame the rubble for the earthquake. Moses Mendelssohn (1729–1786), the Jewish philosopher and leader of Jewish secular enlightenment and Jewish assimilation, complained that to accuse the Jews of immorality was to confuse cause and effect. Extending that thesis, Jews, claim apologists such as Michael Berkowitz, were compelled by Gentile-wrought circumstances to enter into the various realms of crime.[61] Berkowitz quotes Mendelssohn extensively to establish that Jews were forever forced into illicit pursuits and enterprises: "forced to take up such a calling," "shunted into this line because they were 'without refuge or sanctuary,'" and the like.[62] Haumann has it that "The Christians . . . first forced the Jews into fields of [nefarious] economic activity—above all tax farming and money-lending at interest. . . ."[63]

"Jews," said Berkowitz, "did not typically see criminals among themselves as extraordinary or evil individuals, but mainly as 'unfortunates.'"[64] Jewish immigrants to England in the eighteenth century were supposedly forced into thievery and other reprehensible enterprises by government limitations placed on them. Such claims abound, and they are all specious—they are representations of pilpulism. In actual fact, even such luminaries as the founder of modern Zionism, Theodor Herzl, and U.S. Supreme Court Justice Louis Brandeis, acknowledged that Jews as a people have historically been attracted to, not forced into, unsavory pursuits.[65] Whether that aspect of their nature stems from the religious or racial component of their being is argumentative, but it *is* part of their being according to Herzl, Brandeis, and other luminaries whom we will cite in this text.

Pseudojustification of Jewish wrongs is all well enough of course, but one needs to acknowledge that Gentiles, including even Adolf Hitler we may suppose, had legitimate reason to see things otherwise. Moreover, because some Jews tended toward crimes such as fraud, illegal stock market manipulation and such, it frequently happened that a great many Gentiles suffered from their corrupt ventures. Our recent economic hardships are exemplary: they stem in large part from speculation and credit abuses in the lending institutions connected with the U.S. housing market—economic arenas wherein Jews predominate. The free-going credit that created the problem was in no small part due to pressures brought about on the banking industry by the Jewish chairman of the House Financial Services Committee, Massachusetts Congressman Barney Frank. The common criminal may put a bump on your head and thereby earn your everlasting enmity; the fraudulent maneuverings of Jewish stockbrokers affects a broad spectrum of society and thereby engenders the enmity of entire populations. As will be chronicled herein, Jewish critique of Gentile institutions and society, accompanied by Jewish crime and its related economic exploitation of Gentiles, political radicalism, attacks on Christianity (and therefore the organizing and cultural component of Western society), and involvement in social upheavals have long been at the leading edge of anti-Semitism. And they were on the leading edge of Hitler's hate as well.

There was no singularity, as is so often proffered, that caused Hitler's hate. His hate did not stem from being rejected by the Vienna art academy nor from having contracted syphilis from a Jewish whore nor purportedly from having only one testicle nor from his Catholicism nor from any other such inanity. Rather, his hate was founded on a long series of studies and observations—most legitimate, some fanciful—and an actual series of things done by corporatist Jews that brought him to a state of maddening detestation. His hate was like a vast empty cauldron filled by drops and driblets. The totality of Hitler's studies and direct observations of Jewish participation in Austro-Hungarian and German society represented the sociological gathering of a perfect storm that was further compounded and energized by World War I and later events in Germany and Europe, a cumulative radicalization of hate and violence that ultimately ended despicably with the Holocaust.

Chapter 1, About Hitler. In Chapter 1 we will address aspects of Hitler's character that are somewhat out of step with the general mythology about him. Hitler was neither demented nor socially inept. We will emphasize aspects of his being that were important to his success—his positive personality traits, such as his asceticism and idealism. As one writer put it: "To search for the roots of this man's hatred and malice is to delve into the world not of a madman, but of an uncertain and idealistic youth."[66] I subscribe to that contention. Completely untrue contentions about Hitler have been propagated and are still believed by a broad spectrum of people today[67] (but 25 percent of the American population do not know that the earth orbits the sun, so . . .). In Chapter 1 we will provide some correctives with respect to various myths about Hitler.

Chapter 2, About Hitler's Vienna. Chapter 2 begins to highlight Hitler's hate. The time spent in Vienna, Austria, is rightfully credited by historians as the period during which Hitler's fundamental attitudes toward Jews evolved and began to coalesce and congeal into an important element of his worldview, his Weltanschauung. Chapter 2 begins to detail the sources of Hitler's hate and the milieu of Vienna in which it germinated. Many historians assert that by the time Hitler left Vienna in 1913 he was unalterably anti-Semitic; others hold that he was not (I conclude that he was). All concur, however, as did Hitler himself,[68] that the time he spent there was highly influential in molding his worldview. We will examine the milieu of Vienna in Chapter 2 and the influence that Jews and others of that city had on Hitler's psychological, sociological, and political development.

Chapter 3, World War I: The Opening Salvo of World War II. After his stay in Vienna, his participation in World War I was the next momentous event in Hitler's life. In Chapter 3 we will examine his participation in that war and the things that happened that led him to believe that Jews were a fundamental reason for Germany's defeat. World War I not only changed Hitler in several respects (such as leading to his resolve to enter politics), it also served as the basis for massive changes in Germany itself that were to the advantage of Jews and to the detriment of traditional Germans of the Hitler kind. It also provided a critically important source of Hitler's hate.

Chapter 4, Treaty of Versailles. With Germany's loss in World War I, the Treaty of Versailles was imposed on the nation. This treaty, with all of its faults, exerted an oppressive influence on the likes of Hitler and the German people as a whole. In Chapter 4 we will focus on the development of the treaty and its impact on both Germany (its economic, social, and political impacts) and on the psyche of Hitler and the German people en masse. We will also address the issue of Jewish involvement in both the creation and imposition of the treaty.

Chapter 5, The Weimar Republic. In Chapter 5 we will examine the nature of the Weimar Republic, the government that came into being at the close of World War I and remained extant until Hitler's rise to power in January 1933. During the Weimar period (1919–1933) changes to the social milieu of Germany were vast: the country was occupied by foreign troops, insurrections and uprisings of various kinds broke out, Jewish-led Communists were on the march throughout the country, hyperinflation brought financial ruin to the people, and the previously esteemed German culture was cast aside in favor of "progressive" modernist forces that morphed German culture, making it "grotesque."

Chapter 6, Weimar Culture. A great deal of Hitler's devotion to Germany and its people resided in his regard for German culture. At the most fundamental level, Hitler was an aesthetic. As a devout patron of German music, architecture, and culture in general, Nazism developed in no small part as a cultural movement alongside its purely political blossom. In Chapter 6 we will continue our examination of the changes wrought in Germany after World War I, but with a particular emphasis on the vast changes in

German culture and the massive Jewish participation in the leadership of those changes.

Chapter 7, Success of Hitler—Ascension to Power. In Chapter 7 we will discuss the confluence of events that greatly altered the political landscape of Germany and set the stage for Hitler's early success. In this chapter we will reiterate a theme touched upon in several places throughout this text: that the German populace was not by nature anti-Semitic and, in fact, honorably resisted it to the last. Hitler's ultimate successful rise to power did not hinge on German antipathy toward Jews; it was, instead, founded on an overawed people, a people subjected to an accumulation of disasters, stresses, and slights that beat and pummeled them throughout the Weimar period.

*   *   *   *

Hitler hated the Jews, the German people did not, nor did most of the senior members of his government. Historian Sarah Gordon insists that even people such as Hermann Goering (Göring), Heinrich Himmler, Joseph (Josef) Goebbels, Hans Frank, the Strasser brothers, Baldur Von Schirach, Albert Speer, Gottfried Feder, and Adolf Eichmann were not anti-Semites when they joined the party. Many members of the Hitler entourage were perplexed by Hitler's hate. Goering went so far as to forbid members of the German air force from reading the radically anti-Semitic tripe of Julius Streicher's newspaper, *Der Stürmer*. There was at least one good reason for the disjoint: Hitler had studied the Jewish Question in detail, the German leadership and people had not. As put by the Nazi philosopher Alfred Rosenberg, "The Jewish question was one which required a knowledge of history, philosophy, the Greeks, a study of races, music, art and so forth."[69]

As I conducted my research I was again and again struck by the number of parallels between contemporary American society and politics and those of the Weimar era in Germany. Here and there my text departs from the historical narrative to interject and highlight some of these parallels—a practice that I can only hope is worthwhile and not, instead, an irritant to my reader.

Since I devote a considerable amount of text to the anti-Christian issue, let me be clear: I am not a Christian. Nor am I an agnostic. I am an atheist. I am an atheist, but I am not opposed to religion or to those who practice it. I rather like Christmas, am indifferent about Easter, and am frequently disappointed by Christians as a whole, a subset of society of claimed piety but of thin commitment to that piety—a subset of people of cowardly conduct and irrational assertion. Christians, I think, deserve the fate of their demise because their convictions are so very shallow. Christianity has a powerful incentive for remaining nonpolitical and quiet: it must protect its tax exemption, its real god. Christianity deserves its fate.

*   *   *   *

As Dr. MacDonald points out, "It was Jewish historiography with its strong polemical and apologetic bias, that undertook to trace the record of Jew-hatred in Christian history, while it was left to the anti-Semites to trace an intellectually not too dissimilar record from ancient Jewish authorities."[70] Historian Richard Tedor points out that the validity of an argument is often judged less by what is said than by who is saying it. He goes on to mention that "Casting doubt on the personal integrity of an opponent can be more influential than rational discussion to refute his doctrines."[71] Thus, if your pedigree is right, any claim, no matter how ludicrous, is accepted as fact. If, on the other hand, one is lacking in pedigree, even absolute truths are sometimes taken as suspect.

The vast majority of my sources are mainstream historians. If I have here and there cited a source that is biased, even anti-Semitic, it is because it has been left to the anti-Semites to trace the record of Jewish hatred toward Gentiles, Christianity, and Gentile culture. Moreover, as historian Anthony Kauders points out, sources are legitimized or deprecated according the preferences and proclivities of the historian citing them.[72] Former President Jimmy

Carter, I think, is every bit as good (better, actually) a source than someone like the apologist Alan Dershowitz—Carter, though, due to his book about Israeli-Palestinian relations, is now taken by the popular media to be deranged, a political oddball, Dershowitz something of a messiah of apologia.

I have included a great many names of the principal players in my text. I have done this so that my reader, if he wishes to, can rather easily perform independent research to either confirm or deny my narrative.

*   *   *   *

I had originally sought to include many pictures of people and places within this text. However, due to uncertainties with respect to copyrights I ultimately decided against it. I have therefore elected to instead include proposed Google search terms that the reader may, if he chooses too, readily access Web sites that illustrate the point being made. Because such searches produce multiple outputs, I have also included at least one URL resulting from the search which in my judgement illustrates the particular point. Thus, readers of electronic versions of this book may click on the URL to acquire immediate access to the site. Readers of hard copy texts may either enter the Google search criteria or the URL itself (some of which are quite lengthy and complex) to access the material. The date following the URL is the last date that I accessed the site. Proposed Google searches are set off in the text as follows:

Google	URL
Karl Liebknecht	http://en.wikipedia.org/wiki/Karl_Liebknecht 8/2/14

Because some of the URLs are so very lengthy, I have chosen to place the lengthiest ones within the endnotes and include only the reference number for each of the related endnotes within the body of the text.

CHAPTER 1
ABOUT HITLER

In all affairs it's a healthy thing now and then to hang a question mark on the things you have taken for granted.
—British Historian, Bertrand Russell[*]

It is offensive both to our reason and to our experience to be asked to believe that the [young] Hitler... was the stuff of which... Caesars and Bonapartes are made. Yet the record is there to prove us wrong.
—Historian Alan Bullock

Even in art, there is no light without shadows, and no shadows are cast without some light. Even the shadow of Adolf Hitler is accompanied by some light.
—Hans Frank (Nazi governor-general of Poland)

    This chapter seeks to paint a nuanced portrait of Adolf Hitler, an alteration of the common depiction of the man and the broad foundations for his hate.
    Theories about Hitler's hate tend to center on a single event here and there or on a small collection of events. Such accounts picture him as a shallow man, even crazy; a thug with a deep-seated irrational hatred of Jews that stemmed from a pathological hate intrinsic to the German psyche. He is also represented as incorrigibly lazy, though he was certainly otherwise when a task suited his interests. Indeed, as historian Joachim Fest, a man who is often described as Hitler's most perceptive biographer, points out, he often "seemed inexhaustible"[73] from the outset of the DAP—the forerunner of the Nazi Party. Hitler's boyhood friend August Kubizek asserts that when Hitler addressed a task in which he was

---

[*] Quoted from Mearsheimer, John, and Stephen Walt. *The Israel Lobby and U.S. Foreign Policy*. (New York: Farrar, Straus and Giroux, 2007), vii.

particularly interested he would work incessantly, not even stopping to take meals.[74]

Fest was a historian of deserved accomplishment and respect. He was often spot-on, but faltered when he entered his occasional psychobabble mode. Fest also claimed that Hitler had a "complex incapacity for human relationships,"[75] a claim that is simply not true. Hitler had his fair share of entirely normal human relationships, including his close friendship with his fellow aesthetic and opera lover August Kubizek, and later with Albert Speer, his favorite architect. Certainly, Dietrich Eckart, the original founder of the Nazi movement, must be counted as a friend to Hitler and vice versa. We might also count his friendship with his driver Emil Maurice, as well as fellow soldier and later publisher, Max Amann. We should also count the SS General Christian Weber and a number of others. According to Kubizek, even Hitler's Jewish acquaintance in Vienna, Josef Neumann, became "a real friend to Hitler."[76] Neumann helped Hitler sell his artwork. His general conviviality is evidenced by the joy he experienced in the company of a wide circle of close acquaintances such as his photographer Heinrich Hoffmann and the Harvard-educated head of his Foreign Press Bureau, Ernst Hanfstaengl, not to mention such characters as Hermann Goering (Göring), Joseph Goebbels, et al. According to fellow Nazi Dietrich Eckart, he was a "selfless, self-sacrificing, devoted and sincere" man, "forever 'purposeful and alert.'"—a nice guy, if you will.[77] Even the twelve-year-old son of Ernst Hanfstaengl noticed an endearing quality in Hitler. Hitler, he said, "didn't make you remember all the time that he was the Fuehrer."[78] He was a nice enough guy to have had a large number of entirely normal friendships, both before and after he achieved power.

Fest describes a picture of Hitler with other soldiers that supposedly supports a claim that he was alienated from his fellows. "Hitler," says Fest, "sits beside them with a fixed expression, obviously sharing not at all in their viewpoint."[79] Firstly, it is rather difficult in a photograph to have anything other than a "fixed expression." Secondly, it is impossible to discern from the photograph what viewpoint he had or did not have. Of the several

About Hitler

photographs of Hitler during World War I (there are but a few), there is not a single one of which has Hitler looking alienated; on the contrary, he looks entirely normal and his expression in each of them is entirely in keeping with the others pictured with him. There is even one picture that shows Hitler between two war buddies, his arms are affectionately draped about the shoulders of the other soldiers. Alas, Hitler cannot catch a break: the caption for the picture showing him with his arms across the shoulders of his soldier friends suggests that he was a homosexual, which is preposterous.

There is a Web site that includes numerous pictures of Hitler and other personalities. The site includes several pictures of Hitler and his soldier friends during World War I. One may easily access the site, examine the pictures and Hitler's expression vis-à-vis his soldier friends and thereby confirm or deny the claim made by Fest.

Google	URL
Adolf Hitler World War I	https://www.google.com/search?q=Adolf+Hitler+WWI&rlz=1T4GZAB_enUS449US538&tbm=isch&tbo=u&source=univ&sa=X&ei=XLfcU_2YI8WQyATi9oLQAw&ved=0CB4QsAQ&biw=1008&bih=523 8/2/14
Images for World War I messengers Ernst Schmiedl	https://www.google.com/search?q=Adolf+Hitler+WWI&rlz=1T4GZAB_enUS449US538&tbm=isch&tbo=u&source=univ&sa=X&ei=XLfcU_2YI8WQyATi9oLQAw&ved=0CB4QsAQ&biw=1008&bih=523#facrc=_&imgdii=_&imgrc=O0IcrqluFKCbIM%253A%3B0F8mj6Rc4I2zAM%3Bhttp%253A%252F%252Fwww.history.ucsb.edu%252Ffaculty%252Fmarcuse%252Fclasses%252F33d%252F33dWImages%252FHitlerSchmidlLippertWW1-150pxw.png%3Bhttp%253A%252F%252Fwww.history.ucsb.edu%252Ffaculty%252Fmarcuse%252Fclasses%252F33d%252F33d05%252F33d05L03Hitler.htm%3B150%3B148 8/2/14

Fest also had it that "above the base of his nose, between the curve of the thick eyebrows, a clotted bulge bespoke a fanatical will."[80] One should perhaps remember that piece of nonsense each time one encounters some reference to Nazis and their study of phrenology. Is this business about discerning a "fanatical will" on the basis of a "clotted bulge" any more scientific, any more rational, than the study of bumps on skulls? Elsewhere, Fest claimed that Hitler had a "psychopathic face."[81] With Hitler, we find oddity and even demonism on the basis of "exceptionally low standards of proof." Hitler's paintings further illustrate the point. As Frederic Spotts tells us in his book, *Hitler and the Power of Aesthetics*:

> An exhibition of Hitler's paintings—or an exhibition of Hitler's and Churchill's paintings that would show vividly the difference in character of the two statesmen—is unthinkable. In an argument submitted in the spring of 2001 to the Federal Appeals court in Washington, the United States Justice Department maintained that the very brush strokes of Hitler's watercolours have such incendiary potential that they must be guarded from the gaze of all but screened experts. . . . Who is afraid of Adolf Hitler? Just about everyone.[82]

Fest, for all the regard he enjoyed and deserved as a politically correct mainstream establishment historian, could not help but indulge from time to time, as do so many others, in psychobabble with respect to Hitler. His "fear," claimed Fest, made it essential for him to blame the world for his own tribulations. "Fear" was "the impulse behind the fierce dynamism of his whole life."[83] Fest had nothing to say about the nature of Hitler's supposed fear. In actuality, the "fear" that he felt, if any at all can be legitimately claimed, was of a kind that he experienced while living in Vienna. There he perhaps "feared" the danger that he and his people would be caught up in the prevailing corruption and immorality of the city and would finally be "dragged down into the vortex of corruption."[84] And any rational observation of the prevailing political and social conditions in Vienna at that time lent great credence to such fears. It was hardly irrational to "fear" such an eventuality; it seemed to be in the making all around him. Unfortunately, it is largely by way of psychohistorical twaddle of the kind regretfully replicated by Fest that we presume to know the character of Adolf Hitler.

For all of the biased claims to the contrary, Hitler was neither shallow nor, on the whole, irrational. Nor did his authority stem from repression, violence, and terror.[85] In actual fact, the Nazi Party had a rather egalitarian character to it. Hitler sought to unite the people of Germany on a voluntary basis, not by way of truncheons, police surveillance, and the like. "With police, machine guns and rubber clubs, no regimen can be maintained in the long run,"[86] he warned. In 1939, he called for a drastic reduction of the national police force to release manpower to relieve the industrial labor shortage, and, no doubt, to also bolster his military force. That is not to say that he did not deal quickly and harshly with Marxists and other opponents who threatened his people and his regime. He had experienced what tolerance had wrought during the period 1914–1933, and he was not about to let it be repeated.

According to historian Richard Tedor, Hitler sought societal harmony. Tedor puts it as follows:

> The goal of Hitler's policies was to realize a cooperative, harmonious society, a fair and reasonable distribution of national assets, and a life for the working population as free from anxiety and want as possible. In 1942, General Walther Scherff, a military historian in the German army, summarized the popular impression of his Führer during the times: "Hitler's principle of life was the same as that of his role model, Friedrich the Great; that it is not war, but civilized, creative activity such as works of art, social institutions, and travel routes that will bring the German people a practical, carefree and secure future existence."[87]

Hitler was very much like other great men: he had a great capacity for evil, but as historian John Willard Toland points out, he sometimes only "narrowly evaded sanctity."[88] He was deep and complex and demonstrated on innumerable occasions that he was markedly rational. His entire entourage claimed that he was a genius and there were a good many aspects of his phenomenal recall, synthesis, and conceptual insights that supported such claims. We must look deeper for the roots of his hate and anti-Semitism than can be discerned from psychohistorians who explain Hitler by way of "clotted bulge[s]," "transference," and other such absurdities. We can begin by reexamining the concrete character and traits of the man.

* * * *

This chapter paints a picture of Hitler that is different than the one commonly brushed. Hitler was both demon and saint in one. He was capable of much evil, but he also both aspired to and actually accomplished much *good* for his people before the war. He was more complex and multidimensional than any other great leader known to history, full of contradiction and paradox. Spotts highlights but a couple of many enigmas that were central to his being:

> The man responsible for more death and destruction than anyone else in modern times wished to forge a state whose cultural achievements would rival those of the greatest civilizations of the past. And inside that paradox lay another. The warlord who built up the greatest land army since Napoleon regretted having to spend money on weapons that could have been devoted to the arts. . . . "It is a pity that I have to wage war on account of that drunk [Winston Churchill] instead of serving the works of peace. . . ." The whole point of power, he went on to say, was to produce "cultural wonders" . . . he considered war a step towards his final goal of founding a culture-state.[89]

To Hitler, culture and the culture-state was everything—we will expand upon his regard for culture in more detail in a later chapter. He genuinely grieved and lamented over the need to do battle in Italy and Greece because by doing so he had to threaten the culturally iconic cities of Rome and Athens. He even agreed to alter military plans to keep them safe. In particular, he ordered that Florence not be defended because the city was too beautiful to destroy. He told the German ambassador to Italy to "Do what you can to protect it: you have my permission and assistance."[90] He could not countenance the idea that he might be seen by history as having done damage to the great cultural works still evident in those great cities and he therefore took particular care to spare them the ravages of war. He did similarly for Paris: "In the air attack on Paris," said Hitler, "we confined ourselves to the airfields—to spare the city with a glorious past . . . it would have hurt me to be obliged to attack a city like Laon, with its cathedral."[91] Rome was bombed by us Americans to the tune of 110,000 aircraft sorties and 60,000 tons of bombs,[92] the conventional munitions equivalent of 3.75 atomic bombs of the kind dropped on Hiroshima—Germans left the city whole. Obviously, however, he did not hold similar views with respect to Warsaw, Moscow, and Leningrad (St. Petersburg)[*] or other icons of Communism/Bolshevism.

In his book, *Adolf Hitler*, Toland describes Hitler thusly:

> Adolf Hitler was probably the greatest mover and shaker of the twentieth century. Certainly no other human disrupted so many lives in our times or stirred so much hatred. He also inspired widespread adoration and was the hope and ideal of millions.[93]

Unfortunately, for the sake of truth, the adoration that Hitler inspired is typically ascribed to pathological impulses of "the

---

[*] St. Petersburg was renamed Petrograd in 1914, in 1924 it became Leningrad, and in 1991 it again reverted to St. Petersburg.

German mentality," or deep-seated, irrational anti-Semitism that we are assured stemmed from the same source. But prior to World War I, Germans had no reputation whatever for the Jew-hatred that would later be ascribed to their very essence.[94] Indeed, "For the most part," says Lindemann, "the story of German political anti-Semitism from the 1880s up to 1914 is one of marginality and ignominious decline."[95] During World War I and thereafter, the history of Germany was rewritten in much the same way that Soviet Russia commonly altered history in the opening years of Communism there. Facts were altered at will; champions were made out to be villains, and saints were made out to be devils. Some great names and faces simply disappeared. The past was altered to outfit a new identity for the newly installed scoundrels. History was pilpulized.

With specific respect to Hitler, as opposed to the common condemnation of all Germans, the record was greatly skewed by members of the Social Democratic Party (SDP) who departed Germany after the party was outlawed. In exile, members of the SDP operated under the name *Sopade* (also represented as SoPaDe—Social Democratic Party), first in Prague, then Paris, and finally London. The Jewish-German politician Rudolf Hilferding headed up the Sopade organization and published a flood of anti-Hitler propaganda of the kind that had previously been so characteristic of people like the Jewish-German journalist Carl von Ossietsky, a character we will discuss in a later chapter. As stated by historian John Williams:

> While the *völkisch* press exalted him as a war hero and patriot, his left-wing and liberal enemies were prepared to grasp at straws. Without a trace of evidence, it was suggested that he had been a coward, shirker, or draft dodger.[96]

The foregoing was the Sopade depiction of Hitler and remains the popular lore of Hollywood historians. He was labeled a charlatan, and Germans were represented as stupid for following him. He was, according to this line of rationality, a "half-mad deadbeat," a "cowardly, effeminate, pyjama character," a mere "creature of industry," and so on.⁹⁷ We understandably abhor Hitler and we do so for good reason—but the fact of the matter is that he was none of the things that the likes of Ossietsky, Sopade, and Hollywood represented him to be. Hilferding and his organization latched on to and published every conceivable outrageous rumor about Hitler and the Nazis in much the same way that Jews would later skewer Poland after World War II.⁹⁸ As is so frequently the case, such rumors were given over to a highly sympathetic general press with Jews in their masthead and reported as facts that we now call history. The whole of the Jewish reporting about Hitler and his regime was hardly of a kind meant to endear.

The popular image of pathological defects in Germans began with the propaganda of World War I and was then extended and further embellished during the 1930s while Hitler was in power. During and after World War II, still more spurious claims were made against Germany. Prior to World War I, though, "Germany was seen as a peaceful land of fairy tales and dreamy castles, and of industrious, law abiding, disciplined people."⁹⁹ During World War I, history was debased and Germans were represented to be rapacious, bloodthirsty, and uniquely aggressive. Fest correctly puts the issue as follows:

> The first attempts at raising the success of Nazism to a special mentality rooted in German history . . . began early in the thirties [but it actually began during World War I]. The German was pictured as perplexing, full of antitheses, making a principle of his aloofness from civilization and civil conduct. . . . Such "ancestry" was supposed to prove a tradition of latent Hitlerism long before Hitler. . . . William L. Shirer's *The Rise and Fall of the Third Reich*, which has to a large degree formed the world's picture of Germany, made use of it. . . . Seen from this angle, nothing in German history was "innocent." Even in its most idyllic moments, the specters of obedience, militarism, and expansionism were palpably present. . . . Ultimately everything

terminated in Hitler; he was by no means a "German catastrophe," as the title of a well-known book asserted, but a product of German consistency.[100]

William Shirer was a journalist and historian of substantial merit and deserved respect. Still, his *Berlin Diary* and his highly acclaimed, and therefore widely read book, *The Rise and Fall of the Third Reich* (1960), set the stage for sizeable amounts of the diatribe that historians thereafter regularly regurgitated to describe both Hitler and Germans. Many of Shirer's assertions with respect to demonizing German history were taken from an earlier work (1945) by A. J. P. Taylor, *The Course of German History*.[101] Historians *want* to believe Shirer's speculations with respect to the German psyche; and with equal fervor they want to exempt Jews from any association with anti-Semitism. Too many historians contend that both Hitler and anti-Semitism stem from a deep-seated uniquely German historical phenomenon, a sort of psychic cancer that finally and inexorably spread throughout the social and body politic and inevitably led to Hitler and the Holocaust. Albert Lindemann challenges such contentions saying that:

> What has . . . been termed "the gathering storm" or "rising tide" interpretation of Nazism must confront what by now is a massive amount of contrary evidence. It was anything but obvious from the evidence at hand before 1914 that anti-Semitism was growing steadily stronger, especially in Germany, or that Europe was moving toward a mass murder of its Jewish population.[102]

We know Adolf Hitler as the incarnation of evil. His aggressive war (a foggy legal and moral concept), by which we usually mean the inhumanity and immorality that so characterized his conduct of World War II and the Holocaust he unleashed against the Jews and others, are his legacies. There is fairly general agreement that since 1945 it has been en vogue to deride Hitler: "woes to anyone who dares to say something good about him,"[103] says one sage. His former idolaters went mute after World War II.

He is commonly represented as an ex-bricklayer, a failed street-painter, a painter of post cards, a mad orator spitting his hatred while saliva froths at the corners of his mouth. He was indecisive, a draft-dodging coward, a sexual pervert, and a spiteful son. The list goes on.

Nearly everything said about Hitler is subjected to Orwellian newspeak that is fashioned according to his attitude and actions toward Jews. Thus it is that, as Spotts points out, "even if Hitler was an artistic genius (which he was not), the odds that he would be one day accepted as such are very slim indeed."[104] If Hitler had painted the *Mona Lisa* there would be found in it a great many faults of perspective, color, and composition—and somehow, we can be certain, it would be made to represent some aspect of Hitler's supposed sexual aberrations. The *Mona Lisa* smile would be described as proof positive of his craftiness and insincerity.

The popular media frequently paints Hitler as simply an opportunist; a stage player with no actual belief system who exploited the fears of the populace with no objective other than abject power for himself. That depiction, too, is simply untrue. Hitler was a true believer. According to Hermann Goering, "His whole life was dedicated to the German nation."[105] His boyhood friend August Kubizek provided equivalent commentary. Fest correctly puts the issue this way:

> The general view of Hitler as an unprincipled opportunist does not do justice either to his daring or his originality. His courage in voicing "forbidden" opinions was extraordinary. Precisely that gave him the aura of manliness, fierceness, and sovereign contempt, which befitted the image of the Great Leader.[106]

There is no good reason to doubt the sincerity of Hitler as he discussed with his economic advisor, Otto Wagener, his attitude of devotion with respect to Germany and its people. Henry Turner recounts the conversation as follows:

> But I have to deny myself this happiness [marriage]. I have another bride—Germany! I am married: to the

German Volk, to its destiny! I see the Volk suffering, tormented by the accursed provisions of the Versailles Treaty, tyrannized by enemy occupation and by foreign rule in the east and the west. I see how it is despised, defamed, and depraved, this good, sturdy Volk, these honest and industrious people, these heirs to a proud past who are undemanding and willing to make endless sacrifices! This is the Volk to whom I have given my heart, all my thinking and planning, my work, my self! Many a time I have stared at the Gospels and, reading, muttered to myself, Who are my sisters, who are my brothers? No, I cannot marry, I may not.[107]

Fest and Turner are correct on this issue: Hitler was indeed a true believer. He, unlike other politicians of his era, was from a modest background, and he conducted himself in simple ways that helped endear him to his people, and until 1939, he delivered miracles on their behalf. He was not simply a politician, he was a true believer who loved his people every bit as much as they loved him. Indeed, it was at least partially their sense that he loved them that made them love him in return. Hitler was a man of great passion, and his most intense passion was for Germans and Germany.

* * * *

Hitler was born in 1889 at Braunau am Inn, Austria, a small town situated just across the border between Austria and Germany. Austria was at the time, of course, part of the Austro-Hungarian Empire. In centuries gone by, the Germans of Austria were the leaders in both the political and cultural realms there. As Bullock points out, "Both in the Empire and in the Federation Austria had enjoyed a traditional hegemony as the leading German Power. In the middle of the nineteenth century it was still Vienna, not Berlin which ranked as the first of German cities."[108] Fest says that by the time Hitler was born, the German component of Austria-Hungary, representing about one-quarter[109] (Bullock has it as 35 percent)[110] of it, "were ahead of all the other peoples of the empire in education, prosperity, and general development; but their influence was disproportionately small"[111] due to the size of the other races and nationalities encompassed by the empire. It was a fact that enraged the likes of Hitler and others of German stock. The great influence of Jews in Vienna, concluded Hitler and others, was both vast and of a degenerate kind, and was in large part responsible for the precipitous decline in the influence of the German component of the empire.

Hitler and his family moved often. Before he entered the sixth grade they had moved from Braunau am Inn to Passau, Lambach, Leonding, and finally, to Linz. While in grade school at Lambach, the ever-observant Hitler experienced "an excellent opportunity to intoxicate [himself] with the solemn splendor of the brilliant church festivals."[112] Though ultimately an enemy of the church, he praised it for wonderfully exercising man's natural need . . . for something supernatural. "It had, he said, *known how to work on people with its mystical cult, its large sublime cathedrals, with blessed music, solemn rites, and incense.*"[113] (Italics are in the original.) Hitler would later employ these lessons in his torch-lit parades as exemplified by the Cathedral of Light and the Sea of Flags at party rallies, as well as the use of jackboots, the goosestep march, and similar spectacles and devices as a means to emotionally intoxicate the masses.

Google	URL
Cathedral of Light	http://en.wikipedia.org/wiki/Albert_Speer#mediaviewer/File:Bundesarchiv_Bild_183-1982-1130-502,_N%C3%BCrnberg,_Reichsparteitag,_Lichtdom.jpg 8/2/14
Image, Nazi Sea of Flags	http://www.youtube.com/watch?v=xGSnVAjqQFw 8/2/14

His high school education took place in Linz, and it was there that he was heavily influenced by his history teacher, Dr. Leopold Pötsch. In addition to being a teacher, Pötsch was an active politician who led the German Peoples (*Volksdeutsch*) group on the municipal council; he abhorred the multinational Austro-

Hungarian state.[114] He gave lectures to his students titled "Images of German History" wherein he emphasized the great Germans of history and legend. In *Mein Kampf*, Hitler speaks of being "often aflame with enthusiasm and sometimes even moved to tears" by the history narrations of Pötsch.[115] Dr. Pötsch, said Hitler, made history his favorite subject. And it was German history—highly charged nationalistic German history that enamored him most. He would carry his love of history with him throughout his life. He studied it assiduously with a special emphasis on those things that were in any way connected to Germany. Geography was another of his favorite subjects. Later, the history of Jews became still another.

Hitler regarded the Austrian-Hungarian Empire as a polyglot of peoples who were destroying the German component of it. He railed against the Slavic influence in Vienna, a German city polluted, according to his lights, by the presence and influence of Slavs and Jews. He detested the royal house, the House of Habsburg, for having let the lowly Slavs intrude on superior Germanic Austria. And he despised the Jewish press for its praise of Emperor Franz Joseph and his government—praise that was in no small part due to the privileged position of Jews in Austro-Hungarian society, culture, and politics. He also deeply despised the Archduke and Crown Prince Francis Ferdinand because Ferdinand sought to accommodate the Slavs.

Thus it was that Hitler started on the road to extreme German nationalism and irredentism. It would later come to be that anyone or anything that stood in the way of the further accomplishment, glorification, and unification of Germany and its peoples was immediately pegged as an object of Hitler's hate—and there stood the Jews.

By the time Hitler departed Linz and relocated to Vienna, the seeds of his nationalism (but probably not his anti-Semitism) had already sprouted.

Hitler as Seen by His Best Friend

In his youth, Hitler had but one close friend, August Kubizek. Kubizek was a young man he met at the Linz Landestheater in late 1904. The two were compatible souls. Both were serious about life, and both were devotees of the arts, including especially the operas of Richard Wagner. Unlike Hitler, though, Kubizek had been, on the whole, an excellent student, completing his classes with honors.[116]

Because Kubizek knew Hitler so well, and because he seems to have had no particular axe to grind, and because, too, so many historians acknowledge that much of Hitler's personality and ideas were firmly fixed in his youth, it is worth discussing Kubizek's perceptions of Hitler in some detail.

In the realm of music, Kubizek was Hitler's acknowledged superior. Hitler was unabashedly aware of Kubizek's superior musical aptitude and expertise but was not at all jealous of his friend. He heartily encourage and assisted Kubizek's musical ambitions, even convincing Kubizek's father that the young man should be permitted to leave the family's upholstering business to pursue his interests in music. Says Kubizek,

> Adolf recognized my musical talent without the least envy, and rejoiced or suffered with me in my successes or setbacks as if they were applicable to himself. I found him very supportive and the great strength behind my ambition.[117]

Kubizek, far more unassuming than Hitler, served as a sounding board for Hitler's early ideas in the realm of music, architecture, politics, social welfare, and, to a lesser extent, for his occasional anti-Semitic outbursts.

The friendship between the two young men continued when they departed Linz for Vienna where they roomed together. In all, the friendship spanned more than four years (1904–1908).

In 1908, as Kubizek returned to Vienna after a visit at home, Hitler was gone. Kubizek could not fathom why his friend had left; attempts to locate him were fruitless. It seems at least probable, given what both Kubizek and respected historians say about Hitler's personality, that he departed because he could no longer manage his share of their living expenses and was far too proud to accept any form of assistance from his friend. That same sense of pride would also explain why he provided no forwarding address—better to make a clean break in the friendship than be begged to return on the basis of charity. Hitler thereafter sank into abject poverty, living hand to mouth, sleeping on the green bed—on the ground or benches in Vienna—scraping by on a skimpy income from odd jobs and later by way of selling his artwork for meager sums.

After Hitler's departure, Kubizek had no further contact with him until the 1930s. He did, however, follow the news of him as he began to make a name for himself in Munich after World War I. In early 1933, when Hitler became chancellor of Germany, Kubizek wrote to congratulate him. As he wrote, he recalled in his letter a midnight experience that he had with Hitler as they walked and talked after attending a performance of Wagner's *Rienzi*. Hitler had been very moved, claiming that he would one day rise to be *Volkstribun*—the leader of the people, the people's tribune. His rise to the chancellorship made prophetic what had earlier seemed to be youthful bravado[118]—it also seems to deny the claim that Hitler had no political ambitions prior to his experience in World War I. Kubizek received a pleasant reply to his missive but did not reestablish actual contact until 1939 when Hitler invited him to attend the annual Wagner Festival in Bayreuth as his personal guest.

Wanting to exploit Kubizek's remembrances, Nazi underlings pressed him to write about his youthful relationship with Hitler. He ultimately created about fifty typewritten pages of text but never submitted them for publication. Hitler, for his part, never pressed the matter and even sincerely assured Kubizek that whatever he had written and whatever memorabilia he possessed was his personal property and would not be taken from him.

Hitler offered Kubizek a prestigious, bountiful position as a Reich musician, but he would not accept it. It was simply not in the young man's aesthetic nature to exploit a friendship. Entirely nonpolitical, he did not even join the Nazi Party until 1942 when the tide was turning and it was becoming apparent that the war might be lost. As others deserted the ship, Kubizek finally jumped aboard—he was *that* kind of man, *that* kind of friend. After the war, he spent sixteen months in prison but was then released and settled down in simple family life, raising his children and working as a civil servant.

Over the years, Kubizek had many additional opportunities to exploit his friendship with Hitler but consistently declined. Finally, he did write his book, *The Young Hitler I Knew*, which was first published in 1953. The book was a substantially altered and expanded version of the fifty-page manuscript he had created in the 1930s.

Sir Ian Kershaw, the British historian specializing in twentieth-century Germany, says that "Kubizek's book rings true in the portrait of Hitler's personality and mentality."[119] Kershaw also challenges assertions by Kubizek's most vociferous detractor, Franz Jetzinger. Jetzinger made a career out of refuting both Hitler and Kubizek. His refutations were largely adopted by such highly respected scholars as Joachim Fest and Werner Moser. It came to be, however, that other scholars provided correctives: among them, Austrian historian Brigitte Hamann and Ian Kershaw himself. "Hamann especially, managed to convincingly relate personal motives to Jetzinger's tendency to illustrate nearly every statement in Kubizek's book as an ex post modification of facts."[120] As Hamann, Kershaw, and a few others now point out, Jetzinger was, for a time, on good terms with Kubizek but reversed himself when Kubizek's book preceded his own to the bookstores and caused the sales of his own book to falter.

Kershaw convincingly challenges assertions by Jetzinger on several key points and supports his contentions with reliable witnesses. By way of example, Jetzinger claimed that Hitler did not return home even when he knew that this mother was deathly ill. He made this claim on the basis of the testimony of an "old lady" whom he acknowledged was senile.[121] Hitler was, according to Jetzinger's account, a mean son—a claim that was refuted by the consistency of claims by both the Jewish doctor who treated

Hitler's mother, Dr. Edward Bloch, and by Hitler's sister, Paula. Convincing countervailing evidence notwithstanding, it is the mean son version of history that is preferred by Hollywood and the popular press. Dr. Bloch later recalled Hitler's response when he was informed of his mother's pending death. As tears flowed from Hitler's eyes he begged to know if there might still be some chance for her survival. "Only then," the doctor wrote, "did I recognize the magnitude of the attachment that existed between mother and son."[122] Kubizek describes Hitler's presence in the house as his mother lay dying and also describes in some detail both the aid provided by Hitler and the utter remorse he felt over her illness and death. Kubizek, clearly, is a superior source about Hitler's youth than Jetzinger.

And what does Kubizek say about the youthful Hitler?

When his mother first fell ill in 1907 and was hospitalized, Hitler dutifully and faithfully visited her daily.[123] When her illness recurred in late 1908 and she lingered at home, he departed Vienna, hurrying home to attend her. Kubizek describes him as poignantly attentive, anticipating her every wish.[124] He cooked for her, cleaned house, and slept in the same room with her so that he could always be there to immediately service her needs. There was, says Kubizek, a "spiritual harmony between mother and son." In total, Hitler's loving care and devotion created "an atmosphere of relaxed, almost serene contentment [that] surrounded the dying woman. . . . He was nothing but his mother's faithful and helpful son."[125]

With respect to his plans for the future, Hitler's unshakeable will was even then apparent. So, too, was his inclination to be dissatisfied with the status quo—it was an "ineradicable" part of him to want to change things, to improve them.[126] That he remained faithful to his early precepts was evidenced after he attained power: Hitler's impulses toward bettering the lives and culture of his people underpinned his success.[127]

The youthful Hitler, recounts Kubizek, expressed his conceptions of Socialism as he developed explicit plans for new buildings and bridges in and around Linz and Vienna. Detached workers' housing units conceived by Hitler featured separate bedrooms for parents and children, light and air and gardens and baths and children's play areas nearby—it was all entirely revolutionary for the time. And, says Kubizek, "What the fifteen-year-old planned, the fifty-year-old carried out."[128]

> Indeed, the plans which the unknown boy had drawn up for the rebuilding of his home town Linz are identical to the last detail with the town planning scheme which was inaugurated after 1938.[129]

Kubizek also recounts various outbursts from Hitler with respect to a variety of subjects but emphasizes that they were never of a nature that made him take offense. With respect to argumentation, says Kubizek, "He liked to convert by persuasion."[130] Others have commented similarly. Among Hitler's outbursts were his expositions on "professional landlords," people who created and exploited the awful housing conditions of the masses. "The poor tenant usually never meets his landlord," claimed Hitler, "as the latter does not live in these tenements he owns—God forbid!—but somewhere in the suburbs, in Hietzing or Grinzing, in a luxurious villa where he enjoys an abundance of that which he deprives others."[131] Hitler's outburst was a thinly disguised criticism of Jews—both Hietzing and Grinzing were relatively exclusive Jewish neighborhoods on the western and northwestern outskirts of Vienna.

All of Hitler's thoughts during this period were concentrated on ways to help the German masses, "the simple, decent but under-privileged people with whom he identified himself—they were ever-present in his thoughts,"[132] says Kubizek.

Kubizek also remarked that one of Hitler's most striking personal characteristics was that of "unparalleled consistency in everything that he said and did."[133] "Hitler was 'immovable' and 'rigid,'" says he, "he could not change his mind or his nature."[134] Yet as one would expect, Hitler did evolve over time. His interests, focus, and attitudes shifted slowly as he discovered more and more: for example, "the Linz years," observes Kubizek, "were under the star of art; those in Vienna were under the star of politics."[135]

On the whole, Kubizek found Hitler so very considerate that "sometimes he made me feel quite ashamed."[136]

Hitler also remained constant in his attachment to both Kubizek and Kubizek's parents. As late as 1944, he sent a food package to Kubizek's mother on the occasion of her eightieth birthday.[137] "However intensely he was occupied," wrote Kubizek, "he would always have time for the affairs of those people in whom he was interested."[138] As we will later recount, this characteristic of Hitler would also be evident in his relationships during the 1920s and 1930s.

Kubizek recounts at some length Hitler's infatuation with a young girl from a good family, Stefanie Isak. He only admired her from afar, never developing an opportunity to actually be introduced and to properly court her. His relationship with the pretty young Stefanie reads like something out of a Jane Austen novel—the young couple had an "affair" during which "nothing happens."[139] Kubizek emphasizes that Hitler's relationship with Stefanie was entirely normal for the time. Though Hitler despised the bourgeois he was nevertheless entirely faithful to its conceptions of etiquette and mores. His behavior was always absolutely correct and always in keeping with the etiquette of the times, a point that Kubizek several times reiterates.[140] Hitler's early reticence with the ladies was also in keeping with his time, a time when it was common for proper young men to feel obliged to keep themselves pure for marriage.[141]

Types of Hitler

Hitler was many-a-man-in-one. Historians frequently compare him to other famous personalities as a sort of shorthand for giving substance and understanding to certain of his traits. It is a measure of his complexity and breadth of influence that he has been compared to so many different characters. The following are figures that are commonly used in similes, analogies, and metaphors of Hitler:

Pericles. Pericles is an apt analogy that is employed to represent Hitler as a prominent statesman, orator, and populist—and also, according to some, a demagogue and a hawk. The death of Ephialtes in 461 BC enabled Pericles to consolidate his power much as Hitler would do upon the death of President Paul von Hindenburg. As a politician, Pericles managed to eliminate his opponents and thereby enhance his own ability to act independently of others: Hitler did likewise. Like Hitler, Pericles promoted the arts and theater, even proposing that the poor be permitted to attend plays with the cost being borne by the state—a policy actually implemented by Hitler in Germany. But perhaps most importantly, Pericles was responsible for massive construction projects without concern for the cost: the buildings of the Acropolis—the Parthenon, the Propylaia, the Erechtheion, and the temple of Athena and Nike. Hitler, said Albert Speer, thought of himself as a ruler in the mold of Pericles and regarded his autobahns as his Parthenon.[142] Like Pericles, Hitler lived a frugal life and kept himself untainted by corruption as a way of setting an example for his people. Both men were also warriors with expansionist ambitions. Pericles chalked up successes with attacks on Sicyon and Acarnania but met his match when he attacked Oeniadea. Hitler's early successes at war would be undone by his attack on the Soviet Union.

Augustus. Augustus, who entered Rome when it was a city of bricks, would leave it as a city of marble. Hitler planned and fantasized over doing likewise in Berlin, Munich, Linz, and Hamburg. Berlin was to be the greatest city in the world, Munich the cultural center of Germany, Linz the center for the arts, and Hamburg the world's greatest port.[143] Unlike Augustus, though, Hitler left his capital in utter ruin, in rubble and ashes rather like Nero.

Richard Wagner. Richard Wagner is often cited by way of analogy with Hitler because of Hitler's devotion to him and his musical works, the characters within those works, and similarities between the two men with respect to politics, anti-Semitism, and personal histories. Wagner was idolized by Hitler for his personal courage, the heroic characters of his operas, and most especially for the quality of his music. Moreover, Wagner was regarded as a man who, like himself, believed intensely in his own destiny and would permit nothing to deter him from achieving it.[144] Spotts tells us that some people see Hitler's talents as Wagnerian. He justifies the claim by quoting Emil Ludwig as follows:

> Endless parades, continuous music, oaths of loyalty, praise of heroism—"all this fulfilled the [stereotypical?] German dream of obedience and music, discipline and worship, a combination of *Lohengrin* and the Brigade of Guards." Such was the comment of the historian Emil Ludwig who, like most other exiles, admitted that at the simplest level Hitler was providing the sort of excitement and pageantry that was totally lacking in the Weimar Republic and that, however irrational the means, he succeeded in his objective of arousing a deep sense of national pride.[145]

From Hitler's perspective, the above was actually a representation of rationalism in grandeur. The whole of it was a form of Gentile Freudianism. Hitler understood his people. He knew the objective facts of the suffering the German people had undergone, knew that they longed to return to a sense of community and national pride, and he provided both the stagecraft and statecraft to bring it about. He employed symbols (which we must readily grant were themselves largely irrational) to win and hold adherents; it was an exceedingly rational thing to do.

Even many eminent German exiles—Heinrich Thomas and Klaus Mann, Emil Ludwig, Ludwig Marcuse and Bertolt Brecht, says Frederic Spotts, claimed that there was something "Wagnerian" about Hitler's relationship with his audiences.[146]

Wagner's Siegfried is frequently made to represent Hitler's love of combat and his conduct as a soldier during World War I. He is also discussed in terms of Siegfried in that he escaped death on so very many occasions, both in World War I and during his political career (there were over forty attempts on his life). Siegfried was made invulnerable by bathing in the blood of a dragon, but a single leaf from a linden tree (in German folklore, the linden tree is the "tree of lovers" but also one that could "unearth the truth," and therefore, a tree associated with jurisprudence) alighted on his body leaving him with a bare spot untouched by the blood of the dragon. It left him with a single point of vulnerability in the manner of Achilles. The favors of Providence had enabled Hitler to escape death on numerous occasions. His vulnerability was failure; with the loss of the war he took his own life, an act that was both soldierly, given his time and German tradition, and Wagnerian.

Wagner's *Rienzi* is from time to time made comparable to Hitler's self-image as a simple man who is driven by a sense of mission, by an Annunciation, a tool of Destiny to restore greatness to his people and their capital: Rome, in the case of Rienzi, Berlin in the case of Hitler. Hitler himself, according to Kubizek, compared himself to Rienzi.[147] There were indeed many historical parallels between Cola di Rienzi and Hitler in both their rise to power and their use of that power; and, at the end, they both came to ruin and death in a last futile stand as their capitals burned around them. Ultimately, too, the populace turned against the two of them.

Finally, there were also similarities in Hitler's and Wagner's personal histories. Both were somewhat uncertain as to their ancestry, both failed at school (Hitler had to repeat a grade),[148] both were vegetarians, and both possessed a furious will to power and despotism and pomposity and hugeness—one of Wagner's choral works required 1,200 male voices and an orchestra of 100; Hitler's was monolithic with respect to his architectural pieces.[149]

Alexander the Great. Alexander the Great, the youthful Greek conqueror of the ancient world, was tremendously admired by Hitler and historians use that admiration to claim that he viewed himself as a modern-day Alexander, as he certainly, in fact, did.

Frederick the Great. Frederick the Great, the "first servant of the state," was one of Hitler's heroes for having brought so much glory to Germany in both the arts and on the battlefield. He was also an icon of the kind of leadership principles that Hitler sought to emulate.[150] When confronted with opposition to some of his more ambitious building projects Hitler would cite Frederick as having built the beautiful (though rather modest by standards of his time) Sans Souci Summer Palace without regard to cost. Historians often point out that toward the end of World War II, the death of U.S. President Roosevelt was momentarily grasped by Hitler as directly analogous to Frederick's salvation during the Seven Years War (1756–1763) upon the death of Russia's Elizabeth.

King Ludwig II. The Mad King Ludwig II of Bavaria is used as a way of illustrating the craziness of Hitler's grand building projects. Yet Hitler himself, from time to time, made reference to Ludwig as a way of defeating critics of his projects: Ludwig's castle building was still paying huge dividends to the Bavarian people as tourists flocked there to view such places as the fairy-tale castle, Neuschwanstein, the castle that served as a model for the iconic Cinderella Castle of Walt Disney theme parks. He also built the beautiful Herrenchiemsee, Linderhof, and the Residenzy Palace in Munich. Moreover, like Hitler, King Ludwig, too, was an excessive devotee of Richard Wagner, and a "protector of the arts."[151]

Nero. Nero is often invoked to paint Hitler as egomaniacal. Some of his building plans are compared to the notorious Golden House of Nero. The Nero analogy is apt in comparing his obsession with examining models of his building projects even after it had become obvious that the war was lost. Like Nero, he figuratively fiddled as his capital was aflame. Like Hitler, Nero conceived of himself as an artist. As everyone knows, Nero purportedly exclaimed just before his death, "What an artist dies in me!" Nero also began the first Roman-Jewish War.

Woton. Shirer has Hitler representing Wagner's version of the pantheistic Norse god Woton as Berlin undergoes the flames of destruction.[152] In this analogy, Berlin is to be Hitler's funeral pyre.

Bismarck. Otto von Bismarck, an owner of Hitler's great admiration, is sometimes used as a way of highlighting Hitler's conquest of new Germanic territories. Also, like Bismarck, Hitler thought of himself as a fearless Iron Chancellor who united the German people, as did Bismarck. Still more in keeping with the Bismarck analogy, Bismarck's Germany (i.e., Prussia) was the weakest of the five major European powers when he took office, as was unified Germany when Hitler assumed power. Both individuals managed to raise Germany to a position of awesome power.

Satan. Satan is not infrequently used to represent the essence of Hitler and his Holocaust.

Martin Luther. Martin Luther's extreme rhetoric and equally extreme anti-Semitism, as well as his belief in the duty of citizens toward their government, is called upon from time to time to illustrate various fundamentals of Hitler's being. Hitler revered Luther for his genius and courage and for having led Germany away from Catholicism and into the arms of German nationalism.[153]

Lueger, Schönerer. Vienna Mayor Karl Lueger and Vienna's Pan-Germanist George Ritter von Schönerer are invariably cited as two individuals from whom Hitler took a great many political lessons. Certain aspects of his life as a political are seen as having been molded by his studies of Lueger and Schönerer and consciously employed by him in later years. Von Schönerer, like Hitler, was also a fanatical Pan-Germanist. Moreover, Schönerer's concern for German peasants, artisans, and shopkeepers, was, like Hitler's own, "manifestly heartfelt."[154]

"Young Werther." Goethe's "Young Werther" (from *The Sorrows of Young Werther)* is sometimes called on to represent Hitler's romanticism or his regard for the German literary period known as *Sturm und Drang*.[*] Analogies with such characters as Young Werther also serve to emphasize the anti-Enlightenment, irrational, romantic side of Hitler.

---

[*] ***Sturm und Drang*** (the conventional translation is "storm and stress"; a more literal translation, however, might be storm and urge, storm and longing, storm and drive, or storm and impulse) is the name of a movement in German literature and music taking place from the late 1760s through the early 1780s in which individual subjectivity and, in particular, extremes of emotion were given free expression in response to the confines of rationalism imposed by the Enlightenment and associated *aesthetic* movements. Source: http://en.wikipedia.org/wiki/Sturm_und_Drang

Machiavelli. Niccolò Machiavelli's name is sometimes further and unjustly sullied by applying the Machiavellian appellation to Hitler. Those wanting to represent Hitler as ruthless, deceitful, and lusting for power by any means employ the Machiavellian shorthand. On the other hand, Hitler was indeed very much like Machiavelli in that he, too, identified unifying themes related to politics and power. He discovered and described rational political truths. Political realism, Realpolitiks, was characteristic of both men, and both understood the need for the exercise of brute force when necessary. The comparison also holds true when one considers that both Hitler and Machiavelli understood that it was far better to be loved by the people than either hated or feared by them. Similarly, both Machiavelli and Hitler subscribed to the idea that a leader should strive to present himself as being merciful and humane, frank and religious, but should only seem so; the leader must only seem to have these qualities because he must also, from time to time, act in opposition to such belief systems. There are a number of other parallels between Hitler and the qualities of leadership espoused by Machiavelli.

Gaius Marius. Hitler sometimes compared himself to Gaius Marius, the Roman general and representative of commoners in opposition to fellow general Lucius Cornelius Sulla Felix. In that conflict, Sulla prevailed. Hitler claimed that he, as Marius, would triumph the next time out. Hitler was several times fatefully wrong.

Paladin, Tribune, Nemesis. Sometimes Hitler is cited as a deranged Paladin, a Tribune, or Nemesis.

As it happens, there were bits and pieces of Hitler that were indeed representative of all of the above and more, such as Napoleon and Julius Caesar. For all the erudition of the great historians, however, one of Hitler's personal secretaries, Christa Schroeder, a lady who fundamentally admired him, described him about as well as can be: "There was not just one Hitler," said she, "but several Hitlers in one person. He was a mixture of lies and truth, of faithfulness and violence, of simplicity and luxury, of kindliness and brutality, of mysticism and reality, of the artist and the barbarian."[155] "His religion," said Schroeder, "was the Law of Nature."[156] Schroeder had him pegged.

Fiendish Qualities

Hitler's fiendish qualities are well-known to all. He is typically portrayed as a brooding, antisocial loner. He yells at everyone, pounds his fist again and again. He is totally bereft of social skills.

On the whole, establishment historians represent Hitler as almost entirely evil, and his rise to power as having only been enabled by the lockstep, rabid anti-Semitism of Germans; this aspect of historiography is especially prevalent in histories that target mass audiences—it is the case, regretfully for the sake of truth, that the mass of our people do indeed learn their history from Stephen Spielberg and his epigones, and we learn our contemporary history and sociology from an exceedingly biased news media.

The 2003 made-for-TV movie, *Hitler: The Rise of Evil*, is illustrative of the movie genre related to Hitler. The script was written by John Pielmeier and G. Ross Parker. It was directed by Christian Duguay. It stars Robert Carlyle. Both the movie and many of its participants won wide acclaim and a number of prestigious awards. It is represented on Web sites as "Biography, Drama, History." Drama it might be, biography and history it most certainly is not.

There is hardly a single thing in the movie that is representative of the actual Hitler. Every possible device is used to portray Hitler as entirely demented: spittle runs from his mouth, cake crumbs stick to his lips and moustache, he eats in such a way that the food is visible in his mouth. He cannot even consume a glass of water without it running out of his mouth and down his chin. Upon learning of his mother's breast cancer his only comment is that "She'll do anything to ruin my career!" He whips his dog, shouts at everyone, and points his pistol at cowering women as well as an image of himself in a mirror. Facing a momentary defeat, he retires to his bedroom where he assumes a fetal position. His relations with his flighty niece, Geli Raubal, are presented as incestuous, which is preposterous and entirely based on groundless psychohistorical speculation. He makes lurid, obsequious overtures to Helene Hanfstaengl, the wife of his friend and follower, Ernst

Hanfstaengl. These images, like so many others about Hitler, are entire falsifications. Hitler was devoted to his mother, and to his dog, too.* He treated women chivalrously. He was the protector of his niece, and he never made such a pass at Helene Hanfstaengl.[157]

The Jews in the movie are all entirely sympathetic characters: there is the kindly Jewish doctor, Dr. Edward Bloch, who treated Hitler's mother for cancer, a friendly adjutant during the war, and a few others. On the whole, though, Jews hardly exist. The constant object of Hitler's rhetorical hate are nowhere to be seen, Jews do nothing to earn naught but praise, while Hitler is depicted as entirely irrational and demonic. The dramatization of the fight for Munich after the Communist takeover there has Ernst Roehm (Röhm) killing people indiscriminately—there is nothing whatever about the Jewish leaders of the Marxist government that had done its own share of killing before the arrival of Roehm and the *freikorps*. The movie goes on in a similar vein until the credits appear. Several points are highlighted in the movie: Hitler was crazy, and the German people were not much better; they all seem to love a character who is clearly both demented and despicable; Jews are kindly and deserving of sympathy—they were all just standing around being good and patriotic and generous and humorous and helpful when rightist forces pounced on them. Save irrational anti-Semitism, there was no reason whatever for Hitler's attitude toward Jews.

Still another movie, *Hitler*, is entirely based on Hitler's supposed Oedipus complex. As one would expect from such a movie, it represents Hitler as a sexual deviate.

"For the last half-century," says author Frederic Spotts, "and for obvious reasons writers have written about Hitler the maniac."[158] "Describing him simply as a 'lunatic' or 'raving

---

* Hitler revered animals and therefore objected to hunting them for sport or table. Indeed, he became a vegetarian "out of a profound concern for animals." He even objected to cosmetics because they contained animal by-products. His regime instituted a host of laws for the protection of animals that were highly advanced for their time and remain in effect in Germany to this day. Src: "Adolf Hitler and Vegetarianism," Wikipedia, http://en.wikipedia.or/wiki/Adolf_Hitler_and_vegetarianism

maniac' obviates the need for an explanation—though it of course leaves open the key question: why a complex society would be prepared to follow someone who was mentally deranged, a 'pathological' case, into the abyss,"[159] says Kershaw. Unfortunately, the all-too-frequent means of overcoming the foregoing dilemma is to simply ascribe the answer to the supposedly pathologic German mentality or to Christian pathologies. It is established, respected historians who tell these tales. They know the truth, of course, but they publish the lie, and they do so "for obvious reasons."

It is too rarely acknowledged that Hitler had pleasant qualities, but, in fact, he did and serious historians (on the whole, Spotts, Toland, and now Tedor and Stolfi are illustrative) do make mention of them here and there (this chapter is written largely on the basis of various positive commentary by mainstream historians). In creating this book your author has examined a great many historical texts: those of the great authors and those of the novelists who purport to be writing history. Of all the texts examined, the one by R. H. S. Stolfi is by far the most objective and courageous. When one sees the all-too-common literary and cinematic depiction of Hitler as a wide-eyed, screaming, and expectorating madman, we are expected to fault the German people for having embraced him. To return to Kershaw's query, one must ask how it was that the German people could ever have permitted such a man to come to power. Here is the answer: the common depiction of Hitler is not what Hitler was.

Positive descriptions of Hitler are often discarded or derided out of hand. Author Frederic Spotts, for example, in contrast to his general willingness to allow that Hitler had *some* respectable qualities, asserts that a great deal of the anecdotal information provided by Hitler's friend, Kubizek, was bogus. Nevertheless, he explains that Kubizek was contacted in 1948 by the anti-Nazi leftist librarian of the provincial archive in Linz (Jetzinger). Kubizek offered up a stream of praiseworthy commentary on Hitler. The Kubizek commentary exasperated Jetzinger, who then broke off relations with him.[160] It happens that in 1948, it took a great deal of courage to utter anything positive about Hitler. It was not Kubizek who needed to be doubted, as explained above; it was, rather, all the former idolators who had by this time experienced a new, anti-Hitler revelation of sorts.

Still, as mentioned, there are here and there attempts at balance. Authentic historians almost uniformly acknowledge, for example, as even Hitler biographer Joachim Fest puts it, that Hitler "remained always the alert master of his emotions,"[161] which belies his popular depiction. He was very much like a theatrical stage manager: on occasions when he did employ shouts, rants, and physical gesticulations he nevertheless remained, as Fest emphasizes, entirely in control.[162] Hugh Trevor-Roper reminds us that Hitler was both a visionary and a revolutionary: "Hitler," says Roper, "had a brain."[163] We will highlight this and other such aspects of Hitler's person and character throughout this narrative.

The Real Hitler

Even the lowly members of Hitler's staff had it that he was a gracious, "congenial *gemütlich* host."[164] The Austrian historian Brigitte Hamann demonstrated a sizable bit of literary courage by saying in her book, *Hitler's Vienna*, that "It turns out that Hitler was sort of full of . . . small kindnesses."[165] She went on to point out that the father of Hitler's boyhood friend, August (Gustl) Kubizek, was happy that Gustl "had such a well-behaved and polite friend as Adolf."[166] He was a serious young man without even "a grain of the superficial, carefree idler in him."[167] He was both studious and inquisitive, and not without charm. That the young Adolf Hitler took the time during his youth to create outlines for an idealized German[168] state and to make sketches for a proposed opera house for Linz[169] were exemplary of his serious nature. The activities and deep concerns of the young Hitler are reflective of the intense National Socialism that he felt even then. Here was a young man, a teenager, who was on the brink of starvation. What does he do with his spare time? He genuinely frets over workers' settlements! Hitler was not all and forever bad. Moreover, as Stolfi emphasizes, "In his formative years, from 1889 through 1908, we see Hitler without a trace of evil in his conduct."[170] Let us here return momentarily to the assertion of Hugh Trevor-Roper cited in the Preface hereto, "I do not believe that men are born sour and inhuman: if they are so, it is because they have been made so; and what I look for in Hitler's . . . character is evidence not so much of the result as of the process of its formation." There were a too large number of things that made Hitler sour and inhuman—those things do not excuse his inhumanity, but they do help to explain them, however feebly.

Hitler could also be quite selfless and generous, even in the face of his own poverty. While still struggling in Vienna, he voluntarily surrendered the survivor's pension that he had received subsequent to the deaths of his father and mother. The money was then applied to the care of his sister, Paula.[171] In later years, he provided support for her until his death. Shortly after giving up his pension money he was so impoverished that he had no choice but to take to the streets where, as described by James Giblin and Robert Payne, "Wrapped in his overcoat, he slept at night in one or another of Vienna's parks. The next morning he lined up outside a Catholic convent, where the nuns distributed soup and bread to the homeless."[172] He did manage to make a little money here and there as he shoveled snow or carried bags at the train station, but such income was woefully inadequate for acquiring both food and lodging.

Hitler's gift to his sister goes to a larger issue as well: he was a proud, chivalrous young man. He would not let his sister suffer poverty, nor would he accept food gifts from his wartime comrades because he did not expect to be able to repay them. He similarly refused an offer of money from one of his officers. He could not give much to others, but he neither wanted nor could accept charity from his friends. He had a sense of honor about him in his youth that was both genuine and endearing, and it remained evident in his adulthood to all who were close to him.

Later in life, as reported by Hitler's personal SS valet, Heinz Linge, Hitler would occasionally inquire of Franz-Eher-Verlag, his publisher, as to the status of his account, which sometimes contained as much as 8 million marks. When the amount was sufficient he would send large sums of money to organizations such as Mother and Child, the National Socialist Welfare, or various youth institutions. Having done so, he would relax: "Now it's all gone again, and I have peace of mind." Linge goes on to say that Hitler's largesse stemmed from heartfelt sympathy for people who were short of cash due to no fault of their own.[173]

It was entirely in keeping with Hitler's nature that he would never let his chauffeur eat worse than himself.[174] At the Obersalzburg Berghof, the so-called Eagles Nest, and elsewhere, he insisted that everyone, from the lowest staff member to the highest dignitary, enjoy the same fare as that served in the main dining room.

Once, while on a road trip shortly after assuming power, he had his chauffeur stop to pick up a couple of young hitchhikers. He provided them with a ride and engaged them in friendly conversation as they rode. Upon reaching their destination, Hitler cautioned the two young men to keep themselves warm in the bad weather. One of them indicated that he could not: he was unemployed and could not afford even a hat. Hitler immediately removed his own trench coat and gave it to him.[175] Hitler was just full of "small kindnesses."

Hitler's secretary, Traudl Junge, said in the late 1990s that Hitler had been paternal and protective toward her, "a father figure." He was, said Junge, "a kindly old gentleman." She describes him in terms of his low voice and friendly smile, the flattering modulated tone of his voice, his courteous manner, and so on. "He wasn't at all frightening—there was a harmless, peaceful atmosphere" in his offices. In describing her first interview with *Der Führer* she recounts how he put her at ease saying, "My child, don't be nervous. You can't possibly make as many mistakes as me." She also describes how Hitler would sometimes take his meals with his secretarial staff and sit with them for tea in the evening. She describes, too, his devotion to his dog, Blondie, and it is apparent from her narrative that she, too, greatly admired the dog.[176]

Hitler was forever fussing and fretting over his secretarial staff, always doing his best to put them at ease. "Are you comfortable?" "Are you warm enough?" He was both kindly toward them and solicitous of their well-being. To Junge, he was the "best employer" she had ever had.[177] For her, Hitler was personable, paternal, and protective; a kindly old gentleman—a father figure who spoke in a low voice and with a friendly smile that provided a peaceful atmosphere for all.

Shortly after Junge had been hired, she was informed that she was to be brought to Hitler. She thought that she might have to undergo some form of swearing-in ceremony or provide evidence of some kind with respect to her loyalty to National Socialism. It was nothing of the kind. Hitler was simply concerned about her youth and naiveté in the presence of so many soldiers and other men on his staff. He had called for her to assure her that if any untoward comments, suggestions, or pestering were experienced by her, she was to inform him irrespective of the position or importance of the person doing such things. He would protect her.[178] Hitler was *that* kind of man.

Late in the war (1945), the wife of Heinz Linge was visiting Munich. Hitler inquired of Linge if she and his children had a place to stay while they were there. If she did not, he said, she and the children could use his flat in Berchtesgaden.[179] It was perhaps incidents of the kind just described that made Linge conclude that "Scarcely anyone could ward off his likeability and the charm he radiated."[180] It was still another example of his many small kindnesses.

Hitler was even courteous and considerate of his jailers at Landsberg prison in the aftermath of his Beer Hall Putsch. The prison warden, Leybold, described him as "easily content, modest and desirous to please. [He] [m]akes no demands, is quiet and sensible, serious, and quite without aggressiveness. . . ."[181] Referring to the World War I years, Max Amann, who served with Hitler in the war, described Hitler as "selfless in the extreme."[182]

Hitler's Vienna neighbors remembered him as the polite young gentleman that he was. His Munich landlady, Frau Popp, described him as "an Austrian charmer," a pleasant, helpful young man.[183] Herr Popp saw in Hitler "a personality whose abilities entitled him to the highest hopes."[184]

The waitress at a restaurant that he frequented was deeply impressed by him "because he was very reserved and quiet, and would read books, and seemed very serious." "She esteemed him so highly," reports Toland, "that she always gave 'Dolferl' an extra-large portion of *Mehlspeisen*, a meatless flour-based dish."[185]

Later in life, in 1932, the then German Chancellor Franz von Papen sent one of his closest aides (a close friend from the war years, Joachim von Ribbentrop) to see Hitler in order to sway him toward Papen. Papen hoped that with such support he might be able to better claim widespread support from the populace. Instead, due to Hitler's congeniality and his powers of persuasion, Ribbentrop switched sides and became a fervent disciple of Hitler. He soon thereafter joined the Nazi Party.[186]

Ernst Roehm, who would later head Hitler's infamous Brownshirts (the *Sturmalbteilung*—SA) was dispatched to the early Nazi Party (then the DAP—the German Workers' Party) as a spy. He quickly came under Hitler's thrall and for long thereafter was one of his most loyal and effective lieutenants. To many at that time, Hitler was a heck of a nice guy. We can be miffed or even angry that such was the case; nevertheless, it was so.

In his youth, Hitler spent a great deal of his time in libraries and museums and at the opera and reading. In Linz, he had book lending privileges at multiple libraries.

He fretted about social conditions. Even in his youth, he had utterly utopian ideas: he sincerely thought that "To keep the flame of life pure and unsullied would be the most important task of [the] 'ideal state,'"[187] that he envisioned. And he was a young man for whom what he preached he practiced: there was no difference.[188] He possessed a "fervent enthusiasm for everything that was beautiful and noble."[189] As recounted by Kubizek, not only did Hitler suffer with the disinherited and downtrodden, "he lived for them and devoted all this thoughts to the salvation of those people from distress and poverty."[190]

Hitler was a teetotaler and later in life a vegetarian. He abhorred cigarettes. Yet he was tolerant of others who smoked and consumed alcohol and meat products. He most often presented his arguments in a quiet, coherent, rational, and convincing way.

According to Field Marshal Wilhelm Keitel, "he had soft and touching emotions."[191] Joachim von Ribbentrop commented to psychologist Leon Goldensohn at Nuremberg that Hitler had a great personality. "How charming, diplomatic, magnetic he was," said Ribbentrop.[192] "Sometimes, . . ." said Ribbentrop, "when he spoke of all his plans, the good things he would do for the *Volk*, vacations, highways, new buildings, cultural advantages and so forth, tears would come to my eyes."[193] He genuinely loved animals and children, and they delighted in romps with him. Later, when he was an established political face, British Prime Minister David Lloyd George, a man who was among Germany's staunchest enemies during World War I, fawned over him for a time. Lloyd George said that "The old trust him, the young idolize him. It is the worship of a national hero who has served his country."[194] Sir Anthony Eden, who would later become Britain's prime minister, had fought opposite Hitler's regiment during World War I. When they met, Eden and Hitler reminisced about the war years—drawing each of their battle lines, they signed each other's drawings. Eden felt a comradeship with Hitler.

The great American automobile manufacturer Henry Ford and the celebrated aviator Charles Lindberg admired him; many other notables as well. Viscount Rothermere described his politeness and the way "he disarms men as well as women and can win both at any time with his conciliatory, pleasant smile." He is a man of rare culture, said Rothermere, "his knowledge of music, the arts and architecture is profound."[195]

The racist intellectual Houston Stewart Chamberlain* was enamored by him. Even Winston Churchill praisefully cited him with respect to his courage and perseverance in fighting for the German heart.[196] A good many other intellectuals expressed affection and confidence in him even before he became the Reich chancellor. "Even in defeat," says author Ron Rosenbaum, "he was

---

* Chamberlain, like Hitler, had resided in Vienna for a time (for the twenty years beginning in the year of Hitler's birth, 1889), and like Hitler, he was devoted to the music of Wagner. Also like Hitler, Chamberlain evolved many of his racialist ideas on the basis of his observations of the multinational Habsburg Empire.

a titan to those around him, a demigod, a celebrity beyond parallel."[197] Some saw him as a marvelous demagogue, fanatical but also logical. He was the political Elvis of his day. For Germany, he was Destiny walking.[198]

Truman Smith, a Yale man, West Pointer, and at the time an assistant military attaché in Berlin, was dispatched by the American ambassador to assess Hitler's qualities. Hitler, said Smith, was "the unmistakable soldier in mufti,"[199] thereby suggesting that he had qualities of both a brave man of the people and of a great intellect.

He was a fascinating personality. It was not his Caligari eyes, as historian Trevor-Roper and others assert that attracted people to him; it was the magnetism of his personality, his attention to people, his many small kindnesses, his *gemütlichkeit*.

His hold on the devotion of his people is perhaps best exemplified by what was said of him by Foreign Minister Joachim von Ribbentrop while he was awaiting trial at Nuremberg for war crimes: "Do you know," he said to G. M. Gilbert, a psychologist at the trial for Nazi war criminals, "even with all I know, if Hitler should come to me in this cell now, and say 'Do this!'—I would still do it.—Isn't it amazing? Can't you really feel the terrific magnetism of his personality?"[200] Field Marshal Keitel, even as he was being tried for his life at Nuremburg, remained an unabashed admirer of Hitler. It was, he said at Nuremburg, "impossible to prove any error on his part . . . I must admit openly that I was the pupil and not the master."[201] In a word, Hitler was charismatic. It was the charismatic person of Adolf Hitler along with the Nazi political program that brought the masses to his side. And while it is certainly true that the Nazi political program was entirely of Hitler's making, suggesting a Hitler-party equivalency, it is also true that other parties offered up similar policies and objectives without achieving anything even approximating the ultimate political success of Hitler. The Nazi Party was hugely dependent upon Hitler for its success.

The newspaper proprietor Viscount Rothermere described Hitler's "supreme intellect," comparing it to the renowned intellects of Lord Northcliffe and Lloyd George. Hitler's response to questions, claimed Rothermere, were "immediate," "brilliant," and "clear." Rothermere went on to say that:

> No words can describe his politeness; he disarms men as well as women and can win both at any time with his conciliatory, pleasant smile. He is a man of rare culture. His knowledge of music, the arts and architecture is profound.[202]

Throughout the 1920s while he was struggling for power, Hitler lived the life of a Spartan. He never attached any importance to the acquisition of wealth.[203] His Munich apartment was sublet from a widow, a bijous residence, scantily furnished. Its floors were covered with linoleum.[204] It is true that once in power he was ensconced in the grandeur of his position—but that was for the sake of his position, not himself.

Even while in power, he reveled in simple things and the simple life and his lifestyle served to further endear him to his people. He enjoyed walks with his dog and friends and wandering about the Bavarian countryside in lederhosen, the traditional leather shorts of that region. Being outdoors had tremendous appeal for him. "He was never so collected and concentrated as when walking."[205] Kubizek observed that "His love of nature was pronounced."[206] Walking among the trees in the forest was just the kind of thing that everyday German families also thoroughly enjoyed.

During World War II, a vast, lavish bunker was built on his behalf: he utterly rejected it. He would not live in opulence while his troops suffered in the field. The stark simplicity of the Berlin bunker in which he took his own life is also representative of his desire for relative modesty and rejection of the ostentatious in his personal living habits. Similarly, throughout the war he denied himself several of his most enjoyable pastimes such as viewing films or listening to his favorite operas. According to Linge, "Hitler was strong on rationing and even accepted that it applied to himself."[207] Hitler was a man of the people, and the people that he so admired were of a nature that fully deserved his admiration and devotion.

Linge recounts engaging moments during road trips with Hitler prior to 1939 as follows:

> Before 1939 Hitler liked to picnic near and far. I always accompanied him on these excursions and knew the Hitler we preferred: jovial, comradely and unproblematic. When a good spot was found the column of vehicles would halt. Rugs would be laid out in shady woods or on pastureland, beer and wine served. People ate and drank what they fancied, told anecdotes and jokes (in good taste), recounted experiences and made future plans.[208]

For people like Propaganda Minister Joseph Goebbels, and presumably for a great many others as well, Hitler's human qualities were especially endearing. He was the symbol of their hopes and was therefore regarded as a great man, but his true greatness, for them, lay in the simplicity and sincerity of his ways.[209]

"He was a kindly conversationalist, kissing the hands of ladies, a friendly uncle giving chocolate to children, a simple man of the people shaking the calloused hands of peasants and workers," says Ian Kershaw. "As many attested," Kershaw continues, "he could be charming—particularly to women—and was often witty and amusing."[210]

As Kershaw also points out:

> He was invariably correct and attentive in dealings with his secretaries, adjutants, and other attendants on his personal staff, who for the most part liked as well as respected him. He could be kind and thoughtful, as well as generous, in his choice of birthday and Christmas presents for his entourage.[211]

The foregoing portrayal of Hitler does not sit well with our images of him as presented by the popular media. Heinz Linge states the issue matter-of-factly:

> [W]e are kidding ourselves if we imagine that Hitler was some one-dimensional monster—all rolling eyes and rabid ranting. He was not . . . he could be affable to his staff, kiss his secretaries' hands and be kind to his dog. If this apparent humanity offends our preconceptions, then perhaps our preconceptions need altering.[212]

As suggested earlier, if we actually seek to learn from history then we must not look for a madman when we seek to discern our next potential dictator: we need to look, instead, for a charismatic charmer, a replica of the *real* Adolf Hitler.

Hitler had an excellent, "spongelike"[213] memory, and he read avidly. Historian John Toland says that Hitler's bookshelves overflowed with volumes related to the world war, German histories, an illustrated encyclopedia, *Vom Kriege* by von Clausewitz, a history of Frederic the Great, Houston Stewart Chamberlain's biography of composer Richard Wagner, the memoirs of Sven Hedin, a collection of heroic mythism, von Wartenburg's world history, and so on.[214] Kubizek says of the young Hitler, "Whenever he went out, there would usually be a book under his arm."[215] Kubizek also relates that Hitler "never read books simply to pass the time; it was a deadly earnest occupation."[216] Veritably all of the major Nazis imprisoned at Nuremberg after the war commented on the excellence of Hitler's memory. According to German Admiral Karl Donitz, "Hitler could remember things in a phenomenal sort of way. He had the ability to recall everything he had ever read."[217]

Several historians have attempted to record the authors and book titles read by Hitler. Taken in total, the list is simply exhausting. If he was interested in the subject matter he would read and assess all that he could on the subject.

Aided by his superb memory and innate intelligence, he was able to synthesize what he read and observed to arrive at rational conclusions and make assessments based on things he acquired from diverse sources. And it was just by way of such reading and observation that Hitler would objectively underpin his anti-Semitism.[218]

Hitler's blitzkrieg concept, claims Spotts, as awful and effective as it certainly was, "was in part the result of novel strategic concepts that historians credit Hitler with having grasped and supported against military orthodoxy."[219] We might also credit Hitler's ability to arrive at unique perspectives for his daring advance through the Ardennes Forest in 1944, the maneuver that initiated the Battle of the Bulge. As Fest has it, "Hitler's originality manifested itself in his ability to force heterogeneous elements together."[220] Intellectuals in his entourage such as Albert Speer, his minister of armaments during the war, as well as Dr. Joseph Goebbels, his minister of propaganda, and others were duly impressed by his grasp of both concepts and details and his sometimes uncanny ability to synthesize and provide fresh insights. Spotts quotes Hitler's finance minister as having claimed that Hitler was able to "recall statistical data about the most arcane topics with amazing precision." He could, said the finance minister, "get right to the heart of a problem, to draw concise conclusions from long discussions and to throw new light on a matter that had been the object of lengthy deliberation."[221]

The Battle of Fort Eben-Emael, which was part of the Battle for Belgium, the Netherlands, and ultimately France, highlights Hitler's ability to synthesize information and data from diverse sources, consider its application to current events, and to then devise ways and means to overcome obstacles. Measuring 200 by 400 yards, Fort Eben-Emael was the largest such defensive fort in existence at the time. It was protected on one side by a canal to its east and by minefields and 20-foot ditches on its landed sides. Its top and sides were composed of 5 foot thick reinforced concrete. Steel turrets atop the fort provided defenders with a 360-degree field of fire. Its weaponry included 120 mm and 75 mm artillery pieces, twelve 60 mm antitank guns, and twenty-five machine guns. It was also outfitted with searchlights. The fort was manned by a total of 2,000 Belgian troops, of which about half were actually present there at any particular time.

Because it was so very formidable, Fort Eben-Emael was thought to be impenetrable, but it was also essential that the Germans be able to overcome it in order to press their attack through Belgium, and then on to the Netherlands and France. Hitler personally intervened and mapped out the essentials for the concept of operation for the attack plan. Because Belgian early warning systems depended on sound rather than radar, Hitler chose to employ gliders rather than parachute troops to enable the attackers to better achieve surprise. He also conceived of a means to breach the defensive turrets—for this task he chose to employ special-shaped charges—explosives shaped much like a cone that invert their power and heat to send a very high-temperature molten blast of kinetic energy through many inches of steel. Shaped charges are commonplace today but were largely unknown at the outset of World War II.* On 10 May 1940 the attack commenced. It consisted of only seventy-eight German troops (a few hundred others attacked nearby bridges but only seventy-eight the fortress itself). German losses were six killed and twenty-one wounded. The Germans took over 1,000 prisoners. It was an astounding victory for the Germans, and it can be credited to Hitler himself, along with the immense courage and daring-do of the German soldier, that this tactical masterpiece employed such innovation to succeed.

Hitler's knowledge in matters of architecture was an expression of both his love for that field of endeavor and his internal skill set. His architectural knowledge was nothing short of amazing. "He knew by heart the size and ground plans of every significant building in the world" said his personal secretary, Christa Schroeder. "I observed important architects and experts being absolutely dumbfounded by his ability and his unanticipated

---

* The basic concept had been known since the late 1700s, but it was not until World War II that the modern, highly effective versions of the concept came into being.

imagination," she said.²²² Albert Speer, himself an architect, was no less stinting in his praise of Hitler's competence.

> "Hitler," said Speer, "repeatedly demonstrated a professional understanding of designs and could easily combine a floor plan and renderings into a three-dimensional concept. Despite all his other responsibilities, he was able to keep track of the work on as many as fifteen projects in various cities. . . . In [his] sketches he was able to draw outlines, cross sections and renderings to scale, demonstrating a good sense of architectural dynamics and proportions. . . . An architect could not have done better."²²³

Hitler was also masterful at applying his innate talent in political circles. He debated rationally and convincingly, winning agreement from British Prime Minister Neville Chamberlain on the righteousness of his cause with respect to Sudeten Germans and his desire to join together (*Anschluss*—annex) the countries of Germany and Austria. Chamberlain was not the cowardly appeaser of history's regard; he was a rational man who knew very well that Hitler had a solid case for his arguments in demanding the Sudetenland and later for the submission of the entirety of Czechoslovakia.

Hitler's stupendous effect on women was no less than it was on men. "In almost every city," says John Toland, "Hitler was besieged by adoring women";²²⁴ his manner toward them was one of inordinate politeness and chivalry. He adopted the practice of kissing the hands of ladies in a manner customary in former court circles, and then remaining habit of the officer-nobility class.²²⁵ Some historians demean Hitler's practice of hand-kissing saying that it made him look foolish. Still, it did seem to work for him, and for him, what worked is what mattered. The mother of Deputy Fuehrer Rudolf Hess's fiancée, Ilse Pröhl, was initially none too fond of either Hess or Hitler. As recounted by historian John Toland, upon meeting Hitler, all that changed. "My mother," said Ilse, "was totally unpolitical but as soon as she got back from Munich she joined the party—all because of the hand-kiss."²²⁶ His practice of hand-kissing had a similar effect on other women as well.

Ernst Hanfstaengl was a confidant and acolyte of Hitler throughout much of the 1920s and 1930s. He later defected and worked for Franklin Roosevelt's S-Project, which was created to provide revealing information about Nazi leaders. The two met and became close in the early 1920s when Hitler was still very much the vagabond, but he was apparently even then fully able to favorably impress his social betters. Hanfstaengl's father was a German aristocrat and respected publisher, his mother was from a prominent New England family. Ernst was a graduate of Harvard. His beautiful wife, Helene, was an American of German descent.[227] Hanfstaengl observed the reaction of women to Hitler's rhetoric, describing it as "devotional ecstasy."[228] After hearing Hitler some women went so far as to name his Nazi Party as the beneficiary in their wills.[229] Hitler, observed underling and governor-general of Poland, Hans Frank, had "an amazingly large number of women followers,"[230] as he most assuredly did.

During Hitler's trial stemming from his November 1923 Beer Hall Putsch, the assistant prosecutor reported that women bearing flowers for their idol filled the room while awaiting pronouncement of the sentence. Women purportedly even asked permission to bathe in his tub.[231] Journalist-historian William L. Shirer commented on the reaction of women as Hitler appeared on a balcony at a 1934 rally: "They look up at him as if he were a Messiah . . . I think many of the women would have swooned from excitement."[232] The term "messiah" takes on special meaning with respect to Hitler's putsch for it was at about this time that he indeed began to sound like something of a messiah with the holy mission of saving his beloved Germany from Marxist scoundrels, a point that he would announce during his trial in 1924. Prior to the Beer Hall Putsch, Hitler had seen himself as little more than a drummer boy in support of such people as General Erich Ludendorff. Infuriated by the petty implication that he had launched his putsch so that he might acquire a ministerial position in the new government, Hitler exploded: "I aimed from the first at something a thousand times higher than a minister. I wanted to become the destroyer of Marxism. I am going to achieve this task."[233] It was statement as to his messianic mission.

Upon hearing him at a rally in 1932, Leni Riefenstahl, who later directed the famous film *Triumph of the Will*, described the experience in glowing terms: "remarkable rhetorical ability," "a *Gesamtkunstwerk*, a total artwork," "a skilled [verbal or rhetorical] violinist,"[234] she said. Upon meeting Hitler early in 1933, Frau von Ribbentrop was immediately won to his side: "a marvelous man, a true gentleman," she confided to her diary.[235]

In the voting cycles between 1930 and 1933, women were Hitler's staunchest supporters.

Hitler's political oratory is, of course, well-known to all. Hanfstaengl, like many others, provided admiring commentary on Hitler's ability to influence and handle a crowd. In the early days of Hanfstaengl's relationship with him, he was taken by Hitler's "clear blue, guileless eyes."[236] He also shared the assessment of others in saying that "There was honesty, there was sincerity, there was suffering and dignity of mute entreaty" in the person of Adolf Hitler.[237] In observing Hitler's speech making he was especially taken with and commented on Hitler's masterful handling of hecklers. "Every so often," said Hanfstaengl, "someone would shout out an insult and he would calmly raise his right hand slightly as if catching a ball or fold his arms and spit out a brief rejoinder that would crush the heckler." Continuing, Hanfstaengl commented that:

> His technique resembled the thrusts and parries of a fencer, or the perfect balance of a tightrope-walker. Sometimes he reminded me of a skilled violinist, who, never coming to the end of his bow, always left just the faint anticipation of a tone—a thought spared the indelicacy of utterance.[238]

Hitler was something of both a born and studied politician. He was most at ease when engaged with small parties of friends but was, of course, also masterful in front of large assemblies.

He assiduously studied various forms of government and various government leaders. The governments of monarchs, Catholicism, Judaism, Communism, Fascism, and more came under his scrutiny. His studies covered the full range from the ancient historical to the contemporary. He also scrutinized and assessed political personalities for their strengths and weaknesses. His assessment of the German kaiser and the Junker ruling class was that they were frozen in time and attitude, that they clung to stubborn conservatism, and that they were both arrogant and unimaginative. "Recognition of its failures was one of the major perceptions Hitler drew from this period of German history,"[239] says Fest. Fest also points out that Hitler was free of the class prejudice and the self-centeredness that was so characteristic of the abdicating ruling class of Germany. Hitler thought only in terms of effects.[240]

As always, Hitler picked and chose from among the various strengths and weaknesses of institutions and individuals and synthesized his choosings into concepts, constructs, organizational structures, practices, principles, dogmas, and programs that would work for his objectives.

The innate political animal within Hitler made it easy and even inspiring for him to mix with crowds, shake hands, kiss babies, and sup with the common folk.[241] In this respect, he was much like his Viennese political idol Karl Lueger (discussed in some detail in the next chapter); also like Lueger, Hitler's personal popularity carried his political party—when Lueger died, votes for his party declined markedly. We cannot doubt that if Hitler had died any time prior to 1939 his Nazi Party would have faltered badly. Hitler invariably wrote his own speeches and even practiced the theatrical gestures by which he is so infamously portrayed in movies and historical newscasts. He was at once both a consummate actor and an equally consummate politician.

Establishment historians often emphasize Hitler's political dishonesty of one sort or another, such as his disregard for the Treaty of Versailles or his pledge to seek no further territorial gains after his acquisition of the Sudetenland and Czechoslovakia. Yet, it was actually the case that Hitler was particularly open in declaring his intentions. He openly proclaimed his intentions with respect to Lebensraum in the East, and even that once achieving power he would destroy the Weimar constitution and implement a dictatorship. He certainly made no secret of his disgust with the Treaty of Versailles and his determination to utterly discard it; indeed, it was the mainstay of his political rhetoric. He also made no secret of his intention to create a Pan-German union of various states and recover continental German territories lost at the end of World War I, including Danzig. He also promised to brutally crush the Communist Party of Germany and ban all political parties except his Nazis. There is hardly a politician in the history of the world who was so honest and transparent with respect to his intentions. Hitler was a man of many bad things, but he was not, on the whole, a liar. It was not that Hitler was a liar: it was rather that no one chose to believe his pronouncements. Even in the days and weeks leading up to his ascension to power, both opposition and neutral parties almost uniformly assumed that all of his radical rhetoric and writings would be abandoned once he actually took power. They predicted that he would tone down his speeches and make amends with his opponents. They did not understand the true believer devotion of Hitler to his ideas, his worldview.

*   *   *   *

A lot of what has been written about Hitler's abusiveness in dealing with others is nonsense. He fanatically believed in the goodness of his cause and therefore believed as well that eventually even his most ardent and strident opponents would one day see the way according to his own illumination. He reached out to various opponents, not so much because he *needed* them; it was rather because he *wanted* them; he wanted them to join with him in advancing the cause of Germany as he saw it. In Russia, the Marxist revolutionaries murdered their opponents wantonly. On the whole, Hitler charmed his opponents to his side but was likewise entirely willing to execute those he could not bring to his side and remained dangerous to him, his party, and his objectives—Roehm and various would-be assassins illustrate the point.

Hitler could also be tolerant beyond all expectation. His cantankerous chauffeur, Julius Schreck, refused to be overly impressed with the humbug homage paid to the führer. He would even openly mutter in Hitler's presence about the swell-headed party big shots . . . people who forget where they came from and so on. Hitler tolerated it all with mirth and equanimity. Upon the death of Schreck, Hitler placed a picture of him in his private office at Obersalzberg, side by side with one of his beloved mother.[242]

One of his bodyguards, Bruno Gesche, once openly and bitterly complained about the sorry state of the security services provided by elements of the SS. His boss, Heinrich Himmler, the leader of the SS, thereafter tried to have Gesche immediately demoted. Hitler protected Gesche, admiring his willingness to speak out even in the face of likely reprisal. Gesche had several times been fired from his day jobs due to his affiliation with the Nazis but remained loyal to the cause and rose through Nazi ranks. He was also a heavy drinker and therefore forever in serious trouble with Himmler. Himmler several times tried to relieve him from duty due to antics stemming from drinking bouts but Hitler again and again interceded to protect him. Himmler finally succeeded in firing Gesche; he was then sent to the eastern front where he distinguished himself in combat. After being wounded, Hitler repatriated and reinstated him. But Gesche was not a man who could easily be restrained. He again got into trouble due to his heavy drinking and Himmler was finally successful in getting rid of him, but not until 1944. Gesche survived the war and was only briefly interned by the U.S. after it. He died in 1985.

Upon discovering that his niece, Geli Raubal, was in love with and expected to marry his own companion, Emil Maurice, Hitler was initially outraged. He fired Maurice but later reinstated him.[243] Still later, when Himmler tried to have Maurice removed from the SS because he was partly Jewish (a Jewish grandfather), Hitler protected him.[244] Maurice had fought bravely at Hitler's side during a brutal fight with Marxists in a beer hall in early November

1921. In 1923, he was imprisoned with Hitler after the failed Beer Hall Putsch. Hitler could not forget such acts—his resulting loyalty toward Maurice and others like him could not be torn from his mind and soul.

Deputy Führer Rudolf Hess had performed in much the same manner as Maurice and also shared Hitler's imprisonment, and he, too, thereby won Hitler's lasting loyalty, even as Hess later slid perilously close to insanity. He shunted Hess to the outer environs of power as he realized that Hess was losing touch with reality, but he kept him in the government, if only in harmless posts. He was initially outraged when Hess flew to England and was captured, but he later softened and began speaking of Hess's courage in undertaking such a dangerous mission and commented to associates that his former aide and one-time second in line of succession had meant well.[245]

Hitler was also exceptionally tolerant in the face of known deficiencies of people in his entourage. Goering once complained that Hitler only saw what was good in people, that he could see the bad only if it was particularly obvious—Hitler was naïve about people.[246]

He tolerated the homosexuality of SA leader Ernst Roehm and even Roehm's opposition to his priorities with respect to the use and objectives of the SA, the infamous Brownshirts. Even after the "Night of the Long Knives" when he purged the SA, he genuinely anguished over the need to execute his old friend from the beer hall days.

He stood by Field Marshal Goering though he knew well before the end of World War II that Goering was drug dependent and little more than a bloated caricature of his former dashing and daring fighter pilot self.

In the early years of the NSDAP, Dietrich Eckart served as Hitler's supporter and mentor though he was known to be a morphine addict—anathema to a teetotaler like Hitler. Hitler, nevertheless, admired him for a host of other reasons. Hitler dedicated his second book, written in 1928, to the by then dead (1923) Eckart.

Throughout the 1920s, Hitler tolerated the aberrant liberal political views of Gregor Strasser, a man who was nearly Hitler's equal in popularity for some time but who was more inclined to want the socialism of the movement to dominate its nationalism. After a particularly heated exchange between Strasser and Hitler in 1926, an exchange won by Hitler, he was careful to not let the incident sour their relations—in the presence of others at the exchange he went over to Strasser and put his arm around his shoulders in a gesture of friendship, an act that favorably impressed everyone present.[247] Strasser was murdered, along with many others, during the Night of the Long Knives (June 30, 1934)—Hitler could be tolerant, and he could just as well be intolerant.

Joseph Goebbels was, in the fashion of Strasser, far more radically socialistic than Hitler. Hitler worked on him for days to bring him to his side, and he did so without threats or abuse; he won him over with calm logic and what Michael Fitzgerald called a "barrage of charm."[248] Goebbels finally succumbed; he experienced his Damascus moment and was thereafter Hitler's most devoted apostle, even committing suicide with him in the Berlin bunker in April 1945.

Hjalmar Schacht, Hitler's minister of economics, had been a founding member of the pro-Weimar and largely Jewish DDP. Sepp Dietrich, the leader of the Waffen-SS, had been the chairman of one of the Marxist Soldiers' Councils in November 1918. Hitler's chauffeur, Julius Schreck, had served in Germany's Red Army at the end of April 1919. Hermann Esser, an early Hitler supporter, had been a journalist for the SPD. Hitler embraced the lot of them.

Hitler's dedication to Albert Speer did not waver even when Speer disobeyed his direct order to destroy the German infrastructure in the face of the Allied advance.

His attachment to Italy's Benito Mussolini stemmed from the latter's support as Hitler sought to unify Austria and Germany, and it never wavered thereafter. He even undertook a daring and successful rescue of Mussolini after his arrest by the Italian king in

1943. His *Table Talk*[*] was full of encomium by him of individual supporters and contributors to himself and his Nazi cause.

At a group level there is the example of what Hitler did for his earliest supporters, the farmers. German farms and other possessions were being seized all over the country as banks failed and the unfortunate farmers, crushed by the Depression, were unable to meet interest payments. Hitler placed a ban on land speculation, provided debt relief to peasants, and low-interest loans to aid their recovery, and he infuriated creditors by making it illegal for them to foreclose on farms due to indebtedness. The totality of his actions saved the German farmer from extinction. Historian Michael Fitzgerald credits the combination of land security, debt relief, and the readily available low-interest loans as having "transformed the future of the German farmers overnight."[249] Hitler revered these people.

Even a few Jews won Hitler's grudging admiration: musical conductor Gustav Mahler and film and theater director Max Reinhardt were among them. "He was not always impeccably doctrinaire in his personal treatment of artists who were Jewish or partly Jewish," said Goebbels in one of his interminable diary entries. "The opera singer Margarete Slezak, despite Jewish grandparents, was such a favourite that he promoted her career at the German Opera in Berlin after 1933 and often invited her to official receptions at the chancellery."[250] Hitler also liked the works of the partly Jewish Johann Strauss.[251]

There is still another extraordinary example of Hitler's tolerance. Johann Georg Elser tried to assassinate Hitler in 1939 by planting a sizeable bomb of his own making at the Bügerbräukeller where Hitler was to speak to the party faithful. Several Nazis were killed and dozens were wounded. "Elser's background as an excellent worker, and 'artistic carpenter,' sociability, and double-bass musician intrigued Hitler," said his aide-de-camp, Heinz Linge. Hitler prevented Himmler from executing Elser. He instead

---

[*] Trevor-Roper, Hugh. *Hitler's Table Talk, 1941–1944.* (New York, Enigma Books, 2000.)

instructed him to provide the would-be assassin with a workshop in a prison concentration camp. Hitler purportedly claimed that Elser's abilities could be useful to the war effort, which was, of course, preposterous. Linge had it that the claim was an excuse: the truth, according to Linge's assessment, was that Hitler admired Elser's "quiet dedication and consistency." He was a man who Hitler would like to have seen active in his SA or his SS.[252] Establishment historians say that he was "executed" five years later. If we can believe such claims we must think that the Nazis were exceedingly indecisive.

Hitler also had a sense of humor and wit. Humor was hardly a defining feature of his personality, but it did exist, though his use of it has been very much muted in historical accounts of his rhetoric. While serving in the trenches of World War I, he would occasionally delight his soldier buddies by drawing cartoons of the men and their life. He was also known to amuse his friends with his mimicry of various officers who were not liked. He would also do such things as read "housekeeping" regulations in a deadpan manner—such regulations almost require humor given the circumstances of mud and filth under which they were supposedly to be applied. His soldier friends laughed and delighted in it all.

On one occasion he and his fellows humorously tricked one of their friends. The man had shot a rabbit that he then wrapped to take home with him as he was about to go on furlough. Hitler and his buddies switched the rabbit with pieces of rubble. The victim of the prank was provided with two sketches done by Hitler: one showed the hapless victim opening the rabbitless package, the other showed his friends eating the rabbit at the front.[253]

During the war Hitler sometimes drew humorous sketches to amuse himself and his friends. One such sketch, *On the Way to Cannes*, shows the ruins of war as he and his friends jauntily march through the rain. One viewer comments that the sketch was "comic, bold, full of life and movement";[254] that same observer describes the self-portrait that Hitler created as illustrative of his gift for caricature and "admirably conveys the jaunty, irascible, somewhat aloof quality of the man as he was known to his fellow soldiers"[255]—a description that is wholly out of step with common depictions of him as a mean, angry, gesticulating, and brooding misfit.

On road trips Hitler would sometimes entertain his guests with his conviviality and wit, and especially with impersonations and improvisations of various other Nazis such as Rosenberg, the overly committed volkist propagandist and leader of the Nazi cultural bureaucracy; he even mocked himself to get a laugh from time to time. Hanfstaengl had it that Hitler's comedic routines sometimes had the party in tears of laughter.[256] During one of his many *Table Talk* sessions he once deadpanned that "In principle, I'd be inclined to permit dueling between priests and between lawyers."[257] Hitler could be a witty guy, if only sardonically.

On at least one occasion his humor extended to the political arena as well. The Hindenburg political camp devised the 1932 election campaign theme: "He hath kept faith with you, be ye faithful unto him."[258] Historian John Toland points out that Hitler's clever thematic response was made in jest: "Honor Hindenburg: Vote for Hitler."

Hitler sometimes made light of the idiosyncrasies of senior members of his entourage. Field Marshal Goering, for example, was notoriously known for his penchant to award medals to himself. Hitler once humorously played with that personality quirk saying that Goering had once been found waving a baton over his underwear in his bedroom. His wife inquired as to what he was doing: "I am promoting my underpants to OVERpants," Hitler joked.[259]

Goebbels, too, was something of a droll humorist. He was a quick wit and often made good use of humor in his propaganda both before and after the rise of Hitler. During one of his early speeches he was interrupted: "'Capitalist swine!' yelled a heckler. 'Here is my purse,' retorted Goebbels, 'You show me yours. The one who has the most is the capitalist swine!' The miners and textile workers roared with laughter and allowed him to speak on."[260]

*   *   *   *

For about the first half of his period in power Hitler was exceedingly successful. He saved Europe from Bolshevism, unified the German people, reoccupied the Rhineland, engineered the annexation of Austria, recovered the Germans of the Sudetenland, eliminated class divisions (replacing them with racial ones, to be sure), restored and expanded the ruined economy even in the face of both the Depression and a potentially devastating worldwide Jewish boycott of German goods, set about doing many worthy building projects, restored Germany's place as a great power in the diplomatic world, commenced building the autobahns, participated in the design of the Volkswagen, constructed housing and vacation spas for workers, greatly improved worker benefits, outlawed child labor, and all but eliminated corruption in public and business life.

He improved health care for all, but especially for women. Infant mortality rates were significantly reduced, and birth rates were significantly increased. He provided interest-free loans for newlyweds and families as well as subsidized housing for them—each with its own garden. He also made significant improvements in the realm of education, adding, for example, two-thirds more kindergartens. A classless form of achievement was emphasized with the slogan "[W]e bring one to respect the spade, another to respect the compass or the pen."[261]

It is sometimes claimed that when Hitler achieved power he had no real plan for the accomplishment of his many promises and especially those concerning the economy. Still, from the very outset of his chancellorship he set upon implementing a flurry of both cultural and economic reforms that all met their objectives. Richard Tedor, in his excellent book, *Hitler's Revolution*, discusses in some detail many of the various reforms implemented by Hitler starting as early as April 1933. In just 1933, he enacted the Labor Procurement Law, the Building Repair Law, and the Motor Vehicle Tax Law, all of which served to stimulate the economy. By September of that year he had commenced work on the autobahns. Tedor records the 1938 comments of the Soviet diplomat Kristyan Rakovsky, a man schooled in the intricacies of Wall Street and economics in general:

Hitler, this uneducated ordinary man, has out of natural intuition and even despite the opposition of the technician Schacht, created an especially dangerous economic system. An illiterate in the theory of economics driven only by necessity, he has cut out international as well as private high finance. Hitler possesses almost no gold, and so he can't endeavor to make it a basis for currency. Since the only available collateral for his money is the technical aptitude and great industriousness of the German people, technology and labor became his 'gold'. . . . As you know, like magic it's eliminated all unemployment for more than six million skilled employees and laborers.[262]

Hitler was not an economist and had no interest whatever in the machinations of economic theory, but he was, nevertheless, able to brilliantly receive and wisely assess the potential success of the various economic proposals put to him and to invariably select the correct one. Germany was very soon on the march again economically while all other nations affected by the Depression wallowed in economic despair.

*   *   *   *   *

When Hitler's army "marched into Austria," as historians like to put it, they did so with the overwhelming support and ecstatic enthusiasm of the people, both German and Austrian.* Their march was spearheaded by a marching band. The troops were pelted with flowers. Hitler entered the country standing erect in an open car and to the cheers of the multitude.[263] Austria and Germany had previously (1919)[264] tried to unite but were prohibited from doing

---

* Much earlier, in 1919, the Austrian parliament voted overwhelmingly to join with Germany. There was but one dissenting vote, and it was cast by a Jew, Robert Sticker of the Jewish National Party (JnP). The vote was discarded by the victorious Allies. President Wilson's promise of self-determination was not to be applicable to Germany and her people.

ABOUT HITLER

so by the victors of World War I. In a special election on April 10, 1938, 99.02 percent of the Germans and 99.73 percent of the Austrians voted in favor of the union that was ultimately accomplished by the march into Austria.[265] Hitler was greeted by a crowd of 100,000 in Linz. In Vienna, people cheered themselves hoarse. The march into Austria was not one of fear, conquest, or invasion; for both Germans and Austrians it was glorious. And why not? It was a time after which Hitler had already done so much seemingly good things on behalf of his people.

Google	URL
Images of Hitler's march into Austria	https://www.google.com/search?q=Images+Hitler's+march+into+Austria&rlz=1T4GZAB_enUS449US538&tbm=isch&tbo=u&source=univ&sa=X&ei=CLrcU8fVGMGeyATDnIKACw&ved=0CB4QsAQ&biw=1008&bih=523 8/2/14

As early as 1936, the high unemployment rate was turned into a labor shortage in some sectors of the German economy; by 1938, the unemployment issue had been entirely overcome. This, we should be reminded, was while the U.S. and most other countries were still trying to recover from the Depression; U.S. unemployment was at or above 14 percent throughout the 1930s[266] and did not recover until we went to a war economy. It should be noted, too, that it was exemplary of Hitler's innovativeness that he began employing Keynesian economic theory even before Keynes published his magnum opus, the *General Theory of Employment, Interest and Money*, in 1936. As stated by Avraham Barkai in his book, *Nazi Economics, Ideology, Theory, and Policy*:

> The historical truth is that the Nazis and the economists attached to their movement were almost the only figures in the pre-1933 political arena to present genuine employment projects to be financed by unconventional measures and to realize these projects successfully after assuming power.[267]

Taxes were lowered on large families, workers' wages, and productivity skyrocketed as did industrial production. Paid holidays were instituted, as was Social Security. Inexpensive ocean cruises proliferated for common workers and families on holiday. German workers were able to take their families on a one-week holiday for a pittance: 12 to 16 marks (some have it that it was 60 marks), and that included fares, lodging, and entertainment. National income rose from 41 billion marks to 56 billion. German trade prospered. Deficits of all kinds all but disappeared.[268] Germans enjoyed vast expansions in available housing, automobile ownership, and medical care. Job security, workplace safety, vacation time, and pensions were all vastly improved—and all of this while employer-employee relations were simultaneously made harmonious.

Importantly, Hitler also reinvigorated Germanesque culture. Quite understandably, there was nary a peep of opposition from the populace as the likes of Beethoven and other German icons were returned to prominence at the expense of the modernists, the avant-garde. Indeed, while the Nazis appropriated Beethoven's music for party rituals, they also sponsored concerts, festivals, and radio programs that were thoroughly enjoyed and embraced by the masses. The internationally renowned Beethoven Cycle that was first broadcast in January 1934 serves as but one example. Author Richard A. Etlin points out that:

> By banning so-called degenerate music (jazz, swing, atonal music, and music by Jews, "Negroes," and Bolsheviks)[*] and by cultivating "pure" German music by composers like Beethoven, Mozart and Wagner, the Party . . . [fashioned] itself as the legitimate heir, if not the savior, of Germany's rich cultural legacy.[269]

Perhaps most importantly, though, Hitler moved souls. He inspired devotion. He provided incentives for sacrifice. "All misery

---

[*] In actual fact, Hitler and his Nazis did not quite ban what they thought of as degenerate music, but they did discourage its consumption by the masses and did ban it from all public functions.

of body was . . . exchanged for work, bread, and a good livelihood. . . ." says historian Otto Friedrich.[270]

> Men's spirits changed. Early in his reign a wild national jubilation broke out. Banners, garlands, testimonials, laudatory telegrams, worshipful orations, changes of street names became as commonplace as parades and demonstrations. The glorious sensation of a new fraternity overwhelmed all groups and classes . . . all of them suddenly learned what seemed to be the greatest discovery of the century—that they were comrades of one race, one fellowship, one "*Volksgenossen*."[271]

Let us not be even a little surprised that the German people adored Adolf Hitler, and that that adoration had nothing whatever to do with his anti-Semitism—it had everything to do with his magnetic personality and even more with his stupendous accomplishments. "Indeed," as historian Anthony Nicholls observes, "If a party leader were only to be judged by the extent to which he carried out his promises, Hitler would have to be put in the highest class."[272] If Nixon had done as much we would today all be singing his praises, Watergate forgiven. The whole of Hitler's chancellorship was correctly and succinctly characterized by Youth Leader Baldur von Shirach thusly: "Before 1934 he was *menschlich* [human]; from 1934 to 1938 he was *übermenschlich* [superhuman]; from 1938 on he was *unmenschlich* [inhuman] and a tyrant."[273]

As Joachim Fest observes, "If Hitler had succumbed to an assassination or an accident at the end of 1938, few would hesitate to call him one of the greatest of German statesmen, the consummator of Germany's history."[274] Given the successes of the Hitler regime up to that point, it could not have been otherwise.

In 1936, Hitler, as promised at the outset of his regime, submitted himself and his policies to a referendum by the people. Nearly every qualified voter participated. Hitler and his party won 98.8 percent of the vote, and there is no good reason to think that the results were anything other than what was entirely expected and heartfelt by the populace. By that time the entirety of the people adored him; they were understandably in awe of him and his *good* deeds. There was, of course, only one party by that time, the Nazi one. The same applied to the Soviet Union. We must wonder what the vote might have been if such a referendum had also been offered in the Soviet Union three years after the Bolsheviks took power. Such a vote could never have taken place in the Soviet Union, of course, but had it been possible, we can readily presume that the populace would have vehemently chased out that government due to its many atrocities. Not so, the Germans. The Germans were experiencing a national renewal, and they loved every aspect of it. The vote for the Nazis was heartfelt and quite understandable given the times, the turmoil, and the prospects for the future.

Hitler's emphasis on the importance of mother and child along with morality and general family values won him the unbending devotion of women. With socially progressive influences removed from the cultural milieu, families were able to return to the theater to enjoy films and concerts, operas and operettas. Germany was on the move. And it was happy as it had never been before; it was deliriously so.

In his book, *Inside the Third Reich,* Albert Speer relates a story of his travels with Hitler that exemplifies the happiness that people felt toward him. Townspeople stopped Hitler's car so they could savor a moment with him. They did everything they could to delay him for as long as possible. "Slowly, under a rain of flowers, we reached the medieval gate. Juveniles closed it before our eyes; children climbed on the running boards of the car. Hitler had to give autographs. Only then would they open the gate. They laughed, and Hitler laughed with them."[275] "This enormous popularity," says Speer, "was only too easy to understand. The public credited Hitler and no one else with the achievements in economics and foreign policy of the period. They more and more regarded him as the leader who had made a reality of their deeply rooted longings for a powerful, proud, united Germany."[276]

Herman Goering, Hitler's second in command, while imprisoned after the war at Nuremberg, commented to Speer: "At the moment the Germans won't admit it, but of course they know that they were never so well off as under Hitler."[277] Presumably, Goering was referring to the prewar years. We dislike the source of that observation, and dislike its truth even more. Still, it was both unquestionably and justifiably so.

It mattered not a jot what other factors in the world contributed to Hitler's astounding success (such as the beginning of the end of the Depression); to his people he was a miracle worker.

Economists cite the worldwide economic recovery as a prominent stroke of luck that enabled Hitler to succeed in the early years of his reign, and they are undoubtedly partially correct in their assessment. Still, it also needs to be recognized that Hitler faced enormous obstacles during his early years in power: Germany was financially destitute, there were threats of invasion by its neighbors and threats of internal revolution by the Communists, and the worldwide boycott of German goods was potentially devastating. Hitler and his countrymen overcame it all. It needs to be recognized as well that the recovery of the German spirit, of its confidence, was also of profound import. To the extent that consumer confidence matters in a national economy—and it matters immensely—it was Hitler who provided it. He also employed remarkable innovations to overcome problems of the day. For example, because foreign capital was so short due to the Jewish-led worldwide boycott of German goods, he employed a bartering system that enabled him to directly exchange finished goods of Germany for critically needed raw materials from various sources and thus obviated the need for gold reserves or foreign capital to back the German currency. Presented with myriad obstacles, he consistently innovated to overcome them—he figuratively forced his way through every trench and vaulted every obstacle.

Hitler had won the battle for the German heart. He boasted at one point that "In five years we have transformed a people who were humiliated and powerless because of their internal disruption and uncertainty, into a national body, politically united and imbued with the strongest self-confidence and proud assurance." By 1938, he was able to say with complete truthfulness that "the world around us suffers from the anxiety which the unemployment of millions brings with it. In Germany we begin to be anxious because we have not enough workmen."[278] These were hardly idle boasts; if anything, they were self-effacing. He had at that point seemingly done *so much good*! Moreover, he achieved these vast accomplishments without resorting to a war economy—the charge of his having done so is fallacious. His armaments buildup did not begin in earnest until the late 1930s. In support of this point it should be remembered that it is broadly acknowledged that when Hitler remilitarized the Rhineland in 1936 his forces were still so pitifully weak that they could easily have been overcome if France had had the will to eject them. The same can be said of his takeover of the Sudetenland in October of 1938. When war broke out in 1939, the country was still without a single heavy bomber. The cavalry of the day was still too largely of the horseback kind.

Hitler diminished or did away with the most licentious cabarets, with jazz, and with the swill that we now embrace as great art. He reenergized the German people. It can be said that rejuvenation of the German people was an evil all by itself. It was not. The Germans of that time were most assuredly not the *Willing Executioners* of Goldhagen's account of things.

Romanticism, Volksgeist, and Modernity

The dominant personal characteristics of Adolf Hitler—his stereotypes—were related to his intense nationalism and, of course, his equally intense anti-Semitism. His nationalism, in turn, derived in part from the romantic spirit that he so emphatically embraced. Romanticism has ancient roots but was revitalized toward the end of the eighteenth century and produced a movement from which our current understanding of the term derives. The movement stemmed largely from its dissatisfaction with the Enlightenment, which emphasized rationality and the scientific method. The romantic movement emphasized emotion and an affinity for nature, heroism, the mysteries of the soul and the individual, and faith in the great men. The movement's icons stemmed from such sources as Greek tragedies, ancient gods, great battles, and national personalities. The belief in individual genius and individual creations and acts as the force behind epic events were also characteristic of the movement[279]—beliefs that were hailed by Immanuel Kant, who had written that a genius "was naturally endowed with the talent that gives the rule to art."[280] It was by way of such thought processes that Ludwig van Beethoven became *the* symbol of romantics; but the same processes were the ones that also included such people as Goethe, Schiller, Wagner, and other leading lights of the movement.

Hitler was a romantic through and through. Like so many others, including religious believers, he picked and chose aspects of the belief system that most suited his personal being and rejected others. Thus, he could be either an enlightened modernist or a medievalist romantic depending upon circumstance. Like the romantics, he believed that art should hold a central position in society, much as it had in the great city-states of ancient Greece,[281] but he could be decidedly unromantic with respect to such matters as the value and exploitation of industrialization. He ardently and romantically believed in the mystical volk—a term that is more complex than its common translation as "nation" or "people." In German, the term carries with it a sense of community bond based on blood and soil. World War I reinforced the commitment of rightist elements to their volk: "the German notion of *Volk* underwent a postwar inflation no less dramatic and no less portentous than that of the German currency" says author Anthony Kauders[282]—and there was no one who experienced that inflation more so than Adolf Hitler.

The German volk is a romantic notion. It is akin to what a good many American Southerners feel for their land, their kin, and their fellow Southerners. It has a connection with the people and with blood and with soil and with nature and with being that is lost in translation to English. And let us not be too critical of Hitler and Germans for the veneration of their volk; the nascent Zionists of that period were every bit as radical as the Germans with respect to Jews and their culture, their traditions, their ardent racism, and Eretz Yisrael—the one group was no better nor worse than the other in this vein.

Romanticism glorified the historical past and its volk as exemplified by writers such as Johann Gottfried von Herder, August Wilhelm von Schlegel, Johann Gottlieb Fichte, Friedrich Melchior Grimm, Guido von List, Ernst Arndt, and Friedrich Jahn, all of whom in their way promoted an exalted notion of German people and claimed that Jews could never be full-fledged constituencies of that people. Von Herder, for example, who is credited with developing the concept of *Volksgeist*, or spirit of the people, "saw a deep-seated corruption in the Jews of his day, deriving from their long-standing status as peddlers, merchants, and moneylenders,"[283] says Lindemann. Von Herder, like his Jewish contemporary, Moses Mendelssohn, believed that Jews could never become Germans,[284] for, among other reasons, they had no share in the German's romanticism and nationalism.

Enlightenment, Reason, Rationality

That some Germans during the Hitler era sometimes accosted Jews was not without justification. A too-large subset of Jews were figuratively kicking Germans on their volkisch shin. Some few Germans responded accordingly.

Other nationalists of the era, including Zionists, held similar nationalistic and racist views with respect to their own people as did the ultraright-wing Germans. Romantic nationalism was reawakened throughout Europe, inspired by the wars of liberation against Napoleon and as a counterculture movement to the Enlightenment. For people like Hitler, romantic nationalism was a touchstone for what he thought were the profound bonds of a naturally united people—their race. The reawakening was no less prominent among Zionists.

While the Enlightenment enthroned reason and rationality, its adherents warped its focus such that any perversion could be reasoned, could be rationalized, could be pilpulized. Reason and rationality proved themselves no better than romanticism and emotionalism, and perhaps they were worse, for reason and rationality enabled charlatans to tint their hate and prejudice in the guise of scientific authenticity: Sigmund Freud serves as a prime example on this point. Lenin's collectivization of Soviet agriculture was entirely rational and was, of course, an abominable failure resulting in the deaths of millions. The rationalized form of life and culture that was foisted on the Germans during the Weimar era was emptied of all ballast of esteemed traditions.[285] Hitler was intent on changing all of that.

In the late nineteenth and throughout the twentieth century science became something of a fetish. The English biologist Thomas Huxley, who coined the term "agnostic," commented on the abuse of science, saying, "You have no notion of the intrigue that goes on in this blessed world of science. Science is, I fear, no purer than any other region of human activity; though it should be."[286] E. Jones points out in *Degenerate Moderns* that as the leftist intelligentsia attempted to make wrongs into rights, pilpulizing all manner of things, they used intellect in the guise of science. "[T]he modern's [used a] truncated form of rationality [science], as a way of delegitimizing the norm or, something which is the same thing expressed differently, of making deviance the norm."[287] The work of Freud, Boasian Anthropology, Margaret Mead's *Coming of Age in Samoa*, the Frankfurt School, and even the *Kinsey Report* of the 1950s are emblematic of such "science." Today we justifiably doubt the claims of climate change scientists because we frequently read or hear accounts of falsified statistics and observations. The iconic precursors to the likes of Mead and Kinsey were people like Freud and Boas and a host of lesser deities who pushed such agendas in Europe throughout the early 1900s.

The Frankfurt School

In Hitler's day, the politically motivated, ideologically Marxist, and Jewish-dominated Frankfurt School (initially located at the University of Frankfurt), formally known as the Institute for Social Research, had criticism of bourgeoisie Gentile culture as the central focus of its work. The city of Frankfurt was at the time being run by its Jewish mayor, Ludwig Landmann. Because of the work done at the school in the area of social theory, as well as work done at the University of Frankfurt and the general liberalism of Frankfurt society, Hitler and his Nazis came to view Frankfurt itself as a "New Jerusalem on the Franconian Jordan."[288]

Jewish philosopher and historian Gershom Scholem described the Frankfurt School as one of Germany's most remarkable and influential "Jewish sects."[289] The members and adherents of the school created concepts and employed such esoteric language that they were intelligible to only a small coterie of like-minded intellectuals.[290] "By the early 1930s," says MacDonald, "the University of Frankfurt had become a bastion of the academic Left and 'the place where all the thinking of interest in the area of social theory was concentrated'. . . . sociology was referred to as a 'Jewish science.'"[291]

The Frankfurt School was established in 1923 by a group of Jewish Marxists with a smattering of Gentiles who were meant to serve as figureheads against charges of Jewish domination. It was created with the financial aid of Felix Weil, himself Jewish, and was later maintained by government funds. Jewish historian Nachum Gidal noted that of the roughly fifty members of the institution's staff the vast majority were Jewish.[292]

The founding members of the school were unorthodox Jewish Marxists and devotees of Sigmund Freud and Franz Boas who employed the theories of both individuals to advance their leftist, specifically Jewish, political interests. At a very general level, the school can be said to have focused on the "pursuit of politics through academic means."[293] It, like other such movements (e.g., Marxism, Freudian psychoanalysis, Boasian Anthropology, and the like), consciously advanced Jewish interests by way of academic pseudoscientific presentations couched in exotic language offered up to non-Jews as universalistic utopianism.[294]

Freud, says Peter Gay, sought "to diminish religion with psychoanalytic weapons,"[295] as did both Boasian Anthropology and the Frankfurt School, and both of these institutions were staffed by devout acolytes of Freud. Max Horkheimer and Adorno, who were both members of the school, held that modern Fascism is fundamentally the same as traditional Christianity, because, they claimed:

> [B]oth involve opposition to and subjugation of nature. While Judaism remained a "natural religion" concerned with national life and self-preservation, Christianity turned toward domination and rejection of all that is nature. . . . Christian self-denial and, in particular, the suppression of sex result in evil and anti-Semitism via projection.[296]

Though initially financed by Hermann Weil, the school was headed by Horkheimer, a philosopher and sociologist. It was Horkheimer, a political animal highly adept at networking,[297] who shaped the focus of the school and was instrumental in developing its worldwide influence over Gentile culture. He made no secret of the partisan nature of the institute's activities: his objective was to transform the school's work directly into propaganda.[298] It was also Horkheimer who so successfully posited anti-Semitism as a purely emotional and irrational psychosis of Gentiles—criticism of Jews, claimed Horkheimer, was a manifestation of a psychological pathology.

Other luminaries of the school were Theodor Adorno, who was a philosopher, sociologist, and musicologist, and a close collaborator with Horkheimer; Herbert Marcuse, the philosopher who coined the phrase "make love, not war"; Walter Benjamin, essayist and literary critic; and Friedrich Pollock, a social scientist and philosopher. Until falling out of favor for being a revisionist of Freud, the social psychologist Erich Fromm, a man who Adorno liked to refer to as a "professional Jew," was also associated with the school. Fromm, in turn, referred to Adorno as a "puffed up phrase-maker with no conviction and nothing to say."[299] Wilhelm Reich, still another member of the school, developed his own doctrine of sexual liberalism as an antidote to political conformism and social psychosis.[300] Lesser lights included Karl August Wittfogel, Richard Sorge, and Leo Lowenthal.

The ostensible purpose of the school was to bring about a rational, humane, Socialist society. At a fundamental level, though, Freudianism, Boasian Anthropology, and the Frankfurt School all had the dilution and weakening of Gentile society as core objectives. An online article by Linda Kimball titled "Cultural Marxism" has the following to say about the Frankfurt School:

> The primary goal of the Frankfurt School was to translate Marxism from economic terms into cultural terms. It would provide the ideas on which to base a new political theory of revolution based on culture, harnessing new oppressed groups for the faithless proletariat. Smashing religion, morals, it would also build a constituency among academics, who could build careers studying and writing about the new oppression.
>
> Toward this end, Marcuse—who favored polymorphous perversion—expanded the ranks of Gramsci's new proletariat by including homosexuals, lesbians, and transsexuals. Into this was spliced Lukacs's radical sex education and cultural terrorism tactics. Gramsci's "long march" was added to the mix, and then all of this was wedded to Freudian psychoanalysis and psychological conditioning techniques. The end product was Cultural Marxism, now known in the West as multiculturalism.[301]

A major tenet of the school was that a principle source of Gentile identity, religion, and its concomitant supports for high-investment parenting, would be conceptualized as an infantile aberration in the utopian, atheistic, Marxist societies of the future.[302] In consonance with its dogma, the school also attacked the patriarchal family. The school's objective in this respect was to break the bonds that were then being reinforced by concepts of nationalism. As Hannu Salmi reminds us:

> European culture was becoming strongly family-oriented. The safe world of the home and of biological kinship surfaced as central starting points of social values. . . . at the centre of this picture was, before all, the nuclear family, the father, the mother and the children, whose solidarity was emphasized in the Christmas celebrations with their family meals and ceremonies . . . the nineteenth century has . . . been

called the century of the family: it marked the birth of the nuclear family in its twentieth-century sense.[303]

Boasian Anthropology and the Frankfurt School saw both nationalism and its effect on breeding family values as threatening things that needed to be defeated, which was entirely in keeping with the objectives of their Russian, Bolshevistic brethren. The Jewish-Russian commissar for education and culture, Anatoly Lunacharsky, was explicit—"That little institution of manners which is the family . . . that entire curse . . . shall become a closed chapter," said he.[304]

Products of Boasian Anthropology and the Frankfurt School have had gigantic impacts on Gentile societies, both German and non-German, up to and including contemporary events. Among its most well-known Marxist bents is critical theory, terminology that was founded in part on the need to have a focus of study that did not include the term Marxism. "Critical theory is social theory oriented toward critiquing and changing society as a whole, in contrast to traditional theory oriented only to understanding or explaining it."[305] The theory is most closely associated with Adorno, Horkheimer, Marcuse, Walter Benjamin, and Jürgen Habermas. Erich Fromm also played a significant role in its early development.[306] Critical theory, for all of its faults, had an enormous impact on the twentieth century, including the radicalism of the 1960s and the New Left social movement of the post-1960s. In particular, it shaped scholarship in contemporary sociology, film, and cultural studies.[307] When Johnny squabbles with Jimmy in the school yard and your child's teacher and doctor recommend behavioral modification steps and drugs of various kinds by saying, "Studies have shown . . . ," be certain of this: the studies to which he or she refers can be traced to the prejudices of critical theory.

In practice, critical theory was and is little more than a means of providing a scientific patina to prejudicial academic rants. Niel McLaughlin cites Jennifer Platt with respect to the origins of such movements as Freudianism, Boasian Anthropology, and the Frankfurt School. According to Platt, "origin myths [of the

Frankfurt School and other such movements] in the social sciences are not about accurate historical reconstruction, but are part of a process whereby 'contemporary preferences' are legitimated by 'providing them with an honorable past.'"[308] Freudianism and Marxism, like Boasian Anthropology and the contentions of the Frankfurt School, illegitimately claimed to be scientific. Like the Frankfurt School, Boasian Anthropology applied pseudoscientific methodologies and academic dishonesty as well (e.g., Mead's 1928 *Coming of Age in Samoa*) to further its sociopolitical aims. That is, both of these schools offered up faux objectivity of the same kind as Freud's supposed Oedipus complex, which was actually, as E. Jones puts it, "Freud's personal history disguised and writ large."[309]

Adorno's concept of *The Authoritarian Personality*, which was published in 1950 but is representative of work at the Frankfurt School throughout the 1920s, was a supposed predictor of one's "potential for fascist and antidemocratic leanings and behaviors."[310] He identified the authoritarian personality type as having characteristics that were wholly in keeping with German stereotypes. Worse, he exempted Jews from the odious tag of "authoritarian"—he instead applied it exclusively to Gentiles.

With Adorno's treatise as a foundation, one can argue against nationalism, Christianity, sexual mores, and indeed, most any socially unifying concept. MacDonald asserts that while it is difficult to fully assess the effect of works like *The Authoritarian Personality*, "there can be little question that the thrust of the radical critique of gentile culture in this work, as well as other works inspired by psychoanalysis and its derivatives, was to pathologize high-investment parenting and upward social mobility, as well as pride in family, religion, and country, among gentiles."[311] Indeed, *The Authoritarian Personality*, and its predecessor, *Studies in Prejudice*, attempt to show that Gentile group affiliations, including Gentile family relationships, are by themselves indicative of psychiatric disorder,[312] of prejudice.

On a broader scale, the whole of the Frankfurt School's objective was to analyze and critique culture, including literature, music, art, high culture, and mass culture. Writings of the school were consistently laced with interpretations of culture that supported Marxist, Freudian, and specifically, Jewish ideologists.

Another product of the school was Herbert Marcuse's *Eros and Civilization*, a synthesis of Marx and Freud, that argues in favor of uninhibited sexual experimentation and godless egalitarianism as being keys to realizing utopia.[313] The book helped fuel the 1960s counterculture.

With specific respect to Germany, Kevin MacDonald points out that:

> There was a general perception among many anti-Semites that Jewish intellectuals were subverting German culture [by way of such organizations as the Frankfurt School] in the period prior to 1933 ... and psychoanalysis was one aspect of this concern. A great deal of hostility to psychoanalysis centered around the perceived threat of psychoanalysis to Christian sexual ethics.... Psychoanalysis became a target of gentiles decrying the Jewish subversion of culture—"the decadent influence of Judaism," as one writer termed it. . ... In 1928 Carl Christian Clemen, a professor of ethnology at the University of Bonn, reacted strongly to *The Future of an Illusion*, Freud's analysis of religious belief in terms of infantile needs. Clemen decried the psychoanalytic tendency to find sex everywhere, a tendency he attributed to the Jewish composition of the movement....[314]

Nationalism is frequently cast as a political belief system, but it was more than that: it was also, as historian Salmi Hannu emphasizes, a "cultural historical phenomenon, loaded with meanings, signs and symbols. It left its imprint on the arts, popular culture, historical understanding, education—and emotions."[315] Adolf Hitler correctly viewed the Frankfurt School as Jewish-Communist and destructive to all that he worshipped: German nationalism, volkism, social propriety, classical art, and more.

Upon coming to power, the Nazis quickly closed the school. It then relocated to the U.S. where it continued to exert its influence in a massive way. It was by way of such entities as the Frankfurt School that the U.S. inherited Weimar culture.

The Frankfurt School has been instrumental in the creation of cultural Marxism in the U.S. and elsewhere and thereby the destruction of nationalism, Christianity, family cohesiveness, high-investment parenting, and other forms of Gentile cohesion in preference to societal atomization. Multiculturalism has a strong link to the Frankfurt School. All forms of Gentile collectivism were deemed pathological by the school while equivalent collectivism of Jews and other minority groups were pilpulized as natural, justifiable, and entirely benign.

In America, the whole of the school's work served to alter the ethnic balance of the United States by promoting large-scale immigration from societies that were, for America, nontraditional. That is, central and northern European immigration was traded for vastly increased immigration from third world countries. The Immigration Reform Act of 1965 was heavily sponsored by Jewish interests; indeed, the legislation was introduced by Jewish Congressman Emanuel Celler of New York. The counterculture of the 1960s and 1970s and today's political correctness have firm roots in publications of the Frankfurt School and Jewish interests. It was during the 1960s, for example, when the United States embraced the concept of dual citizenship, a concept that specifically favored Jews—the Supreme Court case that decided the issue was brought there by a Jewish citizen in the Supreme Court case of *Afroyim v. Rusk* who was seeking both U.S. and Israeli citizenship. The current (2015) Israeli ambassador to the United States, Ron Dermer, is also an American. He is one among many who enjoys dual citizenship of both Israel and the U.S. He was born and raised in the U.S. but represents Israel at the political table.

Author Sarah Gordon quotes George Kren and Leon Rappoport in *The Holocaust and the Crisis of Human Behavior* as saying, "Far from being irrational, the Holocaust can only be epitomized in terms of excessive rationality, an example of logical thought skipping the bonds of human feeling."[316] If one can accept the foregoing as true, one cannot help but also accept the premise that anything, absolutely anything, can be rationalized—the rational is not a twit superior to sensory perception or empiricism, but as Huxley rightly told us, it should be. Today, we decry the eugenics of the Hitler era, but we readily rationalize creating a hole in the skull of babies and sucking out the brain during partial-birth abortions—we rationalize, pilpulize the despicable. Our emotionalism and romanticism abhor such procedures, but we make it right in our conscience with pilulizations and laundered language. We hold that our rationalizations are superior to Hitler's. They are not.

"Rationalists" even today, commonly and convincingly rationalize the suspension of ordinary moral and legal standards,[317] and particularly with respect to Israel. In the right hands, reason can be distorted as well as any other philosophy or theory of knowledge. Until recently, we successfully rationalized the torture of captured terrorists under the pilpulistic term, "enhanced interrogation techniques."[318] To abortionists, babies are not babies, they are instead "potential human beings." Anyone who studies events in the Middle East knows well how Israel and her supporters continually rationalize war crimes and the despicable way that they treat their Arab neighbors. Alan Dershowitz, an Israeli apologist of the first order, manages to elegantly pilpulize all manner of Israeli crimes under international law. He also fabricates a good deal of what he has to say, but his falsifications carry weight due to his academic pedigree. "Dershowitz," says Norman Finkelstein, "can appropriate from a hoax with impunity due to an environment that tolerates such derelictions so long as the conclusions are politically correct."[319] That is the way that abused rationalism—pilpulism—works. And it is very much the way that the Frankfurt School and Boasian Anthropology worked in Germany.

It is not the case, of course, that rationality is inherently bad; it is, in fact, much superior to, say, emotionalism or romanticism when honestly employed. It is the warping of rationality and science to sociopolitical ends that causes problems: irrational radicalism of every form was wrapped in a guise of rationalism and science, and far too much of it was faked. Where absolute fakery was inappropriate, the deliberate skewing of statistics was often made to serve in its stead. An example of statistical skewing will be provided later in this text.

*   *   *   *

Hitler was, without a doubt, fully aware that principles of the Enlightenment, reason, and rationality, were employed in warped form to attack German interests and values, and he sometimes, therefore, made explicit reference to the Enlightenment in challenging critiques of German interests. His response to Enlightenment values was to utterly reject them: "What we need is instinct and will," said he.[320] On a broader level, the German populace would come to see the Enlightenment as something that had been perverted into a merely materialistic utilitarian ideology.[321] For many, the "rationalism" of the Enlightenment era went hand in hand with unconstrained capitalism, licentiousness, and all manner of deviance.

Romantics trusted and championed their intuition, their emotions; their feelings of love for nature and the soil, and most importantly, their volk, their blood. Chivalry was then still an important component of their belief system. Richard Etlin makes the following points with respect to the appeal of blood and volk in Nazi mythology:

> One of the remarkable aspects of Nazi thought was the widespread use of biological base-metaphors, which appeal to deep and primal psychic responses. . . . Blood . . . could have a positive mythical appeal. It was this nurturing association of blood that undergirded the Nazi concept of a culture—and of an architecture and a landscape—grounded in Blut und Boden (blood and soil). Here the deep psychic appeal of blood is conjoined with the base-metaphor of rootedeness, whereby all that seems vital in life is considered as growing from the ground. For the Nazis, the opposite of rooted in the

ground was rootlessness, which they associated with Jews, Roma, and Sinti.[322]

Romantics like Hitler often focused on the episodic adventures of a single individual and his honor and valor, as well as his lofty idealism. During World War II it was Hitler's romanticism that made him consistently refuse, even when Germany was in dire need of labor, to forcibly draft women into work in war production.[323] Rationalists abhorred everything romantic. Hitler's own nationalism and romanticism extended to a fervent desire to become the people's tribune, a thought process that was stimulated by Wagner's *Rienzi, der letzte der Tribunen* (Rienzi, the last of the tribunes).

Nietzsche is sometimes credited with Hitler's belief that "'War and courage have done more great things than charity.' Nietzsche espoused the idea of the superhuman, daring ruler and ruler race—Lords of the Earth. That Hitler considered himself the superman of Nietzsche's prophecy," says William Shirer, "can not be doubted."[324] Hitler read Nietzsche and Nietzsche, was, as Trevor-Roper reminds us, "often on his lips."[325] Hitler's veneration of Nietzsche was bolstered by Nietzsche's disdain for democracy and parliaments. Added to all of this was Hitler's perception of "the great man" as the mover and shaker of history. Not only could individuals make a difference, it was historically the case according to Hitler that the great epochs of history were entirely the work of great individual leaders, of individual heroes. "World-history," claimed Hitler in one of his speeches, "like all events of historical significance, is the result of the activity of single individuals—it is not the fruit of majority decisions."[326] Alexander the Great, Julius Caesar, Frederick the Great, Napoleon ("the real one" as Kaiser William I was wont to say from time to time), Bismarck, Luther, et al., were among Hitler's examples of great individuals who shook and shaped the world. And Hitler himself did likewise: "In him," says Fest, "an individual once again demonstrated the stupendous power of a solitary person over the historical process."[327] Fest supports Burckhardt in saying that

"History tends at times to become suddenly concentrated in one man, who is then obeyed by the world."[328]

In contradistinction to Hitler's heroic conception of historical forces, the Communists had a materialist conception, emphasizing the economic and technical aspects as the prime movers of historical events—it was boring and mundane stuff when compared with Hitler's emphasis on lofty heroism.

Darwin

Charles Darwin's 1859 book, *On the Origin of Species*, had an incalculable impact on the politics of Hitler's day and on Hitler himself. Darwinism, coupled with romanticism and nationalism, was a stout and potent force for radical racists. Darwinism supposedly proved that differences among peoples were biologically determined, and national archetypes were also biologically determined. To racial ideologues, Darwin's survival of the fittest turned on the idea of the history of humanity as a story of racial conflict. His theories of natural selection "rationally" resulted in social Darwinism, and that in turn mapped to racial Darwinism, the idea that in both society and nature the superior peoples naturally dominate and the inferior ones naturally serve.

The survival of the fittest theme became a justification for colonization, imperialism, Manifest Destiny, and the attendant exploitive treatment of a wide range of peoples. In America, the concept of racial Darwinism was particularly strong and served to justify our genocide of Native Americans.[329] Racial Darwinism was not the preserve of just the quacks of society: serious, learned men at the end of the nineteenth century subscribed to it—many Darwinian phrenologists of that time were actual scientists, not the harebrained kooks of today's regard.* U.S. President Theodore

---

* There are a number of false scientific trails that were earnestly examined by great minds, with social Darwinism and phrenology being only two among them. Max Nordau subscribed to phrenology, and even the great Sir Isaac Newton expended impressive amounts of time and effort in an investigation of alchemy. Einstein developed his concept of a "cosmological constant" as a means to avoid the facts of his own calculations—he wanted the heavens to be static so he tweaked his science to fit his prejudice.

Roosevelt serves as but one example of popular world leaders who enthusiastically subscribed to the tenets of social Darwinism, including its racialist aspects. In his book *The Winning of the West*, Roosevelt made it abundantly clear that he fully embraced racial Darwinism.[330]

Joachim Fest addresses the subject of Hitler's support for social Darwinism as follows:[331]

> [T]he component of Social Darwinism in Hitler's thought cannot be attributed solely to his personal experiences.... He was really reflecting the tendency of the age. Science had become the one truly unchallenged authority. As the laws of evolution and selection put forth by Charles Darwin and Herbert Spencer were popularized in numerous pseudoscientific publications, the average man soon came to know that the "struggle for existence" was the fundamental principle of life, the "survival of the fittest" the basic law governing the societal conduct of individuals and nations. The so-called "Social Darwinist" theory served, for a while at least, all camps, factions and parties in the second half of the nineteenth century. It became a component of leftist populist education before the Right took up the creed for its own purposes, and argued the unnaturalness of democratic or humanitarian ideas by appealing to Darwinist principles.[332]

Those who subscribed to social Darwinism were not off on some irrational bent to misconstrue Darwin. Darwin himself made it clear that he believed, on the basis of his science we must suppose, that the "inferior races" were "living fossils." "When two races of men meet," said Darwin, "they act precisely like two species of animals—they fight each other, bring diseases to each other, but then comes the most deadly struggle, namely which have the best fitted organization, or instincts (i.e., intellect, in man) to gain the day."[333]

Some writings that might be today thought of as related to social Darwinism actually preceded Darwin's book. Some of

Hegel's arguments that societies progress through stages of increasing development, or Thomas Hobbes's contentions with respect to societal competition for natural resources are examples of the predilection in seventeenth- and eighteenth-century Europe to see race as deterministic for societal relations. Thus, while Hitler fully subscribed to social Darwinism and the idea that a pure German race was necessary for a pure German culture and further evolution of Germans, he certainly did not originate the thought process; the respectable intellectually elite who preceded him held that distinction.

Darwin's treatise lent credence to those who saw history as the struggle between opposing races—metaphorical species—seeking their own survival, if not dominion. The secular Jewish philosopher and extreme Jewish racist Moses Hess, who for a time worked closely with Karl Marx, concurred with such thought processes. He saw "the distinct and immutable traits, both physical and cultural, of the races of humankind"[334] as the primary force of history and the class struggle as only secondary. Hess also believed, says Lindemann, that the Jewish race was "one of the superior primary races of mankind."[335] Hitler, naturally, viewed Aryans as primary. According to MacDonald, "Freud and other early psychoanalysts frequently distinguished themselves as Jews on the basis of race and referred to non-Jews as Aryans, instead of Germans or Christians."[336]

As pointed out earlier, Hitler held that history is the story of the struggle between races; Marxists had it as a struggle between economic and hereditary classes. Hitler's view was not particularly aberrant: a great many intellectuals tried to explain the entirety of history as the struggle between opposing forces such as race or class, some by a combination of both. By way of example, Lindemann points out that "by the 1840s and the 1850s the great Jewish Prime Minister of Great Britain, Benjamin Disraeli, and the great Scottish anthropologist Robert Knox had made extensive use of race to explain the rise and fall of civilization."[337] Hitler's Nuremberg Laws of the 1930s that are so decried by historians were in their essence a reflection of the dominant belief of the imperial Western powers of his day that had already employed just such laws within their various colonies[338]—such laws were only problematic when they were applied to Jews. Moreover, it was not only Germany that employed such laws within Europe: the Baltic states as well as Poland and Bulgaria also implemented similar restrictions on Jews throughout the 1930s.

Hitler, Man of His Age

Hitler was very much a man of the age into which he was born and in which he was nurtured. To paraphrase Machiavelli, Hitler often traveled paths that were beaten by others. His life was inextricably linked to his time,[339] and as even Fest acknowledges, his life story needs to be told against "the dense pattern of objective factors that conditioned, promoted, impelled, and sometimes braked him."[340] Hitler was, said Fest, a man in "intense attunement to his time."[341] Kershaw echoes the point: "Hitler's impact can only be grasped through the era which created him . . . A convincing study of Hitler must be, therefore, at the same time in a certain sense a history of the Nazi era."[342] Historian Richard Tedor reinforces the foregoing in saying the following:

> One of the flaws in the annals is the superficial assumption that National Socialism was a rootless political program and the product of one man's world view. There was in fact a conscious endeavor by the National Socialists to align policies with German and European customs and practices. They believed their goals corresponded to the natural progression of their continent and found the diametrical Western-democratic concept to be foreign and immoral.[343]

Hitler lived in a time of empire building, industrial modernization, revolutionary conflict, and racialist thinking that stemmed in no small part from Darwin's discoveries. Both physical and political courage were esteemed well beyond our present regard for such qualities. Teddy Roosevelt, for example, was in the Hitler camp with respect to his views on the virtues of violent struggle between nations and between the Anglo-Saxon race and the supposedly lesser races. "Blending 'muscular Christianity,' the 'social gospel'—which sanctified the state as an instrument of moral reclamation—and Darwinian theory, TR believed that human nature evolved toward improvement through conflict."[344] TR also shared several of Hitler's views on the subject of eugenics and the role of women as breeders in service to the state.[345] Supreme Court Justice Oliver Wendell Holmes provided a 1927 Supreme Court decision that sanctioned sterilization for the mentally unfit as a precursor to the Nazi eugenics program.[346] Jewish Socialists in Germany used their newspaper *Vorwarts* to actively campaign on behalf of eugenics. Liberal humanistic writers and social engineers of the period looked ahead to radical new ways of improving the human stock. Eugenics was only one among several processes proposed to achieve their ends; others included mass sterilization and even eradication.[347] The point is that Hitler's views on a wide range of topics that we today find shocking and odious and attribute to defects in his person were, in actuality, largely in tune with the political and intellectual leaders of his time. In Hitler's time, abortion elicited the selfsame abhorrence that the idea of euthanasia has for us and our time. The medical processes employed today for partial-birth abortions would have been universally abhorrent to men and women of his time.

Homosexuality was abhorrent; now it's not. Even Abraham Lincoln spoke out against miscegenation; now it is entirely accepted. Times change and attitudes as well. And we are mistaken if we apply current thinking to times long gone by.

The milieu of Hitler's youth was such that several dominant social forces were competing for supremacy. The Enlightenment still held sway and was joined by Marxism, capitalism, Darwinism, and Freudianism, and each wrought great political, economic, and social change. Change was everywhere, and it was all in the direction of rationalism. Rationalism threw off the cherished icons of old and replaced them with modern, "rational" substitutes. Hitler's romantic streak, however, was in some respects a polar opposite to the Enlightenment.

Small shops and guilds of Hitler's era were going by the wayside as rational economies of scale were realized in the mass production of goods that were then marketed and sold in large department stores, which, by the way, were a Jewish innovation. Peter Pulzer tells us that:

> Whole economic classes which had existed before the middle of the eighteenth century (the peasants and the independent craftsmen) had by 1914 either disappeared or become economically insignificant. Within a generation of the beginnings of the industrialization combines and cartels had concentrated the ownership and control of industry in a remarkably small number of hands.[348]

And to be sure, it was the case that proportionally, a remarkably large number of that remarkably small number were Jews. The exogenous entrepreneurs of Central Europe were largely made up of Jews from the east. As Pulzer points out, in Germany, these entrepreneurs "were disproportionately Jews, in Austria predominantly, in Hungary overwhelmingly so."[349]

The idyllic was being cast off, for the idyllic could do nothing to generate cold, hard, rational cash. In things like architecture, the beautiful ornamentation of the classical period was consciously and purposefully discarded in favor of the flat, the sleek. Art became nonrepresentational, even purposefully ugly and grotesque. Social turmoil was everywhere evident. Both real and fictional heroes of yore were diminished, demeaned, discarded in much the same way that we Americans now diminish Columbus, "heroes" of the Indian wars, and all other icons of West European culture. The new heroes were the capitalists and revolutionaries and anybody who stood in opposition to cherished values and traditions. Traditionalists like Hitler found it hard going. The dynamo of change was overpowering, and it was operating in explicit opposition to all forms of traditionalism. New was in, old was out, and brutally so. And in some places, it seemed increasingly to be the case that Germans were out and Jews were in; the Vienna of

Hitler's youth was a place that was emblematic of that phenomenon.

Hitler's "prudish morals" are sometimes represented not as moral correctness but instead as sexual aberration. In fact though, his moral stance was entirely in keeping with the outward standards of the middle class of his time, standards that were being challenged in Vienna by the libertine literature of people like Jewish writer Arthur Schnitzler[350] and elsewhere by a number of other prominent Jews.

Hitler's Heroes

Hitler's fictional heroes included Old Shatterhand (a character that is said to have influenced the idea of the Lone Ranger), a character from the American Indian novels of Karl May. Hitler read every one of May's novels, as did some other great names of the era. He is also known to have read *Robinson Crusoe, Gulliver's Travels, Uncle Tom's Cabin,* and *Don Quixote*.[351] He studied and took lessons in life, such as the importance of *will* from both the real and fictional characters and from his extensive readings on that subject. He was enamored by the legendary Norse god, Oden (also called Othinn, Wodan, Woton, and Wotan), the god of war and death but also of poetry and wisdom. It was Oden who presided over Valhalla, the majestic hall where slain warriors were delivered by beautiful horse-mounted maidens, the Valkyrie. He certainly did not literally believe in Oden and other such legendary figures; he was not an occultist as is sometimes claimed. Indeed, because he was not an occultist, he immediately scotched Himmler's wacky plan to replace Christianity with old Germanic gods and the cults of Wotan and Thor, but he did take inspiration from such myths. He was fascinated by the Knights Templar of old, by Teutonic heroism, by the characters of Richard Wagner's operas such as Wagner's superhero, Siegfried. Hitler recounts in *Mein Kampf*[352] that at the age of twelve he saw both Guillaume's *Wilhelm Tell* and Wagner's *Lohengrin* for the first time. As we shall see, Hitler would later in life observe satirical Jewish criticisms of the Swiss William Tell legend, a legend held dear by him and other Pan-Germans.

Hitler, said Albert Speer, drew all his heroes from two historical periods: antiquity and the eighteenth and nineteenth centuries, and he frequently referred to various actual and mythical figures in his speeches.[*] His heroes from antiquity included Alexander, Caesar, and Augustus. His heroes of fairly modern repute included Prince Eugene and Napoleon, but his favorite was undoubtedly Frederick the Great[353] who brought Prussia such renowned military prestige and who was so important to German conceptions of duty, honor, and discipline. Frederick, like Hitler himself, was for the German people an enlightened despot. Add to the foregoing Otto von Bismarck who defeated his enemies and expanded and unified the Reich. Hitler also admired, as he made clear in his *Berlin Table Talk*, Joseph II, a man who ranked along with Catherine II (Catherine the Great) of Russia and Frederick the Great of Prussia.[354]

It is not hard to compare Hitler with Frederick the Great, a warrior-aesthetic with a deep love for things of the spirit. Frederick rejected Christianity and believed in the absolute power of the monarch as "the first servant of the state." With respect to religion, Hitler shared Frederick's view that all religions were equally false, but also politically useful. Hitler saw himself in many ways as analogous to Frederick.

Otto von Bismarck was admired by Hitler for his having engineered the unification of Germany and for his performance in serving as the first chancellor of the German Empire, the Second Reich (the first being the Holy Roman Empire of the German Nation). Bismarck had expelled the Jesuits from Germany and had otherwise undermined the political and cultural power of the Catholic Church, achieved supremacy of Prussia in Central Europe, defeated Austria in battle, and added Schleswig, Holstein,

---

[*] Take, for example, Hitler's reference to Roman mythology's Orcus, the punisher of broken oaths, in his Munich speech of September 16, 1930. Other such references by Hitler to historical and mythical figures abound.

Frankfurt, Hanover, Hesse-Kassel, and Nassau to Prussia's territory, overcame political opposition within the House of Deputies (*Abgeordnetenhaus*), and, after two attempts on the life of Kaiser William I by would-be assassins associated with the Jewish-dominated Social Democratic Party, he for a time silenced the politically troublesome SPD.

Prior to the Franco-German war of 1870–1871 Bismarck famously said that the "the great questions of the day will not be decided by speeches and the resolutions of majorities—that was the great mistake [during the revolutions] from 1848 to 1849—but by iron and blood" (later changed to "blood and iron"). This was a rather direct expression of what Hitler would later term the Leadership Principle, the idea of a single, strong, infallible leader with absolute power. Bismarck stated a fact about himself as much as about the German people when he said that "We Germans fear God and naught besides!" It was a thought process embraced by Hitler. "Hitler's eyes sparkled at such words as 'We Germans fear God but nothing else on this earth,'" said his friend from his Vienna days, Reinhold Hanisch.[355] Hitler recounted in *Mein Kampf* how in his youth he had assiduously studied the Franco-German war by which Bismarck achieved German unification and added Alsace-Lorraine to its territory, and how that "great heroic struggle" had become his "greatest inner experience."[356] Hitler knew all the commanders of the war. His studies led him to admire Moltke the Elder highly, but Bismarck above all.[357] Hitler and other German students of his era even "collected devotional objects such as Bismarck busts made of plaster,"[358] says Austrian historian Brigitte Hamann.

It is only incidental to this narrative, but it is perhaps worth mentioning that Hitler would certainly have been aware that the Jewish terrorist Karl Cohen had tried to assassinate Bismarck on May 7, 1866. If one may dare a bit of Freudian speculation, it was perhaps this, along with many similar such incidents in Russia and elsewhere, that caused Hitler to comment to a friend in Vienna that "Jews are very radical and have terrorist inclinations."[359]

Jews of Germany

That Jews were thoroughly enmeshed in negative critiques of German values and culture was succinctly encapsulated in the writings of Rabbi Dr. Manfred Reifer. In 1933, Rabbi Reifer wrote a retrospective about Jews and Jewish actions in connection with Hitler's rise to power:

> They, and in the same measure, the children of liberalism, all those poets, authors, artists, journalists, prepared the present time, nourished Jew hatred, furnished the grounds, the material for the era of National Socialism. They all surely desired the best, but attained the opposite. They were cursed with blindness, they saw not the approach of catastrophe, they heard not the footfall of time, the heavy footfalls of time, the heavy footfalls of the Nemesis of History.[360]

Also in 1933, Mr. Bernard J. Brown commented on how Jews had fallen into their predicament: "Never in the history of the human race has there ever been a group of people who have enmeshed themselves into so many errors and persisted in refusing to see the truth, as our people have done during the last three hundred years,"[361] said he.

Prior to the rise of Hitler, Germany was a good place for Jews. As Sarah Gordon points out in *Hitler, Germans, and the Jewish Question*, "Had the German population been uniquely rabid in its hatred of Jews," as is often charged, "it is inconceivable that Jews could have fared so well, especially compared to Jews in other nations."[362] Nahum Goldmann, the Zionist founder of the World Jewish Congress, described German Jews as follows:

> Their position in the intellectual life of the country was . . . unique. In literature, they were represented by illustrious names. The theatre was largely in their hands. The daily Press, above all its internationally influential sector, was essentially owned by Jews or controlled by them.

> As paradoxical as this may sound today, after the Hitler era, I have no hesitation to say that hardly any section of the Jewish people has made such extensive use of emancipation offered to them in the nineteenth-century as the German Jews. In short, the history of the Jews in Germany from 1870 to 1933 is probably the most glorious rise that has ever been achieved by any branch of the Jewish people.*

The Jews who were so disruptive to German politics, social structures, and cultural norms were a small minority of a small minority. Jews comprised only about 1 percent of the population. Of these, there was only a small subset that directly engaged in everyday politics and matters of culture, with larger numbers engaging by way of their membership in and support of various Jewish social and political organizations. Moreover, the cohesive, international, and oligarchic compass of the Jews was often made apparent by the financial and press support German Jews received from Jews in places like Russia, the U.S., France, and Britain.

As Jews everywhere know well, the pronouncements and actions of prominent Jews attach to the entire community due to the particularism and ethnocentrism that encourage perceptions of unity among them and their various organizational entities. Jewish particularism and ethnocentrism were characteristic of both radical and progressive Jews of the Weimar period, and they remain central to Jewish politics of today. In totality, the various Jewish organizations, and especially the politically oriented ones, serve to support the modern anti-Semitic accusation of Jews as the secret controllers of governments—the ZOG theory, Zionist Occupation Governments.[363]

The ZOG theory has a long list of predecessors such as the accusations in various countries (e.g., Russia, Poland, Austria,

---

*During World War I, he served in the Jewish division of the German Foreign Ministry where he attempted to enlist Kaiser Wilhelm's support for Zionism. The quoted material is from his book, *Mein Leben als deutscher Jude* (*My Life as a German Jew*), (Munich: Langen-Mueller, 1982).

Hungary, and Germany) that Jews represent a nation within a nation. Kevin MacDonald summarizes the theme of Jews as a nation within a nation, a *Völk im Völk*, thusly:

> Jews have often been characterized as "a state within a state." [. . .]. The German Paul de LaGarde (1827–1891) stated that "we simply cannot tolerate a nation within a nation" [. . .]. The view that Jews constituted an alien, foreign nation residing in Germany was not restricted to intellectuals: over 20 percent of the 1,723 petitions from Bavarian communities opposing Jewish emancipation in 1849–1850 emphasized the *Völk im Völk* theme, sometimes referring to Jews as "oriental" or Asiatic and often using such phrases as "foreign in morals, customs, and religion" or foreign in "blood, speech, and religion" [. . .]. Harris [. . .] describes the Bavarian petitions as "spontaneous, extremely broad-based, and genuine"—in effect independent replications of widespread negative attitudes toward Jewish foreignness. Many petitions "stated flatly that Jews could never assimilate" [. . .]. In Germany, the perception of foreignness was particularly directed at Jewish immigrants from Eastern Europe who retained their separatist practices of wearing distinctive clothing, hair styles, and speaking Hebrew.[364]

That Hitler, like so many others, regarded Jews and their organizations as acting like a state within the state is explicitly stated in *Mein Kampf*:

> The Jewish state was never spatially limited in itself, but universally unlimited as to space, though restricted in the sense of embracing but one race. Consequently, this people has always formed a state within states.[365]

To reiterate a point, it is hardly surprising that the successful exercise of Jewish power via coordinated actions of Jewish individuals and organizations, financially supported by contributions from the mass of Jews, associates all Jews with the position of these individuals and organizations and charges of the kind just described. In Weimar Germany (as we will illustrate in later chapters), a relatively small clique of Jews wielded breathtaking influence that encouraged feelings of helplessness among traditional Germans who were experiencing an onslaught of negative changes to their society that in too large a part originated with the Jewish minority therein. Jews were seen as having achieved national rule by proxy.

Power from Small Numbers

It is sometimes claimed that because Jews comprised such a small percentage of the entire population, they could not possibly have greatly influenced events. Just such an argument was fostered by progressive Reichstag deputies in the 1890s. In particular, Deputy Hermes claimed that "it was absurd to picture the small number of Jews in Germany as a threat."[366] In a book review of Amos Elon's *The Pity of It All: A History of Jews in Germany, 1743–1933*, Gordon A. Craig complains that Germans seemingly blamed everything on Jews, "a tiny minority representing 0.9 percent of the population."[367] The clear implication of both Hermes's and Craig's comments is that such a small minority could not possibly be actually troublesome. Such logic is frequently employed. It is the case, however, as Mearsheimer points out, that "there is . . . extensive academic literature on interest groups that helped us understand how small but focused movements can exert influence far greater than their absolute numbers within the population might suggest."[368] As we ballyhoo the "tyranny of the majority," let us at least be aware and reminded that powerful minorities can also constitute tyrannies. Adolf Hitler was a minority of one, and look what he wrought.

By the early 1900s, Eastern Jews within Germany were championed by established Jewish politicians such as Karl Leibknecht and Eduard Bernstein, together with various Jewish-owned newspapers and publishing houses.[369] They, too, argued that because of their relatively small numbers in the population, the Eastern Jews could not possibly be troublesome. But relatively small numbers vis-à-vis a foe can indeed be troublesome.

By 1921, England, with a population of about 38 million people, had established its worldwide empire consisting of 458 million people that existed on one-quarter of the land mass of the earth. More, when one considers England's trade dominance of that period, she had also subjugated Latin America, China, and Siam. England's East India Company secured the entirety of India with less than 4,000 troops, and many of those were not even Englishmen; they were English surrogates—and the political Jews of the Weimar era had prodigious numbers of Gentile surrogates.[370] Francisco Pizarro took Peru with less than 200 men against a force of 80,000.[371] In Sparta, 6,000 Greeks held sway over 45,000 Helots.[372] In Asia, relatively tiny Japan overwhelmed China and the whole of Southeast Asia. Today's Israel has a Jewish population of about 7 million; the total population of its traditional adversaries (Lebanon, Syria, Jordan, Saudi Arabia, Iraq, Iran, Libya, Egypt) totals about 235 million, illustrating that numbers are hardly as important as intellect, finance, weapons pool, and support from powerful allies (in the case of Israel, the U.S. and Europe) in the realm of power.[*] The Middle East aside, Jews have historically used their superior intellect, organization, and riches to subjugate other peoples by way of the purchase of princes, control of what information flows to the people, and by domination of host economies, all of which are "power multipliers." "Money," as American General David Petraeus asserts, "is ammunition." Jews, when they choose to be, can be palpable threats, even in small numbers.

Kevin MacDonald convincingly argues in several places that historically it has repeatedly been the case that radical minorities within the Jewish community have risen to prominence and ultimately succeeded in representing the broader community. By way of illustration, he cites the Israeli settlement movement of contemporary times and their influence on modern American Jews.

---

[*] For an excellent assessment of Jewish power by way of intellect, organization, and money, see *The Israel Lobby and U.S. Foreign Policy* by John J. Mearsheimer and Stephen M. Walt (Farrar, Straus and Giroux, New York, 2007).

From the historical record he cites the Maccabees who rebelled against the Greeks in the second century BC. Says MacDonald, "If Jewish history shows anything, it's that the radicals eventually come to dominate the Jewish community."[373] Any number of Jewish "messiahs" could be cited in support of his arguments, not the least of which was Moses, but also such quacks as Jacob Frank, Israel ben Eliezer, Shabai Tsevi, Nathan Gaza, and Rabbi Dov Baer, to name but a sprinkling of such people. Add Karl Marx to the list.

Jews have recurrently achieved a dominant influence over various societies despite their small percentage of the population. Indeed, such influence has been a theme of Jewish history, most notably in Eastern and Central Europe prior to the Russian revolution, and then throughout Eastern Europe after the revolution. Such dominance, aided by Gentile surrogates, was evident in revolutionary Russia and underscores the importance of philosemitism and building alliances for Jews.

Similarly, the relatively small number of Jews within the German population is not to be taken as an assumption of powerlessness. It is simply a truism that cohesive groups outcompete individual strategies, and Jews have historically been, and continue to be, the most cohesive group of all. Organization, vaunted intellect, great riches, and intense radicalism were more than enough for Jews to overcome their small numbers. In much the same way that a sheepherder with a capable canine can lead an entire flock, so, too, can a few beings with superior financial and intellectual resources lead a nation. A few whites ran South Africa (and many of that few were Jews). A few Englishmen controlled India. It is the biblical objective of Judaism to lead the entire world—to bring universalism to the world.[*]

---

[*]Theodor Herzl, for example, expounds upon this objective in a letter he sent to Meyer-Cohn, telling Meyer-Cohn that Jews needed to "combat the ideal of patriotism" in order to achieve their historical objective of bringing universalism to the world. See Robert John, *Behind the Balfour Declaration* (1988), 29.

Engines of Change

With respect to Germany, as we will show, Jews were *first* the perpetrators of social unrest and self-declared enemies of the state, *then* the victims of the Holocaust. It can be argued, and often is, that Jewish actions in Germany stemmed from historical grievances with Germans, making Jews the initial victims. That as may be, the Jews of Hitler's time were decidedly agents of social unrest, and the unrest that they fomented occurred during a time of great privilege, full empowerment, in a time of war and in a time of peace.

The engines of change were at full throttle in the late 1800s and early 1900s, and Jews were at the controls. As we shall discuss in some detail later, they were exceedingly rich and powerful in both Austria-Hungary and in Germany. They acquired high positions in the military, politics, and the civil service, dominated the labor unions, and were overwhelmingly in control of the banking systems. They also owned all of the most influential newspapers, and thereby dominated in the area of cultural criticism. And, importantly, they stood in direct opposition to the German romanticists and nationalists. Opposition and conflict was inevitable. As Toland put it, Vienna "derided Freud's psychoanalysis, hissed at the too modern sounds of Arnold Schönberg and the too bright colors of Oskar Kokoschka, and found much to criticize in the works of Hofmannsthal and Schnitzler."[374] And the list of Vienna's Gentile grievances goes on and on.

The progress of the era that is so often and so fawningly attributed to Jewish influence was to the traditionalists an attack on their very being—their fatherland, their unity, their high culture, their *völk*, their *Blut*, and their *Boden*. Moreover, there were several recent and ongoing cultural developments of the time that greatly influenced both Jews and Gentiles. The Age of Enlightenment was pressing its influence everywhere and on everything, including Christianity and its mores, an influence that was exemplified by Sigmund Freud. "There is one thing that both the Enlightenment and Freud had in common," says author E.

Jones, "and that was their antipathy toward religion in general and the Catholic Church in particular."[375]

In addition to Freudianism, Darwinism, Zionism, and Marxism, there was revolutionary turmoil in Eastern Europe that was both financed and led by Jews. The chief rabbi of Moscow famously had it that "The Trotskys made the revolutions, but the Bronsteins paid the bill."[376]—Bronstein was Trotsky's name at birth. That is, the Jew was both the agent of all revolutionary ferment and its financial sponsor as well. Herzl, when he was trying to win the support of various government leaders, including Germany's William II, "grasped that he had bait that he could dangle before potential right-wing patrons: 'I explained that we were taking the Jews away from the revolutionary parties.'"[377] The foregoing, of course, is a tacit admission that Jews were the leading lights in the various revolutionary parties. In Soviet Russia immediately after the revolution, nearly all power was given over to the largely Jewish Military Revolutionary Committee. Alexander Kerensky, who many incorrectly thought was Jewish, was in charge of the government and was aided by a host of Jews such as Trotsky, Joffe, Unschlicht, Boky, Ovseyenko, Mekhonoshin, Lashevich, Laximir, Sadovsky, Podvoisky, Molotov, Nevsky, Bubnon, and Skrypnik. Later, Lenin, who was one-quarter Jewish, and Dybenko (married to a Jewess) were added to the Jewish clique there.[378]

Liberal Jews called forth the Marxist revolutionaries of the future and routed Catholicism from the school and courthouse. Catholics, in turn, saw Jews as both Marxist revolutionaries and captains of capitalism. With respect to the latter, it came to be that, as historian Carle Schorske points out, increasingly large segments of the population thought that "liberalism meant capitalism and capitalism meant Jew."[379] Somewhat ironically, but also rationally, it was simultaneously the case that Gentiles viewed both capitalists and anticapitalist Marxists as stemming from a common source: radical Jews. Communists and Jews were increasingly seen as equivalent constructs, as important subsets of Jews in both camps who argued that theirs was the way of the future for the Jewish race.

A Pickpocket in the Market of Ideas[380]

Of the several core traits of Adolf Hitler, surely his willingness and special knack for lifting ideas from others has to be counted high on the list. Fest points out that "He picked up his tactics and his aims, as he later observed, 'from all the bushes along side the road of life.'" He studied and took lessons from both his idols and enemies. "What distinguished the Nazis from conservatives of the old school," says Fest, "was their absence of false pride about the manner of achieving power. They were more than willing to learn from their opponents, and this gave their reactionary notions a cast of modernity."[381] This aspect of Nazism was ultimately something of a distinct advantage over the Marxists. The Marxists had the words of their messiah, Marx, and deviation from his precepts was anathema, sacrilegious. Hitler and his people picked ideas, tactics, and strategies from a host of lesser gods. He could, of course, be dogmatic, but he enjoyed more flexibility than the mainstream Communists who were so inflexibly wedded to Marxist dogma. Just as turning the other cheek has been the bane of Christians, so it was with the Marxists—irrational devotion to dogma limits one's options and opportunities.

Even Hitler's Holocaust lacked originality. According to conservative historian Ernst Nolte, "it derived to some extent from the example of the gigantic massacres already perpetrated in the Soviet Union by Stalin"[382] and his minions, which included too many Jews among them.

Hitler's worldview, his Weltanschauung, was formed on a pick-and-choose basis from a host of personalities and institutions but had extreme nationalism, anti-Bolshevism, anti-Semitism, and Darwin's theory of struggle at its core.[383] His political ideas stemmed in large part from Karl Lueger, the mayor of Vienna, and Georg Ritter von Schönerer, the Austrian politician and rabid Pan-Germanist. His great use of pomp and ceremony—the flags, parades, jackboots, torches, searchlights, and more—he took largely from Catholicism, ancient Rome, and the Fascism of Mussolini whose pomp, rituals, and artifacts also derived from ancient Rome. His governmental organizational concepts were also taken largely from Catholicism.[384] Hitler took other lessons from Catholicism as well: Christianity, he had concluded, was the first creed to exterminate its adversaries in the name of love—its keynote, he said, was intolerance.[385] "One of the secrets of Christianity's success, he was always saying, was the unalterability of its dogmas. Hitler's 'Catholic' streak seldom emerges so clearly as in his respect for rigid, immutable formulas," says Fest,[386] although he might just as well picked up this trait from his reading of Machiavelli, who had as one of his principles the idea that the leader must never appear to have changed his mind on any matter of great import. It was sort of an extreme form of what we today call "staying on the message." Still, for all of his perceived rigidity, Hitler could be flexible when the occasion called for it—it was what worked that mattered most to him.

His party-building strategies and tactics were taken in large part from the practices of his enemies, the Social Democrats of both Austria and Germany and the Communists. The slogan squads, parading bands, workplace politics, the system of street cells, mass demonstrations, and door-to-door appeals were all tactics and practices used first by his opponents. Hitler himself acknowledged that his ideas with respect to a mass party were taken in part from the Social Democrats. In *Mein Kampf*, he describes his impressions as he viewed a mass demonstration put on by them: "I gazed on the interminable ranks, four abreast, of Viennese workmen parading at a mass demonstration. I stood dumb-founded for almost two hours, watching this enormous human dragon which slowly uncoiled itself before me."[387] When Hitler achieved power, similar torch- lit, dragon-like processions immediately followed. Joachim Fest says that "What distinguished the Nazis from conservatives of the old school was their absence of false pride about the manner of achieving power. They were more than willing to learn from their opponents, and this gave their reactionary notions a cast of modernity."[388]

Hitler, says Frederic Spotts, "had an instinctive understanding of the emotive power of symbols,"[389] and he deliberately searched for the best ones for various purposes—he was willing to take them from anywhere; originality and pride of authorship were of little consequence. Again, it was what worked that mattered most.

Hitler's racism was founded on the tenets of such personalities as Martin Luther, Richard Wagner, Heinrich von Treitschke, and H. S. Chamberlain. His social Darwinism was, of course, taken from Charles Darwin. His intense belief in *will* and the power of the individual over the historical process was taken from Arthur Schopenhauer. His ideas about art and architecture were lifted from ancient Greece and Rome and from various classical artists of the eighteenth and nineteenth centuries. Many of Hitler's planned buildings would be influenced by the architectural style of Rome's Pantheon, a structure that he admired no end. His warrior motif stemmed at least in part from such people as Pericles, Alexander the Great, Frederick the Great, Nietzsche, and Otto von Bismarck.

His ideas about the nature and effective use of propaganda stemmed largely from his experience with it during World War I—he particularly admired the effectiveness of the white, black, and grey propaganda put out by the British under the leadership of Lloyd George. The "big lie" form of propaganda did not originate with Hitler; its origins were British. The British propaganda magazine *John Bull* served as a particular influence on his ideas for propaganda warfare.[390] He also studied and improved upon the post-World War I Communist agitprop.[391] Hitler saw the cold, rational, reasoned propaganda of the German government toward the end of World War I as a mistake. Propaganda had to be focused, repetitive, and emotional, and it had to be simple. Stolfi points out a succinct fact with respect to Hitler's messianic character that is also applicable to his propaganda: "The messiah is either a great simplifier or he is not the messiah."[392] Similarly, if propaganda directed to the masses is not simple, it is not propaganda.

Many of the various organizations such as the Hitler Youth and the Nazi sporting and social clubs were taken from concepts and practices employed by one of his archenemies, the Marxist Social Democratic Party.

Hitler's concept of "living space" (Lebensraum, a term coined in 1901 under Kaiser William II) for the German people was little more than a German version of the commonplace thought process of imperialism. He even explicitly stated that "What India was for England, the territories of Russia will be for us."[393] As Finkelstein points out, America's "Manifest Destiny anticipated nearly all the ideological and programmatic elements of Hitler's Lebensraum policy. In fact, Hitler modeled his conquest of the East on the American conquest of the West."[394] Nor was his planned treatment of the Slavs in conquered territory new; it was, in essence, a fusion of Malthusian theory of population and social Darwinism employed by the British in India, but intended by Hitler to be set upon the Slavs of Eastern Europe.[395]

He also took lessons from his extensive readings in history and from his personal day-to-day observation of prominent personalities and events. The crumbling Austro-Hungarian Empire seemed to point out weaknesses in multicultural empires, the various revolutions in Europe, including the French Revolution of 1789, the various revolutions throughout most of Europe in 1848, the Russian Revolutions of 1904–1905 and 1917; and, closer to home, the revolutionary events in Germany and Hungary during the period 1918–1923 all mightily impacted his worldview.

"Tactically," says Fest, "he learned most from the experiences of the revolutionary period. The Bolshevik take-over and the Soviet rule in Bavaria had shown how a handful of determined men [who happened to be Jews] could seize power."[396] Hitler's study of history, combined with his observation of current events, led him to see Jews at the heart of the great many upheavals of his time, including the ones throughout his beloved Germany.

While it is perhaps legitimate to point out that Hitler was bereft of original ideas, it is equally legitimate to highlight the fact that he assessed, combined, synthesized, expanded, and acted upon the ideas of others as had no one else in the history of the world, and in a sense that very synthesis resulted in many new, even startling, ideas. His was not a case of standing on the shoulders of giants. He would take his ideas and concepts from wherever he found them: from Augustus Caesar, Frederick the Great, or Joe Shit the ragman—it was all the same to him. It was only what worked that mattered.

Hitler's Aesthetics

We know Hitler first and foremost as a despicable warmonger. To his own lights though, he was first and foremost an aesthetic. The point is emphasized by Spotts, who correctly claims that the "aesthetic impulse was an essential element of his character."[397] Fest cites Walter Benjamin who called Fascism the "aestheticizing of politics."[398] "The German conception of politics," says Fest, "had always been infected with aesthetics, and Nazism gave a central place to this quality."[399] It alludes us as to why aesthetics should be deemed infectious, but Fest presumably knew why it was so.

The Swiss politician and historian Carl Burckhardt had it that "Hitler was . . . a case of 'dual personality, the first being that of the rather gentle artist and the second that of the homicidal maniac.'"[400] And while he had definitive ideas as to what represented acceptable art, he was certainly not alone in his contentions that the barbarians—the Modernists, the Jews—were already running asunder in Germany's culture and bringing it all to ruin. Spotts describes Hitler's foreboding:

> In an era of collapsing values, economic crisis and political bewilderment—Oswald Spengler's 1920s international best-seller *Decline of the West* well caught the widespread sense of doom—the Modernist movement reflected and reinforced a popular mood of cynicism and anxiety. . . . In speech after speech he urged resistance to the cultural decay of the time.[401]

Spotts goes on to say that "while Hitler was speaking from his own heart, he was also speaking to the hearts of many others,"[402] as indeed he was. Germany was in dire need of positive aesthetic guideposts.

Spotts speaks of Hitler and "biographic orthodoxy" as follows:

> Biographic orthodoxy has it that Hitler now [1907, Vienna], even more than earlier in his life, was nothing more than a feckless wastrel who led "a parasitical

existence," "a drone's life." But in fact he differed scarcely at all from thousands of young people of artistic bent throughout history. Such aspiring artists spend years in tormented struggle trying to realize themselves. Those who achieve success are praised for their perseverance, those who fail are considered lazy drifters. Hitler's problem—in a way his tragedy—was that he confused aesthetic drive with aesthetic talent. Although the difference must have begun to be apparent to him by 1908, he was determined to pursue his muse as best he could.[403]

Brigitte Hamann makes evident in her book *Hitler's Vienna* that, biographic orthodoxy aside, Hitler was to all outward appearance neither a queer nor a quack. He was instead very much like countless others of his time. It would later take both extraordinary circumstances and equally extraordinary innate talent for him to metamorphose from an ordinary bloke to a defiled tyrant.

Hitler was a thoroughgoing classicist. His esteem for art and architecture of the Romans and the Greeks was unbounded, and his own architectural plans reflect that esteem. As previously mentioned, during World War II when on occasion certain Italian and Greek cities were threatened by German forces, Hitler took steps to ensure that the cities, and thereby their cultural treasures, were spared. When German troops entered Athens, Hitler could take no pleasure from it, so saddened was he by Greece's fate.[404] Paris was similarly spared. When the Germans achieved their victory over France, Hitler entered the city not as a conquering hero; he went there as a museum visitor, a tourist.[405] Likewise, Hitler's visits to Rome and Florence enthralled him as an opportunity to admire immortal masterpieces of art and architecture.

A number of Hitler's closest associates, including Goebbels and Speer, frequently recounted Hitler's apparently sincere desire to one day leave politics and thence devote himself exclusively to the creation of cultural monuments. Posterity, he hoped, would know him by way of his positive cultural attainments, not his wars.

On the subject of posterity, he and Speer even gave consideration to the "ruin value" of their structures—that is, designs for their greatest structures were to be such that as they decayed over time they would nevertheless retain the essence of their original awe and beauty in much the same way that Greek and Roman structures had done. A recurring theme of his cultural session at the Nuremberg party rallies was "the timeless significance," the "eternal value," and "the millennial legacy" of his architecture.[406] But by the 1920s, the opponents of such sentiments were successfully at work to bring about the demise of the beautiful, not excluding beautiful architecture: "In the age of physical sciences and industrialization, beauty was replaced by a calculating rationality,"[407] observes Salmi. And the result was both bitter and ugly.

The ultimate objective of political effort, thought Hitler, was artistic achievement.[408] He sought to outdo Frederick II, Wagner, Ludwig II, Napoleon III—even Augustus and Pericles. Hitler was a man who was serious about art, culture, and construction. Joachim Fest wondered if at the bottom of it all Hitler was anything but an artist.[409] Goebbels recorded Hitler's anguish in January 1945 as it was becoming apparent that his military ambitions would soon fail, how he continued to lament that he had been called by destiny to lead his people in war, tearing him away from his cherished aesthetic ambitions.[410]

It was characteristic of Hitler's aesthetic sensibilities that upon becoming chancellor in 1933, the first building he erected was not a monument to his own triumph—nothing comparable to Mussolini's Forum or Franco's Valle de los Caidos—it was, instead, a massive art gallery,[411] a replacement for a gallery destroyed by fire.

Albert Speer wondered if politics ever had much actual import to Hitler: he decided that it had not. Though a masterful politician, Hitler, decided Speer, "was always and with his whole heart basically an artist."[412] Governing, as Hitler often lamented, caused him to sacrifice his artistic interests to the burdens of politics.[413] As he contemplated in Spandau prison his association with Hitler and the Nazis, Speer had this to say about Hitler and Nazi aesthetics:

> Now, evening in the cell, I have been thinking back on the regime's interest in beauty, which in fact was marked. The ruthlessness and inhumanity of the regime went hand in hand with a remarkable feeling for beauty, for the virginal and unspoiled, although that feeling quite often degenerated into sentimentality of a postcard idyll. Today I sometimes read statements to the effect that all this was merely camouflage, a calculated maneuver to distract the attention of the suppressed masses. But that was not so. Of course the regime's craving for beauty also had to do with Hitler's personal taste, with his hatred for the modern world, his fear of the future. But there was also an unselfish social impulse at work, an effort to reconcile the unavoidable ugliness of the technological world with familiar aesthetic forms, with beauty.[414]

It was perhaps a reflection of Hitler's artistic and romantic sentiment that caused him to become one of the leading early ecologists. Hitler was "green" well before the term was used to describe people with a concern for ecological matters. "His interest in ecological and human scale considerations," acknowledges author Michael Fitzgerald, "were completely against the general trend of architecture at that time, and were not to attract widespread support again until the 1980s."[415] He sought to turn Germany into an idyll, "with flaxen-haired maidens and strong Teutonic swains toiling the land."[416] By 1942, Germany was the "greenest" country in the world.[417]

Germanic history, art, architecture, opera, and operettas were among Hitler's youthful passions, and he carried those passions into adulthood. With respect to opera, we are all familiar with his devotion to the grand operas of Richard Wagner. But he was also enamored by the operetta. He ranked Franz Lehár's *Die Lustige Witwe* (The Merry Widow) as equal to that of the finest operas. Other operettas such as *Die Fiedermaus* (The Bat), *Der Vogelhändler* (The Bird Seller), and *Der Sigeunerbaron* (The Gypsy Baron) were similarly seen by him as sacred things of German cultural heritage.[418]

He was enamored with works of realism painted before the 1860s and despised the modern tendency toward expressionism, cubism, surrealism, Dadaism, and other such perversions of reality[419]—he especially abhorred Dadaism. He did not much care for impressionists such as Monet, either.

In keeping with his national Socialist conceptions, Hitler was adamant in his view that artists were not to create for themselves, but rather for the people. His attitude significantly differentiated him from the modernists who believed that it was the artist's "inner soul" that was to be represented in their work. Modern art, which, as Hitler said, "sought 'to kill the soul of the people' by painting meadows blue and skies green,"[420] also abandoned idyllic scenes depicting peasants, the landscape, the village, and wildlife in favor of the emotional angst and jarring compositions of expressionism and its scenes of horror and deviancy. It was all anathema to his sensibilities. And it must be said that whatever the praise given to modern art of Hitler's era, a lot of it was crude and offensive to romanticist sensibilities; it was every bit as degenerate as the Nazis claimed it was. Much of it amounted to little more than arbitrary heaps of scribble with garish swaths of color; it was mayhemic trash that was deemed artistic only by the proclamation of Jewish critics who praised it. It was, in fact, as bad, garish, and grotesque as the Nazis claimed. And the beat goes on as perverse, trashy art now pervades our current art milieu. We now deem junk as art. And worse, we accept it. We offer no negative voice in critique of such trash.

However lurid and irrational modern art of the day was, it was bestowed with praise by the cultural elite who were almost exclusively Jews. It was the Jews of the day who rationalized it. Any scribbling could be made to seem socially meaningful and important; any debasement of tradition could be rationalized as beneficial, even beautiful. Both morality and beauty were prominent victims of such rationalism.

Honor was made a thing of cabaret humor. Only sex, licentiousness, and all manner of deviancy were esteemed by the societal avant-garde of the era, the thought-leaders, the rationalists.

And to Hitler's lights, far too many of the leaders of the avant-garde were Jews.

Hitler's devotion to the traditional artistic realm of society is illustrated by the fact that even after becoming Germany's chancellor he continued to devote time to making drawings for stage designs for Wagnerian operas, some of which he gave to his favorite stage manager, Benno von Arendt, for inspiration.[421] He personally intervened in the appointments to important theatrical posts to ensure that tradition was preserved and to keep out modernist innovators.[422] It might be said that he had no business interfering in so individualistic an endeavor as art; but then, Hitlerites said the same of prominent Jews, that set of people who could never become real Germans or appreciate German values or the German soul. It was Jewish art critics who promoted art as an individualistic endeavor—for Hitler art was nationalistic and racial.

Hitler generously rewarded artists and sculptors of his liking, and he personally invested heavily in works of art. "He took enormous pleasure in bestowing commissions, grants, awards, honorariums, pensions, tax abatements, scholarships, gifts, titles, professorships, studios and even houses," says Spotts, on his favorite artists.[423] As a striking example of Hitler's devotion to German art and culture, he went so far as to exempt various categories of artists from the military in the early stages of World War II, an exemption that even scientists did not enjoy. At least 20,000 exemptions were granted, enabling major orchestras and opera companies to continue to perform throughout the war.[424] If we may be permitted some Freudian-like speculative leeway, it was perhaps this sort of patronage, this very Jewish-like penchant for taking care of fellow insiders, that initially prompted some historians to presume that Hitler had a bit of Jewry in his ancestry.

On a more general level, Hitler implemented steps to address his sincere concern over the degeneration of Germany's high culture by the appointment of Alfred Rosenberg as the head the Combat League for German Culture (*KAMPfbund fur deutche Kultur*). Rosenberg was a rabid anti-Semitic intellectual who also played a role in establishing various philosophical and ideological underpinnings of Nazism, but he was not actually much of a driving force in those spheres. He was, however, instrumental in establishing and solidifying the idea of equivalency between Judaism, Socialism, Marxism, Communism, and capitalism. His fanaticism was so thoroughgoing that even Hitler and his entourage often had him as the butt of jokes.

As to his own paintings from his days in Vienna, Hitler was realistically self-effacing. After becoming chancellor, his admittedly humble paintings skyrocketed in value. Great art, and particularly great modern art, has much more to do with the artist and the hype the artist can engender than the art itself. Hitler well knew that his paintings and sketches were at best of modest worth. In *Mein Kampf*, he acknowledged himself to be no more than a *kleiner Maler*, a minor painter.[425] When his personal photographer Heinrich Hoffmann showed him a Hitler watercolor that he had purchased, Hitler derisively commented that it was insane that anyone should pay more than about 200 marks for such a work.[426] Ultimately, he intervened to put an end to the rising prices of his paintings. In 1938, he entirely prohibited publication of his artwork.[427]

Critics of Hitler's paintings rightfully point out that his depictions of the human form are often poorly rendered; they are nonproportional and sometimes little more than stick figures that seem to lean hither and yon in unnatural poses, and they certainly lack detail. Hitler was open and forthright about his failings at portraiture. He well knew that he lacked both the training and notions of perspective that it needed. In an interview with *Kunst dem Volke* magazine in June 1937, he pointed out that he had painted in Vienna only as a matter of survival and knew that his canvasses were hardly worth exhibiting in the Haus der Deutschen Kuns (German House of Art). While he certainly had youthful fantasies of becoming a great artist, he quickly adapted to the reality that he would never receive the necessary training to achieve his goals in that respect, and he therefore turned his attention and talent to an area in which he showed more promise, architecture. Of course, he would never become an architect either, but in this area he at least showed great potential, as Speer and others of his contemporaries frequently confirmed.

Fest comments on Hitler's artwork by criticizing "The pedantic brushwork with which he rendered every blade of grass, every stone in a wall, and every roofing tile, shows his intimate craving for wholeness and idealized beauty."[428] Fest is simply wrong on this score, and a good many others as well. Fest's claims about "his intimate craving for wholeness and idealized beauty" is simply an example of psycho-twaddle by a historian with a Freudian bent. While he did from time to time create such detailed works, it was hardly a motif. He did not often paint in the way described by Fest, and when he did, so what? Flemish-English artist Sir Anthony van Dyck was also very exacting in his paintings; they were veritably photographic. Who in the art world would describe van Dyck's portraitures as "pedantic" or as "cravings for wholeness and idealized beauty"? Would we say such things of Dürer? If Hitler sometimes paid too much attention to detail, the modernists of his era certainly paid too little. Hitler's renditions were light-years of departure from the Dadaists, expressionists, cubists, and surrealists of his time; and for the less sophisticated in the art world, that was quite enough to make Hitler's renderings pretty darn good.

Fest, of course, is not the only critic of Hitler's art. It seems to be the case that any acknowledgment that some of Hitler's art was actually pretty good might be misinterpreted as Hitler himself being pretty good. We tend to associate artists with high culture and genteel souls: "good art, good man," so to speak. It needs to be the case, then, that Hitler's art must be deprecated: "bad art, bad man."

There is a refreshing exception to the general mode of off-handed criticism of Hitler's paintings. It can be found in the book *Hitler and the Power of Aesthetics* by Frederic Spotts. Spotts, who is severely and justifiably critical of many aspects of Hitler, nevertheless says the following about Hitler's artwork:

> What was remarkable was that he taught himself without anyone's help, much less any professional training. His style was rooted in the naturalistic German tradition—

concrete and identifiable subjects, clean lines and attention to detail. His handling of the material was at times laboured and clumsy, at other times technically competent and visually attractive. . . . His forte was the craftsmanlike precision that he learned to instill in his treatment of architectural subjects. . . . [He] developed the near-professional eye of an architect.

That is not the whole story, however. What is intriguing is that a number of paintings—all of them almost certainly authentic—demonstrate a respectable master of the medium. Works such as *Weissenkirchen in the Wachau* of 1910, *Old Vienna Courtyard near St Ulrich's Church* of 1911–12, *The Main River Gate* of 1913 along with two unfinished wartime works—*Haubourdin* and *The Seminar Church in Haubourdin*—manifest a remarkable technical leap.[429]

In actuality, much of what Hitler painted was pretty good, or at least competently done. John Toland, taking a positive tact with respect to Hitler's occasional penchant for detail, praisefully describes Hitler's rendition of the *Minorite Church of Vienna* as an example of photographic quality. "Technically," said Toland, "his pictures were quite professional—surprisingly so for a young man without formal art training." Toland goes on to say that "A number of his pictures were pleasant to the eye even if they lacked the artistry that separates competence from professionalism. . . . It was apparent by 1912 that he could draw competently with pencil, paint well with water colors and even better in oils."[430] His *Old Water Gate* is calm, quiet, and restful. For all that is said about Hitler's inability to depict the human form, his *Red Pencil Sketch of Germania* has a pleasing cast to it and demonstrates that with the right effort he could render the human form with appropriate proportion and perspective. His *Sailboats at Sunset* is a painting of positive note and certainly cannot be criticized for excessive detail; in fact, it is rather impressionistic. His little sketch of the *Flying Witch on a Weathervane* has a playful quality to it—and represents an extreme lack of detail.

Google	URL
Adolf Hitler painting, *Minorite Church of Vienna*	http://www.germaniainternational.com/watercolorchurchhitler.html 8/2/14
Adolf Hitler, *Old Water Gate*	431
Painting, *Boat at Sunset*, by Adolf Hitler	432
Sketch, *Witch on a Weathervane*, by Adolf Hitler	433
Adolf Hitler, *Red Pencil Sketch of Germania*	434

Architecture

For all of their reputed roots in the past, however, even ultratraditionalists such as Hitler were, from time to time, willing to depart from the older architectural models. To them, however, the building's place and purpose were the predominant criteria as to style and materials. Thus, it was that buildings along Germany's autobahns were often built in modernist styles, as were factories. Airports and bridges were also built along modernist lines. Autobahns were built always with an eye to both practicality and beauty. "I'm in favour of our building roads everywhere," said Hitler, "but it's not essential to always proceed in a uniform manner. The landscape of Flanders doesn't call for roads like ours. These regions should each keep its own character. Let's not kill the picturesque in the world."[435] Bridges built during the Hitler era surpassed all others in their aesthetic appeal, technical innovation, and even the use of modern methods and materials—they were modern, functional, and especially beautiful. Spotts calls out Germany's Paul Bonatz for special praise:

> Paul Bonatz was the master; his bridge over the Lahn River at Limburg and another over a valley along the Stuttgart-Ulm autobahn are examples of how he

harmoniously balanced monumentalism, care for the environment and technical skill to produce a stunning architectural work.[436]

Acceptance by Hitler of the wonderful bridges and building proposals of Bonatz was perhaps all the more striking because, on the whole, his style was so out of step with Hitler's own. On the other hand, it also illustrates the rational side of Hitler: he had concluded that modernism had its place in the right places. He also supported the idea of standardization with respect to architecture. He stated his position as follows:

> To build a house should not necessarily consist in anything more than assembling the materials—which would not necessarily entail a uniformity of dwellings. The disposition and number of elements can be varied—but the elements should be standardized. . . . What's the point of having a hundred different models for wash-basins? Why these differences in the dimensions of windows and doors?[437]

According to Spotts, Hitler stated his position rather emphatically:

> I will have nothing to do with Romantic eccentricity or anachronistic buildings—as, for example, a service station on a contemporary autobahn of all places that tries to give the impression, through half-timber and gables, of being part of the landscape. Instead they should be declaring, "Here autos are fuelled, not horses given water."[438]

The difference between the modernist and traditional camps was that modernists believed in applying their concepts to all structures; traditionalists reserved the modern for modern settings: for them, you do not construct a modernistic glass pyramid in the courtyard of a classically baroque structure—it is just not done!

Demeaning Hitler, Trite Claims

Psychohistorians have written veritable tomes about what most of us would consider trite incidents in Hitler's life. These historians apply generous amounts of erudite psychobabble to conclude that this or that event in Hitler's life explains his temperament and actions. But for all that has been written on the subject, both the origins and the sincerity of Hitler's anti-Semitism remains a mystery to historians of the Hitler period. Alan Bullock and Emil Fackenheim believed that he was simply a cynical opportunist who used anti-Semitism for his own advancement; others, such as H. R. Trevor-Roper held that he was a true believer.[439] Explanations of Hitler abound—Ron Rosenbaum has even written a book (*Explaining Hitler*) to explain the authors who explain Hitler. Ian Kershaw has the following to say about Hitler's anti-Semitism:

> Why and when did Hitler become the fixated, pathological anti-Semite known for the writing of his first political tracts in 1919 down to the writing of his testament in the Berlin bunker in 1945? Since his paranoid hatred was to shape policies that culminated in the killing of millions of Jews, this is self-evidently an important question. The answer is, however, less clear than we should like. In truth, we do not know for certain why, not even when, Hitler turned into a manic and obsessive anti-Semite.[440]

Here again we see that historians seek a single event to account for Hitler's hate. The answer to the foregoing is that Hitler perceived the actions of individual and organized Jews as being detrimental to Gentiles throughout history and in particular during the first decades of the twentieth century, and that perception accounts for the "why" of Kershaw's interrogative. The "when" of the issue cannot be found in a single event, day, month, or year—the "when" of the issue spans the time between Hitler's sojourn in Vienna and his last days in the Berlin bunker.

Kershaw goes on to acknowledge that "Probably no single encounter produced his loathing for Jews."[441] Unfortunately, after offering that acknowledgment, he falls into his psychobabble mode with comments about Hitler's supposed "unresolved Oedipal complex," and possible "sexual fantasies, obsessions," and "perversions" as key to his anti-Semitism.[442] Consumers of popular lore are seemingly willing to accept such explanations without challenge. What we refuse to accept, apparently, is that despite the evidence that we shall provide in subsequent chapters, Jews were indeed the purveyors of degeneration throughout the political and cultural milieu of Europe during Hitler's time, and that Hitler's anti-Semitism was founded on a very long chain of studies, observations, and events.

Historians commonly use phrases like "undoubtedly," "without doubt," or "beyond any reasonable doubt" (as does this author) to describe things about Hitler and his Nazis for which there can actually be considerable doubt. Lucy Dawidowicz, referring to Heinrich Himmler, for example, claims that after completing college, he got a job at a nitrogen fertilizer company, "reflecting, no doubt, a streak of coprophilia."[443] We must wonder if everyone who gets a job with a nitrogen fertilizer company has, "no doubt, a streak of coprophilia." Michael Fitzgerald, who apparently believes in extrasensory perception, says "that Hitler was a willing and enthusiastic soldier of 'Soviet Bavaria' has been demonstrated beyond any reasonable doubt."[444] The claim is fraudulent—Hitler was an abject opponent of the regime, and there are some claims that he even identified and testified against its supporters. In fact, the regime at one point tried to capture him because of his widely known opposition. It is easy enough to dismiss and belittle Hitler for his actual attitudes and conduct, yet establishment historians seem to be irresistibly drawn by personal fantasy to employ patently false accusations that are expressed with certitude.

Beyond the issue of exaggeration of Hitler's faults and gross misrepresentation of what he said and did, it is a common fault of acknowledged establishment historians to also misrepresent aspects of his life and character. Fest, for example, makes an issue of the allegation that Hitler purposefully "falsified the date of his departure from Vienna."[445] It is absolutely true that Hitler asserted in *Mein Kampf* (p. 163) that in 1912 he went to Munich for good. He actually relocated in 1913. Fest offers neither an explanation nor an implication for the different dates: he makes no claim as to what motive Hitler might have had to falsify the date. But he is presumably certain that the date was falsified, not merely given in error. Hitler said 1912; it was actually 1913. So what? Some historians connect the use of the incorrect date to a deliberate attempt by Hitler as a cover for his having failed to register for the draft while in Vienna. The association seems bogus.[*] Hitler hated the Austro-Hungarian Empire. It would not be surprising that he did not want to return there in order to serve in its military. The apparent fact that he registered himself as stateless in Munich is in all likelihood a reflection of his detestation of Austria-Hungary coupled with his lack of German citizenship—a declaration that "if I can't be German I'll be stateless, but I'll certainly not offer my loyalty to Austria-Hungary." Hitler made no secret of the fact that he would never have served in the armed forces of the detested Austro-Hungarian Empire (though he did at one point belatedly appear before the draft board only to be found physically unfit). He had nothing to hide on this score. Indeed, he might have gotten more political traction by openly and unambiguously declaring that he refused to register for such a draft, especially in light of his heroism on behalf of Germany during World War I. No great significance should be attached to the fact that he claimed to have left Austria in 1912 instead of 1913—he could simply have made a mistake as to the date. Hitler had an extraordinary memory, to be sure, but nobody claims it was infallible.

There are severe strictures to explaining Hitler. Emil Fackenheim, the noted Jewish philosopher and rabbi, enjoins us to resist explanations of Hitler saying that "denying Hitler a

---

[*] Historian Alan Bullock is one among several who have concluded that there is no basis for the draft-dodging claims. As stated by Bullock, ". . . Hitler left Vienna and moved to Munich. There does not appear to be any substance in the story that he did so to avoid military service, for which he had failed to register." Bullock, Alan. *Hitelr and Stalin*. (New York: Vintage Books, 1993, 42.)

posthumous victory is the 614th law," referring to the 613 commandments (mitzvoth) in the Jewish Torah.[446] There is, as Rosenbaum asserts, "outright hostility to the process of explanation itself."[447] Rosenbaum holds that explaining Hitler is not only difficult, it is "dangerous, forbidden, a transgression of near-biblical proportions to some."[448] We are veritably commanded by some members of the Jewish community to not ask, "Why?" It is compliance with the 614th law that provides us all with imitation history, texts that are badly skewed versions of Hitler and the Nazi era.

"Not unreasonably," says Fest, "his biographers have tended to look for a particular 'breakthrough experience'"[449] as the source of Hitler's anti-Semitism. If you ask why he hated the Jews, acceptable answers must rest on simplistic, unfathomable anti-Semitism or some single insignificant truth or fanciful happening in Hitler's life, some monocausal event or experience. Let it not be that Hitler had *any* actual and legitimate reasons to hate Jews—that is the underlying essence of the 614th commandment.

Popular rationale has it that historians examining the Hitler era must restrict themselves to what Hitler did, not what Jews did. "When it comes to the millions of Jews who faced liquidation in Hitler's Europe," says Jewish author Michael Medved, "historians make little effort to figure out what, precisely, the victims had done to make Der Fuehrer so terribly angry."[450] The problem with this perspective is that what Hitler did stemmed in very large part from what Jews did: examining the one begs a concurrent examination of the other. To examine only what Hitler did is rather like trying to examine issues in the Middle East only on the basis of what Arabs there have done; which, regrettably, is, in fact, largely the case. To understand why Hitler hated Jews, one must understand what Jews did to arouse his hatred. Establishment historians know this full well, of course, but choose to deny it for fear that it will "justify" Hitler; and worse, threaten their careers.

Establishment historians have no qualms about attributing Hitler's hate to some inherently evil attribute of all Germans but deny that Jews could have any attributes whatever that could offend so thoroughly as to engender hate. Explaining Hitler in no way provides Hitler with a victory of any kind—nothing whatever justifies the Holocaust. Moreover, as the historian and leading intellectual light of Great Britain, E. P. Thompson, argued, "historians should take care to 'avoid the enormous condescension of posterity': we should make judgments on the actions of people of the past on their terms rather than ours." History is supposed to be narrative; it is, instead, too often fantasy and plot, novelistic. Historical truth, however unpleasant, should be precisely that: truth.

History was waiting for Hitler or someone like him. It might well have happened that instead of Hitler, a member of the radical Left could have taken the reins in Germany—and the consequence for the world, with a different object of genocide, would have been pretty much the same. The forces of history that were in play at the end of Germany's Weimar period were awaiting a powerful, decisive leader. It happened to be Hitler. It could just as easily have been a man like the Jewish Communist Karl Liebknecht[*]— had he lived a while longer it could have been Liebknecht himself.

Hitler had little direct contact with Jews, but Jews, nevertheless, played a significant role in his life: he perceived on the basis of his observations and reading that Jews stood in direct opposition to everything that he so cherished. And as we will later discuss, there was a critical mass of Jews of that period who provided definitive support for his perception.

Of particular concern to this book is the explanation of Hitler's anti-Semitism, a subject area that has been wholly skirted by historians. Historians typically conclude that Hitler's hatred of Jews is simply unfathomable. Donald L. Niewyk, for example, says that "The sources of his antipathy for Jews will probably never be known in any final sense."[451] Alternatively, they seek an incident or two in his life to assign all blame for his hate. The rejection of his application to the Vienna art academy, for example,

---

[*] Most authors say Liebknecht was Jewish; some deny it. Others claim he was a half-Jew by way of his mother whose maiden name was Natalia Reh and generally held to have been a Jewess. Both of his wives were Jewesses. The Nazis thought him Jewish, and that is the claim carried forward herein.

is popularly represented to have been so traumatic that he could have, if he had known or thought that Jews were members of the application examining board, become so ardent an anti-Semite as to order the death of European Jewry. As Stolfi pointedly reminds us, "The cause and effect on display in this argument is simply not credible."[452] Never mind that he did not know the composition of the examining board, and never mind that fully a third of the 113 candidates were dismissed in the very first stage of the competition.[453] That Hitler made it past the first hurdle implies that the drawings he submitted were a cut above many other aspirants. That he then failed in the second stage of the completion could hardly have been entirely unexpected by him, his confidence to the contrary notwithstanding—the academy accepted only the elite (only twenty-eight candidates passed).[454] Hitler, who not infrequently compared himself to historical figures, might have taken comfort from Auguste Rodin—he, like Hitler, was largely self-educated, and he, too, failed in his attempts to enter an art academy, and again, like Hitler, his art was roundly criticized during his lifetime.

One hopes that Brigitte Hamann, in her superb book, *Hitler's Vienna: A Dictator's Apprenticeship*, has put to rest the claim that Hitler's hate stemmed from the rejection of his application to attend an art academy in Vienna, Austria. Hamann investigated the composition of the examining board and found that "not one of the responsible men during the examination was Jewish."[455] Nor was there any reason whatever for Hitler to even *think* that Jews were members of the board. He did not have an inkling of who sat on the board—that was *not* the source or even a contributor to his anti-Semitism. Moreover, Hitler seems to have soon concluded that the academy board was right: "In a few days I myself also knew that I ought some day to become an architect"[456] instead of a painter.

From time to time one comes across commentary from historians about what "might have been" if Hitler had been accepted to the Vienna art academy. This much we can assume with great confidence: he would have failed as an artist. He would never have enjoyed any great success in the art world of his time and place. Can anyone imagine Hitler painting in the cubist or abstract style of the mature Picasso (whose career was launched by the likes of Max Jacob, Leo and Gertrude Stein, and the Cone (Kahn) sisters)? Can we see Hitler painting in the manner of Henri Matisse? Hitler, the Dadaist? Can we see him as a Dix or Klimt or Grosz or other such German artist of the era? Never! He would never have succeeded as an artist, not because his art was bad—it was not—but that would have been precisely his problem, because bad art was what was then coming into vogue. And the demand for such bad art was fostered by Jewish patrons, critics, and gallery owners.

* * * *

Historians and psychoanalysts sometimes grasp at a single word that Hitler uttered here or there and make book chapters out of its demonic significance. Others, as in the case of Lucy Dawidowicz, "the doyenne of Holocaust literature,"[457] took things that Hitler said and earnestly concluded that his words really meant something entirely different. She demonstrated a common penchant, as evidenced in her book, *The War Against Jews*, for identifying various anti-Semitic parties and personalities, as well as speculative narrative about their motivations. Nowhere, however, did she mention anything done by Jews that might serve as actual motivations with respect to anti-Semitism, which is entirely in keeping with her assertion that she used "Jewish sources as the lenses through which to view the Jewish community and to analyze Jewish behavior."[458] With that as her means of analysis, Jews do no wrong. Jews, according to Dawidowicz, are hated but they are at the same time nearly nonexistent—they are hated by anti-Semites because anti-Semites are anti-Semites. Hate against Jews exists, says Dawidowicz, "for no reason other than that they [are] Jews"[459]; they do nothing whatever to cause ire. To the extent that some Jews, in fact, acted criminally, she excuses such criminality by saying that "the historian can never quite know men from the inside, because he can never carry his investigation into the interiority of their minds and hearts, where 'the final play of motive and the point of responsibility' are decided."[460] She made exceptions only with respect to Gentiles. Elie Wiesel claimed that "For two thousand years . . . we were always threatened. . . . For What? For no reason."[461] With "histories" like these, myth and saga predominate, reality and truth play only incidental roles in what we know of past events; so, too, does actual rationality. Sociologist Jennifer Platt holds that "contemporary preferences" are legitimated by "providing them with an honourable past."[462] We concur.

The demonization of Hitler by way of trivialities diminishes proper emphasis on his crimes and makes some people doubt the truth of those crimes. Here are some things that are almost certainly true: he did not chew on carpets (in fact, self-control was one of his most striking characteristics),[463] he possessed two testicles, he was heterosexual, to his mother he was a devoted son and he greatly appreciated the efforts of the Jewish doctor who treated her for breast cancer shortly before her death from that cause. Claims to the contrary are replete in populist "history" but are not true.

By and large, historians, and psychohistorians in particular, have provided us with absurd explanations for Hitler's hatred. In keeping with their Freudian bent, many of their elaborate explanations center on Hitler's genitalia. As the result of almost certainly falsified Russian autopsy of Hitler's remains (the Russians sought to diminish Hitler's image), some psychohistorians seriously claim that Hitler's hate somehow stemmed from his having had only one testicle. In *The Psychopathic God*, Robert Waite built a Neuschwanstein-like castle of Freudian interpretive analysis on the slender foundation of Hitler's purportedly half-empty scrotal sac,[464] says Ron Rosenbaum. The story gets even stranger: it was originally proffered by Dietrich Güstrow, a prominent attorney in West Germany, in his widely acclaimed book *Tödlicher Alltag* (Deadly Routine) that a billy goat had bitten off one of Hitler's testicles.[465] Hitler's personal physician has testified that Hitler had both his testicles and that they were entirely normal.

HITLER, JEWS, AND HATE

Joachim Fest says the following about Hitler's hate:

> We can probably no longer plumb the real cause of this ever-growing hatred, which lasted literally to the last hour of Hitler's life. One of his dubious cronies of those years attributed the hatred to sexual envy on the part of a dropout from the middle class. This crony had described an incident involving a model, the essence of Germanic femininity, a half-Jewish rival, and an attempt on Hitler's part to rape the girl while she was posing. The story is as grotesque as it is stupidly plausible. The theory that Hitler's anti-Semitism was connected with pathological sexual fixations is supported by the whole uneven pattern of Hitler's ideas about sexual relations, which from his boyhood oscillated remarkably between strained idealism and obscure anxiety feelings.[466]

Fest's claim of "stupidly plausible" should be abridged to simply "stupid." Fest offers other such far-reaching "repressed sexuality" suppositions as well. Alan Bullock forthrightly acknowledges that the works concerning Hitler from psychohistorians have been deeply flawed: one, because they lack a reliable evidentiary basis for their speculations, and two, because their conclusions about such things as Hitler's purported schizophrenia are totally at odds with the Hitler person and the debilitated schizophrenics that psychiatrists experience in their everyday practices.[467]

Ron Rosenbaum correctly chalks up such theoretical fantasia as "an example of the hunger for single-pointed"[468] explanation for Hitler's hate.

The purported "one-ball business,"[469] as biographer Alan Bullock calls it, has been accompanied by other nearly equal nonsense about the source of Hitler's hate. Such absurdities include claims that his hate somehow stemmed from his authoritarian and abusive father; still others that it was somehow the fault of his loving and attentive mother. There is no profession anywhere that is more adept in the pilpul method of logic than that of psychiatry and psychology. They easily decide upon a conclusion and thereafter make the facts fit their prejudice. Watch a court case that involves these professions and take note of the fact that in every single case one set of expert witnesses invariably propose diametrically opposed conclusions about the psychology of the defendant. They seemingly take the position that in their science there is no single correct answer; there is only the one that is paid for by their patrons.

There is also a theory that Hitler was something of a sissy as a boy and that his hate of Jews somehow stemmed from his femininity, what Toland and others of his ilk call his "homosexual panic."[470] You can, of course, believe that to be true, but if you do, you put yourself on the side of the most irrational of the Hitler theorists. "Too silly" is an apt conclusion about such assertions.

Others, such as Werner Maser, have it that Hitler was a rough-and-tumble kid who held sway at recess,[471] and even Toland has it that Hitler was the leader of his schoolmates. "'We all liked him, at desk and play,' said Josef Kepling, a boyhood friend. 'He had guts.' He wasn't a hothead but really more amenable than a good many."[472] So which was it? Was he a sissy or a ruffian? Or was he just a normal kid who later happened to become a most extraordinary man?

Rudolf Olden says that one of the roots of Hitler's anti-Semitism "may have been his tortured sexual envy."[473] Fest has Hitler as a "sex-starved daydreamer."[474] Any port in a storm.

In keeping with phallocentric explanations of Hitler, such luminaries as Nazi hunter Simon Wiesenthal believed the speculation attributed to Josef Greiner in his book, *Das Ende des Hitler—Mythos* (The End of the Hitler Myth) that Hitler had been infected with syphilis from a Jewish whore in Vienna's Leopoldstadt and that, therein, lay the source of his hatred.[475] It is preposterous, of course, but it illustrates what even highly learned people are prepared to believe.

Nor was Hitler the weak, bumbling, failed painter or "house painter" that he is so often made out to be. The "house painter" myth was originated by Jewish writer Kurt Tucholsky, in *Die Weltbühne*, no. 17 (April 26, 1932) and thence replicated by a highly biased press. It is, instead, the case, as Hamann puts it, the

"Vienna Hitler was a substantial figure."[476] After relocating to Munich, he managed to develop a reliable clientele and did quite well for himself. His watercolors had genuine appeal, showing, as many of them did, a fresh representation of Munich's architectural splendor.[477]

The fault of Christendom is still another favorite of many establishment scholars in explaining Hitler. "It is a straight line, 'a direct connection,' [Jewish scholar Hyam] Maccoby believed, 'between Judas and Hitler.'"[478] Daniel Goldhagen, in *Hitler's Willing Executioners*, draws equivalent conclusions about Christianity and Hitler's hate. There it is. Now you know.

Still other ridiculous claims abound. There is the speculation that Hitler was part Jewish, and as a self-hating Jew, he directed his hate outward at Jews in general. Some argue that he suffered from epidemic encephalitis which he purportedly contracted during World War I and that his encephalitis was somehow responsible for his hatred of Jews.

Even those who acknowledge that Hitler's hate could have been evolutionary in the sense that different incidents and observations in his life could have collectively caused a sort of slow diabolical metamorphosis in his thinking tend to center their theories on just a few traumatic events. One such event was the suicide of his beloved niece, Geli Raubal, who purportedly pined for a Jewish music instructor and was, according to myth, even made pregnant by the man.[479] Else it might have been the trauma he felt due to Germany's loss of World War I and his perception that Jews were responsible for that loss. Take your pick; there is lots of fruit from which to choose. But limit your assignment of responsibility, in keeping with Freudian concepts, to a "this" or a "that."

We point out the foregoing truths about the silly claims because each of them has been used as significant psychological rationale for Hitler's hate. Many more equally silly rationales have been proffered, a personal favorite is the claim that Hitler hated Jews because he was anti-Semitic. The latter is seemingly the argument of Daniel Goldhagen: he argues that Germans were becoming increasingly anti-Semitic during the 1920s but provides no explanation of *why* they were doing so—his argumentation is circular; they were anti-Semitic because they were anti-Semitic, Jews did nothing whatever to call forth or invigorate anti-Semitism.

There is, of course, still another aspect of Hitler that requires emphasis: the Holocaust did happen, and Hitler was its architect. Our understandable hate of him stems from that fact. All other things done by Hitler could be forgiven, or at least tolerably rationalized. Not so the Holocaust. And that is right and proper and should forever remain in our consciousness.

In actuality, Hitler's anti-Semitism stemmed from the nature of his personality (e.g., his fanatical nationalism and romanticism, but also his considerable intellect) and a long series of observations, studies, and events, and rational assessments of those studies and events that collectively compounded his hatred. As we have seen, the seed of his nationalism was planted during his school days as a boy in Linz. It was reinforced by his assiduous study of German and world history and mythology, coupled with observations of the political and social milieu that he was to experience in Vienna between 1907 and 1913.

His participation in World War I and Jewish-German opposition to Germany's participation in that war was the next momentous event to influence his thinking. The various strikes and revolutions in Germany toward the end of the war and shortly thereafter—all of them led or inspired by Jews but often claimed in the various histories as "spontaneous," enraged him. This was the basis for the "theory," as opposed to the "myth" term preferred by establishment historians, that Germany was stabbed in the back by Jews. Jewish involvement in the establishment of the hated Weimar Republic and their involvement in the creation of the oppressive Treaty of Versailles further reinforced his hate. The right wing unjustly blamed the devastating inflationary period of the early 1920s on Jews, providing still another offense to Hitler's sensibilities. Though Jews did not cause the inflation, some few of them did exploit it to the ruin of many a German household. The political struggles throughout the 1920s, but especially those from 1918 through 1923, involved large contingents of Jews and served to further sully the image of Jewish patriotism toward Germany. From the mid- to late-1920s, a series of corruption scandals involving Jews reinforced the historical stereotype of Jews as dishonest and exploitive. All of the foregoing, and more, will be elaborated upon in later chapters.

Even before Hitler attained power, the worldwide Jewish community, in anticipation of his success, declared what might have been a ruinous international boycott of Germany. The boycott action had the explicit objective of bringing down Hitler and his Nazis, and such an action could hardly have endeared him to Jews. Lastly, the overwhelming influence of Jews in Weimar Germany's politics and culture during the 1920s, when combined with all of the other influences on his thinking, created in him a hate so intense, so violent, that he was conditioned by 1942 to institute the Holocaust. That is, as he realized that the war was to be lost, he took actions to ensure that the Jews of Europe would suffer a fate every bit as bad, and worse, than the one posited for Germany (as, for example, by the Jewish U.S. Secretary of the Treasury, Henry Morgenthau Jr.) by the pending loss of the war.

Hitler's ire did not stem from the "one ball business" or any other such inane singularity; rather, it stemmed from a long-term accumulation of causes. Hitler's hate was founded on real people doing real things over a period of many years that he rationally viewed as inimical to his beloved Germany, her culture, and her volk. And regretfully, the people doing these inimical things were Jews.

Jewish-Bolshevik Equivalency

There is one more issue about Hitler that needs to be clarified before we move on to the incidents and influences that engendered his hate.

All historians that write about Hitler point out that he and his Nazis equated liberalism, leftism, Communism, and Bolshevism with Jews, as, in fact, they did. As early as 1920, Hitler "married the images of Marxism, Bolshevism, and the Soviet system in Russia to the brutality of Jewish rule, for which he saw Social

Democracy preparing the ground in Germany."[480] While he was still in Vienna, he began to make such connections. Historians consistently represent this thought process as both irrational and untrue. The Estonia-born Hitler sycophant Alfred Rosenberg was a particularly strong contributor to the idea of equivalency between Marxism, all forms of leftist radicalism, Social Democracy, Communism, and Judaism.[481] For the Nazis, if you spoke of one you were speaking of the other. Historians rarely explain, though, why or how it was that this was so. We are expected to believe that the association was simply another instance of Nazi irrationalism stemming from their equally irrational anti-Semitism that, in turn, stemmed from deep-seated and irrational anti-Semitic German psychosis. In fact, though, Nazis and a good many others made the same connection, and the reason lay in the preponderance of Jews in the first or second tiers of the leadership of the various leftist upheavals of the age. A good many prominent Jews and non-Jews alike made the connection independently of Rosenberg, Hitler, and other members of the radical right wing. By way of example, Chaim Weizmann, the first president of Israel, commented on the attitudes of the Allies shortly after World War I:

> Russia at this time was hardly in the good books of the Allies, for it was soon after the Bolshevik revolution, which on the whole they identified with Russian Jewry; Russians, Jews, Bolsheviks were different words for the same thing in the minds of the British officers in Palestine in those days. . . .[482]

To some extent, the association was self-inflicted. Karl Marx, for all of the claims of his being outside the Jewish brotherhood, believed at the bottom of it all in the ultimate good of his fellow Jews and the general scheme of his ideas were restatements of the central ideas of Judaism itself.[483] As we shall see, the radical regimes in both Hungary and Germany's Bavaria were composed almost wholly of Bolshevistic Jews, as were the leading radicals elsewhere in Germany (e.g., the Spartacists, the KPD, and the USPD).[484]

In the first years after the 1917 Russian Revolution, it was everywhere evident that Jews were at the apex of the revolutionary movement there. As historian Heiko Haumann asserts, there was "Trotsky, Zinoviev, Kamenev, Sverdlov, Ioffe [this name is an alternative translation of Adolph Abramovich Joffe], Radek, Riazanov and many others. . . . This gave rise to hatred in their opponents and fostered the saying that Jews are Communists (and vice versa)."[485] For Hitler, Jews were the midwives of revolution throughout the Continent. And given the presence of so many Jews in such powerful positions, how could any rational being suppose for a moment that they were not the creators and sustaining forces of Communism and its revolutionary movements? They were clearly the Trotskys and Bronsteins of Bolshevism.

Moreover, a few prominent Jews were more than willing to demean their Jewish brethren in widely circulated publications. Writers such as Professor F. A. Ossendowski in 1926 acknowledged the widespread presence of Jews within the various Communist movements and attributed it to characteristics of the Jewish people: characteristics such as their supposed facility for intrigue, stratagem, conspiracy, and want of revenge.[486] The Jewish biographer of the Rothschild family,[487] Marcus Eli Ravage, published a number of outrageous statements concerning Jews. He wrote in the January–February 1928 issue of *Century* magazine about the guilt of Jews in connection with their dealings with Gentiles and assigned responsibility for various Gentile wars to the schemes of Jews, including not only the Russian revolution but every major revolution in history. Jewish publications, such as the *Jewish Daily Forward*, presented Socialism to the Jewish masses as a secular version of Judaism itself.[488] The April 4, 1918, edition of the *London Jewish Chronicle* said that "there is much in the fact of Bolshevism itself; in the fact that so many Jews are Bolshevists; in the fact that the ideals of Bolshevism are consonant . . . with the finest ideals of Judaism. . . ."

During World War I, the apparent influence of Jews to shape world events caused Hitler, like "millions of other patriots . . . to fear Jews and Reds (almost as a single entity),"[489] says the historian John Toland. Several non-Jewish statesmen such as

Winston Churchill and a number of diplomats who were close to the various Bolshevistic cataclysms commented on the dominance of Jews in inciting them. As recently as June 2013 Russian President Vladimir Putin claimed that 80 to 85 percent of the first Soviet government in Russia was composed of Jews[490] and the atrocities there had a similar percentage of Jews as their instigators and directors.

Mikhail Bakunin, a contemporary of Marx, had it that both Marxist Communism and finance capital worked in tandem to promote the interest of Jews.[491] In February of 1920, Winston Churchill wrote the following for the *Illustrated Sunday Herald*:

> There is no need to exaggerate the part played in the creation of Bolshevism and in the actual bringing about of the Russian Revolution, by these international and for the most part atheistical Jews, it is certainly a very great one; it probably outweighs all others. . . . This movement [internationalism/Bolshevism/communism] among the Jews is not new. From the days of Spartacus-Weishaupt to those of Karl Marx, and down to Trotsky (Russia), Béla Kun (Hungary), Rosa Luxembourg (Germany), and Emma Goldman (United States), this world-wide conspiracy for the overthrow of civilization and for the reconstitution of society on the basis of arrested development, of envious malevolence, and impossible equality, has been steadily growing. It played, as a modern writer, Mrs. [Nesta Helen] Webster [author of *The French Revolution, A Study in Democracy*], has so ably shown, a definitely recognizable part in the tragedy of the French Revolution. It has been the mainspring of every subversive movement during the Nineteenth Century; and now at last this band of extraordinary personalities from the underworld of the great cities of Europe and America have gripped the Russian people by the hair of their heads and have become practically the undisputed masters of that enormous empire.[492]

Quoting Pipes, Kevin MacDonald says that "Among gentile Russians there was a widespread perception that 'whereas everybody else had lost from the Revolution, the Jews, and they alone, had benefited from it.'"[493] MacDonald's point is further illustrated by a popular joke in Russia that highlighted the preponderance of Jews in the early Soviet regime. The letters CCCP, the Cyrillic version of USSR, it was said, stood for three Jews and one Russian—C is the first Cyrillic letter of a slang word for Jew, and P is the first Cyrillic letter of the Ukrainian word for Russian. The claim was not much off the mark, especially with respect to the leadership and membership in the various Soviet secret police organizations.

Slezkine also highlights the idea that the Jews and Bolshevism were broadly thought of as equivalent terms. Says Slezkine:

> The special relationship between Bolsheviks and Jews—or rather, between the Bolshevik and Jewish revolutions—became an important part of the revolutionary war of words. Many Whites and other enemies of the Bolsheviks equated the two and represented Bolshevism as a fundamentally Jewish phenomenon.[494]

In Russia, the most prominent Jews were Leon Trotsky, Lev Kamenev, and Gregory Zinoviev. Lenin, who was one-quarter Jewish, was, of course, the most prominent of all. Huge numbers of Jews of lesser disgraceful distinction were also enthusiastic Communist participants of the era. It was the case, in fact, that as it was recognized just how powerful and protected the Jews of Russia became, Jews throughout the world understandably joined the Communist ranks in droves. The Communist Party of the U.S., for example, had a predominantly Jewish hue.

Hitler was fixated on Jews within the ranks of revolutionary Russia. Fate, said Hitler, "handed over Russia to Bolshevism, which . . . really meant handing over Russia to the Jews."[495] For a time, one of Hitler's most devout, if somewhat petulant followers, Otto Strasser, was first drawn to Hitler and Nazism by disillusionment brought on by the influence of Moscow-based Bolshevist Jews. Strasser had been liberal until he attended a speech in Halle given by Grigory Zinoviev, the president of the Third International (Comintern). Zinoviev had come from Moscow to give speeches in Germany during the autumn of 1920 and to thereby draw some 900,000 German Socialists to the far Left as represented by the Moscow-based, Jewish-dominated Comintern. "What he [Zinoviev] said," complained Strasser, "sounded like a new Messiah-doctrine' with Moscow dominating Germany."[496] Strasser was very much like many of the early Nazis: he was, in effect, a "national Bolshevist," bitterly opposed to the aristocracy and capitalists, an extreme Socialist who differed from the Communists only in that he virulently opposed the international aspects of the movement. He, though, like the Communists, would have confiscated all royal properties, nationalized the land and businesses, and would have broken up the large private estates into tenant farms. Hitler, on the other hand, recognized the value of competition and individual initiative and therefore encouraged the continuation of capitalism, but only under conditions that contributed to the advancement of the country as a whole, a thoroughly socialized form of capitalism.

The Jewish heritage of wandering and rootlessness, coupled with the internationalism of many Jewish organizations and the explicitly international Moscow-based Comintern, confirmed for a good many Germans who opposed Communism that German Jews were internationalists, rather than patriots dedicated to the fatherland. Hitler once observed that "The international element of the Communist movement that emanates from Russia [the Comintern] is not really Russian, or Slavic; it is Jewish."[497] And it is simply a truth that internationalism was almost wholly a Jewish affair at the turn of the century and remains largely so today.

Jews were prominent in the Bolshevik movements of the Baltic states as well as Silesia, Poland, Hungary, Romania, Ukraine, and, of course, in Russia proper, as well as in German-Austria and Hitler's beloved Germany.

After the fall of tsarist Russia, the activities of Bolsheviks of the various countries were coordinated and directed by the Comintern. The Comintern was founded in March 1919 by some thirty-four Communist parties. Its stated objective was to fight "by all available means, including armed force, for the overthrow of the international bourgeoisie and for the creation of an international Soviet republic as a transition stage to the complete abolition of the State."[498] The Comintern both directed and coordinated the revolutionary activities of the various international Communist movements, including those of Germany. Adolf Ehrt, in his 1933 book, *Communism in Germany*, was entirely correct in asserting the following:

> The German Communist Party [KPD] is the only one in Germany which is a foreign, alien and hostile group. It is part and parcel of the Soviet Union; as regards organization and finance, it is directly dependent on Moscow to whom . . . it owes theoretically and practically unreserved and unconditioned obedience.[499]

Hitler provided an entirely rational assessment of the Comintern and its objectives in one of his commentaries to Otto Wagener when he said:

> Bolshevism works with the Comintern organization. It lays the groundwork for the revolutionizing of the mind, and its task is to initiate Communist uprisings, subversion—and the rule of the proletariat in the other nations of the world as well. And since, next to Poland, Slovakia, and Hungary, we are closest to the Bolshevik borders, the danger to us Germans is especially great.[500]

The fact that so many Jews were involved in the Comintern itself and its many subordinate organizations in other countries, and that they were so important to the leadership that utterly and literally starved, murdered, and otherwise brutally subjugated the populations of these various countries, caused large segments of the populations to welcome the arrival of German troops during World War II. It was this fact that put the people of Poland, Ukraine, the Baltic states, Belorussia, Bukowina-, and Moldova-Romanians in such fear of the Bolsheviks that they could hardly wait for the Germans to invade. For their part, Jews expressed their hate for local populations and concomitant loyalty to the Soviet Union as they jubilantly welcomed the invading Red Army into such places as Poland, Bessarabia, Lithuania, and Bukowina—all places in which Jews enthusiastically supported the imposition of Communist rule.[501]

In a closing speech at one of the Nazi Nuremberg rallies, Hitler made apparent his awareness of the goings-on in Russia after the Bolshevik revolution.

> We believe that it is a bigger task to put 5 million people back to work than to burn down houses and churches and allow hundreds of thousands of workers and peasants and others to kill each other. We have also fought against Bolshevism on general economic grounds. From time to time the world hears of hunger famines in Russia. Since, 1917, that is, since the victory of Bolshevism, there is no end to this form of distress. That self-same Russia, starving for close to 20 years, was one of the richest grain countries in the world.

Germany itself had long been influenced by prominent Jews and Hitler was acutely aware of and enraged by this fact. The influences, for example, of such personalities as Karl Marx, Heinrich Heine, Ferdinand Lasalle, and Ludwig Börne were simply incalculable. As we shall see in more detail later, prominent Jewish Leftist-Marxists-Bolsheviks-Communists included Karl Liebknecht, Rosa Luxemburg, Leo Jogisches, Paul Levi, Ruth Fischer, Kurt Eisner, Ernst Toller, Béla Kun, Erich Muehsam, Eugen Levine, Max Levien, Towia Axelrod, Karl Radek, Hugo Haase, and Gustav Landauer. A number of other relatively minor figures were also Jewish, the insane Dr. Franz Lipp who participated in the Bavarian Revolution being among them. In actual fact, not a single member of the Bavarian revolutionary leadership was Bavarian by birth; "they were," reports Joachim Fest, "conspicuous types of the antibourgeois and often Jewish intellectual."[502] And several of the foregoing were not even German, much less Bavarian. The foreigners included such prominent personalities as Levine, Luxemburg, Radek, and

Jogisches. Still others, such as Parvus-Helphand and the Russian financier Yakov Ganetsky, worked behind the scenes. The efforts of the various radical leftists among the foregoing were sponsored by the Jewish-Russian ambassador to Germany, Adolf Joffe. Prominent mainstream Jewish politicians of the time included Walter Rathenau and Hugo Preuss. Like the radical ranks, the mainstream political establishment also had a significant number of lesser lights of Jewish extraction. Hitler, and others like him, could not help but be enraged by the Jewish undertakings in Germany during the 1920s.

During World War I it was many of the aforementioned individuals who led the efforts for revolution in Germany and for the defeat of Germany's war effort. The antiwar movement in Germany originated within the radical leftist ranks of the SPD, USPD, and their associated Spartacist movement. All three of these political parties were founded by Jews: the SPD by Ferdinand Lassalle, August Bebel, and Wilhelm Liebknecht (non-Jewish); the USPD by Hugo Haase, Eduard Bernstein, and Karl Kautsky.* The Spartacus League was founded by Karl Liebknecht, Rosa Luxemburg, Leo Jogiches, Paul Levi, Ernst Meyer, Franz Mehring, August Thalheimer, and a smattering of non-Jews such as Clara Zetkin. The USPD quickly managed to install some twenty-four deputies in the Reichstag. These Reichstag members then used parliamentary privilege to circumvent censorship regulations and thereby safely trounce the war effort in virulent terms.[503] Members of the Spartacus League would declare their true colors at the end of the war when they became the Communist Party of Germany (KPD).

In Bavaria, where Hitler observed events firsthand, it was a coterie of Jews who seized the government there in November of 1918 and caused havoc, including executions, until being ousted in early May of 1919. In Hungary, it was the Jew Béla Kun, and he

---

* Some historians claim that Kautsky was not Jewish; others, including the New World Encyclopedia, assert that he was.

was again a player in the disastrous March Action of 1921 in Germany.

Given the absolute numbers of Jews in the various Marxist movements of the late eighteenth century and early nineteenth century, and especially the overwhelming preponderance of Jews in the leadership of those movements, it is hardly surprising that Hitler and vast numbers of others equated all of the various forms of Marxism with Jews. The evidence was plentiful; the perception of a general equivalency between liberalism-Marxism-Communism and Jews was an entirely rational one.

While still a teenager, Hitler relocated to Vienna, Austria. It would be the next significant place and period in which his worldviews were molded.

CHAPTER 2

ABOUT HITLER'S VIENNA

The Vienna through which Hitler wandered in his youth was a melting pot of decadent turmoil, the capital of an empire in decline—a "research laboratory for world destruction"
—Jason Cowley, April 26, 1999,
http://www.newstatesman.co.uk/199904260039.htm

Adolf Hitler first visited Vienna, Austria, in 1906.[*] He returned and took up permanent residence there in 1907. He remained in the city from that point until 1913. He tells us in *Mein Kampf* that it was during his first visit that he was captivated by the splendor of the architecture of the Ringstrasse (Ring Boulevard). According to Brigitte Hamann, he was immediately enthralled: *"[T]he whole Ring Boulevard seemed to me like an enchantment of The Thousand-and-One Nights,"*[504] he said. (Italics are in the original.) He raved about its mix of elegant architecture throughout the remainder of his life as the most beautiful line of streets that has ever been built.[505] The Ringstrasse's classical parliament building was a "Hellenic masterpiece on German soil,"[506] according to Hitler. While there he painted so many pictures of the parliament building that he could create it in detail solely from memory.

Google	URL
Images of Vienna Parliament Building	507
Images of Vienna buildings	508
Images of Vienna Ringstrasse	509

There was nothing in the Hitler of that period to suggest that he was anything other than an entirely harmless romantic aesthetic

---

[*] 1905 according to some authors.

and idealist. There was not even a hint of evil or lust for power of any kind during the early days of his Vienna sojourn.

While there, Hitler spent the bulk of his time reading, drawing, attending the opera, and examining the city's architecture. The whole of the political and cultural milieu of Vienna was for him an education in the ways of the world. He studied the various political and artistic figures, the mix of races there, the pomp of the church, and the art, architecture, and music. He studied, too, the Jews of the city. And the Jews of Vienna had, by that time, according to Fest, "flung themselves into the Socialist movement and became its leaders. Thus, there arose that fateful picture of a grand conspiracy with parts carefully assigned, some to work within capitalism, some within the coming [Communist] revolution."[510]

Already a Pan-German due to the influence of his Linz history teacher, Dr. Pötsch, his Pan-Germanism was reinforced, cured, and made concrete during his Vienna period. He also continued to read and learn about Germany. "As I had always done before," he said in *Mein Kampf*, "I continued in Vienna to follow events in Germany with ardent zeal, quite regardless whether they were political or cultural."[511]

Hitler formed the basis for his worldview, his Weltanschauung, while in Vienna. Inspiration for his worldview was molded by both his studies and observations of life in the city and by writers such as race theoretician Guido von List. He is known to have owned a copy of List's *Deutsch-Mythologische Landschhaftsbilder* (Images of German Mythological Landscapes),[512] and we can be confident that he perused it thoroughly. In 1898, List published his book, *The Invincible: Basics of a Germanic Weltanschauung*, which Hitler also likely read.[513] Houston Stewart Chamberlain and his book, *The Foundations of the Nineteenth Century*, which was written in Vienna, was still another important influence.

It was also there in Vienna that Hitler's Darwinistic philosophy with respect to survival of the fittest matured. It was there, too, that his conceptions of race, of Jews, the nature of the state, the importance of the individual in the making of epic events, of loyalty to the German fatherland and its people came to fruition. By the time Hitler departed Vienna in 1913, the most distinctive traits of his personality had been molded, in particular his intense nationalism and the foundation for his anti-Semitism, which was, at that time, still more intellectual than stridently emotional.

*   *   *   *

Vienna was the primate city of Austria; it was from here that 50 million people, members of ten different nations and races, were ruled.[514] Historically, the Jews of the city, as nearly everywhere else they settled, were, for a time, welcomed and were highly privileged participants in its society.

In Vienna and elsewhere Jewish predominance in finance, the press, theater, literature, prostitution, white slavery, and political radicalism were particularly evident. Hitler would later comment in *Mein Kampf* about his firsthand observations of prostitution and white slavery in the Jewish district of Leopoldstadt.* "When thus for the first time I recognized the Jew as the cold-hearted, shameless, and calculating director of this revolting vice traffic," he said, "a cold shudder ran down my back."[515]

Jews were in abundance in Vienna because the city was so welcoming and broadminded. That there was anti-Semitism there is unquestionable, but Jews from throughout the Austro-Hungarian Empire were attracted to the city precisely because anti-Semitism was so much greater elsewhere. The *Times* of London correspondent Henry Wickham Steed, one of the most penetrating observers of the day, a man who happened to be highly critical of both Germans and Jews, said at the time that "among the peoples of Austria-Hungary the Jewish people stands first in importance. . . . Economically, politically, and in point of general influence they are . . . the most significant element in the Monarch."[516] Steed was describing a reality that was apparent to everyone in the city.

---

* Jewish involvement in prostitution was not limited to Vienna. In Rio de Janeiro their involvement was so pervasive that the term "kaftan," the long gown of Jewish traditionalists, became synonymous with "pimp."

About Hitler's Vienna

Vienna was variously Freud's Vienna, Mahler's Vienna, and Wittgenstein's Vienna. At the bottom of the social heap it was also Hitler's Vienna, a Hitler who was among those who viewed Jews' profound influence upon Austria-Hungary as an attack on his beloved Germandom. As put by author Steven Beller: "Whether it be Freud, Schoenberg, Schnitzler or Wittgenstein, the number of individuals at the top level of Viennese culture—or rather that type of culture for which Vienna is today so famous—who are of at least partly Jewish descent is so large that it cannot be ignored."[517]

Hitler's observations with respect to art and the "Jewish modernism" of art in Vienna made him conclude that it was not, in fact, art at all but only Jewish kitsch that was pushed by the "Jew press" with business sense.[518] As with many of his other observations and conclusions, Hitler was joined by a good many like-thinking members of the German-Austrian population. Among the observations he made, as he told his sister Paula, "trade in works of art [is] in Jewish hands,"[519] as indeed it was.

By and large, it was Jews who were at the forefront of radical innovation of the progressivism in both arts and politics. Artistically, they propounded expressionism in all its various forms. Expressionism was supposedly a metaphorical act of biblically rebellious sons against fathers and fatherland; a theme that was endlessly repeated. According to historian Istvan Deak, "sons strove not only for the destruction of the fathers, but also for the annihilation of everything that the fathers represented; conventional order, dull philistinism, materialism, the capitalistic world order. During the war father and fatherland became interchangeable terms in expressionist literature."[520] That is, Jews and other expressionists supposedly angry with their biological fathers expressed their anger by undermining the metaphysical fatherland, or so goes the tortuous Freudian-transference logic of such claims.

Whatever the rational for expressionism may have been, it produced a gap between the avant-garde and traditionalists that was probably the widest that had ever existed.[521] While difficult to define because of the breadth of its scope, expressionism was characterized by Communistic leanings, the "largely Jewish ethnicity of Expressionist artists"[522] (e.g., Carl Einstein, Georg Kaiser, Gunther and Schultze-Naumburg), a willful divergence from traditional modes of thinking, "a turn away from the notion of aesthetic beauty" and symmetry, and primitivism, which was attributed to Carl Einstein. "Let us murder reason," said Einstein in his book, *Negerplastik* (Negro Plastic), "reason has created the shapeless death in which there is nothing to see."[523]

Expressionism was short-lived, reaching its apex between 1917 and 1923, but it greatly influenced all of the modern artistic isms that followed it—it set the stage for the degeneration of the visual and literary arts. And it was heavily promoted by Jews such as Georg Kaiser, a man who was among the most prolific playwrights of the Weimar era and who was closely identified with the expressionist movement's discontinuity, fragmentation, and discord.[524]

On the whole, Jews of the time were not artists, at least in the visual arts; they were, instead, the dealers and critics of art. They were also the art promoters as exemplified by Paul Cassirer, who did so much to bring French modernism, and French impressionism in particular, to Germany. As Peter Pulzer points out in *The Rise of Political Anti-Semitism in Germany & Austria*, Jews expressed a genius that was interpretive and critical rather than creative.[525] That is, with some notable exceptions, Jews did not create the art; they, instead, selected the art that was to be praised and that which was to be condemned.

The early expressionists held that art must express the artist's "inner experience." With this as the foundation, expressionists could pass off any sort of painting or textual drivel as exemplary of an enlightened "inner experience." Jewish art critics of the day supported expressionists with heaps of literary bile that purported to explain the artist and the inner experience being represented.

Wilhelm Hausenstein, in an article titled "Art at This Moment," shed some esoteric light on expressionism in 1919–1920:

> That no one is an expressionist can be asserted just about as easily as that everyone is, or a few are: because what

constitutes expressionism has not been established. There is something like a signature of expressionism, perhaps a schema underlying it. One could define it roughly like this: form from deformation. That is put negatively. Positively, one could say: form from imagination. [. . .] Obvious, too, the significance of procedure. Obvious, all too obvious, however, a vagueness over the long run; a by now, after a decade, terrible vagueness—gradually, for some, long since profoundly unsatisfying. Where does that come from?

Let me attempt an answer. Impressionism was from the beginning based on a kind of relativity. Therefore, it is impossible to demand from it the absolutism that expressionism claims for itself, wants to offer us. But at the same time a peculiar reversal has obviously transpired: Impressionism has left us a body of absolute art. Acquiescence to relativism produced in the case an absolute. In expressionism, the claim to the absolute has yielded merely the relative.[526]

The art market was, and still is, full of such drivel as the foregoing.

After World War II, the idea of expressionism would be characterized as nonrepresentational and improvisational—that is, abstract expressionism. The final leg of expressionism thus far is neo-expressionism—"crudely drawn, garishly colored canvases depicting violent or erotic subject matter."[527] Given that the expressionist art of the early 1920s was crude, garish and violent or erotic, one is left to ponder what subtle issues, other than the era, actually distinguish expressionism from neo-expressionism. In any event, the art critics of the Hitler era were no more authoritative than was Hitler himself; the dedication and intensity of Hitler's study of art and architecture made him at least as well qualified a critic as any who were popular in the press of his era. And the hate that Hitler had for modern art was at least as justified as the hate that the influential Jewish critics had for traditional German art and the beauty that it strove to represent and reproduce.

* * * *

During Hitler's formative years the new political class of the Austro-Hungarian Empire, within which there were many Jews, pushed Catholicism aside much as they had in France and elsewhere. Albert Lindemann reports that according to the distinguished historian of France, D. W. Brogan:

> In certain parts of the [French] administration, it was rare to find a practicing Catholic in a position of power. A Jewish prefect could, with impunity, observe Passover, but a prefect who was openly zealous in the observation of Easter might find himself under violent attack from a paper like the *Lanterne*, whose main stock in trade was anti-clerical scurrility and whose editor was a Jew, the great "priest-eater," Eugène Mayer.[528]

Politically, Jews of Vienna were largely liberal and members of the Social Democrat Party. As suggested in the preceding, they were also anticlerical, and more particularly, anti-Catholic. Catholic dogma was satirized and otherwise ridiculed. It was because of Jews that it was priests, not Jews, who were insulted on the street.[529] Hitler, hating Catholic dogma as he did, would have had no particular disdain for attacks on priests and Catholicism, but on a more general level, he saw Jewish attacks on Christianity as assaults on the cultural underpinnings of Germandom. He admired Christianity for its "inexorable fanaticism in preaching and fighting for its own doctrine."[530] He saw it as the foundation of the German nation's morality[531] and was therefore understandably radically opposed to Jewish attacks on its being. For Hitler, later in life, Christianity was a culturally powerful unifying force that if channeled according to his wishes could contribute to Nazism. Hitler and his Nazis would embrace most Christians who were willing to return to the practice of "muscular Christianity."[*] He would not turn the other cheek.

          *   *   *   *

The Jews of Vienna, as everywhere, thronged to academic professions and they thereby came to disproportionately dominate the press there. They also controlled virtually all of the local industry, and especially the banks, making the local economy dependent upon them.[532] That being the case, the fault fell somewhat unjustly to Jews as "Tens of thousands of small shops in Vienna went bankrupt in the latter half of the nineteenth century; and thousands of peasant plots in the surrounding countryside were put up for auction."[533] According to Lindemann, "The benefactors of these Gentile misfortunes were frequently Jews."[534]

The Jewish press praised the monarchy which was particularly good to them, having pushed for multiculturalism and Jewish-unique rights. Jewish Marxists freely, openly, and frequently, vilified the German component of Viennese society, a societal component that rationally saw multiculturalism as detrimental to its own interests.

Viennese culture, so fawningly represented as cultural luminance, was seen by many a staid Viennese as dark and foreboding; for them, it was "the world capital of kitsch," a place of many ills. Karl Kraus labeled it "the research laboratory of world destruction." And Jews, on the basis of common observation, were justifiably perceived to be in the vanguard of each of the city's ills. It had not always been so. Vienna had previously been the finest city of art, music, politeness, and civility: and then came the Enlightenment and rationality and increased Jewish influence from the East. A potentially happy ending to the story of Vienna was put on the out.

---

[*] Muscular Christianity can be traced back to Paul the Apostle, who used athletic metaphors to describe the challenges of a Christian life.

Fin de siècle Vienna

Fin de siècle Vienna is perceived by most historians as a period of great and remarkable intellectual and cultural achievement. It is described as a cultural efflorescence. It was a period of economic prosperity, social liberalism, rising capitalism, the dominance of the Jewish bourgeoisie, and, pointedly, the collapse of the Habsburg Empire.[535]

It was a time that lent itself to a perception of the quadriga atop the parliament building flying in all four directions, symbolic of a polyglot nation that was also flying apart. And culture, too, was flying apart. The city was sometimes lamentably referred to as the "joyful apocalypse," a term that gave recognition to the apparent fact that it and the empire were not in a state of transition and renewed hopes spawned by the new century; it was, instead, a city in an empire that was in decline, a place destined for devastation and destruction, a place of cultural and political ruin. Vienna was then at the center of controversies that were by then several decades in their making as to how and why there had been such a marked decline and degeneration in Western culture.[536]

Vienna was at the height of its Jewish-led cultural innovation. It was perceived by some as a city of declining culture and racial and national confrontation and that perception was especially strong within the previously dominant German component of the city. It was a time when the old guilds were losing their influence to capitalism and the Austro-Germans were losing their power in the face of multiculturalism. One acute government leader, Premier Count Eduard Taafe, said that the focus of governance of the Austro-Hungarian Empire was to keep all the nationalities "in equal, well-tempered dissatisfaction,"[537] and that was pretty much so. "The diversity of national ambition among the subject peoples of the Empire," says Peter Jones, "was ultimately a great strength for the Habsburgs, since resentment of Habsburg rule could thereby be diffused."[538] European culture, like its politics, was in the throes of internationalization. It was like a dying, collapsing star—imploding due to a lack of energy to overcome the opposing force of discontent.

The new architecture of the period was stark and bare compared to the ornate elegance of the traditional structures of the city. The influence of the Catholic Church was in decline, as were moral standards. Musically, Jewish dominance was taking the city from the operatic and the waltz* to scandalous jazz and the baffling, "mathematically coded,"[539] oxymoronic atonal music of Arnold Schoenberg. Prostitution was rampant. By the beginning of the new century the press had become dominant as the "shaper of public opinion and as a commentator of artistic phenomena," and while the press came to dominate culture, Jews came to dominate the press.[540] For Jews, it was still another instance of the Golden Age.

There was progress in the city for which Jews justifiably took credit. But there were ills there, too, that were fostered by them, Jewish apologists notwithstanding. For the radical racialist right-wing elements of the city, the cause for *all* of the turmoil was evident—it was the Jews. For example, Jews did not have much direct influence on the architectural changes that were prominent at the time, but extensions could be made to the general influence of Jews in commissioning radical new building styles and the Jewish-owned press that so fawningly supported radical departures from traditional architecture. To the people of Vienna, including even Emperor Franz Joseph, the new architecture, as typified by the 1909 construction of the Goldman and Salatsch Building, was emblematic of Jewish-commissioned architectural abominations.[541]

Google	URL
Goldman and Salatsch Building, Vienna	542

It was Jews who owned the department stores that were the economic bane of the small shopkeepers. They also owned the new factories that were so destructive to the guilds.† Jews supported the

---
* The waltz, when it was introduced in the early nineteenth century, was initially deemed a scandalous dance because it caused body contact between the dancing couples.
† With capitalism came standardization, mechanization, economies of scale, and high rates of high-quality machine production that could not be matched by the guilds.

monarchy until they no longer supported the monarchy. Multiculturalism was divesting Germans of influence. And it was also Jews who were pushing a social agenda that was destroying the high culture of Vienna and bringing it low. Jews were seen by many as the principal culprits in the rampant prostitution, the white slave trade, and for economic and political corruption. And the foregoing perceptions were not the stuff of myth generated by rabid anti-Semites: they were so. As Lindemann observes, it came to be that "Separating liberal corruption from Jewish corruption was in theory possible but in practice difficult."[543]

Jewish Immigration to Austria

In 1860, there were about 6,000 Jews in Vienna; by 1870, their numbers had swelled to 40,000; and in 1910, there were more than 175,000. In just two generations, then, their population in Vienna had expanded nearly thirtyfold. On the whole, only 46 percent of the population of Vienna was native to the city.[544] In Budapest, the number of Jews was even more striking: so much so that the term "Judapest" was disparagingly used by anti-Semites to describe it.[545]

In 1867, Italy broke away from Austria, an event that prodded the emperor to grant equality of powers between the Hungarian and German components of the empire under the so-called Dual Monarchy, the Austro-Hungarian Empire. It was also in 1867 that Jews and Slavs (Czechs, Slovaks, Serbs, Croats, and others) won complete civil rights in the country.

There were push-pull forces at work that encouraged Jewish migration to the city. Jewish participation in antiestablishment

---

Consequently, department stores could offer high-quality goods at much-reduced prices that could not be matched by small business. These and other fruits of capitalism were good for the economy and all of the people, but for some, only in the long run. A ruined shopkeeper with a "right now" hungry family understandably had little sympathy for the "long run." The "big box" store replaced the "mom-and-pop" one. It was an efficient process but lacked the traditional closeness of the little bakery or the butcher or the candy shop, and so on.

insurrections in Eastern Europe provided a push-force from governments wanting to rid themselves of radical elements, and the new social and legal equality in the empire provided a pull-force for Jews and Slavs to go there, greatly upsetting the hitherto dominant Germans.[546]

As Jews filled the city, "They brought anti-Semitism with them in their luggage," says historian Lenni Brenner. "The new immigrants became a 'problem' to the rulers of the host societies,"[547] whether Austrian, German, or otherwise. Theodor Herzl emphasized the foregoing point with specific respect to East European Jews in a tête-à-tête that he had with Lord Rothschild in London. Herzl had gone to London to testify before the British Parliament with respect to the 1902 Aliens Exclusion Bill aimed at Jewish immigrants. Herzl argued that rather than pass the Exclusion Bill, the Parliament should instead simply embrace Zionism to achieve its purpose. He would, he confided to Lord Rothschild, "be one of those wicked persons to whom English Jews might well erect a monument because I saved them from an influx of East European Jews."[548]

Jewish immigration to Vienna was heavily influenced by events in Russia. Jewish participation in the assassination of the liberal Tsar Alexander II[*] in 1881 represents one event that caused them to emigrate. Their even greater role in both the defeat of Russia at the hands of the Japanese, and then in the abortive Russian Revolution of 1905 stimulated repressive actions by both the populace and the tsar and furthered the emigration rush. The attempted revolution of 1905 in Russia directly impacted events in Vienna as well. In the wake of concessions made by Tsar Nicholas in Russia, the Marxist Social Democratic Party of Austria pressured Austria's Emperor Franz Joseph to agree to universal

---

[*] Only a single Jew was directly involved in that assassination. It was the case, however, that since about 1860 Jews had begun to make assassination attempts on Russia's leadership, including several prior attempts on the life of Alexander II. History books often point out the fact that only a single Jew participated in the assassination but fail to acknowledge the background that gave credence to the charge that the assassination was indeed a Jewish one.

male suffrage. The pressure was in the form of nearly a quarter of a million Jewish-dominated trade union workers wearing red armbands marching past the Parliament Building in November 1905.[549]

After Hitler arrived in Vienna in 1907 it is entirely probable, given his penchant for reading about Jews and Socialism, that he read the then popular book by Rudolf Vrba, *The Revolution in Russia*, describing the trouble there in terms of a Christian battle of defense against the Jewish threat.[550]

A fundamental point to the Vienna immigration issue was that so very many of the newly arrived Jews were from the East: from Russia, Galicia, Bohemia, and Moravia. This set of Jews, many of whom were of the Haredi sect, hated Gentiles, and Christians ones in particular.

The newly arrived Jewish immigrants from Eastern Europe were different than their assimilated brethren in the West: they were different in their religious orthodoxy, their dress, their politics, their exploitive business practices, and their staunch immiscibility. They were also far more radical than their deracinated and mostly assimilated Viennese kinsmen. The Ostjuden (Eastern Jews) were unassimilated, and some held, inassimilable. Their dress, facial hair, and political radicalism made them stand out in society. Some traits, though, were shared between the two groups. In keeping with Jewish ethnocentrism, they largely segregated themselves from Gentile societal customs, lived in their own neighborhoods, and their closest friends and acquaintances were exclusively other Jews.[551] Embracing Zionism, they saw themselves in racial and Jewish-national terms.

Hitler recounts in *Mein Kampf* an encounter with one of these Orthodox Jews while he was living in Vienna:

> One day when I was walking through the inner city, I suddenly came upon a being clad in a long caftan, with black curls. Is this also a Jew? was my first thought.
>
> At Linz they certainly did not look like that. Secretly and cautiously I watched the man, but the longer I stared at

this strange face and scrutinized one feature after the other, the more my mind reshaped the first question into another form: Is this also a German?

The established Jews of Vienna did what they could to assist and settle the newcomers in the city. Given the Jewish predominance in the turmoil caused by the various revolutions and social upheavals, the strange-looking Ostjuden became easily identifiable targets for right-wing extremists such as the Pan-Germans. Hitler, some years later, like appreciable numbers of others, was among such extremists.

The Eastern Jews were by and large ultraorthodox Ashkenazi Hasidim, a sect that, as viewed by assimilated Jews and Gentiles alike, was a sorry lot. In the Vienna of the early twentieth century, it was not the Hasidic Jews' dark suits with distinctively long jackets and their strange hats (*shtreimals* and *spodiks*), side locks and facial hair (*payot*) that so set them at odds with the greater populace: it was, instead, their unscrupulous business practices that made them such objects of suspicion and scorn. It was from just such Ostjuden business practices that terms such as "Jewgoods," a "Jew's gross" (100 instead of 144) and "Jew-stuff" came into being to describe their shoddy, substandard weights, measures, and materials. The Ostjuden earned, or at least emboldened, those stereotypes by way of their business practices, and they simultaneously engendered anti-Semitism. In today's Israel, the Hasidic sect remains highly problematic—they refuse, in large part, to participate in the military, they burden the welfare rolls, and they treat the Arabs in the West Bank atrociously. Prominent Israeli statesmen sometimes use brutal language in describing them and their religious and social practices.

Politically, it was the case that the court and the Jews gave Vienna its character, and Jews and liberalism became as synonymous there as elsewhere. The German Viennese were deeply threatened by the influx of outsiders, and the threat from this source spawned renewed devotion to Pan-Germanism as well as to what Karl Schorske called "politics in a new key,"[552] a willingness to use mass demonstrations and to employ physical violence to advance one's social and political agenda.

Professor Kevin MacDonald refers to the writings of author Peter Gay to reinforce the point of Jewish dominance in Viennese culture:

> Regarding the extent of Jewish cultural dominance in *fin de siècle* Vienna, author Peter Gay (born Peter Joachim Fröhlich in Berlin, 1923) quotes the German Jewish novelist Jacob Wasserman as writing that "nearly all the people with whom I came into intellectual or cordial contact were Jews. . . . I soon recognized that all public life was dominated by Jews. The banks, the press, the theater, literature, social functions, all was in the hand of the Jews."[553]

Thus it was that as Hitler observed Viennese society, he was not being particularly irrational in his assessment of society as being unduly influenced by Jews and Jewish interests; it was a simple matter of empirical fact that was there to be observed by all, Jews and non-Jews alike.

*   *   *   *

By the early 1900s, the Jews of Vienna were exceedingly successful. Some of their success, perhaps much of it, flowed from political intrigue and Jewish press puffery on behalf of kinsmen. That Jews were, and are, the principal owners of news and entertainment outlets remains something of a taboo subject; still, it is true that they did, and do, predominate there. As it is today in the U.S., it was also in Vienna and in Weimar Germany. An example of Jewish rule in U.S. press circles was once provided by *National Review* writer and syndicated columnist Joe Sobran, who commented on the Jewish influence in the press as follows:

> The full story [of Pat Buchanan's 1996 presidential bid] campaign is impossible to tell as long as it's taboo to

> discuss Jewish interests as freely as we discuss those of the Christian Right. Talking about American politics without mentioning the Jews is a little like talking about the NBA without mentioning the Chicago Bulls. Not that the Jews are all-powerful, let alone all bad. But they are successful, and therefore powerful enough: and their power is unique in being off-limits to normal criticism even when it's highly visible. They themselves behave as if their success were a guilty secret, and they panic, and resort to accusations, as soon as the subject is raised. Jewish control of the major media in the media age makes the enforced silence both paradoxical and paralyzing. Survival in public life requires that you know all about it, but never refer to it. A hypocritical etiquette forces us to pretend that the Jews are powerless victims; and if you don't respect their victimhood, they'll destroy you. It's a phenomenal display not of wickedness, really, but of fierce ethnocentrism, a sort of furtive racial superpatriotism.[554]

Peter Pulzer informs us that 23 percent of the actors and musicians, 34 percent of the authors, 51 percent of the lawyers, and a whopping 60 percent of the doctors in private practice in Weimar Germany were Jews. Even more important than their dominance in those fields, however, was Jewish domination of journalism in both Austria-Hungary and Germany. Pulzer says that:

> There was no profession which was more completely dominated by Jews than journalism. Most of the leading organs of opinion, the *National-Zeitung* of Berlin, the *Frankfurter Zeitung*, the *Neue Freie Presse* of Vienna, were owned and edited by Jews. The same applied to the independent weeklies such as Karl Kraus' *Die Fackel* and Maximilian Harden's *Zukunft*. Of the twenty-one dailies published in Berlin during the 1870's thirteen were owned by Jews, four had important Jewish contributors, and only four had no connection with Jews. ... The 'Liberal' press, which grew up with industry and parliamentarism and flourished by advertising and

sensational reporting, owed its origins almost entirely to Jews.[555]

Pulzer goes on to describe Jewish predominance in the political, economic, and cultural life of Vienna.

> It is not merely that the Jews provided the patronage, the audience, and by press criticism the canons of taste, they provided also the creators: Arthur Schnitzler, Stefan Zweig, Franz Werfel. Gustav Mahler was appointed Director of the Opera in 1898, which made him musical dictator of the city. Lewinsky and Sonnenthal scintillated on the boards of the *Burgtheater*. Heinrich Freijung [who, interestingly, was a Jewish Pan-Germanist] was the doyen of historians.[556]

Much later, observing the intra-Jewish press relations in both Vienna and in Germany, Hitler and his Nazis concluded that the Jewish press was responsible for the popular success of all manner of nontraditional art forms. In a speech at the Bürgerbäukeller in Munich on April 9, 1929, Hitler reflected on his Vienna days saying, "All this so-called modern art of today would not be thinkable without its propagation through the work of the press,"[557] by which he most assuredly meant the "Jewish press."

The Viennese press wallowed in venality and corruption. "Officials played favorites," says Albert Lindemann, "leaking stories or planting false ones. The 'revolver press' blackmailed prominent persons and business by threatening revelations unless compensated."[558] The terms "journalism" and "Jews" understandably went together. Since Jews had earned a reputation for shady business practices and journalistic corruption, notions of anti-Semitism and antijournalism always went hand in hand. Moreover, capitalist financiers, the stock jobbers, those responsible for the bankruptcies of artisans and small retailers, the robber barons, the plunderers of the countryside, the deceivers of the small investor, were, according to Lindemann, "overwhelmingly made up of Jews."[559] And Hitler was there to observe and assess their conduct.

The Jewish populace was also replete with petty deceivers. Hitler's friend August Kubizek recounted an incident in which Hitler was himself a personal witness concerning one of these individuals:

> One day, when I was very busy with preparations for my exam, Adolf stormed into our room, full of excitement. He had just come from the police, he said: there had been an incident in the Mariahilferstrasse, connected with a Jew of course. A 'Handelee' had been standing in front of the Gerngross store. The word 'Handelee' was used to designate Eastern Jews, who, dressed in caftan and boots, sold shoe-laces, buttons, braces and other haberdashery in the streets. The Handelee was the lowest stage in the career of those quickly assimilated Jews, who often occupied leading positions in Austria's economic life. The Handelees were forbidden to beg, but this man had whiningly approached passers-by, his hand outstretched, and had collected some money. A policeman asked him to produce his papers. He began to wring his hands and said that he was a poor, sick man who had only this little trading to live on, but he had not been begging. The policeman took him to the police station and asked bystanders to act as witnesses. In spite of his dislike of publicity, Adolf had presented himself as a witness, and he saw with his own eyes that the Handelee had 3,000 crowns in his caftan, conclusive evidence, according to Adolf, of the exploitation of Vienna by immigrant Eastern Jews.[560]

Still, it was the case that the greatest part of Jewish success in Vienna stemmed from their intellect, interorganizational cooperation, hard work, and willingness to assume risk. All but one bank in Vienna was administered by Jews. They constituted 70 percent of the stock exchange council; a large majority of all industry was also in their hands. Close-knit Jewish families such as the Rothschilds predominated in banking and other spheres. Railroads were largely in their hands as well. Seventy-one percent of the wealthiest taxpayers were Jews.

The Jews of Vienna were simultaneously assimilationists and cultural separatists. By way of example, they voluntarily created their own exclusive neighborhoods: the mansions along the famously beautiful Ring Boulevard were occupied by them. They at the same time participated in Gentile society as they engaged with royalty, intellectuals, and Gentile business tycoons.

Emperor Franz Joseph, like his predecessors, ennobled and bemedaled his favorite Jews in return for their various favors. Rich Jewish women married impoverished aristocrats and thereby saved them from the awful fate of being reduced to a state of merely ordinary.[561] The Jews of Vienna of the early 1900s had little about which to complain.

Still, the success of Jews in Vienna was not without social cost to them: by the early 1900s, they attempted to take on a lower profile by consciously substituting surrogate Gentiles in positions of leadership in order to deflect attention from themselves. It came to be that notable Jews sometimes refused public office for fear of putting their head above the parapet; the standard argument has it that they, instead, quietly resided in their palaces. That aside, they remained ostentatious in throwing large parties and in showing themselves as the prominent patrons of the opera and theater—an opera and theater that was increasingly of their own making and propensity, and their propensities were in stark opposition to the sensibilities of Gentiles like Adolf Hitler.

Politically, they exercised their power behind the scenes by way of their power within the Social Democratic Party and the press. They were, in essence, the margravial elites of Viennese society. As early as 1890, Karl Lueger, who would later become mayor of the city, gave a speech that was thereafter quoted for decades. Historian Brigitte Hamann recounts the speech as follows:

> "Yes, Vienna, the Jews are as numerous as grains of sand on the shore, wherever you go, nothing but Jews; if you go to the theater, nothing but Jews, if you walk on the Ring Boulevard, nothing but Jews, if you go to the concert, nothing but Jews, if you attend a ball, nothing

but Jews, if you go on campus, again, nothing but Jews. . . . Gentlemen, don't blame me for the fact that almost all journalists are Jews and that they keep a token Christian editor here and there in their editorial offices, whom they can show off just in case someone might stop by and get frightened." On account of the Jewish press, he argued, "the movement against journalism naturally was forced to take on an anti-Semitic character."[562]

However our politically correct desires of today might have it as otherwise, Lueger was, at the time, stating truths. Jews veritably owned Vienna; and Hitler was there to observe their stewardship of the city. He was appalled.

The Habsburg emperors offered high status to Jews without demanding nationality. Until 1788, for example, Jews were exempt from military service, and even when the requirement to serve was established, those in Vienna who were protected by the emperor remained exempt. According to historian Yuri Slezkine, "they became the supra-national people of the multinational state, the one folk which, in effect, stepped into the shoes of the earlier aristocracy,"[563] and the earlier aristocracy had been mostly German.

Austrian emperors relied heavily on their court Jews. These denizens of the court supplied the empire with capital and weapons and thereby contributed to the emperor's retention of power. As bankers to the crown, they enjoyed special protection from the regent. As they did elsewhere, Jews of Vienna served as money lenders not only to the crown but to commoners as well. Frederick II permitted them to charge a weekly interest rate of 8 heller on the pound (87 percent). His father permitted still higher ones.[564] Their financial, political, and social fortunes fluctuated between good and bad times, to be sure (there were periods, for example, when they could not hold public office). Still, on the whole, Jews of Austria were rich and privileged compared to the vast majority of Gentiles. And Jews of Austria, as elsewhere, took up the standard to "mediate the oppression of the peasants on behalf of the nobility and the Crown."⁵⁶⁵ Israel Shahak says of leading rabbis, court Jews, and other Jews of the privileged class that:

> While Gentiles in general were reviled, Jewish laws made an exception for the elite. Jewish physicians, tax collectors and bailiffs could be relied upon by a king, nobleman, pope or bishop in a way that a Christian might not. The Jewish community enjoyed autonomous status and the Jewish rabbis and rich were part of the governing class. Together they oppressed the masses, Jew and non-Jewish.⁵⁶⁶

In the early 1900s, Jews reigned supreme within Viennese culture—and because of that, Vienna had more than its fair share of Jewish purveyors of cultural filth. Cultural icons of the period included Sigmund Freud who was making his mark with his new and highly popular anti-Christian, sex-soaked pseudoscience of psychoanalysis. Psychologists following the Freudian craze of the time were anchored in sex as the root of both healthy and depraved behavior; they maintained that "all crime, from kleptomania to strangulation was a form of sexual discharge."⁵⁶⁷ As Michael Jones asserts, for Freud and others of his sect, sex was to be "disconnected from the norms of Western civilization, for the most part known as Christianity."⁵⁶⁸

Freud's work was little more than a speculative agenda with a pretense of science for subverting the institutions of Gentile society.⁵⁶⁹ Peter Gay labels Freud's work as "subversive." MacDonald points out that:

> There was a general perception among many anti-Semites that Jewish intellectuals were subverting German culture in the period prior to 1933 . . ., and psychoanalysis was but one aspect of this concern. A great deal of hostility to psychoanalysis centered around the perceived threat of psychoanalysis to Christian sexual ethics, including the acceptance of masturbation and premarital sex. . . . Psychoanalysis became a target of gentiles decrying the Jewish subversion of culture—

"the decadent influence of Judaism," as one writer termed it.[570]

Indeed, all seventeen original members of Freud's Psychological Wednesday Society were Jewish, were acutely aware of their Jewishness, and maintained a sense of Jewish purpose and solidarity. That psychoanalysis remains a largely Jewish affair and even now is emphasized by one Jewish psychoanalyst who quips that "The 1990 roster of the International Psychoanalytical Association reads like the membership list of a synagogue."

"In 1928 Carl Christian Clemen, a professor of ethnology at the University of Bonn . . . 'decried the psychoanalytic tendency to find sex everywhere, a tendency he attributed to the Jewish composition of the movement.'"[571] Freud's psychoanalysis movement and its various offshoots sought to relax social controls on sexuality among Gentiles, theorizing that such a move would somehow reduce anti-Semitism.[572] The malignant effect of Freudianism and its epigones continues to be sorely felt in the thought processes and cultures of both Europe and the U.S. A goodly part of the theories relating to supposed sexual aberrations of Adolf Hitler stem directly from Freudianism.

In the realm of music, the renowned composer Gustav Mahler held sway. Mahler, a genius composer and conductor, was admired even by Hitler for his interpretation of Wagner's works. But like so very many of the Jews of Vienna and Germany, Mahler seemingly could not help himself as he applied his energies in the early 1900s to bringing a notorious play by Oscar Wild, *Salome*,[*] to the Vienna Court Opera—a deliberate offense to German sensibilities that seemed to be a modality of the distinguished Jews of that period. The play, which had been banned for religious and moral reasons, concerned itself with the prototype of the sensual man-killing woman and went on to become a cult figure of modernism. Mahler

---

[*] In the Bible, the daughter of Herodias who demanded and received John the Baptist's head as reward for dancing before her stepfather, Herod Antipas.

finally succeeded in his quest to stage the play, premiering it at the National Opera in 1910,[573] much to the consternation of traditionalists. Mahler's efforts were seen as one among many efforts by Jews to break the bonds of traditionalism in favor of the shocking, the irreverent, and the erotic. While Mahler's symphonies were grandiose and innovative, they were also antitraditionalist and challenged the very definition of the genre. Rudolf Louis made the following point in his 1909 book *Die Deutsche Musik der Gegenwart* (Contemporary German Music):

> If Mahler's music would *speak* Jewish, perhaps it would simply be incomprehensible to me. But I find it repulsive because it *judaizes*. That is, it speaks German, as it were, but with an accent, tone, and above all the *gestures*, of Jews from the East, too much from the East.[574] [Italics are in the original.]

Critics responded to Mahler and others of his vein in accordance with the critic's own inclinations for embracing or rejecting modernity.[575] And the cultural critics of the day were almost wholly Jewish and were almost wholly in favor of discarding German traditions throughout the realm of German art: music, architecture, paintings, literature, and theaters were all to be revitalized according to the wants of the critics of the time, critics who were predominantly Jewish. Purity, probity, heroism, and ornamentation were out; the contaminated, the wicked, the-stripped-down-ghastly—the degenerates—were in. Jews, by way of Jewish critics in the press, were seen as being at the forefront of both scientific and cultural contamination.

"The pinnacle of public offense was the fashionable cult some literary figures made of prostitutes around 1900,"[576] says Brigitte Hamann. For them, the whore was an embodiment of a sexuality that never exhausts itself. In his never-ending battle against his self-defined too-prude morals, Karl Kraus, who was widely known for his German culture and German and Austrian politics, pointed out the solidarity between artists and working girls. The influential Viennese writer Peter Altenberg (born Richard Engländer), the

Jewish dandy of Viennese literary figures with a penchant for very young girls, and many others, emulated him.

The famous author Arthur Schnitzler, the "sardonic, amoral voice of his generation," was gaining fame in both Austria and Germany by both living and writing about aimless pleasure seeking. In his *The Affairs of Anatol*, the pleasure-seeking lead character is, among other things, educated "in the beautiful depravity of the jazz age."[577] His work had a Freudian cast to it and was scandalously pornographic, a feature that earned fame, money, and outrage for him in both Austria and Germany. Until the mid-1890s, Schnitzler joined with other prominent Jews to mock moralist culture and further the cause of sexuality and pornography. In 1926, he published his *Traumnovelle* (Dream Novella) which has in recent years been turned into a Hollywood movie starring Tom Cruise and former wife, Nicole Kidman, *Eyes Wide Shut*.

Schnitzler's timing was not propitious: 1926 was the same year that the Reichstag passed the Law to Protect Youth from Trashy and Filthy Writings.[578] The people were by this time to here with the kind of vulgarities offered up by the likes of Schnitzler. "Teachers, clerics, social workers, and all sorts of other conservatively minded people," says Eric Weitz, "fumed about penny novels and other forms of cheap literature . . . the dangers of Schund und Schmutz (trash and filth)" that was being pushed to youthful readers.[579] And the association between the smut and Jewish authors was increasingly and openly propounded; the whole of it was rooted, as one Protestant minister commented in "Jewish Manchesterism," a three-in-one phrase that succinctly blended anti-Semitism, anticapitalism, and anti-British sentiment.[580] He set himself a goal of having as much sex as possible. For several years, he logged his every orgasm and kept yearly totals subdivided by his various mistresses. According to *New Yorker* critic Leo Carey, "Schnitzler's early plays capture their particular epoch so well that, even during their author's lifetime, they came to seem like period pieces—Strauss waltzes drowned out by Schoenbergian discord." Like many of his Jewish friends and contemporaries, he also delighted in assailing the army's officer corps and in hand wringing over the "fraught position of Jews in Viennese society," even as he raked in the money and infamy from writings that helped cause Jews to be "fraught."

Arnold Schoenberg was overthrowing the traditional harmonies of symphonic music, putting in their place, as one online site describes it, "atonal creations of harmonic strangeness and unconventional melody."[581] He would later relocate to Berlin and become one of the several commanding influences in musical polemics and Weimar culture. Schoenberg's "atonal dissonance—the blasting away of classical norms, the rejection of harmony, the destruction of chords—became a global standard in the realm of ideas, one that remains influential today."[582]

Frank Wedekind, a Sartre-Jew and a culturally divisive figure in Berlin as well as Vienna, teamed with the famous Jewish theatrical producer Max Reinhardt (Goldmann) to generate scandal with the perceived pornography of his play about adolescent sexuality, *Spring's Awakening*. Wedekind, it is said, "was an artistic dividing line in Vienna as well as Berlin,"[583] employing "physical grammar," satire, "sexual expressivity," and the grotesque in his expressionist stage events. He was despised by proper society but as an advocate of what was then sexual perversity, he was popular with the cultural leadership of his time. S. Friedlander recounts police attitudes toward Wedekind to illustrate the point: "As a police report put it: One can easily understand that a German who still feels German to some degree and who is not morally and ethically perverted looks with greatest disgust upon the public enjoyment of Wedekind plays."[584] Right-wing Germans referred to Wedekind's work as "Jewish garbage."[585] At one point, Hitler and his friend Kubizek viewed the play.[586] It was one experience among many that helped form a linkage in Hitler's mind between Jews and the rampant prostitution of Vienna.

Peter Altenberg's *Five songs on picture postcard texts by Peter Altenberg* had not yet premiered to riots in Vienna, but that would happen before Hitler departed there. In the meantime, Altenberg enjoyed the fruits of fame as "bohemia's Bohemian" in Vienna, where he lined the walls of his hotel room with photographs of very young girls.

Hugo Bettauer, a writer who is not particularly well-known today, was a prolific, widely read Viennese writer at the turn of the century. He was the son of a Jewish stockbroker. He had served briefly in the Austrian army but deserted at the age of nineteen. He relocated to the U.S. for about ten years, but then returned to Vienna. There he began his writing career in earnest. Sex was his motif. Bettauer became the most prominent member of a mass movement which sought to abolish the norms of sexual conduct and "liberate" the masses from constrained sexual conduct. In this respect, he joined with the mass of similarly thinking Jewish intellectuals in a quest to sexually liberate Gentiles. Sexuality became pervasive. Sociologists, anthropologists, the new "sexologists," politicians, doctors, lawyers, and writers—all applied themselves to this taboo topic as if exploring previously undiscovered territory. In 1925, Bettauer was murdered by a young Nazi as a protest against the perceived immorality of his sexually licentious writings.

Other Jews who were prominent in Viennese life included Victor Adler, Otto Bauer, Hugo Breitner, Robert Danneberg, Julius Deutsch, and Julius Tandler. It would be these people (except Adler, who died in 1918) who would go on to become the caretakers of Red Vienna between World War I and World War II. Red Vienna, which is to say Communist Vienna, was, of course, detested by Adolf Hitler.

The whole of Viennese expressionism was doubtlessly important to the molding of Hitler's attitude toward both that form of art and of modern art in general, and its proponents as well. In 1942, he described the visual form of modern art as "nothing but crippled daubing."[587] At the 1935 party convention, he commented on the visual arts but might just as well have been describing the theater of his era: *"It is not the function of art to wallow in filth for filth's sake, to paint man only in the state of decay, to draw cretins as a symbol of becoming a mother and to portray crooked morons as models of virility."*[588] (Italics are in the original.)

Jewish cultural gurus seemingly demanded that Vienna heel to its cultural dictates, to its modernism, to its "rationality" and sexual licentiousness. And in large part, the city did just what it was told by the overwhelmingly dominant Jewish press. The press of Vienna provided encomium for its compatriots, Jewish or no, and thereby increasingly influenced all areas of culture. Hamann points out that with respect to art, there was "the far-spread accusation that in reality 'Jewish modernism' was not art at all but only artificially pushed by the 'Jew press' with its business sense,"[589]— a charge echoed by Hitler. The charge had merit. Modern art had the advantage of high production: any scribbling could be represented as great art if properly hyped and could then be sold in one or another of the various Jewish art salons at outrageous prices.

Jewish author Stephan Zweig held that nine-tenths of Viennese culture was "promoted, nourished, or even created by Viennese Jewry." The argument goes that the culture then being championed by Jews was somehow superior to the extant one. But to a goodly number of Viennese, jazz was inferior to symphonies and operas and waltzes; and pornography was inferior to romantic heroism. Biting satire was inferior to polite restraint And the distorted, horrific "reality" of expressionism and theater of the absurd was inferior to idyllic realism. To the cultured of Vienna, the Apollonian was superior to the Dionysian. Hitler was among such Viennese, and many millions of people would later join him in his thought process.

*   *   *   *

The vast majority of Viennese Jews identified with the Social Democrats. The Social Democrats, in turn, very much dominated labor unionism. In effect, the Social Democrats were *the* labor party of Vienna as well as in other cities and countries in Europe, including Germany. The unions provided the Social Democrats with a powerful base from which to both win elections and threaten economic and political stability by way of strikes. Union dues were used to achieve political ends, and the ends that were sought were all too often seemingly of a Jewish kind. It will later be seen that as Jews sought to bring down the German government in 1918, and later as Jews sought to bring down Adolf Hitler, Jewish leadership in the labor unions was employed extensively to achieve those objectives.

By way of the Jewish association with the Social Democrats, Jews became inextricably associated with liberalism and socialism. With few exceptions, the leaders of the Social Democrat Party, the Austromarxists, were Jewish,[590] as were the Social Democrats of Germany. The Austromarxists, while powerful, would not gain total dominance during Hitler's sojourn in Vienna, but they would do so later, in 1919. This close association gave still more credence to the all-in-one proposition that Jews, liberals, and communists were one and the same—it was a thought process of reality. Indeed, as Dr. Kevin MacDonald points out, "the Jewish role in Communism has been sanitized."[591] It has often been demeaned as romantic silliness. The connection between Jews and communism was not confined to Vienna or even to the Austro-Hungarian Empire; it was thus throughout Europe.

Victor Adler, the founder and first major leader of the Austrian Social Democrats, was Jewish, as was Otto Bauer, the leading theoretician for the party and Adler's successor. Other prominent Jews in the party's leadership were Friedrich Austerlitz, Wilhelm Ellenbogen, Otto Bauer, Robert Dannenberg, and Max Adler. Overall, Jews comprised almost half of the party leadership. In Germany, the situation was remarkably similar; while Jews comprised less than 1 percent of the population, they accounted for 31 percent of the richest families, and their political and cultural influence approximated their influence in Vienna. In Berlin, their influence was simply overwhelming. It was all but absolute. The Marxist Social Democratic Party of Germany was the party of choice for nearly every Jew, the German equivalent of the Social Democrats of Vienna and the U.S. Democratic Party of today. The SPD was a traditionally Marxist party that had abandoned its revolutionary fervor and therefore sought to achieve Marxist Socialism by way of evolution, rather than revolution. That said, the SPD never did formally reject its long-term revolutionary objectives, but in the years leading up to the outbreak of World War I the party was ideologically radical while many party officials and functionaries simultaneously tended toward moderation in everyday politics.[592]

Vienna and the Revolution of 1848

The Vienna that Adolf Hitler first entered in 1906 was fashioned by several fairly recent historical events that were important to both Jews and to Hitler, including the Revolution of 1848, the establishment of the dual monarchy of Austria-Hungary in 1867, the unification of Germany in 1871, the stock market crash of 1873 (a crash that was blamed on Jewish stock speculation and deliberate manipulation of the market),[593] the influx of Jews after the assassination of Tsar Alexander II in 1881, the abortive Russian revolution of 1905, and the rise of Zionism. Events in Germany significantly influenced those in Austria and vice versa.

The revolts of 1848 stemmed from broad-based societal ills that affected equally broad populations of people. Bad harvests and resulting food shortages, the beginnings of capitalism in industry that so adversely affected the various guilds, and importantly, Marxism and Jewish desires for emancipation from various forms of extant legal constraints on their participation in the various European societies all contributed to the revolutions.

The revolutions were seemingly anticipated by the Jewish prime minister of Great Britain, Benjamin Disraeli, in his 1846 publication, *Comingsby* (this is not to suggest prescience by Disraeli but only that he was acutely attuned to the social and political ills of the time). In it, Disraeli has his fictional character Sidonia saying, "That mighty revolution which is at this moment preparing in Germany and . . . of which so little is as yet known in England, *is developing entirely under the auspices of the Jews*."[594] (Italics are in the original.) Subsequent to the revolutions, Disraeli returned to the subject of Jewish involvement, claiming that *"men of Jewish race are found at the head of every one of them."*[595] (Italics are in the original.)

The revolutions began in Italy but quickly spread to France and thence across much of Europe. Participants included Italians, French, Poles, Danes, Germans, Czechs, Slovaks, Hungarians, Croats, and Romanians. Shortly after the revolution reached Austria, it jumped the border to Germany.

But let this be said: if bellies had been full, if monarchism and capitalism had satisfied all, there would still have been a reason for revolution, whether the revolutions of 1848 or the ones in Russia in 1905 and 1917, or the one in Germany in 1918. It is the way of revolutionists, and countries, for that matter, to seize upon events of the day in order to respond in a way that was desired from the outset. An excuse for war or revolution is easily had. Witness the truth of this claim by considering the U.S. war in Iraq and the Israeli incursion into Lebanon, the Second Lebanon War that was based on three Israeli soldiers having been killed in a border incident. Consider, too, the paltry justification for the U.S. entry into World War I (the sinking of the *Lusitania* was decidedly *not* the reason for U.S. entry into the war, nor was the absurd Zimmermann Telegram). When leaders want to engage in war, a casus belli is an exceedingly easy thing to come by—it can be a fabricated attack (USS *Maine*, Gulf of Tonkin Incident), a political assassination (Crown Prince Ferdinand), Lebensraum, *tuitio fidei* (protection of the faith), or even a mythical threat (Iraqi Weapons of Mass Destruction), or any number of other such "justifications." We go to battle in much the same way as the horse: we are mounted by a stranger, reins pull at our bit and direct our statecraft—we go into battle knowing but little of the actual enemy, the one on our back. As Adolf Hitler once pointed out as he scolded his propagandists over their incompetent exploitation of SA deaths during the electoral campaigns of the early 1930s, "The sailors of the battleship *Potemkin* made a revolution out of rotten food...."[596] Rationales for revolutions and provoking wars are easy to come by; much *too* easy.

Given their desire for full emancipation everywhere, Jews fostered upheaval and understandably sided with the revolutionaries in 1848. It was during this period that Karl Marx issued his famous Communist Manifesto, the birth certificate of

Communism that claimed in its opening line that "A specter is haunting Europe, the specter of Communism." Moreover, he had long been preparing the ground for upheaval and was intimately involved in it—the publication of his manifesto along with agitation by Marx and his followers helped spark revolutionary fervor throughout the Continent. Within a few weeks of Marx's publication in 1848 revolution broke out everywhere. Jewish participation in the German-Austrian revolutions is illustrated by the fact that some twenty Jews were killed as they participated in street fighting in Berlin. Two of five revolutionaries killed in rioting in Vienna were Jews.

Dr. Adolf Fischhof is credited with initiating the Austrian Revolution with a speech he gave in the courtyard of the Lower Austrian Diet. An accomplished orator prodding the masses toward revolutionary fervor, Fischhof was the most prominent Jewish member of the Austro-Hungarian revolutionaries. Ferdinand Lassalle, the Jewish founder of German Socialism and the General Labor Union of Germany (*Allegemeiner Deutscher Arbeiterverein*), also participated. Other leaders included Abraham Halpern from Stanislau; I. N. Mannheimer, chief rabbi of Vienna; and Bär Meisels, rabbi of Cracow. Another man of Jewish extraction, the radical publicist Hermann Jellinek, was shot as a rebel on November 23, 1848.[597] Karl Heinrich Spitzer was shot outside the lower parliament building. Joseph Goldmark, a Viennese student at the time, was sentenced to death for his activities in the revolution, though he ultimately escaped to the United States (a vast number of Jews, it seems, "escaped" to the U.S. during various periods of turmoil in Europe). Johann Jacoby, who was twice tried and acquitted of treason, was the leader of the extreme left element of the Frankfurt assembly, a constitutional convention that was convened in response to the revolution itself. Gabriel Riesser was the revolutionary vice president of the assembly.[598] Robert Blum was an active revolutionary in Vienna. Blum was executed on November 9, 1848, for his activities—in fact, the day of his death marked the beginning of a series of events that led to November 9 being referred to as a "day of fate"[599] for Germany: other such days included the fall of the monarchy in

1918, Hitler's Beer Hall Putsch in 1923, Kristallnacht (night of broken glass) of 1938, and the fall of the Berlin Wall in 1989. In addition to agitation by Karl Marx, Jewish intellectuals such as Heinrich Heine and Ludwig Börne served as major propagandists encouraging the masses to join the revolutionaries. Heine called for the people to "throw off the iron leading strings of the aristocracy."[600] Other such slogans were created with the underlying objective of replacing the need for actual thought on the part of the people with a ready-made mantra, and as was too often the case, the mantras were contrived by Jews. Later, it would be Nazis who served as the source of such mantras.

The masses, however, were not aligned with the political goals of the Jews and other intellectuals who led the revolutions. Except for city dwellers, the Left did not, in any event, much covet approaches to the masses. The intelligentsia tended to address itself, with typical esoterica, to others within its circle. The revolutionaries sought emancipation of the Jews under the guise of more representative government for all; the masses sought employment and full bellies. Moreover, given the Socialist inclinations of the Jewish revolutionaries, the middle class abandoned them as they became increasingly concerned about the protection of their property against the radical Socialists.

Jewish emancipation was a prominent motivation for the revolutions of 1848, and it was one of the central issues in the debates of the various constitutional deliberations that convened to restructure governments. Indeed, "The liberation of Jews from the legal complexity of the old order became one of the principal issues of the various constitutional deliberations."[601]

In Bavaria, during the period 1849–1850, petitions were created opposing Jewish emancipation due to their suspect loyalty and tendencies to undermine institutions of society, tendencies that were made evident during the revolutions of 1848. Jews were also broadly seen as wholly disruptive to societal norms. MacDonald correctly states the issue as follows:

> [A] general cause of increased anti-Semitism was the
> very strong and unfortunate propensity of dissident Jews

to attack national institutions and customs in both
socialist and non-socialist publications . . . These writers
"violently attacked everything about German society.
They despised the military, the judiciary, and the middle
class in general."[602]

MacDonald might have also included the peasantry in his list of things despised by dissident Jews. The right-wing forces of Hitler's ilk who idolized German institutions and people were justifiably outraged by those violent attacks.

We know from Hitler's book *Mein Kampf* that he assiduously studied the revolution of 1848. A couple of Hitler's heroes, including the famous composer Richard Wagner and the architect Gottfried Semper, also took part; both were revolutionaries in Dresden.[603] The fact that the likes of Wagner and other such right-wing German patriots participated in the revolution along with leftist Jews of equal fervor substantiates the broad nature of societal ills that initially made people susceptible to revolution at the time.

Jewish liberals fought against the concept of Christianity as the cornerstone of the state, providing still another reason for broad Jewish participation and for right-wing opposition to them. The following is according to Albert Lindemann:

> The taste for pushing and shoving, the mocking of
> sacred tradition, the sardonic wit and intellectual
> arrogance, the sensuality and sexual immorality—these
> many "Jewish" traits had infected Catholics in Austria
> and were fatally undermining Christian society.[604]

Catholic social theorist Baron Karl von Vogelsang as well as other nobles and notables concluded that the liberalism sweeping Austria in the 1840s vastly favored Jews, allowing them to prosper extraordinarily and unjustly. Lindemann goes on to say that:

> Vogelsang lamented that Austria had lost its Christian
> bearing, had lost sight of the basis in Christian morality
> for social harmony. The country's indigenous Christian

population was being "robbed, dominated, and reduced to pariahs by the Jews."[605]

Jews and their "incredibly insolent Jewish press," said Vogelsang, "worked constantly to undermine the moral fabric of society, as did the atheistic Jews at the head of the revolutionary parties."[606]

In reaction, conservative opponents of the revolution opposed Jewish emancipation, thinking it incompatible with Christianity. Prussia's King Frederick Wilhelm IV wanted to deprive Jews of their very citizenship. Wilhelm IV and his government expressed popular right-wing sentiments in asserting that Jewish emancipation was irreconcilable with Christendom.[607] Thus, opposition to Jewish emancipation served as an important element of conservative opposition to the revolution.

The revolutions succeeded in the short term but most of the immediate gains were quickly invalidated by the various monarchs after peace was achieved. By 1852, the monarchies were fully restored and the gains of the revolutionaries were largely nullified. Importantly, though, the revolution resulted in the permanent repeal of the law restricting Jewish residence in the city of Vienna and provided other extensions of civil liberties to them, liberties that encouraged the first large migration of Jews into the city. In the revolutions of 1848 only Jews came out winners; there were no others.

In Germany, the revolution sparked calls for unification among the thirty-nine (including Austria) loosely confederated individual kingdoms and principalities, and it was to this end that a constitutional assembly convened in Frankfurt at Saint Paul's Church in May 1848. The assembly was composed mostly of intellectuals—of 831 representatives, 569 were academics—and therein, most argue, lay the reason for its ultimate failure. As one would expect in an assembly of distinguished academics, a number of Jews served as representatives. Gabriel Riesser, a staunch advocate of Jewish emancipation, was the most prominent of the Jewish contingent and was named, as previously mentioned, as the vice president of the assembly. That Riesser was named vice president provides a proof that while Jews continued to suffer certain disabilities in Germany at the time, some were, nevertheless, held in high esteem, even in the highest reaches of the country's political leadership.

With little understanding of consensus or Realpolitiks—the "professors parliament" as it is often called, foundered and ultimately failed to achieve its goal of German unification. In the long term, however, the revolution of 1848 and its various consequent constitutional assemblies did serve the purpose of undermining the very concept of absolute rule by monarchs and set the stage for liberalism, Socialism, and Communism—and likewise, for radical nationalism as a counterforce.

German unification remained a prominent objective for both Jews and non-Jews. Jews sought to overcome the liabilities of dealing with so many independent states, and non-Jews saw unification as a path to greater German power. Unification, minus the German regions of the Austro-Hungarian Empire, would finally take place in Paris in 1871 at Versailles after a coalition of German states under the stewardship of Prussia's Otto von Bismarck defeated France in 1870–1871.

Nationalistic tendencies within the Austrian Empire resulted in calls for independence among several of the various peoples, including the Pan-Germans seeking unification between Austria and Germany. Major rebellions broke out in Vienna, Prague, Hungary, and northern Italy, which were then all territories of the Habsburg Empire.[608] The rivalry among the various nationalities served to benefit the Austrian monarchy in that the separatists could not create a united front and the Austrian crown was therefore able to take advantage of the schism between the various factions and nationalities to crush each of the secessionist convocations in turn. The Austrian emperor at the time, Ferdinand I, a weak and befuddled man who also suffered from as many as twenty epileptic seizures per day, abdicated in December 1848. In his place came his nephew, eighteen-year-old Franz Joseph[609] who was still in power when Adolf Hitler first visited Vienna in 1906 and remained in power thereafter until his death in 1916 during World War I.

Broad Jewish involvement in the various revolutions and Jewish leadership in the writing of new constitutions provided an impetus for the anti-Semitic right-wing in Austria and elsewhere. In Hungary, for example, Jews were required to pay a special tax owing to Jewish support for the revolutionaries. In Austria, the revolution signaled the beginning of a racial turmoil between the German- and Jewish-Austrians. More broadly, it signaled the beginning of internecine racism between all of the various peoples of the regime.

To all of the foregoing must be added the burden of the great influx of Jews from Eastern Europe that commenced in earnest shortly after 1848 and was reinvigorated in the early 1880s and still again during, and shortly after, World War I.

Creation of the Dual Empire

The Austrian Empire was divided in two in 1867 owing to its defeat by Prussia and its consequent settlement with Hungary: the dual Monarchy of Austria-Hungary then came into being. The emperor of the Austro-Hungarian Empire and king of Hungary, Franz Joseph, resided in the Hungarian capital of Budapest for several weeks each year. While there he conducted himself as a Hungarian—wearing Hungarian dress and issuing decrees in the Hungarian language in consonance with his Hungarian parliament. The brilliant and beautiful wife of Franz Joseph, Elizabeth of Wittelsbach (known by her nickname Sissi), was radically devoted to Hungary and its people. Rumors even circulated that her son, the tragic Rudolf, had been fathered by the dashing Hungarian nobleman, Count Gyula Andrássy, with whom she was exceedingly close.

For Hitler and his fellow Germans, the German component of the empire started to lose its dominance as Franz Joseph tried to pacify the divergent national aspirations of his people. The Slav, Hungarian, and Czech components of the empire were all vying for independence from the Austrian crown. With the introduction of universal suffrage in 1906, the power of the various national interests increased according to the weight of their populations and consequently further diminished the relative power and influence of the Austro-Germans. German speakers were reduced to 45.15 percent of the Vienna Parliament. As Hamann points out, under universal suffrage the Germans had to relinquish their predominance. They now had to share power with the other nationalities and "ultimately . . . submit themselves to the non-German majority."[610]

Adding to the troubles of the empire was its decision in 1908 to formalize its de facto control over the impoverished and economically backward Turkish provinces of Bosnia and Herzegovina by annexing them. Thus, still another large group of non-Germanic people were added to the empire and competed with German interests. As we shall see later, the annexation of Bosnia and Herzegovina caused other problems as well.

Hitler's Hate of the Austro-Hungarian Empire

The whole of the Austro-Hungarian Empire was despised by Adolf Hitler. He especially hated the accommodations made by the empire with the Slavic components of the regime. In total, the empire had five major religions, ten nationalities, and sixteen languages.[611] "The longer I lived in this city, the more my hatred grew for the foreign mixture of peoples which had begun to corrode this old site of German culture,"[612] said Hitler.

The efforts of Crown Prince Ferdinand to accommodate the aspirations of Slavic peoples of the empire drew Hitler's special ire—he bitterly despised Ferdinand. He hated, too, the diminution of German power, he hated the babel of languages and customs, and he hated Emperor Franz Joseph, the special patron of Jewry, "under whose blessed scepter they had always enjoyed protection."[613]

For Hitler, the Slavs ran a close second to Jews as objects of hate. Said Hitler in *Mein Kamp*:

> Our historical knowledge of the works of the House of Habsburg [the regime of Emperor Franz Joseph] was reinforced by our daily experience. In the north and south the poison of foreign nations gnawed at the body

of our nationality, and even Vienna was visibly
becoming more and more an un-German city. The Royal
House Czechized wherever possible, and it was the hand
of the goddess of eternal justice and inexorable
retribution which caused Archduke Francis Ferdinand,
the most mortal enemy of Austrian-Germanism, to fall
by the bullets which he himself had helped to mold. For
had he not been the patron of Austria's Slavinization
from above?![614]

For Hitler and others who tended to his way of thinking, there was simply no hope of retrieving the state from its sorry condition, no way to reconcile the interests of the various nationalities, and no way that the Austro-Germans could continue indefinitely to subject themselves to such people as the Slavs, Magyars, and Jews. For the Magyars, Slavs, Jews (Zionists), and others, the only acceptable resolution for their status was complete independence from Austria—and indeed, it would be that contention that would finally erupt in declarations of independence toward the end of World War I. Its result would be Yugoslavia, Czechoslovakia, and other such national disasters.

The only viable salvation for the German component of the empire was to somehow join with Germany in a Pan-German nation, a nation that would include the Austro-Germans. Later in his political career, Hitler would seek to broaden Pan-Germanism to include the Baltic Germans and the Germans of Hungary, Yugoslavia, and Croatia. And, of course, he would seek to reintegrate the Germans who were lost to the country due to the Treaty of Versailles, such as those of Danzig, the Sudetenland, the Polish Corridor, Alsace-Lorrain, etc. In addition to those of purely German stock, Hitler also sought to incorporate the Germanic peoples of Holland, Norway, Denmark, and Flanders.[615] He felt that the Germanic peoples of the various states of Europe had developed distinct and special racial stocks that were endearing and needed to be retained as inviolate—the people of these states were not to be "leveled" into a single German cultural milieu. As emphasized by Albert Speer, Hitler insisted that "Holsteiners,

Saxons, Rhinelanders, Swabians, or Bavarians were to keep the characteristics they had developed over the centuries."[616] His attitude in this respect was a form of negative response to what he saw as "Jewish leveling" that "took the soul out of everything,"[617] and for Hitler, Austria-Hungary was the prime example of the effect of such leveling.

When Hitler achieved power and began to implement his Pan-Germanism, Zionists were supportive because he envisioned a community based on ties of blood that transcended the frontiers of states and nations. His vision for Pan-Germanism mirrored those of the Zionists.

The goals of the Pan-Germans of Austria at the time were impossible to achieve even in their most modest form: Germany and Austria-Hungary, along with Italy, were politically bound to each other by the Triple Alliance, an alliance that was meant to serve as a counterweight to the increasingly friendly relations between France and Russia. Germany could ill afford to accommodate the aspirations of the Austro-Germans.

Character of Austria-Hungary, 1907–1913

In the course of observing and studying the turmoil of Austro-Hungarian politics, Hitler also observed what he believed were the natural consequences of this hodge-podge nation. Debased culture was a "feature" of Viennese society of the time. As Hitler's friend Kubizek remarked, "in this sinful Babel of Vienna . . . even prostitution is artistically glorified and celebrated."[618] Hitler would later have the opportunity to assess the excesses of Berlin and other such large German cities and conclude that, like Vienna, Berlin was as sinful as Vienna and more, and that Jews had brought it to that state of being.

The culture of Vienna . . . the *new* culture of Vienna was in the hands of Jews like Freud, et al. Cabarets, a mostly Jewish art form,[619] were popular at the time and although the ones in Vienna had not yet reached the state of caustic, flippant licentiousness and bitter political commentary that would later characterize cabarets in Paris and Berlin, they were nevertheless an early sign of cultural degeneration in the city. The Jews Fritz Grünbaum and Karl Farkas were the Vienna cabarets' most famous acts. "Grotesque dancer" Cilli Wang aimed her routines at the peasant, the village idiot, which, for some, further highlighted Jewish disdain for peasants everywhere—it was an early version of *The Gong Show* of the 1970s in which simpleton goyim were highlighted as fools, a sort of early incarnation of the Jerry Springer television show or the Howard Stern show.

Political happenings in Vienna also included Zionism, a movement that, according to Hitler, confirmed "the national character of the Jews."[620] The movement was at the time led by the Viennese Jew Theodor Herzl.

France

Events in France also influenced attitudes in Austria-Hungary. In 1871, leftist workers of the Paris Commune implemented a policy of separation of church and state, making all church property state property. Concurrently, the Commune excluded religion from schools. Churches were required to serve as political meeting places at night, making the churches one of the main participatory political centers of the Commune.[621] Under the Third Republic, French Catholics felt besieged by regimes that they perceived as increasingly dominated by atheists, secularists, and Jews, who they further perceived were out to destroy Christian France.[622] As early as the 1880s, Jews were seen as playing a prominent role in the destruction of Christianity as evidenced by such things as widespread Jewish support for the anticlerical Ferry Laws of 1881 and 1882.[623] Supporters of the Ferry Laws, says Albert Lindemann, were explicitly anti-Christian, "militantly secular, and vehemently anticlerical. Since French Jews were allied with determined enemies of organized religion, they could be presented more plausibly as both anti-Christian and antireligious."[624]

Perhaps of even more import than the foregoing, however, was the fact that the Jews of France also came into disrepute when it was learned that they were the principals in the infamous Panama

Canal Scandal of 1889—a scandal in which thousands of Frenchmen lost nearly a billion French francs by way of shady practices and political bribes. The scandal was the largest monetary corruption outrage of the nineteenth century.[625]

Individual investors came to learn that they had been bilked out of millions of franks by two leading promoters of the project, Cornelius Herz and Baron de Reinach, both of whom were Jewish.

The bankruptcy of the Panama Canal Company and the resulting scandal caused more than the ruin of thousands of investors; over the next few years the scandal surrounding it touched an ever-widening number of individuals and institutions. It also contributed decidedly to the anti-Semitism just prior to the Dreyfus Affair, to be discussed momentarily. Edouard Drumont, in his newspaper *La Libre Parole,* used the scandal as a battering ram against Jews.

The political class was deeply implicated. When the chain of bribes, slush funds, and influence peddling was traced to its end, 104 legislators were found to have been involved.[626] Journalists were also among those who received bribes. In addition to prominent Jewish conspirators implicated, several Jewish-owned firms in France and elsewhere were found to be leading participants in the corruption. Georges Clemenceau was implicated by way of his close association with Herz, but as his later elevation to prime minister confirms, he did not much suffer for it. It was the case, however, that it was by way of this scandal that Clemenceau was marked as a man with a "Panama in his past"—a charge that would later be highlighted by radical rightists.

Protocols of Learned Elders of Zion

Given the tensions between Gentiles and Jews at the time, it was perhaps inevitable that Gentiles would formulate fantastic accusations against them. *The Protocols of the Learned Elders of Zion* represent one such example that had, and in some quarters continues to have, stupendous impacts. Beliefs in blood libel, particularly among various peasant populations, represents still another such fantastic accusation. We will say nothing about blood libel and its closely related allegations with respect to changelings because we conclude that they are, in fact, the fictions that Jews assert them to be—they are also very much overblown, as is the supposed poisoning of wells, with respect to their hypothetical impact on anti-Semitism. The Protocols were also a fiction that contributed to anti-Semitism but were believed by so many and were seemingly so much in accord with contemporary reality that they need to be addressed.

In Russia, as Jews became increasingly problematic after about 1860, tensions between Jews and the central government became progressively strained. In the late nineteenth century, as Jewish revolutionaries were making progress in Russia, Russian agents concocted *The Protocols of the Learned Elders of Zion*,[*] or simply, the "Protocols" as they have become popularly known. The Protocols were meant to show the populace the dangers from Judaism and thereby rally the people to the cause of the czar. They purport to be the minutes of meetings held by Jews and Freemasons in Switzerland in the late 1890s. The alleged meetings were supposedly comprised of a rabbinical council of conspirators.

The Protocols first appeared in Paris around 1897–1898, then in serialized form in a Saint Petersburg newspaper in 1903. Their appearance in Paris coincided with the ongoing trial for treason of Jewish-French army Captain Alfred Dreyfus and added heat to an already scorching social milieu there.

The Protocols appeared again in Russia after 1905 in response to Russia's defeat by the Japanese and the establishment of the relatively liberal Russian Duma. The Duma was a legislative body forced on Czar Nicholas II owing to Jewish-led revolutionary turmoil. Twelve Jewish deputies were elected to it, though Jews were a minority in all of the electoral districts.[627] A Jewish

---

[*] Various Web sites provide electronic copies of the protocols. Wikipedia provides a good summary of them at
http://en.wikipedia.org/wiki/The_Protocols_of_the_Elders_of_Zion. Some sites provide the full text; one such site is http://www.biblebelievers.org.au/przion1.htm. Be forwarned, they are incredibly boring to read.

Political Office, somewhat like today's AIPAC in the U.S., maintained close contact with the Duma's Jewish representatives to push for approval of specifically Jewish issues. During the failed Russian Revolution of 1905, the Jewish Bund headed the revolutionary movement in Jewish towns, and especially throughout what is now Belarus. In Poland, also in 1905, more Jews fell at Lodz than members of any other group,[628] a fact that further highlights their predominance in the revolutionary events of Russia. Poland was at the time a client state of Russia. The worst of anti-Semitic pogroms occurred within sixty days of the 1905 October Manifesto that created the Duma. Jews were seen as being at the bottom of both the loss to the Japanese and the creation of the Duma, and by way of actual fact, they were indeed indispensable to both. The appearance of the Protocols during this time was intended to underscore Jewish involvement in the defeat of Russian forces and their perceived takeover of the Russian Duma.

The contentions with respect to Russia's defeat at the hands of the Japanese stemmed from the fact that Jewish financiers under the leadership of the German-born financier Jacob Schiff, in concert with other Jewish bankers around the globe, ensured that loans were withheld from Russia that were sorely needed to fight the war with Japan (a similar boycott would be employed throughout World War I, even as it threatened the success of the Allies' war effort),[629] and that Jews had been instrumental in agitating for the overthrow of the tsar and his government, which, of course, they were. Schiff vengefully boasted that "Russia would have to face the fact that 'international Jewry is a power after all.'"[630] The Jewish activist Simon Wolf made similar boasts. Such chest-thumping only added to the already widespread perception, one that was reinforced by the Protocols, that powerful Jews were working in harmony to pull the strings of political puppets everywhere.[631]

A secret investigation within Russia supposedly took place to look into the origins of the Protocols and concluded that they were indeed a forgery. Czar Nicholas II is said to have ordered confiscation of them, commenting that "a *good cause* cannot be defended by dirty means."[632] (Italics are in the original.)

In 1921, investigations by *The Times* of London definitively established that the Protocols were a forgery that were mostly based on an 1864 fictional work by Maurice Joly aimed at Napoleon III. For all of the conclusive evidence of the forgery, however, the Protocols, more than any other publication in history (with the possible exception of the New Testament), carried the anti-Semitic message forward and had a huge impact on anti-Semitic thinking of the late 1800s and early 1900s. They continue as a prominent piece of propaganda among the most radical of anti-Semites even today.

The Protocols, in their essence, are a distillation of the various stereotypes of Jews. They assert a Jewish conspiracy to foist Marxism and other forms of extreme liberalism upon the world, establishment of a Jewish-led world government to exploit Gentiles; use of alcohol, drugs, and the Jewish press to destroy Gentile moral bearings; the takeover of education; the propagation of pornography and the destruction of nationalism and feelings of patriotism. The Jews, claimed the Protocols, would banish God from the heavens and Christianity from the earth. They would "Abolish marriage, family and home, encourage sexual promiscuity, homosexuality, adultery, and fornication." Jewish gold would be used to bribe Gentile leaders. Economies, claimed the Protocols, would be destroyed, and Gentiles would be made to fight wars on behalf of Jews, and so on. Fanciful stuff, all of it.

Regardless of the irrefutable fact of the Protocols as a forgery, their distillation of Jewish stereotypes continued to serve as a devastating indictment of Jews. In Russia, after the revolution, they were outlawed and their very possession became a capital offense,[633] a fact that illustrates their potential for being perceived as formidable evidence of a Jewish conspiracy to undermine religion, nationhood, legitimate government, and property.[634] They were translated into every European language and many others as well.

A former czarist officer, Fyodor Vinberg, is credited with having first brought the Protocols to Germany in 1919 and made them widely available there.[635] In France, copies of them were distributed at the post-World War I Versailles Peace Conference in 1919 as a means to discredit Jews and diminish the power of the Zionist contingent and the plethora of other Jews who served in advisory capacities within the various delegations.

Henry Ford's infamous series of articles titled "The International Jew: The World's Foremost Problem (1920)" in *The Dearborn Independent* was based almost entirely on the Protocols. The articles were later turned into a book.

Both the Protocols and Ford's diatribe, which also included large amounts of reasoned narrative, were widely accepted and believed by Nazis. In interviews with G. M. Gilbert during his Nuremberg trial, Nazi Youth Leader Baldur von Schirach talked about what a boost Ford's "International Jew" gave to the early Nazi Party.[636] Said Schirach:

> This did not impress me [apparent anti-Semitism in the aristocratic circles of his youth], however, until someone made me read the American book, *The International Jew*, at the impressionable age of 17. You have no idea what a great influence this book had on the thinking of German Youth, who did not have the maturity to think for themselves.[637]

For Hitler, the origin of the Protocols was immaterial; what mattered, he said, was that Jews subscribe to their tenets. In *Mein Kampf*, he commented directly on them as follows:

> To what extent the whole existence of this people is based on a continuous lie is shown incomparably by the Protocols of the Wise Men of Zion, so infinitely hated by the Jews. They are based on a forgery, the *Frankfurter Zeitung* moans and screams once every week: the best proof that they are authentic. What many Jews may do unconsciously is here consciously exposed. And that is what matters. It is completely indifferent from what Jewish brain these disclosures originate; the important thing is that with positively terrifying certainty

they reveal the nature and activity of the Jewish people and expose their inner contexts as well as their ultimate final aims. The best criticism applied to them, however, is reality. Anyone who examines the historical development of the last hundred years from the standpoint of this book will at once understand the screaming of the Jewish press. For once this book has become the common property of a people, the Jewish menace may be considered as broken.[638]

Hitler's commentary on the Protocols is a telling thing. The Protocols were believable to large segments of the population precisely because they aligned so well with empirical evidence of stereotypical Jewish acts in contemporary society. Was it not true that Jews used their gold and their power of the press to undermine Gentile society? Did they not spread all manner of depravity and decay in their various publishing houses and theaters? Who owned the liquor distilleries (other, of course, than the Scottish whiskey makers, the French winery owners, the German beer brewery owners, the Italian bootleggers, and, of course, the Kennedys)? Who were the staunchest opponents of Christianity? Who were the revolutionaries and who was sponsoring them financially? Who was bribing governmental officials in Russia, France, and Germany? Had the Jews not induced the U.S. to enter World War I and thereby have a Gentile society fight a war to benefit the Jews? The list goes on. There seemed, especially to those with anti-Semitic leanings, to be an almost perfect alignment between claims within the Protocols and real or imagined Jewish behavior in various societies, and therein lays their importance to this narrative.

As Kershaw points out, "Hitler, like the Protocols, was believable because he spoke to and clarified for his audiences, issues that were everywhere apparent."[639] The point about believability and things that were "everywhere apparent" is well illustrated by a speech that Hitler made in 1920. In it, Hitler read out a protest over an alleged decision to provide 4 million pounds of flour to the Jewish community at a time when all Germans were on the brink of starvation. The crowd erupted in support.[640] And why not? It did not much matter whether a decision had actually been taken to provide the flour to Jews. It was simply a matter of axiomatic—stereotypical—"fact" that Jews had forever managed to carve out special treatment for themselves, and that is what made such claims believable. Jews were thought to be forever making undeserved claims and seeking special compensation and privilege.

Henry Ford initially took a tact similar to Hitler's when the authenticity of the Protocols was challenged. "The only statement I care to make about the Protocols," said Ford, "is that they fit in with what is going on. They are sixteen years old, and they have fitted the world situation up to this time. They fit it now."[641] By 1927, Ford had retracted his public stance on the Protocols and apologized for his support of them. His retraction, said humorist Will Rogers, occurred when he noticed that Jews were driving Chevys.

As late as 1937, the leading British anti-Semite of the time, Henry Hamilton Beamish, was quoted as saying, "If you have never read the Protocols, you know nothing about the Jewish question."[642] The Protocols continue to be trumpeted as authentic throughout the Arab world.

There were a good number of goings-on in Europe of the late 1800s and early 1900s that lent credence to the Protocols. Jews were indeed heavily represented in the various Marxist, Bolshevist (where Bolshevism is taken to be a Leninist extension of Marxism), Communist, and liberal party movements. Jews owned the popular press and publishing houses and used their power in those spheres to advance their kinsmen and offer up puffery of Jewish values and objectives. They were the most powerful bankers who subsidized leftist politics. They were attacking Christianity and offering proposals to enable the publication of pornography. They were prominent in the homosexual rights movement, the women's rights movement, and every other movement that seemingly ran counter to traditional German mores and culture. "The identification of the feminist movement with Jewesses," says Pulzer, "was no doubt inspired by the fact that most of the leading female advocates . . . were Jewish—Anita Auersperg, Lydia Heymann, and Regina Deutsch."[643] Jews were also at the forefront of modern art, licentious cabarets, culturally extreme theater, and abandonment of traditional, revered forms of German music in favor of modern music such as jazz. Moreover, they were seen as having been disloyal to Germany during World War I and of profiteering during it, of causing the inflationary period (an entirely false charge) and exploiting it to cheaply acquire German properties, of ruining German youth with drugs and promiscuous sex, and of otherwise attacking all things sacred to the German volk—and there was more than a smidgen of truth to all of that. In the mid- to late-1920s, Jews were also prominent in financial and political bribery scandals that rocked the nation. In short, Jewish conduct in German society gave weight and credence to the Protocols, forgery or not.

And the Protocols were also important to perceptions held by radical anti-Semites as the Dreyfus Affair was ongoing in France.

Dreyfus Affair

In the late 1890s, Catholicism and the army suffered an upheaval stemming from the Alfred Dreyfus affair. Dreyfus was born into a wealthy Jewish family living in a German-speaking area of Alsace. While a captain in the French army, he was appointed to a position on the French General Staff. While serving in that position he was charged with spying against the French on behalf of Germany.

Dreyfus was accused and twice convicted by court-martials of spying for the Germans. Nevertheless, the Dreyfusards, in a full-court press of Jewish influence and solidarity, ultimately prevailed in winning both his release from prison and his reentry into the army. The Dreyfusards not only freed and reinstated the object of their effort, they also took revenge upon both the army and the church, entities that had frustrated their objectives. The affair ultimately resulted in a significantly diminished role for both the French army and the church in French society. But in the minds of some, the actions and success of the Dreyfusards served only to lend further credence to the Protocols—a rich Jew had again employed wealth and the power of his kinsmen in politics and the press to escape justice. Such a conclusion was entirely rational: Dreyfus was twice convicted by honorable men serving on his court-martial. He was freed by way of political pressures that were entirely in line with contentions about the power of gold and the press that are found in the Protocols. In the case of Dreyfus, heaping amounts of gold and favorable press reports redirecting blame were employed by Jewish friends and relatives to his good avail. Political allies were bought. Scapegoats were duly created. Dreyfus was ultimately freed and returned to service.

The aftermath of the Dreyfus Affair was such that hard-core elements of rightist sentiment were reinforced. George Steiner contended that in the early 1900s French anti-Semitism, stemming as it did from the earlier Panama Canal Scandal (1892) and the Dreyfus Affair, was far more virile, deep-rooted and bitter than that of Germany. Historian George Mosse said that "if someone had come to me in 1914 and told me that one country in Europe would attempt to exterminate the Jews, I would have said then, 'No one can be surprised at the depths to which the French could sink.'"[644]

Even before the Dreyfus Affair there had been charges of treason by Jews that had led to a number of duels. In 1892, such charges led to a duel between the Marquis de Mores and a Jewish army captain, Armand Mayer. Mayer was killed, but his death had the positive effect of helping to discredit French anti-Semites.[645] But for a while, with the Panama Canal Scandal fresh in everyone's memory and now with the Dreyfus Affair, anti-Semites were briefly revitalized, not only in France but throughout Europe.

The Dreyfus Affair was a heated topic by 1898 and served to further illustrate the age-old accusation of Jewish disloyalty toward host nations and peoples. The various political positions, upheavals, and scandals revolving around French Jews in the late 1800s while the Dreyfus Affair was still ongoing were sufficiently severe that the French chamber took action in 1895 to try to prevent further Jewish "infiltration" into France. The action of the

French chamber had a corollary in the legislation proposed by Schönerer in Austria in 1887–1888.[646]

Edouard Drumont inflamed his newspaper readers by warning that Dreyfus, rich Jew that he was, would ultimately escape punishment even though he had supposedly "admitted everything."[647] And as events would unfold, Drumont's claims seemed prophetic.

The Jewish press and Gentile intellectuals, most notably Emile Zola with assistance from Georges Clemenceau, rallied to the defense of Dreyfus. The Social Democrats, a party dominated by Jews and their interests, used their influence within the labor movement to bring working people to the defense of the accused.[648] They collectively pushed for a finding of innocence. Zola's famous letter, "J'accuse" (I Accuse), was published by Clemenceau who was then the owner and editor of the Paris daily *L'Aurore*. Even in the face of unprecedented political pressure on his behalf, however, Dreyfus was, nevertheless, twice convicted of treason by honorable military officers serving on the boards of his court-martials—those officers were subsequently vilified. Zola was prosecuted for libel and found guilty on February 23, 1898. Ultimately, however, public pressure by French intellectuals and the international press managed to get his multiple convictions overturned.

The fight soon escalated to broader spheres. Respect for the truth was abandoned, particularly among leading Dreyfusards: "many of them," says Lindemann, "were quite willing to believe that the justice of their cause made it acceptable to bend the rules—an 'end justifies the means' perspective that is finally difficult to distinguish from that forwarded by some anti-Dreyfusards."[649] Waldeck-Rousseau, the French premier during Dreyfus's retrial, went so far as to contact the military prosecutor and judges to press them to arrive at a not guilty verdict.[650] His action was taken in recognition of the reality that actual guilt was less important than the agitation that the affair had brought to the fore. To the apologist, the action of Waldeck-Rousseau may be taken as an expression of exceptional extrajudicial courage on behalf of righteousness; to others, it was a representation of Jewish gold and the power that it commands.

The army and the church came under heavy attack by the Dreyfusards as institutions of anti-Semitism. The radicals who supported Dreyfus had supposedly begun by seeking justice, but then went on to seek total victory and abject revenge over their opponents.[651] Victory for the Dreyfusards included successful anti-Catholic legislation. Ultimately, the right wing within French society was discredited, the army stained, and the church disestablished.[652] To a great many, it was all an inglorious confirmation of the power of Jews and their gold as called out in the Protocols.

The Dreyfus Affair was resolved in his favor in 1906 after, as mentioned, two separate convictions by military tribunals. Resolution was had only after more than ten years of legal wrangling over his guilt. In 1899, Dreyfus accepted a pardon from French President Emile Laubet, implying his guilt (in the U.S. and elsewhere, a pardon carries an imputation of guilt, and accepting a pardon is an admission of that guilt).[653]

By 1906, the immense political pressure applied by the Dreyfusards bore still more fruit with the annulment of his second conviction by the French Court of Cassation, the French court of last resort. Dreyfus, we have it today, was not guilty. It was all an anti-Semitic plot carried out by a covey of anti-Semitic army officers.

As MacDonald points out:

> The young Jewish intellectuals, and their growing band of radical allies, began by asking for justice and ended by seeking total victory and revenge. In doing so, they gave their enemies an awesome demonstration of Jewish and philosemitic intellectual power. . . . While at the beginning of the affair the media was controlled by the anti-Semites, by the end of it, fully 90 percent of the literature on the subject was pro-Dreyfus. This campaign involved newspapers, photography, and cinema, and gradually it tilted public opinion in favor of Dreyfus.[654]

The Dreyfus benefactor, Georges Clemenceau, though reviled by the right wing as a tool of the Jews, would go on to become France's prime minister from 1906 to 1909 and from 1917 to 1920. He would also be one of the major voices behind the immensely important post-World War I Treaty of Versailles.[655] To the anti-Semite, the elevation of Clemenceau to the post of prime minister was a confirmation of the Protocols where it was said that Jews would "arrange elections in favor of such presidents as have in their past some dark, undiscovered strain, some 'Panama' or other—then they will be trustworthy agents for the accomplishment of our plans. . . ."[656] Clemenceau had been implicated in the Panama Canal Scandal and that association, coupled with the fact that his brother was married to a Jewess, Sophia Moritz Szeps, did not help in matters of perception about Clemenceau's Jewish connections. Sophia's father was a newspaper tsar.[657] At the conclusion of World War I, Clemenceau was a vociferous advocate for the utter destruction of Germany and its power; that fact, along with his Jewish connections, was more than enough to enjoin Hitler's hate of him.

Judaism remained suspect throughout the Continent due to the stock market crash of 1873, the Panama Canal Scandal, the Dreyfus Affair, and a variety of others in which Jews were implicated.

The furor occasioned by the Dreyfus Affair in 1894 was perceived as a test to see who really ruled France . . . the Christians or the Jews. For the right wing, the subsequent election of the Dreyfusards' Georges Clemenceau, that "tool of the Jews," to the country's leadership and the later election of the Jewish Marxist Germanophobe Léon Blum to the post of prime minister, attested to the perception that the Jews had won. Blum quickly surrounded himself with Jewish advisers. In response, the Alliance Israélite Universelle further embraced the notion of Jewish superiority.[658]

The Dreyfus Affair had still another long lasting implication. The affair established for the first time a distinct class of intellectuals who now realized that Jews were both a major power in European society and perhaps even the dominant one. A new issue was raised: who controls our culture? The answer for many was clear: the Jews do.

Meanwhile, in Russia, Jews continued to undermine the tsarist government as they continued there on their revolutionary bent.

Jacob Schiff—Russia

Russia's loss of its war with Japan (Russo-Japanese War, Feb. 1904 to Sep. 1905) had a number of roots, not the least of which was its inability to finance the war because of the boycott arranged by the Jewish financier Jacob Schiff. International Jewish bankers, at Schiff's instigation, withheld loans to Russia by which it could have financed its war. Schiff simultaneously provided Japan with loans totaling more than 100 million dollars, thereby becoming something of a hero in that country that endeared both Schiff and Jews in general to the Japanese. Moreover, on the home front, the Russian Revolution of 1905 had taken place with significant Jewish involvement.*

All of the aforementioned events throughout Europe were studied by Hitler, who was forever searching for the missteps of Jews. With Jewish-led financial scandals, revolutions, treason, and negative influences on Viennese culture as a backdrop, Hitler also studied the personalities and activities of Viennese politicians who stood in opposition to the Jews in their midst.

Hitler's Political Heroes in Vienna

Hitler looked for blemishes in the Jewish character, and he was not alone: two prominent Viennese politicians, George Ritter von

---

* The Russian "Bloody Sunday," the event led by Father George Gapon, a man who was himself piloted by the Jewish radical Pinkas Rutenberg. The event resulted in the death of several hundred workers and sparked the 1905 revolution. Gapon worked in collusion with the Russian police. Rutenberg ultimately betrayed Gapon's connection with the police to the radical, heavily Jewish, Socialist-Revolutionary Party. There is some dispute as to whether Gapon was killed by Rutenberg himself or at the behest of the Jew Yevno Azef, himself an agent provocateur and member of the leadership of the Socialist-Revolutionary Party.

Schönerer and Dr. Karl Lueger, did likewise. Hitler studied them both assiduously.

Google	URL
George Ritter von Schonerer	http://en.wikipedia.org/wiki/Georg_Ritter_von_Sch%C3%B6nerer 8/2/14
Karl Lueger	http://en.wikipedia.org/wiki/Karl_Lueger 8/2/14

George Ritter von Schönerer, the most radical racist and leader of the anti-Semitic parties in Vienna, came to exert a profound influence on the young Hitler. Schönerer was among those who argued that Jewish-Gentile distinctions were indelible, that they were inscribed in the blood of beings, and that Jews, therefore, needed to be excluded from German-Gentile society. As Lindemann points out, "If one is to speak of proto-Nazis at this time, von Schönerer is a tenable example."[659]

The staunch nationalism and Pan-Germanism developed by Hitler in Linz was such that he was predisposed toward Schönerer well before he arrived in Vienna. That Schönerer's influence was all but completely dissipated by the time Hitler actually got to the city does not seem to have affected his regard for the man and his movement.

Schönerer, like his contemporaries Theodor Herzl and Karl Lueger, began his political life as a liberal. His career began in 1871. By the end of the decade he had become an archconservative, establishing his radically anti-Semitic Pan-German Party in 1879. Fundamentally, von Schönerer was a Pan-Germanist seeking union between Germany and the Germans of Austria-Hungary and elsewhere. His brand of conservatism featured anti-Slavism, anti-Catholicism (in sympathy with the anti-Catholic efforts of Bismarck in Germany at that time, the *kulturkampf* period of 1871–1878), and virulent anti-Semitism. He did not originate his "anti" platforms but instead, propounded with genuine sincerity, the existent turmoil in each of these areas. He was supported in his political objectives by the Pan-German Daily newspaper *Alldeutsches Tagblatt*. The *Alldeutsches Tagblatt*, according to author Brigitte Hamann, was probably the first newspaper that Hitler read each day.[660] That paper, in keeping with Schönerer's stand, fought for German-Austria's unification, for German as a national language in Cisleithania (the area that encompassed Vienna), and for the "Away from Rome" movement, which is to say, the anti-Catholic movement. Schönerer was never able to build a truly significant political mass, but he was, nevertheless, exceedingly influential in fanning the flames of Austro-German nationalism and anti-Semitism.

In 1884–1885 he took up the fight to nationalize the Nordbahn, the Emperor Ferdinand Northern Railway that was controlled by Baron Rothschild in accord with his position as its majority stockholder. In submitting his proposal to parliament, he provided a list of 40,000 signatures that he said represented the "scream of the people"[661] against the Jewish threat. He was unsuccessful, but he did manage to cause Rothschild to pay substantially more to retain his railroad contract, and he thereby gained additional supporters—people rarely take account of the fact that such additional costs are ultimately passed on to the consumer.

By 1901, Schönerer reached the peak of his political power when twenty-one members of his party were elected to the parliament. Thereafter, under a barrage of press criticism, he was demonized and reduced to a comic figure. By the time he left office in 1907, all of his previous influence and power were spent. Both he and his rallying cry of "Without Judea, without Rome (Catholicism), we'll build Germany's church and dome!"[662] became laughable. Schönerer's fate was much like that which has become the fate of other leaders who have opposed Jewish domination over Gentiles: he was mocked and slighted in the popular press and thereby diminished to nothingness. When he finally departed the scene, he was a nonentity, an utterly broken man, the Joe McCarthy of his era.

Still, Schönerer and his movement were studied by Hitler, and he came away from his studies with several important lessons learned. Schönerer, for example, addressed himself primarily to the bourgeois. Hitler saw that as a mistake. Schönerer, thought Hitler, should have directed himself and his movement directly to the masses.

Schönerer's position as a racial anti-Semite needs to be highlighted. To him, there was no redemption for Jews within Germanic society: "Concerning the Jew," said Schönerer, "our standpoint remains irreversible: A Jew remains a Jew whether he is baptized or not!"[663] Hitler felt the same way. In actual fact, if one removes the exclamation point, Schönerer's contention becomes less radical: it aligns perfectly with the modern government of Israel on that particular point, a fact that serves to emphasize the racial vis-à-vis the religious aspect of Jewry.

Like Hitler's later accomplishment, Schönerer sought to turn Germandom into a kind of religion of its own. Also like Hitler, Schönerer emphasized Pan-Germanism, the nobility of the German people, the leader-cult and moral and cultural issues. Like Hitler himself, Schönerer conceived of himself as a "militant knight-redeemer of the German Volk."[664] As a militant, he represented "politics in a new key."[665] He railed against the Freemasons, Slavs, the Catholic Church, the monarchy, parliamentarians, and especially the Jews—their street peddlers, their department stores, their capitalistic mass production, their power and corruption in the press and politics, and their overall economic, political, and social clout. But Schönerer's choice to engage so many enemies at once (the monarchy, the church, the Jews, et al.) was perhaps the most important lesson that Hitler took from him: Hitler's assessment of Schönerer's movement was that it had too many enemies and that it failed to even try to bring to itself powerful institutions of society such as the army, the clergy, the cabinet, or the head of state. Hitler would later resolve that his movement would focus its hate to march against a single enemy: the Jews. Unable to gain much traction by attacking Jews directly, Hitler opted to focus most of his attacks on Marxists, which in very large part tidily encompassed the Jews. Unlike Schönerer's movement, it would seek the support of the army, the business class, intellectuals, and to some extent, even the clergy, and especially the Protestant clergy. Moreover, Hitler would pointedly address himself to the masses, not the elites.

While Schönerer ultimately slinked away defeated and demeaned, another of Vienna's anti-Semitic politicians was on the rise and would enjoy a better fate: this was Dr. Karl Lueger.

Karl Lueger was an extraordinary man. Born of peasant stock, he was nevertheless able to win a place at the most prestigious preparatory school in Vienna, the Theresianum.* From there, in 1862, he went on to the University of Vienna where he obtained his law degree four years on. In 1870, he received his doctorate in law. After serving his legal apprenticeship he opened his own law office in 1874. He quickly attained high rank in his profession stemming from his thoroughgoing legal knowledge and his superior judgment and eloquence in handling cases before the court. He quickly became known for his generosity in providing gratis legal services for the poor. While he successfully practiced law until 1896, he never became wealthy;[666] he labored for his people, not wealth. Among his many outstanding traits was honesty: even his bitterest enemies acknowledged his scrupulous integrity.

Lueger was also handsome. His appearance, his grace, and sense of occasion—his aesthetic distinction—won him the moniker *der schöne Karl*. To the ladies of Vienna, he was "beautiful Charles, the spellbinder." To the commoner, he was the "people's tribune." By the time of his death in 1910, he was the "Lord God of Vienna" (*Herrgott von Wein*) for having accomplished so much on behalf of his city and its people. He moved among commoners and royalty with equal ease. Unlike Schönerer,† Lueger was big enough within himself such that he never became envious of the aristocracy to whom he always remained deferential.

---

* "The importance of this academy to the high nobility of blood and service may be gauged by the fact that the establishment of a secure quota of places for the scions of prominent Hungarian families became a matter of high-level negotiations between the Austrian and Hungarian administrations after the establishment of the dual monarchy in 1867 (Eugen Gauglia, Das Theresianum in Wien Vergangenheit und Gergenwart" [*Vienna*, 1912, 156–57]).

† Schönerer had been a member of the nobility until he was stripped of his title for the violence connected with his anti-Semitism; he thereafter demeaned the royal house.

Lueger entered politics in 1872 with his election to the city council. By 1882, he had formed his own anti-Semitic party. It underwent several name changes until it settled on the name Christian Social Party. In 1890, he was elected to the Lower Austrian Landtag where he became a leading spirit against liberalism and corruption, both of which were at the time associated mostly with capitalism and Jews.

Elected mayor in 1895, Emperor Franz Joseph refused to seat him owing to pressure placed on him by Jews and their supporting Socialists.[667] Lucy Dawidowicz and others claim that it was due to objections from the church and the emperor, which is true enough as long as one is willing to concede that their objections, in turn, stemmed from Jewish opposition—a concession that Dawidowicz omits.[668] Still, for Franz Joseph, there were also very practical issues at stake: Jews, who so thoroughly prospered under his regime, were, as Lenni Brenner claims, "conspicuous as regime loyalists amidst a sea of irredentist nationalities tearing the Austro-Hungarian Empire apart."[669]

Eight percent of the empire's generals were Jews. Moreover, they were exceedingly powerful throughout both the empire and the world. They were to neither be taken lightly nor irritated to the point of withdrawing their support from Franz Joseph and his empire.

The Jewish-owned *Neue Freie Presse*, one of the most prestigious newspapers in all of Europe, was staunchly opposed to the satisfaction of the people's will. The Rothschilds, Austria's economic powerhouse—taking their lead from the church and the emperor if one is to believe Dawidowicz—threatened to leave Vienna if Lueger was seated as mayor. They did not carry out the threat. Sigmund Freud, who had in his youth refused to show respect for the emperor, celebrated the action of Franz Joseph against Lueger by smoking a cigar—let us speculate that he also doffed his hat and offered up a toast to the Catholic Church for its role in opposing Lueger.

Neither the power of the liberal Jewish press nor Emperor Franz Joseph was sufficient to dampen the people's enthusiasm for and dedication to Lueger. Lueger was reelected, but Franz Joseph again refused to ratify the election and seat him as mayor. Union workers, under Jewish leadership, were called on during each election cycle to protest against Lueger, but they nevertheless voted for him.[670] After being elected a total of four times, actual democracy finally prevailed and Franz Joseph relented. Lueger's election was confirmed, and he became mayor in 1897. The Jewish-dominated press of Vienna bemoaned the "culture-hostile mass"[671] that Lueger supposedly represented. It is curious that they should have used such language since they were themselves regarded as hostile to culture by the broad spectrum of people who elected Lueger multiple times; indeed, we must think that opposition to extant cultural issues played a significant role in Luger's success as an anti-Semite.

As mentioned, Lueger started out as a political liberal. But liberalism at that time had come to mean alignment with and advancement of the capitalists at the expense of the guilds and small businessmen, and the capitalists were mostly Jews. Lindemann highlights the point, saying that, for Lueger, "the exploiters and deceivers of the people were the capitalists and the liberals—which, in Vienna, meant overwhelmingly the Jews."[672] Liberalism in Vienna was the functional equivalent of Judaism, and it was beset with corruption. Lueger had come to vociferously fight such corruption and the Jews responsible for it.

Early in his career on the city council, Lueger had launched a campaign against an English engineering firm that was attempting to win a contract related to the city's transport system. He charged that representatives of the firm tried to bribe him and other council members. Libel trials followed. Lueger was acquitted. The whole affair, though, as Carle Schorske points out, provided Lueger with a reputation for fighting the "mighty Goliath of 'international capital.'"[673] The term "international capital" was at the time taken by all to mean "Jewish capital."

Lueger's focused anti-Semitism reinforced an important lesson for Adolf Hitler, the lesson being that one should restrict public appeals to a single enemy. "Lueger entirely focused on Vienna's problems, and his enemy, the Jews, with the slogan, 'Greater Vienna must not turn into Greater Jerusalem.'"[674] He assaulted the "money and stock exchange Jews," and the "press Jews." Social Democracy was to him the "Jew protection corps." Intellectuals and members of the press were "ink Jews." Eastern Jews were "beggar Jews." Modern art was Jewish, as was the women's liberation movement. The Hungarian component of the empire was always the "Judeo-Magyars," a term used in recognition of the perception of Jews as being in the vanguard of Magyar society and culture.[675]

Still, Lueger was an anti-Semite with a twist: he had many Jewish friends and never rejected a dinner invitation to a wealthy Jewish home.[676] When it suited his purpose he would even ally himself with Jews such as he did with Ignaz Mandl in leading the fight to extend the suffrage, a reform on which the Liberals were divided.[677] He made exceptions to his anti-Semitism by way of his often quoted quip, "I determine who is a Jew."[678] Moreover, unlike Schönerer and Hitler after him, Lueger's anti-Semitism was based on religion, not race.

For all of his great admiration of Lueger, one of Hitler's several objections to the man was his call for "Germanizing" the Czechs by imposing the German language on citizens. Hitler thought that such an approach was irresolute: *"Nationality or rather race does not happen to lie in the language but in the blood,"*[679] said Hitler. (Italics in the original). Hitler also adamantly opposed Lueger's exceedingly close ties to Catholicism—Pope Leo XIII had even interceded on behalf of Lueger to have him seated as mayor, which flies in the face of the Dawidowicz claim (it is true enough, though, that the local Catholic clergy initially objected to Lueger).

Lueger was fantastically popular with the people of Vienna. Jews continued to stream into the city during his administration for they suffered no actual harm under his form of anti-Semitism. His goal was to retain the German character of Vienna and to reinvigorate Catholicism as a political power in the empire. His devotion to Catholicism provided him with the significant added advantage of being able to exploit church organizations and membership on his own political behalf, much as Jews exploited the labor movement. Hitler, for his part, admired Lueger's recognition that it was important to secure the support of prominent organizations or personages to advance his political position. When Hitler later curried the favor of the army and leading industrialists in the early 1930s, he made use of them in much the same way that Lueger used the church.

Lueger was a German nationalist but not a Pan-German like Schönerer and Hitler. His slogan, says Hamann, was "Vienna is German and must remain German."[680] To that end, foreign settlers in the city had to forswear their national background and promise to uphold the German character of the city.[681] But Lueger's nationalism related to the German language and customs, not to assimilation with Germany itself. In keeping with his anti-Semitism and German nationalism, he railed against Judeo-Magyarism upon reconsideration of the *Ausgleich* (equalization of power) between Austria and Hungary in 1886.[682]

Lueger's dedication to retaining the German flavor of Vienna was not unlike efforts by others in other cities. Budapest was strictly Hungarian and vigorously magyarized other nationalities there. Prague was Czech; Lemberg, Polish; Trieste, Italian; and Laibach was Slovenian. There were national battles everywhere between majority and minority populations.[683] Vienna was just one more city among many that sought to create or maintain a particular nationalistic culture—it might be compared in this respect to today's Jerusalem wherein Israelis seek to marginalize Muslim and Christian influences.

At the time of Lueger's election as mayor, Vienna was a city beset by political corruption and moral decay. It was also the most backward capital in Europe. Its people were enormously overtaxed, and its population had assumed a lazy indifference to matters of politics, economics, and religion.[684] As mayor, Lueger remained true to his roots as he reinvigorated the spirit of the populace and engaged people in marketplaces and beer parlors. He was the first middle-class politician to center his appeals on the masses; he "moved the masses and dug the roots of his power deep into the soil,"[685] says Hamann. And he was hugely successful in both his politics and his administration. He was more directly connected with the people than the common politician of his day and his political messages were more emotional than the dry rational rhetoric of the liberals. Hamann describes what was said of Lueger's speeches as follows:

> If a thinking person read them, he couldn't help smiling. . . . Yet if a thinking person listened when Lueger was talking, then being a thinking person was of no avail at all, then one's own thoughts disappeared, then one was grabbed by an elementary force, and carried along defenselessly.[686]

Hitler took many-a-lesson from Lueger's rhetorical skills.

Lueger's effect was electrifying to the people, including Hitler. Hitler would later write in praise of his oratory and his appeal to the masses, and he would mimic Lueger's approach in both areas. In *Mein Kampf*, Hitler said, "Today I see the man, even more than before, as the greatest German mayor of all times."[687]

Historian William L. Shirer wrote that even his opponents conceded that he was at heart a decent, chivalrous, generous, and tolerant man. Jewish writer Stefan Zweig, who grew up in Vienna, asserted that "His city administration was perfectly just and even typically democratic."[688] It is no wonder that Hitler admired him: everybody did, and not without good reason. His anti-Semitism aside, Lueger accomplished a great deal on behalf of his cherished city and all of the people therein, Jews and Gentiles alike.

During his fifteen years in office, Lueger improved the traffic network and the provision of gas and electricity. He added schools and overhauled, modernized, and otherwise improved the education system. He also added numerous housing units and provided the people with pristine water. He built parks and reserved open areas and forests for public use. He "municipalized the waterworks, the slaughterhouse, and even the brewery."[689] He established municipal banks to provide competition against the Jewish-dominated banking system. He used trash as a source of energy and garbage as a means to manufacturer fertilizer and applied the revenue from these sources to offset the cost of trash collection. He also built hospitals and added trolley cars to the streets. He was instrumental in bringing universal suffrage to Austria in 1907. Over a million jobs were created in the city during the fifteen years of his stewardship.[690] He was also a pragmatic, tactical thinker like Hitler; results were the predominant criteria for his ideas.

Lueger did not, however, diminish the power of Jews in the city, though he may have caused some of them to assume a lower profile. Jews continued to flock to the city. Indeed, it was under Lueger's administration that Jews enjoyed what we now call the Golden Age of Viennese Jewry.[691]

The combination of Schönerer and Lueger cut a deep impression both on Viennese politics and Adolf Hitler. Both Schönerer and Lueger were able to represent Jewish intellectual and esthetic radicalism as root causes of Viennese political and moral decay and resulting decadence. Whatever the truth of Jewish responsibility for Vienna's ills, it was true that, as one *NY Times* source puts it, the "successful identification, in Viennese politics, of the Jews [as the] presumed sources of all social, moral and political evil provided an explosive political formula that would serve later as a model for the Nazis."[692]

The nationalism that was gripping Vienna and other cities during Lueger's reign was not unlike the nationalism then coming into being for Zionists. When Jewish apologists frequent the idea of nationalism's nasty side, they omit the nationalism and ethnocentrism that were part and parcel of Viennese Jewry and have historically been significant causes of anti-Semitism there and elsewhere. Zionism was not yet the historical powerhouse that it would later become, but it even then was stoutly and wholly supported on nationalist foundations, just as was Lueger's Vienna and Hitler's Nazi Germany.

Hitler's Vienna was the Vienna of the little people. Little people like himself who were being led away from their comfortable traditions and culture. The people that Hitler interacted with were not the scions of political and cultural change, they were the people who were reasonably content with their former lot and were dejected and bewildered by modernity. They viewed Viennese modernity with incomprehension and deemed the new culture, the culture that was and is even now so championed by liberals, as too degenerate, too international, too disconnected from the people, "too cosmopolitan and libertine, too 'Jewish'—a dire symptom of fragmentation and decay."[693]

As the Germans of Vienna were marginalized, other nationalities, and especially Jews, advanced. The great power of Jews to mold society to their will was represented by such icons as Sigmund Freud, who, along with his psychoanalysis, attacked the day's sexual conventions and the clergy. In addition to Freud, Wittgenstein, Herzl, Schnitzler, Altenberg, along with the Rothschilds and the various Jewish newspaper editors and cultural critics, were exerting a tremendous, oppressive influence on Viennese culture.

Prominent Jews heaped praise on the monarchy and its embrace of multiculturalism while Austro-Germans seethed in response. Things long held dear by the German populace in the areas of music, theater, art, religion, and its concomitant social relations were all being debased, they believed, by Jewish influences in the city. Hitler, of course, aligned himself with such sentiments. He would later comment on Marxism, and therefore Jewish tendencies toward criticism in *Mein Kampf*, saying that "it *practiced criticism for seventy years*, annihilating, disintegrating criticism, and again criticism, which continued until the old state was undermined by this persistent corrosive acid and brought to collapse."[694] (Italics are in the original.) He would also claim that Jewish influence was "'a ferment of decomposition' among peoples and races, and in the broader sense a dissolver of human culture."[695] Hitler's thought processes, which were planted and germinated in Vienna, would later grow, as we shall see, when he observed and participated in the happenings in Germany during the 1920s.

Hitler's residence in Vienna from 1907–1913 had indeed been the apprenticeship that Brigitte Hamann emphasizes. By the end of his sojourn there he had developed a worldview with Jews at the center of all strife. He had acquired George Schönerer and Karl Lueger as political role models. He had learned the trade of political rabble rousing from the Social Democrats and anti-

Semitism from personal observation, study, and from what was, by this time, his political heroes, Schönerer and Lueger. Still an utterly unknown entity with little formal education and no prospects whatever, it did not much matter what Hitler believed. Hitler was a political nobody, and nobody of importance was going to listen to the likes of him.

He departed Vienna in 1913 and moved to Munich in Germany's Bavarian province. According to his later testimony before a court in relation to his attempted coup, his Beer Hall Putsch of 1923, he was by this time a confirmed anti-Semite.[696]

Munich was attractive to Hitler because it was German, but just as importantly it was the center of German culture. For him and others like him, it was the Mecca of Germandom, an Athens on the River Isar. His time there was the happiest of his life. He was there when war broke out.

CHAPTER 3

WORLD WAR I: THE OPENING SALVO OF WORLD WAR II

One day the great European War will come out of some damned foolish thing in the Balkans (1888).
—Otto von Bismarck

Since the Thirty Years War of 1618–1648 when Germany was transformed into an underpopulated wasteland with upward of half of its previous population dead,[697] it developed justifiable cause for concern about its neighbors. The Peace of Westphalia in 1648, engineered by France and Sweden, partitioned the German states into small wholly ineffectual economic and military entities. In 1800, "Germany" was composed of 314 states and 1,475 sovereign estates;[698] all this on a land mass only about 80 percent that of Texas, a place with only 254 counties.

In the early 1800s, the country was utterly unable to repel the France of Napoleon Bonaparte. It was only due to reinvigorated German nationalism that France was ultimately fought off and Prussia and the other states again enjoyed a semblance of freedom. Even then, though, France was still able to dominate and exploit the small German states along its border. That problem would only be resolved by German unification in 1871 with its defeat of Napoleon III. To the east lay the industrially and militarily backward behemoth of Russia that was, by the early 1900s, allied with France and was rapidly improving its economic and military capabilities with assistance from France.

In response to perceived threats from all sides, Germany's Prussia had developed its social and political system along military lines and won its contest with Austria in 1866 at the Battle of Königgrätz. With its success at Königgrätz, Prussia set itself on its march, as historians never tire in telling us, toward becoming "an army with a nation." After German unification in 1871, the country continued with Prussia's military tradition. It was at this point that Austria turned away from Germany and instead focused its empire on the Balkan states, and thereby set the stage for the Austro-Germans to become a minority within that state.[699]

Lacking natural barriers to attack along much of its border area (e.g., the Fulda Gap is illustrative of the likely route for tank attacks from the East), Germany sought refuge in treaties with other countries to bolster its security. To this end, the Iron Chancellor Otto von Bismarck allied Germany with Russia and Austro-Hungary under the League of Three Emperors in 1873 and again with the Reinsurance Treaty of 1887, and thereby isolated France. This treaty, precluding any threat from the east as it did, put Germany and its might in a powerful position—she was safe from a two-front war. Of particular note, too, was the fact that Bismarck also did everything he could to avoid challenges to Britain's interests, as did Hitler, and to thereby further isolate France: his successor would do neither.

Upon the death of the old Kaiser, William I, Crown Prince Frederick III briefly reigned but soon succumbed to throat cancer. Frederick's son, William II (Wilhelm), was then installed as the German kaiser. With the installment of William II, Jews, claimed the radical Right, became the real rulers of the German Empire.[700] Rightists accused the kaiser of being soft on Jews and claimed, with some justification, that he was completely surrounded by them. In making that charge, the rightists were referring to such powerful advisors as Ballin, Rathenau, Mendelssohn, Arnold, James, Simon, Bleichröder, Godschmidt-Rothschild, Carwow, Kappel, and others of lesser import and influence.[701]

When William came to power in 1888, disputes between him and Bismarck erupted almost immediately. William was a vain, erratic man, a man of whom it was said that "he wanted to be the bride at every wedding and the corpse at every funeral." England's Edward VII called him "the most brilliant failure in Europe."[702] Historian Barbara Tuchman described him as the "possessor of the least inhibited tongue in Europe,"[703] and so he was—his diplomatic faux pas were a frequent delight to his enemies and a bane to his friends. Hitler, ever the artist, opined that William II had artistic taste but all of it was bad. Russia's Nicholas II was of the same mind.[704] Still, though William II was vain and not ready for his post when his father succumbed to cancer, he was not fundamentally bad. He was impetuous and a diplomatic novice, a foolish braggart who was full of bravado, but still a fairly decent sort of man. He was certainly not the evil incarnate that he was made out to be by the Allies during World War I.

Google	URL
Kaiser William II	http://en.wikipedia.org/wiki/Wilhelm_II,_German_Emperor 8/2/14
Otto von Bismarck	http://en.wikipedia.org/wiki/Otto_von_Bismarck 8/2/14

As a youngster, William II had idolized Bismarck, seeing him as the great chancellor that he was and the loyal servant to his grandfather, William I. As an adult, however, the personalities of Bismarck and William II would clash in ways that were fateful for the nation. At the heart of their disagreement was William's desire to supplant Bismarck's power with his own. Under William's grandfather, Bismarck had garnered the power of state to himself, and William was determined to break that hold. He succeeded but was ill suited to the task.

Adding to the dissension was William's desire to accommodate labor, which was the constituency of the Marxist Social Democratic Party (SPD), Bismarck's old foe. The SPD was founded by and was, at the time, still controlled largely by Jews. The party had been founded by the labor leader Ferdinand Lassalle and other Jews in 1875. Shortly after William II took power, the SPD was led by Paul Singer and Hugo Haase, both of whom were Jewish. Bismarck sought a violent crackdown on the SPD leadership and had implemented antisocialist laws that, for a time, suppressed it but also served to further radicalize both its leadership and its membership. William responded to Bismarck's initiative by saying that he would not commence his reign by spilling the blood of his subjects.

In 1890, William dismissed Bismarck and repealed the law implemented by him that forbade political activity by Social

Democrats. In 1891, in an act that flew in face of William's tolerance, the SPD reaffirmed itself as a party of revolution.[705] By the end of the 1890s, William came to sense that both Zionism and the Socialist movement embodied in the SPD were behind his enemies, but he failed to act on the basis of his foreboding.[706] By the end of World War I, he would come to realize the wisdom of Bismarck's ban on such parties. And after his abdication he would several times express his regret that he had been so accommodating toward liberalism and its associated German Jews, and especially those belonging to the SPD and its offshoots.

In 1912, the SPD had refused to fund the creation of three additional army corps (at least six divisions and perhaps a few more), though it was widely known by way of ongoing turmoil on the Continent that Europe would soon be at war. Looking at that funding denial retrospectively after World War I, Hitler concluded that the denial of that funding was tantamount to treason.

In September 1914, during the First Battle of the Marne, the German army was but a few days' march from Paris. There was panic in the French capital, the city's military governor-general supposedly ordered demolition charges to be laid under the Eiffel Tower, and the government was preparing to flee to Bordeaux. The situation was so dire that French troops had to be rushed to the front lines by way of Paris taxicabs (a great propaganda thing but also a thing of little actual effect). Hitler reasoned, and probably quite legitimately, that the additional 120,000 troops from three additional corps would have enabled Germany to defeat the French in that battle. Instead, the Miracle of the Marne occurred. The badly outnumbered German forces (the French had thirty-six divisions to the German's thirty) were brought to a stalemate, and the two sides thereafter settled into the trench warfare that so represents that tragic war and time. In a speech in April 1923, Hitler railed against the SPD for its perceived perfidy calling the decision "unfathomable baseness and folly."

During the monarchy of William II, very little was done to curb press excesses and the press was even at that time largely in the hands of Jewish owners and editors.

Both Germany's Kaiser William II and Russia's Tsar Nicholas II were a good deal more liberal and soft on dissent than they are generally depicted to have been. For example, during the reign of Nicholas II, Russians enjoyed "freedom of the press, religion, assembly and association, protection of private property, and free labor unions—facts that are only rarely mentioned in history books. Sworn enemies of the regime, such as Lenin, were treated with remarkable leniency."[707] In fact, Lenin, as a member of the minor nobility, even continued to receive a state stipend while he was in exile in Siberia for crimes against that very state.[708]

William's attempt to pacify labor had no real prospect for success. Between 1889 and 1916 he implemented a whole series of social and labor reforms that were at their core attempts to pacify the Social Democrats. Indeed, as Stolfi points out, Wilhelmine Germany was by the mid-1890s an exceedingly humane society consisting of extensive social programs that outshined even the popular models of democracies such as France and Britain.[709] So enlightened were Germany's social programs, England would later adopt important aspects of the German welfare system into its own.[710]

William's progressive social policies were all to no avail. Marxists within the ranks of the SPD had no interest whatever in pacific relations between labor and the government, and whatever William did would certainly not have mollified them. The objective of the SPD was to seize power in Germany, not conciliate labor-government relations, and its opportunity to do so would come with World War I. That William II could not see and understand the objectives of the SPD is testimony to his naiveté. As their activities during World War I would prove, significant contingents of the SPD sought the destruction of William's government in order to emplace a Marxist one. As for the Jews on the whole, they had long objected to powerful monarchs of any kind. A strong monarch beholden to no one but God could act as the "first servant of the state" without deference to the special interests of Jews. If the monarchs could not be bought or bent to Jewish interests, if they would not mortgage their sovereignty, they would have to go.

Under William II, Bismarck's successor declined Russia's offer to renew the Reinsurance Treaty. Russia thereafter concluded a treaty with France (1892) and with French financing it embarked on a military modernization program that was schedule for completion in 1917. The refusal of Germany to further ally itself with Russia was a significant blunder that would almost certainly not have occurred had Bismarck retained power. To make matters worse, William and his new chancellor also took it upon themselves to challenge Britannia's rule of the sea. They in this way sought to create a grand fleet that could rival Great Britain and would ultimately enable them to both extend and defend their overseas empire. It would provide a guarantee that in the event of conflict, Germany would continue to have access to the markets of its colonies and the natural resources that those colonies provided. The colonies, in turn, would propel the nation to that of a prominent world power in politics and influence. It was an expression of its desire to engage in what Germans knew as *Weltpolitiks*. Unfortunately for Germany, Great Britain remained the stronger of the two on the waves, and that strength would be fateful for the German people as Britain was able to effectively blockade the shipping of German raw materials and foodstuffs by way of the North Sea.

William's failure to continue to isolate France by continuing his good relations with Russia and his simultaneous challenge to British maritime hegemony would ultimately represent fateful blunders.[711]

Under William's reign, Germany was, according to historian Walter Laqueur, "a permissive country to an almost bewildering degree,"[712] a fact that was particularly so with respect to Jews. Throughout his reign, William acted the part of a liberal in dealing with the SPD and its Jewish leadership and constituency; he even visited Eretz Israel in 1898 and met with Zionist founder Theodor Herzl as a sop to his Jews. The kaiser's liberalism represented fertile soil for the cultivation and growth of Marxism. He catered to them, fatefully, until it was too late to reverse himself.

It was not until he abdicated that he expressed any insight as to the fundamental source for the demise of his monarchy. He departed spewing vehemence toward Jews, his former cronies. By war's end, he would bitterly comment that his "abdication was orchestrated by the 'tribe of Juda.' Let no German ever forget this, nor rest until these parasites have been destroyed and exterminated from German soil."[713] Jews, said William, were a "nuisance that humanity must get rid of some way or other. I believe the best would be gas."[714] The latter was angry commentary of the moment: when he became aware of Hitler's treatment of Jews, he wrote to his daughter in 1938 saying that he was for the first time ashamed to be German.[715] Still, his ranting against the Jews of Germany, England, and elsewhere make it clear that he felt that both he and Germany had been stabbed in the back by them.

William, of course, failed to recount his own culpability in all that happened: his dismissal of Bismarck, his refusal to further align Germany with Russia, his challenges to England's dominance at sea; and his truckling to Jews and the resultant tolerance of the Marxist SPD and its radical offspring, the Independent Democratic Socialist Party (USPD), and the even more radical Spartacists. William had an unwitting penchant to be an enemy to his friends and a friend to his enemies; it would prove to be a disastrous deficiency of character. "Kaiser William II," said Hitler, "was the first German Emperor to hold out a conciliatory hand to the leaders of Marxism, without suspecting that scoundrels have no honor. While they still held the imperial hand in theirs, their other hand was reaching for the dagger."[716] On this score, as with many others, Hitler was essentially right. William did indeed genuinely seek to mollify the highly powerful Jewish component of the German population, and he had many seemingly good Jews about him who were prodding him on.

After the failed Russian Revolution of 1905, a realignment of power took place in Europe. Two camps developed: the Central Powers (Germany, Austria-Hungary, and Italy)† and the Triple

---

† As war was declared, Italy called upon language in the Alliance to avoid joining the fray. The Alliance was to be executed upon one state being attacked by another; that Germany and Austria-Hungary first declared war on Serbia obviated Italy's obligation to participate. In 1915, Italy would join the Allies.

Entente (Great Britain, France, and Russia), which would later be extended and become known as the Allies.[717] Germany was now beset with potential hostility on two fronts, France to the west and Russia to the east. German preeminence in Europe was badly undermined.[718] By now, diplomatic efforts by Germany to counter its veritable encirclement were fruitless. Germany, which by this time was again in good standing with Austria-Hungary, was left with no choice but to back its only significant friend on the Continent in the event of hostilities. For its part, Austro-Hungary was in the midst of great upheaval with its various nationalities and had reason to fear dissolution of the empire as its national components strived for independence. Since Russia was the patron of several major components of Slavic regions in the Austro-Hungarian Empire, any alliance that could thwart Russia was good for the Austro-Hungarian Empire but was simultaneously fraught with the portent of war.

National Humiliations

In 1908, Austria-Hungary annexed the Turkish provinces of Bosnia-Herzegovina. The takeover was engineered by Austria-Hungary's foreign minister Graf Lexa von Aehrenthal in secret negotiation with Russia's foreign minister, Aleksandr P. Izvolsky (Aehrenthal was widely believed to have had Jewish ancestors, but did not). In exchange for Russia's acquiescence to the takeover, Austria-Hungary was to abandon its objections to the opening of the Bosporus and Dardanelles straits to Russian warships, which would, in turn, provide Russia with access to the open waters of the Aegean, Ionian, and Mediterranean Sea and beyond, a long-held objective of Russia. Aehrenthal was to delay the Austro-Hungarian takeover for a time in order to let Izvolsky properly set the stage in Russia for coming events. Aehrenthal breeched the understanding by accomplishing the takeover before Izvolsky had time to set the stage. Strong popular opposition occurred in Russia and Serbia, both of which had ties to Bosnia-Herzegovina. Supported by Germany, Austria-Hungry prevailed. Russia was made to seem weak and to have abandoned her Slav allies. The whole of the foregoing was to embitter relations between Serbia, Austria-Hungary, and Russia. Humiliated by the Dual Monarchy, hostile tensions thenceforth existed between Russia and Austria-Hungary.[719]

* * * *

Between March 1905 and May 1906, Germany was at loggerheads with France and England resulting from the First Moroccan Crisis, which is also known as the Tangier Crisis. The dispute centered on the colonial straits of Morocco. William II visited Morocco in March 1905 and while there made impolitic and confrontational remarks in favor of Moroccan independence from France. France, with the support of England (and later, Spain, Italy, and the U.S.), took a defiant line against Germany. As tensions mounted, Germany mobilized and France provocatively moved troops to the German border. In 1906, the Algeciras Conference was called to resolve the dispute. Among the thirteen nations present, only Austria-Hungary stood at Germany's side.[720] In 1914, Germany would repay Austria-Hungary for its loyalty and support. The issues were settled for the time being, but only temporarily. The First Moroccan Crisis humiliated Germany and served as a precursor for the Second Moroccan Crisis.

* * * *

The weakened position of Germany due to William II's refusal to renew Germany's treaty with Russia was further illustrated in 1911 by renewed disputes between France and Germany over Morocco. Known as the Agadir Crisis or the Second Moroccan Crisis, this one stemmed from Germany's attempt to impose its will on France by flexing the muscle of its new naval assets.

Germany dispatched the gunboat *Panther* to the North African port of Agadir, Morocco, which was then a French protectorate. Germany sought by this action to both challenge British supremacy of the seas and also force France to provide restitution for its takeover of the North African kingdom subsequent to the First Moroccan Crisis. For her part, Britain was concerned that Germany was attempting to further challenge Britain's sea power by establishing a permanent naval presence in Agadir. The crisis served to reinforce mutual concerns of France and England, expressed through a British-French naval agreement, and simultaneous Anglo-German estrangement.

With France again supported by both England and Italy, and implicitly by Russia, Germany could do naught but once again humiliatingly back down. The Morocco disputes as well as several others in the early 1900s helped set the stage for war: other disputes included clashes between England and Germany during the Boer War that led to the Anglo-French Entente Cordiale and England's involvement in Continental affairs; the Dreadnaught Race of 1905–1914 between England and Germany (a race for supremacy of the seas); and conflicts arising between England and Germany as Germany became increasingly able to compete with England's domination of world trade.

* * * *

In 1912–1913, Serbia had gained extensive new territories from the Balkan Wars, much to the chagrin of Germany's ally, Austria-Hungary, as well as Germany's other ally on the Continent, the Ottoman Empire of Turkey. The Balkan Wars, too, served as an important precursor to World War I. Success of the Balkan League (Bulgaria, Montenegro, Greece, and Serbia) in defeating the Ottoman Empire had dire consequences for several important powers. For Russia, it again opened up the possibility of access to the warm waters of the Mediterranean via the Bosporus and Dardanelles straits. For England, the wars represented the potential threat of naval conflict with Russia in the Mediterranean. For Austro-Hungary, the new Serbian territory represented a unified bloc that might threaten trouble with its Slav populations. Germany sought to turn the Ottoman Empire into a client state and therefore supported its integrity. Moreover, chagrin over Serbia was shared in Germany where Serbia was seen as a satellite of Russia. By 1914, Russia itself was in the unhappy position of having to force a showdown with Austria-Hungary or suffer irreparable damage to its relationship with Serbia and other Balkan states. It chose to do the former.

Added to all of the foregoing was the fact that France was still very much smarting from its loss of Alsace Lorraine to Germany in 1871, so much so that the French developed something of a passionate hate against Germany and expressed that hate in its press, schools, theaters, and cinemas.[721] Many prominent Jewish journalists and publishers in Germany tended to champion everything French, which, of course, set them at odds with the radical Right and with Hitler, in particular.

The accumulation of humiliations, rivalries, national interests, and open conflict let each side think itself justified to act decisively against its foes. Moreover, the new alliances, several of which were secret and therefore all the more problematical, encouraged belligerency. Europe knew full well that war was on the horizon.

Each side, not fully aware of the alliances of the other, now thought it possible to exorcise its demons by defeating its antagonists. The Pan-German press, and even Jewish-owned publications of leftist inclination, began calling for war with France, ostensibly to provide Germany with Lebensraum for its burgeoning population. The exceedingly powerful, Jewish-owned anti-Russian *Berliner Tageblatt*, a paper that was always willing to put Germany at risk on behalf of its goal to defeat Russia, began calling for war with Russia. "Traditionally hostile to the Kaiser, the *Tageblatt* now portrayed him as 'peace loving to the core' and praised his efforts to deal with 'an overpowering, fully armed neighbor [Russia]' who sought to deprive Germany 'of light and air.'"[722] The paper reinforced its stance after the assassination of Austria-Hungary's Crown Prince Ferdinand, expressing satisfaction with Austria's decision to attack.

From a German perspective, the time for war seemed propitious. France was not ready for war. Its lack of military preparedness had already erupted into a scandal. England was enmeshed in colonial difficulties, including what Churchill called "the haggard, squalid, Irish quarrel . . . [that] threatened to divide the British nation into two hostile camps."[723] Russia was as yet both ill prepared for external war and simultaneously fearful of internal revolution.[724] The Continent was a powder keg with a long train of gunpowder snaking about in a kindergarten of mean and mischievous children playing with fire. Old scores and scars were not forgotten. All that was needed was a fresh wound, a spark to enflame and explode old grudges. The spark was provided by the radical Bosnian Serb Gavrilo Princip and his assassination of Crown Prince Ferdinand and his wife, Sophie.

All of the foregoing and more would be the causes of the war, the assassination of Ferdinand would be but an excuse, and a feeble one at that.

Before discussing the assassination of Archduke Ferdinand, an additional critical point needs to be made. There were three personalities that were crucial to the outbreak of World War I: Tsar Nicholas II of Russia, Kaiser William II of Germany, and Emperor Franz Joseph of Austria-Hungary. Nicholas II was something of a wimp with liberal tendencies but an absolutist mentality, a man who might have preferred to have spent his life as a country gentleman. He, like the others, did what he could to accommodate his people and his Jews, but to no avail. By way of example, he reluctantly established Russia as a constitutional monarchy and implemented universal suffrage. Count Stolypin, the minister of the interior under Nicholas, implemented far-reaching agrarian reforms on behalf of the peasants. In 1912, Nicholas accorded cultural autonomy to Jewish groups.[725] William II was a wannabe liberal and simultaneously a stooge of the army. Franz Joseph was a strong and generally capable leader who had long been noted for wanting peace at all costs (Austria had not been at war since 1866) but who was by now old and approaching befuddlement. The leadership of the Continent was not in the best of hands. All of that as it may, all three men—even the kaiser and the tsar—were fundamentally good men who were brought low by their liberalism, their concessions, and their penchant to do wrong as they diligently struggled to do right.

Google	URL
Franz Joseph	http://en.wikipedia.org/wiki/Franz_Joseph_I_of_Austria 8/2/14
Nicholas II	http://en.wikipedia.org/wiki/Nicholas_II_of_Russia 8/2/14
Archduke Ferdinand	http://en.wikipedia.org/wiki/Archduke_Franz_Ferdinand_of_Austria 8/2/14

The heir to the Austrian throne, Archduke Franz Ferdinand, was gunned down by Serbian terrorists in Sarajevo, Bosnia, on June 28, 1914. Thus, as cited earlier, it came to be that, as Hitler said in *Mein Kampf*, "the hand of the goddess of eternal justice and inexorable retribution . . . caused Archduke Francis Ferdinand, the most mortal enemy of Austrian-Germanism, to fall by the bullets which he himself had helped to mold."[726] By that, Hitler was referring to the efforts made by Ferdinand to accommodate the Slavs of the regime. Ferdinand was a proponent of "trialism," of adding still another coequal ethnic and national element to the Austro-Hungarian Empire—Ferdinand would have added a Catholic-Slav bloc to the German-Magyar mix.

Serbia had long been troublesome for Austria-Hungary. It had defied the Dual Monarchy during the Pig War (an economic conflict of 1906–1909 in which Austria-Hungary had imposed a customs blockade on Serbia), been labeled as traitorous during the Friedjung Trial (a treason trial in 1909), and had recently debilitated the influence of southeastern Europe's other dynastic empire, the Ottoman Empire of Turkey (1912–1913). Serbian radicals sought Pan-Slavic independence from the Austro-Hungarian Empire and therein lay its fundamental dispute with the realm of Emperor Franz Joseph.

For the Serbs, who were seeking union with Bosnia and Croatia, schemes such as Ferdinand had in mind were troubling. The potential success of Ferdinand's trialism in pacifying the empire's South Slavs would destroy Serbian hopes to expand still further. And since Ferdinand, heir to the throne of the aged Franz

Joseph, was the single most powerful proponent of trialism, his death would potentially put an end to such schemes. Serbian terrorists, therefore, planned his assassination and successfully carried it through. The terrorists did not have the consent or direct support of the Serbian government for their actions, though several Serbian officials were prominent in facilitating the assassination—and Serbia duly executed three of them.

The assassination of Ferdinand and his wife was a momentous event, to be sure, but it was hardly enough to unfurl the colors. Tempers soon subsided just as they had when the wife of Franz Joseph, Empress Elizabeth, was murdered in 1898 in Switzerland by an Italian. On that occasion, of course, no thought of war ensued between Austria and Italy or Austria and Switzerland.[727] Surely the death of Ferdinand at the hands of a few extremist elements that had only tenuous connections with the Serbian government could not justify war. The *National-Zeitung* (newspaper) did not even mourn Ferdinand: its attitude was that Slavs were Slavs, and Ferdinand had made the mistake of forgetting that.[728]

Emperor Franz Joseph himself was hardly so much as aflutter over the death. Ferdinand had always represented something of a thorn in his side. Franz Joseph was glad to be rid of him. He blithely commented at the time of the assassination, that "For me, it is a great worry less."[729] Ferdinand's funeral was as close as one can come to a royal version of a pauper's burial—the Austrian government even attempted to have Ferdinand's children pay for the whole sorry affair. Clearly, Ferdinand was not a favorite at court. So while the assassination of Ferdinand and Sophie (who was also despised by Franz Joseph) was significant and was a trigger in the start of the war, it was not the root cause of it. It was simply the spark in the powder keg of old wounds, alignments, and power politics on the Continent. It was the long chain of explosive politics of slights, humiliations, and new alliances that pulled the trigger, ignited the spark, and exploded the Continent. It was an excuse for those who wanted war. And the outbreak of war was no more Germany's fault than it was the several others. But it would later be Germany that would be blamed for it all, and that blame would lay heavily on the political and social soul of the country, and most especially upon Adolf Hitler.

The assassins were immediately known, and it was immediately known, too, that the killing was not a deliberate act of the Serbian government. Belgrade dutifully dispatched the government's condolences to Vienna. Still, in many quarters, the killing represented an opportunity to settle Austro-Hungarian and Serbian political issues of the time. Germany provided Austro-Hungary carte blanche support in much the same way that England later provided such support to Poland shortly before the outbreak of World War II—support that encouraged Polish belligerence in the face of several quite reasonable proposals by Germany to settle German-Polish issues. Germany's support is seen as having been a mighty inducement for Austria-Hungary to declare war on Serbia, England's not dissimilar support as the gesture of a brave, faithfully ally. The real difference between the supports offered, though, is that Germany lost its war, England won hers.

Events slowly escalated. More than a month would lapse during which diplomacy could have been made to work, until at last Austria-Hungary declared war on Serbia. From that act the dominoes of peace were toppled, and the world fell into war. Russia mobilized in support of its Balkan client, Serbia—and therefore against Austria-Hungary. Count Ulrich von Brockdorff-Rantzau correctly pointed out to the Versailles delegates in May 1919 that "The Russian mobilization made it impossible for the statesmen to find a remedy, and threw the final decision into the hands of military power."[730] It is not widely known, but Germany made a last desperate attempt to avoid war: Germany's chancellor, Bethmann-Hollweg, informed the Russians on July 29 that "further continuation of Russian mobilization measures would compel us to mobilize."[731] Russia ignored him. When Germany became aware of Russia's final decision with respect to mobilization, Bethmann-Hollweg could no longer think of averting the war and therefore upped the ante of brinkmanship. Germany undertook mobilization of her own.

Germany had quite understandably offered its unqualified support by a rescript to Austria-Hungary. It thereafter mobilized against Russia in support of its Austro-Hungarian client, triggering France and England to then justifiably mobilize against Germany on behalf of their Russian client. The Continent was at war.

Given the vulnerability of Germany to attack on two fronts, its generals had developed the Schlieffen Plan by which it hoped it could strike a decisive blow against France in the early stages of a war while Russia was still mobilizing. With success in France it could then turn its might eastward (and the three additional German army corps mentioned above might very well have enabled that plan to succeed).

The Schlieffen Plan called for the quick attack against the French army by way of neutral Belgium and Luxembourg, followed by a vast turning movement back toward Alsace-Lorraine, pressing the French army against the Franco-German border. This, it was hoped, would place France in a position that would force it to sue for peace. The plan called for the defeat of France within six weeks.

Facing the certainty of a war on two fronts, Germany was left with no choice but to quickly execute its Schlieffen Plan as soon as Russia mobilized to take out France, and then turn its attention to Russia. Immediacy was critical. It could not delay for a moment while Russia was mobilizing its forces. The plan did not work, but its necessity and intent were certainly reasonable and rational given Germany's circumstances.

Germany was blamed for the war in the 1919 Treaty of Versailles. Historians now broadly acknowledge that proper blame must at least be shared by the system of alliances and the festering wounds from past indignities to national pride of the various belligerents and to the machinations that underlay the various alliances in Europe at the time. Fears of rival parties and their resultant alliances were called into play and quickly escalated a local tiff into full-scale continental war and then a world war—up to that point the most devastating conflict of all time.

*   *   *   *

Prior to World War I, Germany was successful beyond imagination. She was the Continent's wealthiest nation; she was producing two-thirds of Europe's steel, half its coke and lignite, and more electrical energy than Britain, France, and Italy combined. She was also the world leader in chemicals and pharmaceuticals. She had a far more productive agriculture than any of the European countries. The great German firms of Krupp and Thyssen, Siemens, AEG, Hoechst, and other BASF were famous for their innovations and quality the world over.[732] Fear of German dominance and jealousy over her success reigned in her neighbor's capitals, and especially France and Great Britain. Socially, Germany was stable. Politically, the country was governed soberly and frugally. Germans were governed by an autocracy, but it was an enlightened one that provided substantial freedom, justice, and Social Security.[733] It was on the whole a proud, happy place. Anti-Semitism was virtually nonexistent though fringe groups remained; the anti-Semitic parties, however, had largely disappeared after the turn of the century.[734] All of the foregoing was destroyed by World War I.

Hitler's War

Hitler was in Munich when war broke out. He claimed that upon learning of it he was "overcome with impetuous enthusiasm."[735] He had long since rejected any thought of serving in the army of the hated Austro-Hungarian Empire so he instead immediately volunteered to serve in the German army, or, more particularly, in the Bavarian army which was then still something of an independent entity.

Alan Bullock, in a rather curious construction of logic and blatantly apparent psychobabble, claims that Hitler found a "secure place" in the army. Here was a young man who spent more than four years fighting in the trenches filled with filth and muck, a place where literally thousands of men were being killed and horribly maimed all around him, a place of utter carnage, a place where he participated in a total of eighty-four battles,[736] a place where he twice suffered debilitating wounds: Bullock, an establishment historian of the first order refers to it as a "secure place." Incredible.

The claim is all the more incredulous because before the war Hitler was doing quite well for himself in prewar Munich: he was all but deliriously happy there. He was painting, and his paintings were selling well, and he was thoroughly enjoying the cultural milieu of the city. He was both happy and secure. And he had good and multiple reasons for his high spirits: as Maser and Joachimsthaler suggest, he was well on his way to "a viable career as a water colourist of picturesque urban scenes,"[737] paintings that he was easily able to sell at a comfortable profit. Hitler himself described his stay in Munich as "the happiest and by far the most contented of my life."[738] In fact, he was doing so well that any idea that he might have enlisted in the army for purely pecuniary reasons is every bit as preposterous as Bullock's claim of his having found a "secure place" by enlisting. Some historians suggest that he entered the army as a way to avoid the mediocrity that supposedly represented his life in Munich in 1918. Stolfi challenges such assertions head-on as he points out that such historians apparently fail to grasp that it would certainly have occurred to a man of Hitler's intellect and discernment that "remaining a live mediocrity would be better than becoming a dead frontline soldier."[739]

Hitler was a brave, conscientious young soldier. He liked the army, and he liked to fight, yet there is no record of his having killed any enemy soldiers—his awards for bravery were in connection with his having saved the lives of his commander and comrades, having captured enemy troops, and for his sterling performance in carrying messages about the battlefield. His military service was in many respects the starting point of a Grecian-like epic. It was the first important step of his monomyth, his failed hero's journey. His service was epitomized by his "self-sacrifice, dependability, loyalty, and steadfastness in adversity.... His dedication was total: no task was too onerous and he seemed to welcome danger,"[740] says author John Williams. And all of this risk was endured by Hitler, as Williams points out, though he owned "not a single German stone"[741]—there can be no doubt whatever, Hitler was a true believer and a brave one at that. Later, as chancellor, he would stand tall in his convertible car as he traveled past throngs of people in various cities—and he would do so much to the consternation of his security detail. It was not so much that he was unconcerned about dying or being assassinated, it was more in the nature of his having simply surrendered himself to the vagaries of Fate. He once commented to the effect that he could die standing or sitting, it was all the same to him.

During World War I, he crawled about the battlefield like one of the Indian scouts in the American West stories by Karl May that so consumed his youth. When the fighting was intense, as it was in 1915, "he would leap out of his bunk as soon as the English artillery barrage started at dawn. Eager for action, he would grab his rifle and stride up and down the trench, rousing all the [other] soldiers. . . ."[742] It was the war itself that was Hitler's world, "what lay beyond didn't exist for him,"[743] says Williams. And it was his experience in the war, according to his own account, that changed him from a "self-confessed 'weak-kneed cosmopolitan' into an anti-Semite and ardent Pan-German nationalist,"[744]* though it is a certainty that the seeds of those fervors were already planted in him in Vienna. William Shirer says that "He never asked for leave [but he did take at least two furloughs at the urging of his officers]. . . . He never grumbled, as did the bravest of the men, about the filth, the lice, the muck, the stench. . . ."[745]

Hitler's performance as a soldier is telling in still another respect as well. For those historians who represent him as a crazy, expectorating hysteric, we must wonder how it was that he was able to so calmly endure the hardship and horrors of World War I. While other men understandably succumbed to the newly identified medical phenomenon of "shell shock," Hitler endured. Hitler was no hysteric. Again, Stolfi has it right: far from being a

---

* The evidence has it that both his anti-Semitism and his Pan-Germanism were already seeded during his years in Vienna, as was the inkling that he might one day enter politics. His ability to sway others with speeches was made evident, according to Maser, even in grade school.

high-strung hysteric, Hitler was, instead, an example of "bedrock psychological stability."[746]

It is exemplary of Hitler's dedication to matters of art and culture that when he finally did reluctantly accept furloughs during the war, as in October 1917 and again in September 1918 while his regiment was in reserve, he used his time to visit museums. This oddity was an extension of his habits while in Linz and Vienna. In Vienna, when he was out of work, his friend Kubizek asked where he had been. "I am working on the solution of the housing problem in Vienna, and I am doing certain research for this purpose."[747] As part of that work he had gone outside the city on one occasion, and then spent several days walking back to it so that he could observe it from different perspectives and identify improvements that he thought it needed. Hitler was a different kind of man than the rest of us.

During his first furlough in three years, he visited Dresden, Brussels, Cologne, and Leipzig.[748] He was particularly interested in visiting sites made famous by Luther, Bach, and Wagner. Just as he had in Vienna he visited and took particular interest in architectural sites. It must be said again: Hitler was a different kind of man and certainly a different kind of combat infantryman. Your author spent twenty-one years in the infantry, he knows what infantrymen commonly do after long stretches in the field—visits to architectural sites are not among the items on their bucket list.

Army service was his chance to be the figurative modern-day version of the dragon slayer, Siegfried. Ultimately, however, he would conclude that he and his comrades, like Siegfried, had been stabbed in the back; it was a conclusion that would angrily invigorate him and sharpen his political prejudices[749]—and it would harden his odium toward Jews, that subset of people who he thought of as Germany's Hagen. Jews and their supporting politicians on the home front were assigned culpability for the stab in the back by both Hitler and other elements of the radical right wing. Participants in the successful German revolution at the end of the war earned them the moniker November Criminals from Hitler and other fanatical right-wing elements. The term was also applied to those who signed the armistice and those who were simply insufficiently patriotic or militaristic.

*   *   *   *

Jews were prominent leaders of the German revolution. In particular, Jewish members of the SPD, USPD, and the Spartacus League were its instigators and champions. "[T]he Marxists," said Hitler, "with a band of bums, deserters, party bosses, and Jewish journalists, abruptly seized power, thus giving democracy a resounding slap in the face."[750] While his language was impolitic, it was wholly sincere and essentially correct. A wide range of Jews and Jewish-led organizations and publications contributed mightily to the defeatism to which Germany ultimately succumbed. Contributors to defeatism included such people as the firebrands Karl Liebknecht and Rosa Luxemburg; the writers Kurt Eisner and Richard Grelling, who was the author of the book *I Accuse*, the same title as used by Emil Zola in his published letter in defense of accused spy Alfred Dreyfus; the politicians Richard Witting, Eduard Bernstein, Dr. Oscar Cohn, Hugo Haase, and Kurt Rosenfeld; newspaper editors Georg Bernhard, Friederich Stampfer, Erich Kuttner, and Rudolf Hilferding, among many others. Organizations and publications related to the aforementioned people abounded and produced a cumulative defeatist impact on the psyche of both the German populace and its military.

Hitler's war began in October 1914 at the First Battle of Ypres (and in 1918 it would end there in the Fourth Battle of Ypres), one of the most savage battles in a most savage war. Of the 3,000 men in his regiment, 2,500 were killed, wounded, or missing at the conclusion of this one battle. Membership in a regiment like Hitler's was a virtual guarantee that one would be either killed or maimed. A total of 3,754 of the regiment's men were killed throughout the course of the war.[751] The number of men killed in his regiment, the List Regiment, that "secure place, was almost as many as all of those killed from the entire kingdom of Bavaria during the Franco-Prussian war of 1870.[752] Hitler saw and experienced a great deal of vicious infantry combat, and he utterly despised those who avoided the front along with those who seemingly worked toward Germany's defeat.

He was initially assigned as an ordinary "storm trooper"—a frontline infantry soldier—and it was in that capacity that he served in the First Battle of Ypres. Shortly thereafter, he was appointed to the exceedingly dangerous but highly prestigious position of courier, a position he would retain for the remainder of the war.

As a courier, Hitler was responsible for carrying messages to and from commanders on the battlefield. Couriers were selected for their bravery, intelligence, and initiative—traits that Hitler possessed in abundance. It was critical that these soldiers demonstrate not only courage, but tenacity and initiative to overcome whatever obstacles lay in their path in order to get their messages through. Of the eight couriers assigned within Hitler's regiment, three were killed in a single day.[753] Of the dispatch runners who served with him in 1914–1915, only one, Schmidt, was still actively serving at the close of the war.[754] One was certainly not induced by prospects of longevity to accept such a position. It is something of a measure of the risk faced by these soldiers that the regimental commander once sent out a total of six men with the same message in the hope that at least one would get through.[755]

Hitler loved it. He was a brave man. Hate him as we may, Hitler was a man who was unafraid, a fact attested to by both his awards for bravery and the testimony of his fellow soldiers.[756] He was described as a "born soldier." He never faltered.[757] He was fearless.[758] And his courageous quality would be demonstrated throughout the remainder of his life: it would show itself in the beer hall brawls, in the Beer Hall Putsch, in the court battle after the putsch, and in his fearlessness in face of all opposition as he rose to power, and then in the exercise of that power. And, finally, it would be demonstrated in the Berlin bunker at the end of the war when he chose to stay in the capital and take his own life rather flee or be captured or killed by his enemies.

That Hitler was indeed a brave and resourceful soldier is also supported by the fact that he received the Iron Cross, First and Second Class. His wartime exploits included the single-handed capture of fifteen enemy soldiers. On another occasion he saved his commander from death.[759] The Iron Cross First Class was rarely given even to officers, and it was virtually unheard of for an enlisted recipient.* He also received the Military Service Cross, a regimental commendation for outstanding bravery, the military service medal, as well as medals connected with his war wounds. Upon his death there would be some claims that he had taken cyanide—the implication being that he did not have the courage to shoot himself, the customary way for a German officer to die when faced with capture. Alternatively, it is sometimes claimed that he both took cyanide, and then immediately shot himself. As mentioned in an earlier chapter, it was also claimed that he had but one testicle—that he "didn't have the balls," as it were, to take his own life. History of the victors notwithstanding, there is just no doubt about it; Hitler was an exceptionally courageous soldier. Whatever his faults, a lack of physical and political courage were not among them.

Historians seemingly delight in claiming that "In contrast to others, he had no family; he scarcely received or wrote letters, and he did not share in their commonplace worries."[760] Alan Bullock goes so far as to say that "He received no letters, no parcels from home."[761] Maser, on the other hand, provides the full text of an extensive letter to his Munich landlords thanking them for the parcels they had sent to him. Such claims as those made by Bullock make for interesting commentary in painting him as a

---

* Some historians, Michael Fitzgerald among them, claim that the award was presented to him by the Jewish battalion adjutant, Lieutenant Hugo Gutmann. It is a preposterous claim. No commander would delegate the award of such a prestigious citation to a mere battalion adjutant. At the very least, the award would have been made by no lesser a commander than the regiment, and more likely a higher one still. Similarly, some historians claim that it was Gutmann who recommended him for the award, which is again preposterous. An adjutant is an administrator, a paper pusher—he would have taken the recommendation from witnesses or Hitler's superior officer (probably someone in the Operations Section), polished it, and forwarded it, no more.

brooding and eccentric loner, but they are simply not true. Hitler had his siblings and wrote to them from time to time. He also wrote to his friends and landlords Joseph and Anna Popp, as well as to a Munich associate, the lawyer Ernst Hepp. Other friends included Graf von Schwerin and a man named Baumann. On page 70 of Fest's *Hitler*, Fest mentions a twelve-page letter of his to a Munich acquaintance[762] (Herr Hepp, presumably).

While in Munich he roomed with a friend who had accompanied him there in 1913, Rudolf Häusler.[763] During the war he was especially close to Hans Mend[*] and Balthaser Brandmayer, the latter being one of the very few men close enough in friendship to address Hitler by the familiar *du*. Closer to Hitler even than Brandmayer, though, was his friend and fighting comrade, Ernst Schmidt.[764] It is clear that Hitler was not the brooding loner depicted in Hollywood productions and by some establishment historians. Moreover, his wartime friends trusted him implicitly: they knew him to be a man "who never exaggerated and who expressed himself carefully" even when under great peril.[765] They knew him, too, to be a young man of both solid logic and playful witticism.[766] While he was indeed in some respects something of an introvert during the war he did not stand out as such. To the extent that he was aloof from the relatively crass people he met both in the Vienna hostel and during the war it was not due to any aberration on his part; he was simply on a different moral, ethical, and intellectual plane than such people. He did interact with his wartime buddies and nearly all of them held him in high esteem, thinking him both smart and interesting.

Historical mythology, replicated by such people as Dawidowicz,[767] has it that Hitler was never promoted beyond the lowly position of lance corporal because of his odd ways and his commanders' lack of confidence in his leadership abilities. In

---

[*] Some authors have it that Mend is a reliable source, others that he is not. Mend's book, *Mit Adolf Hitler im Felde*, praised Hitler, so for the anti-Hitlerites it is important to diminish Mend; he is therefore represented by them as a petty criminal. For others, Mend was a "healthy son of the soil," honest and diligent, a war hero in his own right who later saw the light and became an anti-Nazi.

actual fact, his leaders had considerable confidence in him, a fact illustrated by Lieutenant Fritz Wiedemann when he engaged in string-pulling to prevent Hitler's transfer to a crack Bavarian regiment as Hitler recovered from his first set of wounds.[768] Hitler was a great soldier and Wiedemann wanted him back.

Some historians are fond of quoting such people as Hans Mend, who served with him. Mend had it that Hitler's oddities and outbursts against Jews and Marxists isolated him from his fellow soldiers; most, however, now have it otherwise. While Hitler did indeed erupt in outbursts from time to time, most of his fellow soldiers considered him an intellectual of great insight and fundamentally agreed with what he had to say—even Mend acknowledged that much. Ignaz Westenkirchner, a fellow dispatch runner and close friend, observed that Hitler was "a serious young man concerned with serious matters."[769] He would give lectures on art and history and the detriments of smoking and drinking and on the need for fidelity to duty. "'There is almost no subject,' said Westenkirchner, 'about which he did not talk. He mastered each theme and spoke fluently. We simple fellows were very much impressed, and liked it.'"[770] Another of Hitler's friends from the trenches said that "Most of his fellow soldiers considered him a 'levelheaded' companion and his 'comradely' manner earned him the nickname his mother had given him, 'Adi.'"[771] On the whole, the young Adolf Hitler was seen by his retinue of friends in the trenches as something of a luminary, not a quack. Hitler read Arthur Schopenhauer's *The World of Will and Idea* several times over during lulls in the fighting and was greatly influenced by it.[772] The world would later see evidence of Schopenhauer's influence as he further developed his concept of *will*, his idea that will alone rules and that all else is illusion. Serving as his own unofficial executive producer, Leni Reifenstahl's famous 1935 Nazi propaganda film was named *Triumph of the Will* by Hitler and the subject of *will* was an often-used theme of both his writing and speeches.

When not fighting or reading or engaged with his soldier friends Hitler would take out his watercolors and paint landscapes.[773]

While Hitler was certainly different than the average infantryman, there was nothing in his conduct, countenance, or habits that would cause his commanders to lack faith in his ability to lead other soldiers. The preponderance of evidence suggests that he was highly admired by both his commanders and ordinary soldiers. Claims by some historians, such as Fest, that he had a "complex incapacity for human relationships"[774] are simply in error—he had many entirely normal interpersonal relationships and his admiration for his friends was entirely reciprocated by them. The far more likely reason for Hitler's lack of promotion during the war was his own unwillingness to apply for one because it would have removed him from his esteemed job as a courier. Military organizations have "slots," positions held by people of particular ranks, and if one is promoted beyond what is called for by the slot, one is also typically transferred to another slot befitting the new rank. Hitler did not want to be removed from his slot as a courier. Bullock, for example, points out that "There is no evidence that Hitler ever applied or was eager for promotion to the rank of noncommissioned officer, leave alone a commission. He seems to have been content with the job he had."[775] Kershaw relates that late in the war Hitler was actually nominated for promotion by Max Amann, the man who would later become Hitler's press baron. Amann, as well as Wiedemann, who later became one of Hitler's adjutants, made it clear that Hitler actually refused the promotion because it would have meant a transfer from his job as a courier on the regimental staff.[776] Kershaw also makes it emphatically clear that Hitler's officers thought well of him: "His superiors held him in high regard," says Kershaw.[777]

Hitler lived a charmed life as a soldier and as a politician as well. In letters to acquaintances (of which there were many, notwithstanding the claims of some historians) during the war and in conversations after it, he recounted incidences in which he narrowly escaped death. An intuition caused him to move from here to there as an artillery shell killed or maimed everyone where he was previously sitting. A trench area became too crowded so he and another soldier went elsewhere—an explosion ripped into the area they had just vacated.[778] There is even a story claiming that a

British private, Henry Tandy, had gotten Hitler in his rifle sights in October 1914 but failed to fire on him because he saw that he was wounded and did not so much as raise his rifle. The story is suspect in several respects but was apparently genuinely believed and supported even by Hitler himself.

His seemingly miraculous survival against impossible odds provided him with a certain mystique in the eyes of his fellow soldiers.[779] Recognizing his great luck in escaping death, other soldiers would tell him that there was no bullet with his name on it. Events like these, coupled with his readings about various mythical Germanic heroes and *will*, and Fate, could not help but germinate in him a belief that divine Providence watched over him; that his indomitable *will* and the favors of Fate and Providence would ultimately prevail in times of great adversity; that he was walking with Destiny at his side. Later in his life, as he suffered substantial defeats such as the Beer Hall Putsch and the several severe setbacks of 1932, he was able to recall that in his experience seeming defeats and collapses were really only preludes to ultimate victory.[780] Hitler was again and again saved when he himself had all but completely surrendered to the vagaries of circumstance.[781] During his reign as chancellor, some forty attempts were made on his life: it would ultimately require his own hand to finally take that life.

The vast number of assassination attempts against Hitler is revealing in another way too: if Nazi Germany had been so very oppressive and overseeing of its citizenry (if the example of Hollywood depictions were true with the Gestapo and SS everywhere, and everyone denouncing their friends), it seems highly improbable that such attempts would not have been discovered. The assassination plot of Colonel Claus von Stauffenberg involved thousands of conspirators, yet the plot was not discovered beforehand. Nazi Germany was not nearly as oppressive as Hollywood depictions of it make it out to be. Indeed, it was on the whole rather egalitarian for the racially pure German, but a hellhole for anyone in serious opposition to its objectives.

In keeping with his admiration for Hegel, Hitler developed a theory of heroes, of great men who were the guidons for epic events, "great agents . . . fated by a mysterious Providence to carry out 'the will of the world spirit.'"⁷⁸² He was himself being preserved, he thought, for an epic quest.

Ultimately, Hitler would suffer two serious wounds, and perhaps a slighter one at the beginning of the war. The first serious wound was to his leg (or hip by some accounts) caused by artillery fire on October 7, 1916. He pleaded with his lieutenant to let him remain at the front. "It isn't so bad, Lieutenant, right? I can still stay with you, I mean, stay with the regiment! Can't I?"⁷⁸³ Joachim Fest, never willing to surrender an opportunity to diminish Hitler, says that "Hitler was lightly wounded"⁷⁸⁴ on this occasion. The wound required months of hospitalization followed by a brief period of light duty (October 1916 to March 1917),* which certainly suggests that the wound was hardly a "light" one. Moreover, it was not the case that Hitler might have simply exploited his wound in order to delay his return to the front—in actual fact, he was never quite ordered to return; it was rather that he begged to be permitted to do so.⁷⁸⁵

Hitler's second wound was from his exposure to mustard gas† on the night of October 13–14, 1918, which caused temporary blindness and excruciating pain. Fest, again wishing to diminish the seriousness of the experience, speculates, as others have, that the temporary blindness suffered by Hitler on this occasion stemmed from "a hysterical symptom."⁷⁸⁶ In actual fact, temporary blindness—and sometimes even permanent blindness—was typical in soldiers exposed to mustard gas.⁷⁸⁷ It is simply contemptible that a historian of Fest's merit, and other supposed historians of his leaning, would imply that the symptoms exhibited by Hitler's exposure to the gas were anything other than entirely physical and

---

* Some few historians speculate that Hitler also lost one of his testicles by way of this wound. While such speculation is superior to the claim that it was bitten off by a goat, it lacks authenticity. A man that has just lost a testicle does not claim his wound is superficial, not even Hitler, we must think.

† The Swiss-born Jewish chemist Fritz Hober, who is sometimes described as the "father of chemical warfare," developed chlorine and other poisonous gases during World War I. Mustard gas, however, was developed by others and was first used in World War I by the German army.

entirely in keeping with the common effect of that noxious substance. John William says, rightly, that "His fear in 1918, that the effects might be permanent was common enough among soldiers blinded by gas."[788] Readers may Google the following to see and decide what was most likely: was it "a hysterical symptom" that Hitler experienced or a real fear of permanent blindness?

Google	URL
Images mustard gas World War I	https://www.google.com/search?q=images+mustard+gas+WWI&rlz=1T4GZAB_enUS449US538&tbm=isch&tbo=u&source=univ&sa=X&ei=E17dU-b-F8SKyASqjIDQCA&ved=0CB4QsAQ&biw=1008&bih=506 8/2/14

While convalescing after his first wound, Hitler was able to visit Berlin and Munich before returning to the front. In both cities he observed slackers; apparently healthy military-aged males who were not serving. "Everywhere he found 'scoundrels' cursing the war and wishing for its quick end. Slackers abounded and all were Jews, said Hitler. 'The offices,' he found, 'were filled with Jews. Nearly every clerk was a Jew and nearly every Jew was a clerk.'"[789] In *Mein Kampf*, he commented that he "was amazed at the plethora of warriors of the chosen people [on the streets of Munich] and could not help but compare them with their rare representatives at the front."[790] Such rantings on the basis of anecdotal observations can, of course, be easily discounted or discarded as illusionary; but if so, they were illusions that were identical to those of a significant mass of other observers as well.

When Hitler returned to his unit after recovering from his leg wound both his officers and fellow soldiers sponsored a celebration for him. The company cook provided a special meal of *Kartoffelpuffer*, bread and jam and cake in his honor.[791] Hitler was overjoyed by the paroxysms of ecstasy displayed by the little dog that he had rescued from no-man's-land in January 1915. He named the little terrier Fuchsl (Fox) and thereafter adored the little tyke, making him his constant companion.[792] His soldier friends welcomed him back with joy. Here was still another example of the esteem in which he was held—he was no brooding loner avoided by others; he was, instead, a substantial being who was highly respected and befriended by both his officers and fellow enlisted soldiers alike.

Hitler's observation of Jews as clerks was accompanied by other observations of Jews as anti-German revolutionaries. The stance of the pacifists and other antiwar elements was really one of opposition to German victory. They were as much anti-German as antiwar. For Hitler, "This idea of an anti-war conspiracy involving Jews would become an obsession to add to other anti-Semitic notions he acquired in Vienna, leading to an ever-growing hatred of Jews."[793]

Hitler's idea of an antiwar conspiracy involving Jews was not without merit. As we will discuss later, among the issues and activities that would lend credence to Hitler's ideas were actions of the SPD, the USPD, and the antiwar propaganda of the radical Bolshevistic Marxists comprising the Spartacist League. Nor was it imaginary to view all of these groups as Jewish-led; it was mere reality. Added to the foregoing groups was a formidable contingent of Jewish "pacifists,"* including most prominently Albert Einstein. Jews were so prominent in various pacifist movements that Hitler thought of pacifism as an "exclusively Jewish invention."[794] There was also a growing perception, as observed by Hitler and countless others, that in addition to the antiwar, anti-German groups being Jewish-led, German-Jews were not participating in the military effort of the war in proportion to their numbers in the population.

By 1916, Jews of Germany were being accused of war profiteering, political disloyalty, and avoiding military service, or at least service on the front lines. Moreover, as Lindemann points

---

* German "pacifists," and German-Jewish pacifists in particular, exhibited a determination that their pacifism be applied to Germans only. Others could justify their violence, their wars, without too much objection, but the pacifists of the day demanded that Germany abandon its war aims. It was rather like the ultimate pacifist, Albert Einstein, who objected to war as a matter of great principle: his only willingness for exception being wars in defense of Israel once it had been established.

out, the issue of Jews avoiding military service was not confined to Germany:

> In Great Britain, Jewish immigrants from Russia were similarly accused. By 1916 the Jewish Chronicle of England recognized Jewish reluctance to serve as a "major problem." Jewish immigrants preferred to "entertain their girl friends and play billiards." In the following years serious rioting and looting of Jewish stores occurred in Leeds and London's East End. A police official, in explaining the disturbances, pointed to the large number of alien Russian Jews of military age . . . who can be constantly seen promenading about our principal streets and the various pleasure resorts.[795]

During his wartime convalescence and furloughs, Hitler would observe equivalent promenades in Berlin and Munich, and many of the participants would also be Jewish immigrants from Eastern Europe.

The Jew Count

In 1916, in response to public concern, the German War Ministry commissioned a study into the military status of Jews. A number of Reichstag deputies also demanded a survey of employees in the military supply corporations broken down by sex, age, pay, and religion.[796] The prospective result of such a study was disturbing to Jewish-German leaders. Max Warburg, the great Jewish-German industrialist who was one of the founders of the hugely important IG Farben Corporation, met with War Minister Wild von Hohenborn in March 1917. Warburg asked that a statement be issued for public consumption that Jews were doing their full part in the war effort—what Warburg got instead was a lecture about Heinrich Heine,[797] the eminent nineteenth-century Jewish convert to Christianity, who so thoroughly satirized both Christianity and Germany in his writings.

The survey was quickly termed the "Jew Count." The war ministry insisted that the inquiry was conducted in response to widespread complaints and rumors about Jews avoiding military service. It implied that the survey would serve to discredit such anti-Semitic charges.[798] Historians offer several motivations for the survey: it was an attack by anti-Semites; or, perhaps, as stated by historian Donald Niewyk, it was "a means of defusing charges that Jews were successfully dodging the draft and avoiding service at the front"[799] (a refutation of the age-old claim that Jews employ neither the weapon nor the oar), or it was a means by which the War Ministry could defuse allegations that it was itself participating in providing Jews with special treatment that allowed them to either avoid military service altogether or to serve in relatively safe rear echelon jobs.[800]

The results of the count were also ambiguous: some historians have it that the results were never formally published because they showed that Jews served in numbers that even exceeded their percentage of the population. As typically claimed in books that touch on the subject, "the army refused to release the exonerating data."[801] Such historians allege that the data was suppressed due to anti-Semitism—it could not be made public that Jews were confirmed to be serving in such great numbers. To believe that is to believe that Jews of Wilhelmian Germany were essentially powerless, that they could not have forced publication of such a positive finding. But that was not so. Jews were exceedingly powerful, and if they had wanted the statistics published we can be comfortably certain that they would have been. Other historians have it that the war ministry refused to publish the results in order to spare Jewish feelings, and they withheld the survey results due to objections from Jewish leaders, and this was because the census results made it devastatingly apparent that Jews were indeed slackers.

Whatever the actual motivation and results of the census, it ultimately served to focus "hostility," according to Niewyk, "on the Jews as symbols of unpatriotic elements that allegedly stood in the way of total mobilization and victory."[802] The census also produced what Amos Elon terms "an avalanche of Jewish apologists."[803] Representative of those "apologists" was a study conducted by the *Weltbühne* magazine that was supposedly "more thorough and scholarly" than the one conducted by the war ministry.

The idea that Jews were not serving at the front in numbers approximating their proportion in the population was reinforced in the popular mind by the Zionists, among whom, as Niewyk observes, "normal patriotic feelings could be conspicuously lacking"[804] and who "demanded rights from a country [Germany] to which they gave neither sustenance nor ultimate allegiance."[805] Steven Aschheim, in his book *Brothers and Strangers*, points out that a Zionist editorial at the outset of the war proclaimed that the opportunity was now at hand for reversing Germany Jewry's assimilationism. "By October 1914," says Steven Aschheim, "the *Jüdische Rundschau* (Jewish Observer) pronounced that the change was already taking place: 'The barriers that for centuries have divided East and West [Jewry] have already fallen,'" and argued as well that "children of German Jews had to be isolated until they felt 'totally Jewish.'"[806] And those who were "totally Jewish" were simultaneously "non-German."

One apologist, Jewish Reichstag Deputy Ludwig Haas, acknowledged in the Reichstag that Jews were not doing their fair share in the army but then disingenuously claimed that it was all due to non-Jews who had oppressed them for centuries. "We cripple them and complain that they limp," claimed Haas.[807]

Jews have historically fought against serving in the military of any nation and have frequently been granted exemptions from such service by their host governments. Indeed, Jewish opposition to military service remains a significant problem even in Israel.[808] A recent (November 22, 2010) article in the Israeli publication *Haaretz*, which was widely reported in other Israeli publications as well, highlights the problem: the Israeli army has taken to using Facebook to catch Israelis who have evaded the draft by claiming to be observant Jews and to thereby claim draft exemption. "The army hired investigators two years ago to help stem the increase of draft dodgers and have used Facebook to find evidence of those lying to avoid conscription."[809] In still another article, the paper discussed the fact that upward of 50 percent of all military-aged men, those between eighteen and forty years of age, do not actually serve. The Israelis anticipate that the percentage, if current trends continue, will reach 60 percent in another decade. The ultraorthodox Haredim are especially adept at such evasion, inventing religious rationalizations for their unwillingness to serve. The "secular Haredim," says the article, "who include actors, film directors and academics . . . invent 1,001 ideologies to absolve themselves of any responsibility to the collective."[810] It is the case, then, that substantial numbers of Jews will not serve in the military of Israel—yet we are expected to believe that their even more radically ultraorthodox forefathers served in Germany's ranks in numbers that exceeded their percentage of the overall population. It is a highly unlikely prospect.

In the U.S., where Jews represent 2.2 percent of the population, they comprise but 0.003 percent of our military forces.[811] Part of this phenomenon stems from Jewish riches: in Germany and elsewhere (e.g., U.S. during the Vietnam War), the privileged sons of the upper class, a class in which Jews were disproportionately represented, were routinely exempted from service as they completed their educational studies or otherwise prepared for professional careers. They became "professional students." Moreover, as John Williams points out:

> Political ideology rather than military common sense . . . ensured that the typical German conscript in August 1914 was either the son of a landholding peasant or a tenant farmer, since in peacetime *only 6 per cent* of those conscripted came from the cities, where almost 40 per cent of the population lived.[812]

And the cities were the places where virtually all Jews lived as well.

There is nothing particularly untoward in the foregoing statistics: Jewish education, wealth, and inclinations enabled them to avoid service in the same way that the sons of similarly endowed Gentiles did. Those same qualities also frequently enabled such people to serve in rear echelon positions rather than on the front. It was the case, however, that if you were a German of the World War I era, you did not much care to make such allowances. There was a widely held perception in the army that, as stated by the acknowledged Hitlerite Balthasar Brandmayer, "The greatest percentages of base-warriors were indisputably the Sons of Israel."[813] Back then, when you listened to the likes of Brandmayer or viewed the news that your father or son had been killed or maimed and simultaneously saw young military-aged Jewish boys partying, as was common, you had to be outraged.

The ancient Romans exempted Jews from military service, as did Russia, Austria-Hungary, France, and other countries. By the time of the 1905 Russian Revolution, Jews were obligated to serve but avoided service in droves. Often, by way of compromise, Jews were legally permitted to buy their way out of serving in the army, including the U.S. Army during the Civil War. When the legal purchase of exemptions were unavailable, upward of 90 percent still managed to avoid conscription by various devices, not the least of which were generous bribes offered to and accepted by government officials. "'Going underground,' flight, and even self-maiming were the order of the day among poorer Jews who had no chance of buying themselves out,"[814] says historian Heiko Haumann. In Galicia, again according to Haumann, where, unlike Russia, Jews suffered no debilitation, they nevertheless either bought their way out of military service or fled abroad to avoid service.[815]

Jews have consistently been simultaneously the reluctant warriors and the radical insurrectionists throughout the Diaspora. Treitschke had it that Jews have a "profoundly implanted dread of arms."[816] It was an article of faith to Hitler and his friends that Jews who did serve intrigued with others "so that a decoration or promotion was practically a formality in advance," and that they had a "qualification-pass for officer in their pocket."[817] As elsewhere, Jews, to the extent that they did join the ranks, were the reluctant warriors of Germany. In 1835, under Russia's Nicholas I, they were required to serve in the military, but many of them, instead, engaged in passive resistance, hid, bribed officials, or otherwise acted to avoid their military service obligation. Others, when they were made to serve, avoided combat by obtaining employment behind the lines. Sometimes they took extreme actions to avoid military service. Haumann says that "those who had no money, maimed themselves . . . Their clever reasoning calculated that it is better to live lame than to die healthy."[818]

Before Zionism became popular, both Jews and Germans agreed on the idea that Jews on the whole could never become either soldiers or farmers. Even Moses Mendelssohn, the symbol of secular enlightenment and the father of modern Reform Judaism, a man who sought the integration of Jews and Germans, despaired that it would ever occur.[819]

Orthodox Jewry, which had grown markedly in Germany after the assassination of Russia's Alexander II in 1881, opposed military service of any kind. For the Orthodox, Deuteronomy could be called upon to avoid service, for it exempts, among others, anyone who is simply afraid of fighting.[820]

Eastern Jews had long enjoyed exemptions to military service in Eastern Europe and were decidedly unlikely to flock to recruiting offices in Germany, nor were any of the other Jewish groups, save the staunchest assimilationists.

French opponents of emancipation argued that:

> Jews could not serve in the army because they would not eat the food that other soldiers ate. They would not drink wine produced by gentiles [because the very touch of a Christian makes things unclean].[821] They would not wear the same clothes as other soldiers. They would not work or fight on the Sabbath. They could not be depended upon to defend the French nation because they were members of another nation, one that existed in other countries, potential enemies of France.[822]

With respect to working and fighting on the Sabbath, Jews of the ancient world under the leadership of Mattathias chose to stay true to the commandment banning warfare on the Sabbath and paid the ultimate sacrifice for their decision. In the aftermath of that decision changes were made by the son of Mattathias, Judah, to permit defensive actions on the Sabbath, but not offensive ones. Judah would go on to earn the name Maccabee—the hammer—by his exploits.[823] Orthodox Jews of the modern world remained steeped in the idea that neither work nor combat could be conducted on the Sabbath—and most certainly not on behalf of any Gentile state.

Traditionally, it was the case in Europe that if the Jews of Europe were heavily taxed and sometimes pillaged, they were also commonly exempted from the most grievous of all taxes, service in war. In 1808, Napoleon Bonaparte found it necessary to issue decrees, called the "Infamous Decrees," that prohibited Jews from thenceforth using paid substitutes for their military service. "The ability of Jews to buy their way out of military service was a contributing factor," says Lindemann, "to claims that Jews were especially reluctant soldiers and that they avoided military service."[824] In Russia, Nicholas I instituted a draft making Jews liable for military service. It was perceived by Jews of the country as a persecution, a Goldhagen-pogrom as it were.[825]

Moreover, it was not just the Russians and Germans who observed low Jewish participation in the military. By the end of World War I, says Lindemann, a large part of the entire European population "accepted the image of Jews as using their wiles, high-level contacts, or financial leverage to avoid frontline service and profit from the war."[826]

The issue of Jewish disloyalty in Germany was exacerbated by the German Zionists who held the view that Jews owed no loyalty whatever to the German state. It was further exacerbated in the ranks of the many Marxists of the day. Marx had consistently argued that the entire proletariat owed no allegiance whatever to its nationality.[827]

Even before the outbreak of war some prominent Jews were informing their flock that they owed no allegiance to Germany. Chaim Weizmann touched on the subject of Jewish loyalty/disloyalty at a convocation of Jews in Berlin in June 1914. Speaking of negotiations in which he participated in Berlin, he made the point to those assembled that "We were neither German nor French . . . but Hebrew, and those that would support our Hebrew culture would obtain our support in return."[828] That is to say, loyalty to other Jews took precedence over loyalty to host nations.

It was not lost on Hitler that the disloyalty stereotype of Jews stems from long-term observations of palpable Jewish acts against host nations. Jewish disloyalty to the German state was a major theme of anti-Semitic Germans during the 1920s as well and served as a basis for the "stab in the back" claims regarding the outcome of World War I. A subset of prominent German Jews of the era provided abundant evidence for such "mythical" claims to exist. The highly influential Jewish-leftist *Weltbühne* magazine not only admitted to the stab in the back as a fact, it championed it, calling it "the heroic, saving act of a stab in the back."[829] In late November 1918, *Die Rote Fahne* (The Red Flag), which was edited by Jews, championed its opposition to German war ambitions by saying that "From the first day of this war we endeavored to do our international duty [as Marxists] by fighting that criminal government with all our power, and by branding it as the one really guilty of the war."[830]

German Jews during World War I can be viewed from the central tendencies of their organizational objectives and belief systems. Fundamentally, they consisted of Orthodox Jewry, secular assimilationists, Zionists, Socialists, and Communists.

The assimilationists sought total integration with German society and cocommitment to the German state. Zionists espoused a Jewish nationalism that specifically rejected assimilation and therefore had little use for the idea of loyalty or military obligation to Germany. The Jewish Socialists (the Bund), as well as sizeable numbers of Zionists, sought Yiddish-based Jewish cultural autonomy from their countrymen and felt no sense of loyalty to Gentile "outsiders." The Jewish Communists sought the violent overthrow of the German military and government. With the exception of some assimilationists, observes one online source, German "Jews were . . . less enthusiastic about creating a highly cohesive, unitary German society than were Gentile Germans, and this general tendency among Jews would, in the minds of Gentiles, be exacerbated by such salient examples as Jewish-owned publishing companies that were opposed to German nationalism."[831]

In summary, many Jews of the period sought the advantages of citizenship but did not care to share with fellow citizens in the most fundamental responsibilities of that citizenship. Jewish-German theologian Hans-Joachim Schoeps has emphasized the foregoing Jewish behavior as a source of Gentile antipathy toward Jews. Schoeps contended that Hebrew religious tradition and its resulting narcissistic self-image was a source of anti-Semitism—it arose, according to Schoeps, from a Jewish educational system that taught Jews to view themselves as separate, distinct, and superior to their host populace.[832]

Leaks of some of the "Jew census" data was made available to Pan-Germanist Alfred Roth after the war. In 1919, he published a book, *The Jew in the Army*, wherein he claimed that Jews were involved in the war effort only as profiteers and that they had not borne their fair share of military service and frontline combat. He also alleged that Jews had exercised their considerable influence within the war ministry to get phony medical discharges or behind-the-lines assignments. "His allegations," according to Donald Niewyk, "formed the basis of repeated charges that Jews had shown their true colors by shirking their patriotic duty in the war."[833] Low Jewish casualty rates were cited as one basis for the findings.

Conversely, many historians, such as Peter Pulzer, have it that "More thorough and scholarly studies by Franz Oppenheimer and the sociologist Jakob Segall, based on the number of Jews killed or wounded, promoted or decorated between 1914 and 1918, suggest that the Jewish contribution was, if anything, disproportionately high."[834] It is that "more thorough and scholarly" study by two Jews connected with the radically leftist Jewish-dominated *Weltbühne* publication that serves as the basis for the historical record that military participation by Jewish Germans was "disproportionately high" during World War I. The *Weltbühne* was composed almost entirely of Jews who tacitly recognized that Judaism and German patriotism were mutually exclusive propositions.[835]

The "more thorough and scholarly" findings of Oppenheimer and Segall were founded on interviews with various synagogue members who provided names of Jews who served and those who were wounded or killed. This technique, a technique that might be properly termed the Dawidowicz methodology, we are expected to believe, was a "more thorough and scholarly" approach to the issue than was an examination of the people and military records that were used by the authors of the original study. Skeptics must think that Oppenheimer and Segall employed generous amounts of statistical creativeness to arrive at their conclusions. The nature of the Jewish population of Germany at the time, as we have seen, was composed of large numbers of Orthodox Jews from Eastern Europe as well as Zionists and Socialists/Communists, and pacifists—none of whom had any interest whatever in serving in the German military. Moreover, many of the Ostjuden refugees served as wartime laborers in Germany,[836] not direct combatants. And the fact that the hated tsarist regime in Russia was among Germany's opponents in the war was hardly enough to overcome the radical religious beliefs of such orthodox Jews as the Haredim.* Utopian Socialist Charles Fourier was deeply offended by Jews' unwillingness to even dine with non-Jews;[837] it is something of a stretch to believe that such people would have rushed to the trenches of the German army.

Lindemann points out that "Since Jews on the average were notably richer and better educated than the rest of the population, they undoubtedly had greater resources, both material and intellectual, if they wanted to avoid frontline service."[838] Added to the foregoing is the fact that the powerful Jewish organization known as the Centralverein (CV) took up a campaign in 1914 emphasizing Jewish particularism—"its leaders hovered uneasily between the earlier orthodoxy of 'we are Germans like everyone else' and a frank recognition that there could and should not be

---

* In Israel, utraorthodox Haredi Jews demand exemptions from military service, and those who do serve demand a number of special privileges such as serving in multiple short blocks of time so they are less susceptible to contamination by secular Jews. They also have stringent dietary requirements.

only one kind of German"[839]—that Jews should be able to remain separate and distinct from other Germans while still realizing all of the benefits of citizenship. Under nineteenth-century nationalism, it was increasingly clear that many Jews wished to be only economic citizens of the country without having to be burdened with the idea of absolute and singular loyalty to the state and German nation, as had been the case under eighteenth-century absolutism.[840] The CV contributed to the foregoing as it redefined its terms for Jewish assimilation. As Pulzer points out, "It took up a campaign against apostasy, to the extent of branding converts as deserters. It encouraged the study of Jewish religion and history, especially among Jewish children. In other words, by 1914, it was emphasizing the value of precisely those attributes that had in 1870 been regarded as obstacles to German Jews becoming Jewish Germans."[841]

German Zionists, who were headquartered in Germany at the time, had been radicalized prior to World War I and felt no loyalty whatever to Germany and German interests. At their 1912 Posen convention, the German Zionist Federation called for every Zionist to plan for immigration to Palestine. Two years later, the war broke out. It declared its conviction that Jews had no roots whatever in Germany.[842] It is true that only a tiny minority of Zionists actually immigrated to Palestine prior to the rise of Hitler, which seemingly supports the idea that the Zionist call had little influence, but it remains that the position of the Zionist Federation could only have discouraged German Jews from participating in Germany's military. Moreover, for all their rhetoric, Zionists did not actually expect all Jews to abandon Germany and relocate to the wilds of desolate Palestine; their immediate objective was to instead prepare Jews to live as an unassimilated minority within Germany (Jews of Russia, Austro-Hungary, and elsewhere had similar aspirations). If you were a German Zionist in 1914 you did not join the army; you instead did everything you could to avoid service to this country wherein you "had no roots whatever."[843] Zionists were entirely convinced that it was not only the case that Jews *were not* good Germans; they were convinced that Jews *could not* be good

Germans. Zionist nationalism was Jewish nationalism; there was no room for any other form of it.

Hitler was not alone in his observation that there seemed to be a large presence of Jews in various administrative positions during the war.* While such observations certainly do not establish that Jews were, in fact, slackers, that was the impression of a great many observers—observations from which stereotypes are made—and the Jew Count results validated their feelings.

Whatever the apologists and the "more thorough and scholarly" assessments may have concluded, it is a veritable certainty that the survey conducted by the German army was superior to the one conducted by the *Weltbühne*, and that Jews indeed served in the German military during World War I in numbers that were substantially below their representation in the general population.

The charge that Jews who did serve, served disproportionately in rear area positions was also true in all likelihood. As pretty much every infantryman knows, the company clerk is the guy who is among the smartest in the company, can type and write and can organize matters of company administration. If only as the natural result of their vaunted intelligence and organizational abilities, Jews would have naturally been frequently assigned to noncombat positions—that is simply the way that armies operate. Kurt Tucholsky, one of the most important journalists of the Weimar Republic, serves as an example: Tucholsky initially served as a munitions soldier and later as a company writer. According to a Wikipedia article, "Tucholsky saw the posts as writer and field-newspaper editor as good opportunities to avoid serving in the trenches."[844] And who, other than a fanatical nationalist such as Hitler, would not? Tucholsky later went on to become editor of *Die Weltbühne*, the publication that sponsored the "more thorough and scholarly" survey, above.

---

* Leon Trotsky made the same observation with respect to Jews in the early Russian army under Marxism. "In a Politburo meeting of April 18, 1919, Trotsky urged that Jews be redeployed because there were relatively few Jews in frontline combat units, while Jews constituted a 'vast percentage' of the Cheka at the front and in the Executive Committees at the front and at the rear." (http://www.kevinmacdonald.net/SlezkineRev.pdf 04/26/07)

Roth's publication alleged that Jews used their considerable influence in the war ministry to obtain phony medical discharges and behind-the-lines assignments.[845] It was this publication that Jewish apologists hoped to obviate by their claim of a "more thorough and scholarly" survey and conclusion.

Given the historical privileges of Jews to avoid military service, coupled with the obvious presence of many Jews in the war supply industries, and coupled, too, with empirical evidence of young Jewish men on the streets, the belief in Germany that Jews did not provide their fair share of frontline troops during World War I is almost certainly true and is hardly surprising.

German beliefs about Jewish slackers were reinforced by several well-known Jews who bragged about how they individually avoided military service.

Prominent Jews such as Albert Einstein had avoided military service (well before the war) by renouncing their German citizenship and temporarily relocating outside the country, in Einstein's case, to Switzerland. A number of other prominent Jews did likewise.

Among the prominent Weimar Jews who either avoided military service, served in rear areas, or managed to obtain early discharges were Ernst Toller ("physical exhaustion and a complete nervous breakdown"). Toller would later participate in the subjugation of Germany's Bavarian province. Eric Muesham, like Toller, would also play a significant role in the subjugation of Bavaria. He refused induction and instead spent the war years writing anti-German propaganda and organizing labor strikes that were hurtful to the war effort. Popular dramatist Walter Hasenclever simulated mental illness. The famous artist Max Beckmann, then a rising impressionist painter, served in a medical unit on the Russian front for a time, but was discharged in 1915 due to "shattered nerves."[846] Kurt Tucholsky, mentioned above, also served in a barbed-wire depot in a quiet sector of the eastern front and later as a police commissioner in occupied Romania.[847] Emil Gumbel, the famous Marxist statistician, entered the army in 1914 but never fired a shot in anger and was given a medical discharge in late January 1915. The famous movie director Fritz

Lang served in the war but was discharged in 1918 due to "shell shock." The poet Jakob van Hoddis spent the war years in a mental hospital. Famous film director Ernest Lubitsch, twenty-two years old at the outbreak of World War I, managed to avoid military service entirely and spent the war years directing movies. In the 1920s, Lubitsch relocated to Hollywood where he enjoyed a highly successful career producing anti-Hitler propaganda films. Distinguished *Weltbühne* writer, anarchist, and Socialist politician Erich Muehsam simply refused military service. The editor of *Der Dada*, John (Helmut Herzfelde) Heartfield, began military training but "fell sick" and was declared "unemployable." The radical *Weltbühne* founder, Siegfried Jacobsohn, was faced with either military service or compromising his supposed principles by lending the pages of his journal to war propaganda—he choose the latter.[848] Paul Levi, a radical Communist, was inducted but "starved himself out of the army and was discharged in 1916";[849] he thereafter spent the war in Switzerland in the company of Lenin and Karl Radek. Levi would later go on to become the leader of the German Communist Party (KPD) and win acclaim for turning the nascent KPD into the first mass Communist party outside of Russia. Marxist philosopher Georg Lukács served in the army as a clerk in the Budapest censorship shop. Radical Zionist and leftist political lawyer Alfred Apfel was discharged in 1916 due to "illness."[850] The Jewish writer Hugo Bettauer deserted from the Austrian army. The pacifist novelist and playwright Stefan Zweig served comfortably in the Archives of the Ministry of War. Expressionist artist and sculptor Ludwig Meidner served as an interpreter and censor at an internment camp for prisoners of war. The psychedelic artist, poet, and playwright Oskar Kokoschka served a short time in the Austrian army but was then discharged as mentally unstable. The Jewish Spartacist Max Levien, who would later be a prominent member of the Communist seizure of power in Germany's Bavaria, was conscripted into the army and thereafter lectured soldiers on the need for Germany's defeat. "'It is necessary,' he said, 'that Germany be humiliated, that the colonial troops of France and England march through the Brandenburg Gate.'"[851] The revolutionary firebrand Karl

Liebknecht was forced into the army, but then refused to fight. He spent some time burying the dead before being discharged for "failing health." He thereafter led the revolutionary Spartacus Uprising in Germany.

Others, such as Jewish publisher Kurt Wolff took advantage of Jewish patrons to avoid service or at least service on the front lines. The Jewish poet Wieland Herzfelde (brother of John Heartfield), was discharged in 1915 as "unworthy to wear the Kaiser's uniform." Later, when he was again called up, both he and his brother were extricated from the front by Harry Kessler, the powerful non-Jewish "Red Count."[852] *Neusachlich* news reporter Egon Erwin Kisch served as a military reporter in the Austrian army along with expressionist playwright Franz Werfel. Kisch was jailed briefly for his subversive reportage and incendiary speeches while serving. He also joined the Red Guard, a revolutionary cell.[853] He deserted in 1918. Prior to his work as a reporter, Werfel had served as a telephone operator in Galicia, where he spent much of his time writing. "In fact, he was working on a play most of the time he was there."[854] E. Michael Jones, in his book, *Living Machines*, says, "If an artillery shell had fallen there [on the *Kriegspressequartier*—the press office] . . . it would have wiped out most of modern German literature,"[855] which was, at that time, dominated by Jews. Jewish novelist and playwright of note, Lion Feuchtwanger, was drafted but then quickly discharged on "health grounds." Franz Jung, one of the contributors to *Die Aktion* and editor of the prewar Munich *Die Revolution*, deserted. He was later awarded a spurious medical certificate by a Dr. Walter Serner. Still later he was committed to a mental hospital.

As implied by the foregoing, in World War I you would have been hard-pressed to find a prominent Jew in the German trenches. Hitler himself made just such an observation.

Others entered medical school to gain an exemption from military service and dropped out once the war was over. Others still (Max Brod, Leonhard Frank, Ernst Bloch, et al.), relocated to places like Switzerland where they engaged in anti-German propaganda.

For some, Jewishness was not confined to racial Jews. Non-Jews with close associations or perhaps spouses in the Jewish community were "spiritual Jews" according to the likes of Hitler.[856] Thus, it was that some prominent non-Jews also contributed to the idea that Jews did not serve in the military in full measure during World War I. Ersatz Jews such as the hugely popular playwright and agitprop impresario Bertolt Brecht was so connected with Jews in his work and sympathies that many people, including many Jews, thought that he was himself Jewish.[*] Brecht spent his World War I service as a medical orderly in a clinic for venereal disease. Later, he falsely represented his war service as having taken place in a frontline medical detachment where he personally performed amputations and other serious medical procedures.[857]

Another famous "spiritual Jew," the artist-poet George Grosz,[†] is often trumpeted by historians as having been a member of a machine-gun company during the war. He did, in fact, see frontline service at the outset of the war but was soon afterward discharged for what was then called "brain fever." Recalled again in 1917, he went into an "amnesic fit" and was considered a deserter. Count Kessler got him transferred to a mental institution where he "served" for the remainder of the war.[858] After the war Grosz was celebrated by the left-wing intelligentsia for his blatant, gross depictions of the war, its officers, and its soldiers. "If drawings could kill," said Kurt Tucholsky of Grosz's drawings, "then the Prussian military would surely be dead by now."[859] These and other ersatz Jews, all members of the radical Bolshevik left that was, in turn, dominated by Jewish interests and adamantly opposed

---

[*] Some sources, such as the *Boston Globe*, claim that Brecht was Jewish. In 1990, his grave and that of his wife in East Berlin were vandalized and smeared with anti-Semitic slogans. See http://www.highbeam.com/doc/1P2-8172693.html. Wikipedia asserts that Brecht was born to a Protestant mother and Catholic father. See http://en.wikipedia.org/wiki/Bertolt_Brecht.

[†] The Nazis believed Grosz to be Jewish, most historians do not. Still, modern-day Jewish intellectuals sometimes say or infer that he was. See http://www.forward.com/articles/9631/ 12/15/09

to the monarchy, added further credence to the idea that Jews did not serve in proportional numbers in the German army.

For some Jews who did serve in the military, their service was less than sterling. Alfred Redl was a colonel in the Austrian army who had risen to become the head of counterintelligence. Some historians have it that he was blackmailed by the Russians due to his homosexuality. That as may be, he also lived well beyond his means. He supported his extravagant lifestyle by spying for the Russians, a task for which he was lavishly paid. Redl passed plans for a future Austro-Hungarian offensive against Serbia to the Russian Department of Security (Okhrana).[860] He is suspected of having also spied on behalf of France and Italy, but irrefutable evidence of those charges have never been produced. Redl committed suicide upon discovery of his spying activities, so the full extent of his treasonous activities could never be entirely known. Redl also betrayed both his own agents and agents from Russia who had collaborated with Austria-Hungary. The long and the short of Redl's treachery, however, was that Austria-Hungary suffered significant defeats in its battles with Serbia (the Battle of Cer in mid-August 1914 being most illustrative) and Russia in the early stages of World War I that would otherwise have been victories for both Austria-Hungary and her ally, Germany. Commenting to friends in Munich, Hitler said, "Just take a look at the Colonel Redl, Chief of the General Staff, a homosexual, a slut and spy for the Russians. When I left Vienna, this noble man, because of those crimes shot himself with a bullet into his empty brain."[861] Hitler was not alone in condemning Redl, according to a Wikipedia account of him. "Historians of the Habsburg Empire, as well as espionage historians such as the CIA's Allen Dulles and Soviet General Makhail Milstein, agree in calling Redl an arch-traitor."[862] And the loss of early battles due to his traitorous acts contributed to the charges that Germany was stabbed in the back.

In the German navy it was alleged that "the whole of Jewish finance"[863] was behind the opposition to Germany's U-boat offensive. The theory behind this charge was that prominent Jewish shipping magnates such as Albert Ballin were fearful of losses to their ships that were flagged in countries other than

Germany. Whatever the merit of the accusation, and they were likely without much merit (there were better reasons for opposing unrestricted warfare, such as its potential for bringing the U.S. into the war), it gained credence in 1918 as the sailors of Kiel mutinied under the inspirational and conspiratorial guidance of Jewish provocateurs belonging to the USPD, Spartacists, and their labor union minions.

The pacifist movement and the antiwar movement in Germany were led and stoked by Jews. The popular historical record aside (the one that posits that Jews were not particularly prominent in the anti-German, antiwar movement), Jews participated in large numbers and were prominent in the movements. As early as 1907, the Social Democratic Party was charged with subverting discipline in the army.[864] Before the war, the ardent Marxist, August Bebel (non-Jew* with exceptionally close ties to a number of Jewish sponsors) had declared, "Not a man, not a farthing for this system. . . . [All] European Socialist parties were obligated to 'do all in their power . . . to utilize the economic and political crises caused by the war to rouse the people and thereby to hasten the abolition of the capitalist class rule.'"[865] Bebel was, of course, calling on all people of all nations to participate in the noble cause of obstructing war, but it was only the Germans who were hearing his pacifistic clarion. Moreover, his call to use the economic and political crisis to rouse the people in opposition to national objectives could hardly escape analogy with Lenin's often paraphrased claim that the worse things are, the better they are for the revolutionary forces of Socialism. And the revolutionary forces of Socialism to which both Bebel and Lenin were referring, were predominantly Jewish.

At the same time that prominent Jews were decrying Germany's participation in World War I, German Jews were doing everything possible to aid Jewish immigration into the country. As early as 1914, the German Committee for the Liberation of Russian Jews (*Deutsches Komitee zur Befreiung der russischen*

---

* Some few sources assert that Bebel was Jewish, but most that he was not.

Juden—which was presided over by one of the authors of that "more thorough and scholarly" assessment of the "Jew Count") and other Jewish-German organizations were calling for autonomy for Jews in Poland and aiding Russian Jews to immigrate to Germany. During the war, as pointed out by Aschheim, some "70,000 Eastern Jews—workers, prisoners, civil internees—were added to the prewar population of 90,000."[866] That is, the Jewish population of Germany nearly doubled during the war years. The newly arrived Jews concentrated themselves in the large cities where they took steps to avoid military service and thereby lent further credence to the perception that Jews were not shouldering their fair share of the military burden. At the end of the war, still another tide of Eastern Jews entered Germany.

Jews were especially and correctly perceived as being prominent in nonmilitary positions in war supply corporations. Walter Rathenau, the Jewish head of German war production, was the most prominent among them. Rathenau was appointed to his position at the behest of fellow Jews, Ballin, and the bankers Max Warburg and Carl Melchoir. Rathenau was at least in one respect an anomaly: he was a Bolshevistic Jewish-German patriot. He once told the Zionist leader Kurt Bluenfeld that "At night I am a Bolshevik, by day I seek an ethically regulated society."[867] He necessarily found himself aligned with a great many highly capable Jewish producers and suppliers of food and war materials. According to Hitler, by 1917, the whole of production was under the control of Jewish finance.[868] Allegations were made that Rathenau and his cronies were unjustly profiting from the war and some of them assuredly did; no supplier of war materials went wanting for cash at the end of the conflict. Albert Lindemann summarizes the relationship between Rathenau and Jewish war firms as follows: "Among the favored firms were a disproportionate number led by Jews, many of whom made enormous profits during the war...."[869]

Charges of Jewish profiteering were even more widespread in other areas of Europe. Lindemann says the following about Jewish profiteers:

> In Budapest, the business classes during the war were reported to be "singularly gross in profiteering." They were also widely recognized to be around 90 percent Jewish. The noted historian and Jew Oszkar Jaszi was appalled at the contrast between the luxury of the Budapest business world, overwhelmingly Jewish, and the misery of the war front. He sensed storm-clouds of retribution on the horizon.[870]

The anti-Semite, Theodor Fritsch, in relating his experience as a wartime manufacturer negotiating a government contract, claimed that "he met . . . Hebrews—and more Hebrews. . . . [S]urrounded by others of his tribe, sat Mr. Walther Rathenau arranging things. . . . [I]t was no surprise that Jewish firms almost always received preference."[871] We know Fritsch to be an anti-Semite precisely because he had the gall to recount such observations.

Nor was it radical rightist fantasy to see Jews as the leaders of the war corporations and therefore as the beneficiaries of the war; it was, rather, the fact of Jews being both historically and still then closely associated with the arms trade.

German general Erich Ludendorff claimed in his memoirs that the war profiteers were essentially all Jews. Their domination of war operations of the kind headed by Rathenau provided them with the opportunity to enrich themselves at the expense of the German people and take control of the economy. It was certainly the case that significant contingents of Jews (numerically only about 10 percent, but they accounted for vast amounts of war materials trade)[872] were participants in war materials acquisition, production, and provision. Moreover, this subset of Jews tended to be at the head of war-provisioning enterprises. It needs to be emphasized that Ludendorff at that time was no knee-jerk anti-Semite. Throughout the war he often proved that he knew how to use and appreciate Jewish help and cooperation. As Stephen Aschheim emphasizes, "He fostered Jewish artists, conversed with them enthusiastically for hours and let them dedicate their works to him. He also stepped in more than once against anti-Semitic excesses."[873] In the East, Ludendorff quickly repealed tsarist anti-Jewish legislation, dedicated synagogues, and attended Yiddish language theaters with his officers.[874]

At the end of the war statistics were published in Vienna showing that before the war there had been 100 millionaires there. By 1919, the number had jumped to 8,000, 7,200 of whom were Jews. Moreover, some 5,400 of the newly rich Jews were Ostjuden, which reinforced the idea that this particular subset of Jews was especially predatory. Anti-Semites claimed that they had acquired their wealth by scandalously dishonest means. Such claims were believable precisely because of the widely observed lack of ethics displayed by Eastern Jews; abominable ethics were taken to be a salient Ostjuden trait, a stereotype.[875]

Certain high-profile Jews came out against the war very early on and even made treasonous public statements. These statements further substantiated the popular charge of Jewish-German disloyalty to the fatherland. Among such people were the prominent revolutionary Marxists Karl Liebknecht and Rosa Luxemburg. Moreover, in keeping with Jewish ethnocentrism, it could not help but be the case that radical antiwar and anti-German rhetoric by Jews in leadership positions would further discourage Jewish participation in the German military.

Born in Leipzig in 1871, Karl Liebknecht was the son of a prominent revolutionary and one of the founders of the Social Democratic Party (SPD) of Germany, Wilhelm Liebknecht. Karl was even more radical than his father and like his father was several times sentenced to jail for his activities. Viciously opposed to German militarism, Karl developed an extensive antimilitary training program aimed at German youth. His plan was to indoctrinate children in such a way that by the time they became of age for military service, they would be implacable opponents. Adolf Hitler would later mimic Liebknecht's youth training camps in the form of the Hitler Youth, an objective of which was to prepare youth for military service, not oppose it.

At the end of 1914, Liebknecht, along with Luxemburg, Leo Jogiches, Paul Levi, Ernest Meyer, Franz Mehring, Eugen Levine, and Clara Zetkin—all Jews except for Zetkin—formed the radical

Marxist Spartacus League. Several of this same group would, at war's end, rename the Spartacus League and thereby acknowledge its political objectives as the Communist Party of Germany (KPD). They would also serve as the principals in trying to overthrow the government by violent means in the attempted German revolution of January 1919. All of the founders of the Spartacus League would make their mark in revolutionary circles during the coming months and years, but none so prominently or quite so effectively as Liebknecht and Luxemburg. Amongst Marxists, Liebknecht and Luxemburg are even today represented as revolutionary heroes and are venerated by them. In Communist East European countries of the Cold War era, streets, parks, and buildings were commonly named for them. "Luxemburg was an acknowledged giant of Socialist theoretics, and with an international reputation as an antirevisionist revolutionary,"[876] says Watt. Her fame, along with that of Liebknecht, was, for a time, the equal of Lenin's—they were together celebrated in Marxist circles as the three L's: Lenin, Luxemburg, and Liebknecht, the greatest champions of the proletarian revolution.

The first of several votes was taken in the Reichstag in August 1914 to provide war credits (deficit spending) to finance the war. Nationalism ran high in all of the warring nations and there was an initial enthusiasm for getting on with it. Though the SPD opposed the war, its 110 members nevertheless voted in favor of the credits at that point. It agreed, too, that throughout the war there would be *Burgfrieden* (peace in the castle), a term taken from the Middle Ages when those seeking shelter agreed to behave civilly amongst their hosts. That is, there was to be a political truce during which political controversy was to be put aside in favor of winning the war.

SPD motivations for initially voting in favor of the war credits included fears that if they failed to do so, military authorities, who were given dictatorial powers, would destroy them. They also had to worry that a failure to provide the credits would cause a split in the party and that moderate elements might then move to the Right.

The vote for the war credits and the *Burgfrieden* agreement served the SPD well: because of them, SPD leaders who would have otherwise been arrested at the outset of the war remained free. Throughout the war, SPD literature was allowed to be circulated within the ranks of the military.[877] The *Burgfrieden* also enabled the SPD to vastly increase its labor union membership during the war, an increase that exclusively benefited the SPD and its offshoot Marxist parties.

By 1916, Socialist union leaders were incorporated into the political and economic decision-making process. Membership in the labor unions skyrocketed from less than 1 million in 1916, to over 5.5 million in 1919.[878] Hard-core left-wing factions of the SPD took full advantage of the *Burgfrieden* agreement to dispense Marxist, demoralizing, antiwar literature. By 1917, the agreement would be totally abandoned. Jewish-led radical offshoots of the SPD would by then be in open rebellion against the German war effort. Liebknecht would carry the standard. Other prominent Jews also opposed the war effort early on: Eduard Bernstein along with Karl Kautsky and Hugo Haase published an important pamphlet in March 1915 titled *Das Gebot der Stuunde* (The Demand of the Hour) that opposed German objectives in the war.[879]

As a lawyer, Liebknecht specialized in defending other left-wing radicals who were tried for offenses such as smuggling illegal literature into Russia, a venture that he himself engaged in. A popular writer within the SPD, he was forever in trouble for the radicalism of his publications. One of his pamphlets, "Militarismus und Antimilitarismus," led to his imprisonment in 1907. While still in prison he was elected to the Prussian parliament, which is something of a testimonial to his rhetoric, his ability to propagate his views to the Prussian population, his charisma, and the support that he received from his fellow travelers. In 1912, during the SPD sweep of the electorate, he was elected to the Reichstag. In 1914, as the Reichstag was voting for war credits to finance the war, Liebknecht initially went along with the rest of the Reichstag and voted for them. He soon regretted his vote and thereafter not only voted against further credits* but worked tirelessly against the war and in support of a Communist revolution in Germany.

---

* It may be of interest to the reader to know that Karl Liebknecht's father, William, had voted against war credits for the Franco-Prussian War (1870–1871). His vote incurred for

In December 1914, another vote was taken on war credits. The lone dissenter was Liebknecht. His opposition provided him with worldwide fame and notoriety, and notoriety brought him additional power to influence the masses. "In the United States," recounts Richard Watt, "*Harper's Weekly* printed a poem commending his moral courage."[880] By 1915, the SPD was badly split on the issue of financing the war. Of the twenty members of the Reichstag who voted in 1915 against the provision of further credits, six were Jews, with one additional Jew being among a group of twenty-two deputies abstaining.

Hitler fumed at the likes of Liebknecht and others who failed to fully support the troops and the war. While many of his generation came under the thrall of internationalist Marxist ideology and therefore protested Germany's involvement in the war, Hitler, of course, remained steadfastly committed to a German victory and German honor. He reviled those whose propaganda aimed at inspiring German soldiers to lay down their arms or worse—murder their superior officers. Liebknecht was guilty of both, as well as trying to cut off funding for the war and of inciting general mutiny.

By March 1916, the twenty opposition Reichstag deputies, under the chairmanship of the Jew Hugo Haase, formed themselves into a radical left-wing faction that was initially named the Social Democratic Working Group (*Sozialdemokratische Arbeitgemeinschaft*, SAG). The group[†] would soon after become the nucleus of the radical left Independent Social Democratic Party (USPD),[881] a party that soon grew in membership to several hundred thousand. At the time of its inception, the USPD was also the most openly revolutionary party.[882] The USPD represented itself, says Watt, as "the only true believers and the sole apostles of legitimate Marxist dogma."[883] The Spartacus League headed by

---

him the enmity of Otto von Bismarck, a man venerated by Adolf Hitler. The elder Liebknecht was also convicted of treason and spent two years in prison for that crime (1872–1874).
[†] The principals were Haase, Bernstein, Hilferding, Cohn, Davidsohn, Simon, Rosenfeld, Eisner, and Levi.

Liebknecht and Luxemburg also joined the USPD but continued, nevertheless, to go its own way when the USPD was from time to time viewed as insufficiently radical. On the occasion of the kaiser's birthday in January 1916, the Spartacists distributed an openly revolutionary handbill.[884] There would be many more such publications from them in the following months and years. The Spartacists, often with the aid of the USPD, worked assiduously to prepare the German populace for a Marxist revolution.

Thus, by 1916, there were three significant leftist political forces vying for power in Germany: the largest was the relatively moderate SPD, already several times mentioned, the more radically leftist USPD splinter group, and the ultraleft Marxists belonging to the Spartacist League. All three groups were substantially influenced or absolutely controlled by their large Jewish contingents, with the leadership of the most radical factions, the USPD and Spartacists, being most predominantly Jewish. All three organizations had high-profile members who were staunchly opposed to the war, even to the extent of openly calling for Germany's defeat.

The Spartacus League created a publication that was soon declared illegal but was nevertheless published throughout the war, the Spartacus Letters. Ever mindful of the revolutionary opportunities presented by the chaos of war, Luxemburg wrote much of the material for the publication and Liebknecht served as its editor. The Spartacus Letters found their way to the German front lines by a variety of means, not the least of which was by mail. Spartacus sympathizers in the postal service provided information enabling the Spartacists to thereby directly propagandize the troops. At times, the publication was even stuffed into sandbags that would then be delivered to the front lines. The fundamental theme of the Spartacus Letters was that Germany was solely responsible for the war and that the troops should mutiny and create a Socialist state. The letters also railed against the faction of the SPD membership that continued to support the war effort.

It was not only the Spartacists who were propagandizing German troops against the war: the literature of expressionist exiles was also being smuggled to the troops from 1916 onward and spread rapidly. Jewish author Leonard Frank attacked the concepts of patriotism, loyalty, and honor. His novel, *Der Mensch ist gut*, was smuggled into Germany, printed on newsprint by the USPD, and distributed in the trenches to the tune of a half million copies;[885] it was credited with hastening the German revolution of 1918. A host of Jewish-German voluntary exiles in Switzerland, many of whom were little more than draft dodgers, also contributed to the anti-German propaganda effort.

Liebknecht was arrested early in the war for his anti-German, antiwar pronouncements and publications, including his call for the troops to kill their officers. He was put into the army, where, refusing to fight, he served burying the dead. By 1915, however, he was released due to his "rapidly deteriorating health."[886] Back on the home front, he continued to surreptitiously call for German soldiers to kill their officers and commence the revolution. He was jailed still again. By the end of the war, his actions had Hitler saying that Liebknecht was a revolutionary shirker who needed to be killed.[887]

Liebknecht's lieutenant, Rosa Luxemburg, was an extraordinary woman. Born in Zamosc, Poland, in 1871, the year that Germany was unified under Bismarck, she dedicated virtually her entire life to revolutionary Marxism in Poland, Russia, and Germany. Her biographers are fond of pointing out that she achieved her legendary status as a Marxist revolutionary in Germany though she was thrice handicapped: she was a woman, a Pole, and Jewish.

Luxemburg was born to a middle-class Jewish family. Small and not very well proportioned, she walked with a pronounced limp owing to a childhood disease. While she was not particularly attractive physically, it can be said that she had a beautiful mind if one is inclined toward intellectual radicalism. She was scholarly and revolutionary from childhood. She was also both brave and brazen. She eagerly studied the Torah along with German and Polish classical literature. Later she would also study Russian literature and thereby became conversant in that language. Her command of German was such that she was accomplished even with respect to its many nuances. By high school, she was a consummate internationalist and revolutionary Marxist active in radical Polish and Lithuanian politics.

Hunted by police, she fled to Zurich, Switzerland, in 1889, the year that Hitler was born. There she attended Zurich University where she studied philosophy, history, politics, economics, and mathematics simultaneously[888]—clearly, Luxemburg was no intellectual slouch. While studying in Zurich, she met and befriended one of the loves of her life, fellow Jewish radical and Spartacist Leo Jogiches. She also engaged in the revisionist debate stemming from Eduard Bernstein's call for Socialists to abandon revolutionary phraseology in favor of a policy of evolution and compromise with the capitalist class. Luxemburg, ever the staunchest of Marxists, gained her initial fame by way of her writings that berated Bernstein's ideas. She would later even attack Vladimir Lenin's ideas for organizing the Communist Party with an elite cadre at the top of the structure and obedient vassals below. Luxemburg argued for a more decentralized structure.

By 1898, Rosa was living in Germany. A practical woman, she underwent a sham marriage to a German in order that she could acquire German citizenship and thereby avoid deportation while she engaged in radical leftist German politics. She left her husband at the registry office after the wedding and had nothing more to do with him. She continued to maintain her relationship with her brethren in Poland and Lithuania as she simultaneously offered her services to the Socialist Democratic Party of Germany. She was an ever busy lady.

Socialist biographers treat Luxemburg with admiration akin to religious fervor. To them, and to some of her contemporaries, she was the "best brain after Marx,"[889] "the sword, the flame of revolution,"[890] and a "constant advocate of radical action."[891] Even most of her detractors have it that she was a genius theoretician, but they emphasize her less positive qualities as well. Lindemann claims that "Most party and trade union functionaries considered Luxemburg a quarrelsome outsider, a sharp-tongued, disrespectful, impractical troublemaker, and a foreign, eastern Jew to boot."[892] Karl Kautsky, one of her close collaborators in the early 1900s, had it that she was bereft of tact and feelings of comradeship. The Jewish Austro-Hungarian politician Victor Adler had her as a "poisonous bitch" who was "too clever."[893] During her period of involvement in German radicalism that we will describe momentarily, she was variously described as "Red Rosa," "a modern Fury," "a Shrew," a *"petroleuse,"*[894] "that Donna Rosa Luxemburg who believes herself called to be the standard-bearer of the red revolution,"[895] "bloody Rosa, the Jewish sau," and "the syphilitic Luxemburg bacillus."[896] The prominent German Democratic Party (*Deutsche Demokratische Partei*—DDP) politician Max Weber thought that Luxemburg belonged in a zoo, and he thought that Liebknecht belonged in a madhouse.[897] Hitler purportedly liked to refer to Luxemburg as the "red plague" or the "Jewish plague." To all, she was an incorrigible theorist, an ideologue unwilling to compromise with her fellow travelers, and a committed revolutionary. The love and hate directed at Rosa was as complex as her very being.

Revolution was also brewing elsewhere on the Continent. The Russian Revolution of 1905, failure though it was, served as an inspiration to Marxists in Germany. Stimulated by the events in Russia, Luxemburg authored what was perhaps her best theoretical work, *Mass Strike, Party, and Trade Unions (1906)*. In this work she argued that the mass strike had the power to radicalize workers and bring about revolution. Economic hardships brought on by the war could be made to serve, in effect, as both the assault to breach the defenses of the bourgeois and as the maneuver by which that breach would be exploited to obtain victory. As early as June 1916, a one-day strike was called in protest against the arrest of Spartacist leader Karl Liebknecht—55,000 workers participated.[898] By 1917, the Spartacists, under the leadership of Liebknecht and Luxemburg, would be instrumental in inciting workers to strike throughout the country and millions of workers would follow their lead.

Roughly 500 labor strikes occurred in 1917 alone. The strikes stemmed not from wage movements, not from downtrodden workers seeking better hours or safer job sites: they were part and parcel of the revolution. The ordinary worker who participated in the strikes knew not whose cart he was pulling. After the war, in 1919, there were 3,682 labor strikes affecting 32,825 businesses and 2,750,000 workers,[899] and those strikes were among the several contributing factors and economic woes that were to occur in the early 1920s.

Luxemburg's radicalism several times caused her arrest and confinement to prison. Her first experiences with prison occurred in 1904 and 1906. During the war, in 1916, she was again jailed as a political prisoner. As such, she was well-treated during her confinement (much like the lenient treatment of Hitler at Landsberg prison, so decried by establishment historians). Throughout most of her time in prison her cell door was kept open, she was able to receive visitors, tend a garden, and most importantly, she continued to author radical Marxist literature for distribution to the German populace and to German troops in the field.[900]

Luxemburg sought to bring the Gentile proletariat to her beloved Marxism, but she had little patience for the Gentiles whose devotion she sought. She held most non-Jews in contempt. Her references to non-Jewish leaders in the SPD were that such leaders were "shappesgoyim of the bourgeoisie"[901]—people who accomplish work on Saturdays that is forbidden for Jews. Most of her closest friends were Jews, as were the two loves of her life, Leo Jogiches and Paul Levi. But there was a smattering of non-Jews in her coterie as well, the fiery Clara Zetkin being perhaps the most prominent among them.

Google	URL
Karl Liebknecht	http://en.wikipedia.org/wiki/Karl_Liebknecht 8/2/14
Rosa Luxemburg	http://en.wikipedia.org/wiki/Rosa_Luxemburg 8/2/14
Leo Jogiches	http://en.wikipedia.org/wiki/Leo_Jogiches 8/2/14
Paul Levi, KPD	http://en.wikipedia.org/wiki/Paul_Levi 8/2/14

Luxemburg, like many of her radical fellow Marxists, was also an anti-Zionist and "was nearly as contemptuous of traditionalist

Ostjuden as any German-Jewish bourgeois."[902] Zionists were nationalists, Luxemburg a rabid internationalist. One sought the safety of a homogeneous nationalist homeland, the other a multicultural internationalism. The schism between Marxists and Zionists, though, was not as absolute as many historians would have it. Upon successful conclusion of the Russian Revolution, Communist Jews tried again to carve out a Jewish niche in Russian society: they sought, like the Zionists, special privileges for the Jews as a separate, nationalist-like set-aside for Jews that would enable them to continue to express their particularism and ethnocentrism within the Socialist state. While the government outlawed anti-Semitism, even making it a capital offense, Jews exercised their political power to destroy all vestiges of Christianity as a socially unifying force while simultaneously establishing a secular Jewish subculture so that Jews would not lose their group identity, continuity, or unifying mechanisms such as the Yiddish language.[903]

On May 1, 1916, Liebknecht led an antiwar demonstration of some 50,000 people in Berlin during which he called for the overthrow of the government: "Down with war! Down with the government!" screamed Liebknecht.[904] His treasonous public statements served as the basis for his arrest, conviction, and confinement. It was a mark of his influence in German politics, and his influence within the trade union movement in particular that workers went on strike in Berlin and labor demonstrations took place in his support in Stuttgart, Braunschweig, and Bremen. These political strikes, allegedly impossible during peacetime, became commonplace in wartime.[905] The strikes were largely the work of the USPD and the Spartacist League. Luxemburg applied her genius for sloganeering in a propaganda campaign of extraordinary intensity that had the effect of turning Liebknecht into a martyr. She called on the workers to follow his example. "As a result [of Luxemburg's propaganda efforts] many thousands were won for the struggle against the war," says Paul Frölich.[906]

Meanwhile, other prominent Jewish-Germans spread their anti-German, antimilitary, antiwar, and antigovernment messages in the populace and on the front lines. In 1914, Hugo Haase, second only to Friedrich Ebert in the leadership of the first Weimar government, declared that he wanted to undermine the German army in order to set the world revolution in motion.[907] In 1918, Haase and his USPD followers would be credited by some as the spiritual leader of the revolutionary mutiny at Kiel. For a brief period at the end of the war he would share power in the government known as the November Criminals by the likes of Adolf Hitler and other radical rightists.

Jewish journalist, and later the leader of the Bavarian Revolution, Kurt Eisner wrote in 1915 that "there could be no disputing that what we have is a German world war."[908] In 1917, the First Marine Battalion was forbidden to read papers "of Social Democratic and Jewish tendency."[909] Prominent German-Jews such as Hermann Tietz, Felix Pinner, Paul Hirsch, Eugen Landau, Professor Julius Hirsch, Warburg, and others came out against the war aims of the government, as did prominent Jewish-owned newspapers such as the *Berliner Tageblatt* (the selfsame newspaper that had called so stridently for war with Russia prior to World War I) and the *Frankfurter Zeitung*. According to historian Peter Pulzer, the Jewish editor of the *Berliner Tageblatt*, Theodor Wolff, "was one of the most influential cultural and liberal political commentators during World War I and the Weimar Republic. He had been a regular contributor to various exile magazines during the war and thereby became a symbol of Jewish-liberal defeatism."[910] Wolff's truckling to French interests and to others of the Allies was little short of treasonous. Jewish press opposition to the war would later become widely known by the term "treason via the press."[911] After the war, while serving as a foreign policy adviser to both Gustav Stresemann and Heinrich Brüning, Wolff worked toward reconciliation with France, gaining him still further enmity from the Right. Far from viewing the radicals' idealism as attempts to save German lives from the horrors of war, people such as Hitler and General Ludendorff took it for granted that Jews formed part of the swamp of internationalist, pacifist, and defeatist thinking.

In Switzerland, the Jewish-German Richard Grelling wrote two anti-German books: *J'accuse*, previously mentioned, and *Das*

Verbrechen (The Crime) in which he laid blame for the war squarely and solely on Germany; and he supported his contention with thorough and scholarly falsified facts and documents. The books found receptive audiences, especially in the camps of Germany's enemies and in neutral countries.

The Jewish-German intellectual Hermann Fernau relocated to Switzerland where he waged a relentless war upon the dynasty and the military caste of Prussia that he held to be categorically responsible for the world war.[912] After initially supporting the war, Maximilian Harden (born Felix Ernst Witkowski) fought German war policy and made himself the veritable spokesman for U.S. President Wilson. Harden was called "the Judas of the German people" by historian Friedrich Thimme. He later staunchly supported the Treaty of Versailles, a treaty that was vehemently despised by the whole of the German populace. Numerous other Jewish personalities, both within Germany and in self-imposed exile, contributed mightily to the anti-German propaganda effort. Various groups sprang up, both within Germany and without that had German defeat as their fundamental goal, and these groups were invariably led by Jewish personalities who euphemistically called themselves "pacifists."

Not to be outdone by others, Spartacists, even with Luxemburg and Liebknecht in jail, continued with their revolutionary agitation in both the army and the navy. Indeed, Luxemburg's essay, "The Crisis of Social Democracy," says Frölich, "became the intellectual armour of thousands of illegal militants."[913] In tribute to the successes of the Spartacists and their commitment to international Marxism, Vladimir Lenin, who was himself financed by such Jews as Jakub Fuerstenberg and Alexander Parvus (born Israel Lazarevich Gelfand but also given as Helphand), heaped praise on the Spartacists. To Lenin's eyes, the only German political movement of note in Germany was the Spartacist one. At the 1915 Zimmerwald Conference in Switzerland, he made himself clear on the subject: "'For us,' Lenin said, speaking for the Bolsheviks, 'there exists the Liebknecht group only.'"[914] The Spartacists were joined in their effort by the Independent Socialists. Both the USPD and the Spartacists recognized the revolutionary opportunities that were provided to them by the misery of the war-worn populace, and they therefore did everything in their power to enhance social and political turmoil. Between 1916 and 1918, they prepared for their planned general strikes that would catapult them to power.

The famous stab-in-the-back "myth" (*Dolchstosslegende*) was mythical only by acclamation of the victors—for radical rightist Germans it was entirely real and well substantiated. If by the term "myth" we mean "unverified story" or "mistaken belief" then it is a matter of what one demands in the way of facts and proof to validate the story. Certainly a lesser set of facts would be acceptable as proof if the fact of Germany's stab in the back were not so directly linked to acts of Jews. Too many Jews to escape notice were propagandizing both the home front and the fighting front with antiwar and anti-German publications that were intended to sabotage the German war effort. Prominent members of the SPD and its various offshoots, and especially the USPD and the Spartacus League, fought against war credits, and the more radical elements of these political forces called for the violent overthrow of the government. Wartime strikes were used by these political elements as they attempted to realize their objectives. Luxemburg's Spartacus Letters were widely distributed by surreptitious means throughout the war, helping to demoralize the troops. Toward the end of the war, internal dissension, strikes, riots, mutinies, revolutions, and prevention of supply trains from reaching the front by Jewish-led SPD, USPD, and Spartacus League forces further contributed mightily to the "myth" of the stab in the back.

Historian Ernst Nolte noted that for middle-class Germans, "the experience of the Bolshevik revolution in Germany was so immediate, so close to home, and so disquieting, and statistics seemed to prove the overwhelming participation of Jewish ringleaders so irrefutable," that even liberals believed in Jewish responsibility.[915] Hitler commented on the lot of them; the shirkers, deserters, the revolutionaries, and pacifists: "these are the founders [of the new Republic] and their heroic acts consisted in leaving in the lurch the soldiers at the front, in stopping reinforcements, in withholding from them munitions, while at home against old men and half-starved children they carried through a revolutionary coup d'etat."[916] Such actual things as those just cited served as the pillars of the so-called myth of a stab in the back. The stab in the back had substance, and it created purulent wounds in which hate was to fester. Jews were the *Fons et origo malorum* of defeatism and incendiary revolution in Germany both during and after World War I. Whatever one may care to believe about the "myth," "there was more than enough festering support for the idea as a historical fact," says historian John Williams, "that it became a causal factor, 14 years after the armistice, in the ascent to power of Adolf Hitler."[917]

Hitler and his fellow soldiers had suffered four years of dehumanizing trench warfare: bombs and bullets to be sure, but also heat and cold, and fear, and vermin, and filth, and poor rations, and wetness and its resultant mud and trench foot, and disease, and asphyxiation, and death and dismemberment beyond description: lost eyes and limbs—and lost minds as well. Some soldiers were at times reduced to eating cats, dogs, and even rats to sustain themselves.[918] And there was a widely held perception that Jews were acting in direct opposition to their every sacrifice. Jews, according to the assessment of Hitler and many thousands of others, were stabbing the troops in the back. "He and those like him," says Toland, "burned with a zeal to avenge such treachery, and out of all this would come the politics of the future."[919] In his February 1915 letter to a lawyer friend, Hitler provided insight into his feelings at the time:

> I often think of Munich and every man of us has one wish, that we will come to blows and settle the score once and for all with that gang out there. We want an all out fight, at any cost, and hope that those of us who have the good fortune to see their homeland again will find it purer and less riddled with foreign [i.e., Jewish] influences. That through the sacrifices and sufferings which hundreds of thousands of us go through every day, that through the stream of blood that flows here daily against an international world of enemies, not only will Germany's enemies abroad be crushed, but that our

internal internationalism will also be broken. That would be worth much more than any territorial gains.[920]

Very few strikes took place during the initial years of the war, but by 1917, even the SPD, the least radical of the radicals, was no longer complying with its "peace in the castle" promise of August 1914. Inspired by Russian revolutionary activities in early 1917, a huge wave of munitions strikes took place throughout Germany.[921] In keeping with Luxemburg's revolutionary philosophy, these mass strikes were used to achieve political goals. The munitions workers were at the forefront. Roughly 500 strikes were called in 1917 alone; 2 million workers were involved.[922] Similar politically motivated strikes ensued in Vienna. In February, the undersecretary of state, Wahnschaffe, described the problems associated with the strikes in a letter to Ludendorff. He lamented that the situation was hopeless in the absence of support from workers and their leaders. And he lamented as well that nothing could be done to win over the leaders, much less suppress them at this late stage in the war. And the leaders to whom he was referring were people such as Cohen, Siering, Körsten, Hoffmann, Haase, Radek, Liebknecht, and Eisner. "Without these leaders," said Wahnschaffe, "and even more so against them, nothing can be done."[923]

Even Hitler acknowledged that the strikes ended too quickly to have a material effect on the overall war effort, but they did represent a massively hurtful blow to the psyche of German soldiers and the general populace. The German populace was seemingly abandoning its troops in the field. As Germany came close to winning the war with the Spring Offensive of 1918, munitions strikes again broke out, contributing still more fodder to the allegations of a stab in the back. The failure of the offensive was understandably blamed by a people desperate for victory on the strikes in the armaments industry at a critical moment of the offensive, leaving soldiers without the necessary arms and equipment to win the battle. The strikes were objectively seen as having been instigated by the Jewish leaders of the trade unions. Moreover, since so very many SPD and other Jewish-dominated political entities provided party leadership for the strikes, it was not overly irrational to assign a great measure of blame for the strikes to Jews in general.

Hitler would later say that Jews "organized the munitions strike,"[924] as, in fact, they had. Speaking of the strikes, he said that "In my regiment alone hundreds of soldiers lost their lives"[925] due to the strikes. Albert Speer recounted his own feelings about Hitler after Hitler had related this to him: "Never before had I felt so clearly how absolutely essential the figure of the Jew was for Hitler—as an object of hatred. . . ."[926] Government response to the strikes only compounded what damage had already been done. The drafting of thousands of the strike leaders and sending them to the front where they could ply their antiwar propaganda directly to the troops was but one salient example of the government's monumental stupidity. An even greater stupidity was in not crushing the radical dissidents early on.

Hitler's perception of the trade unions as being entirely in the hands of Jewish leadership was founded on fact: the parties with the greatest contingents of Jews were the leaders of the unions. Most trade unions were allied with the SPD, but the USPD and later the KPD were also very strong in union ranks, especially among the industrial workers in Berlin and the Ruhr, dockworkers in Hamburg and Bremen, and coal miners.

> The Jew, claimed Hitler, "divides the organization of his Marxist world doctrine into two halves which, apparently separate from one another, in truth form an inseparable whole: the political and the trade-union movement."[927] "The Jew," he said, "by means of the trade union . . . shatters the foundations of the national economy" and "parallel with this, the political organization advances. . . . Furthermore, it is the permanent financial source from which the political organization feeds its enormous apparatus. . . . mass and general strike, in the service of the political idea."[928]

In a Berlin speech to the Congress of the German Work Front on May 10, 1933, Hitler forcefully made the point that had the

German trade unions been in his hands during World War I such strikes would never have taken place[929]

Balfour Declaration

The years 1916 and 1917 were seminal for several of the warring nations. Great Britain was feeling the strain of Germany's submarine warfare, strains that included severe shortages of both food and ammunition. There were even portents of total defeat. After the war, British Prime Minister David Lloyd George recalled that "The submarine campaign . . . very nearly achieved the destruction of Britain's sea power."[930] In the postwar years, Churchill claimed that victory had been within Germany's grasp in the spring of 1917.

In February 1916, the Germans attacked at Verdun and gained significant early success, capturing considerable territory and key positions. Ultimately, however, the battle was fought to a stalemate with both sides suffering hideous losses, but for the time being, the French appeared to have suffered the greatest harm. This battle led to French mutinies in the field in April 1917. Lord Robert Cecil explained the overall situation to the British Cabinet saying that France was in turmoil, Italy was faltering, and Russia was on the verge of revolution.[931] The dire straits in which the Allies found themselves at this point made it urgent that the U.S. be enticed to enter the war and the means of achieving that objective was the Balfour Declaration.

In March 1916, the Germans defeated a Russian offensive at Vilna-Naroch that was launched as a French-requested counter to German successes at Verdun. The Russians suffered 70,000 to 100,000 casualties to Germany's 20,000. The Russian army was collapsing after suffering horrific losses due to poor equipment, incompetent training, terrible leadership, and successful Marxist revolutionary agitation. Both at home and in the field, the Marxists, 52 percent of whom were said to be Jewish,[932] were propagandizing the populace and the troops toward revolution.

As Jewish organizations inside Germany worked to undermine her cause, Jews in England and the United States worked for her defeat. The Microsoft Encarta Reference Library 2004 entry on the subject of the Balfour Declaration states the following:

> It has been commonly accepted that the Balfour Declaration was a unilateral undertaking by the British government. The immediate purpose was to win for the Allied cause in World War I the support of Jews and others in the warring nations and in neutral countries such as the United States.

That is, the primary rationale for the Balfour Declaration was to use it as an instrument to induce Jews to use their massive press, radio, and political power to propagandize the U.S. and thereby encourage American entry into the war. As put by the Jewish Marxist writer Lenni Brenner, "The Balfour Declaration was the price that London was prepared to pay to have American Jewry use its influence to bring the United States into the war. . . ."[933]

Another role of the declaration was to further encourage the Jews of Russia.

> Another most cogent reason for the adoption by the Allies of the policy of the declaration lay in the state of Russia herself. Russian Jews had been secretly active on behalf of the Central Powers from the first; they had become the chief agents of German pacifist propaganda in Russia; by 1917 they had done much in preparing for that general disintegration of Russian society, later recognised as the Revolution. It was believed that if Great Britain declared for the fulfilment of Zionist aspirations in Palestine under her own pledge, one effect would be to bring Russian Jewry to the cause of the Entente.[934] [Italics are in the original.]

For leftist Jews there was no conflict of interest in working against both the German and Russian belligerents: they had long sought the fall of Russia, and they firmly believed that the fall of Germany was a prerequisite for the worldwide propagation of Marxism; thus, both of them had to succumb.

World War I, The Opening Salvo of World War II

The perspective of the Allies was that if the Jews of Russia could be pacified, Russia would continue with its war effort. The Bolshevik Jews of Russia, however, were in no way motivated to see a Jewish state created in Palestine that was overseen by England, and they most certainly did not wish to see tsarist Russia participate in the victory of the Allies. Thus, this secondary objective of the Balfour Declaration failed: Russia sued for peace with Germany about a month after the Balfour Declaration was issued.

With America's entry into the war in April 1917 came veritably unlimited reserves of capital, manpower, natural resources, munitions, transport, and great productive capacity—the Allies could thereby shoot, move, and communicate as they were never before able, and they could do so with much larger formations provided by the Americans. The side that won America would win the war. And U.S. entry into the war stemmed in large part from Jews in the United States working in concert with Jews in England who were, in turn, acting in response to the Balfour Declaration. Thus, it was that the famous Balfour Declaration[*] made by Great Britain on November 2, 1917, had as its primary objective to draw American Jews to the cause of Great Britain, France, and Russia. While America's entry into the war preceded the publication of the Balfour Agreement, machinations behind the agreement commenced at the end of 1915, and it was not long afterward that Jewish personalities and groups in the U.S. began to pressure the Wilson administration to abandon its pledge to keep the U.S. out of the war.

The declaration was named for British Foreign Secretary Arthur James Balfour who had been instrumental in its development and approval and who had dispatched the final version of it to Lord Rothschild. In this declaration the British

---

[*] The Balfour Declaration, as Arthur Koestler pointed out, was one wherein "one nation [England] solemnly promised to a second nation [Jewry] the country of a third [Palestine]. More than that, the country was still part of the empire of a fourth, namely Turkey." See Robert John's *Behind the Balfour Declaration* (1988, 28).

made public their support for a Jewish homeland in Palestine. The declaration was the product of international intrigue and extensive negotiation. In Germany, it served as a vehicle for reasonable Germans to think that international Jewry had now openly sided with the Allies, which was, of course, indeed the case.

Zionists had since the late 1800s sought practical ways and means by which the long cherished dream of reestablishing a homeland for the Jewish people in Palestine might be realized. In 1915, as the Allies were suffering from fears that they might lose the war, the British cabinet was casting about for ways to draw the United States into the fracas on its side but was making precious little progress. The United States at that time was neutral, and President Wilson was publicly committed to keeping it so. American Jews were largely indifferent as to the potential outcome of the war: if the German side won, Jews would fare well; if the British prevailed, Jews would still do well. For American Jews, it was a choice between six and a half dozen. The Balfour Declaration motivated American Jews to take a stance.

"'It was fortunate for Zionism that the American Jews as a whole showed no enthusiasm for the Allied cause,' wrote Leonard Stein, political secretary of the Zionist Organization from 1920 to 1929, 'if they had all along been reliable friends, there would have been no need to pay them any special attention.'"[935] In fact, as Kevin MacDonald points out, the German-American-Jewish leaders of the Jewish Committee (AJCommittee) actually favored Germany in World War I, but only until the success of the Russian Revolution. The Germans were fighting the tsar and that was all that mattered to middle-of-the-road American Jews. Neither Germany itself nor the United States was of concern to them— their concern was only with their fellow Jews in Russia.[936] What became the Soviet Union was a veritable Promised Land for Jews: "it ended state anti-Semitism, tried to eradicate Christianity, opened opportunities to individual Jews, and preached a 'classless' society in which Jewishness would presumably attract no negative attention."[937]

Lucien Wolf, the secretary of the Conjoint Foreign Committee of the Board of Deputies of British Jews and of the Anglo-Jewish

Association, wrote a memorandum at the end of 1915 to Robert Cecil of the Foreign office. Wolf suggested that the way to obtain American support and involvement in the war was to appeal to American Zionists by promising them a Jewish homeland in Palestine. Wolf was convinced that should such a promise be made, "the whole of American Jewry will enter into enthusiastic allegiance" with the cause of the Allies.[938] Thus, it was reasoned, the way by which one could radicalize American fervor was by radicalizing the fervor of Jewish power in America.

The most prominent American Zionist at the time was the close friend of President Wilson and soon-to-be supreme court justice Louis Brandeis. James Malcolm and Sir Mark Sykes undertook efforts to win the support of Brandeis. This did not take much doing in that Brandeis was already a devout Zionist committed to the cause of providing Jews with a homeland in Palestine.[*] He believed that it was an absolute duty for all Jews to become Zionists. He also pushed for "cultural pluralism" of a kind that would later replicate East European culture in the U.S.[939] Chaim Weizmann, Nahum Sokolow, president of the World Zionist Congress, and the great financier Lord Rothschild, together, created the text of the declaration. The text was coordinated with other Jewish leaders in both England and America.

Germany had also recognized the power of American Jews to influence events and was itself courting the American Zionists. At the time, of course, Palestine was still in the hands of Germany's ally, Turkey. Germany therefore negotiated with Turkey in an

---

[*]"The first object, of course, was to enlist the very considerable and necessary influence of the Jews, and especially of the Zionist or Nationalist Jews, to help us bring America into the War at the most critical period of the hostilities." This was later publicly acknowledged by British Prime Minister Lloyd George. A second objective, according to Lloyd George, was "to enable and induce Jews all the world over to envisage constructive work as their proper field, and to take their minds off destructive and subversive schemes which . . . had provoked so much trouble and unrest in various countries, until their ever-increasing violence culminated in the Third International and the Russian Communist Revolution." Src: John, Robert. "Behind the Balfour Declaration." CODOH. 9 Nov. 2012. http://codoh.com/library/document/2137/?page=4 06/02/14

attempt to arrive at a scheme that would appeal to American Zionists. But for very practical, rather than patriotic, reasons, the American Zionists rejected the Germans. Brandeis and his friends turned a deaf ear to the Germans because, as he explained to Sir Cecil Spring-Rice, "under German control the (Zionist) idea could never be realized and that under English control their idea could be realized." By statements such as the foregoing, Brandeis and others who felt as he did were giving recognition to the fact that if the Jewish homeland in Palestine was engineered by the Germans it would necessarily be by way of its ally, Turkey; and they knew as well that so long as Turkey retained sovereignty over the area Jews were unlikely to fully realize their ambitions for statehood.

We are left to wonder how World War I might have ended if the Germans had been capable of making a more attractive offer to the Zionists.

Right-wing claims have it that upon agreement between the Zionists and the British as to the terms of the Balfour Declaration, the Jewish-owned press of Germany simultaneously redoubled its opposition to the war and labor strikes became more prevalent at the behest of Jewish-run unions. Whether true or untrue, it would certainly have seemed so to the likes of Hitler. The coincidence of timing was simply too blatant to ignore.

Upon completion of the agreement between Great Britain and the American Zionists, Brandeis, Bernard Baruch, and Rabbi Stephen Wise urged President Wilson to enter the war on behalf of the Allies. Wilson would soon thereafter abandon his campaign pledge to keep America out of the war. He would claim that he was motivated by Germany's unrestricted submarine warfare, but make no mistake about it, he was most powerfully motivated by Jews who fervently supported the Balfour Declaration.

The machinations related to the Balfour Declaration and America's entry into the war did not become public knowledge until well after its end, though the declaration itself was well-known toward the end of it as the Allies dropped leaflets to announce it in Jewish areas from Poland to the Black Sea (the area of the Pale of Settlement). The leaflet drops were intended to sway Jews in those areas to intervene in the Allied cause. In the 1930s, prominent statesmen such as James Malcolm and Winston Churchill publicly acknowledged that bringing the U.S. into the war was the principal object of the declaration.

The Balfour Declaration was a subterfuge. Its language was intentionally structured to win British and U.S. support, but simultaneously subsume its actual objective of imposing a Jewish state in Palestine. Even Lord Balfour, in August 1919, acknowledged the artifice: "So far as Palestine is concerned, the Powers have made no statement of fact which is not admittedly wrong and no declaration of policy which, at least in the letter, they have not always intended to violate."[940]

With the announcement and implementation of the Balfour Declaration we took the first steps along the road to the wars and ongoing violence in the Middle East. But more importantly for the moment of its announcement, it was the moment that Jews of America took sides and brought the U.S. into the war on behalf of the Allies. For Germany, the declaration was fateful.

Beyond the importance of the Balfour Declaration in bringing the U.S. into the war, it also invigorated the Jews of Europe. Leonard Stein described the situation thusly:

> In the enemy and enemy-occupied parts of Eastern Europe, and especially in Poland, the Jews were strongly moved by the Declaration. An eye-witness recalls that in Cracow "the Jews received the Balfour Declaration with indescribable joy. It would be no exaggeration to say that they ran amok with joy." A Jewish writer describes as follows the response to the Declaration in his native Galicia: "The Balfour Declaration not only gave courage to the Jews at a time when they were in need of such encouragement. . . . It gained a new ally for England. The hearts of the Jewish people began to beat for England, and we, Zionists, were happier with the victories of the Allies than the victories of the Germans." In Lemberg the local Jewish organ come out openly in praise of England: "The leading European Great Power has extended a hand to the Jewish people in order to lift

it up once more into the ranks of the independent self-governing races."[941]

Germans may be forgiven for having felt betrayed by the Jewish change of sides, for having felt that they were experiencing a stab in the back. Ludendorff and the German army had done everything possible to court the Jews of Eastern Europe. Their occupation of Jewish areas was exemplary in all respects.[942] They were the liberators of the Jews in the east. They quickly removed all hindrances to Jewish progress and engaged them in friendly, supportive dialogue and actions. It was all to no avail: with the Balfour Declaration, Jews of both the east and the German homeland turned their backs on them and went over to the side of the Allies, betraying a homeland that had faithfully embraced and nurtured them. Germany had taken them in when they were subjected to repression in the East, and Germans therefore rightfully anticipated and expected in return at least a modicum of loyalty from Jews. Their expectations proved to be dissapointing.

Beginning of the End

The capital ships of the German navy had sortied in late May 1916, engaging the British Grand Fleet at the Battle of Jutland. Greatly outnumbered and outclassed, the Germans, nevertheless, managed to destroy three British battle cruisers, three light cruisers, and eight destroyers. German losses were one old battleship, one battle cruiser, four light cruisers, and five destroyers. Though the Germans had fared pretty well in the battle, their losses were sufficient to encourage them to thereafter retain their capital ships in port for the remainder of the war.

With Germany's heaviest naval power out of the war, the British blockade of the North Sea was unchallenged and having its intended effect.

Germany had always been highly dependent on imports for both raw materials and foodstuffs. In particular, about one-third of its foodstuffs and roughly 27 percent of its proteins and 40 percent of its fats were from imports.[943] The blockade of the North Sea was devastating and was compounded by the fact that so many farmers had been called to the front. Food was so scarce that the winter of 1916–1917 would be known in Germany as the Turnip Winter, the winter during which Germans had little to eat save food intended for cattle. Average caloric intake had dropped to 1,350 instead of the normal intake of about 2,000.[944] Worse yet, Jews, as the traditional leaders in the grain and cattle trading businesses,[*] were well positioned to withhold such commodities from the market, drive up prices, and thereby enjoy unseemly profits stemming from the restricted supply. The potato harvest of 1916 is illustrative: it had fallen to 23 million tons from the prewar production of 46 million. Six million of the 23 million tons never reached the open market. "The black market," says Pierre Broué and his coauthors, "flourished, and the opulence of speculators was a standing insult to the workers' districts and to the emaciated soldiers who emerged from time to time on leave from the hell of the battlefield."[945] By just such practices and observations, Jews, who were so very predominant as middle men in the realm of agricultural trade, were deemed to be rapacious profiteers.

Still, for all of the problems pressing on the German populace, government, and military, on balance, it seemed that they were still the strongest during this time and the high command remained confident of ultimate victory.

In November 1916, Henry Petty-Fitz Maurice, fifth Marques of Landsdowne, published a call for Great Britain to negotiate a peace with Germany on a status quo antebellum basis. The Lansdowne Letter, as the peace overture came to be known, was rejected by Germany's military leaders, who, given the balance of things in 1916, saw no reason to accept such an offer. Victory could still be theirs. It should be said that in spite of the dire circumstances facing them, British generals continued to feel likewise. Still, the fact that such a call was made by such a

---

[*] Jews have traditionally been intermediaries between the countryside and the city. They would purchase farm products for sale in the city and sell city-manufactured products in the countryside, a function that was "the characteristic quality or trait of the Jews in European history." [Haumann, 27]

prominent figure illustrates the perception of the dire straits in which Great Britain found itself in 1916.

In the fall of 1917, tsarist Russia fell to the Communists. Germany aided Vladimir Lenin's relocation from Switzerland to Russia in order that he could secure the revolution and bring an end to hostilities between Russia and Germany. The German assistance was engineered by Alexander Parvus. Alexander Kerensky, who was at the time the leader of the Russian Revolution, was in favor of continuing the war.

In Germany, the terrible privations of the Turnip Winter of 1916–1917 were exceeded by the miseries of 1918–1919. Neither food, nor fuel, nor medicine was available in adequate supply. Some 730,000 to 800,000 deaths were attributed to the ongoing blockade of the North Sea, and the deaths occurred mostly among women and children. In Vienna, one baby in four died of starvation. Similar mortality rates from starvation were experienced in Germany. The blockade was left in place even after the war ended. The Allies, in still another illustration of the pilpul method, claimed that they were forced to continue the blockade, *after the cessation of hostilities* "by the criminal character to the war imposed on them by Germany."[946]

The outbreak of a devastating strain of influenza in 1918 was especially hard on the weak, starving German populace. On a single day, October 18, 1918, influenza claimed the lives of 1,700 people in Berlin alone.[947] In the field, a total of about 1.75 million German soldiers fell victim to influenza during the period March–July 1918, a period during which casualties due to fighting amounted to 750,000.[948]

For Hitler, there was still another lesson to be learned from the war. The British blockade of the North Sea during World War I was disastrously harmful to the war effort. It starved Germany of raw materials needed for the war and also of necessary foodstuffs for the population. If Germany was to secure its future she needed to have unlimited access to critical raw materials such as iron and oil and farmland. The ability of the British to so easily and thoroughly blockade German imports from the North Sea and thereby literally starve the German nation made it imperative that

Germany find all of its needed resources on the European continent. There were vast food-producing resources in the Ukraine, there was oil in Romania, and the whole of the East was plentiful with various other resources needed in the modern age. World War I provided Hitler with powerful incentives to seek national security by conquering lands to the east. Clearly, he learned an important strategic lesson during World War I. He stated the issue thusly: "I don't want free trade, open borders. That all sounds wonderful. But we've had it if everything depends on the queen of the waves, if we're subject to a blockade."[949] Indeed.

And if he, in his wildest dreams and fantasies, ever managed to achieve power, something would be done about that. He would not forget its import.

Treaty of Brest-Litovsk*

The triumph of the Russian Bolsheviks in November 1917 led to the Treaty of Brest-Litovsk on March 3, 1918, taking Russia out of the war. For all of its difficulties on both the home front and warfront, the treaty gave new hope and vigor to Germany's war effort. Serbia and Romania had already succumbed. The Germans now had the vast breadbasket of Europe, the Ukraine, at their disposal. Over a million German troops could be released from service in the east and applied in the west.[950] Finally, the Germans felt that they were in a position to deal a crushing blow on the western front. It was not to be. Hitler would later recount his perception of events concerning Germany's victory over Russia:

> When the Germans had forced Russia out of the war and transferred their "undivided forces" to the Western Front, the Allied troops "faith in victory gave way to fear."

---

* In negotiating the terms of this treaty, demands were made by leftist USPD elements that "workers" be given a role in the negotiations. The "workers" cover was actually a call by Jewish leftists to participate in sympathy with the Jews who were leading the revolution in Russia.

> At the very moment when the German divisions were receiving their final orders for the great offensive a general strike broke out in Germany. . . . All of a sudden a means had come which could be utilized to revive the sinking confidence of the [Allied] soldiers . . . revolution . . . in the Fatherland.
>
> British, French and American newspapers began to spread this belief among their readers while a very ably managed propaganda encouraged the morale of their troops at the front.[951]

Victory over Russia, initially thought to be the salvation of Germany's war effort, came to naught. Germans did transfer troops westward but politically contaminated troops from the eastern front did little more than agitate on behalf of Marxism and incite mutiny when they reached the trenches in France and Belgium. Troop trains arrived on the western front flying the red flags of the revolutionaries. Hitler purportedly got into a fistfight with one of the young soldiers newly sent to the western front. He took a pummeling at first but ultimately managed to overcome his opponent and thereby won both the fight and renewed respect from his fellow soldiers.[952]

The Treaty of Brest-Litovsk[*] was brutal for the Russians, yet for all of its punitive aspects, it did give the Russian Bolsheviks one significant advantage: it provided for diplomatic relations between Germany and Russia, a fact that would be important to later developments in Germany. The Bolsheviks used their diplomatic status with Germany as a means to install additional revolutionaries there and to provide conduits for financial aid from Russia to the German Marxists. In particular, Adolf Abramovich Joffe, the Jewish head of the negotiating team for the Treaty of Brest-Litovsk, became the Soviet ambassador to Germany. He and

---

[*] Territorial concessions that had as their objective both the security of Germany's borders and also the acquisition of continental sources of farmland and other natural resources of the kind needed in modern war economies.

a large contingent of other Russians (over 300) relocated to Berlin along with gold and cash aplenty. The Russian cash was used by Joffe to sponsor Marxist revolutionary activity in Germany. Joffe and his staff provided both the USPD and the Spartacus League with money and skilled Russian agitators.[953] Pouches that were protected by diplomatic immunity were used to smuggle in revolutionary propaganda.

The Marxists of Germany were thrilled by the revolutionary success and prospects of their Russian brethren and were thereby encouraged to quickly apply Russian revolutionary strategies and tactics to seize power in Germany. In particular, the Spartacists decided to culminate their years of political struggle and agitation for a course of events in Germany that would mirror the successful outcome for Marxists in Russia: revolution in the armed forces and labor strikes at home.

Rosa Luxemburg set out across Germany to conduct innumerable meetings wherein she spoke as a representative of the Russian Revolution and propagated the ideas of that turmoil.[954] Now was the time to bring to fruition all that she and her comrades had worked for so diligently and long. Now was the time to move the Marxists notions so long propagated by the German Left from the heads of the people to their fists.* Now was the time to execute the strategy developed by Luxemburg in 1906: the time to employ the great lessons of the Russian Revolution, to use "general strikes, partial strikes; sabotage in industry, commerce and transport; military uprisings; the stopping of trains by strikers, etc."[955] By January 1918, the labor unions were striking in Austria, Poland, Hungary, and Germany. By late January, there were over 1 million German workers on strike in Berlin and in over fifty other cities.[956] In October, some 50,000 people joined with the USPD in Berlin to demand the overthrow of the government. The home front soldiers, sailors, and unionists were in the vanguard of Germany's turmoil, and they were led on the whole by Marxist Jews. The seeds of ceaseless Spartacist agitation had by now sprouted, matured, and

---

* The notion of moving emotions from "head to fists" was taken from Frölich (105).

were bearing the fruit of angst and discord. Now it had only to be harvested.

The last gasp of the German army was a great offensive that commenced in March 1918. By August, it had fizzled. In the meantime, massive amounts of propagandistic literature was smuggled into Germany and distributed to soldiers, sailors, and workers. Most of the propaganda originated in Russia and was transported to Germany for further distribution by Joffe. By early August, Marxist agitation had rendered Germany's military situation untenable. The kaiser was fretting about reports that great numbers of desertions were taking place and red flags were flying on troop trains arriving at the front. Germany's most powerful ally, Austria-Hungary, was visibly collapsing in the summer of 1918 so that Germany's southern flank was soon to be laid bare. Though Germany still retained some strength at that point,[957] it quickly became clear within Germany itself that she could not hold out much longer.

In August 1918, Ludendorff proposed a defensive strategy that he hoped would break the Allies' morale and cause them to sue for peace or at the very least provide Germany with an armistice based on a position of strength. To pull off such a strategy, though, Ludendorff needed better discipline within the army and the populace.[958] It was not to be.[959] It was by now far too late to suppress the Marxist agitators. By early October, adding to her military woes was the fact that the country was on the verge of a Marxist revolution. One hundred thousand or more desertions had already occurred within the ranks of the badly demoralized troops, and the rate was on the rise. Supply trains to the front were sabotaged by Marxists. Strikes were again breaking out. Major railroad junctions were controlled by the revolutionaries. Still, it was due more to a lack of political will and dissension in the ranks than actual capability that the great army of 1914 was, by this time, utterly incapable of defeating even its opponents on the home front. "To stout spirits like Hitler," says Toland, "the secure and unmolested home front, its laggards, its profiteers, its malingerers, its traitors, its Jews who had no love or respect for the German Fatherland had betrayed the fighting front in its gravest hour",[960] and while our historians proclaim the facts to be otherwise, to stout hearts like Hitler, it had to seem apparent that indeed they had.

Hitler complained that in the closing stages of the war, replacements received at the front were a sorry lot, poisoned by the propaganda on the home front, propaganda that was inspired, organized, and propagated by revolutionary Jewish leaders and their surrogates. He commented on the turmoil griping and sapping German strength as follows:

> [T]he reinforcements coming from home rapidly grew worse and worse, so that their arrival meant, not a reinforcement but a weakening of our fighting strength. Especially the young reinforcements were mostly worthless. It was often hard to believe that these were sons of the same nation which had once sent its youth out to the battle for Ypres.
>
> In August and September, the symptoms of disorganization increased more and more rapidly, although the effect of the enemy attack was not to be compared with the terror of our former defensive battles. The past Battle of Flanders and the Battle of the Somme had been awesome by comparison.[961]

In late September there was a meeting that included representatives of the German army and leaders of the various political parties. The Supreme Command informed the attendees that the army wanted to seek an armistice. Nearly everyone was aghast and speechless. "Only one man, the Jewish Independent Socialist Hugo Haase, could find words," says historian Richard Watt. "He appeared overjoyed at the development. 'Now we have got them!' he exclaimed to a colleague."[962] This was the same Haase who was the spiritual leader of the Kiel Mutiny and who, in 1914, had declared his desire to undermine the German army and set the stage for world revolution.[963] In the new leftist government installed in late 1918, Haase would be appointed to a position of second in command.

Some politicians and generals continued to believe that the army could stand. At the very least, it was thought, the army could quell the revolutionary movements and continue to fight until an acceptable armistice could be had. It was wishful thinking. There were just too many obstacles. The morale of the sick and starving people had been utterly sapped, not the least by the revolutionary agitation that was so prevalent in their midst. In late October 1918, the Jew Friedrich Stamper demanded in the Jewish-operated SDP newspaper *Vorwarts*[*] that Germany strike her colors: "Germany must—that is our firm volition a [sic] socialists—strike her colour's forever without having brought them home victoriously for the last time,"[964][†] wrote Stamper. Hitler took note of the *Vorwärts* position in *Mein Kampf*: "It takes a truly Jewish effrontery," said he, "to attribute the blame for the collapse solely to the military defeat when the central organ of all traitors to the nation, the Berlin *Vorwärts*, wrote that this time the German people must not bring its banner home victorious!"[965] With a stronger government and determined people, such a demand would have been deemed treasonous, and suppressive action would have been immediate and harsh. In the Germany of late 1918, it was seen as inevitable, demand or no demand, from the likes of Stamper.

There was little confidence that the army could be used to suppress the revolutionary turmoil on the home front, much less hold a line against the Allied armies. Any attempt to suppress the leadership of the revolutionary forces at home would have been met by violent upheavals from the labor unions and more sabotage against the troops at the war front. Civil war would have ensued. Only the most obtuse patriots could call for a continuation of

---

[*] With only a single exception, the entire editorial staff of *Vorwärts* (Forward) was Jewish by 1929. Other Marxist publications that were Jewish run included the *Roten Fahne* (Red Flag—Luxemburg and Liebknecht) and *Freiheit* (Freedom—Hilferding and Herzt). In 1923, *Vorwärts* lost a libel trial brought by Adolf Hitler, and was ordered to pay him 6,000,000 marks. The paper had claimed Hitler was financed by "American Jews and Henry Ford." Src: http://en.wikipedia.org/wiki/Vorw%C3%A4rts
[†] This was a Nazi publication.

hostilities. At least one prominent Jew, Walter Rathenau, was among those who wanted to continue the fight.

It was over. The war was lost. There would be some last-ditch efforts to continue fighting, but there was no realistic chance of success. As Stephen Lee points out, "The combined forces of Britain, the [British] Empire [e.g., Canada, Australia, Irland, South Africa, New Zealand, India, etc.], France, Russia and Italy had been insufficient to defeat the Second Reich and it needed the intervention of the United States to guarantee Allied victory"[966]— and that intervention had been orchestrated by Jewry in response to the Balfour Declaration.

Germany might have gone on to fight a defensive war in hopes of attaining a just armistice but even this prospect had little chance of success. America now had in excess of 500,000 troops in France and was increasing that strength at the rate of 10,000 per day. The U.S. was also flooding the Allies with both supplies and renewed vigor. Cargo ships were departing the U.S. for France at the rate of one every five hours. Germany would need to accept an unconditional armistice. It was abject surrender by another name. Hindenburg would later comment in his memoirs that "Like Siegfried, slain by the treacherous spear of the grim Hagen, our exhausted front collapsed."[967]

Germany, according to both Ludendorff and Hindenburg,[*] had been stabbed in the back, and any truly rational assessment of the time could not help but concur with his conclusion. Their assessment of things simply highlighted a broad-based conclusion stemming from the fact that so very many Jews were prominent in government circles and of the revolutionary activities of the Spartacists and USPD during the war. And, too, there was the critical role played by Jews in bringing the U.S. into the war.

Liebknecht, Luxemburg, and their Spartacist followers, along with the USPD leaders and members, had tirelessly agitated both the general populace of Germany and the military services

---

[*] In November 1919, Hindenburg declared, "As an English general has very truly said, the German Army was 'stabbed in the back.'"

throughout the war. With respect to the military it had long been their objective to draw sections of the army and navy into their revolutionary circle, mutiny, and thereby make others parts of the military waver and erode military strength and discipline. As armistice discussions and changes to the government were taking place in Berlin, their organizational efforts, "pacifist" publications, and tireless sloganeering bore fruit.

Kiel Mutiny

On October 7, 1918, the sailors of the fleet at Kiel mutinied. The immediate cause of the mutiny was an order for the navy to at last sortie and engage the British in the North Sea, but the underlying readiness for it stemmed from the many months of tireless efforts on the part of Marxists, and most especially, the Spartacists and Independent Socialists. Taking a lesson from Russian revolutionaries, they had spent several months prior to the mutiny organizing secret action committees of sailors and stokers on ships. When news spread of the order for the capital ships of the German navy to at long last sally forth and actually do battle, the fruit of the revolutionary preparedness was harvested. Mutiny ensued. Only a single ship, the *Koenig*, remained loyal and steadfast and refused to raise the red flag.

By November 4, 1918, some 100,000 mutinous sailors were included in the fray. Factory workers and 20,000 garrison troops in Kiel had joined with the mutineers.

That the Kiel Mutiny and its many offshoots were not "spontaneous" uprisings as so frequently claimed, is evidenced by the subversive planning and actions of the revolutionary parties months prior to the event. It can also be gleaned from the fact that so many of the leaders and participants in the mutiny later acknowledged their close association with those revolutionary parties.

In accordance with other lessons taken from the Russian Revolution of the previous year, sailors', soldiers', and workers' councils (Soviets) were purportedly "spontaneously" formed everywhere and began to exercise governmental authority in a manner that mimicked the experiences in Russia during the 1905 and 1917 revolutions. The councils were instituted by the radical leadership of the sailors and soldiers and, according to historian Amos Elon, "featured a disproportionate number of Jews."[968] While on the whole their general membership was certainly less radical than that of their instigators, had they remained in existence under a Communist regime in Germany, they would doubtless have been no more effectual than they had ultimately been in Russia, their birthplace. The Spartacist view of the council system was that they would be used as tools for the promotion of public ownership of industry and the establishment of a Bolshevistic dictatorship along Russian lines—they were certainly *not* "spontaneous" constructs whose purpose was to further workers' rights as so many historians claim[969]—though many individual members of the Soviets may have thought that to be the case. As in Russia, the soldiers' and sailors' councils of Germany would have been pushed aside and made to conform to the dictates of the leadership. For the moderate faction of the Social Democrats and Friedrich Ebert in particular, the councils were viewed as the very embodiment of radical Bolshevism and were roundly condemned.[970] The various councils pushed positions that were in keeping with the party leadership of the Spartacists and the USPD. That so many artists and writers joined them was indicative of the radical leftist leanings of the leadership, people like Liebknecht, Luxemburg, the poet Rainer Maria Rilke, the sociologist Max Weber, and the anarchist Erich Muehsam, and Gershom and Betty Scholem

Military officers were beaten and killed; one officer was thrown off a bridge and then shot dead as he attempted to swim ashore.[971] Armories were looted, food supplies were forcibly "requisitioned." Artists and writers soon joined the fray, founding collectives and councils and issuing manifestos that called for the overthrow of everything that was old and stultified.[972] By November 3, Kiel was completely under the control of the radical Marxists and other cities soon followed. Renewed sabotage activity was used to block war materials from reaching the front.

The so-called pacifists were everywhere calling for armed rebellion.

Forever drawing parallels between the Russian revolution and their own, the German Communists saw the Kiel Mutiny as the German equivalent of the uprising on the Russian battleship Potemkin in 1905, an event credited with being an initial step in the successful Russian Revolution of 1917. They reasoned that the Kiel Mutiny would now lead to successful Communist revolution throughout Germany. And just such an outcome seemed to be in the offing.

From Kiel, revolutionary fervor fanned by the propaganda of the Spartacists and other members of the radical Left spread to other ports. Soon the cities of Hamburg, Wilhelmshaven, Lübeck, Brunsbüttel, Cuxhaven, Rundsberg, Warnemüde, Rostock, Bremerhaven, and Geestemünde were caught up in mutiny and revolution, and revolutionary fervor immediately spread from those coastal cities to the interior. By early November, Düsseldorf, Frankfurt-am-Main, Stuttgart, Leipzig, and Magdeburg had succumbed. Red rebellions were also taking place at Halle, Halstein, Osnabrück, and Cologne.[973]

Jews were installed in important government positions within the various German states. The imperial flag was retired. The red flag of the revolution was everywhere hoisted in its stead. In Berlin, fabric stores ran out of red cloth due to the demands made by people manufacturing homemade revolutionary flags and banners.[974] After the republic was established, the black, red, and gold revolutionary flag of 1848 was adopted: that decision enraged the nationalists, causing one Freikorps commander to denounce it as a "Jewish rag,"*[975] an epithet that such people also applied to the red flags of the Soviets.

The sailors had been thoroughly radicalized by the USPD and Spartacists and were only awaiting the opportune moment to strike a fatal blow to the German military and monarchy. Wherever the red flag of the Communists was hoisted, it was the hand of a USPD

---

* Today's German flag retains those colors.

member or Spartacist that grasped at the halyard. From the outset of 1918 and with financial aid provided by Russia and fellow Jews, the most radical members of the USPD and Spartacist parties, men such as Haase and Emil Barth, carefully prepared for armed rebellion. Barth, who was among the most radical of the revolutionaries, had long been collecting weapons to serve his revolutionary aims. His intent was to use the workers' and soldiers' councils as the armed soldiers of his revolutionary conception. As things would happen, Ebert, to his great credit, immediately recognized the threat posed by the various councils and took action to ensure that less radical people were included in their ranks, thus marginalizing both the power of the councils and their USPD and Spartacist sponsors. Barth's and Haase's plans fell short of their objectives but were, for a short time, successful in Berlin. The councils there were particularly powerful and radical and armed by Barth.

* * * *

It was eminently clear that if Germany was to sue for peace it would need to do so with a different government, and President Wilson, to whom the Germans were making their armistice overture, insisted on it. Prince Max von Baden, a non-Prussian liberal, was installed by the kaiser as chancellor. The installation of Prince Max was engineered primarily by the efforts of the Jewish politician Kurt Hahn who was a member of the Foreign Affairs ministry and had close ties to the Imperial Foreign Ministry, Wilhelm Solf.

On October 5, Prince Max announced to a crowded Reichstag chamber that he had made an appeal for an armistice to President Wilson. The news was gladly received. Many of the Reichstag members did not consider Wilson to be an enemy.[*] Upon the

---

[*] It is a strange thing, is it not, that the president of a country whose troops are doing battle with your own is not considered an enemy? These were strange times, indeed.

conclusion of the speech, USPD members shouted for an amnesty, which everyone knew was a demand for the release of Rosa Luxemburg, Karl Liebknecht, and other such leftist radicals.[976] The amnesty was approved. The radicals were released, and they immediately thereafter added to the chaos and misery of the German condition.

Prince Max was the chancellor, but real power in the government was still held by General Erich Ludendorff—even the great Hindenburg did his bidding. Shortly after his appointment as chancellor, Max demanded that the kaiser remove Ludendorff. His leverage for such insistence was that if Ludendorff did not go, he and his government would resign, and thereby endanger the peace overtures to President Wilson.

The kaiser and his advisors thought that the removal of Ludendorff would materially improve the chances for the kaiser himself to retain power, if only in a greatly reduced version of that power. It was a certainty that William would no longer be kaiser but it was hoped that he might at least retain his position as the king of Prussia. Kaiser William therefore readily complied with the demand. Ludendorff was removed on October 27. On November 9, 1918, it became the turn of the kaiser himself to step down. The new government, in compliance with further demands by Wilson, required that the kaiser abdicate. The kaiser renounced his crown, paving the way for an armistice.

Google	URL
Prince Max von Baden	http://en.wikipedia.org/wiki/Prince_Maximilian_of_Baden 8/2/14
Gen. Erich Ludendorff	http://en.wikipedia.org/wiki/Erich_Ludendorff 8/2/14
Paul von Hindenburg	http://en.wikipedia.org/wiki/Paul_von_Hindenburg 8/2/14
Friedrich Ebert	http://en.wikipedia.org/wiki/Friedrich_Ebert 8/2/14
Hugo Haase	http://en.wikipedia.org/wiki/Hugo_Haase 8/2/14

Kaiser William II, the man who had dismissed Bismarck before the war and Ludendorff at the end of it, the man who had tried so hard to accommodate the Jewish-led Socialists and was happy to enjoy Jewish society and generosity, left office spitting venom against them: "Let no German ever forget this, or rest until these parasites have been extirpated and exterminated from German soil. This toadstool on the German oak!"[977] As previously highlighted, the causal nexus of his own actions in shaping the disaster did not earn comment from him.

According to historian William Shirer, Hitler had seen the fall of the Second Reich in terms of William II's tolerance of Jews and Marxists and the catastrophic German alliance policy that linked Germany to "the degenerate Hapsburgs [Habsburgs] and the untrustworthy Italians instead of with England, and the lack of a fundamental 'social' and racial policy."[978] He often commented on the need for Germany to establish close relations with England, as he did in one of his many conversations with Otto Wagener which typifies his attitude: "I turned away from a naval policy [against England], even from a colonial policy, to return to a Continental policy such as Bismarck pursued. I do not *want* to fight against England, nor do I want to *act* against England."[979] (Italics are in the original.) He had also frequently commented on the disastrous consequence of Germany's attempt to engage in a two-front war. Upon taking power, he was determined that he would not repeat the errors of the Second Reich. When his turn came, however, he went about, in several respects, doing just that: in particular, he allied himself with Italy instead of England—England would not have him—and engaged in a catastrophic alliance with Japan. Worst of all, he ultimately maneuvered Germany into a two-front war.

On November 9 the monarchy fell and SPD leader Friedrich Ebert was handed the reins of power by Prince Max. Max had been appointed by the kaiser, but now that the kaiser was no longer in power he felt it incumbent upon himself to relinquish his own power to the headiest political party then extant, the SPD and its party leader Frederich Ebert.

The provisional government formed by Ebert included Jewish USPD member Hugo Haase, a man among many who had diligently worked throughout the war to sabotage the German war effort in order to spur a Marxist revolution, and now it came to be that he was installed as Ebert's deputy.

Haase tried to attach conditions for his party's (USPD) participation in the government, conditions that would decidedly favor him and his cohorts. He demanded that the new government be composed entirely of Marxist Social Democrats and that it be empowered as the People's Commissars, a title that reflected his Bolshevik leanings. All political power, he demanded, must lay in the hands of the workers' and soldiers' councils, which, of course, favored the USPD since it was so very influential in their establishment and because it continued to exert such dominant influence over them. He also demanded that the proposed convocation of the constituent assembly be postponed until he, the USPD, and the SPD, were able to consolidate the gains they had realized thus far. Such a move would undoubtedly enable them to put into place barriers to their opponents and thereby enable them to win the day at the assembly. He named himself as one of the three USPD deputies who were to serve in the cabinet.[980] His duplicity was boundless. Jewish SPD member Otto Landsberg and the radical Jewish USPD politician Emil Barth were also among the six people who made up the top leadership of the new regime. Included, too, was the outstanding conservative politician Philipp Scheidemann, whose Jewish wife prompted derision of him as an ersatz Jew—but, as time would tell, was a wholly improper charge. Rounding out the administration were several Jewish department heads and deputies, including Hugo Preuss, Eugen Schiffer, Emanuel Wurm, Joseph Herzfeld, Eduard Bernstein, and Oskar Cohn. As stated by Kauders in German *Politics and the Jews*:

> The events surrounding the Revolution . . . gave rise to questions about Jews in prominent positions of leadership. If before 1914 complaints had centered on "Jewish influence" in the media or the arts, in the period after 1918 it was far easier to preserve, invent, and inculcate anti-Semitic stereotypes. Names like Luxemburg, Eisner, Toller, Preuß [Preuss], and

Rathenau, among others, testified to anti-Semitic suspicions.[981]

As the new government was formed, Rosa Luxemburg and Karl Liebknecht, along with the Jewish leaders in Bavaria, represented the threat of Jewish revolution. In addition to the people just cited above, the nationalists could point to a number of other Jews of prominence within the hated republic to support the contention that the government was indeed in Jewish hands. Among them were Moritz Liebmann, James Goldschmidt, State Counselor of Law Löwenstein, the Prussian Justice Minister Kurt Rosenfeld, Kantorowicz, Gumbel, Freymuth, Werthauer, and others. Rosenfeld garnered special hatred by way of his early and enduring advocacy of full German compliance with the Treaty of Versailles. Rathenau's support for full compliance materially contributed to the motivation for his subsequent assassination, as did his Jewishness.

In Frankfurt, Düsseldorf, and Nuremberg, as well as the entirety of Prussia, prominent Jews were installed at the top of the political leadership. It was not particularly irrational to see Jews at the apex of all German politics. The *Düsseldorfer Sonntagsblatt* complained that Jews had so insinuated themselves into the German leadership that they threatened the "natural order of things."[982] The SPD, claimed the *Sonntagsblatt*, was led by "alien" non-Germans (Marx, Frank, Bernstein, and Luxemburg). Frankfurt, it was claimed, had become a "stronghold of new Jewry [*Neujudentums*]."[983] "The paper," says Kauders, "also associated Jews with prostitution, atheism, and finance capital."[984]

On November 11, 1918, the armistice was implemented. With civil war breaking out everywhere in Germany and the southern flank of its war effort by now in tatters, the German government had little choice but accede to demands made by the Allies. The war was over. Germany and her allies lay prostrate. So ended the Second Reich that Bismarck established in 1871. Ended, too, for the time being, was Germany's place in the forefront of political, social, and military power.

The liberal Jewish leadership welcomed the revolution that ended the war, believing it to be a victory for "'the spirit [of] freedom and justice,' they were confident that 'a relationship of friendship and sympathy would very soon develop between the new Germany and Jewry.'"[985] Such an assessment highlighted the fact that there was at the time—especially among Jews—a perceived disjoint between Jews and Germans. With Jews now so prevalent in the leadership it was presumed by some that the disjoint would now be melded.

In subsequent weeks, German soldiers withdrew from France and Belgium into Germany, and they did so with impressive order and discipline. As Richard Watt describes it,

> These troops were defeated but they were still soldiers, not a rabid mob. The front line soldiers, those who had suffered the most, remained true to their calling. The "home front" soldiers, the sailors, and the unionists were in the vanguard of Germany's toil, and they were led by communist Jews.[986]

Upon return to Germany the troops were quickly ordered to demobilize, an order that was at least in part intended to make it easier for the radicals to carry forward with their revolution. Within thirty days of the armistice, Germany was militarily defunct, utterly powerless.

Upon their return to Berlin, Chancellor Ebert welcomed the returning troops with the declaration that they had returned from the battlefield unvanquished.[987] He would soon regret his words. His declaration seemed to suggest that Germany could have prevailed if only she had held fast—her troops, after all, were "unvanquished." Ebert's words were used by radical rightist elements to support their contention that Germany would have been victorious, or at the very least would have won a better peace—a better fate—if only her "unvanquished" troops had not been stabbed in the back by Jewish-Marxist elements.

At war's end, Adolf Hitler was still recovering from his wounds of October 13–14 at a hospital in Pasewalk, Pomerania. In short order, he learned of the mutiny in Kiel, the fall of the kaiser, and the end to the war. Hitler observed the revolutionaries raise the red flag of Marxism there. According to his account of the incident, it was three Jews, none of whom had served at the front, who hoisted the red flag. He does not provide an account of how he knew they were Jews or how he knew they had not served at the front except to say that they had previously been hospital orderlies at a gonorrhea hospital behind the front.

German troops were everywhere ensconced on enemy soil and no enemy soldier was on German soil, yet it was Germany that succumbed and surrendered. Stolfi puts the whole of it in clear perspective, as follows:

> It must be acknowledged as a remarkable circumstance that the losing army occupied positions almost entirely within the territory of the victors. And the armistice would be forced by armed rebellion in Germany, as it were, in the back of the field armies and not in the face of Allied arms and resultant surrender and captivity.[988]

Hitler was, of course, shattered when the news of the armistice was announced to him and others by a clergyman. He later described his feelings in *Mein Kampf*: "There followed terrible days and even worse nights—I knew that all was lost . . . in these nights hatred grew in me, hatred for those responsible for this deed."[989] Here was a young man of twenty-nine years who had bravely endured the hardships and horrors of more than four years of particularly brutal combat. Twice seriously wounded (and perhaps another time slightly wounded early in the war) and several times cited for his extraordinary bravery, and all for naught: "all the sacrifices and privations, the hunger and thirst . . . in vain the death of two million . . . was it for this [Jewish-led revolution] that boys of seventeen sank into the earth of Flanders . . . was it all 'only so that a gang of wretched criminals could lay hands on the fatherland?'"[990] He later wrote, "What was the pain in my eyes [stemming from the gas attack that hospitalized him] compared to this misery?"

In typical fashion, Hitler's grief for Germany was greater than that which he felt for his own pain and suffering. How could it be that the fatherland adopted by him had entered the war full of confidence and verve and that had both attacked and defended so courageously, how could it now be brought to such a tragic state of being, of defeat? Germany's soldiers had fought every battle with great courage and tenacity. Not a single Allied boot had landed on German soil.* Germany had been shelling Paris only three months prior. The defense lines were still holding, though shabbily. Just that past summer German victory seemed all but assured. According to Fest, even "The defensive battles of that final phase were, in both military and human terms, among the most impressive achievements of the war, and paradoxically added to the myth of the German army."[991] Germany's soldiers had done their duty; they had acquitted themselves in the finest traditions of their people. Now they were suffering in defeat. How could that be? Who was responsible for this calamity? Who was responsible for this awful result? Who was he to hate? For Hitler the answer was clear.

It did not take much for a man of Hitler's intellect to discern the culprits for Germany's ultimate collapse on the battlefield. The disarray and disunity of the political class, the Marxist propaganda, the multitude of labor strikes, the fracturing of the will of the German people: it all had a single source—it was, concluded Hitler . . . the Jews. And however much we may today care to deny it, Hitler's assessment of Germany's political and social condition was rational. It had indeed been Jews who were at the forefront of Germany's internal dissension, whether civil, military, or political in nature. Every radically leftist group was headed by Jews and not a single radically rightist group was led by them. And to the extent that morale is a factor in warfare, certain activist Jews were rightly

---

* This oft-made claim is not entirely true, technically. Early in the war (August 17, 1914), Russian troops briefly occupied territory in East Prussia. Following their losses at the battles of Tannenberg and Masurian Lakes, the Russians withdrew on September 14, 1914.

blamed by Hitler and other right-wing elements for the sorry state of the German psyche of the time, and for the correspondingly high spirits of the Allies who were aware of the chaos in Germany and confident that it would suffer an internal collapse.

For Hitler, the loss of the war was devastating. We cannot know how many other German patriots experienced similar emotions, but at least two, Rudolph Hess and Herman Goering, are known to have aligned almost identically with Hitler's sentiments. Hitler wanted to play his part in rectifying things. He claims in *Mein Kampf* that it was while he was still at Pasewalk that he decided to go into politics: "There is no making pacts with Jews; there can only be the hard: either-or. I, for my part, decided to go into politics."[992]

Several historians date Hitler's virulent form of anti-Semitism to the loss of World War I. The outcome of the war was a significant milestone on his path to hate and the Holocaust, to be sure, but subsequent events, in total, also contributed mightily to his virulent thought process. He was still to live through the difficult days of Germany in defeat, the many Jewish-led insurrections throughout Germany and elsewhere, the Jewish-influenced Treaty of Versailles, the period of hyperinflation during which Jews exploited German citizens, the perceived cultural ruination of Germany in the 1920s that was almost entirely of Jewish making, the crime scandals of the mid- and late-1920s in which Jews were so prominent, and the stock market crash of 1929. And all of the foregoing was capped off by an explicit worldwide Jewish-led boycott of German goods and services that commenced shortly before he took power. All of these events gave additional weight to his hatred. They also provided him with an incentive and opportunity to achieve the power that ultimately enabled him to act, to self-justify his revenge, first by relatively mild means, and ultimately by way of the Holocaust.

Propaganda Lessons

Hitler had previously studied the propaganda of the political parties in Vienna. During World War I, he assessed the propaganda of the Allies as well. Among Hitler's lessons learned during World War I was his regard for the efficacy of "the big lie." It was "the big lie" form of propaganda used by the Allies during the war, and the British in particular, that provided the world with the persistent view of putative German pathologies, the things that make up the stereotypical German even in the modern era: the German as uniquely subservient to authority, aggressive, rapacious, and bloodthirsty. That is, in addition to its other ill effects, World War I served to revise the history of Germany and Germans.

Prior to the war, both Germany and the kaiser were highly admired: thence after, they would be evil and despised.[993] After World War II, histories of Germans continued to be skewed: the noted historian William Shirer, for example, spoke of "the worst qualities of the German—the coarseness, the boisterousness, the fanaticism, the intolerance, the violence" of the German people, and he went on to cite a number of historical figures that placed Germany and Germans in a bad light.[994]

Of particular note was the propaganda employed by the Allies that targeted the longstanding animosities between Germany's Prussia and Bavaria. The Allies attributed the war to Prussian militarism and thereby provided an out for states such as Bavaria. "While the Jew robbed the whole nation and pressed it beneath his domination," said Hitler in *Mein Kampf*, "an agitation was carried on against the 'Prussians.' At home, as at the front, nothing was done against this poisonous propaganda."[995] Hitler further complained about the inaction of the leadership in dealing with the Allies' propaganda and its effects, saying:

> [T]his kind of propaganda began to achieve certain effects in 1915. The feeling against Prussia grew quite visibly among the troops—yet not a single step was taken against it from above. This was more than a mere sin of omission, and sooner or later we were bound to suffer most catastrophically for it; and not just the "Prussians," but the whole German people, to which Bavaria herself is not the last to belong.

> In this direction enemy propaganda began to achieve unquestionable successes from 1916 on.[996]

The Marxists had employed propaganda to good effect on both the home front and in the trenches to demoralize the German populace and its troops. The Allies did likewise. And neither the Marxists nor the Allies fell short in the number and size of the lies that they employed: Germans were accused, for example, of cutting off the hands off Belgian babies, a practice that was actually relevant to the conduct of Belgian troops in the Congo.[997] It was a big lie. It was also claimed that Germans made lamp shades from the skin of prisoners, a claim that was revived after World War II. It was a big lie. Propaganda from the Allies for a time made claims that the Germans were about to crumble on the battlefield—that bit of puffery was proclaimed shortly before the Germans were found to be at the gates of Paris.[998] It was a big lie.

The propaganda effort of the Allies did not stop short of Orwellian historical revisionism. As stated by Harry Paxton Howard:

> Actually, in the literal sense of the word, the biggest job of revising history was done during the first World War when our "histories" were completely revised to show that Germany had always been our enemy, that Germany had started the war in 1914, that Germany had even started the Franco-Prussian War in 1870, and that in the Revolutionary War we had not been fighting the British but the Hessians. . . . This was a real revision of our histories which has distorted the American mind for more than forty years.[999]

The magnitude of the big lie propaganda against Germany during World War I would later serve as a basis for discarding rumors about Hitler's Holocaust—it was easy enough for Germans to think that such claims were just more of the same old big lies of enemy propaganda.

Kaiser William II thought that propaganda was ungentlemanly and he did little to nothing to blunt it within Germany and on the front lines, and nothing to implement a German campaign to effectively employ it as a weapon. What little propaganda that did originate from the German side toward the end of the war tended to appeal to reason instead of emotions,[1000] a mistake of the first order. Conversely, Allied propaganda published all manner of emotion-laden lies, exaggerations, and distortions, and cleverly exploited long-standing animosities between the German provinces of Prussia and Bavaria. Hitler observed and analyzed all of it and would take mighty lessons from the whole of it.

Propaganda associated with the various munitions strikes during the war served to destroy German morale while simultaneously enriching the morale of the Allies and enlivening the prospects for revolution in Germany. According to Hitler, "English, French, and American newspapers began to implant this faith [that internal revolution in Germany would win the day for the Allies] in the hearts of their readers while an infinitely shrewd propaganda raised the spirits of the troops at the front. 'Germany facing revolution!' Victory of the Allies inevitable!"[1001]

The resurgence of a will to win among the Allies, said Hitler, was the result of the German munitions strike. Moreover, said he, "The instigators of this vilest of all scoundrelly tricks were the aspirants to the highest state positions of revolutionary Germany."[1002] We presume that the "instigators" he is referring to are people such as Liebknecht, Luxemburg, Haase, Eisner, Toller, and Ebert—all of whom provided leadership for the strikes. The combination of the munitions strikes and Germany's failure to effectively respond to Allied propaganda that stemmed from them were represented in Hitler's mind as a "spiritual squandering of the army's heroism."[1003]

Hitler was quick to assess and understand the fundamental precepts of propaganda: one such precept was simplicity and constant repetition, embellished by just enough differentiation from one to the next to hold the consumer's interest. Argument and reason were to be eschewed in favor of moral outrage and repetition.[1004]—it is a propagandistic prospect that has not been lost to current-day propagandists. The propaganda lessons he learned from the British in World War I would later serve him well.

By late November 1918, Hitler was back in Munich where he was able to observe and experience tumultuous postwar events firsthand. Events that would further invigorate his hate.

Meanwhile, the Treaty of Versailles was being constructed by the victors in Paris. The Paris Peace Talks would ultimately produce a treaty that would humiliate and impoverish Germany. Several of the conferees, including the great economist John Maynard Keynes, French General Ferdinand Foch, and British Prime Minister Lloyd George predicted that the harshness of the treaty would lead to further war. Foch would say "This is not a peace. It is an armistice for 20 years."[1005] Foch was wrong—but he was off the mark by only sixty-five days.

CHAPTER 4

TREATY OF VERSAILLES

"Nature, constant in her methods, distributes more gifts of beauty than of intellect."
—**Historian Emile Joseph Dillon**

By the summer of 1918, the German army was on the outskirts of Paris. Both the Italian and Russian armies had been defeated. Germany at that point seemed invincible. A week before the armistice was signed, the German army was still drafting new recruits.[1006]

By that time, however, the Austro-Hungarian Empire was collapsing and would soon sign a separate armistice with the Allies. Bulgaria, too, was lost to the Germany war effort. The USPD and Spartacists had spread their defeatist propaganda amongst the troops and the populace and it was having its intended effect. There was great turmoil. Desertions were rampant. Marxist propaganda relentlessly encouraged the troops to revolt against their officers and for workers to engage in sabotage. Army officers were attacked on the streets. What Hitler termed the "acid of disorganization"[1007] was pouring out of the home front and was debilitating to troops in the trenches. Leftist newspapers such as the SPD's *Vorwörts* were clamoring for peace at any cost. Hitler recalled those last months of the war as follows:

> Now, in the fall of 1918, we stood for the third time on the storm site of 1914. The little city of Comines where we then rested had now become our battlefield. Yet, though the battlefield was the same, the men had changed: for now "political discussions" went on even among the troops. As everywhere, the poison of the hinterland began, here too, to be effective. And the younger recruit fell down completely—for he came from home.[1008]

Marxist-led revolutions broke out everywhere: there was the mutiny aboard ships in the port city of Kiel, then revolution in Bavaria and elsewhere, and finally, in Berlin itself. Red flags were flying throughout the Reich and aboard German ships. The USPD and Spartacists had called for a general strike—debilitating to a country at war—as its means of demanding the ouster of the kaiser and installing their councils along the lines of the Russian Revolution. The USPD and Spartacists wanted to establish a system of close cooperation between Germany and Soviet Russia and a transfer of all political power to the workers' and soldiers' councils which were wholly of their making and which they would oversee. They also sought a workers' militia and collectivization of both the agricultural and industrial sectors of the economy. It is not surprising, therefore, that Friedrich Ebert, who had been appointed to head the transitional government from a monarchy to republicanism, quickly abandoned the workers' and soldiers' councils, correctly seeing them as directly linked to the most radical elements within Germany and heavily influenced by experiences in Soviet Russia.[1009]

With the signing of the armistice Germany surrendered so much of its war machine that subsequent calls for continuing the fight amounted to madness. With its troops and people in open revolt it was impossible for Germany to do other than that demanded by the Allies: and what the Allies demanded was that Germany sign an armistice that was tantamount to abject surrender. That done, the Allies later demanded that Germany sign the Treaty of Versailles.

There was a problem with all this: the Allies were not ready for victory. With the U.S. entry to the war, ultimate victory was assured because of the productive capacity of the U.S. and its huge reserves of manpower. The U.S. resources, used in conjunction with those of the French and British, were altogether too much for Germany to long withstand, especially since its principle ally, Austria-Hungary, had already been defeated. Still, in 1918, even the Allies thought that another year or so of warfare would be needed to bring about Germany's defeat. As late as April 1918, under the strain of the great German offensive that commenced in

March, the Allied situation was so dire that French General Foch and American General Pershing had made a panicky joint plea to President Wilson to get more U.S. troops to Europe as soon as possible, even if untrained.[1010] The collapse of the last German offensive in August of 1918, followed shortly thereafter by the collapse of both the military and political will of the nation, was something of a surprise to the Allies. They, in a measure surpassed only by Germans, were not ready for it.

When the victors met at Versailles, little had been decided as to what was to be done with the peace. It was therefore necessary for them to kludge together the peace terms in short order. Dr. E. J. Dillon described the process using the following imagery: it was, said he, "the frenzy of a few epileptics running amuck among a multitude of paralytics."[1011] Moreover, the most powerful delegates, America's Wilson, Great Britain's Lloyd George, and France's Georges Clemenceau, were collectively frogs in a pond who knew naught of the ocean;[1012] they were novices in world affairs. Dillon states their incapacities succinctly: "Geography, ethnography, psychology, and political history were sealed books to them."[1013] Yet, they had to act as specialists in everything.[1014] Collectively, they were architects who disregarded gravity, says Dillon.[1015] Wilson would soon abandon what supposed principles he had hitherto held so dear; Lloyd George would favor one point, then its opposite; and Clemenceau, that man with "a Panama in his past," would restrict his negotiating objective to little more than savage revenge. All three of the principals were guided through the maze of negotiations by Jewish handlers.

Germany aside, they imposed democracy throughout Europe. Within twenty years all of the most important regimes of that democracy had adopted authoritarian regimes: Russia, Italy, Hungary, Poland, Lithuania, Austria, Germany, Greece, Spain, Slovakia, and even France.[1016] And how about all those new countries in the Middle East? Countries like Iraq, Lebanon, and Iran. We are even now observing how well they fared.

The original intent for Versailles was to hold preliminary discussions and come to decisions that would thereafter be further negotiated with the Germans, but the press of time and

TREATY OF VERSAILLES

circumstances caused the talks to become the final terms of the treaty without regard for German input, much less German sentiment. Germans would later claim that the treaty was in actuality a diktat. The claim was factual.

Over thirty countries were represented at the peace talks leading to the Treaty of Versailles—but none from among the vanquished. Jews were heavily represented within the various delegations as advisors to the principals and had, besides, their own delegation. Zionism, though not a belligerent in the war, was, nevertheless, seated at the conference as representatives of Jewish interests, the Jewish nation as it were. Dillon, in recounting the composition of the peace conference shortly after it had concluded its work, made the following observation:

> Of all the collectivities whose interests were furthered at the Conference, the Jews had perhaps the most resourceful and certainly the most influential exponents. There were Jews from Palestine, from Poland, Russia, the Ukraine, Rumania, Greece, Britain, Holland, and Belgium; but the largest and most brilliant contingent was sent by the United States.[1017]

Jews at Versailles wrenched some significant rights and privileges for themselves, much to the consternation of the Eastern European countries that were most impacted by them. It was here, too, that the stage was set for a British mandatory over Palestine. As the Zionists had urged, Britain would protect the Jews of Palestine.

Jews at the peace conference, of course, sought to secure Palestine for a reconstituted Israel and to further enhance the political and economic privileges of Jews everywhere. In particular, the AJCongress demanded that "Jews be allowed proportional political representation as well as the ability to organize their own communities and preserve an autonomous Jewish national culture"[1018] within the states in which they resided. In effect, they were demanding the right to establish an extranational state within each country where they were located.

Their position was a rather extreme form and forerunner of what we now call multiculturalism.

The Zionist delegation at the conference also argued for an Israeli state that was to be much larger than the one that actually came into being in 1948. In particular, they sought the Golan Heights, the Jordan Valley, what is now called the West Bank, and Lebanon's river Litani as the property of the new Israel.[1019] For the great Zionist leader Ze'ev Jabotinsky, the idée fixe of his program was that "One side of the Jordan is ours—and so is the other."[1020] They did not get everything they sought, but they have been fighting mightily since that time to achieve their original objectives, and more. They now, of course, do have the Golan Heights, the Jordan Valley, and the West Bank, and they have achieved absolute control over about 60 percent of the water resources of the region, but that is a different story. We may yet see a final battle in Lebanon over the waters of the Litani River.

Jews represented themselves as having suffered in the war to a greater extent than all others. Chaim Weizmann asserts in his book, *Trial and Error*, that he "pointed out [to the Versailles delegates] that as a group the Jews had been hit harder by the war than any other [people]."[1021] German fields lay untilled and there were severe shortages of seed and fertilizer. Millions had died in both the military and the civilian populations. Everywhere in Europe coal mines were flooded. Fuel for factories and heating was in dire supply. As described by author Margaret MacMillan, "People were eating coal dust, wood shavings, and sand. Relief workers invented names for things they had never seen before, such as the mangel-wurzel disease, which afflicted those who lived solely on beets."[1022] Belgium lay in ruins as did large areas of France. Misery was rife throughout Europe, and nowhere more so than in Germany. Yet Weizmann had the brazenness, the audacity, the rank gall to claim that "In the first few months after the war, the world at large, and the Jews perhaps more than the rest, lacked everything: food, gold, clothes, shelter, medicine."[1023]

Google	URL
Chaim Weizmann	http://en.wikipedia.org/wiki/Chaim_Weizmann 8/2/14

Weizmann had a carrot to offer to the Versailles delegates: if they would grant the wishes of Zionism, Zionism would "transform Jewish energy into a constructive force instead of its being dissipated in destructive tendencies."[1024] Some would have it that that was still another big lie. On the whole, the delegates gave him what he wanted, but, according to some, they did not get relief from Jewry's destructive tendencies.

Given the suffering of the Russians, the French, Belgians, Germans, and others, both during the war and the postwar period, one has to think that Weizmann's ululations represented brazen nonsense, chutzpah. Including deaths from disease and starvation, Germany had lost between 2 and 3 million souls. Cities and towns of France and Belgium lay in ruin, disease and starvation were everywhere rampant. Even as Weizmann spoke at the Versailles conference, malnutrition and starvation remained everywhere present in Germany as the Allies retained in place the blockade of the North Sea. Prior to the signing of the treaty, German Count Ulrich Von Brockdorff-Rantzau, with justifiable, heartfelt indignation, complained to the victors in May 1919 as follows:

> The hundreds of thousands of noncombatants who have perished since November 11 because of the blockade were destroyed coldly and deliberately after our opponents had won a certain and assured victory. Remember that, when you speak of guilt and atonement.[1025]

As mentioned in the previous chapter, the flu pandemic (purportedly carried to Europe by unwitting American soldiers in 1917) ripped through the world's populace, killing many millions.[1026] In Germany and Austria, with their people so weakened by malnourishment stemming from the blockade of the

North Sea, the flu was especially devastating. Over 400,000 Germans died from it[*] in the fall of 1918 alone. Another 800,000 starved. Germany was clearly in a bad way. In fact, if one were to seek the most prominent atrocity of World War I, the ongoing *postwar* blockade of Germany would be a viable candidate.

Child mortality for children under five was up by 50 percent. Birthrates were down by half. Death from tuberculosis was up by 72 percent. Rickets, influenza, dysentery, scurvy, ulceration of the eyes, and hunger edema were common. Malnutrition, smuggling, black marketing, and hording was widespread and attributed largely to Jewish profiteers and speculators. Naught but misery was flourishing throughout Europe, but especially Germany. Yet Weizmann had the unmitigated gall, the cheek to claim before the world that Jews, above all, were suffering. They lacked "gold," he lamented. Incredulous as the claim was on its face, it was a representation of Jewish power that the world listened without objection.

A fundamental objective of the treaty was to make Germany pay for the war. Each of the war's participants had financed the war with deficit spending, confidently presuming that the costs would ultimately be borne by their enemies. Indeed, a significant reason why each side sought total victory over the other was that such a victory was essential if such a scheme was to be put in place: compromise would not let them off the financial hook.[1027] It was now time for the victors to extract their pound of flesh. Thus it was that British Prime Minister Lloyd George had gone to Paris to "squeeze the German lemon until the pips squeak."[1028] France's Jewish minister of finance, Louis-Lucien Klotz, had but one answer to every question regarding the French budget: "The Germans will pay."[1029]

---

[*] The exact number of deaths worldwide from the 1918–1919 influenza pandemic is not known but estimates range from 20 to 100 million, with most being in the range of 20–25 million. The flu was devastating. Some 675,000 Americans died of it in 1918. Compare that with the fact that "only" 53,513 died from battle during World War I.

The humanitarian sensibilities contained within U.S. President Wilson's Fourteen Points were quickly abandoned in favor of the Realpolitik of the day. As the peace talks got underway, demands of participants expanded and were almost wholly unchecked. Various agreements that had been contracted during the war now came to the fore and had to be fulfilled, not the least among them being Great Britain's promise to the Zionists of a homeland for the Jews. In effect, well-intentioned though most of the participants were, the Versailles delegates set the stage for World War II, for the post-World War II Cold War, for the turmoil in the Balkans in the 1990s, and for the Middle East violence that continues even now. But Germany was the central focus of the day—she was to be made to suffer more than she could bear.

The objectives of the Big Three at Versailles (France, Great Britain, and the U.S.) were at odds from the outset. France, of course, had suffered mightily and she was understandably resolved to ensure her future security by rendering Germany militarily effete and economically destitute. Had France had free rein at the talks, Germany would have been atomized into small individual states with no military potential and few economic prospects. The French objective of ensuring that Germany would never again be capable of attacking French soil was to be accomplished by a cordon of potentially hostile states around Germany; states such as Poland, Czechoslovakia, and Hungary.[*] With the creation of Czechoslovakia, Germany's already vulnerable frontiers were made virtually impossible to defend: Czechoslovakia's Bohemia and Moravia's were thrusting into the German heartland like a gigantic spear, and there was speculation that Poland and/or Russia might take advantage of the Czechoslovakian salient to easily attack Germany. These states and some others such as Yugoslavia, Rumania, and Greater Greece would also serve as a buffer between the now rabidly Marxist Russia and Western Europe. France also,

---

[*] Zionists were successfully elected to office in places like Latvia, Lithania, Poland, Hungary, Czechoslovakia, Romania, Austria, and even Yogoslavia where the Jewish population was less than 70,000.

of course, sought to regain her losses to Germany from the Franco-German war of 1870–1871, and most particularly, Alsace-Lorraine.

Google	URL
Map of Germany, 1920	[1030] This URL contains a series of maps of Germany in 1920, including German territorial losses. The Czechoslovakian salient is also illustrated here.
Map of Polish Corridor	[1031] This URL has maps showing the Polish Corridor and the way that it split Prussia into East Prussia and West Prussia.

The problem with France's objectives was that it would render France exceptionally powerful on the Continent to the possible future detriment of Great Britain. Great Britain, therefore, wanted Germany to remain strong as a counterweight to potential French and Russian hegemony. With the surrender of the German fleet at the end of the war, Great Britain had already achieved its main war aim and was now safe from Germany—not so France, which explains why it was the country most strident in its demand for the harshest possible treatment of Germany. The United States wanted a stable peace based on national aspirations of the various contending counties and races (an impossible task) and also wanted financial compensation for its war expenditures on behalf of both itself and its allies.

German expectations for Versailles had been from the outset that President Wilson's famous Fourteen Points would guide the talks and that Germany would be a party to them. The Fourteen Points were as follows:

1. After the cease-fire (November 11, 1918) all peace negotiations would be done in public with nothing held secret. No hidden, private settlements would be allowed.
2. Total freedom for all nations to navigate on the oceans outside territorial boundaries.
3. The removal, so far as possible, of all economic barriers and the establishment of equality of trade conditions for all nations consenting to the peace settlement.

4. Reducing national armaments to the lowest point consistent with domestic safety.
5. Impartial adjustment of all colonial claims.
6. The evacuation of all Russian territory.
7. Belgium was to be evacuated and restored as a sovereign nation.
8. All French territory was to be restored, and the wrong done by Germany in the 1871 war settlement, corrected.
9. Italy's boundaries were to be adjusted according to lines of nationality.
10. The different people in the Austria-Hungarian Empire were to be given the opportunity for independence.
11. Romania, Serbia, and Montenegro would be evacuated, and Serbia given free and secure access to the sea.
12. The Turks of the Ottoman Empire would be assured a secure sovereignty, but all other nationals in the empire would be given independence.
13. An independent Polish state was to be created with access to the Baltic Sea.
14. A general association of nations (League of Nations) was to be formed to protect all nations from aggression.[1032]

Germany expected that it would be treated as one of two high-contracting parties who had concluded in the prearmistice agreement *a pactum de contrahendo* that was legally binding on both sides.[1033] Indeed, in a note provided to Germany on November 5, 1918, the Allies explicitly stated their intention for a just peace based on Wilson's Fourteen Points[1034] and his various elaborations of those points. For his part in German expectations, Wilson had elaborated on his Fourteen Points during the war, saying that at its end there would be "no annexations, no contributions, no punitive damages."[1035] Wilson insisted before the end of the war that there would be no indemnities imposed upon the Germans and their allies—and there were not, for the term "indemnity" was pilpulized, it was "reparations" that were to be paid, not indemnities.

The negotiations that had taken place between Germany and the United States prior to the armistice all focused on Wilson and his high-sounding, damnable Fourteen Points. At the insistence of the U.S., Germany ousted the kaiser and installed a left-center (SPD) government in his stead and forfeited her military potential (giving over her navy and all of her heavy guns to the Allies as part of the armistice) in belief of Wilson and his concepts for peace. Moreover, the new government demobilized the army immediately upon its return to Germany. Surely, it was thought in Germany, Germany had done her part to position herself as a repentant supplicant to Wilson, the honest broker.

All of Europe assumed a vague understanding that the peace would be founded on Wilson's lofty idealism and he was therefore received in Europe as Humanity's hero when he first arrived—huge crowds welcomed and cheered him everywhere. As it turned out, Wilson's Fourteen Points never even became a subject of issue at the conference,[1036] though most of his objectives were nevertheless imposed. Wilson, who Washington columnist George Will describes as "lean, intellectual and pious, particularly about himself—regarded opposition as impious," was a man who was not to be gainsaid. He would broach no opposition. He was as imperious and officious as any monarch. And he imperiously pilpulized his way out of his commitments with respect to Germany.

Germany tried to make a case that Russian mobilization had triggered the war and that at the very least Germany should be permitted to present her case as to its causes. The Allies would have none of it for they soon realized that their entire case for German disarmament and debilitating reparations was linked to the war-guilt issue. Germany would have no seat at the table, except for the German Zionists (Zionism had been headquartered in Germany before the war but had relocated to London in 1916).

Treaty Provisions and Problems

At the outset of the talks all that business about creating a reconstituted Poland with access to the sea, the Polish Corridor as it was called, if considered at all, was given short shrift. Worse, there seemed to be no realization even in Germany that such access would necessarily be made across territory that was indisputably populated by Germans.[1037] When the Polish Corridor was implemented, however, it was seen by Germans as a jagged dagger cutting Prussia in two. Ruth Henig is undeniably correct in offering the words of General von Seekt to support a contention shared by a multitude of Germans: "it must disappear."[1038] For Adolf Hitler, the Polish Corridor was only one among many humiliating provisions of the treaty. That a Judaized rump state like Poland should occupy German territory and lord over people of Germanic blood—of Prussians, no less!—was to Hitler an abomination, an outrage, an atrocity of the first order.

Wilson's various amplifications of his Fourteen Points had emphasized the right of all peoples to "self-determination," a noble if entirely unworkable concept for the time and place in which it was to be implemented. Moreover, as Stephen Lee tells us pointedly, "Wilson's principle of self-determination seemed to operate against Germans everywhere and in favour of Germans nowhere."[1039] Given the mixed populations in various areas of Europe, and for that matter in the Middle East, it was impossible for self-determination of any one people to be had without simultaneously denying the selfsame determination to other peoples. Enforcement of the concept was, of course, a death knell for what remained of the hodge-podge multiethnic Austro-Hungarian Empire. Still, for the German component of the empire, it seemed like something of a potential salvation, an opportunity for a plebiscite leading to annexation with Germany. And why not the same for the Sudeten Germans of Bohemia, Moravia, and Silesia?

Wilson was the man of the day until the light of that day exposed the vermin in the nooks and crannies of his political ideas. When his liberalism was exposed to the harsh light of reality, and when Wilson himself had to face that reality, he and his exalted ideas succumbed to hard-core politics. France was seeking the disintegration of Germany, its atomization—she was not inclined to broach any silliness about self-determination that would create a

Pan-German state. And what about that absurdity in Point 5, that business about colonial claims—what was to be done with that? Would the U.K. surrender India? Would the French abandon Africa and Southeast Asia? What about South Africa?

In actual fact, the self-determination of colonized people was not to be countenanced. A petty, bothersome note submitted to the delegates by a kitchen assistant at the talks was discarded out of hand. The kitchen assistant was Ho Chi Minh. He and his little group of Vietnamese nationalists had the temerity to ask that his little country of Indochina (later Viet Nam) be granted independence from France.[1040] Ho Chi Minh was a political nobody and nobody of importance was going to listen to the likes of him. Ho Chi Minh, we can legitimately conclude, suffered from frustrations that were similar to those of Adolf Hitler.

It is something of an aside but worth noting nonetheless that the Peace Conference paid attention to Weizmann because he represented organization and therefore, power; Ho Chi Minh did not and was therefore ignored. Later, both Ho Chi Minh and Adolf Hitler would be the leaders of powerful organizations, and it would be only then that the world would pay them mind. None of us fear the snowflake. We all fear the avalanche.

Other interested parties, with Jews at the forefront, sought equality for their people. Conference members moved to include religious equality into the treaty. In actual fact, religious equality was far removed from the pressing issues of the twentieth century, and it was recognized by a number of objecting states that the real influence behind such proposals were Semitic. "What the Eastern delegates said [in opposition to the minorities' clauses] was briefly this: 'The tide in our countries was flowing rapidly in favor of the Jews.'"[1041] As stated by Dr. Dillon in his book, *The Inside Story of the Peace Conference*, Jews pushed their agenda as follows:

> [I]n the flush of their triumph, the Jews, or rather their spokesmen at the Conference, were not satisfied with equality. What they demanded was inequality to the detriment of the races whose hospitality they were enjoying and to their own supposed advantage. They

were to have the same rights as the Rumanians, the Poles, and the other peoples among whom they lived but they were also to have a good deal more. Their religious autonomy was placed under the protection of an alien body, the League, which is but another name for the Powers which have reserved to themselves the governance of the world.[1042]

They [the objecting states] confronted the [Wilson] proposal on the subject of religious inequality, and, in particular, the odd motive alleged for it, with the measures of the protection of minorities which he subsequently imposed on the lesser states, and which had for their keynote to satisfy the Jewish elements in eastern Europe. And they concluded that the sequence of expedients framed and enforced in this direction were inspired by the Jews, assembled in Paris for the purpose of realizing their carefully thought-out program, which they succeeded in having substantially executed. However right or wrong these delegates may have been, it would be a dangerous mistake to ignore their views, seeing that they have since become one of the permanent elements of the situation. The formula into which this policy was thrown by the members of the Conference, whose countries it affected, and who regarded it as fatal to the peace of eastern Europe, was this: "Henceforth the world will be governed by the Anglo-Saxon peoples, who, in turn, are swayed by their Jewish elements."[1043]

Poland strenuously opposed the minority clauses of the treaty. It had what it regarded as an indigestible immigrant population of 2.7 million Jews, all of whom were considered by the Polish government as a non-Polish racial, linguistic, and religious national minority.[1044] Their objections were largely founded on the basis of recent history. The treaty called for anyone who had resided in Poland as of August 1, 1914, to automatically be granted citizenship. But at that time there were numerous Jewish-German and Jewish-Austrian spies in Poland. How was it to be that such people were now to be granted citizenship? Moreover, as the Poles pointed out, Jews in Vilna had recently voted as a block against incorporation of that city into Poland. Why should such people now be granted citizenship?[1045] Worse yet, the provisions of the treaty held the threat of foreign intervention if Jews were not satisfied with their lot. They were to have autonomy over and above other Poles, they were to be a state within the state, and they were to be entitled to call in foreign powers (i.e., the League of Nations) "at every hand's turn" against the constituted authority.[1046] This meant, claimed the Poles rightly, that the country would be forever subjected to the authority of an Anglo-Saxon-Jewish supremacy. The Zionists, in tandem with the American Jewish Committee, were virtuosos playing the heartstrings of the Versailles delegates. In very large part they got their way.

The whole of the concessions made to the Jews at Versailles were a blatant expression of Jewish power vis-à-vis that of lesser nations.

Romania's delegate, Premier Bratiano, elegantly made the point that the treaty was setting the stage for its Jewish citizens "to regard the Rumanian state as an inferior tribunal."[1047] He correctly predicted that the majority and minority citizens would ultimately be systematically estranged from each other; "and, seeing this, the elemental instincts of the masses might suddenly assume untoward forms."[1048] Failing in his pleas, the Romanian premier withdrew from the talks.

Others, and the Japanese in particular, desired that the minority language be extended to include racial equality that was couched in the term "equality of nations." The treaty ultimately did contain language related to religious equality, which encompassed Jews, but not equality for Catholics in England. Racial equality was excluded. Moreover, powerful states in any event were implicitly exempted from compliance. The U.S. was not about to provide equality for its Negroes, and England could hardly be expected to provide full equality for its Catholics. At one point, when a majority voted in favor of the Japanese proposal, President Wilson announced that a majority was insufficient[1049]—only unanimity would be sufficient, claimed Wilson. Wilson did so just after he had accepted a majority vote to establish the League of Nations in Geneva. A delegate pointed out that a majority was good enough to carry that motion, why not so this other one? "The two situations are different," said Wilson impiously. It was a snowflake answer: each snowflake is different each from its other, but only slightly—one must sometimes ignore the fact that snowflakes and voting rights are mostly the same in their properties, and Wilson, that grand liberal, did just that.

With the defeat of the Ottoman Empire, the entire Middle East as well as the Balkans became problematic. The Versailles delegates would manage to enflame the disastrous relationships in those volatile regions as well as they did in Central and Eastern Europe.

By the time Wilson left Europe months later, the sheen of his arrival had been badly and justifiably tarnished. He was by then viewed by Europeans and Americans alike as something of an amateur political idealist; a member of the liberal intelligentsia with lofty ideals, thin commitment, and little inherent capacity to do actual good.

Wilson's Mistakes

While blame for the failure of Versailles is rightfully shared by all of the Big Three, President Woodrow Wilson holds a special place. "Wilson had won a staggering victory in compelling the Allies to accept his Fourteen Points as the basis for the peace treaty" observes historian Richard Watt. "His victory had been so overwhelming that he could not possibly expect to gain more; indeed, he could only lose [by personally participating in the peace conference]."[1050] Germany, for its part, depended on Wilson's goodwill and his Fourteen Points. The country had obviously and fatefully misplaced its trust. Hitler would later do nothing more than express the justifiably widespread sentiment of his people when he said that the treaty was founded on a monstrous lie, to wit,

German war guilt. It reduced the nation to that of serfs and slaves.[1051] Wilson contributed immeasurably to that perception.

Wilson and his advisors concocted a treaty that all but guaranteed near-term turmoil, future war, and postwar upheaval—even today we continue to feel its effects. Of most immediate concern was the war-guilt clause. The clause had practical as well as psychological impacts on the German people: it was that clause, Article 231, that was frequently invoked to deny Germans the right to self-determination by denying them the opportunity, for example, to merge with Austria. The same was true with respect to Upper Silesia, which voted overwhelmingly to return to Germany but was instead, awarded to Poland.

The war-guilt clause had been inserted into the treaty because American lawyers at the talks, many of whom were Jewish, insisted that reparations could not be demanded unless it was established that some wrong, some tort had been inflicted.[1052] The result of the guilt clause was to rationalize and legitimize (pilpulize) the imposition of punitive financial reparations on Germany[1053]—it was the linchpin for all of the confiscatory clauses.[1054] For the Germans, it was a moral judgment and a national trauma that would last throughout the Weimar era.[1055] It ultimately contributed immensely to the rise and political success of Hitler and his Nazis.

Having achieved a significant victory, Wilson then set about bringing it to ruin. His decision to personally travel to Europe and to personally participate in the peace talks was his first fateful blunder. Worse, he deliberately slighted the Republicans by leaving them at home where they fumed over their inability to realize their perceived fair share of the glory of the moment. As the controversy of that decision rebounded in the U.S., humorist Will Rogers had it that Wilson was saying to the Republicans something like "I tell you what, we will split 50-50—I will go and you fellows can stay."[1056] Wilson was widely acknowledged as a great imperious intellect, but this was not the smartest moment of his politics.

Wilson could have and should have stayed home. As pointed out by Richard Watt, his worth to the peace process would have been maximized had he assumed the mantle of most principled statesman, a man above the fray, seeking peace and justice for all in accordance with his lofty Fourteen Points. Instead of personally serving as the U.S. plenipotentiary, he could have guided his negotiators from Washington where his "negotiators would have been protected from the certainty of belief by their counterparts that they had the decision authority to make grand gestures of compromise."[1057] That is, instead of being there where he had to immediately respond to the issues pressed upon him by his negotiating partners, he would have been able to better digest issues at home and offer considered guidance to his representatives. "Meanwhile, Wilsonian statements, couched in his superb prose, polished and repolished, would resound from Washington."[1058] All of this *should have*, however, was probably not a realistic expectation. The prime minister of England personally participated as did the prime minister of France—how could Wilson be reasonably expected to opt out of such a momentous event? Moreover, had he remained behind he would have certainly been open to brutal attack from his political foes, most notably the ardent foe of Wilson's beloved League of Nations, Senator Henry Cabot Lodge of Massachusetts. Still, that he seemingly *had to go* only feebly, *in retrospect*, diminishes the hindsight admonishment that *he should not have gone*.

Humiliation and Loss

In addition to the formal objectives and resulting provisions of the Treaty of Versailles, there was an obvious, if unstated, objective: the humiliation of Germany. Of the 440 clauses in the treaty, 414 were devoted to punishing Germany.

Everything was done by the French to ensure that Germans felt the full force of their defeat and that Germans fully understood that France was now positioned to torment them. As the German delegation traveled to the site for the signing of the armistice with their French escorts, the convoy was intentionally slowed so that the Germans were made to see what destruction *they* had wrought—as they traveled to Paris for the signing of the Treaty of

Versailles their train was slowed for the same purpose. The site selected by the French for signing the armistice was a railway carriage in the Compiegne Forrest.* But it was not just *any* railway carriage; it was the personal train car of Napoleon III whom the Germans had defeated in 1870. In 1940, Hitler would use the selfsame train car in the selfsame spot to receive the surrender of the French. The date selected for presenting the terms of the treaty to the Germans was May 7, the anniversary of the 1915 German sinking of the Lusitania, an event that served as one of the pretexts for U.S. entry into the war. The date for the actual signing was June 28, the anniversary of the assassination of Archduke Ferdinand and his wife in Sarajevo—the event that triggered the various actions of parties that led to World War I. Upon arriving in Paris for the signing ceremony, the German delegation was met at the hotel selected for them by the French. Their bags were unceremoniously dumped in a heap on the ground. They were told to retrieve them themselves and carry them to their rooms. The hotel was the same one that was used by the French delegation that surrendered France to Germany in 1871.[1059]

Wilson had preferred Geneva as the venue for the talks, but the French insisted on Paris, and their reason had to do with their desire to bring Germany low. The place for the signing was the Versailles Hall of Mirrors where the German Empire had been proclaimed in 1871. It was said of the actual signing that "The whole affair was elaborately staged and made as humiliating to the enemy as well it could be."[1060] The Germans, as Watts points out, were made to sit in "the seats of the accused" and "[w]ithout opportunity for defense or rebuttal, they would be found guilty."[1061]

---

* The armistice was signed on the German side by Matthias Erzberger, a man who Hitler described as "the bastard son of Jew and a serving girl" (Rosenbaum, 14). Dr. Carl Melchoir, who was Jewish, was one of the five German delegates in chief at the Peace Conference.

Google	URL
Hitler at Compiegne	https://www.google.com/search?q=hitler+at+compiegne&rlz=1T4GZAB_enUS449US538&tbm=isch&tbo=u&source=univ&sa=X&ei=RbzeU4HHCJOLyASwqIHQDA&sqi=2&ved=0CBwQsAQ&biw=1008&bih=506 8/2/14

All of the humiliations heaped on the Germans felt good to the victors. But Germany was a great nation, capable of great things—and among those great things was great hate. A great deal of what Hitler was all about was the redress of the humiliations heaped on Germans by the loss of World War I. Countries, like the individuals of which they are comprised, are willing to sacrifice mightily to overcome humiliation,* whether of the individual kind or the national kind. Under Adolf Hitler, German hate would be directed at those who he and countless others had concluded had cost them victory and subjected the fatherland to such humiliation, the Jewish radicals, most of whom had arrived in Germany from the East.

The cost included the following:[1062]

- Germany lost 13 percent of its national territory, an area of about 43,200 square miles—an area more than twenty times the size of current-day (Green Line) Israel. German territorial losses included the return of Alsace-Lorraine to France, the Eupen-Malmedy area was ceded to Belgium, and Denmark got North Schleswig. Posen, West Prussia, and, as previously mentioned, a piece of the coal-rich and highly industrialized Upper Silesia were promised to Poland. Other parts of Upper Silesia were ceded to the newly created Czechoslovakia. In losing these and other areas, Germany also lost 12.5 percent of her population, 16 percent of her coalfields, and half her critical iron and steel

---

* In the Middle East, some 46% of Palestinian men have at one time or another been humiliated by Israeli checkpoint or IDF forces in the presence of their children. A man may endure a great lot and still not be an enemy: humiliate an honorable man in the presence of his child and you have an enemy greater than any other.

industry. Her overseas colonies were distributed between Italy, France, Belgium, Japan, and Britain.
- Germany was also forced to cede the province of West Prussia to the newly independent Poland, providing Poland with access to the Baltic Sea by splitting Prussia in two. The city of Danzig was designated a Free City under the auspices of the League of Nations, but the practical effect of this arrangement was secession of the city to Poland.
- The result of the territorial losses was that 3 million Germans living in the Sudetenland, Austrian subjects for 400 years, were incorporated, against their wishes, into the new nation of Czechoslovakia—these were the ethnic Germans of Bohemia, Moravia, and parts of Silesia, people who were known collectively as the Sudeten Germans. An additional 6 million Germans found themselves within the borders of Poland, Denmark, Belgium, and France. All of these Germans would soon regard themselves as oppressed minorities. The 7 million Germans of Austria that sought to be united with Germany were denied their right to do so according to Wilson's elaborations on his Fourteen Points. In total, 16 million Germans would be lost to the state. Wilson's vaunted right of peoples to self-determination, so solemnly incorporated into his famous Fourteen Points, was seen as a sham by these Germans as well as those in Germany proper.
- The German Rhineland was designated a demilitarized zone, and the Saarland province was put under the control of the League of Nations.
- Military weakness was to be created and perpetuated. The German army was restricted to 100,000 troops, and conscription was prohibited. Enlistments were to be lengthy (twelve years for enlisted personnel and twenty-five years for officers)[1063] to prevent Germany from building up a large force of trained soldiers. Germany's navy was restricted to 15,000 men with a smattering of ships.

- Submarines were prohibited entirely as were military aircraft and artillery.
- Article 231 of the treaty, the War-Guilt Clause, the most hated article of all, forced Germany to accept sole responsibility for the war and provided the Allies with a clear conscience in the taking of German riches. Apologist historians make the point that the term "war guilt" was not used in the text of the treaty—nevertheless, any fair-minded reading of Article 231 makes it clear that guilt for the war was, in fact, assigned exclusively to Germany. Moreover, assignment of war guilt to Germany was attributable, in the minds of the radical Right, to the likes of the Jew Henry Morgenthau. Morgenthau had alleged that Kaiser William II and his warmongering coterie had conspired to start the war at a conference held at Potsdam on July 5, 1914. In actually, no such meeting ever took place, but Morgenthau's charges nevertheless stuck. A Versailles Peace Conference commission cited the alleged conference of the kaiser and his conspirators as justification for Article 231 of the treaty.[1064]
- Reparation payments by Germany to the victors were set at impossibly high levels (132 billion gold reichsmarks, 38 percent of Germany's national wealth),[1065] and then renegotiated several times during the 1920s to bring them into line with reality. A variety of other payments in coal, steel, lumber, agricultural products, rolling stock, and intellectual property (including, for example, the patent for Aspirin) were also imposed. At a time when Germany was itself starving, she was required to provide 140,000 cows to France. Belgium, too, received some of its payment in livestock.* She also lost important farming regions that had

---

* During the war, Germany had forcibly taken large amounts of livestock and grain from both the French and Belgians as a response to the naval blockade of the North Sea, so these payments were understandably seen as something of a tit-for-tat by the Allies but as theft and oppression by the Germans.

previously accounted for over 20 percent of her production of wheat and potatoes.
- The League of Nations was created by the treaty. On March 19, 1920, the United States Senate refused to ratify the treaty (one of the consequences of Wilson's decision to exclude Republicans from his negotiating delegation). The defeated nations were not initially admitted, and the Soviet Union did not join it until 1934. Thus, the League was in all practical aspects simply an enforcement authority for the victors.[1066] Absent the potentially moderating influence of the United States, the League became little more than an organ for the torment of Germany.

Google	URL
Map, Europe between the wars	https://www.google.com/search?q=Map,+Europe+Between+the+wars&rlz=1T4GZAB_enUS449US538&tbm=isch&imgil=zvcnX-S_cZh9jM%253A%253BCqcjF3Y1biwwqM%253Bhttp%25253A%25252F%25252Fgo.grolier.com%25252Fatlas%25253Fid%2525253Dmh00049&source=iu&usg=__y3Us9UxbXG6t2Zd0VFHJY6W9ceg%3D&sa=X&ei=iL_eU8_eE86eyASIioC4Aw&ved=0CCMQ9QEwAQ&biw=1008&bih=506#facrc=_&imgdii=zvcnX-S_cZh9jM%3A%3BMmU5ZHYCO8pHyM%3BzvcnX-S_cZh9jM%3A&imgrc=zvcnX-S_cZh9jM%253A%3BCqcjF3Y1biwwqM%3Bhttp%253A%252F%252Fgo.grolier.com%252Fmap%253Fid%253Dmh00049%2526pid%253Dgo%3Bhttp%253A%252F%252Fgo.grolier.com%252Fatlas%253Fid%253Dmh00049%3B624%3B400 8/2/14

Germany lost a lot, and she could not do otherwise than want to recover those losses.

However we might care to justify the territorial, economic, and population losses imposed on Germany, or compare them with such losses as those imposed on the Russians by the Germans at Brest-Litovsk (where the enemy was at least included at the negotiating table); we can hardly blame the Germans for having felt that they had been badly treated at Versailles.

* * * *

Prominent Jews had begun preparing for the coming Peace Treaty Conference as early as 1915. Some would say even earlier because Zionist Max Nordau, a close associate of Theodor Herzl, had seemingly predicted the war[*] in the late 1800s and implored his fellow Zionists to prepare for the negotiations that would take place at its conclusion.[1067] In March of 1915, under the leadership of Louis Brandeis, Rabbi Stephen Wise and Judge Julian Mack, the Jewish Congress Organization Committee, was established in order to discuss the Jewish positions to be taken at the conference and to elect representatives thereto. Jews, of course, were not official belligerents in the war, but they were, nevertheless, treated at the peace conference as if they were a sovereign state on the side of the Allies. Italy, an actual belligerent on behalf of the victors, received a short shrift at the talks; not so the Jewish delegation.

Hitler commented on Jews as a state within Germany, saying that "The Jew has now become a steady resident; that is, he settles special sections of the cities and villages and more and more constitutes a state with a state."[1068] It was the furtherance of Judaism as a state within the various states of Europe that was the central issue of the Jewish lobby at the Versailles Conference.

The treaty provisions sought and acquired by Jews were not only upsetting to Germans; every Eastern state hated them and several purposefully voided them.

As has frequently been the case in history, Jews were immensely privileged and powerful at Versailles. In addition to having their own delegation, they served in vastly disproportionate numbers as advisors to the various other delegations.

A total of thirty countries were involved in the talks. If Jewish numbers at Versailles had been proportionate to their numbers within the various populations of the participating countries they would have had but a single representative. As it was, the Zionists alone had 117 delegates and an even greater number served in

---

[*] Nothing conspiratorial is to be taken from Nordau's prediction—it simply offers a highly probable speculation with respect to the rivalries and events in Europe at the time. Any number of politically aware people could have made the same prediction at that time, a predition that highlights the perceived inevitability of war on the Continent.

various advisory capacities. So many Jews participated at the conference that some Frenchmen were given to referring to the talks as the "kosher conference." Zionists, though they did not represent a nation—neither a belligerent in the war, nor a nation with a territorial interest, nor one of the Allied nations—nevertheless got to present its case for a Palestinian homeland for the Jews. The Germans, as emphasized, did not get to speak at all.

Principal Jewish advisors to President Wilson included the jurist and social reformer Julian Mack; financier and stock speculator Bernard Baruch; and jurist and head of the American Jewish Committee Louis Marshall. British Prime Minister Lloyd George was advised by Phil Sassoon, son of one of the Rothschilds. French leader Georges Clemenceau was advised by his Jewish interior minister, Georges Mandel, born Louis George Rothschild, a man who was said to be Clemenceau's alter ego.[1069] The whole of Jewish participation in the talks made it all too easy for extreme rightists to imagine that the principals at the talks were little more than surrogates of Jewish interests.

The primary focus of the Zionists was to now demand that the British make good on their promise of a homeland in Palestine for the Jews. Jews were seen as having upheld their part of the bargain—they had brought the U.S. into the war. It was now time for the British to deliver on the quid pro quo. They got what they demanded. The stage was set at Versailles for the subsequent talks at San Remo where the Jewish homeland in Palestine was formalized in April 1920. Britain got the Palestinian mandate over French objections. Arabs were not represented: Arab riots that stemmed from their treatment at San Remo were treated in the world press as the actions of unenlightened extremists.[1070]

In addition to the objectives of the Zionists in creating the state of Israel within Palestine, Jews sought, as mentioned above, political and cultural autonomy as a separate nation within the various Eastern European societies.[1071] In seeking satisfaction of this latter objective they sought formal recognition of their de facto status as a nation within the nations that they had successfully established throughout the Diaspora. Jews also sought and received special privileges within Germany, though their attainment of these objectives was couched in universalistic terms. As Donald Niewyk puts it:

> The main and real Zionist aim . . . was to convert the bulk of German Jewry to unassimilated life in Germany. This demanded a sharp division of German and Jewish affairs. . . . Hence they welcomed the Weimar Constitution's guarantee of cultural autonomy to foreign language groups in Germany as recognition of the same distinction, lamenting only that it did not go on to acknowledge the special rights of ethnic groups like Jews.[1072]

Elsewhere, such as in Poland and Hungary, the Versailles provisions regarding minority rights—provisions created by the Jewish Zionist Lucien Wolf—translated to the fact of special Jewish rights and privileges and caused great consternation there. "Hungarians declared their treaty day a day of national mourning and the Romanians refused to sign until the clauses guaranteeing Sabbath rights and [state financed] Jewish schools were deleted from their treaty."[1073] Polish delegates complained mightily and cited examples of fictitious pogroms and vast Jewish exaggeration of suffering there. Poland also complained that isolation and particularism stood in stark opposition to the goals of assimilation and citizenship, and the correlate duties connected to them.[1074] The complaints were all for naught. The Jews prevailed.

The foregoing is illustrative of a recurring theme in the actions of various Jewish organizations. "Rights" are demanded, sometimes explicitly Jewish ones but more often ones that are couched in universalistic terms that, because they apply only to subsets of the population, are not rights at all but are instead, privileges afforded to the few. Such "rights" are a feature of identity politics and the Jewish "culture of victimization," though Jews are hardly victims in the modern world.

The powerful Jewish banking executive Max Warburg served as a financial advisor to the German delegation. Warburg would later play a prominent role at every major reparations conference for the next fourteen years—conferences at which, on the whole,

Germany was further humiliated by additional concessions. Additionally, Carl I. Melchoir and four other Jews served on the German delegation, with many more serving in lesser advisory capacities. With respect to Jews in advisory positions of German delegations, Peter Pulzer says the following:

> Another favoured form of Jewish public activity that survived in an attenuated form in the Weimar years was that of the policy adviser. It was a substitute for formal political office or permanent administrative appointment and, as such, convenient and welcome to both Jews and gentiles. It helped to perpetuate the status of many of the German-Jewish economic elite as privileged outsiders. Like direct political activity it reached a brief heyday immediately after the war, in Jewish participation in the armistice and reparations delegations.[1075]

While not direct participants, other powerful Jews greatly influenced events at the Peace Conference. Louis Brandeis, a man who had been an important member of the Jewish cabal that brought about the Balfour Declaration, was one such man. The Zionist delegation to the Peace Conference also included Felix Frankfurter, who helped to found the American Civil Liberties Union and who, like Brandeis, would later become a U.S. Supreme Court justice. Frankfurter, among others, lobbied President Wilson to incorporate the Balfour Declaration into the treaty.[1076]

When objections were raised about the impact of the Balfour Declaration on the self-determination of the numerically greater Arab inhabitants of the area, a rather convoluted bit of logic was constructed by Balfour and Brandeis. It was wrong, they argued, to use mere

> "numerical self-determination:" a great many potential inhabitants of the Jewish home in Palestine still lived outside its borders. "And Zionism," said Balfour, "be it right or wrong, good or bad, is rooted in age-long traditions, in present needs, in future hopes of far

profounder import than the desires and prejudices of the 700,000 Arabs who now inhabit that ancient land."[1077]

With that stroke of ghastly logic, President Wilson's rhetoric about self-determination was nutered to support the establishment of the Jewish homeland. The self-determination of the numerically greater mass of Arabs was made to give way to the self-determination of a minority of Jews. Such was the pilpulized rationality for the imposition the Balfour Agreement.

Given the decisions of the Peace Conference with respect to the reestablishment of Israel, as well as the already well-known British-Jewish-American Balfour machinations, the German right wing was assuredly justified in concluding that the Balfour Declaration had been instrumental in bringing the United States into the war; an event that assured Germany's defeat. It is little wonder that politically astute Germans attributed the armistice and German subjugation to the Treaty of Versailles.

Adding to the foregoing was the fact that it was, after all, the Marxists within the SPD, USPD, and Spartacists organizations who had so encouraged internal dissension, peace at any cost, and finally revolution which was in accordance with their original intent. And given the number and prominence of Jews within German Marxists ranks, it was hardly irrational to highlight their participation among those thought to be traitors; traitors who stabbed Germany in the back. Then, too, there was the massive involvement of Jews at the peace talks. With all of that as a backdrop, there was substantial reason for Germans to be highly upset with Jewry.

While the vast majority of the German population bewailed and cursed the treaty, the exceedingly influential *Weltbühne*, the same publication that had sponsored the "more thorough and scholarly" studies related to Jewish participation in the German military, argued that the terms should have been even harsher. The *Weltbühne* argued that even the pitifully small army of 100,000 was too large, and well before the German government made its first modest moves toward a fulfillment policy in 1921, the *Weltbühne* argued for immediate payment of reparations.[1078] As time moved forward, Kurt Tucholsky, star writer for the *Weltbühne*, along with Carl von Ossietzky, used every opportunity to belittle the Germans and give praise to the fairness of the hated treaty. The *Weltbühne*, like its star, Ossietzky, was a lover of catastrophe, a gourmet of political misfortune.[1079] It was a publication for the intelligentsia that was adept at "striking heroic poses."[1080] It seemed to many that anything that was hurtful to Germans was embraced by the Jews Tucholsky, Ossietzky, and their supporting cast at the *Weltbühne*. The Jewish-owned *Vossische Zeitung* advocated acceptance of the treaty from its outset.[1081] It would not have been hard for the radical rightists to think that the severely weakened condition of Germany played into the hands of the revolutionaries—a disarmed, impoverished, and sorely dispirited, disjointed, and disunited Germany would be ripe for the Jewish-led Marxists.

France, the mortal enemy of Germany at the time, was the darling of the Jewish intelligentsia and it therefore publicly argued for close German-French cooperation and for full compliance with the terms of the treaty. The intelligentsia of the Democrats (DDP)* and SPD tried to convince the German people that the Treaty of Versailles was good for them—rough justice, as it were, that they should not only endure it but embrace it. It required more than a little cheek to take that position. The very fact that the extremist left-wing USPD had participated in the ratification of the treaty made it suspect. The USPD went so far as to vehemently object to attempts to attach conditions to acceptance of the treaty; they readily accepted the war guilt of Germany and cared not a whit about the fate of the kaiser and the army officer corps. Arguments of the ultraleftist USPD did not, of course, go unnoticed by the parties of the Right.[1082] For the USPD and the Marxists, anything that embroiled the German people was good for them: the worse

---

* The DDP was, along with the SPD, a party entirely committed to the Republic. "The party was attacked by some for being a party of Jews and professors (and, indeed, Jews formed one of its most loyal voters—accounting for as much as 64 percent)." The DDP initially opposed the Treaty of Versailles. Source: http://en.wikipedia.org/wiki/German_Democratic_Party 09/28/07.

things could be made to be, the better the prospects for their intended overthrow of the government and installation of a Bolshevistic one.

* * * *

The *Weltbühne* and other such leftists aside, the treaty engendered a large camp of opponents to its provisions. It was, as German delegate Count Ulrich Von Brockdorff-Rantzau stated, "A peace which cannot be defended before the world as a peace of justice...."[1083] Germany's Prime Minister Scheidemann made a proclamation about it in the Reichstag: "What hand must not wither which places these fetters on itself and on us?"[1084] He resigned his position rather than sign such a treaty, a Carthaginian Peace. The brilliant British economist John Maynard Keynes, a participant in the peace talks, adamantly opposed the treaty provisions. His book, *The Economic Consequences of the Peace (1919)*, made a number of specific and dire economic predictions that did not bear fruit but the essence of his objections was nevertheless valid. In particular, Keynes predicted that the harsh terms of the treaty would lead to further conflict in Europe.[1085] Keynes's ominous assessment of the potential for the peace terms to lead to future turmoil was independently concluded by others as well, not the least of whom was British Prime Minister Lloyd George, a principal participant in the talks.[1086]

Still, there were powerful arguments for Germany to sign the treaty. Proposals were afoot to the effect that Germany should be occupied by the Allies until it had paid off the entire cost of the war—as long as 100 years. Had Germany refused to sign, she might very well have been occupied for a very long time indeed, though 100 years is something of a stretch.[1087] France's Marshal Foch had prepared detailed plans for the invasion and occupation of Germany should she refuse to sign. He actually hoped that Germany would refuse so that the occupation could take place and the terms of the treaty could then be bent more to the liking of France.[1088]

Stolfi makes the entirely valid point that the Allies created moral inequities at Versailles that would define the high points of Hitler's foreign policy once he was in office.[1089]

In addition to the various statesmen and experts of various kinds who saw the treaty of Versailles with portents of future war, there was Adolf Hitler. Hitler propagandized on the treaty even more than he did the Jews, and because it was already hated by so many Germans, his propaganda succeeded in winning the hearts of a broad spectrum of the German populace to his cause: aristocrats and workers, civil servants, students, farmers and peasants were his earliest adherents, though they initially came to his cause in woefully small numbers.

Hitler's early successes in foreign affairs were, in large part, due to his ability to act as if he were a simple adherent of Wilson's veritably sacred principle of "self-determination." Czechoslovakia's Bohemia had 2,070,000 Germans as opposed to only 116,000 Czechs. The Sudetenland had nearly 644,000 Germans and only 25,000 Czechs; Moravia had 180,000 Germans but only 12,000 Czechs.[1090] Clearly, Germany had a strong case for uniting these areas with Germany, and particularly so because the German majorities in those areas were being brutalized by Czech authorities.

Given Wilson's position on this matter, Hitler was entirely in keeping with Wilson's principle when he sought union with Austrian and Sudeten Germans and, ultimately, with the Germans stranded in Poland, though his actual objectives there were also more expansive than that of simply rescuing fellow Germans. Poland had forcefully acquired Germany's Upper Silesia in May 1921, even after the population there had overwhelmingly voted to remain German.[1091] Hitler meant to correct all that . . . and more.

It is often claimed, and it is probably true, that without the Treaty of Versailles Hitler would not have been able to succeed in German politics. Hitler, it is sometimes said, "was born at Versailles." In the early years of the Nazi movement, the Treaty of Versailles was Hitler's exclusive subject of derision. Bemoaning his fate as a defendant at Nuremberg after World War II, Hjalmar Schacht, president of the Reichbank from 1933 to 1939, justifiably claimed that there never would have been a Hitler if it had not been for the Treaty of Versailles. Schacht was joined in his opinion by his codefendant, Friedrich Jodl.[1092] Franz von Papen was correct when he told author G. Gilbert at Nuremberg that the failure of the Lausanne Conference in 1932 to give Germany any hope for the further correction of injustices done to her by the Treaty of Versailles contributed immeasurably to Hitler's success. But it must be said that there were many other factors as well. Von Papen also claimed that America shared in the guilt for bringing about Hitler's success: the U.S. refusal to join the League of Nations, he said, let the League become a "club for preserving the Versailles Treaty,"[1093] a situation that would perhaps not have occurred had the U.S. been a member.

The Treaty of Versailles is often described as the single most important aid to the rise of Hitler. "No Versailles, no Hitler." While the foregoing is something of an oversimplification it is nevertheless true that Hitler and other right-wing elements in Germany were able to exploit the abominable treaty as a means of ultimately joining with the great mass of the populace who regarded the treaty with justifiable odium. Moreover, as many historians point out, the treaty played a large part in the causality of World War II. As Hitler reoccupied the Rhineland, annexed Austria, retrieved the German Sudetenland,* and then subsumed the whole of Czechoslovakia, international tensions increased. Finally, when he invaded Poland, ostensibly to regain German territory lost to Germany by the Treaty of Versailles (the Polish Corridor), war ensued.

---

* Hitler had good reason for wanting both the Sudetenland, and then the whole of Czechoslovakia: it had 3.5 million Germans within its populace and was a strategic boarder area between Germany, Austria, Poland, the Soviet Union, and Hungary. Thus, because of its location, its capture vastly improved Germany's ability to defend itself from attack from the east. It was also relatively rich in natural resources—it was the most industrialized nation in Eastern Europe. Moreover, the country had previously represented a salient into German territory, its capture eliminated the salient and fatefully exposed Poland's southern flank.

As discussed above, both in their advisory capacity and as a Zionist contingent, Jews were instrumental in the construction of the Treaty of Versailles. Jewish-owned leftist newspapers such as the *Frankfurter Zeitung* had urged that the treaty be signed and later urged that Germany faithfully comply with its provisions, even the most loathsome ones. To the extent that the treaty had actual supporters within Germany, they were almost exclusively Jewish. Virtually all leftist elements, the USPD among them, called on Germany to fully comply with the treaty's terms, winning for themselves the loathing of right-wing elements.

In the early days of Hitler's movement, initial attempts to blame Jews for all of the misery that had befallen Germany failed to resonate with the electorate. He therefore refocused his emphasis on the Treaty of Versailles and only indirectly implicated Jews in its creation, though it was certainly the case that he was personally convinced that Jews owned a great share of the responsibility for it. The treaty was Hitler's foremost subject in the early days of his career. According to historian Richard M. Watt:

> [H]e delivered practically the same speech again and again in the early days of Nazism. This attack, first entitled "The Peace Treaty of Versailles" and then retitled "The Peace Treaties of Brest-Litovsk and Versailles," invariably fell on fertile ground, and attendance at his early speeches increased from a dozen persons to a hundred, to two hundred, and then to crowds beyond computation.[1094]

He told his listeners the same thing that all members of the right wing were saying, Germany had not been defeated on the battlefield but had instead been betrayed by Jews and other Marxists who had preached revolution and undermined the war effort. The Treaty of Versailles was a natural extension of the perfidy of those Jews and Marxists; it was all, claimed Hitler, the work of international Jewry.

Hitler expounded on the treaty throughout the 1920s, complaining that the product of German labor now belonged to foreign creditors. The loss of Germany's military prerogatives, he said, was a loss of sovereignty. The treaty had the effect of making Germany a colony of the outside world. And he made no secret of his belief that Germany's losses were for the benefit of members of the suprastate, the Jewish Stock Exchange. The democratic form of government that he regarded as having been imposed on Germany by the Allies was not German, it was Jewish, as was the government in Soviet Russia, he said. When the Social Democrats, the November Criminals, took over the government, they agreed to the terms of the treaty, the "disgraceful victory of Versailles," forced upon the losers of World War I by "international powers"—which, according to anti-Semitic propaganda, was the work of "the Jews."[1095]

When the stock market crashed in 1929, helping to finally give Hitler an opportunity to achieve real power, he claimed that Germany's economic troubles stemmed from the Treaty of Versailles.[1096] As he went about defying and violating the treaty after achieving power, he justified himself by saying that he was not violating the law but was instead restoring it, seeing such things as unification with Austria as being in accordance with natural law, and, not insignificantly, with Wilson's lofty Fourteen Points.

In actual fact, the various Weimar governments worked diligently throughout the 1920s and into the 1930s to have the treaty modified in various ways so that it would not be so burdensome to Germans, and, as evidenced by the Dawes Plan of 1924, the Young Plan of 1929, and the Lausanne Conference results of 1932, they achieved considerable success. Still, the treaty was onerous; it needed to be abandoned, not bandaged. The Young Plan, for example, was aimed at the eventual abrogation of the treaty, but it also committed Germany to continue to pay reparations for nearly sixty years, until 1988—two generations of Germans. It was therefore understandably deemed to be not a relief, but rather a compliance policy. According to Joachim Fest, "[E]leven years after the war, the Young Plan exposed the merciless attitude of the victors toward the vanquished. What was more, the plan once again adverted to the war-guilt clause. . . ."[1097]

A significant fallout from the Young Plan was the successful opposition enjoyed by the rightist DNVP party's Alfred Hugenberg who became the "spokesman of radical resentment" and began to sound increasingly like a Nazi.[1098] Largely as a result dissatisfaction with the Young Plan, Hugenberg would join in a short-lived coalition with the Nazis (the Herzberg Front, which was so named after the town in which agreement was reached in 1931) that enabled Hitler to lay claim to a certain amount of respectability and financial assistance. Hitler's alliance with Hugenberg also enabled him to better reach out to the masses via Hugenberg's publications empire.[1099]

Certain provisions of the treaty that SPD government leaders could not get modified, such as the requirement that the German General Staff be eliminated and the prohibition against tanks and artillery, they simply skirted. The General Staff continued to exist by another name (*Truppenamt*), and weapons and training were provided by Russia under secret terms of the Treaty of Rapallo, a treaty laid at the door of the Jewish-German Foreign Minister Walter Rathenau who was accused by rightists of "'treasonous' advocacy of friendship with Russia."[1100] Interestingly, the Jewish-owned, anti-German *Weltbühne* magazine exempted Rathenau from responsibility for the agreement and instead scapegoated a foreign ministry official who was subordinate to Rathenau, Baron von Maltzan.[1101]

All of the marginal modifications to the treaty were of no worth to the Nazis. For them, no modification was acceptable— their platform consistently called for its total abrogation. And because the treaty was so abhorrent to large masses of the German people, the Nazi position resonated with the populace. When Hitler came to power he immediately set about to openly defy and violate it. Among other things, he reintroduced compulsory military conscription (1935), rebuilt the armed forces, including both the air force and navy, reoccupied the demilitarized zone in the Rhineland, and annexed Austria— all in direct but morally justifiable violation of the Treaty of Versailles.

CHAPTER 5

THE WEIMAR REPUBLIC

The war was over. It was time for *"der Krieg nach dem Krieg,"*—it was time for "the war after the war"

Time line, Late 1918 through November 1923

At the close of World War I, Germany was awash with insurrectionists, nearly all of whom existed on the Marxist left of the political spectrum. Revolutionary and counterrevolutionary forces were also at work in Russia, Austria, and Hungary and events in those places influenced events in Germany. Because many events throughout Germany and the rest of Europe were happening concurrently, it may be useful for the reader to view a time line of these happenings before we discuss some of them in detail. The following also serves to summarize the plight of Germany during the first few years after World War I. Events in Germany and Europe that are germane to this narrative are as follows:

- Late 1918: Spartacist and USPD agitation of both the populace and the military are redoubled.
- October 29, 1918: Sparked by Spartacist and USPD propaganda, the Kiel Mutiny occurs and lasts for several days.
- November 3, 1918: Armed insurrections stemming from the Kiel Mutiny commence in other port cities, and then spread to the interior.
- November 7, 1918: The spreading mutinies and insurrections reach Bavaria. Jewish literati Kurt Eisner overthrows the Wittelsbach dynasty and installs himself at the head of the Bavarian Socialist Republic.
- November 9, 1918: The kaiser is ousted and a leftist but relatively moderate republican form of government is installed.

- November 11, 1918: Armistice is signed. World War I ends.
- December 25, 1918: Spartacist-led Christmas Crisis, an attempt at insurrection carried out on Christmas Day, 1918.
- January 6–12, 1919: Spartacist Uprising; another, more serious attempt at revolution.
- January 19, 1919: Elections for installation of permanent government.
- February 6, 1919: National Assembly (Constitutional Convention) convenes in the city of Weimar to create a new constitution for Germany.
- February 21, 1919: Kurt Eisner is assassinated.
- March 17, 1919: The reins of the government of Bavaria briefly pass to the non-Jew, Johannes Hoffmann.
- March 21, 1919: The Hungarian Revolution takes place. The Jewish radical Béla Kun is installed at the head of a Bolshevistic government there.
- March 31, 1919: Hitler returns to Munich (this date is one of several—establishment historians differ on the date of his return: March 1919 according to Fest and Toland, late January according to Schmidt, and mid-February according to Kershaw).[*]
- April 6, 1919: The success of Kun in Hungary encourages radicals in Bavaria to overthrow Hoffmann. Hoffmann is ousted by an incompetent clique of Jews headed by Ernst Toller.
- April 12, 1919: Toller is ousted by the ruthless Jew, Eugen Levine (along with the Jews Towia Axelrod, Max Levien, et al.). Toller stays on in the new government. Hoffmann escapes northward.

---

[*] The dates are a bit confusing because Hitler returned to the city but shortly thereafter relocated to serve as a guard at a prisoner of war camp. He then returned to Munich still again after the camp was closed.

- April 20, 1919: Forces organized by Hoffmann attempt to retake Bavaria but are defeated by the Red Brigade at Dachau, north of Munich.
- April 27, 1919: The Levine government attempts to arrest Adolf Hitler.
- April 27, 1919: Noske's Freikorps attack the Red forces in Bavaria.
- May 1, 1919: Noske's Freikorps breach the defenses of the Marxist forces in Munich.
- May 6, 1919: The city of Munich is declared secure by Noske.
- May 13, 1919: Hoffmann is returned to power in Bavaria.
- June 28, 1919: Treaty of Versailles is signed. North Sea embargo of Germany is finally lifted (nearly eight months after the end of hostilities).
- August 11, 1919: New Weimar constitution becomes law.
- Early 1920: Hitler is discharged from the army (historians differ on the specific date).
- March 13–17, 1920: The Rightist (Monarchist) Kapp Putsch takes place.
- March 1921: The disastrous Communist March Action occurs in the Ruhr.
- 1922–1923: Period of hyperinflation. Savings of the German populace are wiped out. Land, homes, estates, and other valuables are sold off at fire sale prices.
- 1923: French and Belgian troops occupy the Ruhr.
- November 8–9, 1923: Hitler's Beer Hall Putsch takes place.
- Mid- to late-1920s: Several widely publicized court trials ensue that have Jews as their defendants.

Creation of the Republic—the German Revolution

Historian Otto Friedrich cites Germany's aesthetic leftist diarist Count Harry Kessler to effectively summarize Germany's condition at the close of World War I.

> Germany lay prostrate . . . France gave open vent to her desire for our extermination, expressing it monumentally

> in her Prime Minister's words: "There are twenty million Germans too many." The continuation of the blockade after the armistice was rapidly fulfilling this wish; within six months from the armistice it had achieved a casualty list of 700,000 children, old people, and women. . . . The German people, starved and dying by the hundred thousand, were reeling deliriously between blank despair, frenzied revelry, and revolution. . . . Profiteers and their girls, the scum and riffraff of half Europe—types preserved like flies in amber in the caricatures of George Grosz—could be seen growing fat and sleek and flaunting their new cars and ostentatious jewelry in the faces of the pale children and starving women shivering in their rags before the empty bakers' and butchers' shops.[1102]

Germany was defeated. She lay prostrate. The country was a land of misery, of starvation, a land of utter despair and hopelessness. Roughly 2.7 million young men returned home with wounds, amputations, and other life-altering debilities.[1103] The families of the 2 million men who were killed were without fathers, without breadwinners, but were flush with discontent. While the German veterans of World War I were thrown into abject poverty, the government raised taxes so it could pay the reparations demanded by the Allies. And in the minds of a good many Germans, Germany came to its postwar condition by way of traitors, and more particularly by Marxist Jews. The idea of the "mythical" stab in the back was a currency for such Germans; it bought discontent and political allies.

Germany was in the throes of revolution well before the end of the war and insurrectionary activity continued to occur well after the establishment of the republic and the signing of the Treaty of Versailles.

The political foundations for revolution had been laid by Marxists throughout the first decade of the twentieth century but were intensified and brought to fruition during the war years. The revolution proper consisted of a series of events beginning just prior to the end of the war in November 1918 and lasted until

March 1919 with the establishment of a permanent government that was operating as a republic.

There were actually three different sets of revolutionaries vying for power: the monarchists, the Marxist republicans, and the radical, Bolshevistic Marxists. Armed insurrections against the republican government that ultimately prevailed occurred on several occasions during the period 1918 through 1923. With the exception of the one-week Kapp Putsch of 1920 and Hitler's dismally failed Beer Hall Putsch of 1923, the insurrectionists came from the leftist wing of Germany's political spectrum and that spectrum was heavily influenced by its Jewish leadership and constituency. Insurrections from the Left included the Bavarian Revolution of November 1918, the Christmas Crisis of 1918, the Spartacus Uprising of January 1919, the various insurrectionist activities of 1920, the March Action of 1921, and revolutionary turmoil in the Ruhr in 1923.

Importantly, the end of the war opened the floodgates for Jewish power in Germany. Detlev Peukert, in *The Weimar Republic*, states the changed Jewish-German situation as follows:

> The establishment of the Weimar Republic completed the process of Jewish emancipation in Germany. . . . Jews now assumed an important part in post-war public life, in the liberal parties and parties of the left, in universities and the mass media, and in certain branches of business, especially commerce. . . . many Jewish intellectuals embraced modernism and the art of the avant-garde. These were the first glimpses of the possible emergence of a new international, secularized culture which would sweep aside the traditional nationalist barriers on which anti-Jewish discrimination had rested.[1104]

Peukert, like a vast number of others, assigns the blame for anti-Semitism to nationalism. This was supposedly so even in light of the fact that German anti-Semitism was all but eradicated under the nationalistic government of Kaiser William II prior to the onset of World War I; up to that time, anti-Semitism was confined to those who objected to Jews as modernists. Aside from that, most Germans drew no strong distinctions between Germans and Jews. After the war, says Anthony Kauders, "many Gentiles now believed that *the* 'Jews'—and not just a few of them—were somehow responsible for the misery and dislocation that was postwar Germany."[1105] (Italics are in the original.)

Peukert has no complaint with respect to the Jewish nationalism represented by the Zionists. What German nationalism actually represented was Gentile organization and power, and it was those aspects of nationalism that were at the root of Jewish opposition: it was thought that by destroying nationalism one would simultaneously destroy Gentile power and replace it with a Jewish, secular, internationalistic, and communist version of power. As put by Amos Elon in his book *The Pity of It All*, Weimar Jews sought the following:

> With few exceptions, the main thrust of their intellectual and political efforts—and of their reckless magnanimity—was a desperate but vain attempt to civilize German patriotism: to base citizenship not on blood but on law, to separate church and state and to establish what would today be called an open, multicultural society.[1106]

And for people like Hitler, the multiculturalism that was sought was of a kind that he had observed in Austria-Hungary, a hodgepodge nation of diverse elements with only weak, ineffectual connections between them.

Prelude to the Spartacist Uprising

Shortly before the end of the war, in early October 1918, a Spartacus League war council was held in the port city of Bremen. It was decided that agitation was to be redoubled and that workers' and soldiers' councils on the Russian model were to be established everywhere. On October 5, the radically leftist USPD, along with its even more radical splinter group, the Spartacus League, formed a committee of revolutionary shop stewards. The revolutionary shop stewards were organizations of trade union representatives that had existed since the big January 1918 strike that included munitions workers, and it was these organizations that provided the cadre for the workers' councils (Soviets) established later. The committee of revolutionary shop stewards met daily to prepare for the rising. There was nothing "spontaneous" about the quick creation and implementation of such councils throughout Germany, though they are frequently described that way in historical accounts of their creation. In actuality, they sprang up in response to many months of organization and planning by the USPD and Spartacists.

The USPD-Spartacus elements also began the process of collecting weapons and further radicalizing the workers toward revolutionary ends. The intent of these efforts was to initiate a general labor strike to overthrow the kaiser and seize power. The collection of weapons reveals the lengths to which the USPD and Spartacus elements were willing to go to achieve their objectives. Their slogan for the coming events, "All or Nothing," was indicative of the commitment they felt.[1107]

Following his October 1918 release from prison as part of a general amnesty, Karl Liebknecht joined with the revolutionary shop stewards and resumed his revolutionary rhetoric, speaking at factory meetings and inflaming workers against the monarchy. On November 1, Liebknecht issued an unambiguous call for revolution. He explicitly called for soldiers at the front to disarm their officers and to shoot those officers who would not cooperate. He unequivocally called for armed seizure of the government.

With scorching rhetoric, Liebknecht inflamed the spirit of revolution. He did not mention that seizure of the government was intended as the means by which soldiers, sailors, and marines could win power for himself and his cohorts. Liebknecht's rhetoric was straightforward:

> Soldiers and marines! Fraternize! Take possession of your ships. Overpower first your officers. Place yourselves in communication with your comrades on

land and seize all harbours and open fire, if necessary, on loyal groups. . . . Arise, organize, seize weapons and use them against those who plan to make slaves of you after they have made their own peace. End the war yourselves and use your weapons against the rulers.[1108]

On October 29, 1918, the fruits of Spartacist and USPD agitation were realized: the supposedly "spontaneous" Kiel Mutiny commenced and soldiers' and sailors' councils modeled on the successful Russian Revolution were immediately ensconced throughout the country.

Rosa Luxemburg, in coordination with Liebknecht and others, had issued still another call for revolution. In her Spartacus League publication, she demanded the abolition of the individual provinces and the formation of a Marxist regime. All municipal and parliamentary bodies were to be abolished and replaced by workers' and soldiers' councils. She demanded that the entire police force be disarmed and that the revolutionaries seize all stocks of munitions and weapons to arm the Red Guards. She went on to call for punishment of the monarchy and the bourgeoisie. She also called for the confiscation of all foodstuffs, a move that would have put the entire population on its knees before its revolutionary masters.

It is at the very least reasonable to presume that had Luxemburg and Liebknecht and their fellow Communists prevailed, the German monarchy would have suffered the fate of the Romanovs in Russia, and their opponents within the general German population would have suffered the fate of those millions of Russians, Ukrainians, Latvians, et. al., who opposed Communism in the East.

The demands of Luxemburg and her fellow revolutionaries were not going to be satisfied peacefully. Nor were they to be satisfied by any new form of government that was not of their own making and their own leadership. When Communist revolution came it would have to be violent. The only real question that remained was one of readiness for such an undertaking.

Luxemburg believed that the great lesson of the Russian Revolution was the use of the mass strike as a means to bring down a government and secure power for the revolutionaries.[1109] She also believed that the people had to be prepared for revolution by way of propaganda, and that the propaganda task had not yet been completed by the end of 1918. Once having overcome her reticence, however, and once the uprising commenced, no one exceeded her commitment, her personal involvement, or her tireless effort.

By late 1918, the kaiser's government had fallen and the workers' and sailors' councils were in place. The military was almost entirely disarmed and rife with Marxist agitators. The new interim republican government was still weak and ineffectual. Starvation and a host of other miseries were rampant. The time seemed right for the radical Marxists to strike.

By November 8, 1918, the organizational and agitational efforts of the USPD and Spartacists that had been redoubled a month earlier were deemed sufficiently successful to call for a general strike on November 9, 1918. The strike was to be the opening salvo for the German-Bolshevik revolution. As things would turn out, however, counteractions by relatively moderate factions would delay the onset of widespread revolutionary violence.

Also on November 8, the SPD learned of the impending strike and revolution. One of the revolutionary shop stewards, Ernst Däumig, who was later the cochairman of the KPD, had been arrested and plans were found in his briefcase. Ebert's SPD representatives caucused to decide on a course of action. Knowing that it could not possibly prevent the strike, the moderate faction of the SPD leadership decided to do what it could to represent the strike as its own,[1110] an action that would serve to steal the initiative from the USPD and Spartacists. On the morning of November 9, hundreds of thousands of workers poured out of the factories.[1111] All this was happening while Germany was still at war.

Liebknecht was tireless in his activities that day. He rushed about the city, speaking here, directing there, hoping to bring it all together. In the afternoon, along with a contingent of armed revolutionaries, he seized the offices of the *Lokal-Anzeiger*, a conservative newspaper. The editorial staff was thrown out and replaced by Spartacists. Thus was born *Die Rote Fahne* (The Red Flag) newspaper. Luxemburg took charge.[1112] By November 18, the first issue of *Die Rote Fahne* was published bearing the names of both Liebknecht and Luxemburg as editors, but Rosa was the leading light. Contributors to the paper included Paul Levi, August Thalheimer,[*] and Paul Lange.

As soon as the news of the German Revolution arrived in Moscow, Lenin offered two carloads of Russian wheat for the starving German people. This was his gesture of international Socialist solidarity. Friedrich Ebert, leader of the SPD, sent back his response: "Knowing that there is famine in Russia, we request the bread you wish to contribute to the German Revolution be given to the starving in Russia."[1113] Upon learning of Ebert's response, Karl Radek, the Jewish-Polish representative dispatched by Lenin to make the offer to Germany, snorted that "Judas Iscariot has completed his betrayal."[1114] The Bolsheviks apparently expected that Ebert, as a member of the Marxist SPD, would support the ultraradicals of the Liebknecht faction. Radek, along with many others, had been dispatched to Germany by Lenin in order to assist his German comrades with the revolution. Lenin's agents argued for violent seizure of power from the relatively moderate Socialist government of Ebert.

On November 10, 3,000 delegates assembled at a meeting hall in Berlin. The Bolshevistic thought process of the delegates became apparent when they voted to "send the Russian Workmen's and Soldiers' government . . . fraternal greeting."[1115] The delegates demanded immediate socialization of German industry, but the delegates who did so were opposed by Ebert. By the afternoon, events began to turn in Ebert's favor. A proposed

---

[*] Both Levi and Thalheimer, like Liebknecht and Luxemburg, were Jewish. We know well from our history books that Hitler later purged Jews from publishing—the books are mostly silent on the precedents for such action.

SPD-USPD coalition was discussed, and despite protests from the radicals, it was ratified. The Jews Liebknecht and Haase had spoken, as had Ebert. Ebert's call for Socialist unity had been far better received than Liebknecht's attack on Ebert for obstructing the revolution. Liebknecht's Spartacist dialectic was obscure to the delegates. Ebert, by way of more direct language, managed to push Liebknecht into the role of a niggling theoretician. In the end, the delegates elected a twenty-eight member executive council. The membership of the council was equally divided between the SPD and USPD. The Spartacists were left out. After its establishment, the council declared itself the sovereign representative of the German people.[1116]

The armistice was implemented on November 11. The despicable carnage of World War I was now officially at an end. The government was now composed of relatively moderate Marxists (SPD) and radical Marxists (USPD). Both factions were significantly influenced by Jewish cliques within their membership and leadership. The violence of the leftists in Germany would soon commence in earnest.

The great struggle of the times in Germany was between radical leftists (Marxists/Communists) and radical rightists. The leftists founded their hate on the basis of class; the rightists on their hate of international Marxism that stemmed in no small part from the rightists' inherent nationalism. Both camps, though, espoused hate with about equal vigor, and both sides were ultimately about equal in their willingness to resort to violence. Author Eric Weitz points out, for example, that the KPD had a party culture that always pushed "harsh physical engagement" to the top of its agenda.[1117] Political murder became commonplace on both extremes of the political spectrum, though the Left, due to its larger size and better organization at this time, was by far the most violent in the early 1920s. The Right, for its part, acquired a lot of attention due to its assassination of several high-profile political figures (e.g., Eisner, Rathenau, and Erzberger) who were then trumpeted as martyrs by a sympathetic leftist press.

Revolution Everywhere

At the close of the war revolution reigned everywhere in Europe. Germany was almost immediately beset with revolutionary attempts to overthrow the republican government that had itself been established by revolutionary means. Austria, Hungary, and Poland had their share of revolutionary turmoil and upheaval as well. In Russia, of course, battles between the Marxists and the White Russians raged on during the years 1918–1921—and leading Jews throughout the world did all they could to enfeeble the White Russians by lobbying Western governments to deny aid to them.

As a practical matter, it was the parliamentarians and the radical Marxists who were vying for power in Germany. The monarchists, after a feeble attempt to regain power (the Kapp Putsch) were very soon out of play. The hard-right nationalists like Hitler remained effete. General Eric Ludendorff, the hero of World War I and an early Hitler supporter,* ran for president in 1925: he garnered less than 300,000 votes, only a little over 1 percent.[1118] Rightist forces were clearly on the wane.

From late 1918 through 1923, most bets were on the Marxists, especially the Jewish-dominated SPD and USPD/KPD. In the 1919 election, 45 percent of voters supported Marxist parties,[1119] the rest of the vote went to the Center Party and a plethora of small, special interest parties. On the Right, the monarchist German National People's Party (DNVP) also did well as it garnered 20.5 percent of the vote.

Spurred by the success of the Russian Revolution of November 1917, the Marxists achieved a number of early political successes, grew in strength, and appeared to be the wave of the future. The success of Jews in early Weimar political struggles was made

---

*Ludendorff had joined Hitler in his 1923 Beer Hall Putsch. By the time he ran for the presidency, however, he had split with Hitler because Hitler and his party were insufficiently hostile toward Catholics and Freemasons. On a more general level, Ludendorff became increasingly unhinged in his later years, largely due to the influence of his second wife, Dr. Mathilde von Kemnitz.

evident by their dominance of the various Marxist parties as already mentioned and their consequent participation in federal, provincial, and local government bodies.

The political success of Jews in Germany was concretely illustrated in Magdeburg where Brandes was in control. In Dresden, it was Lipinsky, Geyer, and Fleissner. In the Ruhr, Markus and Levinsohn. In Bremerhaven and Kiel, Gruenewalde and Kohn respectively, and in the Palatinate, Lilienthal and Heine.[1120] Jews also managed to take control in Hirsch, where Haase and Herzfeld reigned. In Bavaria, it was Eisner and his coterie. In Saxony, it was Lipinsky and Gradnauer. In Wurttemberg, Heymann held sway, and in Baden, it was Haas. Their violent attempts to secure the Berlin government (the Spartacist Uprising) and Bavaria (Eisner, et al.) soon came to a vicious end.

In Germany's largest and most influential province, Prussia, Jews dominated. Hirsch and Rosenfeld dominated the cabinet, with Hirsch heading up the Department of the Interior and Rosenfeld the Department of Justice. Simon was in charge of the Treasury. The Department of Justice was all but entirely led and staffed by Jews. The director of education was the Jew Furtran, who was assisted by Arndt. Meyer-Gerhard was the director of the Colonial Office. The food supply departments were also dominated and operated by Jews.[1121]

Shortly before Hitler returned to Munich on or about March 31 after a stint guarding prisoners of war, word arrived of the Hungarian Revolution that had commenced on March 21, 1919. That revolution, in turn, served to further inspire the revolutionaries within Germany.

Russia, meanwhile, which was at the time very much fretting about its own continued existence, sought the establishment of Communist regimes elsewhere on the Continent as a way to further secure its own security; it therefore played a significant supporting role in the revolutions in both Germany and Hungary. Hitler, still in the army in early 1919 (the date of his discharge is variously given as late 1918, February 1920, March 1920, and April 1,

1920), observed the unfolding insurrectionary *Sturm und Drang* while he was stationed in his beloved Munich, Bavaria.*

With the end of World War I there were really only two viable political outlooks for Germany: she was to be either a leftist-dominated democratic republic or a radically authoritarian Socialist republic along Bolshevik lines. The Allies would not deal with the monarchy of William II or any other form of autocracy; nor would they countenance a peace treaty with representatives of a German military regime.

Communism was newly installed, though not yet formally declared as such, in Russia, much to the consternation and concern of the Allies. A Communist government was also an option for Germany. Such a government would, of course, have had the enthusiastic support of Russia, but would have been opposed by the U.S., France, and England. Since Russia was not a participant at the Versailles Peace Talks, it would have been left to the Big Three as to whether Germany could have a radically Marxist government, and that was an unlikely prospect. Still, it remains true that the radical leftists of Germany were trying to install just such a government there. And given the turmoil and war weariness of the times, it had at least some chance of succeeding. The success of Jewish interests in stymieing support for the White Russians illustrates the power and success of those interests—it might very well have also been able to support and emplace a Communist regime in Germany even in the face of objections from the likes of the Western powers.

We can only imagine what violence would have ensued had a radically Bolshevistic government been installed. Communist violence in Russia, parts of Germany, and all of Hungary serve as templates for what would have likely occurred. As things would

---

* Of Hitler's stay in Munich, Fest says he "was not altogether unhappy" there (Fest, 62). In actual fact, Hitler was ecstatic there. He reveled in it and its art and architecture. He was happier there than he had ever been previously. He revered the city and his time there.

turn out, however, no matter the odds, Germany would become a leftist republic, albeit a largely ineffectual one.

On November 9, 1918, Prince Max von Baden, a liberal who had a month earlier been appointed to the position of chancellor to negotiate the armistice with the Allies, transferred his power to SPD leader Friedrich Ebert. Ebert assured Prince Max that his government would establish stability within the country and would soon convene a National Assembly to decide on a new constitution. Ebert established an interim government to conduct business while awaiting installation of a permanent one by way of elections in January 1919. Work on the constitution by the National Assembly meeting in the city of Weimar commenced in February 1919. It was ratified and signed into law on August 11, 1919.

Along with Ebert, the other major political contender of the time at the national level was Karl Liebknecht. Ebert favored a parliamentary monarchy as the form of government. Liebknecht would have created a radically Bolshevistic one. Neither Ebert nor Liebknecht would get the form of government he wished. Philip Scheidemann, one of the leaders of the SPD, declared Germany a republic. As other leaders of the interim government were exhausting themselves with talk about the form and membership of the interim government, Scheidemann had, on November 9, interrupted his afternoon meal to address a crowd that had gathered outside the parliament building. He strolled to a balcony area and cried out to the crowd, "Long live the great German Republic!"[1122] His pronouncement proved irrevocable. A few hours later Liebknecht called for the creation of a Marxist-Socialist state, but it was, by then, too late for him to carry the day.

Thus, the republic was born. A single man made an impromptu declaration and the form of governance was established for an entire people. As numerous historians correctly point out, however, it was a republic without instructions for use, a republic void of republicans.

Adolf Hitler abhorred the new government from its outset. Republicanism and its associated democracy was anathema to him. His hate for such a state was exceeded only by his hate of Marxist

Bolshevism. Even at an early age, he despised the very concept of democracy and republicanism. As historian Sarah Gordon tells us, "democracy and political parties were to him the subtle invention of the 'Jewish race' to weaken, and therefore to destroy, other races."[1123] Those who believed in democracy, Jewish or not, were to Hitler, "spiritual Jews."[1124]

Ebert formed a relatively moderate (relative to the Spartacists, for example, but still very much Marxist) Socialist provisional government composed of equal parts of SPD and USPD leaders. Due to the influence the Spartacists had acquired by way of their ceaseless political agitation and their role in bringing about the revolution, Ebert offered a place in the government to Karl Liebknecht as well. Liebknecht declined.

The elections in January 1919 determined the membership of the permanent government. Ebert was elected president[*] and Phillip Scheidemann, the man who had proclaimed the republic, was appointed as chancellor.

Ebert's provisional government included Jews as heads of two of his six ministries: Otto Landsberg and Hugo Haase. The permanent SPD government that followed also had a substantial contingent of Jews.

The republic suffered from a crisis of legitimacy from its infancy. It was a regime that no one loved and too many loathed. Opponents included members of the Left and the Right, Jewish and non-Jewish, but the right-wing nationalists were especially hateful toward the new regime.

The newly formed Communist Party of Germany (KPD) was the first to try to overthrow the government by force; the rightist Kapp Putsch followed it fourteen months later. Besieged by dissension and revolution though it was, the government nevertheless managed to rally from time to time and muddle along from crisis to crisis throughout the period 1919 to 1933. In the

---

[*] Due to widespread opposition toward the new government, Ebert was elected by the National Assembly, not by a direct vote of the people as called for by the August 1919 constitution. Only Hindenburg was ever elected to the presidency by popular vote.

mid- to late-1920s, it actually enjoyed a period of relative stability as German prospects improved on both the national and international fronts. From 1918 through 1923, though, both the government and the nation were racked by revolutionary violence and turmoil.

The Weimar Republic

The phrase *Weimar Republic* is used by historians to name the government of Germany during the period 1919 through January 1933; it was the government that was quickly destroyed when Adolf Hitler became chancellor. The term was not used officially during its existence; the official term was *German Empire* despite the republican form of government under which it operated and the fact that Germany's previous empire, modest though it was (compared, say, to England and France), was by now defunct. The Weimar name stems from the fact that the National Assembly, mentioned above, convened in the city of Weimar to create the nation's constitution after the defeat of the monarchial German Empire of World War I. The assembly had to meet outside the capital because leftist revolutionary activity in Berlin made it impossible to conduct business there. The radical leftists in Berlin were led by people of Jewish extraction—in particular by the Spartacists under the leadership of Liebknecht, Luxemburg, Leo Jogiches, and Paul Levi.

The National Assembly was dominated by leftists, which is to say Jewish and left-centrist (Catholic) political leanings. The Center Party, which was fundamentally a Catholic one, had eighty-eight delegates.[1125] Of the 421 members of the assembly, the Social Democrats had 163 delegates, and the newly formed German Democratic Party (DDP), which was almost exclusively Jewish, had seventy-five. The remaining ninety-five delegates came from a variety of ineffectual special interest parties from across the political spectrum. Thus it was that in Germany, the birthplace of Martin Luther, the fount of the Protestant Reformation, Jews and Catholics held sway (much like the U.S. Supreme Court where we have six Catholics and three Jews (Breyer, Ginsburg, and Kagan), though the vast majority of the U.S. population is Protestant).

The Weimar Republic was established as a thing of paper and process: a constitutional document and an administrative infrastructure, a makeshift democracy.[1126] It was, as Adolf Hitler and his followers called it, the "system," a term that would be revised and reinvigorated during the protests of the 1960s in the U.S. The republic was not, like its predecessors, a thing of devotion; it had no inspirational element, no kaiser serving at the behest of God as the "first servant of the state," no unifying focus, nothing to support the emotional wants of the people. Its constitution, put together in an atmosphere of starvation and revolutionary turmoil at home and the threat of national disembowelment by the Allies, was hurried along in order to get a government in place that was acceptable to the victors. Its development was heavily influenced by the need to quickly have the North Sea blockade lifted. There were fears that the Allies would occupy the entire country, fears of what had happened in Russia, fears of proposals being put forth by the various soldiers' councils, and by the need to simply restore law and order.

Only by installing some form of democratic government could Germany expect the Allies to lift the blockade that was still in place and continuing to starve the German populace several months after the signing of the armistice. Russia had entered into civil war with atrocity a daily fair of life there—there was genuine fear that the same fate would befall Germany. There were already signs that Germany was well on the road to the Russian experience: street battles, chaos, and every manner of public disorder was everywhere evident.

To the extent that the resulting republic had supporters they were supporters of the "system" and such supporters came exclusively from the relatively moderate left; both the far Left and the far Right abhorred the Weimar government. Still, the republic was established and then went about spawning and strengthening the political and cultural avant-garde of the era under conditions of a series of crises, bleak poverty, and political breakdown.

Istvan Deak handily summarizes the difference between the ideals, if they may be called that, of the Marxist and those of Hitler and his Nazis:

> Marxists failed to understand the little man's need which was not for harsh dogmas, but for a mystique, a tempting idea. The Marxists would have their followers deny God and the nation, surrender their traditions, their prejudices, and their entire cultural heritage; the Nazis asked for no such sacrifices but dazzled their followers with an array of colorful promises.
>
> The Nazis, in effect, offered a non-religious spiritual banner; the Marxists demanded rationalism. It was ultimately to prove an unequal match. Hitler had learned his lessons well in Vienna and thereafter—he offered the pomp of the church without its dogma. Hitler worked to strengthen existing prejudices and use them politically; the Marxists sought to eliminate racial prejudice in favor of class prejudice.[1127]

The Weimar Republic was a corporatist solution to a deeply emotional problem. It was rational but emotionally sterile. Like the wire-frame "mothers" used by behaviorist Harry Harlow in his 1950s experiments with monkeys, it could provide sustenance but no comfort; it could not attach to the emotions of the people; it provided no "contact comfort." Who could love such a thing? How could the likes of Ebert and Scheidemann, not to mention Eisner and Rathenau, dare take the place once occupied by the likes of Bismarck? For the rightist it was all too horrible a thing to perceive with equanimity.

Prelude to Defeat of Revolutionary and Insurrectionist Movements

In the early days of his government, Ebert, to his credit, moved quickly to establish dominion over the Marxist workers' and soldiers' councils that were exercising political control in late 1918. Knowing full well that radical Marxist elements would try to seize the government by force, he wisely allied himself with what remained of the army.

Upon the forced resignation of General Ludendorff in October 1918, Lieutenant General Wilhelm Groener stepped into the breach. It had been Groener's unhappy task to inform Kaiser William II that he must abdicate. Groener was a staunch soldier but hardly a rightist radical. During the war he had done himself political harm by fighting against profiteering. Now, however, he had become the de facto head of the army as Hindenburg continued to serve as its titular head.

Immediately after the fall of the kaiser, meetings took place between Groener and Ebert. Ebert was in desperate straits due to the revolutionary agitation of the Spartacists. Clearly, if something was not done soon, his government would fall. For his part, Groener was concerned about maintaining the prerogatives of the army's officer corps as it was then established, albeit at markedly reduced strength. The Jewish politician Hugo Haase, the man who had struggled so diligently to undermine the army throughout the war, now led an effort to enfeeble the peacetime army: he called for steps to abolish badges of rank, turn military discipline over to the civilian courts, abolition of the wearing of uniforms when off duty, abolishment of marks of respect such as the salute, election of officers, and transfer of command to the soldiers' councils.[1128] Just such a scheme had previously been instituted by the Russian army during the revolution and was a major factor in the decomposition of the Russian forces facing the Germans.[1129] In total, it was a call for the tolling of the death knell for the army; but a call that, if successful, would greatly enhance the prospects of Haase and his radical Marxists to overthrow the government.

A deal was struck between Groener and Ebert: Groener would provide the army's support in crushing the radical Marxists in exchange for Ebert's promise that he would support the objective of the officer corps to retain traditional structures of army command, control, and custom.

As with nearly every problem in the early days of the republic, there were problems with this arrangement. The army was in disarray. Significant numbers of troops were no longer loyal as infiltrated Communists had, by this time, bedeviled its ranks. To overcome these difficulties, Freikorps (militia) units were formed from high-quality, disciplined frontline troops.* It would be these troops that would represent the salvation of the new republic from insurrectionists from the radical Left. Workers would later be used to overcome radical rightist elements.

As previously emphasized, both the radical Left and the radical Right opposed the new government. Our emphasis here will be the radical Left, the elements of the political milieu that were so despised by Adolf Hitler. And in any event, the Right did not achieve much in the way of its objectives until very late in the existence of the republic.

On December 10, 75,000 soldiers under the command of Ebert's new ally, General Groener, marched into Berlin where they waited in readiness for further developments on the political front.

The Christmas Crisis

The first national congress of the workers' and soldiers' councils met in Berlin from December 16–20, 1918. In *Die Rote Fahne*, Luxemburg called on the delegates to remove the Ebert cabinet and to disarm all troops who failed to unconditionally recognize the authority of the workers' and soldiers' councils, dismemberment of the White Guards† previously formed by the government, and the emplacement of a Red Guard (Communist militia) in its stead. She also called for the rejection of the National Assembly; an assembly that she knew would divert the revolution that she and her cohorts sought.[1130]

Radical Marxists were incensed that Ebert would not support their extremist objectives for the immediate overthrow of the bourgeoisie and creation of a Bolshevistic government.

---

* Richard M. Watt (*The Kings Depart*) correctly points out that these early Freikorps units were not, as is commonly thought, reactionary gangs formed of White-Guardist types. They were instead composed of the very best troops operating under the very best of enlightened leadership. See Watt, 240–51.
† Remnants of the regular army that were called the "White Guards of Capitalism" by the communists.

Encouraged by defections of soldiers to their cause and by the turmoil of the times, the radicals, led by Liebknecht and Luxemburg, decided to seize the government by force.

As Liebknecht and Luxemburg were planning their counterrevolution, the Polish-Jew Karl Radek[*] was again dispatched to Berlin by Lenin. He arrived there illegally on December 20 and went directly to *Die Rote Fahne* where he met with his fellow Jews, Luxemburg, Liebknecht, and Jogiches. For Radek, terrorism was an essential element of the revolutionary process; he was aghast that the Spartacists had not yet employed it to its full potential. For Radek, a bayonet was an indispensable tool for introducing Communism.[1131] Luxemburg believed that terrorism of the kind that Radek recommended was theoretically deficient. Radek, for his part, argued that terror was essential for the completion of the revolution, and it was entirely justified—it was to be used, after all, against "classes whom history has sentenced to death."[1132]

It was not as if Berlin was not already awash with violence: sixteen Spartacists were killed and another twelve were wounded in early December during a failed attempt to arrest the Berlin executive of the workers' and soldiers' councils.

In late December Ebert and Groener continued to work diligently to form the troops that remained loyal to the government into effective Freikorps units.

Meanwhile, Liebknecht joined with the USPD as well as elements of the People's Marines and revolutionary shop stewards to create an armed fighting force. Weapons had been acquired and distributed with monies provided by the Jewish Russian Ambassador Joffe to Jewish USPD member, Oskar Cohn. Cohn would later be the leader of an investigation against the war heroes Hindenburg and Ludendorff, who would, in turn, thereafter propagate the claim that Germany had been stabbed in the back.

---

[*] Radek was an intimate of Lenin; he accompanied Lenin on the famous sealed-train across Germany in 1917. In 1912, he had been expelled from the SDKPiL on charges of theft.

Cohn was an undersecretary in the Ministry of Justice—that is, he was among the Jewish members of the government who were working diligently to bring about its demise.[1133] The revolutionaries had some 100,000 supporters, 2,000 machine guns, and thirty pieces of artillery—clearly, this was a serious attempt to violently overthrow the government.

The Spartacus League newspaper called on workers to join with them in battle and thousands responded.[1134] Revolutionaries in other cities followed suit. The Spartacus Uprising had begun though it would still be some days before it was to engage in heavy fighting.

As mentioned above, Liebknecht was a participant in the governmental discussions in which Ebert was able to sway party leaders to his way of thinking instead of Liebknecht's. Having failed in a reasonable approximation of the democratic process, Liebknecht looked elsewhere for support. Throughout November, he and his Spartacists harassed the government and did all they could to incite civil war. Among his actions during this period was the creation of a Council of Deserters, Stragglers, and Furloughed Soldiers, an organization that was to be employed as a Spartacist "shock force."[1135] As time would tell, it was a pitiful thing.

On November 11, Russia broadcast a message urging the German people to continue the revolution under the leadership of Liebknecht. A few weeks later, Joffe publicly revealed the details of his having given money to the Independents to fund the revolution. USPD Commissioners were furious—the admission made them appear to be exactly what they were—agents of a heavily Jewish foreign power. They issued a denial of Joffe's assertions, but the damage was already done.[1136]

Shortly after Radek's arrival in Berlin, revolutionary marines occupied the chancellery and took Ebert prisoner. Ebert, nevertheless, managed to secure a telephone to call for help from General Groener's Freikorps. On December 24, the radicals and government troops exchanged gunfire. Fighting continued throughout Christmas Day. The Christmas Day encounter resulted in the death of some fifty-six government troops and eleven

Spartacists. Initially, as the casualty ratio suggests, the forces supporting the revolution gained the upper hand.[1137]

As the Freikorps troops fought in opposition to the Spartacists, they were hailed and cheered by the populace. Clearly, fighting in Berlin would not be a replication of the fighting in Petrograd the year before as was hoped by the Spartacists. Making matters worse, the hodgepodge of revolutionary elements, that sorry lot of Deserters, Stragglers, and Furloughed Soldiers, were poorly led and just as poorly coordinated. They were no match for the trained and disciplined troops of the Freikorps. The violent clashes in December were a prelude to the full-scale uprising that would soon follow.

Following the Christmas Crisis, the USPD left the government in protest. Its departure was a godsend for Ebert. He had only let it participate due to the revolutionary events taking place when his government was formed. Now he could act in open opposition to the USPD.

Prelude to the Spartacist Revolution

On 4 January 1919, Emil Eichhorn, a member of the USPD and simultaneously a Spartacist adherent close to Liebknecht, was fired from his position as Berlin's chief of police. Eichhorn had obtained his position in the heady days of early November by simply arriving at the police station with a gang of leftist revolutionaries and proclaiming himself the head of the police. Preposterous though it seems, here was Eichhorn, a former chief of the telegraph service at the Soviet Embassy, naming himself chief of police of Berlin—a good many equally preposterous things happened during those turbulent times.

Eichhorn went about releasing leftist prisoners.[*] He then began the task of filling the ranks of the police with Spartacists, who, as

---

[*] The German police were complicit on both sides of the political equation. In Bavaria where the soviet period was not forgotten, Police Commissioner Pöhner supported the Nazis; in the north the Spartacists and other leftists were supported by Emil Eichhorn and later by Berlin's Jewish Vice Police Chief Bernard Weise.

Richard Watt points out, "with their chief's approval, took only the most perfunctory notice of riots against the Ebert government."[1138] With the USPD still part of his shaky government, Ebert could do little but accede to the actions of Eichhorn. When the USPD withdrew from the government on December 29, however, Ebert was able to act, and did so by firing Eichhorn. Liebknecht, knowing that he was about to lose an important ally and tool in his struggle, called out the workers in protest. This was the spark that ignited the Spartacist Uprising. An attempt at revolution now commenced in earnest.

The Spartacist Uprising

In early January 1919, the Spartacist Uprising led by Liebknecht, Luxemburg, Leo Jogiches, and Clara Zetkin, commenced. Zetkin was the only non-Jewish radical within the leadership. The Russian Jew Karl Radek also participated as a major drawing card for Spartacist rallies. The Spartacists were again joined by their radical brethren in the USPD to carry out their actions. On the night of January 5–6, the Spartacists distributed arms to their followers and printed a manifesto demanding the dismissal of the Ebert government and appointment of themselves in its stead.

On January 6, a mammoth demonstration, initiated by Liebknecht, began. Some 200,000 workers paraded through the streets of Berlin. The revolutionaries placed riflemen at strategic locations, such as a machine gun atop the commanding heights of the Brandenburg Gate where they could effectively cover the Unter den Linden, Königstrasse, and Charlottenburger Chaussee. They barricaded streets in the manner of Parisians during the French Revolution.

The Spartacist-USPD (by this time the Spartacists were known as the KPD, as they had declared themselves to be the Communist Party of Germany in late December) attacked and seized buildings throughout Berlin, including the Reichstag. Killings were taking place throughout the city. Elements of the fire department went about Berlin retrieving bodies.[1139] The government fled the city.

Defense Minister Gustav Noske used the army and Freikorps under Groener to respond with sufficient force to crush the revolt. The fighting continued until January 12 when the Freikorps troops prevailed. A few days later both Luxemburg and Liebknecht were captured and summarily executed.* Soon after the uprising, on March 10, 1919, Leo Jogiches was also killed. The Spartacus League, its leaders, and its revolution were at an end. But its Communist Party (KPD) legacy lived on. Leadership of the KPD passed to the Jew Paul Levi.

Luxemburg's body was unceremoniously dumped in a canal. It was not found until June. She was buried on June 13 with 20,000 people in attendance.[1140] Karl Radek was imprisoned for a short time, but then released due to his diplomatic immunity and threats from Lenin to take retaliatory actions against German diplomats in Russia. Hitler, who had long considered Liebknecht and his corevolutionaries "ready for the rope," undoubtedly took great satisfaction from the death of Liebknecht and the others of his coterie.

Those who bemoan the fate of the Spartacists are hypocritical. Had the Spartacists succeeded, there would have been a bloodbath in Germany comparable to the one that took place in Russia. Peter Gay has it that the right wing responded to the uprisings by killing "with abandon and with impunity."[1141] In keeping with historians of his type, he has nothing whatever to say about the nature of the killings by Jewish-led leftists. The murderous response of the German Bolsheviks to opposition would certainly have mapped to that of their Bolshevik compatriots, particularly since the German KPD was financed by Russia and was such a willing and enthusiastic sycophant of the Russians.

Were it not for the Freikorps, Berlin, and eventually all of Germany, says respected historian John Toland, would probably

---

* Incredibly, Amos Elon, in his book, *The Pity of it All: A Portrait of the German-Jewish Epoch, 1743–1933*, claims that Luxemburg, "who had played no role in the revolution, was brutally assassinated by fanatical army officers." [Elon, P. 345.] If we can believe that we can believe that Osama Bin Laden played no role in the events of 911 and should not have been assassinated.

have gone Communist.[1142] And if Germany had fallen to the Communists, it is not much of a stretch to imagine that France and Italy would have soon followed suit, and thereafter the whole of Europe.

Though the Freikorps prevailed in Berlin, uprisings continued within several of the various provinces. Jewish leaders were instrumental in establishing revolutionary governments at the state level throughout Germany. Most prominent among them were Paul Hirsch who served as the Jewish prime minister of Prussia, Germany's largest province, and Georg Gradnauer, also Jewish, in Saxony.[1143] Revolutionary activity continued in the North Sea ports as well as the Ruhr, and in industrial cities throughout the country. Each of the many pockets of insurrection and revolution were confronted and defeated in turn by Gustav Noske's Freikorps. In Bavaria's Munich, street battles were a daily occurrence by late January 1919. By March, the Spartacist Uprising had been largely overcome but a separate set of revolutionary events continued in Germany's Bavaria, a subject we will turn to after we discuss some intervening issues.

The Constitution and Early Weimar Republic

An election was held on January 19, 1919, for the installation of a permanent government. The constitution under which this new permanent government would operate would not be put into place for several months, but at least a government was established that could proceed to deal with the Versailles Peace Talks, a precursor for the lifting of the Allies' ongoing and devastating blockade of the North Sea.

It had been only a week since the Spartacus Uprising had been crushed. Ebert and his people triumphed: Ebert retained the presidency and his SPD won 11.5 million votes (38 percent of the total) and 163 of the Reichstag's 421 seats. The Catholic Center Party won eighty-nine seats, and the liberal Democratic Party (DDP) won seventy-four. The USPD, which had been so prominent and seemingly powerful during the street fighting of a week prior, obtained only twenty-two seats.* The right-wing German National People's Party (DNVP) won forty-two seats (see Appendix for a discussion of the prominent political parties of the Weimar era). The Communist KPD boycotted the election and was therefore left out of the new government.[1144] As easily discerned from the foregoing, leftist and centrist parties won a solid majority of the parliament's seats: 348 of the 421 total—this point is important because many apologists claim that the government was heavily composed of rightist factions.

After the election, the new chancellor, Scheidemann, who was appointed by Ebert, formed a coalition government. Landsberg, Preuss, and Schiffer held cabinet posts. Other Jews occupied important positions below the cabinet level.[1145]

On February 6, the National Assembly convened in Weimar for the purpose of creating a new constitution. For all of the Jewish involvement in all of the various revolutions in Europe and Germany in particular, Germans remained largely aloof from anti-Semitism. As the assembly initiated its deliberations it used a first-draft constitution prepared by the soon-to-be minister of the interior, the Jewish constitutional scholar Hugo Preuss. The constitution that he proposed was taken in large part word for word from the one that had been drafted at Saint Paul's Church during the revolutionary turmoil of 1848, but it also incorporated the principles of the first Ten Amendments to the U.S. Constitution and the French Declaration of the Rights of Man, along with twentieth-century refinements.[1146] As put by Peter Gay, "Hugo Preuss, the architect of the Weimar constitution, was a symbol of the [Republican] revolution . . . he, the outsider [Gay's euphemism for 'Jew'], gave shape to the new Republic, *his* Republic."[1147] (Italics are in the original.) Others who were intimately involved in

---

* In a simple plurality system of voting, a winner-takes-all system, the SPD and USPD would have obtained a majority in the Reichstag. This helps belie claims that Germany was awash with rightist sentiment. Such sentiment certainly existed but the Left was nevertheless vastly advantaged.

the creation of the new constitution included the sociologist Max Weber* and Friedrich Naumann.

Among the constitutional proposals put forward by Preuss was the breakup of Prussia into several smaller, impotent provinces.[1148] His effort did not succeed but for a Jewish-German to even make such a proposal was seen by the radical Right as indicative of Jewish desires to fundamentally alter the power structure of the country.

While anti-Semitism played no part in the creation of the Weimar constitution, it would later play a significant role within the radical right-wing that would declare the Weimar Republic a "Jew Republic." As Elon points out, "That the rightists identified the Weimar Republic with Jews was no accident. Jews were among its most ardent supporters."[1149] Zionists welcomed the constitution's guarantee of cultural autonomy for foreign-language groups within the country, lamenting only that the "special rights of Jews" were not acknowledged as such. Zionist obligations to Germany were left undefined but the prevailing attitude for most was that Jews should maintain nothing but the bare minimum of ties to the country. Their attitude was summed up by the militant Zionist Robert Weltsch, who said, "If I am a Jew, I cannot be a German at the same time."[1150] The Zionists, in typical fashion, once again demanded special rights from the German state while giving neither sustenance nor allegiance in return.[1151]

Radical opponents of the constitution denounced it heartily on the basis of its "foreign origins" and "Jewish inspiration."[1152] The Jewish origins of the constitution were not lost on right-wing radicals, particularly since several of its provisions were highly problematic. It did not much matter that several of its most problematic and inherent problems were not of Preuss's making.

---

* Weber, a sociologist, was closely associated with Jews such as Georg Simmel. His parents were exceedingly close to Karl Marx. It was he who defined the state as that "entitiy which possesses a monopoly on the legitimate use of physical force." He was also a proponent of the "charismatic leader" concept (Stribbe, 71).

The constitution suffered from several important structural defects that would plague the republic throughout its existence and provided the constitutional mechanisms by which Hitler was later able to legally assume dictatorial powers. Historians sometimes summarize the unfortunate parts of the constitution as the 25/48/53 formula; the three articles that made presidential government possible. The formula was arrived at by General Kurt von Schleicher, not Pruess.[1153]

- Article 25 allowed the president to dissolve the Reichstag and rule by presidential decree, a provision that would be exercised and abused throughout the republic's existence, culminating with its use by Adolf Hitler soon after he achieved power.
- Article 48 allowed the president to enact emergency bills without the consent of the Reichstag—it could be used rather like the presidential fiats, the Executive Orders that currently plague our own Constitution. This provision was both necessary and badly abused. It was necessary because of the turmoil ripping the country and the inability of the various parties to form a consensus. It was abused as it was called into play on more than 250 separate occasions during the fourteen-year existence of the republic.
- Article 53 called for the president to appoint the chancellor. Thus, the president could appoint a chancellor of his choosing, and the chancellor could rule, in consonance with the president, by way of Article 48. If the Reichstag overruled the president in some area, as it was constituted to do, Article 25 could be invoked to simply dissolve the Reichstag. In effect, then, all real power was ultimately in the hands of the president. Thus, when Hitler became chancellor in 1933, his power was only limited by the aged and by then exhausted and befuddled President von Hindenburg. Added to all of this was the constitutional provision that provided that in the event of the death or resignation of the president, the chancellor was to assume

that office and possess its powers pending the election of a new president.[1154] This latter provision enabled Hitler to further consolidate his already considerable power upon the death of Hindenburg in 1934.

    The constitution had other failings as well. The form of proportional representation embodied in it was such that people voted for a party (actually for a list of people that was put forward by the party) and its platform, and the party then provided a number of representatives to the Reichstag in proportion to the vote attained; one representative was appointed for every 60,000 votes.[1155] This enabled any party that could garner a few votes to take a seat in the Reichstag. The intent of the provision was to reduce the power of the big parties and enable minority groups, including extremists of both the Left and Right, with a degree of representation that would otherwise have been denied them. Importantly, proportional representation also served the long-held objective of the SPD to break the power of the old imperial method of constituency elections wherein rural voters were advantaged over urban ones. It would henceforth be that the city voter would dominate the rural ones. It was clever, but also destructive to the traditional norm.

    The practical effect of proportional representation was for dozens of parties to blossom and to make it nigh unto impossible to form a stable majority coalition by which a government could rule effectively—there were twenty separate coalition governments during the fourteen-year Weimar period. The revolving coalitions contributed to the view that the government was both unstable and in some ways effete, essentially powerless.[1156] Government actions were again and again reduced to what could be had only by way of the lowest common denominator, the line of least resistance; substantive change was all but impossible. The plethora of political parties also contributed to the frequent removal of the chancellor by motions of no confidence, further exasperating governmental stability. There were fourteen chancellors in as many years.

    There was still another problem with proportional representation: because it was the party that put forth the list of candidates, the candidates and resulting office holders tended to be more responsive to party functionaries and financial supporters than they were to the voters. Office holders were largely puppets of background functionaries, who, in keeping with long-standing tradition, were often Jewish financiers serving as "advisors" and "subject experts" (the Jeffrey Katzenbergs, Rahm Emanuels, David Axelrods, and Scooter Libbys of the day). But there was a flip side to all of this as well: as Hitler gained in popularity as the electrifying head of the Nazi Party, voters tended to vote for him and his party rather than bland and relatively unfamiliar lists of people put forth by other parties.[1157] Hitler's notoriety and charisma was reinforced and enhanced by proportional representation.

In both political and social circles of the general population, it was something of a glorious time for Jews. German finance, theater, news, and other forms of publishing were all largely in their hands. The large contingent of Jews belonging to the SPD continued to enjoy success in the government. They were likewise represented in large numbers in the DDP, USPD, and the KPD. Numerous as Jews were in government positions prior to and during World War I, they were twenty times more numerous in such positions by the end of the 1920s.[1158] They were also fantastically rich. According to a History Channel documentary, "Hitler: The Rise," monies confiscated from Jews by the Nazis paid for "at least" 30 percent of the cost of World War II. That statistic, if true,[*] is simply astonishing; here was a community of less than 1 percent of the population with enough money to pay all those troops and purchase all those aircraft, artillery pieces, tanks, ships, submarines, trucks, trains, bombs, guns of all kinds, etc. Incredible.

For all that has been written and said about the underlying anti-Semitism of Germans in the nineteenth and twentieth centuries, it is interesting to point out that none of the anti-Semitic parties were able to gain a foothold with the German masses throughout the 1920s, including Hitler's NSDAP. Anti-Semites vented their

---

[*] The statistic is suspect: at the close of World War II, Jews, and especially those in the Holocaust industry, had a substantial incentive to inflate claims about their losses as they sought compensation from the German government.

spleen against Jewish participation in the Weimar government (Hitler called them the Via Dolorosa of Germany),[1159] their perceived defeatism during World War I, their war profiteering, their participation in violent revolution throughout the Continent and in Germany in particular, and Jews as the source of moral and cultural decay. Still, the radical Right gained little political traction. The SPD and other leftist and centrist parties represented power in the Weimar period—the extreme rightist parties remained comparatively small, frail, and powerless until the waning years of the republic.

Russia's Need for Germany's Fall

Lenin and his followers had long held that Germany must fall to Communist forces if a worldwide Communist revolution was to be achieved. Indeed, the fall of Germany to Communism was thought to be crucial if Russian Communism was itself to prevail. It was the Russian Communists, not the Nazis, who sought world revolution and world government. Hitler's objective was hegemony in Europe* and thereby great influence in the world, but he had no interest whatever in installing Nazism throughout the world. Conversely, as Trotsky wrote in 1918, "The task of the proletariat is to create a still more powerful fatherland with a greater power of resistance, the Republican United States of Europe, as the foundation of the United States of the World."[1160] Churchill accused Trotsky of wanting to create "a world-wide Communist State under Jewish domination."[1161] Fear of just such an outcome provided a powerful incentive to rightist forces trying to stem the tide of Communism.

The importance of Germany to Communism is illustrated by the fact that prior to the Russian Revolution, Marxism had held that the workers in the industrialized state of Germany should

---

* As Hermann Goering stated it at Nuremberg, "Hitler was more of a continental man—not a colonial man. He wanted a union of European states under the leadership of Germany. . . ." [Goldensohn, 112] Keitel expressed similar sentiments. (Goldensohn, 162). Ribbentrop, too. (Goldensohn, 189).

make Germany the first prize of Communism. Russia was thought to be too underdeveloped for a workers' revolution to succeed there. Once the Russian Revolution had indeed succeeded, however, Lenin feared that it would soon collapse unless Germany also succumbed. Lenin claimed that, "Without a German Revolution there can be no salvation for the Russian Revolution, no hope for socialism after this war. There remains only one solution—mass rising of the German proletariat."[1162] Both Liebknecht and Luxemburg expressed similar sentiments. Lenin would therefore do whatever he could to promote Communism in Germany. To achieve his aim, he dispatched the previously cited Adolph Joffe to Germany as Russia's ambassador. Joffe's involvement in financing and arming the German radicals has already been recounted. Lenin provided an idea of the objective of the Soviet Embassy when he described it as that "burning house on the streets of Berlin which would set all Germany alight."[1163] Joffe was accompanied by several hundred Russian agents and prodigious supplies of gold, cash, and propaganda literature to promote the German revolution from behind the protective wall of diplomatic immunity. Members of Joffe's embassy were sent to the cities to incite revolutionary fervor. After coming to power, Hitler truthfully commented as follows on the attempts by Russia to secure Germany for Marxism:

> The first phase in the fight of National Socialism against Communism did not take place in Russia. Soviet Communism already tried to poison Germany between the years 1918 and 1920, and its methods of penetration into this country was much the same as its present-day military efforts in moving the Bolshevik military machine closer and closer to our frontiers.[*]

---

[*] Prior to the outbreak of World War II, Russia began its encroachment into areas of vital interest to Germany. One prominent example of this was Russia's encroachment on Romania, an important source of oil for Germany.

> We have stamped out Bolshevism which Moscow's bloodfiends such as Lewin, Axelroth [aka Axelrod], [Heinz] Neumann, Béla-Kuhn [born, Kohn, aka Kun], etc. tried to introduce into Germany. And it is because we see day by day these efforts of Soviet rulers to meddle in our domestic affairs have not yet ceased, that we are forced to regard Bolshevism beyond our frontiers as our deadly enemy.[1164]

Jews were heavily represented in all of the Socialist and Communist parties of Russia, Austria, and Germany, and held many of the leadership posts in those movements. As the noted Jewish historian Konrad Heiden pointed out: "The relatively high percentage of Jews in the leadership of the Socialist parties on the European continent cannot be denied."[1165] George Mosse, the "American left-wing Jewish gay historian of fascism"[1166] noted that:

> Jews were highly visible in many of the postwar [World War I] revolutions, not only in Bolshevik Russia but also in Budapest, Munich, and Berlin. During the postwar crisis, belief in Jewish conspiracies and subversive activities was not just a curious notion held by professed haters of Jews; in 1918, even Winston Churchill associated Jews with the Bolshevik conspiracy.[1167]

Indeed, Jewish participation in the German revolution that established the republican government very much advantaged the Jews. As Sarah Gordon points out, "After the revolution, Jews were very active in the early Weimar government at federal, state, and local levels. Later, during the operating years of the republic, they became influential primarily in areas that were controlled by the SPD, especially in Prussia,"[1168] that "most German" of the German provinces.

There is, of course, the popular notion that the Jews within the various revolutionary movements did not identify with Judaism, that they were merely participants in secular universalism without reference to traditional Jewish collectivism. If that is one's position, then Jews, as a race, should not be singled out as particular participants in the subversive movements of the day. That was not, however, the contention of Adolf Hitler, nor anyone else, save Jewish apologists. It was clear to everyone that Jews as a race were heavily involved in all of the revolutionary turmoil of the time. Each of the various revolutionary movements claimed to be Marxist, Socialist, or Communist—and all three were understandably seen as fundamentally Jewish-Marxist of one shade or another (revolutionary Marxists or evolutionary Marxists) and of Jewish origin. Lenin himself equated Communism and Socialism by saying that "Communism is socialism in a hurry." The Socialism of Germany's Social Democratic Party—the largest such party in Europe at the time—claimed to be the true heir of Marxism. Other Socialist parties did likewise. It is hardly surprising then that Hitler and many others came to see an equivalency between Jews, Marxists, Socialists, and Communists. Of course, Hitler's party also called itself "socialist"—it was a mark of his genius for propaganda that he was able to delink his form of Socialism from universalistic egalitarianism and internationalism and to instead associate it with strident racists' nationalism.[1169]

Based on his extensive studies of history, Hitler saw Jewish subversion as a continuum that stretched back in history many hundreds of years and was particular to the Jewish race. As MacDonald has it, the political drift of the Weimar era was toward leftism and "The left-wing intellectuals did not simply 'happen to be mostly Jews,' as some pious historiography would have us believe, but Jews created the left-wing intellectual movement in Germany."[1170]

The Bavarian Revolution

As historian Amos Elon points out, "Nowhere were Jewish revolutionaries so visible and prominent as they were in Bavaria."[1171] He then goes on to refer to these people as "dreamers," "abstract philosophers," "unworldly poets," and "some very able, humane politicians." And a few of them, such as

Eisner and Toller, were indeed people of a kind described by Elon; others, such as Eugene Levine, Max Levien, and Erick Muehsam, were decidedly not. Elon does acknowledge that "Armed men roamed the streets, shooting, looting, beating, and attacking innocent bystanders. Strikes and counterstrikes erupted all over Bavaria."[1172] These people seized the government, made a shamble of the economy, murdered wantonly, and caused a civil war. Still, according to Elon, they were actually pretty nice people, "dreamers," etcetera—he seems to argue that only Germans, not Jews, should be held accountable for the killing and chaos in Bavaria at that time.

It is something of a curiosity that a country so long pummeled for being the bastion of anti-Semitism would nevertheless have a very large segment of the population that would, for a time, embrace Jews as their leaders; even, as time and experience would prove, both incompetent and ruthless ones. Kauders describes this fascinating aspect of German-Jewish relations:

> In an article entitled "Civil War in Munich". . . the Centre [Catholic] organ wondered how it was possible for Bavarians [second only to Prussia as Germany's largest province] to tolerate the machinations of a group of shady alien literary figures: "It will remain one of the greatest mysteries how the Bavarian people, usually so insistent on its *völkish* nature, could accept the rule of persons whose unscrupulous practices and whose pernicious [*volksverderblichen*] convictions were apparent from their Russian-Jewish background."[1173]

As we shall see, the Bavarian Revolution was an oddity from its outset to its demise. And it was wholly the work of Jews.

In early November 1918, as Berlin was broiling with the ouster of the kaiser, the revolutionary declaration of Germany as a republic and the internecine warfare between the Marxist factions, Jews in Bavaria, seized the moment to take the government. The stage was now set for Bavaria, that postcard-picturesque province of beautiful landscapes and fairy-tale castles, farmer's fields with haystacks in dress-right-dress, murals and chalets, and beautiful mountains and lakes (the gorgeous Chiemsee, the "Bavarian Sea" among them) and rivers and streams and brooks, to be taken over first by idealistic Jewish incompetents, and then by vicious Jewish terrorists, and all of them people who were seemingly in stark opposition to all things of the soil, beauty, volkishness, and nationalism. A consequence of it all would be quite understandable brutal excess by the Freikorps.

On November 7, 1918, Kurt Eisner, along with fellow Jews Ernst Toller, Erick Muehsam, Gustav Landauer, Eugen Levine-Nissen, Max Levien, Towia Axelrod, Frida Rubiner (aka Friedjung), Arnold Wadler, Hans-Helmuth Knuetter, and others—80 percent of the Bavarian revolutionaries were Jews—[1174] began his overthrow of the Wittelsbach dynasty that had reigned for over 700 years in the heavily Catholic (70 percent) and conservative German province of Bavaria.

Google	URL
Kurt Eisner	http://en.wikipedia.org/wiki/Kurt_Eisner 8/2/14
Ernst Toller	http://www.ushmm.org/wlc/en/article.php?ModuleId=10007168 8/2/14
Eric Muehsam	http://en.wikipedia.org/wiki/Erich_M%C3%BChsam 8/2/14
Gustav Landauer	http://en.wikipedia.org/wiki/Gustav_Landauer 8/2/14
Eugene Levine-Nissen	[1175]
Max Levien	[1176]

It must have taken considerable impudence for a set of Jewish literati, none of whom were even Bavarians and some of whom were not even Germans, to take over the government in a place like Bavaria; nevertheless, it happened. Hitler would later say that he would always "'remember a Jewess who wrote' at the time in the *Bayrischer Kurier*: 'What Eisner's doing now will recoil upon our heads.'"[1177] It was certainly the case that the actions of Eisner, Toller, Leviné, and fellow travelers had a seismic impact on enraged rightist forces. As is often said of Hitler, "if World War I made the man then Munich of 1919 made the politician."[1178] Hitler would never forget the "high treason" of Jews who had seized control of his adopted province of Bavaria and established a "Jew-Republic."[1179]

Hitler had an attachment to Munich that was greater than to any other spot on earth,[1180] and here it was at the end of World War I, subjugated by a race of people that he detested. Hitler's attachment to the city was based on its "wonderful marriage of primordial power and fine artistic mood, this single line from the Hofbräuhaus [a beautiful brewery and beer hall] to the Odeon [concert hall], from October Festival to the Pinakothek [museum of art]. . . ."[1181] "One does not know German art," said Hitler, "if one has not seen Munich."[1182] For Hitler, Munich was "the most German of all German cites."[1183] It was for many, Athens on the River Isar.[1184] And it was now a city in the hands of petty, incompetent Jewish literati. Stolfi provides an excellent summary of what Hitler encountered when he returned to Munich after the war:

> . . . the young man who had fled cosmopolitan Vienna for German Munich; would return to that city to find it under the control of Marxists. Not one biographer points out that, in a single human being the minister-president exemplified the enemy for Hitler: Kurt Eisner, revolutionary Marxist, Jew, internationalist, and fomenter of antiwar strikes in Germany in January 1918 while the field armies were still engaged in combat in the west. Hitler would have been presented by this apparition from hell of the destructor of a German Reich. Yet no biographer develops the Munich visions of Hitler that must have contributed to his conversion from intense, ineffectual, brooding loner into a German political phenomenon.[1185]

Stolfi goes on to comment as follows:

> . . . we must suspect significant outrage on his part in the presence of six Jews holding the seven top positions in the three Marxist socialist revolutions in Bavaria, the

first of which having been sparked while the [sic] Hitler and the army were still in combat on the western front.[1186]

Hitler would not forget that it was Germany's loss of World War I that so enabled Jews to rise to the top during Germany's revolutionary turmoil in Munich and elsewhere: "Before 1914," he said, "how long would it have taken, for instance, in Bavaria before a Galician* Jew became Prime Minister?"[1187]

In the eyes of people like Hitler it certainly did not help that Eisner, principal among the early Munich cliques, had published documents that tried to lay the entire blame for the war on Germany's Prussia, or that he had, in 1918, asserted that Germany had no right to demand the return of German prisoners,[1188] or that he had appealed to Germans to help rebuild enemy territories (which was interpreted as a call for the enslavement of Germans on behalf of the victors and the French in particular), or that he had been one of the principals in leading the strikes by munitions workers during the war.[1189] Hitler, ever the excessive German patriot, had good reason to hate the likes of Kurt Eisner.

Subsequent to the revolution, Bavarians became exceedingly critical of Jews, referring to those in Bavaria, says Peter Pulzer, as "the numerous atheistic elements of a certain international Jewry with predominantly Russian colouring" and as a "terroristic minority" or as a "foreign, politicizing minority, led by elements alien in origin and race."[1190] On a broader scale, special indignation was reserved for the "centralizing Jews"[1191] Hugo Preuss and Otto Landsberg—the two Jewish social theorists who had been central to the development of the Weimar constitution. Centralized political authority at the federal level, it was feared, would be the means by which secular or anti-Christian elements would undermine Bavaria's Catholic educational system and otherwise attack religion and its institutions. And, as evidenced by

---

* The *Bayerische Volkszeitung* repeatedly referred to Eisner as "the Galician Jew" (Kauders, 67). He was actually born and raised in Berlin. His ancestors were from Galicia.

the exceedingly high priority that the various Communist regimes throughout Europe placed on the elimination of Christianity, the German Communists, and the Bavarian ones in particular, would certainly have done likewise.

At least one historian, John Lukacs, conjectures that Hitler's hatred of Jews did not crystallize until he observed events in Munich, "when he witnessed the 'ridiculous and sordid' behavior of Jewish Bolsheviks"[1192] in the post-Eisner regime that was brought down in early May 1919. Implicitly, Lukacs's assessment of things and his condemnation of the "ridiculous and sordid" behavior of the Munich Bolsheviks is a charge against Jews in the brief reign of the Munich Soviet regime.[1193]

Eisner, who had been planning his Bavarian Revolution for weeks prior to the event, was assisted in his takeover by a coterie of fellow Jews and by mutinous sailors who had arrived in Munich from Kiel. On November 7, 1918, Eisner called on a crowd of demonstrators who were celebrating the anniversary of the Russian Revolution* a year earlier, to "Scatter throughout the city . . . occupy the barracks, seize weapons and ammunitions, win over the rest of the troops, and make yourselves [by which he actually meant himself and his fellow Jewish revolutionaries] masters of the government!"[1194] The crowd responded like Shakespeare's version of Mark Antony's Romans; they spread havoc; they accosted anyone who even looked like a member of the bourgeois. The government was overthrown by the next day, November 8. Eisner declared Bavaria to be a Soviet republic. At the suggestion of Landauer, churches were forced to peal their bells in celebration of the great event. The new republic was celebrated at the National Theater. Bruno Walter (born Jewish as Bruno Schlesinger) conducted Beethoven's *Leonore Overture.*

As events were unfolding in Munich, Düsseldorf, Frankfurt-am-Main, Stuttgart, Leipzig, and Magdeburg, all came under the

---

* Russian Revolution: In Petrograd, Russia, Bolshevik leaders Vladimir Lenin and Leon Trotsky led revolutionaries in overpowering the provisional government (as Russia was still using the Julian calendar, subsequent period references show the date as October 25). Src: http://en.wikipedia.org/wiki/Nov_7

control of quasi-revolutionary regimes. The red flag was hoisted over those cities as well.[1195] And in each of the cities, the new Marxist regimes contained heavy concentrations of Jews within the governments. Riots were in vogue in Madeburg, Halle, Halstein, Osnabrück, and Cologne—they were soon all red.[1196] As was common, the Jewish radicals attacked both the bourgeois and Christianity with particular vehemence: thus it was that Jews were blamed for Socialism's hatred of Christianity. In addition to Jewish leadership of the several revolutionary regimes in Bavaria, the apparent hatred of Christianity that the radicals evidenced added still another reason for the widespread support of Gustav von Kahr's 1923 expulsion of Ostjuden from Bavaria,[1197] the expulsion that Detlev Peukert calls "shocking," and about which Goldhagen complains in his book, *Hitler's Willing Executioners*.

Eisner and his cohorts were a curious lot and as unlikely a set of revolutionaries as have ever been, and most especially for a place like Bavaria. Eisner was not himself a Bavarian, having been born and raised in Berlin. He despised Prussia and every success that it enjoyed; he was especially hateful of the fact that Prussia had prevailed in the Austro-Prussian war of 1866 and the Franco-Prussian war of 1870–1871.[1198] While he was an accomplished orator and something of a "charismatic authority," to use a term coined by DDP leader and sociologist Max Weber, he was also an entirely incompetent leader.

Physically, Eisner was also something of a curiosity, a caricature-Jew: a great face-covering beard; dark, runny eyes and pince-nez glasses; wild hair, sallow skin, a shabby coat and an immense *vie de bohème* black hat, the combination of which provided him with an especially untidy appearance. He is aptly described on one Internet site as, "a living cartoon of the bomb-throwing red."[1199] As mentioned in an earlier chapter, Adolf Hitler commented in *Mein Kampf* that upon first seeing an orthodox Jew in Vienna he was taken aback: he could not reconcile such a specter with Germandom. Eisner could have served as an exemplar for such an encounter for he certainly looked the part of an apparition of Jewish orthodoxy.

Still, for all of his physical oddities, Eisner's intellect was first rate. It was also wholly impractical. He was an accomplished author and speaker, and his speeches were both fiery and witty.[1200] He was far and away the most popular of the Munich radicals. He was also, on a practical level, just incredibly stupid.

As early as 1897, Eisner had demonstrated his disdain for the German monarchy by writing a magazine article satirizing the kaiser, an offense for which he was arrested and convicted of lèse-majesté.[1201] This incident brought him to the attention of the elder Liebknecht who recruited him for the SPD and later made him the political editor of the radical-left, Jewish-controlled, *Vorwärts* newspaper. Upon the death of the elder Liebknecht in 1900, Eisner assumed the position of editor.

For all his popularity, he also had enemies, including some within the party: Rosa Luxemburg abominated him, thinking him an insincere student of economics and social theory and too concerned with literature to be an effective Social Democratic functionary. Worse, Eisner was a Bernsteinian revisionist while Luxemburg was a revolutionary Marxist. In reference to Eisner's Kantian flare, Luxemburg wrote to Eisner: "May you drown in the moral absolutes of your beloved *Critique of Pure Reason*."[1202]

Stemming from various disputes within the party, Eisner was ousted from the editorship of *Vorwärts*. He thereafter abandoned his family and relocated to Munich. In what must have been a delicious triumph, Eisner's nemesis, Rosa Luxemburg,* was among the ultraleft radicals who replaced him and five other editors at *Vorwärts*.[1203]

After initially supporting the SPD at the outset of World War I, Eisner quickly took the side of and became a leading member of the USPD political faction, which is to say the far Left. The Spartacists were also allied with the USPD at that time. Among his other activities during the war, he was instrumental in inciting the strikes of the munitions workers, an activity for which he was, for

---

* Luxemburg, in a letter to her lover and fellow leftist, Leo Jogiches, commented: "The editorial board will consist of mediocre writers, but at least they'll be 'kosher'."

a short time, imprisoned, and for which he earned the abiding hate of Adolf Hitler.

Eisner, along with his revolutionary cohorts, were Old Testament prophets of justice, equality, and democracy without an inkling of what institutions and actions were necessary to realize their messianic aspirations. They were intellectual utopians and practical dolts. They were able to take power, but then made a shamble of every opportunity to establish a viable government. Moreover, as members of competing ideological factions, the Bavarian revolutionaries could not much concur even among themselves: Muehsam and Toller were leading figures of the expressionist avant-garde, but the first was an anarchist and the second a left-wing Socialist. The same was true for Eisner and Landauer. Leviné was a leading hard-core Bolshevik.

Muehsam was a German-Jewish anarchist, essayist, poet, playwright, and Communist agitator. He is now remembered as one of the most dangerous anarchist agitators of the period. He also involved himself as a writer for political cabarets and founded his own anarchist journal, *Kain* (*Cain*), and later the *Fanal* (*The Torch*). Ridicule of the German state was his motif. The consummate antipatriot, he had refused induction into the army and spent the war years writing anti-German tracts and organizing labor strikes: his speeches, writing, and actions became increasingly violent and revolutionary over the years.

Eisner was certain that the place of his birth and rearing, Prussia, had to bear the entire responsibility for the war. Keen on gaining the good graces of the French, he sought to convince them to make a separate peace with Bavaria. Watt describes Eisner as a man who "thought of himself as a brilliant diplomat and dreamed of occupying a commanding role in German foreign affairs. He thirsted for recognition by the Allies (particularly by Woodrow Wilson, whom he admired enormously) as the man who symbolized the new Germany."[1204] As early as 1915, Eisner had laid the blame for the war on Germany and his native Prussia, in particular. He wrote at the time that "there could be no disputing that what we have is a German world war."[1205] Hitler understandably took issue with such assertions. On November 24,

1918, Eisner followed up on his accusation by publishing a series of documents that put responsibility for the war squarely on Prussia. He also provided additional data to "prove" the culpability of Germany as the instigator of the war. "Eisner would see, Ebert charged, just how much Germany would pay for Bavaria's anti-Prussianism."[1206]

Ebert was entirely right. Eisner was entirely wrong. Eisner did not get his separate peace by way of France, but Germany would be saddled with the war-guilt clause in the Treaty of Versailles. Hitler saw Eisner's actions in playing Bavaria against Prussia as being representative of his service to Jewish Bolsheviks. According to Hitler, "He used the existing instincts and dislikes of the Bavarian people [dislike of Prussia], to help him break up Germany the more easily. The shattered Reich would have easily fallen prey to Bolshevism."[1207] Hitler was also entirely right on this point as well—the more that Germany could be atomized; that is, the more that it could be fractured into competing interest groups, the easier it would be for the Jewish-led Bolsheviks.

Bavaria had long been at odds with its larger northern cousin. In the Austro-Prussian war of 1867, Bavaria had sided with Austria. When Germany was unified Bavaria demanded and received special privileges: it had its own army which came under the command of the German kaiser only during times of war. It also had its own ambassadors to Vienna, St. Petersburg, and the Vatican as well as its own postal, telegraph, railway, and coinage systems. The Prussian army was not permitted to enter Bavarian territory.[1208]

On November 26, 1918, Eisner took full advantage of Bavaria's animosity toward Prussia by taking the additional step of severing Bavaria's ties to the federal government in Prussia's Berlin. Eisner had determined that he could better conduct the foreign affairs of Bavaria than could the Ebert government. His action, though, was not coordinated within his own government. Erhard Auer, his minister of the interior, opposed the decision. Auer, along with the leadership of the SPD, was insistent that the German nation not be fractionalized. Auer also demanded that Eisner keep earlier promises for an election for the Landtag, which was intended to then become the sovereign power in Bavaria, replacing Eisner's workers' and soldiers' councils. Aurer won the election dispute. Elections were scheduled for mid-January 1919.[1209] The election would set the stage for Eisner's political demise and for the rise of another Jew, Ernst Toller, who at the time had warned against permitting a popular vote because, he said, such a vote would put Bavaria's future in the hands of "ignorant people."[1210] These utopians, these "dreamers," "abstract philosophers," and "unworldly poets," according to Toller's logic, knew what was best for the people and there was no point in mucking things up by having people express themselves in a voting booth.

In trying to salvage his government, Eisner offered a temporary sop to the bourgeoisie who were fearful of losing their property to his radical Socialism. He announced that private property would, for the time being, be protected. While this helped assuage the bourgeoisie, it infuriated his fellow Marxists who were calling for instant nationalization. To them, Eisner's compromise smacked of betrayal.[1211]

Eisner went on to make incredibly insensitive and downright silly decisions. He socialized the theater thinking that such a move was crucially important to the revolutionary struggle of the moment. In this connection he summoned representatives of the actors' guild to his office and asked that they more equitably distribute dramatic roles. He also barred newspaper drama critics from harshly reviewing plays.

Eisner decreed the abandonment of compulsory military service, a move welcomed by many. He also ended compulsory religious education in state schools—a move that was despised by the heavily Catholic majority and provided them with a basis for claiming that Eisner's government was out to destroy Christianity, which was certainly high on its list of objectives. Taken in the context of the times, however, all of his decisions, whatever their motivations, were evidence of his absurdity given the pressing priorities of the sick and starving Bavarians.

Eisner's manner of governance was as sloppy as his manner of dress. His office, open to the public from the outset of his regime, was a mess. French journalist Paul Gentizon wrote that "Diplomatic papers, parchments, revolutionary proclamations and telegrams cover tables and armchairs in a confusion suggesting the backroom of a shop . . . No method and no organization seems to prevail in the working of this strange ministry."[1212]

Opposition to Eisner quickly showed itself, most of it legitimate, some of it fanciful lies. Most Bavarians, including those who cursed Prussia and the kaiser, were unwilling to participate in Eisner's call to sell the rest of Germany down the river. Soldiers returning from the front were incensed by his actions, including Adolf Hitler who was at the time still recovering from his wounds. The Catholic press participated in circulating rumors that Eisner's real name was Salomon Kuchinsky, and that he was a Lenin acolyte.[1213] On the political left there were many who regarded him as insufficiently ruthless due to his unwillingness to immediately seize the property of the bourgeoisie. With his attempts to appease France, Eisner appeared to the ultraleft as the lackey of a capitalist nation, and to the ultraright as a traitor.

The Spartacus League established its Munich branch in early December and was joined by the People's Naval Division. Spartacus League members felt no allegiance whatever to Eisner. They sought power for themselves. By mid-December, there were daily demonstrations against him.

To stem the tide of criticism, Eisner chose to explain his actions at a Fete of the Bavarian Revolution in the opera house. People were starving. Coal could not be had to heat apartments. There were riots in the streets. The transportation system was a shamble. Disease was rampant. Nothing was being done to address these problems. Shouts of opposition to Eisner were at first so loud that he was unable to make himself heard but was finally permitted to speak. His subject? "Education and Democracy." This farcical speech only confirmed for the crowd that Eisner was an impractical idealist with little or no grasp of attitudes and actions needed to service the events of the time—the man was an intellectual luminary of the theoretical but as stupid as can be with respect to matters of practicality.

The growing opposition to Eisner was expressed by the people of Bavaria in the elections held on January 12, 1919. The election was a disaster for him and his government. The SPD polled 1,224,000 people. Parties that appealed to Catholic fears about anti-Christian Socialists also did well. And why not? Russia was in the midst of demonstrating Marxism's hostility toward Christianity, and Catholicism in particular—a foreshadowing of expectations for Bavaria.

Eisner and his absurd USPD clique won a paltry 86,000 votes, less than 2 percent of the total. He was voted out of office but was not willing to leave. He managed to hold on to the government for several more weeks. On February 21, 1919, he finally decided to relinquish power. While on his way to the Landtag where he was to submit his resignation, he was assassinated by a right-wing monarchist zealot, Count Anton Arco-Valley, a half-Jewish superpatriot who tried to use the assassination of Eisner as the bona fides of his nationalistic fervor. "Eisner's death," Hitler later wrote, "only hastened developments and led finally to the Soviet dictatorship, or to put it more correctly, to a passing rule of Jews, as had been the original aim of the instigators of the whole revolution."[1214]

The death of Eisner brought out his supporters. Calls were made for revenge. Armored cars full of Red Army men drove about with mounted bullhorns blaring "Revenge for Eisner."[1215] Several murders ensued. Eisner was now represented as something of a saint, a martyr, a messiah. Bell ringers in churches throughout the city were forced to toll the dead Eisner. Where necessary, priests were forced to the task at gunpoint.[1216] Eisner's place of assassination was quickly covered with floral tributes and red flags. Passersby were forced by security patrols to doff their hats as they passed portraits of Eisner that had been set up in the streets. It all amounted to little more than a leftist parody of Nazism, except that at the time this was happening Nazism did not yet exist. But such things as had transpired during that time served to encourage both the birth and nurturing of adolescent Nazism.

A three-day strike was called that all but paralyzed the city.[1217] A day of mourning was declared for Eisner's funeral on February

26. Gustav Landauer, a bohemian anarchist and fellow Jew who would be a leading member of the subsequent Bavaria Soviet, provided a eulogy. Landauer compared Eisner with Goethe, Jan Hus, Old Testament prophets, "and, for good measure, Jesus."[1218] Favorably comparing Eisner to Jesus and to Jan Hus in Catholic Bavaria seems a bit strange, but these were strange people and strange times. It all seemed appropriate to them, apparently.

The Hoffmann Government

Because of its strong showing in the recent election, the SPD demanded and was granted control of the Bavarian government. On March 17, 1919, the torch was passed to Johannes Hoffmann, a Socialist Protestant. Hoffmann tried to reconcile the various elements of Bavarian political life. His very moderation infuriated the left-wing elements in Munich.[1219] As he was trying to dampen the political fires in the city, news arrived that Hungary had been taken over by Communist forces under the leadership of still another Jew, Béla Kun, a sycophant of Lenin and Bolshevism. Communist forces throughout Germany were rejuvenated by Kun's success, and nowhere more so than in Bavaria. It was thought to be a virtual certainty that what Kun was doing in Hungary could now also be done in Germany, starting with Bavaria. What happened in Hungary and Bavaria not only turned millions of their citizens against the Reds, but because Jews were so very prominent in both places, against Jews as well. The idea that Jews were everywhere insinuating themselves into Gentile governments, was widespread, and it was not a simple reactive response by anti-Semites. Evidence existed everywhere: Jews were dominant among the Russian revolutionaries; Kun's revolution in Hungary was composed almost entirely of Jews; and the revolutionary leadership throughout Germany was composed largely of Jews as well, no less so in Bavaria. Moreover, the worst had not yet been seen: not in Russia, not in Hungary, not in Germany, and not in the province of Bavaria. Jewish radicals, by their horrific excesses, were yet to earn the hate they inspired. And all of Jewry would partake of their legacy.

In Bavaria, the "Russian Jews" (men who were born, raised, or had close family ties to Russia), Towia Axelrod, Max Levien, Eugen Leviné, and others, prepared to move against Hoffman.

On April 5, while Hoffmann was in Berlin trying to garner support, SPD members met to decide on a course of action for Bavaria. Leviné demanded the immediate creation of a Soviet Republic. Moderate SPD members at the meeting decided to delay a decision until Hoffmann returned. The radicals then made the decision for them: with the familiar cry of "All power to the Soviets!" the radical Left declared the Socialist Republic of Bavaria on April 6. Eight of the most influential players among the twenty-seven leaders of the post-Eisner government were Jewish: Ernst Toller, Eugen Levine-Nissen, Towia Axelrod, Frida Rubiner, Erich Muehsam, Gustav Landauer, Ernst Niekisch, and Arnold Wadler.[1220] The relatively moderate non-Jewish SPD leaders slinked out of Munich, absconding first to Nuremburg and thence to Bamberg where they could be protected by a Freikorps detachment. They knew full well that some members of the new regime in Bavaria did not suffer from Eisner's lack of ruthlessness.

The Hungarian Revolution and Its German Impact
(March 21, 1919–August 1, 1919)

We now interrupt our discussion of events in Bavaria to expound further on those in Hungary. The Hungarian Revolution is important to our narrative because it was such a thoroughly Jewish undertaking[1221] and because it provided such great inspiration for Jewish revolutionaries in Germany, and particularly in Bavaria. It also inspired hate and anti-Semitism. We will return momentarily to events in Bavaria.

The Hungarian Revolution under the leadership of Belá Kun (Kohn) was noted for being almost entirely Jewish in composition—wags of Budapest snorted that the lone goy in the government was needed to turn on the lights on Saturdays.[1222] Others had it that the goy was needed there to sign death warrants on Saturdays. The revolution achieved notice throughout Europe for its atrocities. The Jewish commissar for military affairs, Tibor

Szamuely, was particularly ruthless and wanton in his murderous rampage. "Terror is the principal weapon of our regime," claimed Szamuely, a statement that was entirely in keeping with the attitude of Kun himself who had sought to "inspire the revolution with the blood of the bourgeois."[1223] The radical Hungarian Jew who would later help wreak havoc on German politics and culture, Georg Lukács, served as Kun's commissar for education and culture.[1224] Lukács was a man who held that there are several levels of truth: one for the initiated, another for the rank-and-file, and still a third for the masses.[1225]

Google	URL
Belá Kun	http://en.wikipedia.org/wiki/B%C3%A9la_Kun 8/2/14
Tibor Szamuely	http://en.wikipedia.org/wiki/Tibor_Szamuely 8/2/14
Georg Lukács and the Hungarian Revolution	http://iso.org.nz/georg-lukacs-the-actuality-of-the-revolution/ 3/07/15

Kun and his associates traveled about Hungary in trains to carry out their objectives, wreaking havoc and mayhem everywhere. He and his henchmen have been rarely surpassed in their abject cruelty. In the aftermath of the Kun regime, mothers and nursemaids frightened unruly children with tales of murder and mayhem against nuns, landowners, and royal personages by Kun and his clique.

Toland emphasizes the Jewish composition of the Kun regime as he says: "A Jew himself, twenty-five of his thirty-two commissars were also Jews, provoking the London *Times* to characterize the regime as 'the Jewish mafia.'"[1226]

As a Wikipedia entry on the Kun regime points out, the Kun revolution was noted for its barbarity and especially the "anti-Christian atrocities that followed his accession to power."[1227] The aftereffect of the Hungarian Revolution was the outbreak of Red revolts throughout Germany. An unintended consequence of Kun's terrorism was that it later helped swell the ranks of Hitler's SA. According to Hitler, it "brought more people into the SA than would ever have been possible through its own propaganda efforts."[1228]

The Hungarian Revolution illustrates in the person of Kun how he and a number of other Jews traveled throughout Europe to participate in revolutionary movements that resulted in the deaths of untold numbers. The charge that "foreign Jews" were behind many of the problems in Germany was not mythical. Kun, like Rosa Luxemburg, Leo Jogiches, Karl Radek, Eugen Leviné, Adolf Joffe, and a host of others, were part of the elements that substantiated the charge of foreign Jewish involvement in the misery and turmoil of Germany.*

Before the war, Kun was a muck-raking journalist in Hungary. He had also served on the board of directors for an insurance firm where he had been accused of embezzlement.[1229] He was a vain, self-centered man. Adding to his other personal traits was hot temperedness.

Kun had been an Austro-Hungarian prisoner of war in Russia where he eagerly consumed the message of Communism. Upon his release, he traveled to Petrograd where he met and befriended Vladimir Lenin. In November 1918, Lenin provided him with funds and fake documents and sent him to Budapest to found the Hungarian Communist Party, which he did with gusto. While in Hungary, he was imprisoned for his revolutionary activities, including a share in the responsibility for the death of four police officers.

While in prison, Kun was beaten severely by police in full view of a news reporter. News of the beating, propagated by a sympathetic press, provided him with widespread fame and sympathy, veritable martyrdom.

On March 19, 1919, the French issued an ultimatum to Hungary, ordering it to pull back from positions it was occupying. The new line of the deployed forces was to represent the new border of Hungary. The French demand for Hungarian territorial

---

* Adding to all of that, of course, was the widespread perception in many countries that *all* Jews, regardless of their origin, were "foreigners."

concessions caused a surge in Hungarian nationalism and resolution to fight. If Hungary was to fight, however, it had to have allies and Russia was the only potential one on the horizon. Hungarian Social Democrats, knowing that Kun was closely connected to Lenin, offered the government to him (Kun was still imprisoned at this point) in hopes that such a move would bring Russia to their side. On March 21, 1919, a Hungarian Soviet Republic was announced with Kun at its head.

Kun immediately surrounded himself with fellow Jews who then quickly nationalized all private property. Eschewing advice from Moscow he refused to redistribute land to the peasants, thereby alienating a majority of the population. He also unleashed a particularly vicious attack on the church and its clergy.

In a manner not unlike his brethren in Munich, Kun also issued a series of quirky directives. He prohibited alcohol, abolished all titles, implemented compulsory baths, reallocated housing and furnishings, standardized graves, and instituted sex education in the schools. In his 133 days of rule, he thoroughly alienated everyone. Catholics were incensed by his plans to turn churches into cinemas, liberals bemoaned the new censorship; and arbitrary arrests, beatings, and appallingly cruel means of summary execution horrified all. Topping things off, the regime was wholly corrupt.[1230] "Among the many despicable actions of Kun was to offer the historic crown of St. Stephen of Hungary to 'an old curiosity dealer of Munich.'"[1231] According to Dr. E. J. Dillon, he also smuggled from Hungary to Switzerland some "fifty million kronen bonds, thirty-five kilograms of gold, and thirty chests filled with objects of value."[1232]

None of Kun's actions were in keeping with the desires of the people. Kun had come to power because it was thought that he could enjoin Russia to assist Hungary in retaining its territory, not because the populace wanted reforms of the kind he so brutally imposed.

High inflation plagued the Kun government. He exacerbated the situation by printing more money and thereby brought the currency to ruin. To provide food for the cities, he sent what were soon called "Lenin boys" into the countryside where they wreaked havoc and extorted foodstuffs. His attempt to force farmers to provide food was no more successful in Hungary than Lenin's attempt to do likewise in Russia, but it doubtlessly reinforced age-old historic perceptions of Jewish contempt for the peasantry. Severe food shortages ensued.

Responding to a failed anticommunist coup attempt on June 24, Kun took retribution by siccing his "Lenin boys" and Red Terror squads on the populace. He also established revolutionary tribunals to deal with his enemies. Hundreds were tortured and executed, often by extraordinarily vile means.

Hostilities soon erupted between Hungary on the one side and Romania and Czechoslovakia on the other. The Russians, with problems of their own in Ukraine, were unable to help him. The Romanians and Czechs trounced the Hungarians and handed the government back to the Social Democratic Party on August 1, 1919.

In the aftermath of Kun's 133-day rule, Hungarians took revenge on those who participated in the government or otherwise supported it. The Hungarian responses to the Kun regime were deemed anti-Semitic by the world press.

For the time being, Kun escaped into exile in Vienna. He would later be interned in a lunatic asylum. Later still he would control the Cheka* secret police in southern Russia[1233] where he would oversee the deaths of tens of thousands of people. He would also later participate in and become a driving force in inciting riots in Germany's central region during the infamous March Action (the Marzaktion Putsch, another attempt at violent revolution) of 1921, so much so, in fact, that Lenin would refer to the March Action proponents as "Kunists." He was also responsible for killing ten thousand White prisoners of war—troops who were promised amnesty in exchange for their surrender. Lenin scolded Kun for those killings.

---

* The Cheka, the vile secret police of the Bolsheviks, had been founded by Felix Dzerzhinsky who had a Jewish father and a Polish mother.

Kun's revolution and the actions of him and his cohorts became branded on the Hungarian consciousness for years to come and fueled anti-Semitism there. Later, after Hitler came to power, recollections of the Kun revolution were instrumental in encouraging the regime of Miklós Horthy to align his country with Hitler. Horthy hoped that by so doing he would keep the "Asiatic barbarians" at bay. Things did not work out well for Horthy: Hitler eventually crushed him. After World War II, the Soviet Union installed one of Kun's few surviving colleagues, the Jew Mátyás (Rosenfeld) Rákosi, to rule the country.[1234] Rákosi ruled in the manner of a despicable tyrant.

Hitler was still in the army while revolutionary events were unfolding in Bavaria, Berlin, and Hungary. He returned to Munich while both the Bavarian and Hungarian revolutions were ongoing and experienced unfolding events firsthand. He could not help but be both enraged and frustrated: enraged because Jews were now successfully leading their extremist followers to Marxist revolutionary fervor throughout Germany and places like Hungary; frustrated because as a simple, powerless individual, he could do nothing to influence events.

The Toller Government—Bavaria

The Hungarian Revolution reinvigorated the revolutionaries throughout Germany and nowhere more so than in Bavaria. The cry of "Germany is next!" went up everywhere. In Bavaria, a set of ultraleftist Jewish radicals now proclaimed for a Marxist republic there. This set of radicals, like Eisner before them, were utopian Jewish literati who had not an inkling of how to govern. Their utopian inclination was revealed in their announcement that they would transform the world "into a meadow full of flowers in which each man can pick his share."[1235] The pronouncement was something of a poetic rendition of the Marxist chant "From each according to his ability, to each according to his needs." Newspapers were ordered to print poems by Hölderlin or Schiller on the front page along with the latest revolutionary decrees.

If the Eisner government of Bavaria was quixotic, the government that followed bordered on the insane. With the ouster of Hoffmann, Ernst Toller, an accomplished orator, took advantage of his position as a member of the SPD and his association with the now popular but dead Eisner to demand that the Bavarian government pass to him, which it did on April 6. In addition to Toller, the main leaders in this phase of the revolution were Gustav Landauer, Erich Muehsam, Eugen Leviné, Max Levien, and Dr. Franz Lipp. All were Jews.

Toller served as the head of government but Landauer wielded the most power. Toller was a twenty-six-year-old dramatist, Landauer was a theater critic and anarchist. It was Landauer who resolved that he and the others must follow the lead of the Russian example: he decided to "conform to the will of the masses," the less than 2 percent of them who had voted for the Jewish radicals led by Eisner, by declaring a "Bavarian Soviet Republic."[1236] The first proclamation of the new regime was to state that "the dictatorship of the proletariat" was now in being and that it would be retained in power by a Red Army of its own creation. The press was immediately socialized and revolutionary courts established to deal with opposition.

The Toller-Landauer government was not merely incompetent in the vein of Eisner's, it was farcical. It seemed silly that Eisner had addressed the physical and spiritual woes of the people by giving a speech on the subject of education—Toller did him one better.

Toller began his rule with a plea for new art forms in sculpture, drama, painting, and architecture. "To a people seeking liberation from empty bellies and freezing temperatures without fuel, Toller and his government might have at that point seemed somewhat odd," says Richard Watt, wryly.[1237] The famous Jewish sociologist Max Weber commented on the efficacy of Toller's politics, saying: "God in his fury has turned Toller into a politician."[1238]

Toller's commissar for public instruction, Landauer, announced that no special courses of study were needed at college and that the teaching of history, "that enemy of civilization,"[1239] was to be suppressed. He also set his educational priorities: "Every

Bavarian child at the age of ten is going to know Walt Whitman by heart. That is the cornerstone of my educational program."[1240] He did not explain at the time why a homosexual iconoclastic American poet of Quaker origins should be the cornerstone of Catholic Bavaria's educational system.

His commissar for housing declared that no home could contain more than three rooms and that the living room must always be placed above the kitchen and bedroom. Toller's commissar for finances experimented with the idea of free money. Given the quixotic governing philosophy of this group, it is perhaps not too surprising that Dr. Franz Lipp, recently released from a mental asylum, declared war on Switzerland because it would not lend him sixty locomotives. Lipp also purportedly wrote missives to both Lenin and to the pope complaining that his predecessor had absconded with the keys to the washroom.

The Leviné Government—Bavaria

Toller's government lasted but a week, ending on April 13. It was supplanted by still another Jewish-led government but Toller stayed on as member of the new regime. This one, unlike the Eisner and Toller governments, was authentically Bolshevistic and it would employ Bolshevistic violence to prove it was so. The Eugen Leviné government demanded the surrender of all weapons in private possession on pain of death.[1241] It was in full accord with the Russian model, including arbitrary confiscations and outright theft, seizure, and murder of hostages, curbs on the bourgeoisie, revolutionary whim, and the facilitation of hunger.[1242]

A 20,000-man force of released prisoners, factory workers, unemployed workers, and deserters were joined together to form a Red Brigade under the command of the only native German among the upper echelons of the Munich revolutionaries, Rudolf Egelhofer. Brigade members were recruited with promises of high pay, expenditures that rapidly completed the ruin of the Bavarian economy,[1243] along with prodigious amounts of beer, liquor, and free prostitutes. When not engaged in fighting, members of the brigade broke into safe deposit boxes in banks throughout the city and went about brutalizing the populace. As mentioned in the time line, above, the Red Brigade was used to successfully crush Hoffmann's counterrevolutionary forces at Dachau, ten miles north of Munich. That done, they then rounded up and began executing anyone they thought might have right-wing sympathies. To his credit, Toller rushed about the city trying to quell the executions but eight people were executed before he could be successful.[1244] That as it may, right-wing opinion held that the Jewish leadership of the regime was directly responsible for atrocities such as the murder of hostages in the cellar of the Luitpold Gymnasium in Munich. The whole of it, claimed the right wing, was representative of Jewish-Bolshevik terror in Germany.

The Eisner and Toller regimes were both impractical and incompetent. The follow-on regime was brutal. The regime was led by what were known as the Russians,* Russian-born Eugen Leviné and Towia Axelrod. By mid-April, Bavaria was experiencing a civil war.

While civil war ensued, government leaders went about trying to sell Bavarian treasures. This set of Jews included the brothers Hans and Richard Richter, Alfred Wolfenstein, Nelly Sachs, Frieda Rubiner, and Heinrich Davinghausen. Among other things, they arranged for the sale of the contents of Bavaria's royal palaces to foreign countries. Richter and his cohorts would later go on to found the Bund Radikaler Künstler (Association of Radical Artists) and publish a manifesto proclaiming abstract art as the only acceptable form: Hitler, it would seem, was not alone in his desire to control the art of Germans; so, too, did certain Jews.

Leviné, a hard-core Marxist, was a founding member of the German Communist Party (KPD). He was regarded as a "potential German Lenin."[1245] He had been ordered to Munich to take charge of the Communists there by KPD party boss, Paul Levi, who had replaced Rosa Luxemburg after the latter's execution by rightists

---

*Many historians attributed the moniker as being due to family connections. In fact, though, Levien and Leviné were both born in Russia. Levien lived in Moscow until he was twenty-one. Axelrod resided in Russia just prior to the events in Bavaria; he was dispatched to Germany by Lenin and even enjoyed diplomatic immunity there.

The Weimar Republic

in January. While participating in the Bavarian Soviet, Leviné once offered his thoughts about the fact that babies were starving. "What does it matter . . . if for a few weeks less milk reaches Munich? Most of it goes to the children of the bourgeoisie anyway. We are not interested in keeping them alive. No harm if they die—they'd only grow into enemies of the proletariat."[1246]

Leviné was the organizer and man of action in the group. He had thoroughly studied Lenin's activities after the Russian Revolution and sought to copy them. A committed Spartacist, he had openly advocated during the war for an Allied victory over Germany, saying, "It is necessary that Germany be humiliated, that the colonial troops of France and England march through the Brandenburg Gate, that Helgoland [small German archipelago in the North Sea] become the property of the English, that the (German) fleet be taken away. . . ."[1247] But Leviné was best known for his utter brutality, a brutality that was so much a part of his being that it did not much bother him that he was so widely known for his abject sadism.[1248]

The new regime immediately pronounced the severance of all church-government connections but nevertheless demanded that Christian church bells be rung in celebration of the great event, the establishment of the great Bavarian Soviet Republic. Calls were made for Bavarians to join with the new regime and their "Russian and Hungarian proletariat brothers."[1249] It was Leviné who proposed and implemented the establishment of a "revolutionary temple" in Munich—the site of this "temple" was Munich's Roman Catholic cathedral. A woman, some say a Jewess, dressed as the "Goddess of Reason," presided over the opening ceremonies.[1250]

Ultimately, when the Freikorps attacked, the Levine government panicked. Orders were issued that represented such lunacy that Toller resigned his position. Levine instituted a Red Army reign of terror. Red Brigade soldiers created firing squads, lined up people, and murdered them out of hand. The Prince of Thurn and Taxis and the young Countess Heila von Westarp were among them.[1251] A total of twenty royalists and conservatives were executed. The executions were widely seen as quintessential illustrations of vengeance by "Jewish Soviet leaders" and served to impassion anti-Semitism in Bavaria.

It is interesting to see how our establishment historians refer to the foregoing events. Alan Bullock, author of *Hitler, A Study in Tyranny*, a 1952 book that dominated Hitler scholarship for many years, says that the Leviné government "was accompanied by quarrelling, uproar, and utmost confusion."[1252] Bullock's description is a curious one for the murder, robbery, and mayhem that took place under Leviné. He does not fail to mention, however, that "a bloody revenge was extracted"[1253] by the Freikorps units that liberated Munich and the rest of Bavaria. In retaking Munich, the Freikorps lost about seventy of its own men, and it did indeed take bloody revenge: it executed about 700 people.

Witnesses and victims of the events in Munich included Archbishop Pacelli, later known as Pope Pius XII, the pope who would be falsely accused of indifference to the plight of Jews during World War II,* a charge that was fostered in no small part by the Jewish Marxist theater director Erwin Piscator. It was during these times in Munich that Pacelli's hatred of Communism was nourished. In an April 1919 letter written by Pacelli to the Vatican secretary of state, he described conditions at the Communist headquarters.

> An army of employers [sic] were dashing to and fro, giving out orders, waving bits of paper, and in the midst of all this, a gang of young women, of dubious appearance, Jews like all the rest of them, hanging around in all the offices with lecherous demeanor and suggestive smiles. The boss of this female rabble was Levien's [Leviné's] mistress, a Russian woman, a Jew and a divorcée, who was in charge. And it was to her that the nunciature was obliged to pay homage in order to proceed.[1254]

---

* Quoting Franz von Papen, G. M. Gilbert records that "the chief resistance to the Nazis came from the Catholics" (Gilbert, 1995, 180).

Leviné and his Communist cohorts managed to further outrage Pacelli by their discourteous conduct toward him and his aide and by their confiscation of his automobile. Clearly, the revolutionary Jews of Munich were not out to make friends. That they were all indifferent to their own Judaism was of little consequence to those being subjected to their destructive policies and sadistic acts. The commonplace association of Jews with liberalism, Marxism, capitalism, secularism, and now, revolutionary subversion and anti-Catholicism, evoked renewed hostility among German Catholics toward Jews. And not too few of them sought revenge.

Noske to the Rescue of Bavaria

Beginning on May 1, Noske's Freikorps troops were welcomed with jubilation by a beleaguered, but now much relieved, Bavarian citizenry. The people waved cloths and applauded, everyone was cheering.[1255] Noske and his troops quickly defeated the ragtag Red Brigade, and then went on to extract revenge many times over. By May 3, the Leviné government was at an end.

Had it not been for the Freikorps, it is entirely likely that all of Germany would have been subjugated by Communism by 1920.[1256] Later, in the early 1930s, when the Communists had recovered their footing and sought revolution anew, it would be Adolf Hitler and his Nazis who saved the day from a Communist takeover.

History does not record much in the way of Jewish-German leaders or the world press rising in opposition to the excesses of the Jewish Bavarian Marxists during this period. No cries of outrage in the Jewish press. No calls for moderation. No claims of pogroms. No shouts of indignation condemning the revolutionaries or even calling for restraint. There would, however, be historical complaints aplenty that the right-wing forces who defeated the Marxists were brutal and that the judiciary did not afterward met out sufficient punishment to them in the aftermath of the bloodbath of their making. They make these claims as though it would have been different if the Bolshevists had prevailed, that punishment would have been meted out to such thugs as the executioners of Countess von Westarp.

Detleve Peukert, in his book *The Weimar Republic*, complains of the mass expulsion of Ostjuden by the Bavarian government in 1923 and the "shocking" anti-Jewish riots that took place in Berlin.[1257] Both the expulsion and the anti-Semitism were direct popular responses to the Jewish-led upheavals during the period 1918–1923, and it was not at all surprising, much less "shocking," that such actions were taken.

Egelhofer was summarily shot and killed by Freikorps troops. Landauer was beaten to a pulp before being executed. Leviné was summarily tried and executed before a firing squad. Toller, in part because of his effort to stop the killing of hostages, was sentenced to only five years in prison. He later enjoyed a career as a screenwriter in Hollywood. Axelrod escaped injury by claiming, like Radek before him, diplomatic status and by threats from Lenin that if Axelrod was harmed, German diplomats in Russia would suffer a similar fate. The brutality of the leftists was quelled by the even greater brutality of the rightists. On the whole, it was not a happy time for Munich and the rest of Bavaria. Still, it could have been worse; it could have succumbed to Bolshevism.

It was at about this time, as revolutionary efforts were spawned and subsequently overcome throughout Germany that Ben Hecht of the Chicago *Daily News* cabled his newspaper with a fitting description of the totality of events and impacts in Germany: "GERMANY IS HAVING A NERVOUS BREAKDOWN. THERE IS NOTHING SANE TO REPORT."[1258] (Capitalization is in the original.)

Aftermath of the Bavarian Revolution

Ian Kershaw correctly summarizes the impact of the Bavarian revolution as follows:

> It would be hard to exaggerate the impact on political consciousness in Bavaria of the events between November 1918 and May 1919, and quite especially of the Räterrepublik [the Leviné regime]. At its very

mildest, it was experienced in Munich itself as a time of curtailed freedom, severe food shortages, press censorship, general strike, sequestration of foodstuffs, coal, and items of clothing, and general disorder and chaos. But, of more lasting significance, it went down in popular memory as a "rule of horror" (*Schreckensherrschaft*) imposed by foreign elements in the service of Soviet Communism.[1259]

Kershaw goes on to explain that rightist forces saw and represented events in Munich as having been spawned by

> ... alien–Bolshevik and Jewish—forces taking over the state, threatening institutions, traditions, order, and property, presiding over chaos and mayhem, perpetrating terrible acts of violence, and causing anarchy of advantage only to Germany's enemies. Even more moderate press organs painted much the same picture. The mainstream newspaper of Munich's middle class, the *Münicher Neueste Nachrichten*, spoke of the "aims and methods of Russian Bolshevism," "Russian emissaries," "Bolshevik agents," the "practice of Asiatic Bolshevism," and "foreign agitators." It placed the blame for the "criminal atrocities" and the "bestial slaughter of innocent hostages" squarely on the [Jewish] "communist leaders."[1260]

Kershaw claims that the images described above were "more telling than reality." Perhaps, but those who actually experienced that reality thought otherwise. Hitler, too, thought otherwise: he felt a sense of "utter repugnance."[1261] Average Bavarians, and particularly those in Munich, says Kershaw, concluded that "the Jews are at present the greatest danger for all working Germans" and that "only when the Reich is liberated from this malicious, treacherous vermin" could German revival be contemplated.[1262] Hitler was attuned to their wavelength.

During and after the Bavarian Revolution, revolutionaries of Jewish extraction were prominent in upheavals in Magdeburg, Dresden, the Ruhr, Bremerhaven, Kiel, and in Palatinate. The total of these events, including those in Hungary, but especially those in Bavaria, had seismic impacts on the likes of Adolf Hitler and other right-wing extremists. Hitler could not have helped but observe that in late 1918 and early 1919 his dear Munich had, in the course of only six months, as Watt points out, lived under a "monarchy, revolutionary Socialism, moderate Socialism, anarchy, Communism, and, finally, brutal counterrevolutionary suppression."[1263] Bavaria saw a revolutionary Jewish government (Eisner) pass to a revolutionary Jewish government (Toller) and thence to still another, but this time, brutal Jewish revolutionary government (Leviné). Moreover, coupled with the events in Russia, Hungary, and Poland, it was not particularly irrational to conclude that one was witnessing the start of a worldwide Jewish revolution—when you are outdoors in a torrent it is not hard to rationally conclude that you are getting wet. The coming events in Austria, the Red Vienna of the 1920s, would add still more to the thinking that Jewish-led Reds were on the march throughout the Continent, that they were the political torrent of the times.

That Hitler concluded that Jews were at the source of Bolshevistic revolution was hardly a surprising outcome; the evidence was everywhere to be seen. In the aftermath of the Bavarian revolution, Hitler purportedly served as a witness against several participants and provided information to the authorities as to the whereabouts of soldiers and officers who had taken part. His testimony did little. He lost all faith in the legal system as each of the culprits was set free by the liberal courts.[1264]

During the Bavarian upheavals, Red soldiers had tried to arrest Hitler at his barracks—he was seeing things on an up close and personal basis. He turned the Reds away at the point of a gun. He later wrote that "Faced with my leveled carbine, the three scoundrels lacked the necessary courage and marched off as they had come."[1265]* On the whole, the epidemic of revolutions placed

---

* Historian Joachim Fest doubts Hitler's claim. Fest says that Hitler's claim that the "Central Council" ordered his arrest is bogus in that that particular council was no longer in existence at the time Hitler gives. That acknowledged, it remains, however, that

Hitler in a state of ferment and turmoil. Again, Toland provides a good summation:

> His simmering hatred of Jews had been activated by what he himself had witnessed on the streets of Munich. Everywhere Jews in power: first Eisner, then anarchists like Toller, and finally Russian Reds like Leviné. In Berlin it had been Rosa Luxemburg; in Budapest Béla Kun, in Moscow Trotsky, Zinoviev, and Kamenev. The conspiracy Hitler had previously suspected was turning into reality.[1266]

The importance of the Bavarian revolution(s) lays not in its short-lived existence; it lays, rather, in the perceptions that it invigorated. The Bavarian revolutions, all led by Jews, had resounding impacts on perceptions about Jews, their subversiveness, and a perception of their violent leftist revolutionary tendencies. In the case of Eisner, his attempt to document German responsibility for the war contributed to the Allies' cause and Germany's detriment. Many Bavarians contended that Eisner was guilty of treason, not merely insurrection. Such people pointed to his Jewish origins, and by extension, asserted that every Jew in Germany was potentially treasonous, and, like Eisner, incapable of grasping "German sensibilities."[1267] "The *Bayerische Volkszeitung*," says Kauders "repeatedly referred to Eisner as 'the Galician Jew,' whose tribal disposition (*Stammeseigenschaften*) precluded any knowledge of the Bavarian psyche. But not only Eisner, 80 percent of all revolutionaries were 'of the Jewish race.'"[1268]

By May 1919, the Spartacus Uprising as well as the Bavarian Revolution and most of the various insurrectionist movements throughout the country had been quashed. Between 1,500 and 2,000 people were dead and 10,000 were wounded.[1269] The armed struggle was at an end for the time being. There would be further

---

various councils were still in existence that did order such arrests, and Hitler may very well have been the object of one or another of them.

clashes up until the end of 1923 when the German Communists made their last attempt to forcibly overthrow the republic and Hitler staged his Munich putsch, but mid-1919 marked a new beginning. It was a time to renew the political battle for the hearts and minds of the populace. The battle would be a sloppy one, but throughout the 1920s it would go almost entirely to the leftists.

"The Bolshevik take-over and the soviet rule in Bavaria had shown," says Fest, "how a handful of determined men could seize power,"[1270] as indeed it did. As always, Adolf Hitler would take lessons from his observations of people and events, and the events in Munich were most certainly included among them. Hitler himself openly acknowledged that he had learned a great deal from the Marxists: lessons in social history, political struggle, and the efficacy of utter ruthlessness were gleaned from his study of Marxists and their methods in Munich, Hungary, and elsewhere.

It would later come to be that internecine battles within the leftist movement (with the "right-wing" elements of the leftist movement participating in the government and the radical leftist elements trying to bring down that government), that infighting, coupled with various disasters still to be borne by the people, along with corruption in the leftist parties, would ultimately further open the way for Adolf Hitler.

The sufferings of Bavarians under the various Jewish regimes made Bavarians uniquely sympathetic to the rightist cause. As Kolb puts it, this formerly liberal state was "From 1920 onwards . . . an Eldorado for extreme right organizations and leading personalities of militant right-wing radicalism."[1271] It was an example of Stolfi's observation with respect to historical physics: that for every action there is an opposite and equal reaction. In the aftermath of the Bavarian revolutions Munich installed a staunchly right-wing government that was sympathetic to Hitler and other rightists. It also installed a 400,000-man force with 2.5 million weapons as a product of its now mental obsession with the need for protection against further threats from the Left.[1272] That the threat remained real was illustrated by what Hitler related to one of his later confidants and economic adviser, Otto Wagener: "The SA [*Sturmabteilung*]" said Hitler to Wagener, "was made up of those informal militias that were organized after 1919 by communities and countries as well as by the governments as a protection against the Communist terror which, beginning in November 1918, continued to create disturbances in one region or another."[1273] Among the disturbances caused by the Communists was the sometimes violent disruption of meetings held by competing groups; among them, Hitler and his Nazis.

Hitler first established his Storm Troopers, the *Sturmabteilung* or SA (originally known as Brownshirts) organization, as "hall protection" so that he and his party could stage meetings without being disrupted by radical leftists.[1274] Throughout most of the 1920s the SA remained far smaller than competing groups organized by the SPD and KPD.

Like the Nazis' Brownshirts, the KPD organized and employed a paramilitary force, the Red Front, to protect its meetings and intimidate its political opponents. The Red Front organization attracted hundreds of thousands of followers.[1275] Indeed, the precedent for much of the violence we now associate with the Nazi SA was first set by the Red Front. As Joachim Fest states it, "There is a good deal of confirmation for the stories of deliberate riots launched against the NSDAP by the Left."[1276] The Marxists united mind and brutal violence harmoniously. Hitler's SA was but a mimic and counterforce to the violent leftist formations.

Historians frequently point out that the SA membership was composed largely of brutish thugs, and there can be little doubt that many of them fit just such a description. But that mattered not a twit to Hitler—from his perspective if they were effective they were quite good enough. Once, when criticized for his association with such people, he quipped that he would rather associate with a German tramp than a French count.

Nazi brawls with the Red Front were mostly defensive. In the early 1920s, the Reds were far better positioned to employ violence against their opponents than were the Nazis: they were a far larger organization and had the distinct advantage of being able to call upon their labor union membership at a moment's notice.[1277] Hitler was recounting a fair approximation of reality when he claimed in *Mein Kampf* that during 1920, "a national meeting that dared to address its appeal to the broad masses and publicly invite attendance was simply impossible. . . . participants in such a meeting were dispersed and driven away with bleeding heads."[1278] This assessment of things was not only true for Hitler and his NSDAP, it was so for all rightist parties, but unlike the lesser rightist parties, Hitler was sufficiently determined to weather such storms and ultimately build a counterforce that could directly challenge and defeat the Red Front.

Even before Hitler's SA had grown to an appreciable size, his small hall protection organization often clashed with the Red Front. Hitler once vented his frustration about the disruptive tactics of the Left, saying, "in a public meeting a Demosthenes can be brought to silence if only fifty idiots, supported by their voices and their fists, refuse to let him speak."[1279] Hitler's SA was a response in kind. Hitler recounted one such response that took place in November 1921: his fifty SA toughs beat back a force over "400 communists and Jews" who had tried to disrupt his speech in the Festival Hall of the Hofbräuhaus in Munich.[1280]

In 1922, Hitler went on the offensive by taking his SA to one of the home turfs of the Red Front, Coburg. He brought a total of 800* SA men with him into a city populated by many thousands of die-hard Marxists. To get to Coburg, which was 160 miles from Munich, he needed to rent train cars to carry all of his men but had no money to do so. He asked his men to pitch in and pay their own way, which they did. This was a group of true believers who paid their own way to travel into the jaws of an opposing force that outnumbered them by a multiple of at least ten, and perhaps more. They arrived in Coburg, engaged in fights throughout the first day, and then paraded victoriously as they departed on the second day, and to the cheers of crowds who were glad to be rid of their Marxist tormentors. Shortly thereafter, Coburg became the first city to elect a Nazi mayor and city council. Stolfi provides an excellent commentary with respect to the SA and its opposition KPD Red Front Fighters League and the million-strong Reichsbanner of the SPD:

---

* The Nazi Alfred Rosenberg claimed it was 600.

Given the similarly organized Marxist street-fighting formations and the similar toughness of their members, and if we accept the interpretation of SA men as beer-swilling bullies and thugs, we could generalize that a smaller number of beer-swilling Nazi thugs stood opposed to a greater number of beer-swilling Marxist thugs in the meeting halls and streets of Germany throughout the Nazi rise to power.[1281]

Intellectuals, many of whom were supposed pacifists, ignored the brutality of Red Front street fighters as they did the much more drastic brutality of Lenin and Stalin's rule in the Soviet Union and Kun's brief rule in Hungary because it served their political objectives. For them, the brutality of the various leftist regimes represented "historical necessity." Stated otherwise, such brutality was represented by them as pilpulized pacifism.

After the Bavarian Revolution, Bavaria's Prime Minister Eugen von Knilling installed Gustav von Kahr as state commissioner with dictatorial powers. Kahr went so far as to represent himself as one who sought a decisive battle with the "internationalist-Marxist-Judaic front."[1282] Otto von Lossow was installed as the commander of Bavarian troops, and Hans Ritter von Seisser was made head of the Bavarian state police—radical rightists, all. Police Commissioner Pöhner and its Chief Bailiff Frick were particularly tolerant of and even assisted Hitler and his movement (which is why, presumably, Rubenstein assigns to Munich the blame for the birth of the Nazis). It was Pöhner, who, when asked if he knew there were political murder gangs in Bavaria, famously quipped: "Yes, but not enough of them."[1283] Thus it was that in the aftermath of the Bavarian Revolution, Hitler and his nascent Nazi movement enjoyed maneuver room for a time within both Munich and Bavaria as a whole.[*]

---

[*] In Berlin, the Communists had enjoyed similar freedoms under the protection of the Jewish Vice Police Chief Bernard Weise and the non-Jewish Emil Eichhorn. The Nazis also pegged Eichorn as Jewish though he probably was not.

The whole of the excesses of the Bavarian Revolution were coupled in Hitler's mind with such things as the Treaty of Versailles, the capitalistic and Marxist systems, the outrages of modern art, the abandonment of moral precepts, and the perceived struggle between lower and higher races—all of which stemmed, he concluded, from one source, the Eternal Jew.[1284]

Kapp Putsch

On March 13, 1920, troops loyal to Wolfgang Kapp, the monarchist founder of the Fatherland Party, entered Berlin to seize the government. Appeals by the government to the German army to put down the coup were fruitless. That is, the army refused to save Ebert's leftist government from rightist monarchial forces. The government fled the capital.

The SPD and USPD leadership called on the trade unions to defeat Kapp's forces by going on strike. Demonstrating the early schism within Marxist factions that would plague them throughout the 1920s and ultimately play a large part in the downfall of the republic and the successful rise of Hitler, the KPD initially called on workers to remain neutral, treating the Kapp Putsch as a fight between rightists and insufficiently radical leftists. Soon, however, the KPD reversed itself and joined the fray with the SPD and USPD to defeat Kapp.

In the Ruhr a Red Army of some 50,000 men was formed and armed, ostensibly in response to Kapp's putsch. This formation was fully equipped with modern weapons, including artillery. For a time they became the masters of the region[1285] and were supported by 300,000 mine workers. After the Kapp Putsch collapsed, the Red Army of the Ruhr remained and retained its armament; it would later be the source of still more violence and misery for Germany and her people.

The general strike in opposition to Kapp was entirely effective—if Luxemburg and Liebknecht had been able to so thoroughly energize the workers a year earlier their Spartacist Uprising might very well have succeeded.

Berlin came to a virtual standstill. Union leaders called on workers throughout the country to participate, and they responded accordingly. Workers in the Ruhr, central Germany, and Bavaria all went out on strike. All the worse for Kapp and his followers, the well-armed workers in the Ruhr joined with the Red Army faction to overcome Kapp forces. Within a week the Kapp Putsch had fizzled, collapsing entirely on March 17.

Failure though it was, the Kapp Putsch had resounding effects throughout Germany and all of those effects advantaged the extreme Left, not the Kapp Right. Failure of the putsch led to the resignation of Gustav Noske, the hero of the republic when he was putting down the Spartacists a year earlier but who, as war minister in 1920, was unable to rally the army to the government's cause as the Kapp Putsch commenced. Thus, a strong representative of the right wing of the government was lost to the political battle.

Popular reaction to the Kapp Putsch provided fodder for leftist elements. By June 1920, the radically Marxist USPD became second only to the SPD as the largest party in the Reichstag, and in several of the provinces it became the largest one. The radical Right also increased its numbers at the expense of the SPD, but it still remained relatively small compared to leftist political formations. In the Ruhr, where armed workers had succeeded in ousting the Freikorps and Reichswehr during the putsch, the Red Army now refused to lay down its arms.[1286] The central government had to resort to the Reichswehr army, the same army that refused to put down the Kapp Putsch, to restore normality in the Ruhr.

The KPD grew from 3–4,000 members in January 1919 to 78,000 shortly after the Kapp Putsch.[1287] Moreover, Communist forces were very much in ascendency throughout Europe with more and more of the parties joining, and therefore taking direction from, the Moscow-based Communist International (Comintern). Both the KPD and the SPD were members of the International, but unlike the KPD, the SPD was disinclined to take its every direction from Moscow.

By March 1921, the KPD, heavily influenced by theorists in Moscow and ultraleft extremists at home, decided it was time for a showdown with German capitalism. As always within the KPD, the decisions and actions involved several Jews: among them, Paul Levi, August Thaelheimer, and Béla Kun. The KPD, the theory went, would go on the offensive in the Ruhr, a region made ripe for revolutionary action stemming from the actions of the central government (SPD) against the Communists in the region.

March Action

The infamous March Action of 1921 was a dismal failure. Thinking that their violent offensive actions would immediately inflame the workers with revolutionary fervor, the March Action got underway. Hundreds were killed, but with minor exceptions, the offensive was limited to western and central Germany.

In the early 1920s, as the ultraleftist faction of the Russian Executive Committee of the Communist International (ECCI) toyed with the newly inspired "theory of the offensive," a theory that called for offensive action regardless of whether such action had the support of the masses, it hit upon the idea of still another armed insurrection in Germany. A principal in pushing for the new offensive was the Communist leader Grigory Zinoviev. Zinoviev was at the time a confidant of Lenin and one of the most powerful members of the Comintern. He was joined in his push by Béla Kun who was also by then a member of the Comintern executive, Ruth Fischer of the German KPD, and Karl Radek. Kun, of course had been the leader of the disastrous Hungarian revolution in early 1919. Fischer was a member of the leadership of the German KPD and would later become its party leader. Radek served as Lenin's representative in Germany on matters of organization and actions by the Spartacists and the KPD. Zinoviev, Kun, Fischer, and Radek were all Jewish.

The KPD was at the time being led by Heinrich Brandler, a sycophant of the Comintern.

Kun and Fischer were insistent that the KPD act to seize power in Germany and the March Action, to be initiated in the industrial regions of central Germany and the Ruhr, was to be its venue. They did not flinch from deliberate bogus attacks on their fellow

Communists in order to prompt a negative reaction on the part of workers who would then, it was reasoned, come to the defense of those attacked. Sham kidnappings of local KPD leaders, the dynamiting of munitions depots, and blowing up of a workers' cooperative in Halle and blaming it all on the police were part of the Communist operations intended to fuel the anger of the workers.

In mid-March 1921, tens of thousands of German workers, mostly industrial workers and coal miners in the German provinces of Thuringia and Saxony, were duped by the Kun-Fischer Communist organization to take up arms against the police and army. The ostensible provocation for the KPD to initiate the insurrection was an entirely legitimate call by the government's leadership to occupy the mining district of Mansfeld to disarm workers and restore order.

Recall that in the aftermath of the Kapp Putsch of 1920, a 50,000-man Red Front-Fighters' League had been formed. It ultimately grew to 130,000 by 1929. It was that Fighters' League that the government was trying to disarm. The Red Front-Fighters' League was called on by its KPD leadership to violently resist the government's attempt to disarm them, and indeed to carry forward to seize power. Belá Kun himself provided propaganda material in the KPD-owned *Die Rote Fahne* to incite the workers. Actions by workers and the Red Front-Fighters' League included general looting, bank robbery, burning of buildings, and the dynamiting of trains, including passenger trains.

On March 24, the KPD called for a general strike. This time, the call went unanswered. The timing of the strike was as inauspicious as the Action itself. The strike was called a day before Good Friday. Most factories were closed for a four-day weekend. Thus, according to Walter Held who was one of the leaders of the Fourth International, "While most German workers were celebrating Easter, the leadership of the German Communist Party was conducting a revolution."[1288] The hoped-for millions of militant workers who were expected to join the struggle on behalf of the KPD did not materialize, but tens of thousands did. A wave of fighting between the Communists and government forces went on for about two weeks, leaving hundreds of dead workers in its wake. On March 31, the KPD called off the strike and shortly thereafter accepted defeat.

The March Action was a fiasco. The KPD, on a strong upward swing at the time toward becoming a mass party, was made to appear amateurish.[1289] In 1920, the Red Front-Fighters' League was an important element in the outbreaks of violence in the Ruhr—violence that represented a regional civil war. Now, in 1921, the Red Front represented the organized force of insurrection for the March Action. Mainstream Social Democrats backed the regular army against the Red Front; the fracas that this support caused in leftist ranks would never heal. It served to further the internecine warfare between the ultraleftists of the KPD and the relatively moderate leftists of the SPD that would last throughout the decade and into the election cycles of the early 1930s.

In its fundamentals the March Action was just another Communist-inspired insurrection, adding to those of the period between 1918 and 1920. The difference was that the March Action was organized and ordained exclusively by a clique of Jews in Moscow in coordination with other Jews in Germany, rather than stemming primarily from just the radical leftist Jews of Germany.

Within the Comintern, various critiques were forthcoming that finally settled on rejection of the "theory of offensive," which, in turn, led the Moscow clique to opt for unbending opposition to the SPD. With that decision in hand, the KPD was directed by the Moscow Comintern to make the SPD its primary opponent; all others, including the Nazis, were of much lesser matter to them. That is, the KPD abandoned its armed revolutionary fervor in favor of a focused propaganda war with the SPD to win the hearts of the masses. As history would have it, both parties were ill equipped. Hitler did them better.

In the aftermath of the March Action, the government outlawed the KPD for a time and passed a law for the "protection of the *Reich*." Between 1921 and 1933, the law was invoked five times against the Right and 822 times against the Left—and this by an essentially leftist government. The KPD lost upward of 100,000 of its members. KPD leader Paul Levi, who had only recently resigned as the head of the party, blatantly denounced the adventurist policies that led to the Action and the personalities of the clique who had inspired and initially directed it; he was subsequently expelled from the party altogether. Public backbiting between Zinoviev and Radek exposed the Moscow origins of the Action to all. Rightists were provided with still another powerful propaganda tool against both the Communist-Bolsheviks and Jews; it reinforced the notion that Communists, Bolsheviks, and Jews were equivalent constructs and out to do violence against Germans and Germany.

Inflationary Period: 1921–1924

The hyperinflation that gripped Germany and Austria from 1921–1924 stemmed largely from actions by the government in response to the payments demanded by the Treaty of Versailles and governmental responses to the French occupation of the Ruhr. The inflation did not stem from the acts of Jews. Nonetheless, the worthless money that the period produced was deemed by radical right-wing elements as "Jew Confetti"[1290] in recognition of the too many Jewish bankers and speculators who either made the inflation worse or who otherwise unjustly profited from the crisis.

In early 1923, the French and Belgian armies invaded and occupied the Ruhr in reaction to a failure of Germany to make delivery of certain commodities as part of the reparations requirements laid upon it by the Treaty of Versailles.* The government called for passive resistance on the part of workers there but continued to pay them though they were unproductive. This move compounded the problems with the already feeble currency (the beginnings of which were to be found in the deficit spending of World War I).

The occupation of the Ruhr had four significant impacts: firstly, it inflamed German nationalist spirit (Hitler humorously

---

* France's Poincaré used the technical excuse of minor defaults by Germany in the delivery of timber to occupy the Ruhr on January 11, 1923. "The occupation of the Ruhr [the industrial center of Germany] gave the final touch to the deterioration of the mark" (Bullock, 90).

claimed that the government "action" of passive resistance sought to "kill the French by loafing");[1291] secondly, it greatly exacerbated the monetary inflation that was already well on the rise at that point; and, thirdly, it brought adherents to Hitler. The mark plunged from 6,750 to the dollar to 50,000 in just two weeks (in November 1918 it had been 7.45 to the dollar).[1292] The fourth impact of the invasion was to vastly favor the USPD and KPD: the Ruhr strikers were, at that point, radicalized constituents of those parties. The KPD would soon recover its strength from roughly 60,000 in June 1923 to 3,700,000 the following May.

The government sought to pay off its debts with worthless marks and therefore printed vast amounts of bills that debased the currency until it came to be that literally trillions of marks were needed to purchase even staples such as bread and milk. The mark/dollar exchange rate ultimately sank to 4.2 trillion marks to the dollar.[1293] The misery brought about by the hyperinflation was such that there were reports of girls selling themselves for packets of butter.[1294]

Google	URL
Pictures, German Inflation Period	http://www.spiegel.de/fotostrecke/photo-gallery-germany-s-national-trauma-fotostrecke-45217.html 8/2/14

Misery was rife due to the loss of savings and properties stemming from the inflation. And it was in this atmosphere that high-profile Jews such as Siegmund Bosel and Camillo Castiglioni pulled off daring stock market scams, acquired financial empires, manipulated public opinion, speculated against the Germany currency, and purchased the cooperation of corrupt, pliant politicians. Such individuals borrowed large sums from foreign sources where the currency was valuable and stable, such as the U.S., and used those monies to leverage the purchase of various concerns at fire sale prices. Since money was losing value so quickly, they were able to pay off their debts with veritably worthless marks. Other racketeers made huge profits by illicit currency dealing, smuggling, and illegal movement of goods. Out of almost nothing, speculators created enormous economic empires.[1295]

Donald Niewyk, author of *The Jews in Weimar Germany*, quotes Dr. Max Naumann in saying that "German Jews of uncertain commitment [Ostjuden] were only too easily turned into shirkers and leftist revolutionaries, as events during and after the World War had demonstrated. Half-hearted Germans with their pacifist plays, discordant music, and leftist tirades degraded everything sacred to the German soul."[1296] Says, Niewyk:

> The Eastern Jews gravitated to "communist, syndicalist, Jewish-nationalist, or other organizations that stand in opposition to everything German." Using underhanded tactics, they took advantage of runaway inflation to buy property and bonds from desperate owners for a fraction of their real value. Such practices precipitated the November, 1923, riots in Berlin, and insofar as foreign Jews were their victims, they had it coming to them. . . . Bavaria's laudable expulsions of Eastern Jews [which Goldhagen complained about] put the matter in sharpest relief; only prejudice in favor of foreign coreligionists could justify excluding these shady elements from the general ban on immigration at a time when Germans could scarcely provide for their own needs.[1297]

"The black marketer and the profiteer," says Richard Evans, "had become objects of denunciation by populist demagogues even before galloping inflation became hyperinflation. Now they became popular hate-figures."[1298] And it was no more irrational at that time to see Jews as the only beneficiaries of the strife as it is to now muse over the beneficiaries of the recent economic crisis brought about by the devaluation of the U.S. housing market: the trillion dollars spent by the U.S. government to stave off the utter collapse of the economy went almost wholly to the banking and investment communities, a community overly populated by Jews. They were at once both the cause of the collapse and the beneficiaries of the bailout. The traditional multimillion-dollar bonuses to players in the investment community rose by 17 percent at the end of 2009 even as that community accepted government bailouts and worker unemployment hovered at 10 percent of the population. Germans saw equivalent actions in Germany as wholly beneficial to unscrupulous Jewish profiteers.

The black marketers in Germany during both the war years and the inflationary period were composed in no small part of Jews. The whole of the misery of the hyperinflationary period confirmed in the minds of many that at the root of their suffering was the criminal, the gambler, the speculator, the profiteer, "the financially manipulative Jew."[1299] Such attitudes were reinforced by crooks, bribers, political schemers, and black marketers such as Ivan Kutisker and the three Barmat brothers who were wartime food merchant profiteers. The five Sklarz brothers and Jakob Michael and Michael Holzmann stroked the inflation to swell their fortunes. Add to the list Alexander Parvus, the notorious Jewish Communist functionary and war profiteer. Born in Russia, Parvus had tried to gain German citizenship—he wrote to Wilhelm Liebknecht saying, "I am seeking a government where one can inexpensively acquire a fatherland." The hyperinflation enabled men like Parvus to inexpensively acquire the properties and treasures of the fatherland.

As mentioned, debtors were advantaged during the inflationary period in that they could pay off their debts with worthless script. People with access to foreign currencies, such as Jews with relatives and business relationships in other countries, also did exceedingly well. Historian John Toland summarized the period as follows:

> About the sole ones who rejoiced were those deeply in debt who could pay off their obligations with worthless paper. But the greatest beneficiaries were the exchange barons, the profiteers and opportunistic foreigners who bought up jewelry and real estate at ridiculously low prices. Large estates and buildings went to these vultures for a few hundred dollars. Family heirlooms were exchanged for enough to feed a family a few weeks. There were scenes beyond belief: a woman who had left a basket-full of money on the street, returning a moment

later to find the money dumped in the gutter and the basket stolen; a worker with a salary of two billion marks a week able to buy his family only potatoes.[1300]

According to Richard Evans in his book *The Coming of the Third Reich*,

> It was not least as a consequence of the inflation that Weimar culture developed its fascination with criminals, embezzlers, gamblers, manipulators, thieves and crooks of all kinds. . . . Much of the cynicism that gave Weimar culture in the mid-1920s and made many people eventually long for the return of idealism, self-sacrifice and patriotic dedication, derived from the disorienting effects of the hyperinflation. . . . It lent new power to stock fantasy-images of evil, not just the criminal and the gambler, but also the speculator, the financially manipulative Jew.[1301]

Radicalism always flourishes in times of great misery and upheaval. It is not surprising, therefore, that Hitler was able to exploit the misery stemming from the inflationary period to dramatically swell the ranks of his party, though it continued to remain miniscule compared to other parties. Still, between January and mid-October of 1923, 35,000 new members joined the Nazis,[1302] and the inflation of the currency made a significant contribution to the inflation in Nazi ranks.

Camillo Castiglioni, a character we will encounter again later in this narrative, became the wealthiest man in central Europe during World War I. During the inflationary period of 1921–1924, his financial machinations continued, but he was now joined by the Austrian financier Siegfried Bosel. The two were the leaders of the almost exclusively Jewish Phoenix Life Insurance Company. The company's Jewish director was the notoriously corrupt Dr. Wilhelm Berlinar. They collectively managed to purchase politicians and manipulate the public through their newspapers. They also manipulated the stock market. The object of their effort was to add to their already considerable empire of wealth. By

1926, their financial machinations caught up with them. The company collapsed amidst a bribery scandal. They bankrupted their creditors. Castiglioni absconded with securities of high value. The whole of the conduct of Castiglioni, Bosel, and their ilk was to add still more to the widespread perceptions of Jews as profiteers and exploiters of misery.

* * * *

The impact of the inflationary period in Germany was massive. The middle class in particular was devastated. Alan Bullock provides a good summary of the effect that it had on German attitudes:

> Even if a man worked till he dropped it was impossible to buy enough clothes for his family—and work, in any case, was not to be found.[*]
>
> Whatever the cause of this phenomenon—and there were sections of the community, among them the big industrialists and landowners, who profited by it and sought to perpetuate its progress in their own interests—the result of the inflation was to undermine the foundations of German society in a way which neither the war, nor the revolution of November 1918, nor the Treaty of Versailles had ever done. The real revolution in Germany was the inflation, for it destroyed not only property and money, but the faith in property and the meaning of money. The violence of Hitler's denunciations of the corrupt, Jew-ridden system which had allowed all this to happen, the bitterness of his attacks on the Versailles settlement and on the Republican Government which had accepted it, found an

---

[*] While it is true that the inflationary period also increased unemployment, this impact on the economy was not nearly as severe as it would become during the Depression that commenced in 1929.

echo in the misery and despair of large classes of the German nation.[1303]

Jewish Prominence in Politics and Society

The effect of Jewish prominence in the various governments, the many uprisings, revolutions, and political terrorism of 1919 to 1923, as well as its power in the press and other areas of cultural leadership, provided the basis for right-wing claims about the "Judification" of German society. It was a claim made tirelessly throughout the Weimar period. The presence of so many Jews in the ranks of revolution and liberal democracy was heaven-sent for radical right-wing agitators.[1304]

In places like Hungary and Germany's Bavaria, the supposed Jewish Marxist utopians had now demonstrated what their utopia was to look like. It was not pretty. The effect of their action was that Jews were now considered not merely exploiters and profiteers, the worst sort of capitalists, but also traitors working against the national interests of Germany and conspiring with the international Communist revolution, as the KPD was in fact doing.

Referring to Germany's war dead, Adolf Hitler concluded that this "gang of despicable and depraved criminals" had fermented revolution and sacrificed the lives of "two millions."[1305] And who were these Marxists? They were Rosa Luxemburg, Karl Liebknecht, Kurt Eisner, Toller, Leviné, Landauer, Jogiches, Axelrod, Radek, Béla Kun, and their many cohorts, both Jewish and Gentile. They were aided in their aims by Jews in important German government positions such as Walter Rathenau. And the Marxists in Germany were all, thought Hitler, working at the behest of the Jews in Russia, at the behest of such characters as Leon Trotsky, Gregory Zinoviev, Belá Kun, Karl Radek, and others. And in a very real sense the revolutionary Jews of Germany were doing precisely as Hitler charged.

Yet for all this, evidence of German indifference and even opposition to the radical anti-Semitic right-wing groups was recurringly demonstrated at the polls from 1919 through 1932. For all of their anti-Semitic rhetoric, anti-Semitic parties made precious little headway throughout most of the 1920s. The Nationalist Party (DNVP), which was fundamentally a right-wing monarchist party, not a volkisch or particularly anti-Semitic party, did manage at one point to install 103 representatives to the Reichstag (1924), but they thereafter steadily declined in strength and influence. The whole of the radical volkisch movement parties were able to garner only a pitiful 3 percent of the votes; it had previously had thirty-three Reichstag deputies but was reduced to only fourteen as the result of the 1924 election.[1306] Ludendorff, the rightist hero of World War I as previously mentioned, got only a paltry 1.1 percent of the vote when he ran for president in 1924, a lesser percentage than Eisner in Catholic Bavaria.

It remained the case that the thing most hated in Germany during the 1920s was not Jews; it was the Treaty of Versailles. To the extent that Jews were also hated, the hate was confined to small, ineffectual political elements and was based on the actions and attitudes of prominent Jews during and after the war, including both the creation and implementation of the Versailles Treaty and the various insurrections already recounted. By 1928, Hitler was all but finished as a national leader; his virulent anti-Semitism had failed at every turn. The policies of the republic were bearing fruit. Unemployment had fallen to 8.4 percent of the workforce; both the economy and Germany's reemerging place in world politics had put the populace at ease. The people had gained faith in the democratic system and began to find the extremists at both ends of the political spectrum unattractive.[1307]

To the extent that the Nazis gained support, it stemmed from volkisch issues, issues of nationalism and culture, and, of course, the hated Treaty of Versailles. At this point, Germany was no brewing caldron of anti-Semitism just waiting for a Hitler messiah before pouring fire and brimstone on Jews. Throughout the 1920s, Germany honorably resisted anti-Semitism, no matter the actions of a minority of prominent Jews who were widely and justifiably perceived as detrimental to German interests. By 1928, the Nazi Party was only able to muster a pathetic 1.5 percent of the vote, giving them just twelve seats in the Reichstag, twenty *fewer* than they had in 1924. The total vote for extremists of all kinds—Left and Right—garnered only 30 percent of the vote.

Hitler was, of course, far less tolerant than the average German. As he contemplated Germany's loss of World War I and the Jewish-Marxists that he believed responsible for that defeat, hatred grew in him, hatred for those responsible for the deeds. Hitler had a single answer for the dire straits of both Germany and the state of Bavaria: it was the Jews. It may be that enlightened rationality should have prevailed even under such circumstances but it did not; and under the conditions of the kind that then existed, it never, ever does. Emotion reigned: anger, venom, hate—and a thirst for vengeance stirred in the minds of Hitler and his minority-type. There it all was: Jews everywhere at the heart of all turmoil in Russia, Germany, Hungary, and elsewhere. Everywhere there was turmoil there were revolutionary movements that were awash with Jews in positions of leadership and wreaking havoc on already wretchedly demoralized peoples. Every catastrophe, every calamity, every hardship was exploited by Jews to their advantage—no crisis went wasted.

Several times during the 1920s prominent Jews, especially Zionists, broke ranks with the general liberalism of Weimar Jews and condemned their brethren. Their actions in this regard illustrates that while Jews were exceptionally powerful in Weimar Germany their power was neither absolute nor entirely homogeneous. As the history of Jews thoroughly confirms, Jews have never achieved absolute unity in their objectives. Moreover, even when their objectives are relatively agreed upon, the means of achieving them or the lust for factional power often intervenes to frustrate achievement of their goals. By way of example, Jacob Klatzkin, a Zionist ideologue, advocated the undermining of Jewish communities in Germany as a way of encouraging the creation of a Jewish state therein. In 1921, Jacob Klatzkin, a major Zionist writer, wrote that:

> We Jews are aliens . . . a foreign people in your midst and we . . . wish to stay that way. A Jew can never be a

loyal German; whoever calls the foreign land his Fatherland is a traitor to the Jewish people.[1308]

Paul Nikolaus Cossmann, the baptized Jewish editor of the Munich journal *Süddeutsche Monatshefte*, was among the first to spread the story that Jewish Marxists had stabbed undefeated Germany in the back.[1309]

While these individuals were perhaps sincere in their criticism, they were, at the same time, unwitting contributors to radical rightist propaganda. Hitler would observe it all: he saw and assessed the characters in the various revolutions and other turmoil in the country; he read voraciously and he concluded that Jews were at the source of all of Germany's ills. From the leftist propaganda that he had seen and heard during the war to the leftist push for peace at any cost, to the stab-in-the-back theory for Germany's defeat, he consumed it, assessed it, rationalized it, and concluded—that was his way. When Hitler spoke of Jewish plots and enemies of the state, as he often did, he was recalling those Jews who had made a battleground of his beloved Munich. He also learned there that power must be used to crush political opposition.

Hitler's observations and experiences concerning Jews would continue into the coming years. The Treaty of Versailles and the cultural wars of the Weimar years further solidified his assessments and conclusions. He also took note of the impact that Jews were having on Germany's culture. He did not like it.

CHAPTER 6

WEIMAR CULTURE

> In a world where Jews are only a tiny percentage of the population, what is the secret of the disproportionate importance the Jews have had in the history of Western culture?
> —Ernest van den Haag, *The Jewish Mystique*, p. 13.[1310]

> The cultural Heritage of the West [along with Truth] was one of the first casualties of the Great War.
> —Michael Jones, *Living Machines*, p. 16.

The Weimar era is represented by most historians as a period in which German culture advanced: it came into alignment with modernity in art, literature, and thought, it is said. Such claims are made even in the face of the fact that it was a period during which Dadaists declared their war on art with their explicit antiart manifestos and Bolshevists brutally attacked and altered esteemed German culture. It was still another instance of a Golden Age—a veritable chazzanut of Jewish proponents and apologists. Hitler thought otherwise.

As one delves into the Weimar cultural scene and gets past the windy rhetoric of the Golden Age tripe, a sober assessment causes one to conclude that there is just no escaping the fact that Jews were the predominant catalysts for Germany's precipitous cultural decline. Jews of Berlin, like the ones Hitler had experienced in Vienna, were prominent in the prostitution trade, white slavery, fraud, usury, criminal bankruptcy, bribery, and illegal drugs. They were both plentiful and powerful in Berlin, and they were particularly so in the realm of German culture. Heinrich von Tretschke had once offered an angry quip with respect to the predominance of Jews in Berlin: "One knows one has entered the city when one sees a synagogue." The synagogue reference was offered with specific respect to Berlin's Oranienburger Strasse synagogue and its gilded dome and prominent Star of David that claimed a commanding height on the city's skyline;[1311] it was representative of Jewish power there. Author Emily D. Bilski comments that "Jewish modernism"[1312] was imposed on the big cities of the country, especially Berlin. The Jewish philosopher Martin Buber saw the trends of the time as part of internationalized Jewish Renaissance, a "renaissance of humanity," a great "modern national-international cultural movement."[1313] But all of this was contrary and highly offensive to the German mind-set. For many, the culture being imposed on Germany was a tyranny of taste.[1314] The subject of culture was a banner carried by the political armies of the era, armies that engaged in battles over culture and the very nature of the state.[1315]

Lucy Dawidowicz, in one of her few encounters with an approximately correct assessment, said the following about Germans and their culture:

> This commitment to the past explains the German preference for *Kultur* over *Zivilsation*. Culture was for them something innate, intrinsic, inherited, a tradition handed down from the past. Civilization was external, an artificial product of modernity, lacking the essence of a specific people, race or culture.[1316]

An important and influential subset of Jews in Germany at that time were wholly at odds with those perceptions.

As put by historian William Grange, Germans of the Weimar era saw not only the economy enter a cataclysmic decline, they were also among the first to observe the modernist tendency toward the disappearance of order: "lawlessness enveloped the streets, theaters, museums, concert halls, and even churches."[1317] He goes on to say the following:

> Germans gawked in astonishment at previously unthinkable spectacles: Previously suppressed plays, films, and books flooded the market; choruses of protestors sang songs of disrespect for the defunct Kaiser, and broadsheets calling for revolution were hawked openly on the streets.[1318]

Culture was everywhere being "commodified," commercialized. According to Hermann Goering, Jews in Berlin "controlled almost one hundred percent of the theaters and cinemas..."[1319] and he was not far off the mark.

The radical left-wing German economist and social activist Werner Sombart claimed that "Jews are incorrigibly Jews, an Asiatic clan bent on insinuating themselves through the ploys of urban civilization and subverting the culture and life of the native population."[1320] They were shattering every bound of decency.

In 1919, the predominance of Jews in European culture was lauded by the American social philosopher Thorstein Veblen. With specific respect to Germany, he observed with palpable admiration that Jews "count for more than their proportionate share in the intellectual life" there, and "they count particularly among the vanguard, the pioneers, the uneasy guild of pathfinders and iconoclasts, in science, scholarship, and institutional change and growth."[1321] All of what Veblen said was incontrovertibly true. What was also true though, was that Jews accounted for the rapid decline in Germany's culture, whether in the area of the visual arts, stage, theater, music, literature, architecture, crime, prostitution, fraud, bribery, political shenanigans, or moral rightness in general. It is harsh to say, but Jews were the pathfinders for Germany's moral and cultural descent.

By 1933, when Hitler assumed power, Jews accounted for 30 percent of the drug traffickers, over half of the illegal gambling, and a whopping 82 percent of the international pick pocketing gangs. Their representation in the pornography and prostitution trades was nothing short of astounding; it was veritably absolute. Hitler's complaints about Jews were not without merit. It was certainly true that only a subset of Jews who were so very troubling, it was not *the* Jews, it was simply Jews, most of whom were of the East European, Hasidim strain. But who was to make such allowances? The answer is, not many—and certainly not Hitler.

Around 1910, Jews reached a new apogee in both Berlin and Vienna. With the end of World War I there was yet another surge of Jewish influence, but 1910 is important because it was at about then that German culture began to migrate toward degeneracy. It was the year that marked the beginning of the expressionist decade, 1910 to 1920, and expressionism was especially attractive to and promoted heavily by Jewish culture-critics.[1322] "That year," says author Frederic Spotts, "marked an arbitrary but as good a dividing line in the evolution of the arts as any, and a remarkably diverse variety of artists likewise singled it out as the juncture when the old gave way to the new. 'In or about December, 1910,' Virginia Woolf famously wrote, 'human character changed.'"[1323] It was then that artists shifted their role in society from traditionalist realism to the role of "prophet without honor."[1324] A host of new art groups sprang up, all of them heavily influenced by the Jews within them who were seeking to build a new "cathedral of socialism."[1325] The year 1910 set the stage for the mottled, grotesque themes of twentieth-century art. The artist's alienation from the general public came to dominate. "Artists," says author Emily Bilski, "sought to overcome their anomie through mysticism, theosophy, and a religion of art."[1326]

As important a marker as 1910 is, the movements that characterized culture from 1910 onward did have antecedents. Historian Walter Laqueur cites cultural happenings in 1908 as follows:

> The real break [with Germany's cultural traditions] came after 1908 with the appearance of atonal music, such as Schönberg's *Drei Klavierstüke* and Alban Berg's String Quartet op. 3, and with Stravisnsky's *Sacre due Printempts*, which provoked a scandal at its Paris première. In 1909 the first Futurist Manifesto called on its followers and well-wishers to live dangerously, to destroy museums and libraries, to awaken literature from its long sleep and to turn it into a "mad movement."[1327]

The events described above were but a few of the many goings-on just prior to the eventful year of 1910. The rapidity of cultural changes from 1910 onward was remarkable. It was at this time that the expressionism movement and a host of other avant-garde cultural upheavals came to the fore. And while expressionism only lasted until the early 1920s it had profound influences on its successor movements such as the Dada Movement, New Objectivity, and a host of others whose impact we continue to experience even now. It was a time when, seemingly with one fell swoop, long accepted aesthetics were dismembered and discarded. Ugliness came into vogue, harmony in music was discarded, dissonance was championed, and the poets and playwrights began to preoccupy themselves with madness, sex, horror, and mayhem. Patriarchalism was roundly attacked—explicit calls were made for the destruction of the family.[1328] For people like Hitler it was all very Jewish in its attitude and angst.

Hitler, too, specifically called out 1910 as eventful: "Up to 1910 we displayed an extraordinarily high level in our artistic achievement," he said. "After that . . . everything went ever more precipitously downhill."[1329] As Hitler was painting *Weissenkirchen in the Wachau* and *Old Vienna Courtyard near St Ulrich's Church* around 1910, Max Pechstein was organizing the New Secession movement, throwing out old standards of artistic representation and introducing the new ones: the Modernists. The powerful Jewish critic Samuel Lublinski, who died in 1910, had already published his critique of the Naturalist Movement and its associated pessimism, and it was having telling effects.

Between 1871 and 1910, the Jewish population of Berlin almost trebled, going from 36,000 to 90,000, and as late as the 1920s, nearly a quarter of Berlin's by then 175,000 Jews were aliens. There was a growing feeling that Jews were causing Germany to become soulless and commercial.[1330] And degenerate, too. In 1910, the impact of so many Jews in the art world, and particularly in the choice and marketing of artistic works, began to become sorely evident.

Jewish objections to early Marxism took on a character of nearly universal support when Marxism and its offspring, Communism, achieved success. It was then that Marxism was widely reputed in the Jewish community to be entirely compatible with Judaism. To many European Gentiles, Marxism was the feared precursor to a comprehensive assault on all traditional ideas, an assault that would horribly disfigure the accustomed cultural framework of life.[1331]

The replacement of traditional cultural norms were explicitly called for by the Bolshevists. Marxist-Bolshevism was seen as a precursor to a comprehensive assault on tradition. It was a declaration of war on the European idea of culture.[1332] An article in *Die Aktion* on September 4, 1920, addressed the issue thusly: the proletariat, it said, must "cast off all bourgeois concepts of culture, morality, ethics, and aesthetics."[1333] And so it did. And it was replaced first by secularism and degenerate art, and racy literature, and atonal music, and corrupt politics; and ultimately, in accordance with political physics, by Adolf Hitler and his cultural policies of *Blut und Boden* and all that that implied.

Shortly after the war, Prussia became the political province of the Marxist SPD, which quickly instituted censorship in schools even as it championed freedom of the press (rather like today's elite colleges in the U.S. wherein opposing views are shut out even as administrators champion academic freedom of speech). It also replaced administrators of court theaters and opera houses with SPD functionaries, many of whom, such as the exceptionally divisive Leopold Jessner, were Jewish.[1334] The *Arbeitsrat für Kunst* (Working Council for Art) was founded under Bruno Taut, the Jewish architect and city planner—the council published a manifesto calling for a "socialist art" to "benefit people everywhere."

Kevin MacDonald persuasively supports claims that Jews have everywhere created conflict within host cultures: "they are adept at other activities, such as influencing culture, developing political and intellectual movements, and advocating specific policies, such as immigration policy, that results in conflicts of interest with segments of the gentile population."[1335] Nowhere was this characteristic of Jewish interaction with its host people more evident than it was in Germany and Austria in the 1920s. As historian Albert Lindemann points out:

> Members of the Gentile lower-middle class . . . encountered malicious caricatures of themselves in the

liberal Jewish press, mockery of the traditional, petty-bourgeois values they cherished, often accompanied by a complete lack of sympathy for their dilemmas and insecurities. Catholic leaders encountered articles by liberal Jews that encouraged anticlerical students, that indeed even incited them to violence.[1336]

Even as early as the 1860s and 1870s, divergent observers, Right and Left, philo-Semitic and anti-Semitic, Jew and non-Jew, attacked the ever-increasing Jewish influence. Germans had long been expressing concern about the rising Jewish influence on their cultural bearings, and with the loss of World War I, that influence became overwhelming.

The revolution of 1918 and the postrevolutionary period brought with it a vicious frontal attack on German ideas and ideals. With respect to culture, history books often read more like novels; they heap praise on the "heady enthusiasms," "artistic experimentation," the "vibrant, kinetic energy" of the era. Germany underwent a "moral renewal," and "inner transformation," and "a new birth" according to such books.[1337] "Luminaries" of Jewish-German culture during the period, say such texts, included Martin Buber, Gershom Scholem, Rabbi Leo Baeck, Dr. Max Hodann, Dr. Lothar Wolf, Martha Ruben-Wolf, and Alfons Godschmidt, among others.[1338] The whole of such claims are spurious: Germany was instead put on a path to moral and cultural degeneration. By the 1920s, when Jewish influence in German society came to predominate and concurrently came under attack, German critics like Theodore Fritsch, Hans Blucher, and Adolf Bartel were influential in highlighting the scope and breadth of the new order, the domination of Jews in German culture.

Loyalty, divine rights, and nationalism were pummeled and overlain with democracy gone wild: nudism was introduced, along with arrant naturalism and companionate marriage.[1339] And that was only at the outset of the 1920s: things would become much worse before they got better. And there is just no escaping it, Jews were the leading culprits in the demise of German happiness and idealism. They created the Cesspool Republic, the despoiler of all that was noble and healthy.[1340] Hitler viewed Jews as advocates of the bastardization of races, that they poisoned nobility, that they glorified fratricide, fomented civil war, and that they were the "wirepuller of the destinies of mankind."[1341]

The Weimar era, which was ushered in by Germany's defeat in World War I, was a glorious period for Jews, and Jews of that period and place missed no opportunity to abuse the rights and privileges they had acquired. As Dr. Nahum Goldmann, president of the World Zionist Organization, said: "No Jewish minority in any other country, not even that in America could possibly compete with the German Jews."[1342] Jews of that period were wont to comment that they had founded a new Jewish homeland—a new Jerusalem; its name was Berlin.[1343] It was, claimed political theorist Ernst Block, a "Periclesian Age," with the Jews mimicking the influence of Pericles.[1344] While the claim of Jewish influence is just, the influence they wielded was hardly of a Periclesian kind. It was instead of the degenerate kind.

Jews were not suppressed in Germany of that time; they were instead the owner-operators of the country. They were inordinately powerful, and they led German thought by way of their dominant position in politics and all forms of publishing, radio (which was still an infant medium, but by 1929 had risen to 3.1 million units), and the theater. They were the real leaders of Germany, not Germans—it was sometimes said that Jews ruled, Germans reigned.

As Istvan Deak asserts, "[Jewish] participation in literary criticism and in literature was enormous: practically all the great critics and many novelists, poets, dramatists, essayists of Weimar Germany were Jews."[1345] Maximilian Harden, Siegfried Jacobsohn, and Otto Brahm all published journals that participated in cultural criticism. Other critics included Kurt Tucholsky, Carl von Ossietzky, Fritz Engel, Alfred Kehr, Max Osborn, and Oskar Bies. Siegried Breslauer, Emil Faktor, Norbert Falk, and Joseph Wiener-Braunsberg were all Jewish newspaper editors who had cultural critique as a focus of their journalism. As he recounted his years in Vienna, Hitler observed in *Mein Kampf* that "the transfigured ['encomiastic,' in some translations] raptures of their theatrical critics were always directed at Jewish writers, and their disapproval never stuck anyone but Germans."[1346] It was not the Germans who were so intolerant; it was instead the Jews of Germany, many of whom were of Polish, Hungarian, Lithuanian, Estonian, or Russian origin—in a word, the Ostjuden.

For all of the foregoing and more, the focus of Jewish apologists is consistently centered on claims of German discrimination against Jews. Historian Sarah Gordon, after pointing out that "not a single law was passed between 1869 and 1933 to rescind the new freedoms granted during the foundation of Germany," goes on to say that, "Of course, in practice there were many instances of job discrimination. . . ."[1347] Given the prominence of Jews in the government, the judiciary, banking, medicine, entertainment, publication, finance, education, etc., one must wonder about just what jobs were left for the application of discrimination. Hod carrier?

While German Jews abhorred German nationalism they exercised it amongst themselves. On the whole, they lived in exclusive neighborhoods, befriended fellow Jews, belonged to leftist political parties, promoted other Jews to positions of prominence, and participated in various Jewish organizations. The Jewish nationalism propounded by Moses Hess (1812–1875) was rationalized and later advocated by Zionists. Said Hess, "Jews are not a religious group, but a separate nation, a special race, and the modern Jew who denies this is not only an apostate, a religious renegade, but a traitor to his people, his tribe, his race."[1348] A good many Jews of the Weimar era seemed to subscribe to just such a tenet. Meanwhile, nationalism among Germans was viciously attacked—a double standard commonly found in Jewish critiques of Gentile society.

Given the role of Jews in the anti-German propaganda movement during the war, their leadership and participation in the various revolutions at the conclusion of and shortly after the war, and their obvious and overwhelming predominance in matters of German culture, it was not surprising that by 1919 the radical right-wing press, such as it was, became obsessed with the "judification" (*Verjudung*) of German society. Moreover, the

Jewish dominated left-wing of German politics and social criticism provided support for right-wing obsessions as the leftists took it upon themselves to fight for the abolishment of capital punishment and for greater sexual freedom. More specifically, they called for the abolishment of paragraphs 175 and 218 of the penal code dealing with homosexuality and abortion, respectively.[1349]

One of the explicit objectives of radical Marxists was to destroy the idea of the family and its values, which they considered to be politically reactionary.[1350] As Sarah Gordon informs us, "many of them [Jews who were prominent in German culture] tended to use their works as vehicles to oppose or criticize prevalent German values."[1351] This German-Jewish cultural symbiosis had few adherents but many enemies; and the enemies were strengthened by works of the Jewish filmmakers and the broad spectrum of Jewish critics of German culture.[1352]

Jewish influence on German politics and culture was most starkly apparent in Berlin but permeated all of the other big cities as well. Berlin in the 1920s was a city of grandeur, but also, as Peter Gay points out, "a city of crooks and cripples."[1353] The Berlin press was cruel, pitiless and aggressive, critical and nonconformist, and it was all but wholly Jewish. The startling rise of Jewish influence was summarized in a Nazi pamphlet written by Dr. Friederich Karl Wiehe, in a retrospective published in 1938:

> At the time of the German Empire the Jews had not yet played any leading role in the political life, at least not as far as the appointments to leading offices goes. At the time of the revolution in 1918 and the introduction of a new constitution this situation changed radically. . . . [F]rom November 1918 a regular Jewish onslaught on the leading positions in the country and the provinces was made.[1354]

As we shall see later in this chapter, Wiehe's claims were accurate reflections of reality. As put by Peter Gay, outsiders—"democrats, Jews, avant-garde artists and the like—became insiders, decision makers in museums, orchestras, theaters, private centers of scholarship."[1355] Gay assures us early on in his book (on page vi) *Weimar Culture: The Outsider as Insider* that the Weimar Republic "was not a 'Jewish' republic, as its enemies have so often proclaimed it to be."[1356] He then goes on to use the remainder of his book to establish that the republic was indeed a Jewish one, or at least so influenced by Jews that it was certainly reasonable for its enemies to have deemed it so. Weimar culture of the time was the creation of "outsiders,"[1357] the creation of its Jewish constituency. Denials notwithstanding, Walter Laqueur's assertion that "without the Jews there would have been no 'Weimar culture,'"[1358] was correct, and the culture they created was absent of virtue and traditional moral values.

Germans were understandably claiming that Jews, as Lindemann points out, "were taking over the new German nation, its economy, its political institutions, its art and music. Jewish or Semitic traits were undermining and corrupting German traits."[1359] That such claims owned merit is emphasized by Istvan Deak in his book, *Weimar Germany's Left-Wing Intellectuals*. Deak emphasizes Jewish leadership in German culture by way of their ownership of the greatest newspapers and publishing houses in the country as well as all of the distinguished literary magazines and art galleries. They also played a dominant role in theater and film: in the film industry they were the producers, directors, and actors. In an article titled "Performing High and Low: Jews in Modern Theater, Cabaret, Revue, and Film," Peter Jelavich proudly proclaims that "the theatrical culture of prewar Berlin would have been unimaginable without the participation of Jews."[1360] And the foregoing was a fact that did not escape the mind-set of the aesthetic romanticist, the staunch traditionalist, Adolf Hitler.

Prodigious numbers of Germany's composers, musicians, artists, sculptors, and architects were Jews, says Deak. "Their participation in literary criticism and in literature was enormous: practically all the great critics and many novelists, poets, dramatists, essayists of Weimar Germany were Jews."[1361] Thirty-one of the sixty-five leading expressionists and neo-objectivists were Jews.[1362]

Those members of the cultural milieu who were aligned with Jews did well. Those who were faithful to traditional German ideals were relegated to waste in a dung heap on the outskirts of their nation's cultural happenings. They had lost all power; they and their history and traditions were left to rot, figuratively turned and watered by Jewish cultural critics to facilitate their decomposition. Ultimately, however, repeated assaults on the German character and psyche reinvigorated German determination for change, reinvigorated calls for a return to traditional values and culture and for strong leadership provided by actual Germans who would make an exigency of Germany's political and cultural landscape.

An army officer born in 1878 spoke for a good many people when he provided a heartfelt commentary on Weimar culture as follows:

> Returning home, we no longer found an honest German people, but a mob stirred up by its lowest instincts. Whatever virtues were once found among the Germans seemed to have sunk once and for all into the muddy flood . . . Promiscuity, shamelessness and corruption ruled supreme. German women seemed to have forgotten their German ways. German men seemed to have forgotten their sense of honour and honesty. Jewish writers and the Jewish press could "go to town" with impunity, dragging everything into the dirt.[1363]

In addition to their direct involvement in the degradation of social norms, prominent Jews were severe critics of all things German, and thereby nourished both the cultural decline and anti-Semitism stemming from it. Kevin MacDonald, quoting S. Gordon, points out that "a more general cause of increased anti-Semitism was the very strong and unfortunate propensity of dissident Jews to attack national institutions and customs in both Socialist and non-Socialist publications."[1364] These writers, says MacDonald, "violently attacked everything about German society. They despised the military, the judiciary, and the middle class in general. . . ."[1365] Hitler represented a counterattack against such tendencies.

Germany: the Culture Nation

Historian Peter Pulzer and several others correctly point out that "Germans had been a cultural nation before they became a political one; a shared language and literary and philosophical tradition is what united Prussians and Bavarians, Saxons and Hamburgers, Protestants and Catholics."[1366] Stated otherwise, as it is by Spotts, "Culture, which historically defined German identity in the face of disunity and ambiguous borders, played a vital role [in Hitler's cultural worldview]."[1367] Indeed, even in the face of French annexation of various German territories over the centuries that stretched well to the east of the Rhine River, German cultural solidarity prevented such incursions from taking permanent hold.[1368]

The high culture of classical art, music, and literature were renowned and were shared by all Germans even before the country was politically unified in 1871. We Americans, with our polyglot culture, find it difficult to grasp how very committed Germans were with respect to their culture. When Spain's Philip II sent his armada to England he was confident of victory because he thought that God was on his side; at the outset of World War I Germans thought that the war would go their way because they represented "a higher culture fighting in the service of human history." For them, culture was godlike. Some ninety-three German intellectuals signed a declaration, an appeal "To the Cultured World" (*Der Aufruf an die Kulturwelt*), wherein they stated that "We shall wage this fight to the very end as a civilized nation [a] nation that holds the legacy of Goethe, Beethoven and Kant no less sacred than hearth and home."[1369]

While on trial for their lives at Nuremberg after World War II, each of the major Nazi leaders addressed the centrality of culture to their thought processes. German culture was not simply important, it was *everything*. According to Goering, "German culture, even now, with Germany in ruins, is the highest in the world because we had the greatest art, music, industrial capacity, and so forth."[1370]

Germans called themselves *Ein Volk der Dichter und Denker* (a people of poets and thinkers) to underscore their cultural achievements. Jewish author Kurt Tucholsky demonized that noble inkling by characterizing Germans as *Ein Volk der Richter und Henker* (A People of Judges and Executioners).[1371]

Germans took justifiable pride in the conception of themselves as poets and thinkers. They had the largest reading public of any country in the world.[1372] Their outstanding universities included those at Tübingen, Göttingen, Marburg, Berlin, Freiburg, and Heidelberg. All Germans could bask in the glow of such intellectual mandarins as Goethe, Schiller, Kant, Luther, Ranke, Niebuhr, and Nietzsche, in poetry, literature, and history. German scientists, scholars, and artists were universally acclaimed. Germans were seen by others as supremely cultivated, and their achievements in that sphere were shared by the cultural elite of Europe—German culture, it was widely asserted, was a triumph for European civilization.[1373] They dominated science and because of that German was still the language of science well into the twentieth century. Their visual art emphasized classical beauty in mystical and pantheistic settings. Their renderings were realistic. German craftsmen and their guilds were honored everywhere for their superb engineering innovation, exactness, and other markers of exceptionally high quality work. The German love of nature, of the soil, was akin to religiosity; it centered on, says author Roderich Stoltheim, the "sacredness of nature, the loftiness of art, the value of the earthy."[1374] Jews, conversely, "journey[ed] through life without any intimate connection with nature,"[1375] said he.

Germans were attached to the past and to small towns and rural living, and the lifestyles of rural and urban populations differed enormously. In the countryside, Sunday was still a holy day, a day of rest on which families enjoyed a quiet existence. Nature took on a liberating sensuality of peace and calm. For the rural peasant, a family walk in the forest with all members of the family in their Sunday best, followed by a visit to the local *gasthaus* where dad would drink beer with friends and mother would socialize with the ladies was still an endearing tradition well into the 1960s. Peter Gay acknowledged (even as he excoriated) that theirs was a "deep yearning for the inner unity and harmony of all laws of life and events in life."[1376] Soil and blood, real and mythical heroes, community and camaraderie were belief systems as strong as those provided by the church. Germans loved their own nearly as much as Jews theirs. For the urban dweller, rationality was the focus; sentiment was largely abandoned, except in its darkest, meanest motifs.

The battle over Germany's culture was as serious as serious gets: the oft-used line of Nazi leaders was, "when I hear the word culture, I reach for my gun."* During World War II, Hitler commented in all sincerity that "the power we to-day enjoy cannot be justified, in my eyes, except by the establishment and expansion of a mighty culture. To achieve this must be the law of our existence."[1377] With specific respect to the visual arts, literature, and music, it is a truth cited by Spotts that "in no other country in the world—not even in France or Italy—was there such popular respect for the arts and so broad a participation in them"[1378] as in Germany. It is indicative of the regard that Germans had for their culture that even such people as Wilhelm Liebknecht made it a point of reference as he excoriated anti-Semites in a Reichstag speech: such people, said Liebknecht, represented *Anti-Kultur*.[1379] The accusation was presumably the most severe that could be had to demean such people.

As E. Jones correctly observes, "the great rebellion against fixed moral norms and religious beliefs that began before the First World War . . . reached its high tide—at least in certain circles—in the 1920s,"[1380] and Jews were the principals in the rebellion's leadership. So prominent were Jews in this culture war, it was the case that during the 1930 election cycle Gregor Strasser formulated a propaganda theme around the negative influence of Jews on

---

*The line derives from a line in a play related to Nazi hero, Albert Leo Schlageter, who had been executed by the republic for his role in conducting terrorist activities against the French during their occupation of the Ruhr in 1923.

German culture: "We demand protection of our cultural goods against Jewish arrogance and aggression,"[1381] said he. Albert Lindemann comments on the Jewish role in the destruction of culture as follows:

> [T]he image of modernist Jews as "culture destroyers" reflected an undeniable reality, however much exaggerated by anti-Semites. The disproportionate numbers, visibility and volubility of Jews in modern art roughly corresponded to the disproportionate numbers of Jews in journalism, medicine, law, banking, and revolutionary parties. These were all arenas that saw attacks on the traditional status quo, that were restlessly innovative and often destructively dissatisfied with the past....[1382]

The high values and esteemed traditions that represented the core of German culture were represented in idolatry of nature and its things—motherhood, companionship, field labor, church, and community. At the highest level, the purpose of culture was to preserve and elevate the very best in mankind. Physical representations of German values were found in paintings and architecture and literature. Music, too, centered largely on the things of nature and mythical, heroic beings. Actual and fictitious heroes served to further bolster German admiration for their culture. Germans, probably more than any other people on earth, were steeped in the superiority of their culture over all others. The superior man, according to German legend, lived in the realm of art, the realm of the sublime.[1383] Hitler himself carried such an idea of culture even further: "There was absolutely nothing that mattered outside of art, he would say; even as a general, only an artistic person could be successful."[1384] Such was Hitler's regard for culture that we can be confident in his sincerity when he said that "Wars come and go. What remains are the values of culture alone."[1385]

German culture, however we may demean German militarism and hate the Holocaust, was arguably the world's best. Germans were proud of their culture precisely because it was so thoroughly deserving of pride. Germans were the *Kulturträger*, the culture-bearers of Europe.[1386] But Jews and Jewish perceptions of culture reigned over Germans during the Weimar Republic. Karl May's brave and resourceful Old Shatterhand and the noble Apache Winnetou were made to give way to Kafka's nightmarishly bizarre Gregor Samsa. There would be no more beauty or happy endings. Modernism and its adjunct, surrealism, would be imposed on the arts under Jewish auspices. The aim of the newly imposed cultural milieu seemed to be exactly opposite the traditional German conception of culture: it was no longer a means for the elevation of mankind—it was instead morphed into a means for the degeneration of man.

Nazi ideology was largely culture-based so it is not surprising that the subject of culture was one that Hitler visited frequently. For him and other Germans, culture was, as Matthew Arnold put it, "the best of which has been thought and said."[1387] During the Weimar Republic, all of "the best" was regularly demeaned and overlain with Eros. And it was Jews, concluded Hitler, who brought German culture to its nadir. Nazism represented a powerful counterforce to the cultural ills of the nation.

Prussian Militarism

We cannot leave the subject of Germans and their culture without commenting on a negative aspect of that culture. On the flip side of great German culture was, of course, Prussian militarism. It is true that Germany's Prussia had a military tradition that historians, even today, delightfully revile—politically correct speech is accepted when one speaks of the dark side of Germany. German parades were "gaudy," says Peter Gay. Gay, a champion of "Weimar culture," describes Wilhelmian taste as devoted to "glittering medals" and "sentimental heroic portraits."[1388] Marble statues on the Siegesalle in Berlin, he asserted, were an "ambitious double row of marble statues commemorating the unmemorable."[1389] It was just that sort of slight to the heroes of the people, to things held dear, to cultural icons, to things and people loved that ultimately turned the largely apolitical Germans against

Jewish critics, many of whom were far more severe than Peter Gay. For it was indeed Jews, even well before Mr. Gay, who made light of—nay, eviscerated—all things that defined German culture and its venerate volk.

To the German volk, their military was the stuff of honor and legend. They were the first to defeat a Roman legion, doing so at the Battle of Teutoburg Forest in AD 9. As recently as the late 1800s, the German army had defeated the Danes, the Austro-Hungarian Empire, and mighty France: they had been indispensable in the defeat of Napoleon Bonaparte at Waterloo and the Napoleon III at Sedan. And Germans, like all other people who achieve victory over others, took pride in their military triumphs (Jewish holidays, let us be reminded, are largely celebrations of the defeat of their enemies—they are flippantly summarized as: "They wanted to kill us. We won. Let's eat.").

Jewish disdain for German military victories was besotted when Israel achieved its victory over the Arabs in 1967 and Jews throughout the world rejoiced wildly in celebration. For once, at least, Jews were just like Germans. In both finance and war, winning is better than losing—except that in war it is not only better, it is everything. Israelis know that. Germans did as well. But a too large subset of German Jews, it seemed, could not credit Germans with legitimate emotions that Jews themselves would experience thirty-some years after the Weimar period.

Hitler, His Nazis, and Regard for German Culture

Germany's cultural degeneration could hardly be ignored by people of the kind that joined the Nazi Party hierarchy. The leadership of the party was composed of men of discerning taste, educated and conditioned in the traditional mode of German thought and culture. They were men from prominent families with deep-seated cultural traditionalism.

The Nazi leadership was composed of men who appreciated and sought to promote the high European culture that flourished prior to 1910. While the party certainly had its fair share of misfits and social outcasts, the leadership was composed primarily of idealistic men of high culture. Hitler himself, as we all know, was a devotee of opera, a serious student of history, a middling artist and wannabe architect. Gregor Strasser, so important to Hitler's movement until the early 1930s, relaxed by reading Homer in the original.[1390] Hermann Goering, Hitler's second in command and the commander of the German air force, was a bona fide war hero (a recipient of the coveted Blue Max) who came from upper-class stock. He was the successor to the famous German ace, Baron von Richthofen, the Red Baron, as he was known. His father had been the first governor-general of the German protectorate of South West Africa. He was related to the German aviation pioneer Count Ferdinand von Zeppelin and other notables, and he was educated by tutors and later at private schools.[1391] He was married to a millionaire countess, was fluent in the Italian language, commonly vacationed at the exclusive Schloß Veldenstein, and had attended the prestigious Lichterfelde Akademie. The father of Heinrich Himmler, leader of the infamous SS and often described by populist historians as a "chicken farmer," tutored a Bavarian prince and continuously maintained ties to the Bavarian royal house of Wittelsbach (which, as we have seen, was overthrown by Kurt Eisner). Baldur von Schirach, leader of the Hitler Youth, came from nobility. His father oversaw the royal theaters in Germany and Vienna. On his mother's side he was a descendant of two of the signers of the U.S. Declaration of Independence. Von Schirach was also an accomplished swordsman, author, and poet. Rudolf Hess, Hitler's deputy, was born in Egypt as the son of a wealthy importer-exporter. His family maintained a luxurious Egyptian villa and summer homes in Germany. Joseph Goebbels, Hitler's minister of propaganda, attended several esteemed universities, obtaining his doctorate from the prestigious Heidelberg University. Hitler's ministers, such as Franz Joseph von Papen, who played an important role in the appointment of Hitler to the chancellorship and subsequently served as vice chancellor and later still as ambassador to Vienna, was a member of German royalty. Others in Hitler's entourage tended to be university graduates, doctors, and high civil servants. Albert Speer, Hitler's architect and later his minister of armaments, was himself the son of a prominent

Heidelberg architect. Jonathan Petropoulas, in his *Art as Politics in the Third Reich*, comments on the Nazi leadership in saying that "[A]mong the seventeen Reichsleiters [district leaders] who were members of the elite, all but three or four were so well established socially that they would certainly have succeeded in their chosen occupations."

Petropoulos asserts that "The Nazi elite were ambitious men. They stemmed from milieus that provided them career advantages and instilled in them a respect for both high culture and traditional social order."[1392] However badly they ultimately went astray, these were men of intelligence and devout scions of high culture.

For those who survived World War II and were tried by the Allied Court at Nuremburg, IQ testing demonstrated the intelligence of the Nazi leaders. Most historians tend to represent Albert Speer as the most intellectual of the men comprising the Nazi hierarchy, yet Speer's IQ was found to be only in the lower half of the twenty-one prisoners tested.[1393] Both the minister of economics, Hjalmar Schacht, and Arthur Seyss-Inquart (who served the Nazi cause in both Poland and the Netherlands) had IQs over 140; geniuses. Air Force Minister Herman Goering and Naval Commander Karl Doenitz had IQs of 138. These men were certainly not dullards. Dr. Joseph Goebbels committed suicide at the close of World War II and was therefore not subjected to the IQ testing, but given his academic pedigree we can be certain that he, too, would have scored high. Goebbels is described by Ian Kershaw as "among the most intelligent of the leading figures in the Nazi Movement,"[1394] as indeed he was.

Germany's cultural degeneration could hardly be ignored by people of the kind who joined the Nazi Party hierarchy. The leadership of the party was composed of men who were educated and conditioned in the traditional mode of German thought and culture. They were men from prominent families with deep-seated cultural traditionalism.

It is a telling thing that Hitler "saw himself, like Richard Wagner," says Richard Etlin, "not as a politician but as a cultural revolutionary. He himself once described Wagner as his only predecessor."[1395]*

*   *   *   *

While Germans took justifiable pride in the breadth and depth of their entire culture, German accomplishments and traditions in the sphere of music was held above all others. Composers, conductors, and orchestra musicians were a kind of aristocracy within the German cultural milieu.[1396] Music, the most German of the arts, was revered. "One spoke of the Germans," says Etlin, "as the chosen music-nation and of music as the special expression of its emotional world, its soul."[1397] Serious music was first among the cultural assets of the German and Austro-German people. Bach, Brahms, Mozart, Beethoven, Schubert, Schumann, Weber, Wagner, the Strauss brothers, Bruckner, and others were pantheons of German musicality.† As early as 1837, Robert Schumann gave expression to German musicality when he remarked that "when listening to Beethoven, 'a German feels in spirit that he won the battles lost to Napoleon.'"[1398] While the U.S. at the time had two permanent opera companies, Germany had seventy-four,[1399] a fact that serves to illustrate German devotedness to high German culture and to serious music in particular. For Germans, their music was central to their national identity, their very being.[1400] Opera was not the sole possession of the upper crust; it reached out to and was revered even by commoners such as Hitler. It was an expression of his dedication to that art form that made him joyfully give up the wages of some seven hours of work as a construction

---

*It must be added, though, that Hitler has been similarly compared to Martin Luther, Frederick the Great and others.
† According to some, Hitler did not much care for either Brahms or Beethoven; others, such as Goering, claim that he did. Whatever the truth may be, Beethoven in particular was the musical idol of the Nazi Party, and his music was thoroughly exploited by its leadership.

laborer in Vienna to purchase a standing-room ticket at the Vienna Opera.[1401] At times, he bought opera tickets in lieu of food.[1402]

To Germans, their music tradition was like the painting on the ceiling of the Sistine Chapel, the Creation of Adam, in which the hand of God reached out to them, touching their very essence, their soil and their soul. Hitler, devoted as he was to architecture and to the music of Wagner, referred to architecture and music as the "two queens of all the arts."[1403]

To some prominent Jews, German musicality was fraudulent; Arthur Rubenstein commented in the 1930s that Germans "are not a musical people. They accept the heavy, pedantic music of Pfitzner, Reger and Bruckner with their long-winded 'development,' just as they enjoy a stodgy meal of sauerkraut and sausages."[1404] Rubenstein's criticism was all too typical of all too many Jews in its tone, its language, its meanness, and its error.

Into this milieu, some ten and more years earlier came Viennese composer Arnold Schönberg and his "atonal" musical dissonance. With the aid of fellow Jews, Schönberg was appointed to the directorship of a master class in composition at the Prussian Academy of Arts. To the considerable consternation of a good many seriously music-minded Germans, Schönberg, "blasting away [at] classical norms," exerted strong influences on virtually all Weimar composers, "including three young Jews, musical rebels, Kurt Weill, Hans Eisler and Paul Dessau,"[1405] all of whom would make their own marks as musical polemists in direct opposition to Germany's revered music tradition.

One Web site declares that Schönberg's "rejection of harmony, the destruction of chords—became a global standard in the realm of ideas, one that remains influential today."[1406] Richard Evans in *The Coming of the Third Reich*, addresses developments in German musicality as influenced by Schönberg and several others:

> Instead of losing themselves in portentous thoughts inspired by the mythical world of Wagner's *Ring* cycle or the ritual religious music-drama of *Parsifal*, dress-suited bourgeois opera-goers were now confronted with the Kroll Opera's production of Paul Hindemith's News

of the Day, in which a naked diva sang an aria sitting in a bathtub. . . . audiences were now treated to Alban Berg's [Berg was a student of Schoenberg's] Expressionist masterpiece *Wozzeck*, set among the poor and downtrodden of the early nineteenth century and incorporating atonal music and everyday speech patterns. The conservative composer Hans Pfitzner struck a chord when he denounced such tendencies as symptoms of national degeneracy, and ascribed them to Jewish influences and cultural Bolshevism. The German musical tradition, he thundered, had to be protected from such threats, which were made more acute by the Prussian government's appointment in 1925 of the Austrian-Jewish atonalist Arnold Schoenberg to teach composition at the state music academy in Berlin. Musical life was central to bourgeois identity in Germany, more, probably, than in any other European country: such developments struck at its very core.[1407]

Other prominent Jews who took on and applied themselves to the revision of German musicality included Gustav Mahler, a man who, interestingly, was admired by Hitler for his renditions of Wagner's operas. Leo Kestenberg was still another revisionist, who, as the musical adviser in the Prussian ministry of science, culture, and education until 1930, was able to, in typical ethnocentric fashion, call fellow Jews to positions of prominence. It was Kestenberg who called upon fellow Jew and musical adventurist Franz Schreker to head the formerly conservative Berlin Hochschule für Musik (Academy of Music). He also supported the nominations of Artur Schnabel and Carl Flesch as professors and had Otto Klemperer, Paul Hindemith (non-Jew with a Jewish wife and exceedingly close ties to the Jewish community), and Arnold Schönberg relocate to the German capital.[1408] Jewish music critics fawned over the musical direction of their fellow Jews and spiritual Jews. Right-wing critics fumed over the destruction of their cherished musical traditions. Anyone opposed to the new directions in music were pegged as ignorant traditionalist dullards, or worse, as anti-Semites.

Throughout the Weimar era jazz was offered up as a proletarian replacement for the music of Mozart, Beethoven, and other such traditional purists. It was especially popular in cabarets, and the cabarets were almost exclusively Jewish. Jews, alleged some, were the leading dancers in the "cancan of vulgarity."[1409] The Jew, claimed Roderich-Stoltheim, "calls this descent into vulgarity 'Progress,' and designates, on the other hand, everything of an aristocratic or noble nature, as out-of-date or reactionary."[1410] The Jew, he said, "practices 'Raubbau' (predatory culture)."[1411] The waltz was out; flappers, the black bottom, the fox-trot, and the Charleston were in. It was somewhat prophetic that the Jewish composer Oscar Straus staged his operetta, *Der letzte Walzer* (The Last Waltz) in 1920, for by that time the waltz was being replaced by jazz. If one likes jazz, one may rightfully think that it was all just as it should have been. If not, one might think it was all degenerate: Hitler and his hangers-on thought the latter.

Jews in the entertainment industry such as Kurt Weill and Friedrich Hollander, as well as many others promoted and celebrated such musical genres as jazz, much to the consternation of traditionalists. Frederic Spotts observes that the promoters of modern music were deemed by their opponents to be "cultural poisoners of the German people."[1412] In spite of the fact that many of the cultural battles during the Weimar Republic centered around music, jazz withstood Nazi opposition and continued to be heard in the various clubs throughout the 1930s, albeit not at government-sponsored functions.

Hitler angrily denounced modern music on both aesthetic and political grounds. For him, it was an example of degeneration paralleling the nation's political decay. That even opera was subjected to modernism was a ghastly thing—he was infuriated by the Kroll opera performance in 1929 in which the seemingly naked soprano sang in her bathtub about the wonders of modern plumbing.[1413] Jewish involvement in modern music was writ so large that Hitler complained of "the complete judification of music."[1414]

Clearly, Jews were in the vanguard of movements to radically alter Germany's historical conceptions of music, architecture, literature, religiosity, sexuality, mores, and more. Hitler was being entirely rational as he assessed the negative impacts of Jews on German culture: Jewish authors, editors, composers, architects, educators, and politicians all provided copious evidence that they sought to demean and alter German culture of the day. In matters of law, Jewish-German leaders proposed all manner of loosening strictures with respect to homosexuality, same-sex marriage, bigamy, prostitution, and the like. Hitler regarded their objectives as grotesque—and that, in all truth, is precisely what much of it was.

Spotts, in his otherwise excellent book, *Hitler and the Power of Aesthetics*, complains that under Hitler, "art became a national affair."[1415] But art has always been something of a national affair. When kings and princes were governmental leaders, it was they who influenced the direction of artistic endeavors. When the Catholic Church was still a meaningful entity, it was the pope who did so, as for example Pope Julius II and many others. In the United States, we have the National Endowment for the Arts by which art is made a national affair and by which the nation has acquired such pieces as the provocative *Piss Christ* by Andres Serrano, the winner of the National Endowment for the Arts "Awards in the Visual Arts." One may very well prefer the *Piss Christ* by Andres Serrano or the *Dung Madonna* of British artist Chris Ofili to, say, the Nazi's *Farm Family from Kahlenberg* by Adolf Wissel, or *Eos*, by one of Hitler's favorite sculptors, Arno Breker, but that would only be one's expression of support for one nation's artistic direction over that of another—all are iconic of national art.

Google	URL
Piss Christ	http://en.wikipedia.org/wiki/Piss_Christ 8/2/14
Dung Madonna	https://www.mtholyoke.edu/offices/comm/csj/991008/madonna.html 8/2/14
Farm Family from Kahlenberg	http://thecensureofdemocracy.150m.com/art7.htm 8/2/14
Arno Breker's Eos	http://commons.wikimedia.org/wiki/File:Arno_Breker_Eos_(1939).jpg 8/2/14

As everyone now knows, in the realm of music, Hitler was a fanatical devotee of Wagner. Hitler's friend in Vienna, Kubizek, claimed that Hitler read everything available about the master "'with a feverish heart,' studying Wagner's work and biography 'with incredible tenacity and determination . . . as if he could become part of his own being.'"[1416] Hitler himself claimed that he heard Wagner's *Tristan* thirty or forty times while in Vienna.[1417] Even some music experts claimed that his knowledge of music, and Wagner's in particular, was equal to or in excess of various impresarios. In some respects he saw himself as the embodiment of Wagner's Cola di *Rienzi*,† the late medieval rebel and People's Tribune. It could not be otherwise that a man of Adolf Hitler's sensibilities could look at Weimar culture and not be enraged by what he saw.

Influenced by Hitler's interest, prominent members of his inner circle were art connoisseurs and invested heavily in the medium. As the regime matured, exchanges of art among its leaders became commonplace ways of showing appreciation and affection, and of obtaining favors. Hitler himself honored favored cronies with gifts of artwork, sometimes art of his own creation from the pre-World War I era. Goering, Bormann, Speer, and Heinrich Hofmann were all honored in this way. Hitler knew very well that his own artwork was unexceptional and therefore ultimately took steps to keep them from public view, but by bestowing one or more of his works on his subordinates he represented to them a personal attachment and shared with them a touching vulnerability.[1418] Such gifts were representative of the many "small kindnesses" that endeared him to both the party leadership and the lowest echelons of his staff.

Some of Hitler's entourage, to be sure, chose to pilfer what they did not care to purchase. By 1943, Goering had collected some 1,375 paintings, 250 sculptures, and 168 tapestries. He spent over RM 100 million on art.[1419] What he could or would not purchase, he simply confiscated. Goebbels, Speer, and others also

---

† An operatic character who, ironically, makes his last stand in the capital (Rome) as it burns around him. Hitler would do likewise in Berlin.

spent prodigiously on art. Hitler himself not only spent prodigiously, he also personally contributed to the support and work of his favorite artists.

Hitler favored the nineteenth-century Austro-Bavarian genre of paintings. His early art collection efforts centered on works by Carl Spitzweg (noted for paintings of restrained, classical architecture) and Eduard Grützner (humorous, anecdotal subjects such as happy, drunken monks). He also admired and collected works by Rudolf von Alt (views of Vienna). He collected works, too, of the old masters along with limited holdings of contemporary art to his liking. Eventually he "amassed art at the most rapid pace in history,"[1420] asserts historian Jonathan Petropoulos in his book, *Art as Politics in the Third Reich*. In addition to Spitzweg and Grützner, Hitler coveted prints by Albrecht Dürer (paintings in the tradition of Rembrandt and Goya) and the massive sculptures by Rodin for his private collection. His partiality to Rodin was transferred to his architectural taste for massive, gigantic structures. Rodin's *The Thinker*, while of course not massive, was also a favorite. By the time of his death Hitler had amassed over 7,000 pieces of art and sculpture[1421]—clearly, this was a man who was serious about serious art.

"Hitler's love for . . . particularly German art," says Petropoulos, "derived in part from his cultural nationalism. Providing his own interpretation of theories of art developed during the Romantic period, he postulated that all art was national. He believed that race formed the basis of both nationhood and culture and therefore linked these concepts in an inseparable manner."[1422] His cultural deity, Richard Wagner, believed that art was necessarily political. "If an artist shaped the views of the nation and national objectives, it was necessarily a case of political action: the artist became a politician."[1423] For his part, Hitler fully appreciated the political potential of the arts, but he did not much exploit that potential when he gained power—he instead insisted that art was above politics. Thus it was that while much of the art in the Nazi era had a national or racial aspect to it, it was not blatantly political.

Modernists deny that art has a national dimension, emphasizing, instead, its universal aspects. We nevertheless easily speak of Jewish art, Greco-Roman art, Chinese art, Japanese art, Egyptian art, African art, and so on because it is not particularly difficult to see national peculiarities (or in the case of African art, continental peculiarities)[1424] in individual pieces of art from those cultures. Even today, art critics acknowledge that during the Weimar era, "Jewish sensibility" replaced artistic subject matter as a crucial factor in Jewish art criticism.[1425] The modernists stood in stark, angry opposition to the sentiments of people like Hitler. Modern culture was casting aside the national past.

All of the peoples of Europe, it seems, were interested in their own origins and interested in differentiating their own character in a positive way from that of all other peoples. As people like Hitler were rediscovering Germanic culture, the Czechs, Hungarians, Poles, Serbs, and other members of the former Austro-Hungarian Empire were doing likewise. The nascent Zionist movement was offering Jews a form of nationalism and racism that was every bit as virulent as Germany's right-wing. Hitler's version of nationalism, coupled with his intense interest in history and his resultant assiduous study of German antiquity, led him to take inspiration from both real people and mythical ones, as did the Zionists. Art, for Hitler, was a way by which Germans were to celebrate themselves—it was to emphasize German maidens and farmers and landscapes and heroes and other such iconic representations of the nation and its people.

Even after Hitler became personally involved in the standards to be applied to art, the regime was decidedly indifferent to art that sought to glorify Nazism. That Hitler's dedication to art placed it above politics is illustrated by his rejection of paintings that glorified National Socialism. He despised political art.*[1426] Art was

---

* There is a painting that depicts Hitler astride a horse. He is wearing medieval armor and carrying a Nazi flag on a staff. At least one historian claimed that he purchased that particular "art object." If that is so, he most certainly did so to get it off the market—it is a 1930s equivalent of presidential candidate Mike Dukakis in a tank with a helmet. It makes him look ridiculous. He knew that, of course, and had explicitly said so to one of

to be beautiful and was to represent the sacredness of nature, loftiness, and the value of the earthy.[1427] It was to appeal to the imagination, to heroism, to the greatness of the German people, to the *völk*, to *völkisch* mythology, and to *völkisch* blood and soil. It was to serve a social purpose and be healthy, solid, and decent. It was to be German.

Having emphasized that the art of the Hitler regime was politically neutral (though examples can be found here and there that were not), an important exception is in order: Hitler's architecture was highly political. It was ideological. It was politics in stone.[1428] Public buildings such as the Reich Chancellery, museums, government ministries, and his proposal for a gigantic People's Hall (*Volkshalle*, also known as the Great Hall (*Große Halle*) or Hall of Glory (*Ruhmeshalle*)) and the like bespoke German greatness and Nazi power. Nazi architecture was political ideology and power made concrete and visually manifest.

For all of the emphasis and sincere dedication that Hitler placed on volkishness in the field of culture, he was not irrational about it. Excesses of German romantics as represented in "Teutonic art" were demeaned by him for their absurdity. Observing the excesses of some adherents to the spirit of volkisch culture, he criticized and even mocked the ideas of the extremists, calling their program "Teutonic nonsense."[1429] In a 1938 speech, he lambasted "Teutonic tomfoolery,"[1430] which was reflective of his general scorn for extremist volkisch sects and cultism.[1431] Beneath all of what Hitler is represented to be by too many historians there was a rational man, albeit, a rational man who was simultaneously capable of horrific irrationality.

As we have here emphasized, it was the case that on the whole, the Nazi regime had a high regard for traditional art, for beauty. Albert Speer, whose favorite painters included Philipp Otto Runge (mystical, pantheistic), Hans von Marées (country scenes in

---

his aides, Heinz Linge. Moreover, the painting's origin was that of a cartoon on the cover of the satirical magazine *Simplicissimus*. It was a cartoon, not a serious art rendering. Hitler knew that as well and took it in good humor (Stolfi, 217).

realistic style), Wilhelm von Kobell (landscapes), and Anselm Feuerbach (leading classicist), effectively summarized the Nazi regime in this regard:

> Now, evening in the cell [Speer was at the time serving a post-war twenty-year prison sentence at Spandau Prison in Berlin], I have been thinking back on the regime's interest in beauty, which in fact was very marked. The ruthlessness and inhumanity of the regime went hand in hand with a remarkable feeling for beauty, for the virginal and unspoiled, although that feeling quite often degenerated into sentimentality of a postcard idyll. Today I sometimes read statements to the effect that that all this was merely camouflage, a calculated maneuver to distract the attention of the suppressed masses. But that was not so. Of course the regime's craving for beauty also had to do with Hitler's personal taste, with his hatred for the modern world, his fear of the future. But there was also an unselfish social impulse at work, an effort to reconcile the unavoidable ugliness of the technological world with familiar aesthetic forms, with beauty. Hence the ban on corrugated iron roofing for farm buildings, hence Autobahn maintenance buildings in half-timber style, hence birch woods and man-made lakes at army camps. As chief of the Beauty of Work Office, I was responsible for a part of this program, and I still take unabashed satisfaction in what we accomplished.[1432]

With their understanding of art and music as an expression of the "racial soul," the Nazis quickly excluded the Jewish race from all matters touching on German culture. As Richard Etlin emphasizes, "Neither as interpreter or composer, nor as publisher, teacher, concert manager, or culture policymaker were any opportunities left for Jews after 1933."[1433] Both Jews and philo-Jews were entirely excluded from the realm of art.

*   *   *   *

Hitler's regard for art is perhaps best represented by the fact that in 1937 he decreed a huge arts budget and even put his royalties from *Mein Kampf* into that budget,[1434] and the royalties from that source were by then gigantic.

Art was so dear to him that he readily forgave some artists who held views contrary to his own. Albert Speer recounted Hitler's reaction when he was informed that one of his favorite sculptors, Josef Thorak, had signed a Communist proclamation in 1933:

> Oh, you know I don't take any of that seriously. We should never judge artists by their political views. The imagination they need for their work deprives them of the ability to think in realistic terms. Let's keep Thorak on. Artists are simple-hearted souls. Today they sign this, tomorrow that; they don't even look to see what it is, so long as it seems to them well meaning.[1435]

The openly Communist, avant-garde artist Käthe Kollwitz painted clearly subversive artwork for the satirical journal *Simplicissimus*. Her art centered on the downtrodden, the homeless, and dredges of society. Her political work was in direct support of revolutionary Russia. Later she joined with others in direct opposition to Hitler. Yet for all of that, Käthe Kollwitz was granted membership in the Reich Chamber of Culture, continued to paint throughout the early years of the Third Reich, and was even permitted to hold public exhibitions of her work[1436]—Hitler, as previously emphasized, could be highly tolerant of artists.

He was also lenient about artists' membership in the party; "They were, after all, his fellow artists, and remembering his hardships as an artist," he said, "My artists shall live like princes," and the leading artists of the Reich did precisely that.[1437] The painter Sepp Hilz received a personal gift of 100,000 reichsmarks from Hitler to build himself a studio.[1438] Others received similar largess.

Cultural Counterrevolution

That Hitler's Nazi movement was in some respects a countercultural revolution was emphasized early on by Hitler himself. The Weimar Republic's "destruction of our whole cultural life"[1439] was one of his arguments before the court in justifying his coup attempt, his Beer Hall Putsch of November 1923. "The much vaunted 'National Socialist revolution' was . . .," says Spotts, "far less a social than a cultural revolution—or, rather, counterrevolution."[1440] It sought to redeem mankind from degenerate modernism.

Even while he resided in Vienna in his youth Hitler fumed over what he believed was the diminution of German culture brought about by the multicultural society there, and especially Jews. As stated by Joachim Fest, "it craved the past's system of values, the style, the austerity, the morality, as a defense against the forces of dissolution thrusting from all sides."[1441] Moreover, as Martin Kaes observes, the cultural counterrevolution was in direct response to the stated objectives of the Marxists to "cast off all bourgeois concepts of culture, morality, ethics, and aesthetics" and to put "real culture" in its stead.[1442] And it was by way of such Marxist objectives that Germany was imposed upon to accept unrestrained licentiousness, moral cretinism, and Freudianism; and in the arts, Dadaism, expressionism, cubism, surrealism, abstractionism, and a host of other culturally degenerate "isms" as "real culture." Much of the Western world would be made, by way of propagation by Jewish interests, to follow the cultural dictates of the Russian and German Marxists.

With respect to morality at least, Hitler shared the observation made by Kant: "it is not morality that makes the Jews bad, but the Jews make bad morality."[1443] The Jew, claimed Hitler, scoffs at Germany's history and "drags everything that is truly great into the gutter." Commenting on Jews and culture in general, Hitler claimed that:

> Culturally, he contaminates art, literature, the theater, makes a mockery of natural feeling, overthrows all

concepts of beauty and sublimity, of the noble and the good, and instead drags men down into the sphere of his own base nature. . . . Religion is ridiculed, ethics and morality represented as outmoded, until the last props of a nation in its struggle for existence in this world have fallen.[1444]

And as it happens, evidence in support of Hitler's conclusion was plentiful. Some prominent Jews of the Weimar Republic seemingly sought to uproot every rose so that weeds might flourish. The Jews, claimed Hitler, "cannot do otherwise than to try to blacken what is shiny and to pull the lofty into the dust."[1445]

Berlin and the other big cities of Europe had been polluted by a "moral plague,"[1446] a perversion, thought Hitler, and his assessment of things had substantial support in both the historical record and contemporary thought and observation. As recounted by Fest, German ideals of loyalty, divine rights, and love of country were, "extinguished mercilessly in the storms of the revolutionary and post-revolutionary period. In their place had come 'democracy', the nudist movement, arrant naturalism and companionate marriage."[1447] In a book by E. Friedländer (*Sexual Ethics of Communism*), marriage was presented as an "evil spawn of capitalism." The Marxist revolution would do away with such evils as well as prohibitions against abortion, homosexuality, bigamy, and even incest.[1448]

Berlin became the "national sewer." Rainer Metzger, in his book, *Berlin in the Twenties*, describes the degeneration of the city as follows:

> Greek tragedy uses a pair of terms to describe the revenge of circumstances on the state of affairs with which its heroes have to engage: hubris followed by nemesis. This was genuinely the case with Berlin. The hubris of the city's mass culture was followed by the nemesis of its mass politics. The slide from arrogance to degeneration happened in a plainly vulgar fashion, with a devastating lack of regard of its tragedy.[1449]

It was clear to Hitler who was responsible for the moral plague that swept Berlin and other German cities: it was Jews. Modern art was distinguished by its ugliness and its perversion of naturalism, and it lacked national character; in a word, it was internationalistic[1450] and what were Jews if not internationalistic? Stated otherwise, the Modernists were corrupting society, claimed Hitler, and Jews were the avant-garde of the Modernists; society was therefore being corrupted by Jews.[1451] His rants along these lines were only slightly overstated. The point is emphatically made by Spotts:

> Leaving aside personal taste and racism, Hitler spoke true—truer than he knew—in analysing Modernism and its place in the cultural crisis of the time. Modernists differed significantly in their artistic intentions; avant-garde painters did not always work in the same direction as their counterparts in music, literature or architecture. But by and large Modernists were guilty as charged....
>
> Modernists were indeed revolutionaries.... It was permissible for art to be "ugly" and to emulate the blunt energy of "primitivism".... Modernists celebrated disorder and uncertainty. Far from shunning the epithet of elitist, they raised it to a high principle that artists were independent of society and that culture was a sphere unto itself.... Nothing could have been more foreign to the Modernists than the idea that they had an obligation to society.[1452]
>
> [Their art was] shocking, abstract, pessimistic, distorted, cynical, enigmatic, disorderly, freakish....[1453]

Hitler and his Nazis had a single word to describe Weimar art: the word was "degenerate."

Upon achieving power Hitler had a great many challenges: there was the Depression, the Jewish-led worldwide boycott of German goods, the Reichstag fire, and the ongoing threat of the Communists, to name but a few. It is indicative of the centrality of culture to his being and objectives that just two months after taking office he highlighted that centrality in a speech to the Reichstag in Berlin on March 23, 1933. "[T]he Government of the Reich," said Hitler, "will undertake a thorough moral purging of the body corporate of the nation. The entire educational system, the theater, the cinema, literature, the Press, and the wireless [i.e., radio]—all these will be used as a means to this end and valued accordingly."[1454] In the same speech Hitler went on to speak of a "profound revival of religious life," and addressed the destruction of moral values. His speech was a poignant counterpoint to the cultural objectives stated by Eisner and Toller in Bavaria in 1919: Germany was to return to its esteemed culture. Cultural Bolshevism was to be utterly crushed.

The Jews of Germany, or at least the prominent ones in the press and theater, seemingly did everything in their power to besmirch and bring low Germany's civilization—its literature, its music, its visual arts, its customs, and its morality and mores. S. Friedlaender says that "The 'pernicious' influence of Jews on German culture was the most common theme of Weimar anti-Semitism,"[1455] as, in fact, it was.

Hitler contended that the Jewish-controlled press in Germany was responsible for the promotion of the modern art of the era and that it promoted it as a means of quickly reaping huge profits. Indeed, it was frequently claimed that the only interest Jews had in art was to sell it.[1456] In April 1929, Hitler claimed that "All of this so-called modern art of today would not be thinkable without its propagation through the work of the press,"[1457] by which he was most assuredly referring to the "Jewish press." Art in Germany, claimed the Nazis, had been taken over by Jews, and they were facilitated in the takeover by their brethren art critics who were, in turn, supported by the Jewish-dominated press. The term "kitsch" came into being in the 1860s to describe such tasteless art.[1458]

Unlike classical art, modern art could be produced ("manufactured," said Hitler in *Mein Kampf*)[1459] very quickly and in great volume. Artistic renderings of classical artists could take many months or even years (take, for example, the *Mona Lisa* or the art of the Sistine Chapel) while those of the modernists could be produced in an afternoon. Art became a high-volume, high-profit enterprise. Much like what has traditionally been done in the realm of women's fashion, protean art helped establish the momentary "in" art and thereby overcame issues of too much supply. The quick succession of cubism, Dadaism, surrealism, and other such art world isms illustrate the point. Expressionism, the catchall term for the artist's inner experience and angst was such that there were seemingly no limit to the ways in which it could be altered to represent something new and different, and therefore a new art market niche.

*   *   *   *

As early as 1919, Hitler had assessed the cultural and spiritual degeneration of the nation and wrote about the need to achieve the rebirth of the "nation's moral and spiritual forces"[1460] which were under heavy attack. In *Mein Kampf* he returned repeatedly to the subject of German culture and his perception of the role played by Jews in its debasement. Later, in 1937, and often in the intervening years between 1919 and 1937, he railed against degenerate art. He proclaimed that "From now on we will wage a merciless cleansing war against the last remaining elements of our cultural disintegration."[1461]

Hitler's assessment of modernism and its place in the cultural crisis of the nation was a correct one. And his assessment of the role of Jews in modernism was also correct. The evidence for his assessment was to be found everywhere and in every realm of German culture. The correctness of his oft-expressed complaint that the art world was largely in the hands of Jews was perhaps best exemplified by the fact that when he and his Nazis raped Europe of its art treasures, he found it necessary to employ Jews to identify what art objects were the most valuable and where they existed.

Modernists, says Spotts, were revolutionaries. It was they who made it permissible for the ugly, the primitive, the shocking, pessimistic, distorted, cynical, enigmatic, disorderly, and freakish to be celebrated as great art.[1462] Art was made entirely elitist: if you could not understand the beauty of the ugly, you were stupid or a fool or unfit to appreciate the inner experience of the artist. They were the modern messiahs; society was to follow their dictates. They were the tailors of *The Emperor's New Clothes*. Hitler was out to change all that.

"Perhaps most remarkable about Weimar art," say the editors of the book, *The Weimar Republic Source Book*, "was its syncretism; a propensity for blurring styles and genres which was as ubiquitous as the hyperbole of its manifestos."[1463] The Nazis would have no more such claptrap foisted on the people.

Hitler was insistent that German culture be retrieved and that it triumph over the trends of late. He saw his actions as a form of cultural protectionism. He did not place outright bans on various forms of art and music, but he did extract a high price for those who continued in the modernist vein, a sociocultural tax as it were. Let us not be too surprised or too critical of his actions in this respect—we Americans do exactly the same thing with a wide array of "politically correct" issues.

At least one historian has it that:

> It was with undoubted sincerity that Hitler . . . paid homage to the German ideal of *Kultur* and made it the foundation of his entire ideological system. . . . In undertaking the creation of the largest art museum in the history of mankind, and in the process of dictating a new hierarchy of values for the artworks, in which the "Germanic" occupied an exalted position, Hitler attempted to realize his cultural-based ideology.[1464]

In the early years of his dictatorship, Hitler gave little personal attention to the art of his regime, no doubt due to the more pressing economic and political conditions needing attention. Initially he was satisfied to leave all matters related to art to his underling minister of propaganda, Dr. Joseph Goebbels. Heinrich Himmler, leader of the SS, would also directly participate in matters of art and culture, especially with respect to the Degenerate Art exhibitions in the late 1930s.

Goebbels, for his part, rather admired much of what he saw in modern art and even showed considerable antipathy for the volkisch art of the radical, even by Nazi standards, Alfred Rosenberg.* When Hitler began to express himself on the subject, however, Goebbels wisely concluded that all modern art—the totality of it—was abhorrent. By late 1935, Goebbels, after Hitler made a scathing speech about modern art,[1465] was exhibiting decidedly antimodernist tendencies, and purging modern art from German museums.[1466] Until then, various forms of modern art had continued to thrive, as exemplified by the works of avant-garde artist Ernst Ludwig Kirchner. Kirchner had no inkling that his days of participation in the modernist movement were numbered. He believed until 1935 that the Nazis viciously attacked him out of error.[1467]

Hitler attacked Dadaists, cubists, the international art market, and the Jews who he felt were responsible for it all. Dadaist Raoul Hausmann (non-Jew with a Jewess wife) provided one of the many outrageous claims of Dadaists in a 1920 article as follows:

> We wish to organize the economy and sexuality rationally, and we do not give a hoot for culture, which was no tangible affair. We wish an end to it and with it an end to the philistine writer, the manufacturer of ideals that were nothing but excrement. . . .
>
> Down with the German philistine![1468]

In contravention to the rants and objectives just cited above, Hitler's underlying objective was to encourage the beautiful, an admiration for life, and for the strong and noble, all of which was in alignment with his romantic theory of the heroic character, for the protection of healthy people from degenerates. He sought to

---

* Rosenberg's involvement in a variety of endeavors prevented him from excelling at any one thing. "Goebbels maliciously [but one must admit, humorously] referred to him as 'almost Rosenberg' because he was almost a scholar, almost a journalist, and almost a politician—'but not quite.'" (Petropoulos, 34)

explicitly delink art from the intelligentsia. Art was henceforth to be a property of the commoner, the people of his volk. It was to mirror the German soul; its iconography was to be wholesome, and it was to esteem Germany and Germans. The character of art was to be calm, realistic, and earthy. Paintings would be "finished" and "beautiful." Music would be "healthy." Politics would be had on the political stage, not on the canvas of artists, the writings of authors, or the strings, percussions, and wind of musicians.[1469] Artistic renderings would be such that they could be universally understood without reference to tomes of intellectual twaddle: people, said Hitler, were accepting every mockery of true art in order that they would not be considered lacking in artistic understanding.[1470] He would put an end to art that could not be understood and appreciated on its own merit. Artists were to entirely reject the pessimistic negation and abstraction of expressionism, cubism, and other such Jewish-inspired artistic movements. "If the age of Pericles seems embodied in the Parthenon," said Hitler, "the Bolshevistic present is embodied in a cubist monstrosity." Referring to modern artists, Hitler said that:

> These cultural disciples, it is true, possessed a very simple means of passing off their nonsense as something God knows how important: they passed off all sorts of incomprehensible and obviously crazy stuff on their amazed fellow men as a so-called inner experience, a cheap way of taking any word of opposition out of the mouths of most people in advance. For beyond a doubt this could be an experience; the doubtful part was whether it is permissible to dish up the hallucinations of lunatics or criminals to the healthy world. The works of Moritz von Schwind, or of Böcklin, were also an inner experience, but of artists graced by God and not of clowns.[1471]

The realism or naturalism of paintings made under his regime would make them instantly comprehensible—one would know without study which end was up. Nazi art would emphasize beauty without sensuality. Women would be rendered, he said, as potential mothers and visions of Nordic purity. Nazi art would represent a clear departure from art of the Weimar Republic: it would be absent the tawdry, decadent aspects of being.[1472]

Google	URL
Joseph Thorak's *Monument to Work*	http://www.google.com/imgres?imgrefurl=http://www.oberlin.edu/images/Art265b/Art265b.html&tbnid=ABP39jF8UuSVfM:&docid=ZIzDlKUkeGB7XM&h=639&w=828 8/2/14
The Courtyard of the Old Residency in Munich, Adolf Hitler	http://en.wikipedia.org/wiki/Paintings_by_Adolf_Hitler#mediaviewer/File:The_Courtyard_of_the_Old_Residency_in_Munich_-_Adolf_Hitler.jpg 8/2/14
You and I, by Arno Becker	http://www.ilovefiguresculpture.com/masters/german/breker/brek11.jpg 8/2/14
Woodland Meadow, Hans Thoma	http://www.allposters.com/-sp/Woodland-Meadow-1876-Posters_i1343624_.htm 8/2/14
Painting, *All Their Worldly Goods*	[1473] Depiction of dastardly Jews taking peasant property.
German painting *Farm Girls Returning from the Fields*	[1474]

All of Hitler's objectives with respect to art and culture in general were anathema to leftists. John Heartfield, in concert with George Grosz, published an article in 1920 titled "The Art Scab" in which they gave vent to their own objectives:

> Workers! By representing things in their painting that the bourgeois can cling to, things that give you a reflection of beauty and happiness, they sabotage your class consciousness, your will to power. . . . Today the cleaning of a gun by a Red soldier is of greater significance than the entire metaphysical output of all the painters With joy we welcome the news that the bullets are whistling through the galleries [Dresden Art Academy, where, on 15 March, a masterwork of Rubens was damaged by a bullet] and palaces, into the masterpieces of Rubens, instead of into the houses of the poor in the working-class neighborhoods. . . . We

summon all to oppose the masochistic reverence for historical values, to oppose culture and art![1475]

For those of us who have it that burning the books of such people as Felix Salten was akin to literary genocide, the destruction by leftists of art masterpieces, churches and other such icons of culture—and traditional culture itself—might merit some little contemplation.

Even Hitler acknowledged that in earlier times there had been aberrations of taste, but such times were, according to him, artistic derailments of a kind that at least retained in them a certain historical value; conversely, the artistic products and prophets of Germany during the Weimar period represented a spiritual degeneration. The body of art then being produced, he concluded, was a reflection of the political and cultural collapse of the nation that was rendered visible in Bolshevistic art: cubism and Dadaism were indicative of his point. And for him, Bolshevism and cubism and Dadaism were representative of Jewish art. "Jewish art" of the period included the following and contrasted sharply with traditional German art.

Google	URL
Art of the Dada Movement	http://en.wikipedia.org/wiki/Dada#mediaviewer/File:Hoch-Cut_With_the_Kitchen_Knife.jpg 8/2/14
Marzella, 1909, by Ernst Ludwig Kirchner	[1476]
Actresses, Max Beckmann	[1477]
Lovers, Auto Dix	http://www.moma.org/collection/browse_results.php?criteria=O%3AAD%3AE%3A1559&page_number=14&template_id=1&sort_order=1 8/2/14
Images German cabarets	https://www.google.com/search?q=Images+German+cabarets&rlz=1T4GZAB_enUS449US538&tbm=isch&tbo=u&source=univ&sa=X&ei=0dffU9qMDpG0yASJ6IHgDw&ved=0CB4QsAQ&biw=1008&bih=523#facrc=_&imgdii=_&imgrc=6MH-j050xzqeAM%253A%3BAX40ACwJ7k32OM%3Bhttps%253A%252F%252Fwww.iphotocentral.com%252FPhotos%252FVi

	ntageWorks_Images%252FFull%252F13524_Schall.jpg%3Bhttps%253A%252F%252Fwww.iphotocentral.com%252Fsearch%252Fdetail.php%252F256%252FRoger%252BSchall%252F0%252F13524%252F1%3B800%3B844 8/2/14
Images for degenerate music, Germany	https://www.google.com/search?q=images+for+degenerate+music,+Germany&rlz=1T4GZAB_enUS449US538&tbm=isch&imgil=6pXr0XRLRy0zIM%253A%253BQAPIXh0LItq2jM%253Bhttp%25253A%25252F%25252Fappleswitcher.com%25252Fforum%25252Fviewtopic.php%25253Ff%2525253D7%2525252 6t%2525253D5522&source=iu&usg=__VGj6_ZCTlNJkHBskb=YMPr17VYw%3D&sa=X&ei=B9nfU_LfAcSayATdo4CQAg&ved=0CCEQ9QEwAA&biw=1008&bih=523#facrc=_&imgdii=_&imgrc=6pXr0XRLRy0zIM%253A%3BQAPIXh0LItq2jM%3Bhttp%253A%252F%252Fwww.reichslieder.com%252F0862_degenerate_music.jpg%3Bhttp%253A%252F%252Fappleswitcher.com%252Fforum%252Fviewtopic.php%253Ff%253D7%2526t%253D5522%3B255%3B380 8/2/14
The Hero by Georg Grosz	https://www.google.com/search?q=The+Hero+by+George+Grosz&rlz=1T4GZAB_enUS449US538&tbm=isch&imgil=adEVGBdNS_UhcM%253A%253BSigHXGBx5obKgM%253Bhttp%25253A%25252F%25252Fwww.moma.org%25252Fcollection_ge%25252Fobject.php%25253Fobject_id%2525253D72585&source=iu&usg=__CgG5SOtCyZYlQer9W6ASQ9kUJXo%3D&sa=X&ei=vNnfU7mLOpClyASCxYKwAg&ved=0CCwQ9QEwAQ&biw=1008&bih=523#facrc=_&imgdii=_&imgrc=adEVGBdNS_UhcM%253A%3BSigHXGBx5obKgM%3Bhttp%253A%252F%252Fwww.moma.org%252Fcollection_images%252Fresized%252F455%252Fw500h420%252FCRI_113455.jpg%3Bhttp%253A%252F%252Fwww.moma.org%252Fcollection_ge%252Fobject.php%253Fobject_id%253D72585%3B300%3B420 8/2/13
Apocalyptic self-portrait by Ludwig Meidner	http://weimarart.blogspot.com/2010/07/ludwig-meidner.html 8/2/14
Cover of the Degenerate Art Exhibition program, 1937	http://www.google.com/imgres?imgrefurl=http://www.answers.com/topic/degenerate-art&tbnid=4x_sxK27v4Ic4M:&docid=OqB6s-9Ko1kNAM&h=249&w=175 8/2/14

Hitler's charges were true. The Dada movement, for example, was not simply one of literature and visual art: it had deep political and social implications in that it was both libertine and antitheistic. Dadaists claimed that their poems of a "brutish" nature ought to be read in all churches and that sexual relations should be organized by the state. Other such extremism was common to the movement. Germans should not be faulted for having rebelled against such lunacy.

Dadaism influenced surrealism. Former Dadaist-turned-surrealist, Louis Aragon, and his cohorts published a pamphlet in 1931 that "applauded the burning of churches [by Communists] in Spain and made an appeal to the French to do likewise. 'Only the proletariat has the power to sweep God from the surface of the earth,'"[1478] claimed Aragon and his fellow surrealists. "Sixty years ago," said Hitler, "an exhibition of so-called Dadaistic 'experience' would have seemed simply impossible and its organizer would have ended up in the madhouse, while today they even preside over art associations."[1479] There was to be no more such hokum art under Nazism.

There can be no doubt that the success of Hitler in the realm of art was built on a genuine desire of many to see art that told a story and could be easily understood by the commoner, the constituents of the volk. All of this was, of course, anathema to the elites of society; it failed to represent the "rational" truth of their calculation, their version of "real culture."

Jews and German Culture

To this point we have emphasized the perceptions of culture that were held by many ordinary Germans and by Hitler and his Nazis in particular. We have also emphasized that Hitler and his cronies saw themselves as engaged in a countercultural battle with the influence of Jews in German society. In this section we address the particulars of Jewish influence on German culture.

Even before World War I the conventional culture of Germany was being pushed in new directions, but with the loss of the war the floodgates opened. Camp trivialization of long-cherished values was championed by opinion makers as Jewish immigrants to Germany assumed elite positions in society. By way of their prominence in radical politics, psychoanalysis, anthropology, and cultural studies, Jews called into question, says Dr. MacDonald, "the fundamental moral, political, cultural, and economic foundations of Western society,"[1480] and of German society in particular. Writing in 1958, former minister of the army (Reichswehr) Otto Gessler bravely observed that the pacifists, progressives, and modernists of the Weimar era, who were predominantly Jews, "tore down, with cold cynicism, everything that healthy German national sentiment held sacred; because they hailed, as a sign of progress, every symptom of decadence."[1481]

The new regime in place in Germany after World War I was especially sympathetic to Jewish proclivities. Jewish cliques within the SPD, USPD, and KPD exercised their power to excoriate nationalist opponents while at the same time providing havens for Jews and like-minded progressives such as the modernists and the internationalists.

It was the case that traditional German culture was despised by the literati precisely because it was embraced by broad masses of the public, the commoners, the volkisch peasants: be it music, art, architecture, sexual mores, religion, bratwurst or beer; if it was venerated by the common German it was despised and eviscerated by the literati, and most especially the Jewish component of that literati. They chided officialdom and the people, says Peter Jelavich in an essay, for "clinging to outmoded taste," and called on them to "be open to the new"[1482]—their new.

The political power of Weimar Jews, including their dominance in German publishing, provided radical Jews of the era full rein. To reiterate a point made in an earlier chapter, the prominence of Jews in revolutionary Berlin was illustrated by the new postwar Prussian cabinet, which had a Jewish prime minister, Paul Hirsch (SPD); finance minister, Hugo Simon (USPD); and minister of justice, Kurt Rosenfeld (USPD). Of the four People's Commissars who governed the city of Berlin, three were Jews: Rosenfeld, Hermann Weyl (USPD), and Hugo Heimann (SPD), who became chairman of the city council.[1483] In January of 1920, the Jewess Cora Berliner was named councilor of the Rich Finance Ministry, the first woman to hold that post.[1484] Jews had risen to such dizzying heights of power that they were, by the 1920s, in a commanding position with respect to the politics of the country, its economics, and the sociology and mores of its people.

Jews were overpoweringly influential in all matters of cultural life in Germany and charges with respect to their pernicious influence were common themes of the Weimar era's anti-Semites. S. Friedlander makes the point that "Their participation in literary criticism and in literature was enormous: practically all the great critics and many novelists, poets, dramatists, essayists of Weimar Germany were Jews."[1485] The climb to the top of the social ladder and influence over the arts was aided in no small part by Jewish power in the politics of the period and even more so by the stranglehold on publishing outlets of all kinds. Jews and their like-minded fellow travelers were nurtured to prominence by Jewish editors and their subordinate Jewish cultural critics.

The Jewish critics of the time could only faintly grasp the peasant's worldview—which was often limited to a circumference of ten or so kilometers. As a Zionist of the Weimar era put it: "our productive stock comes from other provinces, is supplied from different depths, watered from different springs." Prominent Jewish critics of Germany, some of whom we will discuss later in this section, were especially venial in their excoriation of Germans and their culture, and they and their ilk indelibly inscribed on the Weimar German's consciousness that their esteemed culture was being debased. Such people thereby contributed immeasurably to the anti-Semitism of the time. The totality of Jewish power and actions during the Weimar period seemed to confirm for the radical right wing that Jews were attempting to destroy German culture and simultaneously atomize German society while they themselves remained tightly cohesive. It was a point of truth that we now care to put in softer terms; the Jews, we say, were simply, "ethnocentric"—racialists, inoffensively named.

Jewish dominance of Weimar culture was emphasized by Jewish scholar Werner Mosse who said, "What today we are apt to call Weimar culture was largely the creation of left-wing intellectuals, among whom there was such a disproportionate number of Jews that Weimar culture has been called, somewhat snidely, an internal Jewish dialogue."[1486] "To a very considerable extent," says author Friedrich Otto, "the spectacular culture of Berlin in the 1920's, the culture dominated by men like Max Reinhardt and Bruno Walter and Albert Einstein, was a Jewish culture."[1487] Hitler, when speaking of Walter, liked to add, "alias Schlesinger" to highlight the fact that Walter had changed his name to a more Gentile-sounding one.[1488]

Spartacist Franz Mehring assessed Jewish influence in Berlin as "awe-inspiring."[1489] Jewish literary critic George Steiner hails the Jewish intellectuals of Germany as "meta-rabbis." He has the following to say about them:

> The Jewish element had been largely dominant in the revolutions of thought and of sensibility experienced by Western man over these last one hundred and twenty years.... Without Marx, Freud, or Kafka, without Schönberg or Wittgenstein, the spirit of modernity, the reflexes of argument and uncertainty whereby we conduct our inner lives, would not be conceivable.[1490]

Jews were the prophets of modernity, but for some they were "prophets without honor."[1491]

Some authors flatly deny the negative influence of Jews in Weimar Germany. Donald L. Niewyk, in his generally excellent book, *The Jews in Weimar Germany*, says flatly that "The charges that Jews ran the German economy, manipulated anti-German political movements, and fostered decadent cultural trends were patently false."[1492] That is the PC answer, but it falls short when subjected to historical reality and reasoned analysis. Mr. Niewyk provides no real support for his contention, other than some esoteric psychological scapegoating theories that are as farfetched as their Freudian roots. He makes some claims having to do with Freudian-based displacement theory and the "German's primitive impulses" as explanations for German anti-Semitism. Jewish behavior for him, as for so many others, is exonerated as a cause for anti-Semitism because such acknowledgment "blames the victim" for his fate. It is a neat piece of pseudologic that skirts a most basic premise for German anti-Semitism, the actual conduct of Weimar Jews.

Some Jews seemed determined to continuously reinforce the idea of Jews as opponents of Germandom. Jewish professor of philosophy at the Hanover Technical Institute, Theodor Lessing, created a political uproar during the 1925 presidential campaign with a tasteless attack on General Hindenburg. Similar outrages were the products of other insensitive Jews such as Friedburg University law professor Hermann Kantorowicz, and Breslau University faculty member, Ernst Cohn.

Historically, other Jews had brazenly and brutally criticized Germans and their culture, and it was not to be without cumulative effect: Heinrich Heine* was accused by Heinrich von Treitschke for "mocking German humiliation and disgrace following the Napoleonic wars" and for having "no sense of shame, loyalty, truthfulness, or reverence."[1493] Napoleon, of course, was a great benefactor to the Jews, but even he bemoaned their lack of civic morality and the "state of abasement in which they have long languished."[1494] Treitschke had previously taken Ludwig Börne to task for his "brazen manner of speaking about the Fatherland irreverently, like an outsider who does not belong to the Fatherland."[1495] Treitschke had also condemned the famous Jewish historian Heinrich Graetz's "deadly hatred of the purest and most powerful exponents of the German character from Luther to Goethe and Fichte."[1496] Commenting on what might even today be justifiably said of Jews within cultures such as the U.S., Treitschke said that "the conflict [between Jews and Gentiles] will soften when the Jews, who speak so much of tolerance, really become tolerant and show respect for the faith, customs, and feeling of the German people. . . ."[1497] It is also worth noting that Graetz had himself written that "Börne and Heine had 'renounced Judaism,

---

* Heine had been baptized but soon regretted it (and later redeveloped a strong Jewish consciousness) as baptism did not seem to provide him with any material benefit. Soon afterward, his writings exhibited very negative attitudes toward Christianity. Christianity was "a gloomy, sanguinary religion for criminals," "a religion that repressed the healthy sensuality of antiquity," said he. (MacDonald, SAID, 220)

but only like combatants who, putting on the uniform of the enemy, can all the more easily strike and annihilate him.'" "[W]e must above all work to shatter Christianity," said Graetz.[1498] Treitschke also complained that "what Jewish journalists write in mockery and satirical remarks against Christianity is downright revolting."[1499] As we will discuss later in this section, Weimar, in the persons of Tucholsky, Ossietzky, and a host of others, were Weimar equivalents of the historic personalities highlighted by Treitschke.

As is very much the case in the United States today, it was the case in Weimar Germany that Gentile critics of Jews were ravaged in the Jewish-owned press. As was said by Treitschke:

> about the shortcomings of the Germans [or] French, everybody could freely say the worst things; but if somebody dared to speak in just and moderate terms about some undeniable weakness of the Jewish character, he was immediately branded as a barbarian and religious persecutor by nearly all the newspapers.[1500]

In addition to Treitschke, notables such as Wagner and Chamberlain had railed against Jewish criticisms of things embedded in German hearts. Germans recognized that Jewish-German intellectuals and members of the press had created a culture of critique that was entirely negative toward Germany and Christianity but protective of Jews and Judaism. It was a culture of critique that sought to shatter the social bonds of Germans, and most particularly the organizing forces of the church while maintaining those of Jews. Such observations by prominent Germans on the shortcomings of Jews were not lost on Hitler.

As the 1920s advanced, the efficacy of these tendencies became apparent; traditional morals collapsed, hedonism ascended. And because Jews were so prominent in the propagation of such hedonism, they were widely regarded as social deviants.

Nationalism was giving way to Marxism and its advocacy of internationalism. Institutions of all kinds that promoted organization and group ties among Gentiles were actively opposed and subverted while Jewish separatism and autonomy were championed, maintained, and strengthened.[1501] Hitler was not being irrational when he claimed that Jews were at the center of Germany's tendency toward disunion.[1502] In 1928, says author Istvan Deak, "when the Weimar republic congratulated itself for having weathered ten stormy years, Kurt Tucholsky," a character that we will discuss later, complained that "the Church still rides Victory's wing."[1503] The church represented organization and therefore Gentile power—it had to be defeated.

It was a phenomenon not limited to Germany; the Jewish-dominated Polish government campaigned against nationalism and against the cultural power of the Catholic Church, the main force of social cohesion in traditional Polish society.[1504] Hitler, political and historical animal that he was, could not help but conclude that the actions of so many prominent Jews in the degeneration of German culture and unity—and indeed the entirety of European culture—had to be halted.

* * * *

In the first quarter of the twentieth century the Jews of Europe were concentrated in the East, with Poland and Russia accounting for about half of the 9.5 million total. Romania had a million, and Hungary a half million. Germany had 565,000, a large percentage of whom (about 20 percent) had migrated there in recent years (1881–1918) from the East. After Germany's defeat in 1918, still another surge of immigration of eastern Jews occurred there. The statistics, however, are somewhat misleading. They were based on census data that relied upon claims of people belonging to the Jewish faith. Thus, ethnic Jews who often did not make such claims, were not included in census data. Moreover, the settling of Jews was by no means uniform throughout the country. They instead settled heavily in Prussia and in Berlin in particular.

Germany took in the Jews as they fled Russia and other East European countries. Germans of the day were dismayed. The vast majority of East European Jews were never fully assimilated and created a culture that was clearly set apart from and in direct opposition to the non-Jewish population: some wrote in Hebrew or Yiddish or employed, to the mind of the Gentile, esoteric Jewish analogy, simile, and allegory in their works. Artists such as the highly influential modernist Max Liebermann painted what at first looks to be an entirely traditional painting, as were many of his early works. It depicts himself in a kitchen scene. He is wearing a chef's cap. There is a great basket and cooking pot along with a variety of vegetables to be cooked. On the table there is a dead chicken. A small red tag hangs from its neck, a sign of kosher slaughter. "On the surface," comments Inka Bertz, "the painting portrays a bourgeois domestic scene, but those familiar with Jewish customs may perceive other meanings and contexts."[1505] Karl Schwarz, the first director of the Berlin Jewish Museum, viewed Liebermann as "the most important representative of impressionism in Germany: his penetrating intellect and his typically Jewish instinct for the psychological contributed to his extraordinary talent as a painter."[1506]

German Jews, and particularly those from the East, remained a people distinctly apart from their hosts, but even assimilated Jews tended to maintain close but closeted ties to other Jews and Jewish organizations. Jews on the whole championed Jews and all things Jewish and simultaneously eviscerated Germans and all things German. They were a people that dwelled alone but exerted titanic negative influences over Germans and Germany. "Moses Mendelssohn, Heine, Börne, Mendelssohn-Bartholdy, Meyerbeer, and Liebermann represent in Germany the summit of racial power," says essayist Chana C. Schütz in the book *Berlin Metropolis, Jews and the New Culture, 1890–1918*. Schütz goes on to say that "German Jews had formed their own subculture in the midst of modern German society"[1507]—a stereotypical tendency that they have demonstrated everywhere in the Diaspora, present-day American not excepted. But they not only fostered their own subculture, they pressed what Hitler thought was their deviancy upon the previously esteemed German culture.

The right wing of German society during the Weimar years continued to champion nationalism even as it came under ruthless attack by leftist internationalists who were then in power. As correctly stated by Peter Pulzer, nationalism—and German nationalism in particular—"coincided with the romantic movement, with its emphasis on the cultural component of nationality and the sanctity of unique traditions."[1508] Internationalism explicitly abhorred all nationalistic sentiments. Adolf Hitler, the most nationalistic of the nationalists, observed what was taking place in the cultural scenery of Germany and was, of course, appalled.

The Jewish leadership of Weimar Germany was out to change society, and it thoroughly succeeded. In the minds of people like Hitler but also in the minds of far less radical Germans, the Jewish ascent and success was horrific. Jews in large number were in the vanguard in producing cultural wreckage that was offered up as "voluptuous";[*] its essence was bitter stuff for the German psyche—it was entirely offensive to nationalism and traditional German sensibilities.

MacDonald makes the point that "A common component of Jewish intellectual activity since the Enlightenment has been to criticize gentile culture."[1509] Indeed, as the president of the Silesian Provincial Supreme Court pointed out in a 1911 report, Jews "seek to impose their ways of thinking on the Germans," but "they strictly preserve for themselves their own peculiarities." He also mentions that the Jewish "way of life, moral concepts, attitudes and outward customs . . . contrast with German culture to a degree that cannot be underestimated."[1510] These were not outrageous claims of anti-Semites; they were simple statements of empirical fact. "A striving for Bildung (culture/education) had turned the Jewish bourgeoisie into the self-appointed (and ecstatic) carrier of German culture,"[1511] says S. Friedlander. And according to Hitler's assessment of the things, the place to which they carried it was the swamp.

---

[*] I am here using a term employed by Mel Gordon in his book, *Voluptuous Panic: The Erotic World of Weimar Berlin*.

In the 1920s, the people who dictated public taste and morals, says Istvan Deak, "who enlightened, entertained, or corrupted their customers were not only Germans but Russian refugees from the Red and Hungarian White terror, voluntary exiles from what was now a withering poverty-stricken Vienna, Balkan revolutionaries, and Jewish victims of Ukrainian pogroms."[1512] No matter from whence they came though, the meanest critics of German cultural achievements were exclusively Jewish.

Among the foreign Jews of that place and time were the Hungarian Marxist philosopher György Lukács, the Austrian theater director Max Reinhardt, the Czech citizen and Prague journalist Erwin Kisch, the operetta singer from Budapest, Gitta Alpár, and the Polish embezzlers Leo and Willy Sklarek. In places like Berlin these Jews joined German-born Jews such as Kurt Tucholsky, Karl von Ossietzky, Emil Gumbel, and a myriad of others. In the political field there were the foreign-born Jews such as Eugen Leviné, Max Levien, Karl Radek, Rosa Luxemburg, Leo Jogisches, Towia Axelrod, Adolph Joffe, Belá Kun, and many more to advance their causes. Together, both native- and foreign-born Jews worked in concert to ravage the church and its clerics, the army, traditionalists of every stripe, and each and every noble inkling of Germandom.

The dichotomy between the Jewish and German mind-set was illustrated by perceptions within each group that denied that the other could understand its outlook. For many, Jews and Germans were polar opposites. Jews claimed that Germans lacked the necessary roots and traditions of Judaism and could have no understanding of the Jewish qualities of *yiddishkayt*. Such claims were accepted by all with equanimity. Conversely, German claims that Jews did not and could not have deep and genuine roots in German culture, that they did not and could not share the aesthetic experience with volkisch Germans who had been part of traditional Christian culture for centuries,[1513] were deemed anti-Semitic.

The "Red Count," Count Harry Kessler, already several times mentioned, was an avid chronicler of his times. He was a man whom Peter Gay described as a "liberal statesman and indefatigable diarist, eminently well-informed and remarkably free from caste prejudice."[1514] Kessler was on the whole a philosemite who unwittingly illustrated the dichotomy between German and Jewish cultural mind-sets in one of his numerous diary entries. In it he recounted an evening spent at the home of one of the Rothschilds in 1929:

> Dinner at Baby Goldschmidt-Rothschild's on the Pariser Platz. Eight to ten people, intimate party, extreme luxury. Four priceless masterpieces by Manet, Cézanne, van Gogh, and Monet were handed round with cigarettes and coffee. Poor van Gogh! I saw red and would gladly have instituted a *pogrom*. Not out of jealousy, but disgust at the falsification and degradation of intellectual and artistic values to mere baubles, "luxurious" possessions.[1515] [Italics are in the original.]

Kessler's response to the tasteless display was entirely Germanic: how could people, thought Kessler, reduce such artistic treasures to "mere baubles." It was, to Kessler's lights, a disgusting display of riches with no appreciation for the sanctity of art. It was also indicative of Jewish attitudes toward Gentile cultural icons.

In Weimar Germany the anti-Christian themes of popular artists sponsored by Jewish interests were so extensive that the Nazis had to set aside an entire room to display the collection of anti-Christian art at the infamous Degenerate Art Exhibitions in the late 1930s. Jewish apologist Peter Gay describes some of this art as "magnificently repellent";[1516] Germans of the era can be forgiven, one must think, for having dropped the adverb. It was, to average people, elitist, morally suspect, and incomprehensible, and it needed to be displayed with at least an equal measure of the anger and schismatic intent as that of its originators. A Boston art critic summed up the breadth of feeling about it by acknowledging that "There are plenty of people, art lovers, in Boston who will side with Hitler in this particular purge."[1517] The art show was a stupendous success; millions attended and the spectators were there to bury, not to praise, the displayed works.[1518]

The term "Degenerate Art" was not one of Nazi making. The term comes to us from the famous Max Nordau, a German-speaking Jew from Hungary who, as previously mentioned, was a cofounder of the World Zionist Organization. Nordau authored a book titled *Entartung* (Degeneration) attacking degenerate art:

> We are now fully infected by a serious popular mental illness, a sort of black plague for degeneration and hysteria. . . . The degenerates babble and stammer instead of talking . . . They draw and paint like children who with useless hands dirty tables and walls. They make music like the yellow people of East Asia. They mix together all artistic genres.[1519]

Without attribution one might suspect that claims like those above had originated from the radical Right because they align so well with Hitler's perspective. On the subject of degenerate art Nordau was one of very few Jews who saw such art as disgusting—the vast majority of the Jewish elite—the avant-garde, the modernists—supported and praised it, and most them did so with wrathful vigor.

* * * *

Jewish intellectual opinion makers of the period in Germany and elsewhere often sought humor in the peasant's filth and ignorance, his implied bestiality. Jewish-Polish author and Holocaust survivor Norman Salsitz sympathetically noted that "all across Poland the peasant was held in almost universal contempt."[1520] The same could have been said of German, Russian, or peasants elsewhere. In an 1847 Lantag speech, the young Bismarck described the relationship between German Jews and the peasants:

> I know a rural district where the Jewish population is numerous, where there are peasants, who cannot call a single object on their farms their own property, where the entire furniture, from the bed to the stove, belongs to the Jew, and where the peasant pays a rent for each

separate piece of furniture; the growing corn and the corn in the barn belongs to the Jew, and the Jew sells the corn for bread, seed and feeding purposes back to the peasant again, by the peck. I, at any rate, in the course of my professional duties, have never come across nor even heard of a Christian practicing usury comparable with this.[1521]

*   *   *   *

The affinity between Jews and modernism has long been a controversial one: Jews engaged in the various modernist movements in numbers that far exceeded their proportion within the population, and they thereby demonstrated their self-conscious rejection of Gentile tradition.[1522] Their participation has been a rallying cry for the opposition to such movements and simultaneously a source of ethnic pride for themselves.[1523] They were the leaders and purveyors of the culturally dissident media. The whole of their form of modernism demonstrated that while they were certainly well-versed in German culture they nevertheless remained strangers to it—they were aliens who were full-fledged members of society but were simultaneously outsiders who confronted every aspect of it.[1524] Their influence was spectacular. Historian Peter Gay observed proudly that "Jews, it is said, making themselves at home in Berlin, transformed it, and imprinted upon it something of their rootlessness, their alienation from soil and tradition, their pervasive disrespect for authority, their mordant wit."[1525] There can be little wonder as to why culturally conscious Germans rebelled against such people. German publicist Philipp Stauff responded to the goings-on by denouncing the perceived Jewish threat to German culture in the art world. He charged that the cultural modernists were "driven by the innate Hebrew motives of greed and cultural hate" and were destroying "the native values by which the Germans had lived since the Teutonic tribes first confronted the Romans."[1526]

The Jews of modernism in Germany were not just fighting for their own niche in the marketplace of the visual arts, theater, and literature—they fought simultaneously for the utter destruction of all of traditional German culture that had come before them. Their goal was to challenge and destroy, says Carl E. Schorske, "the validity of traditional morality, social thought, and art."[1527] In literature, as in the visual arts, Jewish opponents of German orthodoxy such as Rainer Maria Rilke dedicated themselves to the destruction of the "dilapidated building of Naturalism"[1528] and all other such forms of German tradition. For these people, hatred of traditional German culture was palpable. As internationalists, which is to say Communist when put in the context of the time, they likewise despised German nationalism in the field of art.[1529]

In 1923, Carl Einstein, writing in admiration of Otto Dix in the Jewish-owned *Das Kunstblatt*, had this to say in praise of art trends of the time:

> If a German wants to represent reality, he no longer thinks of spring, flowerpots, and the chattily ordinary salon. Spring forces not only the still lifes of the charmingly marketable; bedsores, abortion, and multiplying venereal diseases work best of all; sweet spring satirizes malicious plots, outrages, and budgetary details; winter gets soiled by wet feet, black-market galoshes, overheated houses of fornication, and murderous price increases—these simply routine tidbits of the stinking panorama.
>
> [Otto] Dix gives this era—which is only the caricature of one—a resolute and technically sound kick in its swollen belly, wrings confessions of vileness from it, and produces an upright depiction of its people, their sly faces grinning an array of stolen mugs. A great, old painter lives in Paris—[Georges] Rouault—who spits on the present in a similar fashion: bridal wreaths, shirtfronts, and medals. These painters are waging civil war; their repulsive subject matter draws opposition, whether opponents refuse and demolish it as adherents of objectlessness or as observers. Both are now expedient.

Dix's pictures are an assault, sober, without the improper
assertion of a beloved, false personality that always sells
smirking Calembourg [a word game] instead of fact.
Personality that accumulates in jokes and sly anecdotes
is a defect and a sellout of the bankrupt. Whoever paints
like Dix could easily turn into [Lothor] Meggendorf
[satirist, illustrator of children's books, famous for his
creation of "pop-up" books]. Dix dares to produce a
suitable kitsch, namely, the ridiculous world of the
cleverly stupid bourgeois splashing properly about in
stifling ordinariness.[1530]

The foregoing has the tone of a person that has perhaps been unjustly wronged in some significant way, someone lashing out at his oppressors. But that was not the case. Jews of the period were not suffering from oppression or even anti-Semitism; they were rolling in Gentile clover, what Hitler called a "Jews Paradise,"[1531] and to Hitler's lights they were simultaneously befouling it. And they were rolling in cash. And power. And arrogance. And Germans justifiably resented them for it.

In the visual arts, Jews predominated as patrons, gallery owners, critics, and to a lesser extent, creators. Jews were the owners of Germany's greatest art galleries—an artist wanting to sell his work had to, in effect, be vetted by Jewish art connoisseurs. And the art that was selling during the Weimar period was modernistic, hedonistic, and propagandistic, and was seen by a broad segment of the German populace as an act of aesthetic violence against the German spirit.[1532] Artists as well as various stage managers, authors, publicists, producers, directors, and cinematographers had Marxist politics at the core of their artistic endeavors, and it was Jews who provided the fife and drum corps for the Marxist-Bolshevist assault on culture and politics.

Hitler's claim to his sister that Viennese art was in the hands of Jews was doubly so in Berlin—Jews owned art, artists, and artistic direction there. One study of the era concluded that thirty-one of the sixty-five leading German expressionists and neo-objectivists were Jews.[1533] Classical motifs by Gentile artists in the mold of Albrecht Dürer were on the out; the harsh, ruthlessness of New

Objectivity and the repulsive subject matter of Otto Dix and the savage caricatures of Georg Grosz were all the rage. Jewish writer Egon Erwin Kisch's writings reflected the new "rejection of all personal, 'lyrical sentiments,'"—it defined the new, hard-core literature that was deemed "thoroughly modern."[1534] The visual arts and literature were now part and parcel of a cultural civil war.

The popular press was obsessed with deviance, murder, atrocity, and crime. Graphic depictions of violent scenes of murder and rape and serial sex killers were everywhere. Jewish director Fritz Lang's *M*,[*] Bertolt Brecht's *The Threepenny Opera*, and novels such as Jewish author Alfred Döblin's *Berlin Alexanderplatz* became standard fair. Lang would later go on to make a number of anti-Nazi films. The stage and novels became, says historian Matthew Stibbe, "littered with the bodies of raped and murdered women."[1535] Sensationalized newspaper reporting of serial killers such as Fritz Haarmann and the "Düsseldorf vampire," Peter Kürten, were nationwide media sensations.[1536]

Jews owned the direction of all German art forms. Many of Germany's most prominent authors, composers, musicians, artists, sculptors, and architects were Jewish. In all of these areas if a non-Jew had any hope of success he needed to pass a vetting process within the Jewish community. Amos Elon, in his book *The Pity of It All*, comments on Thomas Mann and Jewish influence in the arts as follows:

> Thomas Mann, who in many ways was ambivalent about Jews (though he was married to one), hailed them as Germany's finest judges of literature and the arts. Amongst all things "German" in the arts, he claimed, only those that also passed the acid test of approval by Jewish critics were truly valuable.[1537]

---

[*] Jewish actor Peter Lorri played the lead in *M* (1931), which was based on the serial child murderer Peter Kürten. The Nazis would later quote Lorri's *M* character in their famous film, *The Eternal Jew*.

By way of analogy with current U.S. politics, in Germany of those days it was rather like the vetting that takes place today in the U.S. as one seeks national political office: one must first obtain the blessing of AIPAC; failure there means all but certain defeat, and it is by way of such vetting that Jews have become the casting directors of our political leadership. And so it was with artists and other cultural gurus of the Weimar era.

Because Jews were also so very prominent in advertising agencies (Rudolf Mosse alone had 275 agencies worldwide) they were also able to ensure that even non-Jewish means of news distribution mirrored views that were important to the Jewish community. Publications that offended Jewish sensibilities were quick to lose their advertising revenue, a situation that is mirrored in American society today.

According to Hitler, the press made an absurdity of morality and ethics as derisive petty bourgeois concepts. As put by Istvan Deak, "The German intellectual ferment in the first years of the twentieth century was above all a revolt against conventional morality."[1538]

During the Weimar period, the radical leftist press was heartily embraced for the most part. The press was permitted to violate things that had been previously inviolable: the church, the army, matters of culture, the peasant, and the whole of German culture in general. The press itself provided the justification for its outrages against German sensibilities: the "value of the press," its importance to society, its "educational mission," and so on. Hitler, seeing every negative aspect of the press as having Jews at the apex, commented that "as for the Jews, they took all this with a crafty smile and acknowledged it with sly thanks."[1539]

Modernism in the visual arts was introduced in Berlin by Carl and Felicie Bernstein in 1882. The Bernsteins had acquired a large collection of impressionist paintings by Manet, Monet, Sisley, and Pissarro. They then used their home as a salon that was frequented by notables in the art world to arrange for an exhibition of the works under the auspices of the Jewish-owned Berlin Galerie Fritz Gurlitt.[1540]

Later the cousins Bruno and Paul Cassirer led the way in bringing French Modernism, which was then impressionism, to Germany. The stage was set to further the attack on German traditionalism in favor of various hues of modernism. Expressionist poet Jakob van Hoddis (Davidsohn) created his works in a purposefully grotesque style. The cultural rebel Georg Heym relocated to Berlin from Silesia in 1900 and there joined with others such as Simon Guttmann, Kurt Hiller, Jakob van Hoddis, and Erwin Lowewenson in propagating political and aesthetic upheaval.[1541] The theater critic and plagiarist Siegfried Jacobsohn, who learned his trade from the likes of Maximilian Harden, Fritz Mauthner, and Paul Schlenther, published his brutal critiques in Berlin's *Die Welt am Montag* and Vienna's *Die Zeit*. He later created his own publication, *Die Schaubüne*, which supported the criticisms of other like-minded leftists, many of whom were Jews such as Julius Bab, Lion Feuchtwanger, Kurt Hiller, Walter Mehring, and Kurt Tucholsky, to name but a few. Theater manager and director Max Reinhardt (born Maximilian Goldmann), in league with a covey of other Jews, including the composer Hugo von Hofmannsthal and film producer Paul Davidson, was by far the most dominant figurehead for erotic stage productions of the era; and as such, he furthered the careers of a great many Jewish writers, actors, composers, and set and costume designers. One of Reinhardt's protégés was famous film director and "sexual theater" precedent setter, Ernst Lubitsch. Lubitsch started out as an actor in Reinhardt's Deutesches Theater but later went on to become a director in his own right. Both Reinhardt and Lubitsch, like many other German Jews of the period, would later enjoy great success in Hollywood. Lubitsch's casting precept was: "Write Yiddish—cast British."[1542]

Kurt Hiller, known by many of his contemporaries as among the most troublesome of the political agitators and self-promoters, founded several political cabarets after the war. He had been among the early members of the wartime German Peace Movement. "As a homosexual, Jew, political agitator, pacifist, and antinationalist, he aroused the ire of several groups throughout the Weimar period,"[1543] says historian William Grange.

The Jewish poet, artist, playwright, and bohemian expressionist damsel Else Lasker-Schüler wrote poetry without regard for the rules of poetic form or even the rules of language (neologisms were a mark of her "poetry"). Her "art" was expressionistic and of the degenerate class—scribblings deemed "art" by the cultural scribes. Her wide-ranging acquaintances and relatives within the art world and publishing business ensured that her works were distributed and widely known. As expressed by Sigrid Bauschinger in an essay within the book, *Berlin metropolis: Jews and the new culture, 1890–1918*, Lasker-Schüller was the darling of her Jewish promoters:

> When Lasker-Schüller wrote *Die Wupper* [written in 1909 and first performed in 1919], she was at the pinnacle of her productivity. She stood at the center of the modern movement in Berlin, which was most evident then in the newly established publishing houses and art galleries where primarily Jewish editors and gallery owners were turning Berlin into a capital of modernity.[1544]

Publisher, art dealer, poet, composer, Communist, and cultural impresario Herwarth Walden (born Georg Lewin), the polemicist and "grand patron of Berlin's avant-garde,"[1545] was an unapologetic "eraser of boundaries."[1546] Along with a host of others like himself, he promoted modernist artists and writers through his publication, *Der Sturm*.[1547] Walden is credited—or accused as the case may be—with having been one of the most important and successful promoters of German avant-garde art in the early twentieth century: expressionism, futurism, Dadaism, and magic realism. Walden opposed traditionalists as "agrarian painters," as despicable peasants, and sought to supplant them with painters who would instead depict life in the big cities.[1548] According to Emily Bilski, he sought to have artists "paint strange and grotesque structures as gently and transparently as you paint streams; boulevards like flower beds!"[1549] Many of the Jewish artists of the day used their brushes to portray pessimistic visions, negative epiphany, and fractured forms in apocalyptic landscapes.[1550] Traditionalists were outraged by the newest trends. People like Max Liebermann and a number of others were attacked as having too much influence and were "birds of doom," and "servants of the Talmud" who were corrupting German culture.[1551]

"[T]he theatrical innovations of directors like Otto Brahm and Max Reinhardt; the pioneers of early film, such as Ernst Lubitsch; and the quest for modern Jewish art and culture undertaken by philosopher Martin Buber and artists like Lesser Ury and E. M. Lilien"[1552] exerted enormous influence on German culture—and all of that influence was, according to the radical right wing of German society, degenerate (but some of their works were actually quite attractive). Theater productions emphasized social radicalism and the subversive tendencies of the production directors; they emphasized gutter themes but described them pretentiously.

Jews of that place and time, claims Peter Jelavich, "Lacking long-standing ties to German 'high' culture . . . could enter the cultural realm with open, unprejudiced eyes."[1553] But that, alas, was still another big lie. They were highly prejudiced—they despised the traditionalists and everything they represented and they were out, with clear purpose of mind, to destroy them. They were anything but "unprejudiced." They were instead, hateful and vengeful, and determined to do cultural ill.

An artist of genuine ability, impressionist Max Liebermann, departed from his traditionalist style in the early 1900s and became the premier advocate for the avant-garde. He was one of the founders of the Berlin Secessionist movement, which, in turn, incorporated and heavily promoted modernist tendencies. He also became president of the Berlin Secessionist movement and the Prussian Academy of Arts, so he was ideally positioned to both popularize the movement and to advance the careers and sales of Secessionist artists. He was accused, with some validity by traditionalists, of having turned art into a purely commercial venture, "hiding behind big words about art."[1554] In 1911, Carl Vinnen emphasized the foregoing attitude in a pamphlet, *Ein Protest deutcher Künstler*, wherein he emphasized the manipulation of the German art market to favor modern French art.[1555] Paul Cassirer responded to Vinnen by asserting his attitude that the bringing of French impressionism to the German art market was a "cultural deed" for which he gladly took both the credit and pride. From the perspective of the cultural purist Adolf Hitler, he was assigned blame, not credit.

Along with the Cassirers, Liebermann, Lovis Corinth, and Max Slevogt became the principal proponents of impressionism in Germany, much to the chagrin of the traditionalists. Indeed, without the likes of Liebermann and the Cassirers the highly influential Berlin Secession movement would hardly have been possible; it was those men in concert with a "fluid network of relationships that supported the growth of modernism"[1556] in German cultural circles. They were financed by their connections within the Jewish community and thereby managed to open their own galleries in both Berlin and Vienna. The efforts of these people were also supported by the various other Jewish-owned galleries and critics such as Karl Kraus (who hailed from Vienna) and Lothar Brieger-Wasservogel, and by dominant publishers such as Rudolf Mosse, Leopold Ullstein, Kurt Wolff, and Samuel Fischer, as well as a number of lesser publishing moguls. The lot of them were self-styled opponents of what they called the "vulgarities of Wilhelmine Germany."[1557] Jewish artists in Berlin, such as Hermann Struck, Louis Tualillion, Walter Bondy, Eugen Sprio, Max Oppenheimer, and Lesser Ury were sponsored by and promoted by their fellow Jews. Ury developed an entirely intentional style of "archaic coarseness"[1558] that became representative of a wide clique of Jewish arts of the time and also their non-Jewish brethren. The radically modernist artist Gustav Klimt was heavily promoted by the aforementioned cultural rabbis and is exemplary of the point. Wolff's publishing firm marketed first editions of numerous modernist authors and thereby pushed that genre into the public sphere—among the authors he championed were Franz Kafka, Karl Kraus, Carl Sternheim, and Franz Werfel,[1559] all of whom were Jewish.

During the early years of the modernist movement in Germany Ludwig Meidner began painting his deeply depressing apocalyptic landscapes, paintings that are now deemed to be among the purest of expressionist works: they portray terror, fires, rage, and deformed screaming men in modern cities, his favorite catastrophic setting.[1560]

Max Oppenheimer, a Jewish-Austrian painter and printmaker, joined with the likes of Oskar Kokoschka and Egon Schiele in the furtherance of expressionism, with "psychological portraits" as a motif. He also frequented Christian themes and not to the delight of Christians. Shocking subject matter was deliberately employed as a supposed "weapon in the fight against a reality that is felt to be unbearable."[1561] Oppenheimer experimented with futurism and cubism as well—anything but traditionalism.

Standards of probity and moral conduct came under attack by Jewish critics as did every other realm of German culture. Probity mattered to Germans of those days, including most especially Adolf Hitler. And, in fact, Germans had always exhibited exceptional moral conduct. The Roman historian Cornelius Tacitus had, in AD 98, described Germans and praised the prowess of German men and their courage in battle as well as the virtue of German women and their strong family values. "Good morality," said Tacitus, "is more effective in Germania than good laws are elsewhere."[1562] But Germans who clung to idyllic conceptions of probity and of hearth and home, of kith and kin, had little chance to have their versions of virtue and decency and loyalty and love known and championed except in the relatively small and relatively feeble volkisch press.

Children of traditional Germans were expected to behave. Honesty was honestly important.* On the whole, women were the loyal helpmates of their hard-working husbands. Sexual mores were founded in the church. Chastity, and upon marriage, fidelity, were respected—they were cherished as social norms.

---

* One can only wonder at how many other Americans such as your author marveled at the honesty of German children as our troops encountered them in the countryside while on military maneuvers there. Give a German child 20 DM and ask that he go to the local village to buy and return with breads and meats and cheeses and such and it would be done: the child would return with the items and every phenning of change. That was a Germany that is now but of yore.

Homosexuality was still an aberration. Far too many Jews of the Weimar era set out to change all that.

* * * *

It was then, in the postwar years, that the homosexual Magnus Hirschfeld's Institution for Sexual Science could flourish for the purpose of opening wide the gates for the attack on the sensibilities of staid Germans who still viewed such issues as homosexuality and companionate marriage as perversities. The institute was founded by Hirschfeld and several others, among them Iwan Block, the man who discovered and published *The 120 Days of Sodom.**

Google	URL
Magnus Hirschfeld	http://en.wikipedia.org/wiki/Magnus_Hirschfeld 8/2/14

The focus of Hirschfeld's "science" was homosexual licentiousness. Hirschfeld organized Berlin's first Sexological Congress, the International Meeting for Sexual Reform on a Sexological Basis. Obscenity laws were attacked. Abortion, homosexuality, and prostitution flourished and were defended and championed by Hirschfeld and other Jewish interests. Major cities of the Weimar Republic, with Berlin at the forefront, became tourist attractions for sexual deviates of every stripe. Mel Gordon, a champion of the era, its participants, and its conduct, says that, "[S]ex—in all its untraditional, transgressive, and anti-familial manifestations—had become a religion as well as a pastime."[1563] Gordon goes on to say that in Berlin,

---

* For a rather good summary of the personalities involved in the Institute for Sexual Science, see the following Web site: http://me.in-berlin.de/~magnus/institut/en/personen/pers_01.html)

> Police estimated that prostitutes in the 1920s numbered over 25,000—many were preteen girls and high school boys. Observers saw pimps everywhere offering anything to anybody: "little boys, little girls, robust young men, libidinous women," even animals. . . . There were approximately 10,000 pimps. This was Babylon on the Spree. . . .[1564]

The magnitude of the Berlin prostitution trade is made somewhat more concrete when compared to present-day Amsterdam, which has long been regarded as the "sex capital of Europe"—Amsterdam has only about 1,000 prostitutes.

In 1928, a Nazi propaganda sheet referred to Berlin as "a melting pot of everything that is evil—prostitution, drinking houses, cinemas, Marxism, Jews, strippers, negroes dancing.'"—and it had come to that condition, thought the Nazis, by way of Jewish influence of the Hirschfeld sort.

The Hirschfeld institute had a tremendous impact within Germany and even a bigger one internationally. He built up a wide range of international contacts and organized the World League for Sexual Reform. His institute and its offshoots were veritably saturated with Jewish names and influence. In those days one would search in vain for a non-Jewish sexologist.

Hirschfeld was the driving force behind efforts to spread access to birth control methods, sex counseling, and moves to abolish homosexual acts as criminal. He was supported by the Communists and other "progressives."[1565] The institute, funded by the leftist government of the time, argued vigorously for decriminalization of homosexuality and helped set the stage for abortion rights advocates and for attacks on traditional marriage. He and his institute were prominent in the ongoing public debates regarding birth control, procreation, motherhood, marriage, sexuality, and family values.[1566] In 1927, he was successful in having abortion reduced from a felony to a misdemeanor, an action that was later overturned by the Nazis.[1567] His institute was the subject of frequent attacks during the 1920s; it was denounced as Jewish, social-democratic, and offensive to public morals. Given that homosexual rights, abortion rights, and the redefinition of traditional marriage are now accomplished facts in the U.S., it can easily be argued that the Institute for Sexual Science was simply ahead of its time. However, given the long-standing traditions in Germany of *that* time, such proposals were understandably seen as detestable assaults on German mores.

It is not an exaggeration to claim, as did the Danish chargé d'affaires at The Hague, that Jews turned Germany into the world's pornographic center. Peter Gay emphasizes the influence of Austrian Jews on the sexual orientation of both Austrian and German populations:

> And in all areas Austrians—poets, novelists, psychologists, cultural critics—transmitted to their German audience their obsession with decadence and their attempts to come to terms with Eros; Sigmund Freud, Hugo von Hofmannsthal, Karl Kraus, and Arthur Schnitzler had as many readers in Berlin, Munich, and Frankfurt as they had in Vienna—perhaps more.[1568]

With respect to prostitution, Jewish involvement was writ so large that Jewish organizations became greatly concerned with its effect on Gentile perceptions of Jews. MacDonald correctly observes that "The 'extraordinarily large representation of Jews among traffickers and their victims' . . . in international prostitution from 1870 to 1939 was a major source of negative stereotypes by gentiles."[1569]

"The sweet qualities of Gallic porno," says Mel Gordon, "were supplanted in Berlin studios by the psychopathic scenarios from Krafft-Ebing.* Forced, intergenerational, scatological, and

---

* Richard Freiherr von Krafft-Ebing (August 14, 1840–December 22, 1902) was an Austro-German "sexologist" and psychiatrist. He wrote *Psychopathia Sexualis* (1886), a famous series of cases studies of sexual perversity. The book remains well-known for his coinage of the term "masochism" using the name of a contemporary writer, Leopold von Sacher-Masoch, whose partially autobiographical novel *Venus in Furs* tells of the protagonist's desire to be whipped and enslaved by a beautiful woman. Source: http://en.wikipedia.org/wiki/Richard_Freiherr_von_Krafft-Ebing

obsessive fetish sex prevailed.[1570] It was hardly irrational of Germans to conclude that attacks on their previously exemplary moral bearings were being directed by Jews, and Hitler did just that.

*　　*　　*　　*

Austrian pornographers of the day were also largely Jewish. They were exemplified by Felix Salten (Siegmund Salzmann). Salten, born in Budapest but raised in Vienna, is best known to the world as the 1923 author of the coming-of-age story (or, as some few would have it, an allegory on the plight of Jews between the world wars)[1571] of *Bambi* which was released as a Walt Disney feature animated film in 1942.

Salten gained initial fame from his laudatory obituary for French novelist, social critic, and Dreyfusard Emile Zola in 1902. Zola was, by that time, perceived by many as something of a Judeophile. He was later tainted with something of infamy by the radical right wing for his highly critical 1910 obituary relating to the beloved anti-Semitic mayor of Vienna, Karl Lueger. Given his affection for Lueger and his penchant for reading things contrary to Jews, we can be certain that Hitler was aware of Salten's criticism of his political hero, Lueger.

In addition to *Bambi*, Salten was known for the pornography he produced, such as his 1906 *Josefine Mutzenbacher: Die Lebensgeschichte einer wienerischen Dirne, von ihr selbst erzählt* (Josefine Mutzenbacher: A Viennese whore's life story, told by herself). The story recounts the reckless sexuality exhibited by the "heroine" during the period when she was between five and twelve years old. At the age of twelve, she enters the prostitution trade as a professional. The book unabashedly catalogs the sexual antics of incest, rape, and homosexuality to child prostitution, group sex, and fellatio. According to a Wikipedia entry on the subject, the book's content of taboo sexual antics was "entirely pornographic and unmistakably deviant in nature."[1572] It is a testimony to the marketability of appeals to lower instincts that Salten's *Josefine*

Mutzenbacher sold over 3 million copies.[1573] Hitler had Salten's books banned in 1936, not because he wrote *Bambi* but because he wrote such stuff as *Josefine Mutzenbacher*. The book was recently (1990s) a cause célèbre in Germany. Though several courts had found the material to be pornographic and a danger to children, leftists successfully convinced the Federal Constitutional Court of Germany to deem the book both pornographic and art, with the latter trumping the former. It is now available for reading by German children.[1574]

Like Salten, others were at work to diminish the moral standards of the German people. Among them were the members of an almost entirely Jewish group of intellectuals to which Salten belonged, the Young Vienna group. Members of the group would meet at the Viktor Zauner Café where they would plan, organize, and network—or, it may be said, to conspire.

* * * *

It was a common practice of left-wing cultural agitators of the Weimar period to edit, distort, and otherwise bastardize the great classics to fit the exigencies of their propaganda.[1575] The classical plays of Shakespeare, Shaw, Molière, and others were typically reconceptualized and reduced to elemental political or moral conflict. Such plays were then staged against stark, highly symbolic expressionistic backdrops.[1576] Often the plays were rewritten into didactic agitprop renditions that supported Communist Party objectives.

Leopold Jessner, an exceedingly important Jewish leader in the field of culture, was among the many producers and directors who maimed the original intent of famous works and skewed them for sociopolitical, agitprop purposes. He became the director of Berlin's Prussian State Theater in 1919. He opened the theatrical season with an expressionist version of Friedrich Shiller's *William Tell*. It caused riots. Jessner resigned his post in January 1930 after right-wing pressure had intensified due to his many "Jewified" productions and the "cultural Bolshevism" that he promoted throughout the 1920s.[1577] His assaults upon traditional European conceptions of humanity, along with those of the Blaue Reiter, the Brücke, the Dadaists, and others, were seen as great menaces and were collectively branded as "cultural Bolshevism."

Both Shiller and the legend of William Tell were icons of German romantics. Shiller was somewhat like Wagner in expressing his intense nationalism and alignment with the German people and he was therefore exceedingly popular among Nazis.[1578] A contemporary and friend of Germany's greatest literary demigod, Johann Wolfgang von Goethe, Shiller was a poet, historian, dramatist, ethicist, and aesthetic; he was named for the hero of Prussian militarism, Fredrick the Great.

William Tell was the well-known mythical hero of Germanic Switzerland who is famous in legend for having been forced by the tyrannical bailiff, Hermann Gessler, to shoot an apple from the head of his son with a crossbow. Tell subsequently kills Gessler and thereby inspires a rebellion leading to the formation of the Swiss Confederation. Swiss history and German mythology treat William Tell as a great patriotic hero celebrated in all manner of romanticist art. He is celebrated to a lesser extent by the French and Italians as well. Italian composer Gioachino Antonio Rossini, most famous for his *Barber of Seville*, also wrote *Guillaume Tell* (William Tell), and the now famous "William Tell Overture" made familiar in the U.S. in the 1950s as the music that opened each episode of *The Lone Ranger* television series.

Hitler's regard for Schiller was developed during his school years in Linz. Brigitte Hamann describes Hitler's attitude thusly:

> [I]t was a matter of "German" honor to be familiar with Schiller's life and works, in particular *William Tell*, and always to be able to claim the Germans' right in a classical manner, for example, by quoting, "The nation is worth nothing that doesn't gladly put everything at stake for its honor." Or, "By virtue of owning it for a thousand years, the soil is ours!" Or, "He must expel who does not want to be expelled,/That is the point, and only strength will win."[1579]

Hitler had first seen Schiller's version of the *William Tell* play when he was but twelve years old; he commented on the play in *Mein Kampf* saying:

> In such a case [when the fate of a people may be decided in a favorable sense by a single act of murder, as in the case of William Tell killing Hermann Gessler], a self-sacrificing man may suddenly spring forth from a people, to plunge the steel of death into the breast of the hated individual. And only the republican sentiment of petty scoundrels with a bad conscience will regard such a deed as horrible, while our people's greatest poet of freedom [Shiller] has dared to give glorification of such an action in his *Tell*.[1580]

Jessner, whom Peter Gay calls "the most powerful man in the Weimar theatre," deliberately distorted Shiller's *William Tell*, cutting all patriotic references to the fatherland and converted it into a call for revolution. Both of the leading roles in the play, the roles of Tell and Gessler, were played by Jewish actors. Jessner's version of the legend had the villain dressed in a uniform with medals much like those of a Junker general, and for good measure he had the cheeks of this villainous representation of Prussia rouged bright red. Upon presentation of the play, the first of the theater riots ensued in Berlin.[1581] Here was an instance of a Jew in a high position of government who deliberately affronted the German mind-set by attacking at once an icon of Germandom, Shiller's *William Tell*, and a sacred institution of Prussia, its army.

"Affront" was thematic of Jewish conduct with respect to all matters of culture throughout the Weimar period, and each affront was noted and accumulated in the mind of Adolf Hitler.

Hitler looked at the desecration of Germany's culture and the culprits of that desecration and commented as follows:

> Was there any form of filth or profligacy, particularly in cultural life, without at least one Jew involved in it?.... What had to be reckoned heavily against the Jews in my eyes was when I became acquainted with their activity in

> the press, art, literature, and the theater . . . It sufficed to look at a billboard, to study the names behind the horrible trash they advertised. . . . The fact that nine tenths of all literary filth, artistic trash, and theatrical idiocy can be set to the account of a people, constituting hardly one hundredth of all the country's inhabitants, could simply not be talked away; it was the plain truth.[1582]

Jessner was ousted from his position in 1933. He then emigrated to the U.S. where he spent the rest of his life working anonymously in film in Hollywood until his death in Los Angeles in 1945.

*   *   *   *

Even before the mass immigration of East European Jews to Germany, Jews were an exceedingly powerful force in Austria and Germany. In Austria, the *Neue Freie Presse,* the most prestigious newspaper in Central Europe, and the *Wiener Tagblatt* were both owned by Jews. The readership of the *Neue Freie Presse* was primarily Gentiles, but it managed to subtly and consistently push interests on behalf of the Jewish community. Wickham Steed attacked it as a "journal that embodies in concentrated form and, at times, with demonic force, the least laudable characteristics of Austro-German Jewry."[1583] Among the charges leveled by Steed was that it aimed constantly at influencing the stock exchange.[1584] In the 1870s, thirteen of Berlin's twenty-one daily newspapers were owned by Jews. And as Jews became more numerous in Germany due to immigration from places like Poland and Russia, they quickly increased their power to overwhelming, even awesome proportions.

Many leading liberal and avant-garde publishing houses in Germany were in Jewish hands such as S. Fischer, Kurt Wolff, the Cassirers, Georg Bondi, Erich Reiss, and Wieland Herzfelde who owned the Malik Verlag. The Malik publishing house was the leading promoter of the Dada movement and became the most influential distribution center for left-wing and Soviet literature. Its directors were the draft-dodging Jewish brothers Wieland Herzfelde, the company founder, and John Heartfield who had Anglicized his name from Herzfelde.[1585] Many leading theatre critics were Jews, and Jews dominated light entertainment. Virtually the entire press was owned by Jews, and especially the national press, says Metzger and Brandstatter:

> It has been calculated that in Berlin in 1929 there were 2,633 magazines and newspapers, of which at least 147 were daily newspapers. Three companies divided the lion's share between them: Ullstein with the flagship papers *Vossische Zeitung* and *Berliner Morgenpost*, Mosse with *Berliner Tageblatt*, and Scherl with *Berlin am Morgen* and *Berliner Nachtausgabe*. In addition, there were the political publications such as the Communist paper *Der Rote Fahne* and the Socialist paper *Vorwärts*. A new genre of photo-journalism was developing, led in particular by the Berliner *Illustrierte Zeitung* published by Ullstein, its proletarian counterpart *Arbeiter Illustierte Zeitung*, which was published in the agitprop multinational Willi Münzenberg, cultural magazines like Ossietzky's *Die Weltbühne* and, finally, numerous regional newspapers from the provinces, especially Kracauer's *Frankfurter Zeitung*.[1586]

The *National-Zeitung* of Berlin as well as the *Grenzboten* and *Ostedeutsche Post* were all also owned and operated by Jews. Leopold Ullstein and Rudolf Mosse were the Jewish publishing giants of the era. Ullstein's power, says Peter Gay, was almost frightening: "for a writer without a private income, the favor of Ullstein meant luxury, its disfavor, near-starvation."[1587] Stated otherwise, any writer who was unwilling to align his text with the proclivities of Ullstein had little hope of getting published. It was Hollywood on the Spree. Veritably, all information that was transmitted to the people at large was done so by a small subset of a small subset of people—a subset of a subset comprising only 1 percent of the country's population. And it was a subset of people who were largely at odds and out of touch with the deep-seated values of the German masses.

Some of Ullstein's publications pushed racy reportage and photographs of naked girls—this, at a time well before the 1939 movie *Gone With the Wind* achieved notoriety for having its star, Clark Gable, use the word "damn." His tabloid, *Tempo*, was quickly renamed by Berlin wits as *Die jüdische Hast*, Jewish haste or nervousness.[1588] Late in the Weimar regime, in an attempt to lower the profile of Jews as cultural critics, Ullstein ordered that such things as film reviews be published anonymously; it was common as well to employ Gentile-sounding pseudonyms to accomplish the same purpose.[1589] Thus it was that Jews continued to ravage German culture, but by then they increasingly did so anonymously or through the use of Gentile-sounding names.

To the extent that non-Jews held positions of influence within Jewish-owned publications, they were most often overshadowed by Jewish owners or their Jewish underlings, as was the case at the *Frankfurter Zeitung*, which was operated by Theodor Wolff, the nephew of the paper's owner, Rudolf Mosse.[1590] Wolff was well-known and seen as someone who actively combated German geopolitical interests; he was therefore specifically called out by virtually every commentator assessing Jewish abuses of German trust.

The commercial press aside, Jews were also ensconced in the highest reaches of the Prussian government's press departments. The German Press Association, the Berlin Press Union, and the freelance German writers association, the German Writer's Protection Association, were all composed almost entirely of Jews.

With support from Jewish-owned publishing houses and government-operated press associations, Jewish journalists enjoyed notoriety and influence across the entire spectrum of the liberal, left-wing German press. The House of Mosse and the House of Ullstein published a wide range of books and popular magazines with which they influenced public opinion, and they nurtured Jewish authors and sympathizers into prominence; Thomas Mann, Gerhart Hauptmann, and Hermann Hesse, among others. Racy tabloids, offensive to the tastes of cultured Germans, were made widely popular to the masses by Jewish publishers. Indeed, the Jewish press of Germany, much like the Jewish press of the U.S. today, served up a full platter of sensationalist, sex-soaked, antireligious publications directed at the lower instincts of the masses. And, as always, Jewish publishers represented liberalism and pluralism for Gentiles in both the social milieu and politics, while at the same time decrying opponents of Jewish autonomy and ethnocentrism.

There were here and there a few Gentile publishers that were at odds with the predominant Jewish press. In an example of Freudian "transference," Peter Gay accuses right-wing publisher Alfred Hugenberg of being possessed by "hatreds masquerading as convictions"—an accusation that is actually far more compelling when applied to the left-wing, anti-German, anti-Christian, anticulture, politically radical icons of the Jewish press of the period.

A great many Germans responded negatively to the Jewish radicalism in their midst and to the debasement of their esteemed culture. That it was a small minority of Jews who were largely responsible for the daily affronts to Germania was of no matter: they had the cumulative effect of breeding anti-Semites and of compounding Hitler's hate.

* * * *

The stage and theater were likewise dominated by Jews. By 1930, Jews of Berlin represented fully 80 percent of the theater directors and wrote 75 percent of the plays. Over 37 percent of the actors were Jews. The influence of the theater directors, writers, and actors was both hedonistic and obscene. "The theater during the twenties staged celebrated provocations, treating of parricide, incest, and crime,"[1591] says Fest. Fest goes on to say that in typical fashion, the closing scene of the Brecht-Weill opera *Mahagonny* had the actors display placards reading "Up with the chaotic state of our cities," "Up with love for hire," "Up with honor for assassins," or "Up with the immorality of vulgarity."[1592] To the mind of too many a staid German, it was all very Jewish.

Jews had played an ever-increasingly important role in the theaters of Imperial Germany and came to dominate them by the early 1920s. They were everywhere in the forefront of modernist metropolitan entertainment. They were the prominent theater owners, actors, writers, composers, scriptwriters, producers, set designers, and performers. The same was true in the realm of film products. Demigods of this realm included such people as the theater critics and directors Otto Brahm (Otto Abrahamsohn) and Max Reinhardt (Max Goldmann), the cabaret composer Ruldolf Nelson, and the critics Julius Freund and Viktor Hollaender. In film there was Ernst Lubitsch and others.

Playwrights like Carl Sternheim, Arthur Schnitzler, Ernst Toller, Erwin Piscator, Walter Hasenclever, Ferenc Molnar, and Carl Zuckmayer, as well as producers such as Max Reinhardt, dominated the stage with "sexually daring" productions.[1593]

Nightlife in the city was horrifically transfigured. In the early days of the degeneration a variety of cultural disguises were employed. Naked Dance was represented as exercises in Naturalism or high art, a faux intellectual cover. Mel Gordon proudly describes one technique for pulling off such disguises: "Studious lectures, ornamental theatrical backdrops, and accompaniments of classical or modern music were typical strategies to hide the prurient enterprise."[1594] With stack upon stack of prurient precedent set in this way, promoters of licentiousness were finally able to abandon such pretense by the end of the inflationary period and could present their prurience in open form. The Golden Age of Weimar culture was at hand.

Attacks on culture and standards of morality occurred on multiple fronts: there was the obvious shift in emphasis from the idyllic to the grotesque, but also attacks by way of various journals, the courts, subterfuge, and creeping grotesque cultural precedent. Jews devised an array of ways by which their proclivities could be brought to the stage while simultaneously avoiding the censors. One such scheme was to mount so-called closed performances to which only "invited" guests could attend.

Theater scandals became commonplace. The German censors, consistently accused by historians for being radically prudish, initially objected to Frank Wedekind's play, *Frühlings Erwachen* (Spring Awakening), a play about masturbation and homosexuality. In the early 1900s, the censors were approached with packets of letters from prominent personalities who praised the artistry of the work. Reinhardt was thereby able to overcome their objections and was permitted to stage the play. "The explosive subject matter guaranteed the play an extremely long run,"[1595] says Emily Bilski. Still another precedent was set.

In 1918, Roda Roda, Sandor Friedrich Rosenfeld staged her drama, *Der Minster*, which glorified the revolution.[1596] In the 1920s, Germans were given *The Threepenny Opera* and thereby the song made popular in the U.S. by Louis Armstrong and Bobby Darin, *Mack the Knife*, but without the embedded reference to Lotte Lenya, the High Camp bisexual protégé of Anita Berber and wife of the Jewish composer of the song. *The Threepenny Opera* was hailed by virtually the entire Berlin press corps as a brilliant rendering. Walter Kerr called it "The most wonderfully insulting musical I have ever come across."[1597] As William Grange observes, it "became the internationally recognized cultural emblem of the Weimar Republic and remains so to this day."[1598] Psycho-twaddle established its worth as a cultural icon. In actual fact, the musical was, as Mel Gordon pompously proclaims, "Girl-Culture in song."[1599]

In film, *The Cabinet of Dr. Caligari*, *Metropolis*, and *Nosferatu* were hailed as modernist treasures; and perhaps they were, but they were hardly fitting replacements for the old-fashioned moralistic paganism of *The Ring of the Nibelung*. Other popular titles of the era included *Sundige Mutter* (Sinful Mama), *Wenn Ein Weib Den Weg Verliert* (When a Woman Loses Her Way), *Zieh Dich Aus* (Get Undressed), and *Tausend Nackte Frauen* (One Thousand Naked Women). These were not titles created by Germans of that era, they were Jewish through and through. And they enraged the likes of Hitler and others of his mind-set.

Theater criticism was an all but entirely Jewish domain. Istvan Deak has this to say about the theater critic of the time:

> The Berlin theater critic at the turn of the century was not simply a frustrated playwright and professional grumbler; he was a priest assisting the dramatist and the theater director in the performance of a sacred function. That function was to inculcate culture and progress in the heart of the Wilhelmian *Bürger*, by definition servile, materialistic, pompous, bigoted, and conventional, was to be persuaded to become a modern and, therefore, better man. He was to stop prostrating himself before the higher orders and through a moral and aesthetic regeneration become a self-respecting bourgeois.[1600]

They were indeed "priests," but priests of the queer sort, deviants from the moral norm.

More and more theater critics waxed political, enlarging their sphere of influence through a combination of culture and politics.[1601] Alfred Kerr (born Alfred Kempner) was among the most prominent Jewish theater critics, so much so, in fact, that he was nicknamed the Culture Pope (*Kulturpapst*).[1602] Along with fellow Jew Paul Cassirer, he founded the publication *Pan* and was important to the promotion of expressionism. Still another important critic of the period was Walter Benjamin "who demonstrated his zeal for the new with the first publications in the journal *Der Anfang* (The Beginning)."[1603]

To the extent that non-Jews participated in directing Weimar culture, they were left with no choice but to respond to the leadership of the Jewish intelligentsia; anyone doing otherwise was marginalized or successfully attacked as anti-Semitic.

Hitler assessed what was being presented to the public by contemporary producers, directors, and critics. "Our whole public life today," he said, "is like a hothouse for sexual ideas and stimulations. Just look at the bill of fare served up in our movies, vaudeville and theaters, and you will hardly be able to deny that this is not the right kind of food, particularly for the youth."[1604] Current culture, he claimed, was a manifestation of a rotting culture, a moral plague of big-city "civilization." He saw the cities as "hotbeds of vice and shamelessness" that were "populated by white slavers." Love, he said, had been "perverted to a commodity, 'nothing more than a deal.'"[1605] He left no doubt as to the source of the cultural rot.[1606]

The cultural rot that was so very much a part of Weimar Germany's culture, today hyped as its Golden Age, was rightfully placed at the feet of Jews. We may not like the accusation, and a good many Jewish apologists have created tomes of offsetting arguments; still, it was so. Gentile aberrations and pathologies were at the actual roots, say apologists of such contentions. The arguments are false. Jews were indeed at the root of the cultural degeneration of Germany. And, as Peter Gay makes apparent in his several books on the subject, they at the time took pride in their great influence over German culture, even the most gross aspects of that influence.

It is often mentioned in the literature, sometimes happily and sometimes derisively, that without Jews there would have been no Weimar culture. If one speaks of Weimar culture in terms of the Golden Age, Jews celebrate their unique influence and take justifiable credit for it; if one speaks of it in terms of its degeneracy, authors tend to downplay or even deny the Jewish role.

Jewish influence on German culture became massive as Jews rose in prominence after World War I. The Nazi, Dr. Friederich Karl Wiehe, provided a retrospective summary in 1938, thusly:

> This strong sexuality in Jews, chained in the ghetto of the Middle Ages was flooding into the public life of the states as a result of the emancipation. But it didn't get a completely free line until all barriers in the form of police surveillance and censorship were removed in Germany after the defeat in 1918. Then a flood of immoral litterature, immoral films and theatre plays poured out into Germany, primarily nourished by Jews. Concerning the field of litterature it has already been mentioned, that the publishers and writers of the immoral litterature, that were flooding the book market, was Jews and Jews again. In the hundreds of thousands of volumes that were seized in 1933 we find the same names repeatedly. Aside from publishing houses like

Benjamin Harz, Richard Jacobsthal, Leon Hirsch, M. Jacobsohn or Jacobsthal & Co., we mention here above all the Vienna-Jewish "Verlag für Kulturforschung" (Publishing House of Cultural Research), the production of which could fill whole libraries. The names say everything: "Sittengeschichte des Lasters" (The history of morals and vices), "Sittengeschichte der Schamlosigkeit" (The history of morals and shamelessness), "Bilderlexikon der Erotic" (Picture Lexicon of Eroticism), "Sittengischichte des Geheime und Verbotene" (The history of the secret and the forbitten (sic)) etc.[1607]

* * * *

The women's liberation movement in Weimar Germany—what Hitler called "the degenerate women's emancipation fit,"[1608] was strong for a time as women sought equality and respect in both the home and workplace. Between 1918 and 1920, the SPD enjoyed a vast wave of female support: party membership of women rose from 66,000 to 207,000. The USPD experienced similar spikes in membership and support. Such support, however, was short-lived. German women would soon realize what their "liberators" had in mind for them and would thereafter abandon both parties in favor of the traditionalism represented in the Nazi Party.[1609]

Hitler and his Nazis considered the women's movement to be a Jewish, social-democratic, immoral, and degenerate battle.[1610] The movement was soon transfigured by its very adherents into a vile sort of subjugation, placing women in the position of sex objects of a kind far worse than those of traditional mores. Berliners rebelled against beefy philistinism, libertines fought old-fashioned moralists. "Girl-Culture," gushes Mel Gordon, became mainstream: "Here, the New Woman was automated, made trainable, streamlined, remolded into a robotic doll. Both aspects of Girl-Culture—the Demonic Sex Object and the Rationalized Sex Object—enthralled and animated Berlin."[1611] The foregoing provides one with a pretty firm understanding of what was really meant by the term "liberated woman." The cultural gurus of the period were leading women up the ramp to the blue door, to the kill-floor of morality's slaughterhouse.

The women of Weimar Germany were a dominant force in the electorate due to the deaths and disablement of so many men during World War I, and they initially voted in support of the Weimar government. By the end of the 1920s, however, women had had quite enough of the republic and its cultural flotsam. By 1932, they were the fastest-growing group of Nazi supporters.[1612] An account by a young female urbanite illustrates the disenchantment of women:

> No wonder that both physical and moral resistance are on the wane; the entire environment is directed at destroying it.... [T]he city most certainly does not harbor Germany's soul, despite the restless thought and incessant activity that takes place there. The soul of Germany rests in the countryside, in the grace of its rolling hills where man is still part of the land which instills him with the strength to defend himself against the developments of our time that are infringing on our lives.[1613]

By 1926, women were increasingly disillusioned with the claims of equality that were such a vast departure from traditional notions of German womanhood. They no longer experienced exhilaration at the prospect of the new ways of life; they, instead, experienced dismay and exhaustion and they increasingly rejected the new, "imported" models of femininity.[1614] And just as traditional femininity was being revitalized, there was also a growing movement of people toward a political reorientation; it was toward the provinces and away from the city.[1615] Traditional women's issues and the degradation of their being ultimately turned women away from the culture of the time.

The supposed liberation of women during the Weimar era was not unlike that of liberated American women of today, especially the drug-laden ones with penchants for tattoos, facial iron, and low-investment parenting that seems to go hand in hand with that manner of liberation. Women who only *think* that they *think* as they readily succumb to the incessant beat of the tom-toms of faddism. Like their respectable contemporary American counterparts, German women wanted respect in both the home and the workplace. They sought to break free of their traditional narrow lot. They wanted recognition for their accomplishments, capabilities, and intellect, and equal access to good jobs and power. Their wants were then morphed into what is now represented in the persona of libertine Hollywood sluts and their breed.

German women were wise enough such that their enamorment with the perverse liberation being offered up did not last as long as it has in the U.S. As pointed out in *The Weimar Republic Sourcebook*, "A great many German women sought a return to traditional roles and family values and they expressed their desires by voting heavily on behalf of right-wing parties."[1616] This desire among women to return to more traditional fold of cultural norms was so encompassing that even the strong feminist agenda of the KPD, its prominent female party leaders, and its relatively large number of women candidates could not sway the women's vote for the Communists. German women, formerly deemed "liberated German women," became an exceedingly important voting block for the Nazis. Hitler courted them.

Architecture

Above even his regard for painting, music, and sculpture, was Hitler's love of architecture. Big architecture. Really big, big, stripped-down-neoclassic-monolithic-gargantuan architecture.[1617] Germany was to have the widest streets, the biggest bridges and airports, the biggest enclosed meeting place, the biggest and fastest ships. Its highways were to be the most impressive, its trains both the biggest and fastest. Frederic Spotts correctly emphasizes, as did Albert Speer, that Hitler had "a passion for the colossal,"[1618] which was true enough, but he also helped design the petite Volkswagen which illustrates an eminently practical aspect of his being. It also illustrates his connection with the people: he sought a Peoples Car, a Volkswagen, not an ostentatious heap of iron.

Hitler's views on architecture stood in stark contrast to the most influential architectural movement of the time, the Bauhaus Movement. For Hitler, says Spotts, "great architecture [was] the outward sign of inward political greatness."[1619] Modernist trends in architecture, driven largely by market forces instead of culture and beauty, were anathema. The architecture of great cities was supposed to be of the kind in Athens and Rome and Paris, the kind that were constructed by Pericles, Augustus, Frederick the Great, Bavaria's king Ludwig, and Napoleon III. The Bauhaus Movement stripped architecture of all of its ornamentation, its beauty. It created architectural abominations that were despised by Hitler.

The Bauhaus was a Marxist-oriented group that drew much of its early membership from the German Socialist Revolution, the Workers' Council for Art, and the leftist student group, *kostufra*. According to Bauhaus modernists, many of them Jewish, building ornamentation was criminal; it had to be eliminated. The nonfunctional, while beautiful, was unnecessary and was to be discarded, eliminated. Pillars and portals and arches and ornaments were out; flat, sleek, square, or rectangular, was in. Modernists of the Bauhaus mold used flat roofs, modern technology, glass, and metal, all of which they considered suitable for any type of building, and it was with that stance that they departed most markedly from the traditionalists. "The traditionalists," as Spotts tells us, "held to the 'true Germanic tradition' of gabled roofs and old-fashioned design concepts and materials."[1620] Building design became a socially and politically charged activity, particularly since upward of 80 percent of Bauhaus funding came from public coffers.[1621] Some prominent architects faulted the Bauhaus School, accusing it of promoting cultural and racial decline. They decried replacement of the traditional German abode with what Kaes and others called mechanical "dwelling machines."[1622] Such dwellings were roundly decried by traditionalists as "designed and executed in complete ignorance of all the things a family needs to make a dwelling a home,"[1623] which, as many such structures illustrate, was uncomfortably close to the truth. Hitler abhorred the entire

Bauhaus Movement but was entirely willing to employ some of its principles in what he considered to be appropriate settings.

Jewish architect Bruno Taut, who was one of the most prominent Jewish polemists associated with the movement, was close to the Bauhaus founder Walter Gropius. Taut proposed that public funds be expended on behalf of radically inclined architects and even that architects be chosen for public works on the basis of their radicalism. For Taut, architecture was to be used to bring about "a complete revolution in the cultural sphere."[1624] He went so far as to propose melting down public monuments and breaking up triumphal avenues as a source of funding for his type of architecture.[1625] The Taut-types would not be of use in Hitler's new building schemes. The Nazis viewed Bauhaus as a haven for Jews, Bolsheviks, and cosmopolitan non-German viewpoints.

The architectural monstrosities of modernism were all too depressing for an aesthetic like Hitler—Modernism itself was an expression of contempt for traditional aesthetic norms.[1626] Bauhaus architecture was sometimes called "jailhouse style," a style that represented hostility to tradition and thus spawned a "back-to-the-country" movement within Germany.[1627]

The Bauhaus Movement, which stood most markedly in opposition to Hitler's conception of architecture, "wasn't a new style of architecture," says E. Michael Jones. "It embodied a new way of living in conscious revolution against traditional values."[1628] It was, as Jones also asserts, a fork in the road where architecture made a wrong turn. He supports his contention by pointing out that Bauhaus structures throughout Germany are now being demolished and replaced by the old architecture, the stuff of traditional Germany.[1629] The political aspect of Bauhaus architecture is also well captured by Jones, who says that, "It was, to coin a phrase, politics by design."[1630]

As previously emphasized, the element that Hitler loved most in classicism was the opportunity for monumentality. "He obsessed," said Albert Speer, "with giantism. . . . But his real preferences were for arched passageways, domes, curving lines, ostentation, always with an element of elegance—in short, the baroque."[1631]* Hitler's love of the baroque stood in stark contrast to architectural trends of the 1920s; the architectural direction of the time was to totally eliminate ornamentation of the kind so prominent in baroque structures. It should be added, however, that whatever his regard for the baroque (Kubizek says Hitler actually disliked it as too ornate),[1632] much of the architecture planned by Hitler was not much burdened with overly ostentatious ornamentation. Ornamentation was present, but only in subdued forms. Still, as emphasized earlier, he did like the buildings of the Ringstrasse. Hitler was not always dogmatic and unbending in his likes or actions.

Hitler's love of the gargantuan extended to sculpture as well. The monumental sculptures of Arno Breker—"a continuum that proceeded from Rodin" as he phrased it, was extolled, as was the sculpture of Georg Kolbe, Fritz Klimsch, and Josef Thorak,[1633] and the art of Emil Nolde.

In his several books, Speer related many engaging stories of his times with Hitler as they planned the rebuilding of great cities like Linz and Berlin. Speer satisfied Hitler's desire for massive edifices, carrying it to an extreme in his design for the Great Hall in Berlin—a structure so massive that it probably could not have actually been built due to that city's sandy soil.

Speer also created models for Hitler's city-building plans; models that Hitler studied in detail in his Berlin bunker even as Germany collapsed around him, bringing to mind Hitler as a modern-day Nero. The Nero analogy has a number of sources in Nazi lore, but Goebbels's diaries are perhaps the most telling. Even as disaster loomed over Hitler's war with Russia, he could not tear himself away from the subjects of art and culture. Spotts discusses Goebbels's diary entries concerning that time:

---

* Several authors deny that Hitler was enamored by the baroque. The simple lines and lack of excessive ornamentation in the structures he built certainly seems to support such contentions. That said, it is also a certainty that in his youth he admired the baroque structures of Vienna's Ringstrasse—his penchant for constancy, though strong, was not absolute.

> [T]he battle of Stalingrad was now at its height, Goebbels noted that "despite the gravity of the situation, the Führer remains as devoted as ever to the arts and cannot wait for the moment when he can devote more time to them." On this occasion the conversation began with Hitler speaking of his pleasure in Bruckner's symphonies and concluded with his comparing the philosophies of Kant, Schopenhauer and Nietzsche. In early May of that year—when aerial bombing was shattering German cities, the Wehrmacht was in retreat in Russia and the German military had been thrown out of Africa—Hitler returned briefly to Berlin and met with Goebbels on four successive days, dealing on each occasion with "a variety of cultural and artistic questions." What was on his mind this time? In the visual arts, it was the need to encourage individuals to buy paintings for themselves and not leave it up to art museums to acquire them. He also wanted art galleries to be run by the community not the Reich.[1634]

It is true that Hitler could sometimes act rather like Nero, and sometimes even rather like the crazy Jewish character, Dr. Franz Lipp.

Architecture, like all other forms of art in the early 1900s, was under attack by modernism, and modernism of the era was attributed mostly to Jews, the culture-critics. In Vienna, Hitler had observed firsthand the architectural influence of the Secessionists, who were mostly non-Jewish experimentalists praised in the Jewish press for their modernist innovations. For example, the famous architect Adolf Loos was non-Jewish but his clients, supporters, and primary friends, including fellow pedophile Peter Altenberg, were Jews. In 1910, Loos built a house of men's fashion directly opposite the court castle at the Michaelerplatz in Vienna. It was a deliberate provocation of contrast with Viennese architectural tradition. It was quickly termed "a monstrosity" and "a house without eyebrows" because it did not have any form of traditional window ornamentation. Emperor Franz Joseph was both appalled and outraged as were other traditionalists of the city.

When Hitler drew the Michaelerplatz he pretended that the Loos House did not even exist by replacing it with a rendition of an eighteenth-century structure.[1635]

After World War I, it was the Novembergruppe and the Bauhaus School that took up the cause of modernism in architecture.

The Novembergruppe, founded by Max Pechstein and run by him and other Jews and ersatz Jews, was heavily involved in both architecture and politics. Authors Rainer Metzger and Christian Brandstätter say the following about them:

> The Novembergruppe (November Group) proved more successful [than the Rat geistiger Arbeiter], as it put a greater emphasis on the here and now. Taking its name from the month of the Weimar Revolution, this group was primarily formed by [Jewish] artists and architects, and included Die Brücke (The Bridge) veterans Otto Mueller and Max Pechstein, Erich Mendelsohn (the pioneer of new building methods), and more moderate representatives of the modern style such as Otto Freundlich and Rudolf Belling. Soon the group attracted most of the well-known Berlin artists of the day. The Novembergruppe wanted to exploit the political situation by offering themselves as a kind of pool of potential artists willing to work for the state, should the new Republic find itself in need of them. In addition, they demanded to have their say at every political-cultural opportunity, be it on art education, the foundation of museums or the design of public spaces. The group was allocated its own spaces in the annual Berlin art exhibition and increasingly became a professional association.[1636]

Clearly, the Novembergruppe was not lacking in the hubris stereotype.

Jewish Novembergruppe member Erich Mendelsohn would in 1921 build an observatory that became known as the Einstein Tower. One source describes the tower as a "cheerful concrete sculpture, a rampant, swelling expanse of curves and lines, like a

Hitler, Jews, and Hate

living organism . . . a building whose architectural character combines both pride in a new style of building, the scientific institute, and a philosophical conviction of the importance of progress."[1637] Well, maybe. For all of the forgoing, though, it looks very much like a depiction of the residence of the Little Old Lady Who Lived in a Shoe.

The "superficial approach to buildings was the result of architecture's own search for self-definition. . . . the architectural skeleton was 'working its way to the surface,'"[1638] say Rainer Metzger and Christian Brandstätter. A prominent example of such architecture, of the architecture's skeleton working its way to the surface, is perhaps now best exemplified by the Pompidou Center in Paris, about as ugly a piece of construction as can be had by way of purposeful, entropy design. It is Bauhaus architecture on amphetamines.

Google	URL
Einstein Tower	https://www.google.com/search?q=Einstein+Tower&rlz=1T4GZAB_enUS449US538&tbm=isch&imgil=YyavDdhsix-eWM%253A%253B3S6WsPdZGcukDM%253Bhttp%25253A%25252F%25252Fen.wikipedia.org%25252Fwiki%25252FEinstein_Tower&source=iu&usg=__fL52_ks_99i-cr94pIhgJ4oxulI%3D&sa=X&ei=bqzgU8_UKJWryASp44DwDQ&ved=0CDUQ9QEwAg&biw=1008&bih=523#facrc=_&imgdii=_&imgrc=YyavDdhsix-eWM%253A%3B3S6WsPdZGcukDM%3Bhttp%253A%252F%252Fupload.wikimedia.org%252Fwikipedia%252Fcommons%252F3%252F36%252FEinsteinturm_7443.jpg%3Bhttp%253A%252F%252Fen.wikipedia.org%252Fwiki%252FEinstein_Tower%3B819%3B614 8/2/14
Pompidou Center, Paris	https://www.google.com/search?q=Pompidou+Center,+Paris&rlz=1T4GZAB_enUS449US538&tbm=isch&imgil=7OIPTuS__wf5FM%253A%253BVprNELYDMf4ddM%253Bhttp%25253A%25252F%25252Fvacation-tours.blogspot.com%25252F2009%25252F02%25252Fcentre-georges-pompidou-paris.html&source=iu&usg=__6vEcqmYiFXG5I3Ic_j9sobHYoCg%3D&sa=X&ei=yqzgU5eqFdifyATlyoGYDw&ved=0CEUQ9QEwBQ&biw=1008&bih=523#facrc=_&imgdii=_&imgrc=7OIPTuS__wf5FM%253A%3BhtR6xqig8len5M%3Bhttps%253A%252F%252Ftowerofaifel.files.wordpress.com%252F2013%252F04%252Fimg_0744.jpg%3Bhttps%253A%252F%252Ftow

	erofaifel.wordpress.com%252Fcategory%252F%2525CE%2525B1%2525CE%2525BE%2525CE%2525B9%2525CE%2525BF%2525CE%2525B8%2525CE%2525B5%2525CE%2525B1%2525CF%252584%2525CE%2525B1%252F%3B3456%3B2304 8/2/14
Bauhaus House am Horn	https://www.google.com/search?q=Bauhaus+House+am+Horn&rlz=1T4GZAB_enUS449US538&tbm=isch&imgil=jFUUsoo1Twtc2M%253A%253B3Xf63nduxQGUxM%253Bhttp%25253A%25252F%25252Fnl.wikipedia.org%25252Fwiki%25252FHaus_am_Horn&source=iu&usg=__e24v_-3wEss8j8LlM15rNdugzxY%3D&sa=X&ei=Ba3gU6HJF4uvyAT44YDgBw&ved=0CDQQ9QEwAg&biw=1008&bih=523#facrc=_&imgdii=_&imgrc=jFUUsoo1Twtc2M%253A%3B_N0YL1OkrYwb2M%3Bhttp%253A%252F%252Fupload.wikimedia.org%252Fwikipedia%252Fcommons%252F8%252F8c%252FHaus_am_Horn%252C_Weimar_(Westansicht).jpg%3Bhttp%253A%252F%252Fde.wikipedia.org%252Fwiki%252FMusterhaus_Am_Horn%3B2236%3B1660 8/2/14
Bauhaus Building, Dressau	https://www.google.com/search?q=Bauhaus+Building,+Dessau&rlz=1T4GZAB_enUS449US538&tbm=isch&imgil=esNL9qnLTU_UsM%253A%253BbS_7unB1ubJeUM%253Bhttp%25253A%25252F%25252Fdimarieilarraza.com%25252Fvideo-documentary-bauhaus-building-in-dessau%25252F&source=iu&usg=__s_IH3sq-PopuP8GTuHMoS0dDWoI%3D&sa=X&ei=Ka3gU43gHcKQyASIxILgDQ&ved=0CCQQ9QEwAA&biw=1008&bih=523#facrc=_&imgdii=_&imgrc=esNL9qnLTU_UsM%253A%3BbS_7unB1ubJeUM%3Bhttp%253A%252F%252Fwww.dimarieilarraza.com%252Fwp-content%252Fuploads%252F2009%252F08%252Fbuhaus.jpg%3Bhttp%253A%252F%252Fdimarieilarraza.com%252Fvideo-documentary-bauhaus-building-in-dessau%252F%3B500%3B327 8/2/14

Bauhaus was founded by Walter Gropius as an art school 1919. Gropius eventually came to exert an extensive influence on design currents in the creation of furniture, and most notably, building architecture. Before the war, says E. Michael Jones, "Gropius had built modern factories and houses in the vernacular style. After the war, he built houses that looked like modern factories."[1639] The celebrated Bauhaus Building built by him in the early 1920s in Dessau is offered up as exemplary of what the Bauhaus School represented. For all the praise given to its technical innovation, it looks awful. The structure is remarkably familiar to anyone who has ever had the opportunity to experience the architecture of a modern army barracks at any-army-fort-USA.

In the U.S., where the Bauhaus style took hold in the late 1930s with the relocation of its Jewish-German advocates to the U.S., the apartment-box became a symbol of social failure. As Jones emphasizes recurringly, modern architecture is fundamentally the box. All of the post-World War II buildings of Eastern Europe are representative of this style, as are the many high-rise buildings in the U.S. that were originally planned as a means to address the housing needs of the urban poor. The box used by the homeless bum on the streets is remarkably similar to the box employed by modern architecture to house the urban poor. Drive across the George Washington Bridge from New Jersey to New York—what you see before you is representative of Bauhaus architecture.

Some of the modern architects of the Hitler era were deliberately provocative. Albert Speer recounts in his book *Spandau, the Secret Diaries* how various architects created designs that resulted in social uproar. "As a matter of fact," says Speer, "I always felt that a good many of these works were deliberately aimed at outraging the public. . . ."[1640]

All of this was an abomination to the likes of Hitler, a youthful devotee of baroque architecture, and then the simpler and more austere neo-Doric; but still, architecture that on the whole had "eyebrows." After World War II, the Bauhaus influence could be seen most starkly in the structures of East Berlin. The Stasi Building (East Germany's Ministry for State Security) at Berlin-Lichtenberg was amongst the best examples of Bauhaus ugliness, of architectural brutality. The Palace of the Republic was an architectural revulsion that underwent demolition precisely because of its ugliness. Built along Bauhaus lines and ugly though it was acknowledged to be, it vied with the Stasi Building for the title of "ugliest building in Berlin," which is saying something because East Berlin of the Cold War era had some god-awful ugly buildings. Hitler thought that the whole of Bauhaus creations were abominations, and he despised both the movement and the many Jews who both participated in it and praised it. The Stasi Building and the Palace of the Republic stand in stark contrast to the architecture of the type admired by Hitler such as the Semper Opera House in Dresden, which was designed by one of Hitler's favorite architects, Gottfriend Semper.

Google	URL
Stasi Building, Berlin	https://www.google.com/search?q=Stasi+Building,+Berlin&rlz=1T4GZAB_enUS449US538&tbm=isch&imgil=1_m5eAJGMOJdJM%253A%253BUH0_zK0xL07szM%253Bhttp%25253A%25252F%25252Fandberlin.com%25252F2012%25252F04%25252F30%25252Fthe-stasi-museum%25252F&source=iu&usg=_-XPjYDwvi2ogGqNl_xBTNFmxRMw%3D&sa=X&ei=6K7gU8-eLY2pyASVrYCQBw&ved=0CD4Q9QEwAw&biw=1008&bih=523#facrc=_&imgdii=_&imgrc=1_m5eAJGMOJdJM%253A%3BUH0_zK0xL07szM%3Bhttp%253A%252F%252Fandberlin.com%252Fwp-content%252Fuploads%252F2012%252F05%252Fthe-stasi-museum-berlin.jpg%3Bhttp%253A%252F%252Fandberlin.com%252F2012%252F04%252F30%252Fthe-stasi-museum%252F%3B3877%3B2582 8/2/14
Palace of the Republic, Berlin	https://www.google.com/search?q=Palace+of+the+Republic,+Berlin&rlz=1T4GZAB_enUS449US538&tbm=isch&imgil=vi4-ahsI8XlrNM%253A%253BnirdRMYk4TZlfM%253Bhttp%25253A%25252F%25252Fwww.lilano.de%25252Fcatalog%25252Fpalace-of-republic-c-21_23.html&source=iu&usg=_Ng9Jr58-YMaN5IVSG1J4twMbBl4%3D&sa=X&ei=gK_gU6evHcukyATntoDgAg&ved=0CHwQ_h0wCw&biw=1008&bih=523#facrc=_&imgdii=_&imgrc=vi4-ahsI8XlrNM%253A%3BnirdRMYk4TZlfM%3Bhttp%253A%252F%252Fwww.lilano.de%252Fcatalog%252Fimages%252FPalastderRepublik_200511DSC8225.jpg%3Bhttp%253A%252F%252Fwww.lilano.de%252Fcatalog%252Fpalace-of-republic-c-21_23.html%3B515%3B332 8/2/13
Semper Opera House, Dresden	https://www.google.com/search?q=Semper+Opera+House,+Dresden&rlz=1T4GZAB_enUS449US538&tbm=isch&imgil=HyMS6a-5iqIp0M%253A%253Bozd01bsOusTXKM%253Bhttp%25253A%25252F%25252Fwww.tripomatic.com%25252FGermany%25252FDresden%25252FSemper-Opera-House%25252F&source=iu&usg=__cOt_t5b4Dd2HXmzQ_

	i_DgIRqXAA%3D&sa=X&ei=xa_gU7ebGsilyATekoG4BQ &ved=0CDsQ9QEwBQ&biw=1008&bih=523#facrc=_&im gdii=_&imgrc=HyMS6a- 5iqIp0M%253A%3Bozd01bsOusTXKM%3Bhttp%253A% 252F%252Fstatic.panoramio.com%252Fphotos%252Flarge %252F1367412.jpg%3Bhttp%253A%252F%252Fwww.trip omatic.com%252FGermany%252FDresden%252FSemper- Opera-House%252F%3B1024%3B682 8/2/14

In architecture, the Bauhaus Movement was in. There was to be no more of those criminal, decorative facades of old; straight, sleek, unadorned structures were the wave of the future—the new architecture was to be the stuff of Ayn Rand's Howard Rourke (from *The Fountainhead*, a book greatly admired by your author). The International Style was to be the new form of architecture even as it was, as an artnet.com commentary asserts, "indifferent to the particularities of human use."[1641]

Complaints about Bauhaus structures centered on such things as the Bauhaus's apparent "ignorance of all things a family needs to make a dwelling a home"; storage problems, structures that were difficult to clean, limitations on what could be done with furniture in the spaces provided; and flat, ugly, leaky roofs.[1642] Such structures were bereft of the things that Hitler thought important to the home: things such as gardens, garages, and child play areas. Some of the Bauhaus structures looked "like strangers from another planet. They seemed to have been influenced by science fiction as well as machine ideology,"[1643] says Donald Kuspit in "A Critical History of 20th-Century Art." Controversies surrounding the new architecture of the Bauhaus Movement were as acrimonious as was the criticism of atonal music and abstract painting,[1644] and deservedly so. E. Michael Jones, author of the book *Living Machines*, comments on modern culture and in particular the Bauhaus boxes that covered all of post-World War II Eastern Europe:

> Where, I wonder as we drive through Masuria [in northern Poland], is saturation bombing when we really need it? Saturation bombing would have been fine with me if it had only been used on the works and pomps of

the twentieth century. But, like the Oedipus Complex, Bauhaus architecture, moral relativism, contraception, deficit spending, the automobile, and cubism, saturation bombing was used as the twentieth century's revenge on the cultural legacy of the West.[1645]

Jones goes on to refer to the Bauhaus structures as "toxic waste."[1646] Such structures, as he also points out, had an air of "scientific rationality" so beloved by the Bolshevistic ideologues. Bauhaus was, as many claimed, *Kulturbolschewismus*.[1647] Nazis lumped all of the Bauhaus works under the terms "Bolshevik" and "Jewish." The flat roofs of the Bauhaus designs, claimed the Nazis, looked like Palestinian buildings, a claim that had credence because it was so.

Fest describes the new style trends as follows:

> Prefabricated housing, Le Corbusier's machines for living, the Bauhaus style, tubular steel furniture [so common during the 1950s]—the "technical matter-of-factness" on which such creations plumed themselves were a further threat to the traditionbound, who spoke of all this as "jailhouse style." The romantic hostility to the modern world also give rise to a large back-to-the country movement in the twenties.[1648]

Today, the city of Tel Aviv, built largely by some 130 Jewish-German architects who fled Nazi Germany, is the most concentrated representation of Bauhaus architecture of any city in the world. There is a Bauhaus museum in Tel Aviv that opened in 2008 to display Bauhaus-designed furnishings. The museum itself is built in a featureless Bauhaus style. A Bauhaus structure on Rothschild Boulevard is highlighted in several Tel Aviv tourist brochures. Bauhaus architecture is often termed "international style" and early Bauhaus adherents were internationalists who intentionally placed themselves in stark opposition to German nationalists.

All of the foregoing and more took place under the considerable influence of Jews in positions of political, social, and cultural authority during the Weimar Republic.

Adolf Hitler was appalled. And, we might ask, apologetic argumentation notwithstanding, why should he not have been?

Berlin, a Cesspool

For rightist Germans who regarded the various changes to their culture as detrimental, Jews were seen as being responsible for undermining both patriotic commitment and social cohesion. Jewish Dadaists were popular in cabarets shortly after the war, and they were not unstinting in their irreverence, derision, black humor, absurdity, and tastelessness in attacking traditional values. According to art historian Emily D. Bilski, "Sally Pinkus [a character who goes from social failure to renowned success] in 1916 would not have been out of place in one of the 'Jewish' skits of *Saturday Night Live* shown in New York in the 1980s."[1649] As one academic put it, Jews and their influence on politics and culture were seen as "the classic party of national decomposition."[1650] In 1923, Joseph Goebbels described the new cultural phenomenon of Berlin as follows:

> The heart turned to stone of this city. Here in the niches and corners of cafés, in the cabarets and bars, in the Soviet theaters and mezzanines, the spirit of the asphalt democracy is piled high. Here the politics of sixty-million diligent Germans is conducted.[1651]

Berlin was reduced to a cesspool of sexual licentiousness, a haven for aberrational misfits gathered from around the globe. Present-day child prostitution in Thailand is but nothing when compared to its popularity in Weimar Berlin; sexual tourism became a primary industry there. Transvestite balls were held, both women and boy prostitutes engaged in every form of perversion. Tourist guides highlighted the various dissolute establishments. Between 1921 and 1933, the city developed a reputation for debauchery unrivaled by any city before or since.

Author Otto Friedrich says that "Even the Rome of Suetonius had never known such orgies as the pervert balls of Berlin. . . ."[1652] Rightist speakers throughout Germany were able to rouse their crowds as they called for apocalyptic conquest of Berlin, that "Great Whore."[1653]

Unlike other European capitals such as Paris, Barcelona, and Amsterdam, where brothel districts were extensive but discreet, Berlin's debauchery was everywhere and was everywhere evident.

In the cabarets, drugs and prostitution were virtual monopolies for Jewish business interests. Jewish intellectuals celebrated the new cultural altering drifts. The mass media magnified the impact of everything from fads to radically leftist political ideas. Subcultures and club cultures nurtured gender-bending fashions and lifestyles, the Weimar era's equivalent of today's drug use, body piercing, tattoos, etc. The focus of cabarets was literary, mercilessly satirical, and politically aggressive. The Jewish role in the cabarets was that of owners, producers, and writers and performers who shaped and sustained the genre. Rudolf Nelson (Rudolf Lewysohn) was one of most prominent and influential composers and producers for cabarets.

It was also commonplace for product marketing to go hand in hand with stage productions in both legitimate theater and cabarets, reemphasizing the stereotypical focus of Jews on matters of profit. Bilski describes the marketing focus:

> Couture was not only central to the economy of Berlin, but it also was an area of business clearly dominated by Jewish firms, in terms of both manufacture and retail. . . . Thus is was hardly surprising that the Metropol [theater] revues did their best to promote the latest trends in outer and underwear. The height of glamour in the Metropol was embodied by Fritzi Massary (1882–1969), a dazzling soprano from a Viennese Jewish family who was the star of the shows. She not only displayed her great talents as a singer and comedienne, but she also appeared in the latest *haute couture*. . . . The performers of lesser parts likewise had a role to play in the fashion show. A song like "What the Fashionable Lady Needs" was not just a tentative striptease number that showed the style of shoes, stockings, garters,

chemises, and corsets that "a woman of the world" and "a woman of today" were expected to have.... It also promoted the types of commodities that were manufactured and retailed in the most "Jewish" sector of the Berlin economy.[1654]

The writer Erich Kastner succinctly described the whole of the happenings in Berlin: "In the east there is crime; in the center the con men hold sway; in the north resides misery, in the west lechery; and everywhere—the decline." It was all *so* depressing, and it was seemingly all *so Jewish* in its making.

Goebbels expressed his thoughts on the subject as follows:

> The eternal repetition of corruption and decay, of failing ingenuity and genuine creative power, of inner emptiness and despair, with the patina of a Zeitgeist sunk to the level of the most repulsive pseudoculture: that is what parades its essence, what does its mischief all around the Gedächtniskirche. One would so gladly believe that it is the national elite stealing day and night from the dear Lord on Tauenzien Avenue. It is only the Israelites.[1655]

Goebbels also vented his frustration when he wrote that:

> The German people is alien and superfluous here. To speak in the national language is to be nearly conspicuous. Pan-Europe, the *Internationale*, jazz, France and Piscator—those are the watchwords.[1656]

Gay, in his book *Weimar Culture: The Outsider as Insider*, quotes Austrian writer Stefan Zeig, who summarized Berlin's cultural degeneracy during the inflationary period like this:

> Berlin... transformed itself into the Babel of the world. Bars, amusement parks, pubs shot up like mushrooms. What we had seen in Austria proved to be merely a mild and timid prelude to this witches' Sabbath, for the Germans brought to perversion all their vehemence and love of system. Made-up boys with artificial waistlines promenaded along the Kurfüstendamm—and not

professionals alone: every high school student wanted to make some money, and in the darkened bars one could see high public officials and high financiers courting drunken sailors without shame. . . . Amid the general collapse of values, a kind of insanity took hold of precisely those middle-class circles which had hitherto been unshakable in their order. Young ladies proudly boasted that they were perverted; to be suspected of virginity at sixteen would have been considered a disgrace in every school in Berlin.[1657]

Zeig assigns blame for the cultural degeneracy to German perversion. He is wrongheaded on that score—the source was Jewish exploitation of human perversion. There was nothing whatever that was particularly German about it, but there was lots that was Jewish.

Otto Friedrich, in *Before the Deluge,* quotes English essayist Sir Stephen Harold Spender as saying: "Nothing expressed the cynical relationship between the grim architecture of the feckless population more than the belief of the Berlin population that one of the stone lions outside the palace at the end of the Unter den Linden roared whenever a virgin walked by."[1658] Spender's comment is not unlike current-day U.S. humorists who contend that a virgin is an ugly second-grader.

Anita Berber—A Personification of Berlin

The cabarets and sexual licentiousness that attended them were personified in the person of Anita Berber in the early to mid-1920s. Berber, under the tutelage of her many Jewish friends[*] and her

---

[*] Her Jewish friends included Richard Oswald, Leo and Lotta Lania (of Mack the Knife fame), Fred Marion, Charlotte Berend-Corinth, Ludwig Levy-Lenz, Valeska Gert, Magnus Hirschfeld, Fritz Grünbaum, Dora Kallmus, Vicki Baum and Henri, Baron Sebastian von Droste, Dr. Henrich Klapper. Gordon, Mel, *The Seven Addictions and Five Professions of Anita Berber: Weimar Berlin's Priestess of Depravity,* Feral House, Los Angeles, 2006, 169–71. The foregoing characters all made individual contributions to the corruption of Weimar culture.

Jewish husband, was briefly famous for her outrageous, sexually explicit dance routines and equally outrageous lifestyle (Marlene Dietrich was one of her many sexcapades).

She was something of an exotic, drug-laden, bisexual "saint of whoredom"[1659] with a cute body. She was also entirely without moral fabric. Mel Gordon describes her thusly:

> Berber consciously broke every social and theatrical convention of her time, and then proclaimed some startline [sic] theory to justify her provocative, outlaw behavior. She haunted the Friedrichstadt quarter of Berlin, appearing in hotel lobbies, nightclubs, and casinos, radiantly naked except for an elegant sable wrap that shadowed her gaunt shoulders and pair of patent-leather pumps.[1660]

She once urinated in the drink of a club patron who was paying insufficient attention to her dance routine.[1661]

Google	URL
Anita Berber	http://www.google.com/imgres?imgurl=http://www.wornthrough.com/blog/wp-content/uploads/2011/01/berbercocaine380.jpg&imgrefurl=http://www.wornthrough.com/2011/01/11/anarchists-of-style-anita-berber-part-2/&h=307&w=164&tbnid=4YEBSMbDQIZnjM:&zoom=1&tbnh=186&tbnw=99&usg=__tJo1dI1mvYGqBA4QrKyZY3ASFuA=&docid=gzx8O_j4FvMQDM&itg=1&sa=X&ei=QLHgU5WPIYqhyAS2sILIDQ&ved=0CH8Q_B0wCg 8/2/14

Richard Evans, in *The Coming of the Third Reich*, comments on Berber and her milieu as follows:

> Visiting big bands and chorus lines such as the Tiller Girls enlivened the Berlin scene, while the more daring could spend an evening at a club such as the Eldorado, "a supermarket of eroticism," as the popular [Jewish] composer Friedrich Hollaender called it, and watch Anita Berber perform pornographic dances with names such as "Cocaine" and "Morphium" to an audience liberally sprinkled with transvestites and homosexuals,

until her early death in 1928 from drug abuse. Cabaret shows added to all this an element of biting, anti-authoritarian political satire and aroused pompous conservatives to anger with their jokes about the "nationalist and religious sentiments and practices of Christians and Germans," as one of them angrily complained.[1662]

Berber, like today's cultural icons, knew how to get attention—to use the proper marketing term, she knew how to "differentiate" herself, she knew how to be unique. Gordon approvingly asserts that "Among Central Europe's countless femme fatales, only Anita Berber was noted for her unvarnished belief in artistic authenticity and her rootless, nearly unquenchable, lust for ineffable sensations." Adolf Hitler would not have seen her antics as "artistic authenticity;" he would have seen them for what they were, an all-too-familiar representation of the degeneration of vaunted German values and probity, and he would have seen Jews in the background of it all.

Gordon informs us in his book *The Seven Addictions and Five Professions of Anita Berber: Weimar Berlin's Priestess of Depravity* that Naked Dance was rooted in the late nineteenth-century Germanic revolt against all things rigidly bourgeois and "hypocritically Christian."[1663] He might have added that it was Jews who led the revolt, and it was Jews as well who determined what things were "hypocritically Christian." It all happened in Germany, but it was not German, nor was it Christian.

Weimar Berlin was perhaps the place where the beginnings of a modern trend emerged: the trend toward the celebration of the antics of sexual deviates. "For us," says Gordon in another of his books, *Voluptuous Panic*, "she [Berber] was the first postmodern woman: a vibrant Marilyn Monroe with the devious, adolescent mind of Norman Mailer [Monroe's Jewish playwright husband]. Her life needed to be celebrated." Indeed. We must suppose that what Gordon calls the "artistic authenticity" and "sophisticated choreography" she brought to nude dancing along with her "smutty poetry-recitations-in-the-nude," and "sacred dildos and morphine syringes as props,"[1664] somehow stemmed from Berlin's previous staidness. Or perhaps, as Gordon records elsewhere, she needed to be celebrated in recognition of her "Depravity, Horror, and Ecstasy," or her "enduring 'Repertoire of the Damned.'"[1665] The woman was a toy for perverts.

By the late 1920s Berber was utterly spent. She was used up and all but completely abandoned. Taken ill with tuberculosis and the cumulative effects of illegal drug use while performing in the Middle East she called upon her Berlin friends for assistance. They took up a collection providing her with enough money to return to the city but that was the extent of their generosity. She died in 1928 at the age of twenty-nine. "The cult goddess Astarte, the avatar of female desire and perversity," Gordon laments, "had finally succumbed to the stimulants and addictions that made her the single most decadent personality in a world without moral boundaries or legal restriction." But at the bottom of it all she was actually just a cultist of the superficial: she was the Weimar era's version of beautiful womanhood discarded by the "freedoms" of liberalism.

Berber was buried in a pauper's grave outside Berlin. The lease on her grave site eventually expired and her very gravestone was thereafter removed. Her worth had been depleted. She no longer had any commercial value. Neither her husband nor her friends would be put to the cost of doing her a better resting place, nor a permanent one. By the time of her death she had become a "carrion soul that even the hyenas ignored."[1666] She deserved her fate. Many of her friends later relocated to Hollywood where she was created anew.

The point to be made in the foregoing is not that of the slutty antics of a single performer—the point is that Jewish interests created the foundation for, the celebration even, of moral cretins of the Berber type.

It was the owners of the cabarets, the theaters, and the popular press and its cultural critics, entirely Jewish, that so encouraged society to replace German probity with unbridled licentiousness. Apologists provide us with a wide array of reasons for Berlin's and Germany's moral decline, the loss of the war being high among them (the cause-effect of that contention is not clear except by way of Freudian transference claims, which are themselves inane), but it is a rarity indeed for the popular press to acknowledge the leadership role of Jewish interests that provided Berlin with the title of "wicked Berlin, the international sex-tourist Mecca of the Twenties and early Thirties."[1667] It was the Jews of Weimar Germany, not the Germans, who created what Gordon delights in calling the "human swamp of unfettered appetites and twisted prurient proclivities," this "prime breeding ground for evil."[1668] This was Berlin, a city that had previously been best known for its staid morality, and, of course, militarism by way of its Prussianism. And it was Jewish dominance of this culture that so enraged right-wing Germans, including, of course, Adolf Hitler.

* * * *

Purely cultural issues aside, Jews were also the leading dissidents with respect to common political values and the German psyche. A Jewish professor of constitutional law became the subject of riots after remarking to his students that the Treaty of Versailles was no worse than the treaties of Brest-Litovsk and Bucharest. It was a true enough assertion, but it was badly out of touch with German sentiment of the times.[1669]

Similar wounds to the German psyche were salted by such people as Freiburg University law professor Hermann Kantorowicz with his ex post facto criticism of Bismarck's seizure of Alsace-Lorraine by Germany after the Franco-Prussian War (Alsace-Lorraine had been annexed by France in the seventeenth century and had been retaken by Germany in 1871). Another Jewish university faculty member, Ernst Cohn, created political outrage with his proposal to offer asylum in Germany to Leon Trotsky.[1670]

Among the most prominent dissidents of the day were Theodor Lessing, Emil Julius Gumbel, Carl von Ossietzky, and Kurt Tucholsky, who make up our next subjects of discussion.

* * * *

During the election for Reich president in 1925, the noted Jewish philosopher and professor at the Hanover Technical Institute, Theodor Lessing (Lessing is credited with coining the term, "Jewish self-hatred," the attempt to kill the Jew within oneself), created a scandal when he published an article in a foreign newspaper in which he brutally attacked Field Marshal Paul von Hindenburg's presidential candidacy. Hindenburg, by then aged seventy-seven and still venerated by many a German as a war hero, was attacked by Lessing as a "moronic zero," "inhuman," a "simpleton," and a "ferocious wolf." He went on to claim that if elected, Hindenburg would prove to be a Nero in office. In actual fact, Hindenburg served honorably and constitutionally and was to the very last, even in his last befuddled state, among the most steadfast opponents of Hitler's rise to power.

The radical right wing made political capital with Lessing's words, using the article to further the cause of anti-Semitism throughout the nation.[1671] Their task was made easier because to the average German Hindenburg's election to the presidency was seen as an opportunity to stabilize the republic. He was seen as something of a kaiser-substitute. A good many ordinary Germans also thought that he would be able to protect the country against Bolshevism and its violent Socialist rabble-rousers as well as unscrupulous Jewish financiers;[1672] and it must be said that those categories of people were the most strident opponents of his candidacy.

* * * *

Emil Julius Gumbel was a Jewish professor of mathematical statistics at Heidelberg University. His political essence was that of Communism, and he battled tirelessly and sometimes untruthfully against his nationalistic rightist opponents.[1673] In 1926, he worked for several months in Moscow and for a while considered permanent residence there. He again visited Moscow in 1932 but ultimately decided not to remain. Gumbel was not averse to statistical misrepresentation to make his point. His readers, dazzled by his statistical brilliance, expected and believed that he painted truthful statistical pictures.[1674] But Gumbel was a Communist through and through; if ever he told the truth it was only by way of a slip of the tongue.

Gumbel published a series of pamphlets for which he gained notoriety by way of lawsuits against him after he came out with a paper titled "Germany's Secret Rearmament" (*Deutschlands geheime Rüstungen*), revealing the Weimar government's noncompliance with the Treaty of Versailles. The paper was passed to the French, English, and Polish governments by the Jewish front organization, the League of Human Rights, an organization of which Gumbel was a member.[*] Picking up on his notoriety, Gumbel also gave speeches at French universities in which he blamed and pummeled Germany for starting World War I. It was claimed that he declared at a public gathering in 1924 that "dead German soldiers had *'fallen on the field of dishonor'*"[†][1675] (Italics are in the original). As Gumbel was attacked within Germany by right-wing elements, he succored protection from people such as Albert Einstein and Georg Bernard.

In the political realm, Gumbel is best remembered for his statistical analysis of the German judiciary system after World War I. He claimed, and supported with appropriately biased statistics (creation of "facts," that for both our historians and popular media moguls, "are too good to check"),[1676] that the German judiciary was bloated with radical rightist members. The charge was false. Gumbel managed to create his statistical "proof" by including such people who had fallen as the result of revolutionary turmoil, such as Rosa Luxemburg and others: such people were deemed to be "victims of the rightists"[1677] in Gumbel's account of things. Moreover, it was common during the Weimar years for the leftists to make outrageous charges against opponents in order to bleed

---

[*] The league was directed by the Jews Witting, Grelling, Bernstein, Hirschfeld, Heymann, Gumbel, and Wulfsohn—it was a Jewish clique.

[†] The charge is somewhat misleading. Gumbel had asked for a moment of silence to honor the war dead, saying "who, I shall not say, fell on the field of dishonor, but who died in the most horrible way."

them financially and politically. The Nazi Party was subjected to 40,000 such lawsuits during the six-year period between 1921 and 1927.[1678] Such charges, when exposed to the demands of evidence, often fell far, far short and resulted in light sentences or dismissal of the charges. Gumbel bemoaned such findings and ascribed them to a rightist judiciary. The numerous charges brought against the Nazi Propaganda Minister Joseph Goebbels in the late 1920s and early 1930s are also illustrative of such numerous and highly inflated charges—Goebbels was often faced with dozens of criminal and civil lawsuits at a time, but the courts commonly discharged them or imposed particularly light fines, and this outcome occurred even when the judges were Jewish.[1679]

As early as January 1919, the two leftist parties, the SPD and USPD, not to mention the KPD, had roughly 50 percent of the electorate behind them. According to historian Walter Laqueur, "the left-liberal intelligentsia predominated during the 1920s."[1680] By the time Hitler came to power, fully 50.2 percent of the lawyers were Jews,[1681] as were 30 percent of the judges,[1682] which, given their leftist leanings, seems to suggest the direct opposite of Gumbel's charge and statistical findings.

While it is true that the civil service was not purged of people disliked by the radical Left, it is also true that these people did little or nothing to further rightist causes. As was seen during the rightist Kapp putsch, the civil service, many of whom were military veterans, remained entirely aloof—neither the judiciary nor the civil service was inclined toward anti-Semitism or even antisocialism at that time. The civil service, as Walter Laqueur puts it, "was not so much anti-democratic as a-democratic."[1683] The worst charge that can be laid at their door is that they were simply indifferent to the political machinations of the various parties, causes, and thrusts: they functioned on behalf of the state whether that state was led by a kaiser, a president, or a führer. The position of such people was handily summarized by Field Marshal Wilhelm Keitel at Nuremberg: "I am a soldier," he said, "and I worked for the Kaiser, under Ebert, Hindenburg, and Hitler, all the same way. . . ."[1684] Leftists, and therefore Jews, claimed Gumbel, could not get a fair hearing before a German court; a charge that was wholly untrue. According to Sarah Gordon, for example, Jews as early as 1903 represented only 0.74 percent of the labor force in Prussia, yet 27 percent of all Prussian lawyers, 10 percent of apprenticed lawyers, 47 percent of magistrates, and 30 percent of all higher ranks of the judiciary were Jews.[1685] They and their sympathizers in these desirable and influential jobs could only have increased during the Weimar years when the floodgates for Jewish dominance were opened wide. Prussia was dominated throughout the 1920s by the SPD and its numerous Jewish functionaries.

Gumbel's claims, on close examination, are fallacious. Donald L. Niewyk, in his book, *The Jews in Weimar Germany*, points out that the courts of that period were especially harsh with Jew-haters: "Every known case brought to harass Jews or to cripple their self-defense activities," says Niewyk, "was thrown out of court."[1686] Such treatment could hardly have been the case if the courts were so dominated by radical rightists as claimed by Gumbel.

Yet it remains that Gumbel's claims serve as a sort of semiofficial representation of the German judiciary after World War I. Gumbel, an accomplished statistician to be sure, used his stature as such to offer up a USPD, *Weltbühne* version of reality. Jewish apologists frequently quote Gumbel in support of their anti-German contentions. It should be noted as well that Gumbel had little compunction about placing his eminence as a statistician in the service of his political objectives: the application of statistics, wrote Gumbel, "belongs to the ideological class struggle."[1687]

* * * *

Die Weltbühne

Before going on to discuss the characters Kurt Tucholsky and Carl von Ossietzky it will be helpful to first understand more about the journal with which they were so intimately connected, to wit: *Die Weltbühne* (The World Stage). The magazine was founded, funded, and run by Jews, many of whom were not even German;

they were instead natives of Austria, Hungary, Ukraine, and Poland. "The famous 'Berlin style' of the 1920's," says Istvan Deak, "was largely a product of these non-Berliners who forged new traditions in the theater, in art, in literature, and in journalism"[1688]—*Die Weltbühne* was emblematic of that observation. At least forty-two of its sixty-eight permanent staff writers were Jewish, and perhaps even more. Two staff members were half Jews. Several of the non-Jews on the staff were married to Jewish women. Like their number at other leftist publications, however, only a few openly acknowledged their Jewishness.[1689] *Die Weltbühne* conducted a campaign of media violence directed at German culture.[1690] Like the rest of Weimar's left-wing intellectuals, writers for the *Weltbühne*, says Deak, "combined all the characteristics repugnant to the Germanic ideologists: Francophile, Jewish, Western rebellious, progressive, democratic, rationalist, socialist, liberal, and cosmopolitan."[1691] With respect to culture, Deak points out that the *Weltbühne* sought to have Germany mimic France:

> [F]riendship with France was sought for the beneficial effects that French culture might have on the Germans. With a nostalgia, envy, and admiration so characteristic of the Central European literati, the writers of the *Weltbühne* looked to Paris for salvation . . . they admired the French for all that they felt the Germans lacked.[1692]

Put another way, *Die Weltbühne* was, from the moment of its founding and throughout its existence (1905–1933), entirely anti-German.

The journal was typical of leftist intellectual publications that preach workers' gospels while simultaneously viewing them with contempt for their lack of intellect and discernment—for these people the workers were mere tools by which they hoped to achieve power. While they railed against the Nazis and other rightists as beholden to big business (which was untrue), they were themselves beholden to Moscow and to rich Jews who provided much of their financing. In the 1930s, they all admired and justified Stalin, which is a telling thing about their own discernment.

"Die Weltbühne!" wrote gay rights activist Kurt Hiller . . . "It wasn't a journal. It was an institution!"[1693] Carl von Ossietzky was the editor in chief (1927–1933) of this almost exclusively Jewish and most prominent cultural magazine of the Weimar era. Under his leadership the magazine served both the cultural and political milieu of Weimar Germany. "Around 1930 . . ." continued Hiller, "it was considered uncouth not to have read the latest issue of the *Die Weltbühne*." Like Hiller, who was himself one of the journal's contributors, the readership of *Die Weltbühne* were intellectuals, "pacifists," antimilitarists, and antinationalists; people, who, like the authors themselves, came from bourgeois backgrounds and had little or no contact with the masses in their daily lives. They did not know any actual peasants or soldiers, but they knew with certainty that all peasants and all soldiers were ruthless clods. Bourgeois themselves, it was nevertheless the case that, in accordance with their Marxist convictions, it was only the bourgeois that they despised more than the peasant. They supported the works of people like Otto Dix and his depictions of stupid bourgeois and their stifling ordinariness.[1694] Their hate was as great as the Nazis but less focused—they created too many enemies. These were people who thought that Judaism and German patriotism were mutually exclusive. They sought a united, internationalized Europe and were therefore disdainful, to say the least, of German nationalism.

Other popular Jewish-left publications included *Die Zukunft* (The Future) and *Die Fackel* (The Torch)—"both were highly controversial and their [Jewish] editors fiercely hated,"[1695] says historian Istvan Deak. And both of these publications, like *Die Weltbühne*, shared a predilection for savage commentary. Still, *Die Weltbühne* stood well above the rest in terms of importance in cultural criticism. It was *the* cultural journal. The publication only reached about 1,500 subscribers, but they were exclusively members of the literati and therefore the thought leaders of the country, the creators of "social facts." With such a meager number of subscribers, the magazine was dependent upon contributions from owners and sympathizers such as Eduard Goldbeck for its operations. Goldbeck was the Jewish editor of the German *Wochenblatt* (Weekly News) in Chicago.[1696]

According to a Wikipedia article on the subject:

> More than 2,600 authors wrote for the paper between 1905 and 1933. In addition to Jacobsohn, Tucholsky, and Ossietzky, the contributors included prominent writers and journalists like Erich Kästner, Alfred Polgar, Arnold Zweig, Lion Feuchtwanger, and Else Lasker-Schüler. Other regular contributors included Julius Bab, Erich Dombrowski, Axel Eggebrecht, Hellmut von Gerlach, Moritz Heimann, Kurt Hiller, Erich Mühsam, Rudolf Arnheim, Richard Lewinsohn, Fritz Sternberg and Heinrich Ströbel.[1697]

That is, almost all of *Die Weltbühne* writers were Jews, and to Hitler's mind, they were birds of feather, cultural vultures.

The literati of the period, and most prominently Kurt Hiller, had argued as early as 1915 that the literati alone, who were predominantly Jewish, was entitled to world leadership. He went so far as to publish a manifesto that demanded the immediate transfer of power to the literati. The manifesto also called for freedom of the press but only with the stipulation that the rightist opposition press first be suppressed; he sought, that is, a Bolshevistic conception of a free press,[1698] one without opposing views. Hiller also called for government protection of the psychiatric profession, the suppression of parliaments if they opposed the will of the intellect, and a House of Lords composed of intellectuals, and Logokratie, the rule of philosopher-kings.[1699] Such were the thought processes of these *Weltbühne* men.

Soon after the armistice, *Die Weltbühne* demanded an immediate peace treaty at any cost and recognition of Germany's responsibility for the war.[1700] Both of these demands were, naturally, vehemently opposed by the right wing. After the treaty was signed, *Die Weltbühne* called for full compliance, in part in order to befriend France and thereby have Germans benefit from "superior French culture," again enraging right-wing opposition.

The truckling of leftist Jews toward France was limitless. It is exemplary of *Die Weltbühne* logic that it bemoaned Germany's outrage at the French-Belgian incursion in the Ruhr:

> Germany could have fulfilled her obligations in the past, Morus [Richard Lewinsohn] wrote in the *Weltbühne* during the first days of the Ruhr occupation, if only she had worked harder and placed her wares on the world market. To satisfy France would have been both a moral obligation and a good strategy. . . . France erred morally by ordering a violent measure; it was up to the Germans to score a point by showing more generosity.[1701]

The foregoing is roughly equivalent to asking present-day Palestinians or Gazans to show "more generosity" toward Israel. The New Testament version of *Die Weltbühne's* position on the French incursion into the Ruhr would be that Germany should not only have turned the other cheek, she should have given fishes to the French. Right-wing Germans thought otherwise. Hitler was among them.

Throughout World War I and the 1920s, *Die Weltbühne* took an unyielding pacifist position. The veil of pacifism so long held by *Die Weltbühne* was finally lifted in the early 1930s as it advocated the creation of armed antifascist units in the factories and the trade unions.[1702] The *Weltbühne* position of "we must violently attack fascists," moreover, was a call for Gentile unionists to do the fist-to-fist stuff on behalf of Jews. In effect, the *Weltbühne* was singing "Onward, Christian Soldiers."

*   *   *   *

Carl von Ossietzky was a committed "pacifist" and the editor of *Die Weltbühne*. When the war broke out he immediately denounced it in Marxist language saying it was a "manifestation of imperialism and of predatory capitalism."[1703] When the Marxist revolution of November 1918 broke out, he was brought to "paroxysms of enthusiasm" and called for struggle without compromise.¹⁷⁰⁴ Later, when he broke with the republic, his stated positions paralleled those of the KPD, and he actively participated in Communist-inspired undertakings.¹⁷⁰⁵

Like Albert Einstein, Ossietzky was willing to compromise his pacifism on behalf of Jewish interests: Einstein was willing to abandon his pacifism in defense of Israel; Ossietzky advocated violence against the Nazis.¹⁷⁰⁶ The connection between Einstein and Ossietzky was that they were both pacifists with a twist— according to their stance, armed violence should never be countenanced except in defense of Jewry.

Ossietzky campaigned mightily against Prussia's voting system and the church. As a militant anticlericalist, he desired that the state be based on unconditional atheism.¹⁷⁰⁷ Both the church and the army, he claimed, were corrupters of society.¹⁷⁰⁸ A weak church, he thought, would deprive the Prussian government of its strongest support. His attitude toward Germany as a whole is probably best summarized by his widely acclaimed criticism of the German demigod, Goethe; saying that Germans celebrate Goethe "not as poet and prophet, but above all as an opium."¹⁷⁰⁹ He denounced Germany's participation in World War I in 1915, praised Rosa Luxemburg's stance, and otherwise remained an unyielding critic of everything German while simultaneously proclaiming a great love for it.

Ossietzky, like several other Jews of the era, also earned historical fame for publishing revelations about Weimar Germany's secret rearmament program. In March 1929, he published an article by Walter Kreiser that was part of his campaign in opposition to Germany's secret rearmament. From the viewpoint of the post-Nazi era we can, of course, look upon his actions as representative of great moral courage (he was a 1935 recipient of the Nobel Peace Prize),* but given Germany's situation

---

*The prize was at the time highly politicized, and it remains so, as evidenced by it having been awarded to President Barak Obama before he had done anything to earn it. Ossietzky's candidacy was pushed by Berthold Jacob and the German League for Human Rights (a Jewish-led league that featured Ernst Toller and Albert Einstein in its leadership). Hellmut von Gerlach orchestrated a worldwide letter-writing campaign—all

of abject weakness at the time, coupled with the fact that the program was—like it or not—a closely guarded military secret, Germans were understandably outraged by his treasonous act, or at the very least, an act perceived as treasonous.

When Ossietzky was accused of treason for having published details of the secret rearmament program, the worldwide Jewish press came to his defense with a full-court press of journalistic outrage. The *Neue Zürcher Zeitung*, the *Manchester Guardian*, *The Times*, *Le Monde*, and *The New York Evening Post* were among the members of the influential foreign press that came out in support of him.[1710] Thus, apologists were aplenty when Ossietzky was charged. The press's defense of him and others was not dissimilar to its defense of other Jews charged or found guilty of various crimes: Alfred Dreyfus, the Rosenbergs, and now Jonathan Pollard and Roman Polanski, among them.

In August 1929, Ossietzky was charged with betraying military secrets, was tried in November 1931, found guilty, and given the exceedingly light sentence of eighteen months in Spandau Prison. He was released after only seven months.[1711] While in prison, he was treated with great courtesy, even to the extent of being provided with books and paper by the warden, enabling him to continue to write and publish. Interestingly, while writing from prison, Ossietzky took on the pseudonym Thomas Murner, the name of a Franciscan polemicist (1475–1673) who satirized Lutherans in his writings. Murner also abused the Catholic Church.[1712] It was Ossietzky in his purest form.

In addition to his excoriation of everything German, Ossietzky championed German pluralism, the "emancipation" of German women, birth control, and drastic change in the sexual mores of the country. On rare occasions when he offered praise, it was inevitably praise in support of fellow Jews or spiritual Jews such as the brothers Mann.

---

of which influenced the award of the prize to Ossietzky. Two members of the prize committee resigned in protest. Joseph Stalin was twice nominated for the prize, 1945 and 1948. The organization of the prize committee was later altered to depoliticize the award—it apparently did not work.

Ironically, Ossietzky's rearmament revelations were responsible for bringing down General Hans von Seeckt. Seeckt was replaced by General Kurt von Schleicher who would ultimately be appointed chancellor, and then make a mess of things, not the least by setting the precedent for a military dictatorship in Germany. Schleicher was eventually fired, calling Hitler to power; Hitler then built on the dictatorial foundation that had been laid by Schleicher.

* * * *

Another of the most prominent Jewish critics of German society was Kurt Tucholsky. Tucholsky was a journalist and satirist about whom the Nazis would justifiably claim: "Nothing which was sacred for the German people was sacred to him." He wrote for a number of Jewish-owned publications, *Die Weltbühne* being the most famous and influential. Walter Laqueur, in *Weimar–A Cultural History 1918–1933,* says that "Tucholsky was the most brilliant and most fertile German satirist since Heine."[1713] It was also said of him that his very lack of German patriotism is what made him a "true European." Tucholsky scolded his fellow literati for their patriotic scruples.[1714] According to MacDonald, he was a man who "wore his subversive heart on his sleeve"[1715] and he was at the forefront of *Die Weltbühne's* attacks on Germans. Niewyk tells us that "In the words of Naumann's newspaper: 'A single Tucholsky breeds millions of anti-Semites.'"[1716] He was best known for the way in which he "flayed Germans and German values mercilessly."

Like so many of his Jewish compatriots of the period, Tucholsky's fiction tended to the erotic and lurid. His very first book, *Rheinsberg*, was published in 1912 when eroticism was still essentially taboo; the book was an account of an erotic escapade of a young Berlin couple. It was one of many books of such genre that contributed to the "revolution of naturalness."[1717]

Istvan Deak says that Tucholsky "was obsessed by the idea that the Germans 'deserved' a tyranny."[1718] His attitude in this respect was entirely in keeping with his utter abomination for the entirety of German citizenry: "These people, he felt, were too deeply committed to their estates and institutions to be viewed individualistically."[1719] They needed to be condemned en masse—it was a stance to which Hitler adhered to with respect to Jews. It is a stance that Israel now applies in the West Bank and Gaza. It was said by one articulate enemy of Tucholsky in 1937 that: "of all the Jewish literati, who, between 1918 and 1933, molded public political opinion in Germany, none could equal the effectiveness, in breadth and depth, of Kurt Tucholsky."[1720]

"[W]e have fought . . . hate with hate, violence with violence, fist with fist," wrote Tucholsky in 1919.[1721] But let us be clear: Tucholsky did not actually fight "fist with fist." His was a fight of pen and paper, a fight confined to the written word. He, like other intellectuals of his era, says Deak, could "plan a revolution, proclaim that God was dead, propagate the most dangerous ideas, but always and only on paper."[1722] Even during the war he did not actually fight: drafted into the army in 1915, he served as a manager of a barbed wire depot on a quiet sector of the eastern front, as a librarian at a school for aviators, and as a police commissioner in occupied Rumania. He never fired a weapon or was ever in serious danger.[1723] Fist with fist? Not that man.

Some of Tucholsky's writings bring to mind his racist bent. In one article, "Face of a German," he describes Germans stereotypically as inherently evil with certain physical characteristics that highlight their evilness: a "rather thick-set head, a none too high forehead; cold, small eyes, a nose that likes to lower itself into a drinking glass,"[1724] etc. Tucholsky's position on this and other matters, of course, was not to be taken as anti-German or anti-Gentile or even stereotyping—he was a Jew writing about an "other," a stranger, a Gentile, a goyim; his pronouncements were to be accepted by readers as simple fact. We need not wonder about the reaction of the Jewish community if similar phraseology were applied to Jews by a prominent Gentile. Naumann's newspaper had it right: Tucholsky was a man who bred millions of anti-Semites.

In addition to Tucholsky, fellow Jews Siegfried Jacobsohn and Kurt Hiller joined with others to attack everything that German patriots and moderate republicans held sacred.[1725] Jacobsohn was an Old Testament fanatic who molded the image of the radical cultural leftists. He was also obstinate, ruthless, and unduly suspicious—his extremism, says Deak, was genuine.[1726] Hiller was influential in support of the early German gay rights movement. In 1929, he assumed chairmanship of the Scientific Humanitarian Committee from fellow gay activist Magnus Hirschfeld.[1727]

Tucholsky and the others were also closely affiliated with the SPD, campaigning for it in 1911. His writings, especially his incessant excoriation of the German military, earned him huge commendations in leftist circles. His writings also earned for him the abiding hatred of Adolf Hitler and other radical rightist Germans.

Blasphemy and biting sarcasm were central to his repertoire. He was also militantly anticlerical. In addition to the churches and the military, he viciously attacked the police and the legal system. His contempt for German culture and tradition was palpable. Ultimately, however, he was but one among many of the left-wing Jewish intelligentsia members of the SPD and USPD/KPD who were active political participants therein. While Tucholsky's writings inflamed hatred for him personally, they also served to impassion the radical right wing against Jews as a whole; for Tucholsky was a Jewish writer writing exclusively for Jewish-owned publications with anti-Germanism as their veritable mastheads.

Tucholsky, it was said, sought to "sweep away with an iron broom all that is rotten in Germany."[1728] And for Tucholsky, everything dear to a German was rotten. He wrote that the German spirit was poisoned beyond recovery and could not be improved. Of the German military, he said, "There is no secret of the German army I would not hand over readily to a foreign power."[1729] He and his cohorts, of course, were to be the arbiters of good and bad in German society. In 1921, he wittily claimed that "Germans had two passions: beer and anti-Semitism." "The beer," he said, "was twenty-eight proof, but the antisemitism was a hundred proof."[1730]

To the extent that some Germans were indeed anti-Semitic, Tucholsky and his ilk only served to reinforce their thought process. At the bottom of it all, Tucholsky was an exemplar of hate.

Like Walter Rathenau, and the Protocols of the Learned Elders of Zion, Tucholsky believed that the world was ruled by a small clique of people: "'Travel across the world from the North Pole to the South Pole'—wrote Tucholsky—'you will find that everything takes place among two hundred people.'"[1731] Rathenau thought it was three hundred. Herzl believed that the political history of humanity is made by only a few people, leaders who arrange among themselves, and then impose on others the content of political history.[1732] Such drivel from Tucholsky could not help but be connected to similar claims by Rathenau and the Protocols, except that Rathenau and the Protocols specified the race of the rulers: they were Jews. Hitler, too, thought that the world was ruled by a select subset of Jews: "300 Rathenaus who all know each other, who guide the history of the world over the heads of Kings and Presidents."[1733] Tucholsky helped ferment and reinforce such nonsense. The totality of his rants had no effect other than to breed still more anti-Semites. In 1935 he killed himself.

Education, Judiciary, and the Economy

It was common throughout Europe in the seventeenth and eighteenth centuries, as well as the first half of the twentieth century, for education to be closely tied to religious teachings. Great debates and political upheaval occurred in France as that country sought to rid itself of the dominance of the Catholic Church in the sphere of education. In Germany, the *Kulturkampf* instituted by Bismarck in 1871 and lasting through 1887 was the German equivalent of France's struggle to rid itself of the power of Catholicism in both education and society as a whole. While Germany was mostly Protestant, Catholics nevertheless continued to hold great sway in both matters of education and in German culture, generally. This was especially so in Bavaria but was also true to a lesser extent elsewhere in the country. As Christians squabbled with Christians about which faction was to be dominant in molding the minds of children, they remained united in the idea of a need for "Christian teachers for Christian pupils."[1734] Religious Jews already enjoyed Jewish teachers for Jewish pupils but secular Jews fumed from their inability to hold teaching positions for Christian students in the primary schools. There were some such strictures at the university level as well, but the restrictions there were not nearly so absolute. To breech such barriers, Jewish-dominated municipalities like Berlin sought to appoint teachers according to merit[1735] rather than religiosity. There were not, of course, any Christian teachers with merit of the kind that would enable them to teach in Jewish schools, since, for example, such candidates could not read or write in Yiddish or Hebrew. The merit issue, then, was entirely one-sided and entirely to the benefit of Jews.

At the university level, even in the presence of what strictures that did exist, Germans hotly complained that the sons of Germans were being excluded from prestigious schools in favor of Jews. Tens of thousands of Germany's talented sons, it was claimed, could no longer go to school. Christians wailed against raising an "alien people" at the expense of Christian children.[1736] Their complaints went unanswered. The whole of it was not much different than the U.S. today, such as at Harvard where Gentiles, who make up 73 percent of the population, comprise only 45 percent of the student body, while Jews who make up 2.4 percent of our population make up 27 percent of the student body. Jews in higher education was once touched upon by Albert Einstein, who remarked that "the Israelites had spent the past two millennia of the exile preparing for their university exams."[1737] Germans often quipped that *"Doktor ist ein jüdisher Vorname,"* Doctor is a Jewish first name,[1738] emphasizing the dominant place that Jews had achieved in the country's academia and society, but even more so the emphasis that Jews placed on education and their aptitude to benefit from it.

Jews campaigned emphatically for the principle that all career areas, including those in education, should be open to those with the requisite talent—that is, on the basis of meritocracy. "The paradox that this campaigning created," says Pulzer, "was that effective pressure required organization, and organization drew attention to [the] peculiarity and separateness"[1739] of Jews. With time, organization, and the power of money, politics, and cultural suasion, Jews became increasingly prominent in Germany's educational system at a cost to its Christian adherents. As Jews became prominent in the higher reaches of German academia, certain of them used their positions of prominence to ridicule German customs, German politicians, and the Christian foundations of German culture; Theodor Lessing, previously cited, serves as but one such example of such tendencies.

* * * *

In matters of law, liberal and Marxist Jews were as prominent as they were in all other spheres of culture. They held important posts at the Ministry of Justice and elsewhere in the government. At the federal level, Oskar Cohn and Curt Joel, for example, were able to exert significant influence. Georg Gradnauer was minister of justice in Saxony, in Baden the post was held by Ludwig Marum. In matters of criminality, Jews were prominent as both jurists and defendants.

Right-wing Germans were angered and depressed by propositions forwarded by influential Jews. Kurt Rosenfeld, Prussia's Jewish minister of justice (1918) and Reichstag member in the period 1919–1933, proposed that treason, sodomy, and homosexuality be exempt from punishment. Jewish educationalists successfully proposed and implemented sex education in the schools. Peter Gay recalls that fellow Jew and expressionist playwright Carl Sternheim's "acidulous comedy of 1926, *Die Schule von Uznach*, which was subtitled *Die neue Sachlichkeit*, took exception to the new cynicism and caricatured the 'realism' of progressive educators as an excuse for promoting sexual license."[1740] Sternheim's satire was aimed squarely at "bourgeois morality . . . cynical mockery of the ethical nihilism and sexual license that postwar German youth took for emancipation."[1741] The cynicism of which both Gay and Sternheim wrote, did exactly that: it served as excuse for sexual licentiousness. Chastity was ridiculed; what was at the time sexual perversion was championed. The advancement of homosexual rights was seen by traditionalists as looming over and foreshadowing the decline of the family.[1742] Sexual license was also aided by findings of the judiciary.

*   *   *   *

Clearly, Jewish influence in German culture had become overwhelming. Fifty percent of the Social Democrats on the Reichstag Judiciary Committee were Jews. On the Committee for Reforming the Criminal Code, they comprised 43 percent.[1743] The Workers Educational Institutes were 81 percent Jewish. In medicine the story was the same: over 50 percent of the faculty of medical schools was made up of Jews, as was about a quarter of the student body. They were overrepresented in the ranks of the economic elite by a staggering factor of 33.[1744]

Politically active Weimar Jews often leveraged their strength in the judiciary by applying to magistrates to ruin their opponents financially and socially. Judicial issue shopping and judge shopping were as much in vogue in Weimar Germany as they are in today's America, and the staunch Jewish presence in the judiciary was seen as a boon to their overall influence. Just as in today's America, the judiciary was often employed to overcome plebiscites (what we call ballot questions or referendums) or legislation that reflected the will of the people. If one cannot win a majority of legislators or the populace to support an objective, one goes to the courts and shops around until a judge is found that supports the desired position: that is precisely how we came by abortion rights, companionate marriage, and a host of other initiatives that the majority of people opposed.

Jews of the radical Left often used the courts to good avail to harass and impoverish their opponents. As previously highlighted, Dr. Joseph Goebbels, among many others, was several times a target of such Jewish judicial partisanship. Attempts were also made to legally prohibit his publications, actions intended to silence him; he was even jailed for six weeks because of things he said.[1745] Editions of Julius Streicher's *Der Sturmer*, claims a stormfront.org[*] article, were "banned or seized thirty times between 1923 and 1933, and in one eleven-day period, he was hit with five lawsuits. He served a total of eight months in prison for defying court orders to cease distribution of banned issues of *Der Sturmer*."[1746] Ultimately, the writings of Streicher were found to be so odious at the war crimes trials in Nuremburg that he was sentenced to death for them. He was neither a member of the government nor the military, he killed no one nor ordered anyone killed, but he wrote and said awful, malicious things about Jews. He was hanged for it. We might easily agree that the anti-Semitic claptrap of Streicher's publications was odious and therefore deserving of such treatment; but if that is to be our position, then we might want to also express a bit of sympathy for the Nazi suppression of leftist publications—they, too, were odious. It is a goose and gander proposition.

In addition to attempts to silence right-wing publications, Jewish organizations and associations of lawyers took it upon themselves to challenge the laws of the republic having to do with matters of tradition and morality. Professor Dr. K. Klee, the president of the Senate, fumed that "Everywhere they (the Jews) were fighting in the front most ranks when it was a matter of blunting the sword of punishment in the struggle against crime." Klee specifically mentioned a small clique of individuals who he thought were leading the fight to diminish criminal law and thereby orderly society. Among those he accused were "'penal law theorists' such as Moritz Liebemann, James Goldschmidt, State Counselor of Law Löwenstein, the Prussian Justice Minister Kurt Rosenfeld, Kantorowicz, Gumbel, Freymuth, and others." Some Jewish members of the judiciary, such as the Communist Johannes Werthauer, claimed that the state had no right to punish at all; he demanded decriminalization of all offenses that were concerned

---

[*] Stormfront.org is clearly an anti-Semitic site.

with morality (e.g., abortion, homosexuality)—let us again be reminded that this was during a period when even the public use of the word "damn" was a bit shocking. The aforementioned were joined in their pursuits by Jews associated with Magnus Hirschfeld's Institute for Sexual Science, men such as Werthauer, Kronfeld, Otto Juliusburger, Max Alsberg, Kurt Hiller, and, of course, Hirschfeld himself.[1747]

* * * *

Jews were also conspicuous in all matters of the German economy. Thirty-six percent of the largest corporations were owned or managed by them. In banking, Jewish ownership and management was overwhelming: In 1913, fifteen Jews held 211 seats on boards of German banks; by 1928, it was 718. They also represented 80 percent of the leading members of the stock exchange and a similar percentage of the department stores were owned by them. Jewish dominance of the stock exchange would be a factor for the anti-Semites when the economy collapsed in 1929. In the general economic arena, like other areas, there was a small minority of Jews who caused widespread condemnation of Jewry in general.

* * * *

It certainly must have seemed to Hitler on the whole that the totality of Jewish influence on German culture both historically and during the 1920s justified the admonition issued by Baden State Councilor Johann Ludwig Kübler in 1847 that Jews were of such a nature that "excludes any gradual progress toward higher culture."[1748] Treitschke had written that "Jewish cosmopolitanism was incapable of understanding occidental nations; the Germans 'innocently accepted as German enlightenment and German progressivism what in truth was Jewish hatred of Christianity and Jewish cosmopolitanism.'"[1749] To that might be added the idea that

Jews were, by way of their overrepresentation in Marxist political parties, committed to internationalism and therefore diametrically opposed to German nationalism.

Kurt Münzer, in *The Way to Zion*, a 1910 novel, says: "We have ruined the blood of all the races of Europe, defiled them, broken their strength, made everything tired, lazy and rotten with our corrupt culture." In the first two decades of the twentieth century such claims did not seem novelistic, they seemed entirely real. Hitler had it in mind to change all that.

In a retrospective after Adolf Hitler had assumed power, Rabbi Dr. Manfred Reifer, oft-quoted by historians, said in 1933:

> We played with the most holy possessions of the people and at times made fun of all that was sacred to the nation. We trusted to the imperishable rights of democracy and felt ourselves as equal citizens of the state within the Germany community. We posed as censors of the morals of the people, and poured out full cups of satire upon the German Michel.* We wanted to be prophets in the pagan fields of Germania and forgot ourselves so far that all this had to draw destruction upon us. We made revolutions, and ran as eternal God seekers, ahead of the masses of the people. We gave to the international proletariat a second Bible, one that was adequate to the times, and we roused the passion of the third estate. The Jew Marx from Germany, declared war on capitalism and LaSalle organized the masses of the people in Germany itself. The Jew Eduard Bernstein popularized ideology, Karl Liebknecht and Rosa Luxemburg called the Spartacist movement to life. The Jew Kurt Eisner created the Bavarian Soviet Republic and was her first and last, president. And against that the German nation rose up, rebelled. She wanted to forge her

---

* A figure representing the national character of the German people in much the same way as the English John Bull. Michel, though, "also represents the innocent and simple person who must endure and fight against tyranny and injustice." Src: http://en.wikipedia.org/wiki/Deutscher_Michel 02/20/09

> own destiny, determine the future of her own children—
> and she should not have been blamed for it.
>
> What we objected to first of all was the world
> citizenship, the cosmopolitanism, which had Jews as its
> front fighters. These uprooted persons imagined they
> possessed the power to transplant the ideas of Isaiah into
> the alleys of Germania, and to storm Valhalla with
> Amos.[*] At times they succeeded in that, but they bury
> themselves and the Jewish people under the ruins of a
> world that has collapsed.

Donald L. Niewyk, in *The Jews in Weimar Germany*, asserts that Hitler improperly assigned blame for the nation's cultural issues to Jews. He acknowledges, though, that its Jewish participants in the cultural life in Weimar Germany would have "lost much of its richness and diversity"[1750] had it not been for Jews. What Mr. Niewyk calls "richness and diversity" was thought by Hitler and ultimately by millions of other Germans to be culturally grotesque, disfiguring mayhem, and degeneration. It was decadence of the first order and it was rightly and justifiably called that by Hitler and his Nazis.

Germans, says Mr. Niewyk, were bewildered by Marxian Socialism, pacifism, internationalism, expressionism, psychoanalysis, atonal music, and organic architecture, and they undeniably were. But, says Niewyk, "Without the contributions of a single Jewish intellectual, Weimar Germany would still have produced a remarkable and energetic cultural life not substantially different in its broad outlines from the one for which it is known."[1751] That German culture would have undergone change is to state the blatantly obvious, but the character of the changes that took place were most certainly and dominantly influenced by Jews. What was Marxist Socialism without Jews, without Marx? Pacifism of the day was led by Jews of such prominence as Albert Einstein and virtually the entirety of the leftist, which is to say,

---

* Amos: an eighth-century Jewish prophet.

Jewish, press. Internationalism was then and continues today to be a wholly owned subsidiary of Jewish interests. Jewish artists, gallery owners, and cultural critics were at the forefront of expressionism and its associated "isms," and it likely would not have gotten off the ground had it not been for Jewish praise of it. Psychoanalysis and its various epigones cannot be imagined without Sigmund Freud and his camarilla. The Frankfurt School was a wholly Jewish institution based on Freudianism, and it and its various offshoots would not have existed except for its creation and sponsorship by organized Jewry. The "organic architecture" of the Bauhaus Movement could not have long endured without Jewish membership and patronage. Jewish patronage of the Bauhaus Movement is illustrated both by Albert Einstein's defense of it in 1924 and by the fact that Israel's Tel Aviv was built almost entirely on the basis of Bauhaus architectural concepts.[1752] Atonal music was a concoction of Arnold Schoenberg—it would not have occurred without him. Mr. Niewyk is wrong on this score: Jews made Weimar culture, and its development would have been vastly different had they not participated.

    In actual fact, much of what passes for "Weimar culture" was little more than the success of the effects of the brutal Jewish critique of German values. The cabarets, the biting satires, and anti-Christian motifs, the various forms of "sexual liberation" and the revolution, as well as the political and labor union unrest had Jews at the forefront. After becoming chancellor, Hitler provided an observation that must have seemed increasingly apparent to all: *"This race simply has a tendency toward ridiculing everything that is beautiful, and it frequently does so by way of masterful satire."*[1753] (Italics are in the original.)

    The cleansing of German culture was of enormous importance to Hitler and his regime. The Nazis became engaged in a "grand spiritual mission to demolish the vestiges of Weimar culture."[1754] As early as September 1933, Propaganda Minister Joseph Goebbels had instituted the huge Reich Chamber of Culture (*Reichskulturkrammer*) to redress what was by then Germany's sorry state of cultural being. The subject of culture was institutionalized in Hitler's annual speech at the Nuremberg Party congress where he made it clear that he intended henceforth to be the arbiter of the aesthetic disputes that raged in the period prior to 1936. Norman Rich argues correctly that "It was with undoubted sincerity that Hitler . . . paid homage to the German ideal of *Kultur* and made it the foundation of his entire ideological system."[1755] His ambition for a gargantuan Kulturhalle was an expression of the seriousness that Hitler assigned to such matters.[1756]

Purging German Culture

There were few objections to Hitler's new cultural policies among the common people; they had had quite enough of the cultural swill offered up during the Weimar years. Very early in his administration, Hitler began his culture purge, the purge of what he called *Kulturbolschewismus*. The primary objects of these early steps were the Marxists and were in keeping with his oft-repeated theme of stamping out Marxist-Bolshevism. That so very many Jews were caught up in these early purges was simply indicative of how very many of them were prominent in the various Marxist movements. Shortly thereafter, Jews were removed from positions of power of all kinds.

After 1933, the non-Jewish liberal intelligentsia that had been so important to the success of Jewish efforts during the 1920s now found that they no longer subscribed to the propositions that they had previously embraced with such verve. The submission of the Gentile intelligentsia to Nazism was summarized in a statement by the denazification court in 1947: "As National Socialist barbarism took over in 1933, it was deeply disappointing that the intellectual elite, instead of opposing," said the court, "one by one collaborated with National Socialism."[1757] "They assisted in the book-burnings, Aryanization of publishing and media outlets, confiscation of Jewish property, and the establishment of censoring boards."[1758] Even Bauhaus founders Walter Gropius and Ludwig Mies, the darlings of the Jewish press in the 1920s, "unhesitatingly joined the visual arts section of the Reich Culture Chamber and participated in the Nazis' early architectural competitions,"[1759] says Spotts. The feebleness of intellectual honesty and courage was made manifest by their alacritous abandonment of such concepts—there would be no fist-to-fist stuff from this crowd.

Getting control of the artistic community was easy; their commitment to ideals was as shallow as the ideas they had previously proffered. It must be presumed that many of these intellectuals had long harbored the cultural aspects of Nazism but had been cowed by Jewish power in expressing themselves. With the rise of Hitler their innermost feelings were apparently liberated. We need to suspect that if similar circumstances came about in the U.S. many a current senator would make similar conversions—we must suppose that they are as stymied by Jewish power as were Weimar intellectuals.

"According to Michael H. Kater, 'physicians became more thoroughly Nazified and much sooner than any other profession, and as Nazis they did more in the service of the nefarious regime than any of their extra-professional peers.'"[1760] "By 1935, almost a third of the non-Jewish German physicians belonged to the Nazi Party. From 1925 to 1944, the percent of medical doctors in the party was almost three times as high as in the population as a whole."[1761] With the fall of Hitler the intelligentsia, of course, once again did a backflip; they reverted to condemnation of Hitler, his Nazis, and everyone who aided them, but on the whole excepted themselves. We now have it that the Nazis were, on the whole, illiterate thugs when, in fact, the party was comprised of vast numbers of highly capable, though highly cowardly, intellectuals.

CHAPTER 7

SUCCESS OF HITLER—ASCENSION TO POWER

The National Socialist revolution, they proclaimed, was not just political but cultural; indeed, cultural above all.
—**Historian Frederick Spotts (153)**

[T]he Weimar Republic is best measured by the legacy it bequeathed to other cultures after its death, "part murder, part wasting sickness, part suicide."
—**Historian William Grange (xii–xiii)**

Setting the Stage for Hitler's Success

As Joachim Fest emphasizes,[1762] to imagine and assert that Hitler came to power by veritably magical or conspiratorial or even brutal means is to betray an understanding of the course of events in Germany between World War I and the early 1930s. Ultimately, Hitler came to power by way of his consummately skillful politics and his "indomitable will." When he finally achieved power he did so in precisely the same way as his predecessors: he was appointed to the position of chancellor by President Paul von Hindenburg and in full accord with the German constitution. When Hindenburg died and Hitler took over his position, he did that, too, in accordance with the constitution and the approval of the people. Upon the death of the president, the constitution called for the chancellor to temporarily assume the position. To make his appointment permanent, a special election was held in August 1934. Owing to the remarkable success of his first eighteen months in office, almost 90 percent of the German people voted their approval of Hitler as Hindenburg's permanent successor.[1763]

Hitler did not "seize power" as is so often claimed (though even the Nazis themselves sometimes used the term). Indeed, as Fest correctly emphasizes by use of the term "so-called," Hitler came to power quite legitimately. "The so-called Seizure of Power by the Nazis," says Fest, "was soon being hailed as a 'miracle' and a 'fairytale.'"[1764] As historian John Williams points out "The Germany of 1870–1933 had been divided by 'parliamentarianism' and weakened by Judeo Marxism and Social Democracy. Political parties had encouraged class war, which tore at the fibre of the old Reich and enfeebled its ability and will to overcome [its] enemies."[1765] The foregoing facts, along with others that were connected by political and social ills of many kinds were the foundations upon which Hitler was able to construct a broad-based movement.

From 1918 onward, there was a confluence of political misstep, scandal, societal exhaustion, and economic hardship that set the stage for the final political thrust of Hitler and his Nazi Party. All of these issues were added to the series of blows that the German people had suffered since the loss of World War I. A review of those hardships is appropriate:

- The war had been lost along with a ghastly number of German soldiers killed and maimed.
- Revolution and counterrevolution had poisoned the political well and pummeled the Germany psyche.
- Vast tracks of Germany's farm and industrial base were placed in the hands of other countries and there seemed to be no hope or prospect whatever for their recovery.
- The country carried a massive financial debt to the world and was scheduled to remain indebted for some sixty more years into the future.
- The whole of the agriculturally rich Rhineland was no longer under Germany's control.
- Germany's industrial heartland, the Ruhr, had been invaded and occupied by the French, and the people of that region had been treated by them with utter brutality.
- The Polish Corridor split Prussia in two, and the German port city of Danzig had been put in Polish hands.
- Some 6 million Sudeten Germans lived under an oppressive regime in Czechoslovakia and were crying out to their countrymen for salvation.

- Germany was forbidden permission to join (*Anschluss*) with Austria.
- The inflationary period of 1921–1923 had brought the middle and lower classes to financial ruin.
- Scandal was rife, as was political murder. By the late 1920s, deadly street battles were again a daily spectacle in Berlin.
- German culture had been brought to ruin, or so it seemed in the minds of tradition-minded Germans.
- The "democratic" government was, by the late 1920s, being operated on a dictatorial basis under Article 48 of the constitution.
- Communists continued to represent a threat from violent revolution.
- With the 1929 crash of the stock market the economy was again in ruins and the people again plunged into abject despair.

By the late 1920s, the people of Germany were utterly sapped and the Weimar government was seen as the primary culprit in the dismay, the discouragement, befuddlement, and misery felt by the commoner. It was by this time clearly evident that the German attempt at democracy, the Weimar Republic, was a dismal failure. The Marxist and centrist parties had had fourteen years to show what they could do; they produced nothing, save ruination: ruination of the economy, ruination of the culture, and ruination of the spirit and noble instincts of the German people. As Tedor points out, "It was a disillusioned and destitute nation that Hitler inherited when he took office on January 30, 1933,"[1766] as indeed it was.

* * * *

Several political missteps occurred in the late 1920s and early 1930s that further contributed to the anger of the masses; among them was the 1929 passage of the Young Plan, already touched upon in a previous chapter. The Young Plan committed Germany to continue with its reparation payments for some sixty years into the future, two generations. For many, the reparations represented an ongoing form of German slavery on behalf of its powerful masters, the League of Nations. While the plan offered several advantages to Germany, it also, at the bottom of it all, was seen as still another example of Germany's base helplessness and therefore its inability to strike a decisive blow against the hated, oppressive Treaty of Versailles.

Still another political misstep occurred in 1931 when Germany again tried to form an Austro-German Customs Union. Again, however, the Treaty of Versailles intervened to dash both German and Austrian hopes of improving their economic lot through such a union. The customs union was opposed by France with the support of both Italy and Czechoslovakia, countries that understandably saw the union as a backdoor attempt to bring about political and territorial solidarity between the two states. But to the German, the unsuccessful attempt to form the union represented still another humiliation and again highlighted Germany's weakness vis-à-vis other states. Failure of the customs union further inflamed national resentment toward what ardent nationalists perceived as both the weak-kneed, limp-wristed Weimar government and Germany's opponents.[1767] Clearly, if Germany was ever to shake off the fetters of Versailles it would first need to regain its military strength—the Young Plan and the failed attempt to form a customs union with Austria illustrated the fact that there could be no hope that negotiations from a position of weakness would ever break the shackles of Versailles.

*   *   *   *

Zionists of the late 1920s were increasingly sounding very much like right-wing nationalists except that Palestine, not Germany, was the focus of their fervor. Moreover, attacks on Christendom and its moral precepts by the Jewish intelligentsia throughout the 1920s was taking its collective toll, not so much in converts to secularism but in hardening attitudes toward the perceived anti-Christian stance of Jews.

In the 1920s and '30s, German peasantry had a contemporary hero. It was, of course, Adolf Hitler. Though never close to the soil himself, he could nevertheless smell it; he could revel in it; he could champion it. Hitler's experience with the soil was much the same as Kafka's experience with the ghetto: it was removed from his own experience but was nonetheless figuratively owned by him. Hitler knew the nationalistic peasant as the metropolitan internationalist could not. And the peasant was there to be had by anyone willing to speak to him.

The leftist political parties (SPD, USPD/KPD, DDP) paid scant attention to the rural population, its peasants, and its miseries; indeed, they had little but contempt for such beings. It was indicative of the intellectual mandarins of German culture to hold the farmers and peasants in vile contempt.[1768] Their focus was understandably on the cities and the labor unions, the place of Jews and Jewish strength. The other major rightist party, the Nationalists, also failed to make appeals to the peasantry, favoring, instead, the landed gentry and middle classes in the northern districts of the country.

The peasantry had been experiencing misery for years prior to the stock market crash. After the war, when food was scarce and farmers could have benefited from that fact, price controls on food remained in effect and were not lifted until the summer of 1921. The good harvest of 1923 had to be sold for worthless paper due to the ravages of the hyperinflationary period. The following crop, however, when the value of the mark had been restored, had to be financed with hard currency. Some 4.5 billion marks of agrarian savings were wiped out.[1769] It was entirely understandable then, that retreat from support for the government was first evidenced in the patchwork of small towns and farming communities where the majority of Germans still lived and where Hitler's Nazi Party made its greatest early inroads.

In the countryside, symptoms of retreat from the republican form of government had long been apparent by the end of the 1920s. The agrarian crisis of 1927–1929 saw sharp declines in agriculture prices that presaged the stock market crash of 1929. The Weimar government, always more attuned to the cities than the countryside, exasperated rural hardship by its trade treaties with countries such as Poland from which Germany imported agricultural products in exchange for finished goods and thereby further depressed German agricultural prices.[1770] Rural artisans and small traders were also hurt by such governmental acts.

The stabilization of the German currency was a godsend for putting an end to the period of hyperinflation, but it simultaneously put an end to what had been ten years of rising agricultural prices and set the stage for financial collapse in agricultural communities. The real income of German farmers increased a mere 4.5 percent while the national average was 45 percent between 1913 and 1928. The farming community constituted 25 percent of the total population but realized only 8 percent of the national income. The dire straits of the farming community was exasperated between 1925 and 1933 when it experienced crop failures, credit shortages, low prices, rising taxes, and resultant bankruptcies.[1771] Hitler, unlike the others, sought to woo the masses. His initial focus in that respect was to concentrate on support from the peasants. Farmers and their rural brethren, due to the multitude of hardships they were facing in the late 1920s, became radicalized well before the onset of the Depression.[1772] Because the "Jewish parties" focused on urban populations, Hitler was able to easily differentiate his Nazis from the big-city politicians and parties and win their votes. Moreover, important as the cities were, Hitler was able to overcome his relative weakness in the big cities by appealing to the rural areas that still accounted for the majority of the population.[1773] This segment of the population was sneeringly referred to by big-city intellectuals as the "backwoodsmen" (*das platte, allzu platte Land*), flatlanders.[1774] Intellectuals of that time had the same disdain for the rural population as many current American intellectuals have for traditionalists in the American South.

When Hitler and his Nazis began to represent a mass movement it was initially the rural peasants of the Protestant north, not the workers or Junkers or civil servants or financiers or the businessmen who clambered onto his movement.[1775] The election of 1928 confirmed the support of rural areas: in that election year the vote for the Nazis varied inversely with the size of the community from which it was drawn.[1776] To the extent that the Nazis received support in the big cities it was from the most affluent suburbs that cast the highest number of votes for them,[1777] which, of course, contributed to the myth that such people voted for Nazis because they were jealous of Jewish success. The Nazis also competed successfully with the KPD to become the party of the youthful, and the unthinking enthusiasm and energy of youth was exploited to the fullest: "of its 130,000 members in 1930, nearly 70 percent were under 40 and 37 percent were under 30."[1778] The party was also aided by the policy position of the largest party, the SPD, which was emphatically opposed to raising tariffs on imported foodstuffs, much to the consternation of the farmers and other rural citizens. The number of local Nazi branches was up to 1,378, emphasizing its rural presence as it simultaneously continued to vie for the support of the workers in the cities.

Still, even in the late 1920s, the electorate remained essentially immune to the appeals of Nazism as evidenced by the election results of 1928.[*] The Nazis did well only in the countryside, that place of the socially underprivileged that felt itself smothered by parasitical metropolitan Berlin and was made aghast by the failures of the central government.[1779] Kurt Tucholsky described these rural environs as "permeated by romanticism, empty talk, and surreptitious Catholicism," which he claimed was more dangerous than the open variety. For Tucholsky and his fellow Jews, the provinces and their peasant populations represented darkness; Berlin was the city of Jews, of light.[1780] His attitude represented still another example of the disdain Jewish intellectuals had for all peasants, their Christian belief system, and the misery they were suffering. The peasants themselves were by now increasingly embracing Nazism as a means of relief from their oppressive plight.

---

[*] It was the disappointing result of this election cyle that made the Nazis reassess their campaign tactics to place still more emphasis on winning the rural voter.

Success of Hitler—Ascension to Power

There was a feeling throughout the country, but especially in the rural parts, that the German people needed to declare war on the pernicious and corrupting influences of modern metropolitan life that was so typified by Berlin and the likes of Tucholsky and his ilk. The spirit of the people, their *Volksgeist*, was in revolt against the spirit of Berlin and its Weimar government, not Jews per se.[1781]

Anthony Kauders, in his book, *German Politics and the Jews*, argues in opposition to Ian Kershaw's conclusion about the "relative indifference of most Germans towards the 'Jewish Question'" before 1933. Kauders, in keeping with the politically correct views of post-World War II historians, seems to want to assert that anti-Semitism is and always has been embedded in the German soul and psyche but fails to provide much in the way of argument to support his dissension. The Germans, claims Kauders, showed "widespread support" for the rightist parties: they did not; they instead showed widespread support for the leftist SPD and USPD/KPD, and the Catholic Center Party as evidenced by every voting result between 1919 and 1928. Indeed, at the very outset of the republic, in the January 1919 vote, the parties dedicated to a pluralistic republican state won a full four-fifths of the vote. In the parliamentary elections that took place eighteen months later, the three largest and most centurist parties won 43.6 percent of the vote and the ultraleftist USPD won another 20 percent.[1782] The conservatives won only a paltry 10 percent.[1783] Kauders also mentions that Germans by this time held views with respect to the volk and the fatherland that made them susceptible to Nazi racism.[1784] Translation: nationalists are by nature, racists; and German nationalists, by nature, anti-Semites. Kauders is wrong, Kershaw had it right. Germans were largely indifferent to Nazi racism. More telling even than the foregoing is the fact that the Nazis all but entirely abandoned the anti-Semitism theme in the election cycles of the early 1930s. The theme had no legs. For the vast majority of Germans much bigger issues held sway.

Even in the first years of the 1930s the Left and Center still constituted a numerical majority (a fact illuminating the widespread support they received from the populace), but one that could not be converted into a unified political force: the ongoing, Moscow-enforced fratricide between the KPD and SPD prevented such a union of purpose.[1785]

In 1929, the KPD had again resolved to continue attacking the SPD as its primary political foe. The SPD, though Marxists like the KPD, was insufficiently radical for the Bolshevistic Communists of the KPD. Moreover, in the early 1920s, there had been several defining confrontations between the two parties, not the least of which were the Spartacist Uprising of 1919 and the March Action of 1921. The cleft between the two most prominent and powerful Marxist parties could not be closed. Both of them assumed unalterable positions aimed at the other: a joint candidate for the upcoming elections was therefore a political nonstarter. When they finally went down in defeat, observes Istvan Deak sagely, the "Social Democrats and Communists could look back on fourteen years of working-class disunity, unmitigated by a single instance of genuine interparty cooperation."[1786]

The KPD resolution against the SPD was taken in conformity with the position adopted by the Soviet Union under Stalin's leadership. By 1930, the KPD and affiliated parties were mere bureaucratic extensions of Soviet foreign policy, its strategies were developed in Moscow, and its objectives were geared to the needs of the Soviet Union.[1787] Its leaders were appointees of the Kremlin;[1788] they represented a major source of the international and foreign influences about which Hitler railed incessantly.

For the elections of 1932, the KPD, after considering possible candidates such as Albert Einstein, Ernst Toller, Alfons Goldschmidt (the KPD leadership was comprised of people who were not in close contact with political reality), and others, settled on its party leader and 1925 candidate Ernst Thälmann as its candidate for president against the venerable President Paul von Hindenburg. A KPD ally, the *Weltbühne*, proposed Heinrich Mann, who was married to a Jewess, because "he would be acceptable both to Moscow and Paris,"[1789] and therefore, implicitly acceptable to the Jews of Germany. Hitler also ran for president that year. The candidacy of Thälmann split the center-left vote and thereby significantly weakened the anti-Nazi forces. The result was that the

Thälmann's candidacy markedly contributed to Hitler's rise to power.

As Hitler was eschewing his anti-Semitic rhetoric in the several election cycles of the early 1930s, the KPD and several prominent German Jews, and even the Zionists, espoused anti-Semitism as a means to swing anti-Semitic voters to their cause.

Additionally, Hitler had been deemed a fool in 1928 as he predicted economic disaster that he said would stem from Germany's heavy reliance on short-term loans from the U.S., but given the stock market crash he was now seen as a prophet.[1790]* The crash did for Hitler and his Nazis what the war had done for the Marxists; it served as an enabler for upheaval and revolution.

As correctly observed by Bullock, when the prosperity of the mid-1920 was brought to an unhappy end in 1929, "All the fears and insecurity of that postwar period were revived and made the harder to bear by the brief interlude of recovery, now seen to be a treacherous illusion."[1791] By the 1930 election campaign Hitler's claim that he would abolish unemployment had some credence due to his foresight (luck) in predicting the economic disaster. Moreover, the matter of unemployment was made even worse as the government constricted various welfare programs at a time when such assistance was most in need. Germany was "starving on democracy."[1792] Due to the unemployment relief provided by the government, wrote American journalist H. R. Knickerbocker wryly, it would take ten years to starve.[1793] "The government," according to a popular quip of the time, "was administering misery instead of relieving it."[1794]

Hitler's appeal was in consonance with the desperate straits and hopes of the people. He correctly sensed that people were by now conditioned to hear his appeals for a seminal spiritual transformation, "a national renewal, drawing on Germans' pride in their nation's historic destiny, and his own passionate conviction

---

* This was still another stroke of luck for Hitler—anyone can predict a coming crash in the market: if one waits long enough it is a certainty that it will occur.

that will and faith could overcome all difficulties."[1795] He would, he said, demand still further sacrifice from the people, but he would also abolish the ineffectual democratic political system and the Treaty of Versailles; he would in their stead bring decisive leadership, unity of purpose, national pride, and a return to the vaunted moral precepts of yesteryear; and, importantly, he would bring full employment back to the masses. Hitler's call for additional sacrifice from a people who had already endured so much pain and loss was both heartfelt and genius. His aims and slogans did not champion a class revolution—he sought nothing less than the redemption of Germandom. He was to restore the past's system of values and morality, he would defeat the forces of dissolution thrusting from all sides.[1796] As Bullock points out:

> Hitler was shrewd enough to realize that such demands, far from being resisted, bound those who accepted them more tightly to the party, developing an attachment that was as much religious as political in character, "the faith of the church combined with the discipline of an army."[1797]

Hitler also openly proclaimed that he would totally discard the Weimar constitution. As outrageous and brazen as such a statement seems, it was not particularly untoward for the tenets of the time. In actual fact, the constitution could be legally abrogated. As Joachim Fest points out, "One of the people's rights was to give up its sovereignty."[1798]

*   *   *   *

The relationship between the Nazis and the Communists was in some ways a curious one. They each sought the abject destruction of the other, but they each in their way also admired the other and took lessons, one from the other. Both parties were ruthless, despised the ruling classes of the country, and both were radically committed to Socialistic ideology. These commonalities were such that throughout the "period of struggle," it was not at all uncommon for supporters to switch from one party to the other, often several times.[1799] Such switching illustrates still another point: it was the very radicalism of the parties that attracted people, and especially the young. The KPD was heavily influenced and led by Jews, so it would seem that anti-Semitism could not possibly have been at work as Nazis left their party in favor of the KPD.

As the various parties entered the several election cycles of the early 1930s, some of Hitler's closest supporters were still showing their staunch Socialistic (or even Communistic) leanings, and others their conservative, nationalistic ones. Gregor Strasser would have liked to unite the Nazis with the Communists and Social Democrats. Gregor's brother, Otto, wanted to again seek to capture power by way of a coup. Goering and Hanfstaengl pushed for a moderate conservative platform in order to overcome the perception of Nazis in some quarters as crazed radicals.[1800]

Hitler, as always, chose his own strategy. He would stick to his strategy of strict legality. He would win power by winning the people. His campaign centered mostly on opposition to the Marxists. He realized and espoused an unmitigated fact in the campaigns of the early 1930s: the fact was that the Nazis were in a life-and-death struggle with the Marxist parties; they were not about to become an appendage of such parties as advocated by Gregor Strasser. If the Nazis were to win, Marxism in Germany would be utterly annihilated; if the Bolshevist faction of Marxists (the KPD) won, Nazism would suffer the same fate. "We know no tolerance," said Hitler, "[w]e shall not rest until the last newspaper is crushed, the last organization destroyed, the last educational institution eliminated, the last Marxist converted or exterminated. There is no middle course."[1801]

Hitler's campaign successes did not stem from his anti-Semitism; they instead grew out of the campaign strategies jointly conceived by Goebbels and Hitler himself. With those strategies in place he undertook a tireless and unique campaign effort. The Nazi campaign strategies and methodologies had never before been seen. Airplanes showered leaflets on the populace. Fifty thousand propaganda recordings were mailed to people known to own record players. Sound movies of Hitler's campaign appearances and speeches were projected in public squares in all of the major cities. Hitler traveled everywhere by airplane, making it possible to hold multiple rallies at distant locales in a single day and to also provide him with an aura of modernity The Nazi slogan for these flights was "Hitler Over Germany,"[1802] a slogan that was at once both literal and metaphorical. Hitler also monitored the pulse of the people by establishing a reporting system from his Gauleiters. He had them send agents into the populace to find out what people were saying. He then used such reports in developing campaign literature. It was an early version of what we today call polling.

There was still another aspect of Nazism that drew people to its cause: the Nazis acted upon their principles. They readily engaged in populist causes that were in accord with their own preachings. By way of example, in the farming districts of Franconia, East Prussia, Pomerania, and Schleswig-Holstein, they organized and participated in farmers' protest movements. In both Pomerania and Schleswig-Holstein, they joined demonstrations that opposed government litigation against farmers. In Oldenburg, they joined in the large-scale demonstrations demanding agricultural price stability. In Bavaria, they protested against banks that charged excessive interest rates on loans to farmers.[1803] They also sought extensive tax and land reform. The foregoing is only a smattering of the many proposals and actions taken by the Nazis on behalf of their constituency. Unlike the other parties, it was apparent that the Nazis meant what they said and practiced what they preached.

The success of Hitler and his Nazis was gotten in the old-fashioned way—it was earned by superior strategies, techniques, organization, slogans, and tireless effort.

Jewish Criminality

As emphasized in previous chapters, it has regretfully been the case that Jews have long been perceived as principals in the economic exploitation of Gentiles, often by way of fraud. German philosopher Johann Gottlieb Fichte highlighted the circumstances of Jewish exploitation as follows:

> In a country where even the King may not, of his own
> free will, deprive me of the cottage, which I inherited
> from my father, and where I have my legal rights against
> the all-powerful minister, the first Jew, nevertheless,
> who takes it into his head, can plunder me with
> impunity.[1804][*]

"Before the Nazi rise to power," says Michael Berkowitz, "Germany and other European states had had a long history of recognizing the phenomenon of 'Jewish crime.'"[1805] Karl Marx had emphasized the criminal vocations that were seen as lending themselves to the special expertise of Jews.[1806] Just as was the case in both Germany and Austria in the 1870s and the financial scandals in France in the 1880s, the German scandals of the 1920s involved prominent Jewish culprits.[1807] Beginning in 1925, a series of scandals involving Jews rocked Germany and toward the end of the decade still another series of affronts to German sensibilities became public. Germany, it seemed, like Austria and France before it, was in a state of endless crisis,[1808] and all too many of the crises originated in Jewish ranks.

Several corruption scandals ripped the nation in the mid- to late-1920s. Jews themselves wrote openly about their dominant role in the corrupt happenings of the time. Exhaustion from the saturation of society with sexual licentiousness was being felt, too; people were tired of the excesses that so marked Weimar culture. Coupled with Zionism in the popular German mind-set was the large population of Jewish refugees who engaged in shady business dealings near or beyond the edge of the law. "In defending or excusing their coreligionists from exaggerated versions of these charges," says Donald Niewyk, "German Jews betrayed profound uneasiness over the impression that they left on the masses."[1809] Adding to the image of dishonest Jews, the

---

[*] In 1993, the people of New York City voted to limit the terms of the mayor to two: in 2011, Mayor Bloomberg, a billionaire, by way of a vote in the city council, ignored the will of the people and was able to stand for a third term. Votes by the people are of no consequence to the powerful.

Centralverein (CV) had published a pamphlet in 1925 alleging that a "significant minority of Eastern Jews had become 'racketeers, swindlers, currency and stock cheaters, and thieves and fences.'"[1810] The CV acknowledged that "many of our Christian neighbors, who otherwise have made every effort to be objective, have lost confidence in German Jewry as a result of the Eastern Jewish question. It cannot be denied that in the hour of our greatest need many of these people engaged in dealings that were highly dangerous for the national economy."[1811]

* * * *

One of the scandals came to light in the mid-1920s; it centered on the corrupt shenanigans of the Jewish Sklarz brothers and members of the SPD leadership. The brothers, by way of bribes provided to SPD leaders, had created a monopoly for supplying what was left of the German military. They garnered enormous profits. After lengthy trials ending in 1926 only one of the brothers was convicted but awareness of the scandal was widespread, contributing to both anti-Semitism and damage to the SPD.

* * * *

The Kiev-born Jewish Barmat brothers, of whom there were four (Julius, Herschel, Solomon, and Isaak) was still another big corruption scandal that beset the republic in the mid- to late-1920s. It came to light at the close of 1924. Their trial commenced in 1925 and did not conclude until 1928 when two of the brothers were sentenced to eleven years and six months imprisonment for bribery.

The brothers had defrauded the Weimar government out of roughly 15,000,000 marks. They defrauded the Prussian State Bank of several million more. A special commission constituted to investigate the scandal found evidence that SPD politicians at all levels of authority had been involved in the schemes and accepted bribes from the brothers, including ex-Chancellor Gustav Bauer (1919–1920) whose government had agreed to sign the Treaty of Versailles. Bauer had helped the Barmats to win food supply contracts and also with a scrap-metal deal for which he had received commissions. Bauer, to his discredit, was caught in several perjuries about his connection to the Barmats. The malfeasance of the political class, it was alleged, had been paid for by the Barmats. The scandal reinforced the idea of Jewish corruption, including bribery of the kind called forth in the *Protocols of the Learned Elders of Zion* and the briberies in France connected with the Panama Scandal.

Politicians linked to the Barmats were said to be as "crafty as the craftiest Ostjuden."[1812] The idea of Jewish bribery in Germany was made all the more believable due to its widespread use in the East. Bribery of government officials became a veritable way of life for Eastern Jews as they sought exemption from various special laws concerning them. "Many millions of rubles a year," says Lindemann, "moved into the pockets of officials who had authority over Jews. Many conscientious police officials and members of the judiciary came to consider the Jews a troublesome and corrupt people, forever importuning the authorities with petitions, protests, and bribes."[1813] Such bribery was now afoot in Germany's political parties and its previously venerable civil service. Corruption in the civil service was most prominent in Prussia, which was then wholly the province of the SPD.

Rumor had it that the Jewish leader of the SPD's delegation to the Prussian Landtag, Ernst Heilmann, accepted bribes from his acknowledged friend, Julius Barmat, a man of "less than perfect character."[1814] These rumors were later dismissed by the special commission constituted to investigate the affair. Still, such facts and fancies, as Kauders reminds us, "disclosed the moral corruptibility of the system, and reminded [people] of the early months after the war, when such shady business deals had been common practice"[1815] and, lamentably, Jews were the common practitioners.

Among the various crimes of the Barmat brothers was their involvement in food imports during and shortly after World War I.

Food distribution during that period was a subject of great controversy, with accusations of rampant profiteering and hoarding of food to drive up prices being widespread.

The KPD exploited the Barmat scandal in order to weaken the SPD, but did so in a way that failed to highlight the Jewish background of the brothers.[1816] The right-wing parties, however, made and publicized the connections.

The breaking of the Barmat scandal also brought to light the help provided to the Barmats by fellow Jews. In particular, it became known that Heilmann, mentioned above, and the notorious Jewish war profiteer Alexander Parvus had aided the brothers.

After serving his sentence, Julius Barmat relocated to Belgium where he again employed bribery and fraud to bilk the Belgium government. The whole of the scandal seemed to confirm for many the charges from some elements of the right wing that the republic had been made wholly corrupt by Jews; and such people were thereby also reminded of the widespread corruption so evident shortly after the war.[1817]

Later, Nazi propagandists cited prominent Jewish swindlers of the Weimar era to indict all Jews as corrupt. In addition to the Barmat brothers, Nazi publications made specific mention of Michael Holzmann, the brothers Rotter, the brothers Sklarz, the brothers Sklarek (not to be confused with the brothers Sklarz), and Ludwig Katzenellenbogen.

A widespread perception of corruption by Jews was a dominant subject by the early 1930s. The whole of the Barmat scandal provided a semblance of authenticity to the right-wing charge that the Weimar government, and especially its SPD component, were part of a "corruption economy."[1818] At the conclusion of the scandal the SPD abandoned its participation in the government and instead went into opposition against the Center, DVP, and DNVP. The perception of widespread corruption fueled by the various scandals, coupled with equally widespread perceptions of Jewish dominance in the cultural decline of the republic, materially contributed to large-scale rejection of the Jewish-dominated liberal parties in favor of the Nazis in the elections of the early 1930s.

* * * *

In 1925, the Jew Jakob Michael, a man who was both feared and hated, was arrested on suspicion of having defrauded the Prussian State Bank. Michael, only thirty-two-years-old, was the owner of vast metallurgical interests, a shipping magnate, proprietor of vast estates, a chemical producer, and a tsar of finance. While the charges were ultimately discharged, the damage of continued suspicion about the truth of the allegations could not be so easily dismissed. There remained the suspicion that still another rich Jew had bought his way out, that justice had been subverted. The Michael affair was one more scandal among several to be aggregated in public perceptions.

* * * *

In 1932 Kurt Meyer was sentenced to fifteen years in prison for killing his father's non-Jewish maid, and then dismembering her body, pieces of which were later found about the nearby countryside. The Meyer murder affair provided grist for the mills of people who still gave credence to the age-old legends of ritual murder, blood libel, by Jews.[1819]

* * * *

Georg Bernhard, Jewish author, leading liberal publicist, and editor of the *Vossische Zeitung*, was found to have connections to French interests who in the early 1920s had tried to detach the Rhineland from Germany. French occupation of the Rhineland provided France with a springboard from which to also occupy the Ruhr. The French had iron, Germany had coal—the objective was to improve French economic prospects by marrying French iron with German coal. For radical rightist forces in Germany the scandal was representative of still another instance of Jewish perfidy, another stab in the back, another instance of Jewish disloyalty. The scandal was of such magnitude that Bernhard was forced to give up his publishing business in the early 1930s. He subsequently became a leading member of the foreign press whose focus was on bringing down Hitler's government, which for Hitler and his Nazis, represented still more perfidy.

Contentious Books

In 1929, Jewish author Rudolf Schay published his book *Juden in der deutschen Politk* (Jews in German Politics), in which he claimed a dominant role of Jews in carrying out revolutions and rejections of democratic-republican order. It represented still another nose under the tent of dissatisfaction.

Also in 1929, Erich Maria Remarque published his vastly popular but highly contentious novel *All Quiet on the Western Front*. The pacifist theme of the book and its characterization of the military opened him up to charges of having sullied the honor of soldiers and added still further to the cultural polarization that was underway.[1820] The book was ultimately translated into twenty-five languages and sold over 30 million copies.[1821]

Remarque had served in the army during the latter part of the war. Never exposed to the fiercest combat, he was nevertheless wounded by a grenade. A committed pacifist, his novel was seen by the Nazis as particularly unpatriotic. He was "accused" by them of being a Jew (he was not, he was a Gentile Catholic). Still, given his nature and his pacifism, Remarque was heartily embraced by the Jewish press, adding to the association between him and Jewry.

Antimilitarist though he was, Remarque had nevertheless posed as a German officer after the war, complete with Iron Crosses. It was his way of acquiring unearned valor. His misrepresentation of himself was a forgivable act among his left-wing friends but not his right-wing detractors.

Ultimately he went on to write many more novels and was embraced by the Jews of Hollywood. In Hollywood, he enjoyed the status of a playboy. While there, he engaged in an affair with Marlene Dietrich (as did, it seems, everyone else in the Hollywood universe) and a host of other starlets.

Our point here is that Remarque was neither the brave pacifist of liberal commentary nor the evil traitor of Nazi description. His fame stemmed from his works, not his character, but his works and his associations were of a kind that in Nazi circles elicited enduring hatred and incorrectly painted him as Jewish. Rightist sentiment over *All Quiet on the Western Front* remained one of outrage. Remarque's book was a poison in the wound of a lost war, a bellow on the fires of hate.

Threat of Bolshevism

Fear of yet another Jewish-led attempt at a Communist revolution was again on the wind in the early 1930s. As stated by Kevin MacDonald, "the experience of the Bolshevik revolution in Germany was so immediate, so close to home and so disquieting, and statistics seemed to prove the overwhelming participation of Jewish ringleaders so irrefutably, 'that even many liberals believed in Jewish responsibility.'"[1822] Hitler's Nazis hammered away on the theme of the threat posed by the Communists. One Nazi slogan stated the issue succinctly: "If the party breaks up tomorrow, the day after tomorrow Germany will have 10 million more Communists,"[1823] a slogan which emphasized the fact that many people were seeking a radical solution to their plight and it did not much matter to many of them whether that radicalism emanated from the Left or from the Right.

With the success of Hitler's Nazis in the elections of the early 1930s, many German Communists switched to the Nazi Party, enormously alarming the KPD leadership. The KPD responded by raising the political stakes: it began to again openly call for violent revolution.[1824] While some historians pshaw the threat, it is a fact that there was a real, substantial, immediate threat of violent revolution from the Communists just before and just after Hitler came to power.

As late as 1932 at the twelfth plenary meeting of the Executive Committee of the Communist International (EKKI), the Communists again called for renewed armed revolutionary struggle in Germany. "[T]he German Revolution will decide the fate of the proletarian revolution in Western and Central Europe,"[1825] declared the EKKI. Its position was that the world was to be captured by first marching through Germany. When Hitler came to power their efforts were redoubled, issuing fighting orders to their terrorist-fighting organizations.[1826] To aid its revolutionary objectives, the Communists smuggled weapons into Germany from Czechoslovakia, Belgium, and Holland.[1827] Large thefts of explosives took place and detailed plans for conducting the revolution were prepared.[1828] Indeed, in March 1933, the Communists even managed to hijack 150 tons of explosives.[1829] Moreover, they explicitly threatened to burn the Reichstag.[1830] There can be little doubt but that they were both capable and willing to create still another violent German upheaval, disclaimers by leftist historians notwithstanding.

Shortly before Hitler came to power, there was justifiable fear within the populace that either or perhaps even both the Communists and the Nazis might again try to violently seize power or that they might even do so simultaneously. Such an event, it was thought, would likely trigger civil war within Germany and attacks on her soil by the Poles. In such an eventuality it was also assumed that Russia, France, and Poland would do all they could to exploit the situation. It was a dangerous time. During its conflict with Poland in 1920, Russia had gone so far as to prepare leaflets in German that were to be distributed after Russia had secured Poland, and then advanced into German territory. That plan was only abandoned after Russia was so thoroughly trounced at the Battle for Warsaw, or, as it is also known, the Miracle at the Vistula.[1831]

After Hitler had actually assumed power, the palpable threat and fear of still another attempt at Communist revolution prompted a good many Germans to see Hitler's crackdown immediately after the Reichstag fire in February 1933, says Kershaw, as "a long-necessary act of liberation"[1832] for the people. Reports within Germany were widespread that the KPD was planning still another coup and horrifying reports of atrocities in the East were being confirmed by credible witnesses, reports that added still more to fears of a Communist takeover.

The KPD launched a campaign to bring down Hitler. Shortly before the Reichstag fire they were making particularly threatening moves with calls to their union members to revolt. "Workers, to the barricades! Forward to victory!" proclaimed Communist publications.[1833] And, according to James Giblin and Robert Payne, "Put fresh bullets in your guns! Draw the pins of the hand grenades!"[1834] Clearly, the threat from Bolshevistic KPD was real enough and held the potential for enormous, disastrous consequences. Concern for the fate of Germany and Europe was understandably at something of a new apex.

Hitler saw a distinct connection between the threat of Bolshevism and the Jews. He commented on the subject and revealed his thinking for conduct toward Jews in the early years of his regime. In a discussion of the matter with Otto Wagener he revealed the following:

> Which is the more dangerous enemy—I mean, the one that threatens us most immediately? Without a doubt it is Bolshevism—we can safely call it Jewish Bolshevism. For if it were not Jewish, it could be given a different format. In that case, we might even be able to come to terms with it at some later date. But we will never be able to come to terms with Jewish Bolshevism without signing our own death warrant.
>
> Once we have recognized *it* as the primary enemy, however, we must avoid rousing the remaining Jews in the world against us *until* the Bolshevik danger has been removed. That is why we may *not* expel the Jews who live in Germany, we may *not* expropriate their goods, we may not harm a hair on their heads; and that is why we may not go public with our social economy and with other problems and plans, with which we would rouse liberalistic world Jewry and the entire liberalist world against us. *Rather, we must live peacefully with them!*[1835] [Italics are in the original.]

In December 1928, the SPD chief of police in Berlin had banned all public demonstrations. In March 1929, the ban was extended to encompass the whole of Prussia. The ban meant that the Communists would be prohibited from public demonstration on their traditional International Workers' Day, a name used interchangeably with May Day, May 1. In addition to being a day of celebration, the day was also one that was commonly accompanied by street protest and demonstration, and, frequently, violent riots. The Communist Party of Germany, which was by this time nearly equal in strength in Berlin to the SPD (in the May 1928 elections, the KPD captured 24.6 percent of the vote, the SPD 28.4 percent), challenged the ban and demonstrated in defiance of it. The SPD responded by calling out the Berlin police garrison. By the end of the day some thirty-two demonstrators were dead and another eighty were wounded. The events of the day highlighted the threat still posed by the Communists and further deepened the rift between the SPD and the KPD.[1836] Even the eventual installation of Hitler as Germany's chancellor in 1933—an appointment that was in no small part due to the internecine combat between the Marxist parties—could not heal the breach between the SPD and KPD. KPD leader Ernst Thälmann's proposal for a joint SPD-KPD-led general strike that was intended to bring down Hitler came to nothing.

After 1929, fears of Communists were of vast import in bringing Hitler a mass following. Their militant labor strike on May 1 and their calls for civil war fizzled after several months but those acts further hardened the populace against the KPD. Hitler was speaking for a multitude when he expressed concern that the fate of Russia might befall Germany. Joachim Fest quotes him as saying, "I tremble at the thought of what would become of our old, overcrowded continent if the chaos of the Bolshevistic revolution were to be successful."[1837]

The Bolshevists had made no secret of their intentions. The Jewish chief of the Cheka, Latvian M. Latsis, had proclaimed at the end 1918 what was in store for the bourgeoisie enemies of the Bolsheviks:

> We are engaged in exterminating the bourgeoisie as a class. You need not prove that this or that man acted

against the interest of Soviet power. The first thing you have to ask an arrested person is: To what class does he belong, where does he come from, what kind of education did he have, what is his occupation? These questions are to decide the fate of the accused. That is the quintessence of the Red Terror.[1838]

Communist and Nazi Clashes

Our establishment historians tend to emphasize the violence of the Nazis but on the whole say little of the violence from competing camps. Political murders carried out by the KPD in the late 1920s and early 1930s intensified popular fear of Communism. The various Marxist parties had formed paramilitary units such as the SPD's Reichsbanner with over a million members. The Communists had the 130,000 men of the Red Front Fighters League[*] and used it extensively, especially toward the close of the Weimar era. The SA was but a mirror image of the various leftist paramilitary formations. In November 1922, Hitler compared the actions of the Marxist formations with those of his SA:

> The Marxists taught—if you will not be my brother, I will bash your skull in. Our motto shall be—if you will not be a German, I will bash your skull in. For we are convinced that we cannot succeed without a struggle. We have to fight with ideas, but, if necessary, also with our fists.[1839]

The Marxists, says Fest, even as much and more than the Nazis, "united mind and brutal violence harmoniously."[1840]

Germany's Marxist violence is highlighted by the fact that 2,400 of Hitler's SA troops were wounded or killed in fights with them in just the first four months of 1931.[1841] Nazi meetings and parades were often the object of Communist violence. During the first three weeks of July 1932, there were numerous clashes in the

---

[*] The league was banished in 1929 but continued to exist under a different name, *Kampfbund gegen den Faschismus*—Fighting Alliance Against Fascism.

streets; in the five weeks before July 20, there were 500 clashes in Prussia alone, resulting in ninety-nine dead and 1,125 wounded.[1842] On July 17, 1932, a particularly bloody confrontation took place in Hamburg-Altona when Communist snipers atop roofs fired on a Nazi parade. The Nazis answered in kind. A total of seventeen people were killed that day and many more severely wounded.[1843] The general populace concluded that most of the violence stemmed from Communist initiatives, and they were therefore highly in sympathy with the counterviolence by the Nazis.

In August 1932, Chancellor Franz von Papen promulgated an emergency presidential decree imposing the death penalty on anyone who killed a political opponent out of rage or hatred, a Weimar version of Hate Crimes. Von Papen's decree was aimed squarely at the Communists, a fact that highlights the culprit for most of the violence of that time.[1844] The Jewish-led Communists were every bit as bullying as Hitler's SA; in those days even more so. The SA and SS lost over 350 dead and 40,000 wounded[1845] by their Communist counterparts during the period 1919–1933. Voters justifiably saw the violence of the Nazi SA as a countervailing act to the violent aggression of the Communists.[1846] It was also in response to Communist violence that Papen ousted the government of Prussia and assumed the leadership role himself. In a wholly unconstitutional act he appointed himself as Reich Commissar for Prussia. As we bemoan and condemn the constitutional excesses of Hitler we should keep in mind the precedents established for him under "democratic" rule.

Anti-Semitic Rhetoric

The Communists, appealing for support from the Right, tried to sell a form of National Bolshevism. They sought to emplace the idea of a possible merger between German nationalism and Russian Communism. In doing so, they excoriated Jews.

For all that the Nazi leadership thought of "Jewish sexual perfidy—as violators of Aryan women, . . . traffickers in white slavery, abortionists, homosexual pederasts,"[1847] and purveyors of pornography, they did not make any of it an electioneering theme.

To the extent that such electioneering did occur, it, too, was on the part of the SPD and the KPD as they tried to woo right-wing anti-Semitic voters to their cause. This was done in spite of the fact that it was the Communists themselves who were allied with the hedonists of the period—the KPD was the gay movement's ally in the Reichstag.[1848] For all of their effort to win votes from the Right, however, the SPD and KPD could not overcome their identification with the avant-garde, an association that served to validate anti-Semites in their claims that the Weimar government was a Judaized Republic.

The KPD, though heavily populated by Jews, was not reticent about attacking its opponents with anti-Semitic slurs. While Hitler had toned down his anti-Semitic rhetoric in order to attract the broader populace, the KPD continued to contribute to anti-Semitism with its political work. Hitler at the time presented himself as a moderate on the Jewish Question, speaking of an "anti-Semitism of reason," a nonviolent version of anti-Semitism that only sought to mollify Jewish influence through political measures.[1849] Attacks on "capitalist Jews" were as intense from the Left as from the Right—the theory being, as Jewish Communist Ruth Fischer had put it, "anyone who exhorted others to join the conflict against Jewish capitalism was participating in the class war, even if he did not know it."[1850] The idea was that German nationalism could perhaps be melded with Russian Communism on the basis of common hostility to Western culture and capitalism. Previously, Fischer had gone so far (in 1923) as to make a demagogic appeal to volkisch students to hang Jewish capitalists from street lamps.[1851]

Both the KPD and the SPD employed all manner of propagandistic devices of the kind that we normally associate only with Hitler. The SPD symbolism was awash with red banners, sashes, and flames.[1852] The KPD, of course, had its red flags and hammer and sickle as well as various slogans such as "Workers of the world, unite!" The influential ADGB trade union employed a three-arrow motif to symbolize its three main principles: *Einigkeit, Aktivität, Disziplin* (unity, action, discipline) against its three enemies: *Kapitalismus, Faschismus, Reaktion* (capitalism, Fascism, reaction).[1853]

The SPD, for its part, deliberately abandoned issues of reason and instead appealed to the emotions of the populace. It went so far as to hire Sergei Chakhotin, a psychologist and former student of Ivan Pavlov, to aid them in making propaganda. Party members wore party badges, used a clenched-fist greeting with each other, and shouted "Freedom!" or "Red Front!" as its equivalents to the "Heil Hitler!" salute. Street processions, uniformed marches, and collective demonstrations of *will* were also employed in much the same manner as the Nazis;[1854] indeed, much of what the Nazis did in those days was learned by them from the acts of the various leftist formations.

The right-wing *Völkischer Beobachter*[*] was by now reaching the masses and trumpeting the right-wing cause, highlighting and hawking Jewish involvement in all of the misery and decline suffered during the decade, but without connecting its claims to Hitler. The newspaper, for example, began running reviews of art exhibitions in 1928, attacking Jews as the harbingers of modern art and generating heated controversy.[1855]

Squalidness in film, art, and other areas of culture that were so highly influenced by Jewish interests continued. By the late 1920s, it seems that many Germans who had previously supported or at least tolerated the absurd crassness in film, literature, and social mores were at their end. Tolerance had been stretched to the breaking point. The women's movement had by then reversed itself; German woman were then seeking an end to flagrant licentiousness and a return to traditional values of hearth, home, family, and marital fidelity—of moral certitude. Celebration of the hooker, the insane, the degenerate was still hefty but in decline; distortion was giving way to normality, to rectitude, even as the severe economic and social problems of the era were pressing

---

[*] The radical right-wing *Völkischer Beobachter* had been cheaply acquired by the Nazis in 1920 after the paper had approached a state of bankruptcy stemming from various lawsuits brought against it by its Jewish opponents. The newspaper became a staple of Nazi propaganda.

down on the necks of the populace. Mockery and desecration of Christianity and its tenets, though, remained high on the list of progressives. It was becoming increasingly apparent to Germans that the godless school policies of the Bavarian revolutionaries at the outset of the previous decade, the ongoing attacks against probity such as the attacks against pornography and homosexuality laws, was not for them.

In 1926, controversy over the need for antipornography laws had again surfaced, stimulated in large part by performances of the always controversial Jewish author and playwright Arthur Schnitzler's *Reigen* (Round, Hands Around or Merry-go-round, a sex comedy),[1856] a play which had been written in 1897. According to an online article by Gareth Lewis, "The play was so appalling to the society, that the actors were taken to court. The play became so famous during the trial that no other writer could have wanted a better promotion for his novels and plays. The actors were prosecuted and the play was banned again."[1857] Schnitzler was branded as a pornographer as the result of *Reigen*, and rightist leaders exploited his notoriety by using his works as examples of "Jewish filth." Popular outrage that was stimulated by *Reigen* and other cultural affronts had accumulated in the mind-set of voters. In 1929, Magnus Hirschfeld resurfaced the pornography issue as he successfully proposed liberalization of the 1925 antiobscenity law, again highlighting Jewish power and involvement in the subject of obscenity.

Also in 1929, Jewish politician and playwright Walter Mehring, in association with the Jewish theater director and producer, Erwin Piscator, produced his drama, *Der Kaufmann von Berlin* (The Merchant of Berlin), depicting an Eastern Jewish immigrant who goes from rags to riches. The play created a scandal due to its brutalization of Germans. The Jewish characters in the play are manipulators of capital, an incarnation of the Eternal Jew. With plays like this, Hitler and the extreme right-wing had found an unlikely ally. At the end of the drama, street sweepers sweep away German symbols that are represented as junk: steel helmets, the dead body of a German soldier. A chorus sings: "Dreck, weg damit!" (Filth, away with it!)

Adding still further insult to the social milieu of 1929, Kurt Tucholsky published his book, *Deutschland, Deutschland, über alles* (Germany, Germany Above All—the title of the German national anthem). In keeping with everything he represented to the right wing, Tucholsky again attacked the churches, denounced the police, further excoriated the German officer corps, and heaped still more derision on Field Marshal von Hindenburg. He emphatically declared that "What . . . judges call treason, does not concern us, what they consider high treason is not to us a dishonourable action."[1858] All the while that Tucholsky was attacking Germany and her venerated icons and institutions he championed pacifism and sexual promiscuity. Dissatisfied with the strength of pacifism at the time, Tucholsky assigned responsibility for its relative failure to its abstract and philosophical loftiness; he recommended "infiltration of the family" as a means to strengthen its position.[1859] The sort of extremist criticism of Germany and Tucholsky's declaration of willingness to commit treason was stuff made for the propaganda mills of radicals of the ultraright wing.

But if Tucholsky knew the power of propaganda, so, too, did Hitler. Here was "proof" of the stereotypical Jewish tendency for disloyalty toward host countries in the Diaspora as well as their souring effect on matters of culture. Tucholsky's treasonous statements and acts, as well as his general loathing of everything German, provided loathsome subject matter for Hitler and his Nazi propaganda mill.

Zionism Joins the Nazis in Spirit

The rise of Hitler to power was taken by a few Jews as good for Judaism precisely because Hitler was such a devout and radical anti-Semite. The then world famous Emil Ludwig commented to an interviewer that "Thousands who seemed to be completely lost to Judaism were brought back to the fold by Hitler, and for that I am very grateful to him." Chaim Nachman Bialik, the poet laureate of Zionism, was a man who "thought of the Jews as a pocket-sized master race." He "could not hide his happiness that Hitler had come just in time to save German Jewry from its own destruction" by assimilation. Bialik even shared some of Hitler's extremism: "I, too, like Hitler," said Bialik, "believe in the power of the blood idea."

The popularity of the nationalistic Zionist movement in Germany had by the late 1920s become a force of both great power and controversy. Robert Weltsch, according to Niewyk, commented in 1928 that "the whole of Jewish life orients itself around Zionism"[1860]—a claim of only mild hyperbole. Their antiassimilationist thrust was highlighted in 1929 when Zionist leaders in Berlin condemned intermarriage as a threat to the racial purity of the stock[1861] of Jews, thus putting themselves squarely in the Nazi camp in terms of racism and its facilitator, endogamy. Similarly, German Zionist assertions about creating a closed brotherhood of Jews over and against all other communities on earth[1862] lent credence to Nazi propaganda about both racialism and the threat posed by Jewish organizations. Zionist assertions often included specific rejection of assimilation and all things German, adding to suspicions already prevalent that Jews were disloyal and a threat to Germany.

Mainstream Jewish opposition to Zionism centered on the idea that Zionism's emphasis on cultural separatism, and especially the Eastern Orthodox ones, would further inflame anti-Semitism because Jews would be viewed as aliens and would be perceived not as a religious group but as an ethnic/national entity. That is, it was not the case that opposition Jews did not want to participate in the separateness and particularism that has historically characterized them, it was, instead, that they did not want their penchant for separateness and particularism to be perceived by Gentiles. Zionists, on the other hand, trumpeted Jewish separatist inclinations—the "foreignness" of Jews within the German populace.

Events in Russia and Elsewhere

Events in Russia and elsewhere in Eastern Europe were alarming and Jewish involvement in them was increasingly known. The events of the early 1920s in Poland and Hungary were, of course, widely known within the German populace, and likewise the Red Terror* in Russia during the period 1918–1921. At the close of the decade there was renewed awareness of atrocities in what was by this time the Soviet Union. The face of Communism again came into focus; it was vicious—and too largely of Jewish making.

One of the most Jewish of all Soviet institutions[1863] was the notorious NKVD, the secret police organization formally known as the People's Commissariat for Internal Affairs. Peasant farmers were starved and otherwise brutalized under Jewish NKVD leader Lazar Moiseivich Kaganovich, "the Butcher of Ukraine." Beginning in 1929, cattle and crops were confiscated; widespread starvation ensued, culminating in the starvation death of some 7 million Ukrainians. Jewish-Russian writers and human rights activists pilpulized the Ukrainian famine as "historical necessity."[1864] Soviet writer Lev Kopelev, says Kevin MacDonald, "shed no tears for the Ukrainian and Russian peasants and nationalists who were murdered in the name of international Socialism even as he mourned the loss of Jews murdered because they were Jews."[1865] To the extent that such happenings were known to the German populace in the 1920s, they both created revulsion toward Communism and further reinforced the thought process of an equivalency between Jews, Communism, and brutality.

When Hitler finally came to power world leaders credited him above all else with having defeated Communist aims in Germany. So abhorrent were the acts of leading Jews in the Soviet Union, it was the case that for many, Hitler's defeat of Bolshevism in Germany was alone quite enough to embrace him and his Nazis. England's Lord Rothermere published an article in the *Daily Mail* in September 1930 that praised Hitler as the bulwark against

---

* The brutal campaign of Red Terror was initiated upon the assassination of the Jewish leader of the Cheka for Northern Russia, Moisei Uritsky (Boretsky) and the attempted assassination of Lenin in August 1918.

Bolshevism. He had, said Rothermere, eliminated the grave danger posed by the Soviet campaign against European civilization.[1866]

Death of Stresemann

Without question, the most influential events in Germany during 1929 were the death of Gustav Stresemann and the October crash of the stock market. Stresemann was an admixture of staunch nationalist sentiment but with liberal leanings. He, like countless other nationalists, including Hitler, was inclined to everywhere see "reds under the beds."[1867] He had been a central figure in what little progress and stability Germany managed to achieve during the 1920s. It was he more than any other who had finally stabilized the currency in 1923, and it was he who had carefully negotiated a path between the strictures of the Treaty of Versailles and international goodwill for Germany. He had served in multiple governments, even serving as chancellor for a short time. Most of the work for which he rightly earned great credit, however, was as the minister of foreign affairs under four different governments; it was in that position, for example, that he helped end the French occupation of the Ruhr in 1924 and thereby saved the nation from the radicalism that the occupation had unleashed. He also negotiated the 1924 Dawes Plan that recommitted Germany to compliance with the Treaty of Versailles, rescheduled her debt, and resulted in massive foreign investment coming into the country to the great benefit of the economy. He finalized the Locarno Treaties in 1925, thereby helping to reestablish Germany's place among the world's nations, including its admission to the League of Nations in 1926—the year in which he shared the Nobel Peace Prize.

Though a liberal in some respects, Stresemann was more nationalistic than the typical members of the Weimar government leadership. He asserted that 33,000 Marxists held sway in Prussia and that consequently, Prussia's domestic politics were purely Marxist and that the policies went counter to the natural order of things in that they were oriented toward compulsion, agitation, demagoguery, and street fighting. German foreign policy, he said, had become internationalized and that those who controlled it were out to ensure that Germany would never again achieve power. With respect to the foregoing, at least, Stresemann's thought process was well aligned with that of Hitler.[1868] Like Hitler, he also yearned for the repatriation of the 10 to 12 million of his kindred who were then under foreign yokes and flags. Similarly, he sought to recover Danzig, the Polish Corridor, and Upper Silesia, and, too, to create a union with Austria[1869]—in these areas, too, he was in total alignment with Hitler and other staunch nationalists.

The death of Stresemann and the onset of the Depression signaled the demise of Hermann Müller's Grand Coalition cabinet, which was comprised from the membership of the SPD, DDP, DVP, and Center Party, one of the most stable governments since the election of 1928. The liberal German People's Party, DVP, the party to which Stresemann belonged, broke with the coalition, and the government was therefore forced to resign in March 1930. Stable government would thenceforth not be had until the advent of the Nazis. It was the figurative, but not yet the actual, end of the Weimar period.[1870] With the resignation of Müller, who was chancellor from 1928–1930, the chancellorship was passed in quick succession to Heinrich Brüning (March 1930–March 1932), Franz von Papen (June 1932–December 1932), Kurt von Schleicher (December 1932–January 1933); and finally, and fatefully, to Hitler on 30 January 1933. But it is worth noting at this point that the Brüning-Papen-Schleicher system of rule by presidential decree from 1930 onward served as a prehistory for the Third Reich.[1871] That is, an ineffectual dictatorship was already in place by the time Hitler assumed power.

U.S. Recalls Loans

The stock market crash caused the United States to recall its many short-term loans made to Germany, resulting in a rapid decline in the economy and skyrocketing unemployment. Fest claims that the recall of loans stemmed from rumors of a pending Nazi coup. Other authors have it that it was rumors of a Communist coup that caused the recall. Whatever the truth or falsehood of those claims, it can certainly be assumed that financially influential Jews, such as investment bankers, contributed mightily to the outflow of German capital. If only because Jews were so plentiful and prominent in both the banks and the stock exchanges, it was axiomatic to associate the miseries of the Depression with Jewish machinations in the financial machinery of nations, and most especially Germany's. Hitler was therefore all the more able to assign blame for the economic depression to Jews and to Germany's compliance with the Treaty of Versailles.[1872] Moreover, with the Jewish and radically Marxist economist Rudolf Hilferding as the German minister of finance when the Depression hit (Hilferding was a former member of the USPD and one of the November Criminals), fault for the economic conditions was rather all the more easily assigned to Jews.

The Great Depression actually stemmed from two significant events, not one. The first, of course, was the collapse of the stock market in October of 1929; the second was the collapse of the Austrian bank, Creditanstalt, in 1931. The bank had been founded by the Rothschilds in 1855. It was the largest bank in Austria-Hungary. It was the failure of this bank, not the stock market crash per se, which was the proximate cause of the global financial crisis in the world's banking system. Indeed, it was this crisis that touched off the sea change of bank failures that resulted in the Great Depression. Given that the bank had been founded by the Jewish banking family of Rothschilds, and given as well the prominence of Jews throughout the world's banking system, it was not much of a stretch to lay the blame for the misery of the Depression, however illegitimately, on Jews and Jewish interests.

The onset of the Depression was certainly a major factor in Hitler's ability to rise to power, but it did not stand alone: Germany was in exhaustive psychological shock that was brought about by the accumulated effects of the lost war, revolutionary turmoil, hyperinflation, ineffectual government, widespread scandal, and, importantly, a complete collapse of Germany's hitherto exemplary views and practices concerning matters of morality and culture in general. And all of the ills, with only a pittance of irrational logic, could be pretty easily ascribed to Jews.

More rhetoric by the effete government concerning the need for reason went unheeded. What was wanted was a seachange and determined leadership that would overcome the governmental and societal floundering of the past ten and more years.[1873]

William Brustein, in his book *The Logic of Evil*, maintains that Nazi success "resulted largely from its superlative success at fashioning economic programs that addressed the material needs of millions of Germans."[1874] While it is easily conceded that economic motivations are important when selecting a party, we may suspect that it did not hold quite the importance it assumes in the work of Brustein and some others. The broad-based nature of Hitler's program encompassed national and international issues (e.g., Treaty of Versailles, lost lands), political philosophies (democracy vs. autocracy, Socialism vs. capitalism, nationalism of the Nazis vs. the internationalism of the KPD), religious, cultural, rural and urban, and differing objectives of the various classes (urban vs. rural workers, exporters vs. manufacturers for domestic consumption), and social and cultural issues, as well as societal atomization along with a host of others. When the economic crisis of 1929 hit the German economy, many Germans were already prepared to embrace autocratic government, whether from the Left or the Right, and they were prepared for such an outcome due to a storm of hardship and humiliation they had endured under democracy. The economic crisis might be likened to the assassination of Archduke Ferdinand and World War I—it set to flame an already highly volatile kindling. Democracy paved the road for the Nazis, and it did so on a broad range of issues that pulled at the kith, kin, and the heartstrings of the populace. The economic issue was only one among many that drew people to the Nazi Party and we may justifiably suspect that its importance was not nearly so great as it is often claimed.

People often select a political party or candidate for quite irrational reasons. In America, Blacks voted overwhelmingly for Barak Obama though many had not an inkling of his political stance; the same can be said about Hillary Clinton and women. A dear friend of this author voted for Barak Obama because "he seems like such a nice man," as indeed he did and does—but she had not an inkling of his politics. None.

In Weimar Germany the anomic character of the Weimar government and society served as a powerful incentive for people to abandon it in order to try a new, radical one. It could just as easily have been the Communists who had won the day. It was the superior understanding of humanity and the resultant emotional messaging that enabled the Nazis to win the ideological struggle. Moreover, the very fact that the Nazis had not participated in previous governments put them outside the circle of blame for the anomie engendered by the ultraliberalism of the Weimar government.

Reichstag Elections, 1930

As several times emphasized, in 1928, Adolf Hitler and his Nazi Party were still little more than curiosities, political backwater extremists with virtually no hope of success. Two years later, in 1930, they experienced the luck of gargantuan political shifts in the voting populace. From a mere 800,000 votes, 1.5 percent of the vote overall total, resulting in twelve Reichstag seats, they now soared to over 16.5 million votes, 18 percent of the vote and 107 seats. They were now solidly the party of the rural villager and the traditionalists, if not yet the national conservatives (large landowners and monarchists—the Junkers). The vote was an expression of the intense polarization of the electorate, an electorate that now advantaged both of the extremist parties: the Nazis and the Communists. The Communists climbed to seventy-seven seats in the Reichstag, mostly at the expense of the SPD. Hitler's Nazis benefited by defections from the conservative DVNP but also brought aboard a broad coalition of new voters and won a surprising number of votes from the middle classes. In essence then, the Left moved further to the left and the Right further to the extreme right. It is all easy enough to identify now with more than eighty years retrospective consideration plugged into the political equations, but at the time it was not so simple as that: only emotion stemming from repeatedly shattered hopes could adequately account for the voting patterns of the early 1930s. And, regrettably, a small subset of Jews provided enormous inputs into the shattered things of Weimar Germans in the late 1920s and early 1930s.

Many historians examine the rise of Nazism with respect to particular groups within German society such as the upper and lower middle class, the new and old middle class, rural and urban populations, workers and capitalists, religious affiliation, geographical aspects of the population, men, women, youth, etc. Economic interests are often seen as the primal motivator for going with the Nazis. In actual fact, as already emphasized, there was a broad spectrum of things that joined with the economic woes that encouraged commitment to Hitler's ideas.

Hitler explicitly set out to encompass every class, region, and religion: he was of a mind that although you may presently oppose him, you would eventually see things his way and embrace him, his policies, and his party. This attitude of Hitler was not entirely a matter of political strategy; it was, instead, simply in keeping with his regard for the greatness of the German people—rich, poor, leftist, rightist, capitalist, or Marxist—he sought to convert the lot of them to restore German unity and greatness. Hitler had a religion: it was Nazism and he was every bit as effective as its proselytizer as any apostle. As Fest states it, "The significant fact is that the [Nazi] party attracted people of every origin, every sociological coloration, and developed its dynamism as a movement unifying antagonistic groups, interests, and feelings."[1875]

The basic reason for Hitler's success was much simpler than conspiracy theorists would have it: The people were by then simply desperate for leadership that could revitalize the nation. Such leadership seemed to be embodied in Adolf Hitler. It was the party membership—the downtrodden and disaffected, the true believers who sponsored the Nazis. According to Bullock, "Police agents were quoted as reporting that the sums people of modest means were prepared to give 'bordered on the unbelievable.'"[1876]

In the early years people joined the Nazi Party at great risk to their livelihood and careers. Author William Brustein highlights the fact that "studies of the early Nazi Party ignore the numerous personal costs and risks that the act of joining the party entailed."[1877] There were, for example, governmental bans on teachers and civil servants from joining the party, and those who did were fired. "During the years 1920–1933," says Richard Tedor, "many universities banned SA men, Hitler Youth leaders and NSDAP members, a substantial percentage of whom were combat veterans of World War I, from enrolling or teaching."[1878] In places like Cologne, the University of Cologne had banned the presence of the National Socialist German Student League from university property. Civil servants in SPD-controlled Prussia were threatened with termination if they joined the Nazi Party. But even as the social and political boycott of the Nazis was enforced, the party continued to grow. As many as 12 percent of party members lost their jobs or had their business ruined after they joined the party.[1879] Bruno Gesche's experience with democracy and its willingness to terminate his employment due to his political beliefs has already been recounted. Sepp Dietrich, another intimate of Hitler and the chief of his security detail, suffered a similar experience after Hitler's Beer Hall Putsch. Kurt Gilisch, still another member of the security detail, was similarly sacked from teaching jobs due to his Nazi affiliations. It was easy enough for the rural peasant to ignore such strictures; there was nowhere in the countryside any political entity to punish them for their voting patterns, and they were therefore free to join and vote for the Nazis.

By the early 1930s even the many strictures and risks in the big cities were no longer enough to keep the educated classes from joining with the Nazis. The depth of dissatisfaction within those classes is evidenced by the fact that members of those classes joined the party in spite of the considerable risk to their careers and livelihood. They had had quite enough of Weimar "democracy."

William Brustein, in his book *The Logic of Evil*, illustrates the risks as follows:

> One of the most frequently cited examples of the potential costs of joining the Nazi Party, as far as

> employment went, was the government's pronouncement in 1932 that membership in the NSDAP was incompatible with employment in the German civil service. All teachers and government employees, like public transport workers, had to sign a declaration asserting that they were not members of the NSDAP and had not participated in NSDAP activities. Thus, before 1933 many civil servants who sympathized with the Nazis probably decided to vote for the party and forego joining it.
>
> Between 1925 and 1932, governmental policy often served as a major impediment to Nazi Party recruitment. In particular, state and central governments frequently instituted bans on Nazi Party activities. Nazi Party recruitment fared relatively ill in Prussia, Baden, and Bavaria, where governmental hostility toward the NSDAP eventuated in an array of official bans on Nazi Party activities, active police enforcement of those bans, and police harassment.

It was democracy in farcical garb—a democracy in which the constitution was ignored, for the constitution explicitly sought empowerment of the minority parties, even the radial ones.

While Nazi Party membership entailed numerous costs it simultaneously offered very few offsetting rewards. Party members were not only obliged to pay membership dues, they were also required to distribute party literature, attend party meetings, and take part in public rallies, all at their own expense. What they got in return for their sacrifice was nothing more than the staunch belief that the future would be better than the past—and that was quite enough. Stated otherwise, they got precisely what the rich industrialist got when they finally embraced the Nazis: they got the party platform and nothing more.

After expending several pages of text (pages 169–71) to illustrate the many examples of risk endured by Nazi Party members, Brustein concludes the subject by saying that "In the face of so many disincentives associated with membership, it is certainly remarkable that the Nazi Party grew into a mass movement."[1880] He is quite right.

For all that has been said about the evil motivations of the Nazi leadership and its membership, it is refreshing to, from time to time, encounter an author who acknowledges the practical reasons for joining the Nazis. Brustein does just that and his assessment is worth quoting at some length:

> [W]e have overlooked the plausibility that millions of Germans may have consciously voted for or joined the Nazi Party because they believed the Nazi programs reflected their interests. It was not because they were evil that Germans flocked to the Nazi Party *before 1933*, nor did they perceive the NSDAP as representing evil. Rather, many Germans calculated that of the competing Weimar political parties, the Nazis offered them the best prospects for a better life. In particular, in the midst of the Great Depression, the Nazi Party alone crafted economic programs that in the perception of many Germans could redress their grievances or provide the means to greater mobility.
>
> [I]rrational leitmotifs such as anti-Semitism, hypernationalism, and xenophobia played a marginal role in the rise of the NSDAP. Because the collective result of Nazism was so horrific and irrational, the literature has naturally focused on the nonrational nature of Nazism and thus tended to overestimate the importance of nonrational themes to the rise of Nazism. In attempting to understand the Nazi phenomenon, we err if we fail to distinguish its origin from its outcome. The average German who voted for or joined the NSDAP before 1933 did not envision Auschwitz, World War II, or the destruction of Germany.[1881]

After the Reichstag fire in February 1933 the Nazis proposed the infamous Enabling Act that gave plenary power to Hitler. Otto Wels of the SPD rose to object to passage of the legislation. Among the claims advanced by Wels was that opposition to the government was salutary and needed to be protected. Hitler thereafter rose to challenge Wels's assertions with an impromptu speech of invective that recounted the treatment of the Nazis when they were the opposition party. In particular, he recounted the repression meted out by the Berlin Police Commissioner Albert Grzesinski (purportedly Jewish), as well as Prussian Minister-President Otto Braun, and Prussian Interior Minister Carl Severing, all of whom were from the SPD. Hitler also recounted the following:

> You talk about persecution. I think that there are only a few of us here who did not have to suffer persecution from your side in prison You seem to have forgotten completely that for years our shirts were ripped off our backs because you did not like the color. . . . We have [progressed beyond] your persecutions. You say furthermore that criticism is salutary. Certainly, those who love Germany may criticize us, but those who worship an Internationale cannot.[1882]

Where he could, Hitler emphasized that all of the nation's troublemakers, all of its revolutions and financial woes and hardship stemmed from a single sinister force, the big-city Jew who was usually attacked, not as a Jew per se, but instead, as a Marxist. And his task was made all the easier by the abundant evidence that a great lot of it actually was.

* * * *

By 1930, Germany's industrialists had concluded that the system of parliamentary democracy was not up to the tasks facing the nation. In particular, the SPD was seen as corrupt due to the numerous scandals of recent years, wrongheaded with respect to fiscal policy (the SPD wanted additional unemployment benefits while employers were calling for less), and ineffectual with respect to foreign policy, as exemplified by the Young Plan. Calls were increasingly made for stronger "presidential style" government and even for the exclusion of the SPD from political power.[1883]

Now, with the demonstrated polling success of the Nazis the industrialists began to clamber aboard the Nazi bandwagon, but even by this late stage, the party remained primarily dependent upon party membership for its finances. There has long been a tendency among historians, and especially those who wrote in the first forty or so years after the war, to associate Nazi success with the financial largesse of German businessmen and industrialists. Even now, there are hangers-on for that idea. Amos Elon, whose book *The Pity of It All*, which was published in 2003, continues the myth by incorrectly claiming that Hitler's early financial support came from businessmen, landowners, and church leaders.[1884] Elon's claim is in error: he did not receive meaningful support from such sources and it's now the case that even most establishment historians readily acknowledge that fact.

There is a famous cartoon that was drawn by the Jewish Communist John Heartfield in 1932 that shows Hitler with his hand above his head, his palm up, while a businessman is placing money into the hand. The cartoon is titled "Real Meaning of the Nazi Salute." The cartoon was meant by Heartfield to create an image of Hitler and Nazism as dependent on the right-wing forces of capitalism.[1885] The image is propagandistic and powerful but wholly false—Nazi money came from the people, and not for anti-Semitic reasons. The mythology that industrialists such as Hugo Stinnes were critical to the electoral success of Hitler is also untrue. There is nowhere any convincing evidence that Hitler received substantial subsides from big business.[1886] Indeed, claims to the contrary provided the Nazi Party with a substantial infusion of cash: a newspaper had claimed that Hitler and his Nazis were financed by Henry Ford. Hitler sued the publication for that liable and won a settlement of 6 million marks. As American historian H. A. Turner has conclusively demonstrated, the NSDAP received only modest, inconsequential support from industrialists until shortly before he came to power.[1887] Industrialists supported Hugenberg's DNVP, not Hitler's NSDAP. Hitler's support came from pitifully small donations from true believers, the sale of Nazi publications, and admission fees at Nazi rallies and speeches.

It is sometimes stated, sometimes just implied, that when businesses finally did contribute to the Nazis in large numbers and amounts, it was due to the ingrained anti-Semitism of the donors or stemmed from their supposed jealousy over Jewish successes in industry and commerce. Again, though, the problem with such assertions, like similar ones concerning their importance to Hitler's electoral success, is that they are simply not true and contemporary historians are increasingly willing to acknowledge as much. Michael Fitzgerald comments on this subject as follows:

> In spite of all the reams of paper which have been wasted by conspiracy theorists in a vain attempt to "prove" that the Nazis were a party of the upper and middle classes, the facts simply do not bear this out. Most party members were very ordinary people, from working-class or lower middle-class backgrounds. Also contrary to the myths, the amount of money which the Nazis received from business sources has been grossly exaggerated. The bulk of the party's income up to 1934 came from membership subscriptions and donations by party members, by no means always the better off ones either. To these ordinary Germans, bewildered and angry at a country that seemed to have no use for them, Hitler's sudden appointment as Chancellor, which had been totally unexpected, came as if a miracle had delivered them from their sufferings. They went wild with joy.[1888]

It is true that the Bechsteins, Bruckmanns, Hanfstaengl, Stennis, and a few industrialists had hitherto made contributions to the party, but these were minuscule given its expenses of roughly 2.8 million marks per week.[1889] And such contributions, modest though they were, had nothing whatever to do with anti-Semitism on the part of the contributors. Moreover, if it were only money that enabled the politics of the day, the KPD, financed by Moscow, would have won the day handily. Money is certainly important to an election effort but so too are feelings of helplessness and misery in the populace.

Hitler was not only a true believer, he was scrupulously incorruptible. Stolfi correctly points out that historians have been unfailing in seeking evidence of corruptibility on Hitler's part but have failed in their quest, though they have conducted the search for more than a half century. But they do have an explanation, though a pilulized one: they explain their failure simplistically; the Nazis, they say, were secretive.[1890] Elsewhere, Stolfi goes on to say the following about Hitler's incorruptibility:

> For most men and even the greater ones, real power must usually destroy them through the corruptive temptations of pleasure. Hitler was impenetrable to such temptation and was characterized by the legend of his monastic frugality with its quality of the pitiful, saintly, and awe-inspiring.[1891]

The Nazis even occasionally sent the SA on to the streets as common beggars, Nazi *Schnorrers*, as it were. They had become the "rainbow coalition of the discontented,"[1892] and it was those discontents who were the sources for Nazi finances. And the monies that these discontents provided were exceptionally well monitored and managed. All income and expenditures were duly logged and thoroughgoing annual audits were conducted to ensure that money was not misspent. The party treasurer was empowered to examine the books of any branch without prior notification.[1893] Nazis were not just politically radical; with respect to party finances at least, it seems they were scrupulously honest as well.[*]

Still, some few industrialists did begin to support the Nazis in the early 1930s, particularly a small but powerful group of coal and steel producers in the Rhineland and Westphalia. A few bankers

---

[*] Power corrupts. While the Nazi Party was scrupulous with respect to its finances, it is certainly easy enough to identify too many members of the party who later exploited their power in office to obtain great riches—Hermann Goering is most exemplary but certainly not alone in the category.

also provided funds.[1894] With additional monies now made available to them from the aforementioned sources, improved organization and themes, Hitler's temporary coalition with the DVNP, and by now a very large base of support (the SA alone numbered 100,000 in 1931, a year later it was at 300,000),[1895] the Nazis were finally positioned to at last get their message across to the broad spectrum of people who had previously been sitting on the political fence. Interestingly, as emphasized above, Hitler accepted contributions without any semblance of a tit-for-tat. Emil Kirdorg, an eighty-year-old maverick industrialist, at one point made a single donation of 100,000 marks to the party—a little more than a year later he resigned from the party because Hitler had viciously attacked the coal cartel which he and others had founded.[1896] Hitler and his Nazis, according to Fest, unlike the other large parties, gave their backers nothing more than the party platform in return for their largesse.[1897] They made the same deal with Germany's youth—great demands for sacrifice with no promise of offsetting individual rewards. You had to believe in the greater good that would eventually derive from your support, and that, and only that, was to be your reward. For its part, the Nazis would do what they claimed in their political platform and would manage contributions efficaciously.

That the Nazis were able to sustain themselves through donations from essentially impoverished supporters says a great deal about the commitment that those supporters felt. The Nazis, even more so than the Communists, were by now heartily radicalized and willing to risk their all on behalf of Hitler and his party. They were impoverished versions of America's Founding Fathers, people who were willing to risk their all in hopes of a better tomorrow.

Success at Last

In 1932 the Nazis more than doubled the huge success of a year earlier, by now garnering 37.3 percent of the vote, providing them with 230 seats in the Reichstag. Even as their election results in 1928 seemingly served as a confirmation of the incorrectness of their political posture, the accumulation of collective misery, and coming events (death of Stresemann, the stock market crash, ongoing scandals, shifts in voter attitudes about the state of German culture, and leftist interparty conflicts) set the stage for their surge and success. Success also came from the fact that Hitler campaigned exhaustively. His famous Flights Over Germany are typically portrayed by historians as gimmicks, but the fact was that he, far more effectively than all others, employed modern electioneering methodologies, and they paid off handsomely. Such methods represented both foresight and a keen willingness to embrace modern technologies to get his message to the people.

The elections of 1930 and 1932 had devastating effects on the republic. They established the Nazis as the largest party in Germany and all but demanded that Hitler be given the chancellorship. By March 1933, shortly after Hitler was indeed named chancellor, the Nazis, along with their allies in the Nationalist and Center Parties, in still another vote, managed to establish a majority coalition in the Reichstag. By that time, the political scales of the German Reichstag were weighted as follows: Nazis, 288; Nationalists (DNVP), 52; Catholic Center, 74; SPD 120; KPD, 81; and others, 32. That is, while the Nazis did not themselves achieve a majority, their coalition with the Nationalists and Center parties did: the Nazi, Nationalist, Center Party coalition represented a total of 414 votes in what was by that time a 608-seat Reichstag. Moreover, taken together, the Nazis and Communists garnered over 50 percent of the vote—thus, a majority of the people voted for the two parties whose objective was the overthrow of the extant government. It was a powerful expression of the people's dissatisfaction with the status quo.

*   *   *   *

As emphasized earlier, the elections did not revolve around anti-Semitism: Hitler and his party made almost no mention of Jews throughout the campaigns and his supporters were motivated by other issues. Richard Evans, in his book *The Coming of the Third Reich*, makes the point as follows:

> Among ordinary Party activists in the 1920s and early 1930s, the most important aspect of Nazi ideology was its emphasis on social solidarity—the concept of the organic racial community of all Germans—followed at some distance by extreme nationalism and the cult of Hitler. Anti-semitism, by contrast, was of significance only for a minority, and for a good proportion of these it was only incidental. The younger they were, the less important ideology was at all, and the more significant were features such as the emphasis on German culture and the leadership role of Hitler.[1898]

As a matter of campaign electioneering, anti-Semites, including Zionist and Communist ones, gleefully quoted from *Die Weltbühne's* destructive criticisms of everything German as typical of Jewish opinions. Recent attempts to rehabilitate publications such as *Die Weltbühne* notwithstanding, there can be no question but that it and its counterpart publications aided Hitler as they heaped abuse on the people and the republic at a time when it needed every possible morsel of encouraging support.[1899]

Moreover, says Niewyk, "As case studies of specific groups of Nazis have shown, anti-Semitism rarely played an important part in bringing new converts to National Socialism."[1900] Rather, it was the cumulative effect of crisis upon crisis, slight upon slight, and the collective effect of cultural corruption and an effete and wrongheaded central government that sounded the clarion for change. Adding to those ills, there was now the economic and political crisis stemming from the stock market crash that wiped out the middle class for a second time in the span of six years. It was altogether too much.

Hitler emphasized three important themes in his electioneering: The first was the threat from Bolshevism already discussed. The second was a highly viable economic plan to end the suffering from unemployment, including such innovations as the application of Keynesian economic principles even before Keynes published his treatise. The third was an emotional call for a national renewal, a renewal of Germany's esteemed culture. With respect to the economic situation, Hitler established in 1930 a Nazi Department for Economic Policy headed by Otto Wagener. Between 1930 and 1933, he laid out a series of important programs that defined the party's general economic philosophy: these included the 1930 agrarian program, the 1930 employment program, the 1931 WPA (*Wirtschaftspolitisches Sofortprogramm*), and the 1932 Reconstruction Plan (*Wirtschaftliches Aufbauprogramm*).[1901] The economic themes were intended to assuage the millions of people who were now out of work, but the emotional appeal was the one that most demonstrated his genius. Hitler addressed the emotional exhaustion of the people: their weariness with democratic rhetoric, and its constant appeals to reason and sobriety. The people were fed up with such pleas; they wanted to let their emotions run rampant—Hitler was there to accommodate them. Bullock effectively summarizes Hitler's approach as follows:

> Hitler never made the mistake of supposing that the best way to exploit its [the economic Depression] impact for electoral purposes was by making economic policy promises the centerpiece of the party's appeal. He grasped, as no other German politician did, that the effect of such economic factors on people's lives was one of psychological shock and that it was the emotions this created—fear, resentment, despair, the longing for reassurance and renewal of hope—to which a political leader should address himself.[1902]

Fest makes an argument that aligns with Bullock's:

> Hitler's great trick was to leap over the economic contradictions and offer instead high-sounding principles.... For his key weapon was his understanding that the behavior of human beings is not motivated exclusively by economic forces or interests. He counted instead on their need to have a suprapersonal reason for living and trusted in the power of an

"alternative culture" to dissolve class limits. This alternative was a package of slogans—an invocation of national honor, national greatness, oaths of loyalty and readiness to sacrifice.[1903]

Unable to explicitly satisfy the conflicting interests of several important voter factions (such as the farmers who wanted higher prices for food and urban dwellers who wanted lower ones), he substituted "national renewal" themes instead of addressing explicit grievances.

It was not the logic or particular policies given in Hitler's speeches that electrified his audiences, nor was it the pithiness of his slogans that captured their hearts and minds, it was instead the shared experiences—shared sufferings and hopes drew people to Hitler and his party.[1904] He would call for further work and sacrifice from the populace, he said, but he would also put an end to class war and everything that had happened to Germany since the war. He did not just offer empty promises, he demanded sacrificial participation by the people in the renewal of the country. He promised to renew Germany's moral and political strength and throw off the fetters of Versailles. His government would emphasize the Prussian virtues that had previously brought Germany such renown: culture, order, authority, sacrifice, service, discipline, and hierarchy. He would establish the heroic man in place of the economic man.[1905]

By the early 1930s, the voting populace was conditioned and attuned to hear and embrace his messages.

Composition of the Nazi Vote

In 1930, Hitler garnered support from all of the various classes but none so disproportionately as the upper and middle classes;[1906] not even the peasants moved to Nazism in such proportions. Support from these sectors of society is frequently assigned to German jealously of Jewish riches and consequent attempts by the merchant class to better compete with Jewish success. There is an alternative rationale: these were the people who were the best informed and most politically astute—and by this time they were so utterly dejected that even "democratic" threats against them for aligning themselves with the Nazis had little effect.

Hitler's upper- and middle-class supporters were, like everyone else, exhausted, and they understood the totality of the negative effect of leftist behavior in German society. They voted for rightist forces who were promising a return to the norms of traditional conduct and values. Hitler was openly promising that he would utterly destroy the Weimar government and relieve German suffering by discarding the Treaty of Versailles. He would, he said, bring about a new beginning. He would unite the people in what Kershaw refers to as an "ethnically pure and socially harmonious 'national community.' It was a complete counter-vision to the image of the 'leaderless democracy' of Weimar and its divisive system run by contemptible 'politicians', mere party functionaries."[1907] Sarah Gordon correctly observes that:

> Many Germans hoped Hitler could pull Germany out of the depression and others thought he was the only man capable of restoring dignity to the nation after its humiliating defeat in World War I and the Treaty of Versailles. Still others counted on his giving precedence, both economically and politically, to their own special interest groups; and some were merely fed up with the Weimar government and wanted a change. In short, there was a myriad of reasons for joining the Nazi party or voting for Hitler.[1908]

The people, badly fatigued and dispirited by a decade and more of strife, hardship, and disappointment, had had enough of progressives, of liberalism, and its leaders. The election of 1930 was more than anything else a plea, a scream from the people for an honest government that would act decisively and firmly and in the interest of the mass of Germans: that both the Nazis and the Communists improved their polling numbers in 1930 speaks to this issue. The people wanted decisive, effective government—even if it was wrong, rightist, or leftist.

Increasingly, rightists and moderates sought a resolute government that could and would provide jobs; a return to an honest, vaunted civil service; an end to the belittlement of previously cherished things—they wanted an end to the "politics of despair,"[1909] a return to probity and moral rightness; peace in the home, the heartland, the world. Hitler offered it all, and Germany, in its exhausted state, could not help but welcome him. People were finally willing to follow him for the sake of their repeatedly shattered hopes, their lost dignity, their disillusionments, their deep despair and exhaustion. They wanted community and unity.

As Detlev Peukert points out in *The Weimar Republic*,

> many anti-fascist historians . . . have mistakenly concluded that the central thrust of German social thought was the "destruction of reason" that a reactionary tradition of hostility to modernization led in a straight line from Nietzsche [or Judas or Luther or Catholicism, or Christianity] to Hitler. Yet in fact the "politics of cultural despair" cannot be properly understood unless the accuracy of many of its criticisms of modernization is also acknowledged.[1910]

The sixteen or so parties clamoring for votes were willing, it seemed, to backstab any opponent or friend alike. Disunity was emblematic of both the German political system and its supporting social milieu. The very existence of so many parties was one of the attractive features of Hitlerism—he assured the populace again and again that he would eliminate such diffusion of power and purpose.[1911]

Otherwise good young people without hope of selling themselves in Berlin and other major cities to Jewish supported misfits of the day became too much to bear. The rejection of good—of happy endings—was all too depressing. The scandals, political infighting, the incessant attacks on culture, it was collectively overpowering. Why not a determined leader figuratively rooted in the soil of the German soul? Why not someone with the "unshakable will"* to cast off the shackles of

---

* "Unshakable will" was a term used by Hitler ad nauseam.

Success of Hitler—Ascension to Power

Versailles and its oppressive dictates? Why not someone of the national kin who would trumpet the national spirit, culture, and people, its volksgeist? Why not accept a German patriot, a hero of World War I who was willing to put Germans and age-old German values and culture at the forefront of government? Why not Adolf Hitler and his Nazis? What could be wrong with that? What could be wrong with confidence, jobs, full bellies, morality and social harmony, and Germany as a full and equal partner at the table of great nations?

As previously emphasized, initially even some Jews celebrated the ascension of Hitler to power. "Joachim Prinz, a German Jew who later became the head of the American Jewish Congress, celebrated Hitler's ascent to power because it signaled the end of the Enlightenment values which had resulted in assimilation and mixed marriage among Jews."[1912] Even polar opposites to Hitler were singing his praises: the Jewish lesbian writer and avant-garde devotee Gertrude Stein was calling for the award of the Nobel Peace Prize to him.[1913] At the time, Hitler seemed good for everybody, but especially for those who held traditional values and desires, however extreme those desires might be. There was no one at that time, almost certainly not even Hitler himself, who knew that he would one day unleash anything so horrific and despicable as the Holocaust.

Fall of the Weimar Republic

The Weimar government could no longer form a viable majority in the Reichstag. During the period 1930–1932, Chancellor Brüning tried to govern with the help of the president's emergency decrees and clearly unconstitutional means as exemplified by his entirely unconstitutional takeover of Prussia. He thereby created the precedents that set the stage for later, similar actions by Hitler. Brüning would be followed by Schleicher who would further expand the dictatorial power of the "democratic" Weimar government.

Believing that a reduction in public spending would revitalize the economy, Brüning slashed state expenditures, including Social

Security payments. It was precisely the wrong thing to do both economically and politically; what was needed, according to classic Keynesian economic theory, was an infusion of capital. But this was the early 1930s and Keynes had not yet published his economic treatise (which occurred in 1936). Given the hyperinflation of the early 1920s, it was entirely understandable that the government was unwilling to print more money and Brüning and others were horrified by the prospect of renewed inflationary pressures. And with the financial burdens of the Versailles Treaty still about its neck (though much reduced), it could hardly take on more debt. Whatever the ill wisdom and constraints of government actions to address the Depression, the Weimar Republic lost all credibility with the populace.[1914]

The second election of 1932, wherein Hitler and his Nazis lost momentum and were driven to near bankruptcy, nevertheless enabled him to retain his position as the head of what remained the largest party in the country. Moreover, with some industrialists now finally in tow, Hitler and his party managed to survive to fight another day.

Large as the Nazi Party had become shortly before it achieved power, its strength of 12 million was matched by the combined strength of the Left, wherein there were 6 million belonging to the KPD, which was growing stronger daily, and another 7.3 million in the SPD. As already emphasized, with the KPD being directed from Moscow by a policy of opposition to the SPD instead of the Nazis, their combined strength could not be combined and harnessed for the defeat of Hitler.[1915] For the time being, then, the only thing keeping Hitler out of power was the ongoing opposition of the noble President Paul von Hindenburg to his appointment as chancellor.

As a sop to Hitler, an attempt was made to have him accept a lesser position than chancellor. Hitler was adamant that he would have none of it. He saw his mission as nothing less than the salvation of Germany from Communist Bolshevism, and for that task, he needed to be chancellor. Offered the position of vice chancellor, Hitler purportedly responded contemptuously: "There is no such person as the vice-savior."[1916] Some historians represent

Success of Hitler—Ascension to Power

Hitler's refusal to accept the post as the stubborn demand of the ultimate gambler's instinct to risk everything he had achieved to that point. Stolfi has a more reasoned perspective: "Hitler's unbending demand for the chancellorship," he says, "reduced the options of the president and the intriguers to an eleventh-hour choice between Hitler and civil war."[1917]

No one understood Hitler. Politicians of his day saw politics as a profession. It was a thing of parties and people jockeying for positions by which they could advance themselves—for Hitler it was a messianic mission. He was out to save Germany and could be satisfied by nothing less.

By late January 1933, even Hindenburg's opposition to Hitler was frazzled by the combined pressure of various industrialists, the army, the leadership of the Center Party, and even his family circle. These forces argued that the appointment of Hitler to head a new government was the only viable means of breaking the deadlock with the Reichstag and combating the very real menace of Bolshevism, the Communists.

On January 30, 1933, Hindenburg finally relented and appointed Hitler to the position of chancellor. The stage was thereby set for him to exploit coming events to secure his dictatorship. It was at this point, too, that the Nazis finally acquired a truly mass following—people quickly deserted their former party affiliations and joined with the Nazis. It was a time when, as Fest correctly observed, "the axiom was proved that in revolutionary times principles are cheap, and perfidy, calculation, and fear reign supreme."[1918]

In February 1933, the Reichstag was set ablaze by the Dutch Communist and serial arsonist, Marinus van der Lubbe, an act that was initially seen as an opening act on behalf of the threatened KPD revolution. Some historians claim or at least speculate that the fire was actually the work of the Nazis. It is a claim that, given the whole of the evidence, can be safely discarded as false. Stolfi makes the point emphatically: "There was not a factual hint of conspiracy on the part of Hitler and the Nazis in the event."[1919] It is also false, in light of the evidence, to assume or imply that van der Lubbe acted at the behest of Communist leaders. The evidence is that he acted alone, but that fact does not diminish the justification for the genuine fear at the time that it was the work of the Communists and that action needed to be taken on the basis of that supposition.

Hitler used the Reichstag fire to acquire broad new powers under the Enabling Act,* powers that enabled him to pass laws without reference to the Reichstag, control the press, and otherwise oppress all opposition, and with masterful persuasion he also convinced the moderate Reichstag deputies to participate in a majority coalition on his behalf. A little more than a year later he used the death of Hindenburg in 1934 and the device of a plebiscite to permanently combine the office of president and chancellor and to thereby position himself for absolute dictatorial power. It was all accomplished in accordance with strict legality.

The Boycott

When Hitler attained power and was about to carry out his objectives, Jews of the Diaspora, acting as a supranational body, declared a worldwide boycott of German goods. Hitler and his regime were at this time by no means secure. He was at that time the head of a coalition government (Hitler's Nazis occupied only three of the cabinet posts while the conservatives from the DNVP occupied eight), he was not yet comfortably ensconced as an unchallenged dictator. He had thus far made a lot of claims and promises but had accomplished nothing. He had no experience whatever as a leader, save that of the Nazi Party. He had to show the people that he could handle such things as running the economy even as it strained against the Depression and the worldwide Jewish boycott of German goods.

Germany was mostly a have-not nation with respect to both industrial raw materials and foodstuffs. It was exceedingly dependent on external sources for some of its energy (e.g., oil) and other raw materials and on world export markets for its finished

---

* An Enabling Act had been used previously (1923–1924) by the Weimar government that enabled it to fight inflation; thus, a precedent existed for Hitler's action.

goods and overall economic well-being. And given that Jews were powerful in the emporiums of Germany's largest trading partners, Eastern Europe and America, Hitler's anti-Semitism was a matter of some significance to Germany's economic prospects.

The boycott was initially led by Rabbi Stephen Wise of New York City, a man who, as said by Jewish author Edwin Black, "rattled the boycott and protest saber at Germany."[1920] Wise was joined in his early efforts by the Zionist American Jewish Congress (AJC). Mainstream Zionists would soon thereafter take an entirely different tact. Wise actually initiated his boycott effort even before Hitler came to power. In 1932, he called together in Geneva Jewish leaders from various nations to organize the boycott and establish the anti-German propaganda effort that was to accompany it. This was a period during which Germany was in dire need of exports in order to continue to provide jobs at home during the Depression and to thereby acquire critically needed foreign capital. The boycott, then, was a weapon that Hitler justifiably feared. To many, it was an act of war: and even if we reject that premise, it was certainly nothing short of Jewry's figurative declaration of war on Hitler, his Nazis, and the German people.

It was not lost on the Nazis that leaders of the anti-German boycott were orchestrating the redirection of goods acquisition to countries and suppliers of their choosing. There was more than a smattering of boycott enthusiasts whose underlying objective was not so much the destruction of Nazism as getting for themselves a piece of the lucrative markets that Germany had traditionally dominated, such as gloves, toys, cameras, and shipping.[1921] Save certain Jewish elements within Germany itself, there were virtually no Jewish protests to the boycott. The boycott of Germans against Jewish businesses, on the other hand, was, and continues to be, represented as something of a pogrom. History books that discuss the Nazi era rarely fail to mention that Hitler imposed a boycott on Jewish establishments. It commenced and ended on Saturday, April 1, 1933, the Jewish Sabbath when many Jewish shops were not even open for business. Moreover it was largely ignored by the German populace.[1922]

The German boycott of Jewish shops was imposed in direct response to the worldwide boycott imposed on Germany by international Jewry. If our reader was unaware of the events leading up to the German boycott of Jewish shops we need not be surprised—our history books and popular media only rarely mention actual Nazi motivations. Their motivations are typically simply chalked up to Nazi irrationalism—or worse, German anti-Semitism.

The prominent Jewish attorney from New York, Samuel Untermyer, was among those who were openly calling for a Jewish holy war against Germany.[1923] Many others did as well. "Judea Declares War on Germany!" shouted the *Daily Express* headline on March 24, 1933. The *Daily Express* went on to say that:

> The Israelite people of the entire world declare economic and financial war on Germany. The appearance of the Swastika as the symbol of the new Germany revives the old war symbol of the Jews. Fourteen million Jews stand as one body to declare war on Germany. The Jewish wholesale dealer leaves his business, the banker his bank, the shopkeeper his shop, the beggar his miserable hut in order to combine forces in the holy war against Hitler's people.[1924]

Bernard Lecache, president of the World Jewish League, was also explicit; he declared that "Germany is our public enemy number one. It is our object to declare war without mercy against her."[1925]

In August 1933, the supranational Jewish congress meeting in Amsterdam called for a holy war against Germany and for Germany's utter destruction.[1926] Jewish organizations throughout the world trumpeted their boycott prowess. They were confident it would soon topple Hitler and his regime.

In 1933, at the Eighteenth Zionist Conference in Prague, the extreme right-wing Zionist Vladimir Jabotinsky,* founder of the Irgun Zvai Leumi terrorist organization and for a time the close friend of Chaim Weizmann, referring to Hitler and his Nazis, said, "[we must] destroy, destroy, destroy them."[1927] Jabotinsky, whatever his rhetorical excesses against Hitler, was a man who shared at least some instincts with him. He believed, like Hitler, says Lenni Brenner, in the importance of the "national ego" as being "deeply ingrained in a man's blood," in his "racio-physical type"; things within beings that remain "unchanged and immutable so long as the physical-racial type is preserved."[1928] In keeping with that attitude, he also believed that Jews could not become true Germans or truly at one with any other nationality; Jews, according to him, were made different by their Jewish blood.[1929] He was also highly nationalistic and openly in favor of Jewish segregation.[1930] By 1934, Jabotinsky was not limiting his wrath to the Nazis; he was by then out to destroy the whole of Germany and its people. He wrote in the January 1934 issue of *Mascha Rjetach*, as follows:

> For months now the struggle against Germany is waged by each Jewish community at each conference in all our syndicates and by each Jew all over the world. There is reason to believe that our part in this struggle has general value. We will start a spiritual and material war of all the world against Germany's ambitions to become once again a great nation, to recover lost territories and colonies. But our Jewish interests demand Germany's total destruction, collectively and individually. The German nation is a threat to us Jews.[1931]

Emil Ludwig Cohen wrote in 1938 that "Even if Hitler at the last moment would want to avoid war which would destroy him he will, in spite of his wishes, be compelled to wage war."[1932]

---

* Jabotinsky was an exception to mainstream Zionism with respect to the boycott of German goods. He supported the boycott while mainstream Zionists did not.

In October of 1940, the Jewish magazine *Sentinel* of Chicago claimed that "When the National Socialists and their friends cry or whisper that this [war] is brought about by Jews, they are perfectly right."[1933]

The radicalism of Jewish publicists extended even to such respected and widely circulated and magazines as *Time*. A 1941 diatribe by New York businessman Theodore Kaufmann titled "Germany Must Perish," also called for sterilizing Germans. *Time* endorsed that thought process saying that it was a "sensational idea."[1934]

The Jewish newspaper *Natscha Retsch* wrote:

> The war against Germany will be waged by all Jewish communities, conferences, congresses . . . by every individual Jew. Thereby the war against Germany will ideologically enliven and promote our interests, which require that Germany be wholly destroyed.
>
> The danger for us Jews lies in the whole German people, in Germany as a whole as well as individually. It must be rendered harmless for all time. . . . In this war we Jews have to participate, and this with all the strength and might we have at our disposal.[1935]

The foregoing is the stuff of the *Protocols of the Learned Elders of Zion*. The document is chock-full of such language.

The worldwide Jewish opposition to Germany throughout the 1930s and into the 1940s continued to fire Hitler's hate. The boycott, moreover, exemplified Jewish worldwide organization and supranational power, "After all, was not the [boycott's] . . . avowed goal to smother Germany's industries, choke off its foreign exchange, and topple its government?"[1936] says Edwin Black. Was it not the case, then, that the boycott was entirely in keeping with several of the claims of the *Protocols of the Learned Elders of Zion* as to how organized international Jewry would use its power? Was the boycott not an explicit example of how world Jewry could demonstrate its supranational power against a national state?

Success of Hitler—Ascension to Power

Throughout the 1930s, Jews the world over continued their attacks on Germany in the press. In 1938, the French Communist and journalist Bernard Lechache, who was the president of the Jewish World League, wrote that "It is our task to organize the moral and cultural blockade of Germany and disperse this nation. It is up to us to start a merciless war."[1937]

By 1939, the Jewish newspaper *Central Blad Voor Israeliten in Nederlands* was making it clear that Judaism's war with Germany was to be fought with the utter extermination of the German nation as its objective:

> The millions of Jews living in America, England, France, North Africa and South, not forgetting Palestine, have decided to carry on the war in Germany to the very end. It is to be a war of extermination.[1938]

Much of the preceding language can be attributed to excesses that are common in tense political epochs, but it is worth noting that the language and actions of Jewish organizations during the 1930s was every bit, and more, as virulent and vile as that of any of the Nazis. Should we have expected a Jewish-led genocide against Germans? Should Germans have expected one against Jews?

Zionism to Hitler's Rescue

As Hitler implemented and carried out his purge of Jews from German society to the understandable outrage of the world's Jewish community, he also found a friend there: mainstream Zionism, and in particular, the World Zionist Organization (WZO). The WZO was willing to help him overcome both the boycott of goods and the moral condemnation of various nations. Jewish-Marxist-American writer Lenni Brenner says that "of all of the active Jewish opponents of the boycott idea, the most important was the WZO. It not only bought German wares; it sold them, and even sought out new customers for Hitler and his industrialist backers."[1939]

Of the hundreds of powerful Jewish organizations, none has been more powerful or had more impact than Zionism on Gentile perceptions of Jewish power. The Zionist Organization (ZO), which would later become the World Zionist Organization (WZO), was established in 1897 under the leadership of Theodore Herzl and the Jewish racist[1940] Max Nordau (born Simon Maximilian Südfeld). It would ultimately grow in size and influence until, in the early 1930s, it was the most influential Jewish organization in existence for impacting world events. Over time, Zionism took on several hues: there is Cultural Zionism, General Zionism, Labor Zionism, Revisionist Zionism, Synthetic Zionism, and a host of others. Whatever the hue, however, the whole of it was an implacable foe of Gentiles, East or West. "The West," said Chaim Weizmann, "preached liberty, the East practices repression; but East and West alike were the enemies of the Zionist ideology."[1941]

Of particular note for our purposes are Zionist attitudes, pronouncements, and actions between about 1900 and the onset of World War II.

As several times already emphasized, early proto-Zionists were not seeking to relocate their people to Palestine; they, instead, sought to formalize the status of Jews as individual states or tribes within the borders of the various countries of the Diaspora. "In fact," says Brenner, "the average Zionist never thought of himself as leaving civilized Europe for the wilds of Palestine."[1942] In Germany, Austria, Russia, and elsewhere, the real Zionist aim was to convert the bulk of Jewry to unassimilated life[1943] in those countries. Thus, it was that Jews in Austria attempted, through the courts, to establish Judaism as a "tribe" or nation within the nation, a legal expression of their de facto status as a state within the state. Similar attempts were made in Russia both before and after the revolution there. Before the revolution the Jewish Bund sought, among other things, to have Jews granted recognition as a nation therein with a legal minority status; that is, a legally formalized nation within the nation.[1944] It was this stance of early Zionism, in fact, that caused Russia's von Plehve to reject Herzl and his early form of Zionism: Herzl sought to have von Plehve set aside an area for a Jewish nation within Russia. It was rather like asking a high

U.S. official to give over New York to the Jews. Von Plehve would have none of it. In the Soviet Union, Jewish nationalism was partially successful; it was in 1934 that the Jewish Autonomous Oblast, a Soviet Zion, was established wherein Yiddish was adopted as the national language and Jews practiced their particular culture but not Judaism as such.[1945] The oblast was not populated entirely by Jews, however; the majority of the population remained non-Jewish, just as it had in the former Pale.

As Zionism became a movement for the return to Israel, great debates occurred within the Jewish community. Assimilationists argued that the Zionists were fulfilling anti-Semites' wishes by their attitude that they owed no allegiance whatever to their host country but only to their own Jewish nation, and that by encouraging emigration they were achieving the goals of anti-Semites, a *Judenrein* (Jew-free) Europe.[1946] None of this sort of debate much mattered to the Zionists. They were fanatically focused on their goals and absolutely nothing would deter them. In pursuit of their goals, they enthusiastically and knowingly benefited the Nazis as well.

Given their new focus on Palestine, the WZO felt nothing for the Jews who chose to remain in Germany—they did nothing to aid them unless they were able and willing candidates for relocation to Palestine. Nor had they any interest whatever in German Jews who were old, infirm, poor, or unskilled. Between the years 1933 and 1935, two-thirds of the German Jews who applied for permission to emigrate to Palestine were turned down—not by the Nazis and not by the British. They were instead turned down by the Zionists in Palestine.[1947] Brenner, in *Zionism in the Age of the Dictators*, says that while Zionists today blame the British and Arabs for the low number of refugees admitted to Palestine, it was in fact the Zionists who were responsible—at that time they were not interested in seeing Palestine become a genuine place of refuge for all Jews. They were willing to accept only those refugees who could most benefit their goals of the moment.[1948] They wanted only the "Tiffany's window" Jews.[1949]

Zionists were entirely willing even to accommodate—indeed, to embrace—anti-Semitism in its most extreme forms, the *un bon tyran* rulers of Fascism and Nazism, if such accommodation furthered their goals.[1950]

Revisionist Zionism had nothing but contempt for democracy; they were themselves Fascists through and through, and they were eager to support Fascist regimes, Mussolini's Italian Fascists, in particular, but even Hitler under the right circumstances.[1951] In effect, says Brenner, Revisionist leader Jabotinsky "became Mussolini's defence attorney within the Jewish world."[1952] Georg Kareski, a classic Revisionist and Nazi collaborator, foresaw a Jewish state that stretched from the Mediterranean Sea to the Euphrates with Mussolini as its mandatory protector.[1953] With respect to the Nazis, the Revisionists were wholly in agreement with Nazi claims that Jews could never be real Germans and did not want to be.[1954]

The Transfer Agreement: Its Origins and Players

Almost from the very moment that Hitler came to power, Zionist elements enthusiastically cooperated with him and his Nazis in creating and executing what quickly became known as the Transfer Agreement. Zionists openly congratulated Hitler on his success in overcoming the forces of liberalism.[1955] In particular, Dr. Joachim Prinz, a friend of Golda Meir (who in 1969 would become the Israeli prime minister), who would ultimately rise to the leadership of Zionism and Israel, published a book in 1934 that heaped praise on Hitler's revolution because it ruled out further mixed marriages.[1956]

Germany was in particularly dire economic straits stemming from the worldwide Depression. Adding to the economic woes was the aforementioned Jewish-led boycott of German goods. Zionists were willing to help on a quid pro quo basis. They were willing to become the scabs of the boycott movement.

Sizing up the situation in both Germany and Palestine, the original scheme for the Transfer Agreement was launched by Sam Cohen, a Polish-born profiteer who had managed to acquire a large fortune during World War I. He was at the time residing in an opulent castle in Luxembourg.[1957] Cohen's scheme was to now use

SUCCESS OF HITLER—ASCENSION TO POWER

the current crisis to further compound his wealth. If successful he would gain control of many millions of dollars, thousands of people, and large tracks of land.[1958] To many Jews he was an evil rogue, a traitor, a collaborator, a liar, and a fraud.[1959] To others, and particularly to the Labor Zionists, he was a munificent man who could save the day in terms of aiding Jewish immigration to Palestine.

In May 1933, Cohen concluded a Transfer Agreement deal with the Nazis for a modest 1 million reichsmarks.[1960] Edwin Black, author of *The Transfer Agreement*, asserts that "It was almost as though Sam Cohen had become a part of the German diplomatic and trade apparatus, selling German goods, arranging for the emigration of German Jews, supplying foreign currency, stimulating German employment and breaking anti-Nazi boycotts."[1961]

The Transfer Agreement operated essentially like this: German Jews would deposit their money in a Zionist-controlled bank account in Germany. Money in the account would then be used to purchase a wide range of German goods for use in Palestine and also for resale elsewhere by Jews already in Palestinian. The resale of goods was conducted by the Ha'avara (Hebrew for "transfer") company in Tel Aviv. The proceeds from the sale (whether to Jewish settlers in Palestine or to foreign countries) would subsequently be deposited in a Ha'avara-controlled bank account. Jews who had made the original deposits in the account in Germany would then immigrate to Palestine and would there be provided with most of the proceeds realized from the sale of the goods. The arrangement enabled tens of thousands of German Jews to relocate to Palestine with the bulk of their money intact. Germany benefitted from the arrangement in a number of ways: the Zionists provided Hitler's Nazis with a gateway to Middle East markets, supported German exports, and, ultimately, as goods were sold and transferred to various foreign countries on German ships the arrangement also provided sorely needed foreign capital. Finally, on the propaganda front, Hitler could both remove the Jews of Germany and simultaneously be seen as assisting Jewish national aspirations.[1962] The whole of the deal was as morally corrupt as it was financially and propagandistically beneficial.

Cohen was soon pushed aside and his place was taken by Dr. Chaim Arlosoroff who was then the head of the Political Department of the Jewish Agency, the official representative of the Jews in Palestine under the British Mandate. Dr. Arlosoroff, a prominent Zionist second only to Dr. Chaim Weizmann, was one of the early leaders in the creation of the Transfer Agreement and Weizmann himself was intricately involved. Arlosoroff demanded that all Jewish sentimentality about negotiating with the Nazis be rejected[1963]—an example of reason and rationality at its worst.

Arlosoroff was assassinated by Jewish radicals in Tel Aviv on June 16, 1933, for his part in instituting the Transfer Agreement. By that date, however, he had concluded his negotiations with the Nazis and managed to strike a deal just two days prior to his assassination. Upon his death, coordination and cooperation with the Nazis was carried on and expanded by other Zionists under the leadership of the man who would become Israel's first prime minister, the "father of Israel," David Ben-Gurion (born David Grün).

So connected were the Zionists and Nazis, Zionism was for a time supported by the German SS, the Gestapo, and Hitler himself. In the 1930s, with the full cooperation of Nazi authorities, Zionists in Germany organized a network of some forty camps where prospective settlers were trained for their new lives in Palestine. As late as 1942, Zionists operated at least one of these officially authorized kibbutz where they proudly flew the blue and white banner that was later adopted as the national flag of Israel. By way of the Transfer Agreement, Hitler and his Nazis, claim some, did more than any other government during the 1930s to support development in Palestine and to thereby further the Zionist goals.

Zionists were adamant that only Jews relocating to Palestine could benefit from this arrangement. Those who desired to go to other nations were left to their own devices. Zionists did their level best to prod the Germans to only permit emigration of Jews if their destination was Palestine.

An example of the radicalism of the Zionists exists in the efforts of Rabbi Michael Dov-Ber Weissmandel. Weissmandel had led an effort to clandestinely bribe Nazis to spare the lives of Slovakian Jews. The Zionists resisted Weissmandel's efforts on the theory that it was preferable that such Jews be killed.

As Hannah Arendt claimed: "it is certain . . . that during the first phases of National Socialist Jewish policy situations developed in which it seemed suitable to the National Socialists to accept or advance a pro-Zionist attitude."[1964] Arendt explicitly accused the Zionists of abandoning the wider Jewish community and of directly aiding the Nazis. "This role of the Jewish leaders in the destruction of their own people is undoubtedly the darkest chapter of the whole dark story," said Arendt.[1965]

Arendt was speaking of the Transfer Agreement in making the foregoing charges. It should be added that the arrangement was not restricted to "the first phases" of National Socialism as stated by Arendt; it continued even into the early 1940s. Indeed, the provisions of the agreement expanded with time. It soon became clear, as Black records, "that the success of the future Jewish Palestinian economy would be inextricably bound up with the survival of the Nazi economy . . . The German economy would have to be safeguarded, stabilized, and if necessary reinforced . . . If the Hitler economy fell, both sides would be ruined."[1966] Nazi exports to the Jews of Palestine soon flooded that market so the Zionists thereafter supported a variety of Nazi efforts to boost exports by way of Tel Aviv to third-party countries. The whole of the effort served to help stabilize the weak reichsmark and support the German workforce, and thereby the Hitler government. Importantly, it also greatly diminished the effectiveness of the worldwide boycott of German goods. It was good for the Nazis. It was good for the Zionists.* It was terrible, ultimately, for European Jewry.

---

* Sixty percent of total investments in Palestine for the period August 1933 to September 1939 were via the Transfer Agreement.

The Jews of the boycott leadership remained loyal to the aspirations of the Zionists even as the Zionists worked with Hitler in opposition to the boycott's aims. In New York, the Labor Zionists enthusiastically supported the boycott in the United States while simultaneously providing tacit support for the Transfer Agreement. They were running with the fox and hunting with the hounds. They held that nobody should break the boycott except for the Jews of Palestine, and nobody should deal with Germany except for the Zionists in Palestine.

The Zionist position was something of a hard sell in world capitals. In Britain, the newspaper (the *Blackshirt*) of Fascist sympathizer Sir Oswald Mosley's editorialized on the subject as follows:

> Can you beat that! We are cutting off our nose to spite our face and refuse to trade with Germany in order to defend the poor Jews. The Jews themselves, in their own country, are to continue making profitable dealings with Germany themselves. Fascists can't better counter the malicious propaganda to destroy friendly relations with Germany than by using this fact.[1967]

German Zionists were in league with, in business with, Hitler. It was not Pope Pius XII who was indifferent to the plight of German Jews; it was the likes of Cohen, Arlosoroff, Weizmann, and Ben-Gurion. Zionists apparently felt that it was up to the pope, not themselves, to save Jewish lives; their focus was on saving Jewish gold. The whole of the arrangement also served to reinforce the stereotype of Jews as being solely concerned with money, the idea that even when it comes to a choice between morality and business, business wins out.

An expression of the fanaticism of the Zionists is given by a 1938 statement made by Ben-Gurion shortly after the infamous *Kristallnacht* and England's offer to accept 10,000 Jewish children from Germany and Austria: "If I knew it was possible to save all the children in Germany by taking them to England," said Ben-Gurion, "and only half of the children by taking them to Eretz

Success of Hitler—Ascension to Power

Israel, I would choose the second solution."[1968] Ben-Gurion's assertion was entirely in keeping with the fanaticism of the Zionists of that time.

While the world press was excoriating Germany's every dealing with other countries, Jews of the million-strong WZO were working hand in glove with the Nazis. And in doing so they were also providing critically important support for the Hitler regime. For the Zionists, the Jewish boycott of German goods was something of a godsend; without it there would not have been a Transfer Agreement and perhaps no state of Israel. The motives of both the Nazis and Zionists were less than pure, to be sure, but the effect was to benefit them both.[1969] The extent of benefit—whether Zionists or Nazis came out ahead—is a matter of argument. Some have it that without Zionist support the Nazi regime would have collapsed. Others have it that without the Nazis there would have been no Israel. Both of those extreme claims are probably wrong. Whatever the truth of the matter, it remains a fact that the Zionists provided significant aid in helping Hitler get through some very tough economic and political times.

Hitler's Successes

Historians sometimes claim that Hitler offered no concrete proposals to recover the economy during his election campaigns in the early 1930s—which is true enough, because specific proposals are more easily attacked than generalizations. Still, he clearly had specific plans in mind, and he implemented them in a flurry beginning in June 1933, only five months after coming to power.

Hitler had only rudimentary qualifications as an economist. He claimed in *Mein Kampf* that he took inspiration on the subject from the right-wing economist Gottfried Feder and had even read Karl Marx's *Kapital* so that he might understand it better. Whatever his qualifications or lack thereof, he did have the good sense to assess the arguments of his various advisors and unfailingly select the ones that were most promising for implementation. By way of example, the Labor Procurement law of June 1, 1933, financed vast new construction projects to repair or remodel public buildings, businesses, residences, farms, and the like. All of the materials for such projects were to be German made, which stimulated demand, added to the tax coffers, and revitalized the workforce. Hitler also significantly reduced interest rates, an act that one might think would damage financial institutions but did the reverse since they thereafter realized greatly reduced defaults on loans. He also freed businesses from having to pay unemployment benefits which freed up capital for new purchases and personnel hiring.[1970] In the same vein, the government offered low-interest loans for newlyweds to buy furniture and other household wares which stimulated demand for those items. As children were born to the couple, the loan amounts were reduced, and upon producing four children, forgiven entirely. In September of 1933, Hitler began construction of the autobahns, an initiative that added 200,000 laborers to the workforce.[1971] Because Germany had no gold whatever on which to base the value of its currency, Hitler and his regime created innovative bartering schemes to obviate the need for large holdings of gold and other precious metals.

Importantly, Hitler also revitalized the people. When he came to power the nation was immediately filled with jubilation. The effects of the stock market crash were still being felt, and there was still misery aplenty but now there was also hope. Friedrich Otto captures the mood of the people in his book, *Before the Deluge*. Says Otto:

> The glorious sensation of a new fraternity overwhelmed all groups and classes. Professor and waitress, laborer and industrialist, servant girl and trader, clerks, peasants, soldiers and government workers—all of them suddenly learned what seemed to be the greatest discovery of the century—that they were comrades of one race, Volksgenossen.[1972]

Until the outbreak of World War II Hitler would be for Germany what his hero Karl Lueger had been for Vienna: he would reinvigorate and reenergize the nation; he would replace shame with pride and dissension with common purpose and solidarity. As early as mid-1933 the Germany economy had improved markedly, Germans were going back to work, the streets were free of beggars. Clearly, better times were on the horizon.

By 1935, unemployment was largely overcome, the mark had been stabilized, autobahn construction was underway, the VW was in its design stages, working conditions had been vastly improved, as had health standards. Infant mortality and infectious disease rates were down markedly. Farmers were thriving again, and policies were put in place to improve the productivity of the soil. Land reclamation programs were initiated, as were flood protection measures. The term "organic farming" was invented under Hitler, and its methods were developed and honed to reduce reliance on costly artificial fertilizers. Food quickly became plentiful and affordable again. "By 1936 Germany had become 81 percent self-sufficient in food."[1973]

People were able to take family vacations at government subsidized resorts and on government subsidized ships. The spirit of the people was revived and German cultural values were restored. It was the reinvigorated spirit of Germans that contributed so markedly to their leaving the field of friendly competition at the 1936 Olympic Games[*] with the most gold medals (thirty-three) as well as the most silver and bronze. In total, Germany won eighty-nine Olympic medals that year, more than any other nation. The U.S., with more than twice the population, ranked second with fifty-six medals. Hitler had revitalized, reenergized the German people.

Soon the Rhineland was restored to Germany, then came union with Austria, then the recovery of the Sudetenland. Germany was on the move. It was a happy time indeed, and all of these good things were attributed directly and solely to Adolf Hitler by Goebbels's propaganda ministry. Who at that time in Germany

---

[*] It was at these games that the modern practice of running the Olympic Torch from Greece to the site of the games was instituted—still another example of Hitler's penchant for innovation and celebratory display.

(other than Jews and die-hard Marxists) could help but love such a man as Hitler?

It was not long before the former cultural gurus of Germany emigrated to the U.S., which thereby inherited Weimar culture. There they continued to work against the interests of Germany via the press, political arm twisting, and propaganda movies out of Hollywood (*Confessions of a Nazi Spy*, starring Jewish actor Edward G. Robinson serves as but one of many examples of that genre).

Hitler eliminated smut and restored Germany's high culture. Beginning in the mid- to late-1930s, he renewed Germany's military strength and discarded the Versailles diktat. The economy began to boom again; there was soon a chicken in every pot. At last the German people were deliriously happy—if only for too tragically brief a time.

Why Did Hitler Hate the Jews?

In the preface to this text we posed the question, "Why Did Hitler Hate the Jews?" We now seek to recapitulate our conclusions in response to that query.

The construction of Hitler's worldview began at school in Linz where he was exposed to the teachings of his history teacher, Dr. Leopold Pötsch. It was there that he developed his love of history and also his commitment to Pan-Germanism. It was also there that he was instructed on and developed a sense of loathing for the non-German components of the Austria-Hungarian Empire. He was convinced before leaving school there that Germans of Austria-Hungary were undeservedly losing their previously dominant influence in the empire. The extreme nationalism that he began to acquire in Linz prompted him to study any and all political and social groups that seemingly opposed Germans—and there, most prominently, stood the Jews.

Throughout his five-year sojourn in Vienna he observed and studied both the social and political milieu of the city. In particular he observed the vast power of Jews to dictate policies in both the social and political realms of Viennese society. He also observed

Success of Hitler—Ascension to Power

the influx of the Ostjuden to the city and the abhorrent business practices of that clan. He took note of the power of the "ink Jews," as well as Jewish Marxists and Jewish financiers in propagating what he thought were harmful social and political policies. Moreover, it was here that his anti-Semitic inclination was either founded or reinforced due to the pronouncements of his political hero, Vienna Mayor Karl Lueger. By the time Hitler departed Vienna in 1913 he was a committed anti-Semite based on his total assessment of the histories he had read and on his firsthand observations of the Jews of the city.

World War I reinforced Hitler's hatred toward Jews in that he knew very well that the principal leaders of the various labor strikes and anti-German propagandists throughout the war were Marxist Jews who had the defeat of Germany as the objective of their efforts. These same Jews desired the overthrow of the monarchy so that they might themselves assume power in the country.

While on furloughs during World War I he visited various cities of Germany and made firsthand observations of the home front: he decided that prominent Jews not only opposed Germany's war objectives but that they also failed to serve in the trenches and protected their brethren from doing so as well. He observed that "nearly every clerk was a Jew and nearly every Jew was a clerk"; that is, that they were avoiding military service in droves. The "Jew Count" conducted by the German military reinforced his perception.

Adding to his animosity at that time was the fact that prior to the war the Jewish-led Social Democratic Party had refused to fund three additional army corps. These corps, totaling about 120,000 men, would have almost certainly been decisive in winning the opening battles of the war and would probably have brought it to an early close with Germany as the victor—as early as September 1914. As the war dragged on and Hitler experienced the horrors of trench warfare over a period of four years he was acutely aware of the anti-German propaganda being widely published by the various Marxists on both the home front and the battlefront, and he knew full well that the leaders of those Marxists were Jews, people such as Liebknecht, Luxemburg, Eisner, Toller, Eisner, Haase, and a host of others.

Adding still more to his hatred was the fact that the Jewish archtraitor, Colonel Alfred Redl, who had been the head of the Austrian military's counterintelligence, betrayed his countrymen and caused Germany's ally, the Austro-Hungarian Empire, to lose the opening battles of the war.

We do not know at what point Hitler became aware of the Balfour Declaration and its effect on drawing the United States into the war, but we know that he learned of it at some point. For him, this was still more Jewish perfidy in that the declaration had been initiated and pushed by Zionists who had, until 1916, been headquartered in Germany. With the entry of the U.S. into the war, Germany's fate was sealed: she would lose the war. Who sealed that fate? It was of course the Jews.

When the war ended in German defeat Hitler was, naturally, deeply affected. He pieced together the causes of that defeat and saw Jews as the primary culprits. In Berlin, the kaiser had been ousted and the government taken over by the hated SPD and USPD—parties that had been founded by Jews and was still under their thrall. Revolutionary turmoil was everywhere in the streets. In January 1919, the Jewish-led (Liebknecht and Luxemburg) Spartacus League, now under the banner of the Communist Party of Germany, attempted an armed revolution which resulted in widespread death and turmoil.

Shortly after World War I, the National Assembly convened an Investigation Committee on the causes of the war. The committee was headed by the Jewish Reichstag member Georg Gothein. He, together with fellow Jews Oskar Cohn[*] and Hugo Sinzheimer, investigated the conduct of Generals Hindenburg and Ludendorff.[1974] The committee's treatment of Hindenburg was brutal. The Jewish tint to the committee was expressed by the

---

[*] Cohn had been a principal member of the revolutionaries who participated in the Spartacist Uprising of January 1919. It was Cohn who received money for the acquisition of weapons to support the uprising from the Jewish Soviet ambassador, Adolf Joffe.

widespread slogan, "Cohn versus Hindenburg." It was by way of this committee that Ludendorff first made the charge that Germany had been stabbed in the back, a charge that was embraced by Hitler even before it was espoused by Ludendorff. Hitler said of the committee's work:

> It required the whole bottomless falsehood of the Jews and their Marxist fighting organization to lay the blame for the collapse on that very man who alone, with superhuman energy and will power, tried to prevent the catastrophe he foresaw and save the nation from its time of deepest humiliation and disgrace. By branding Ludendorff as guilty for the loss of the World War, they took the weapon of moral right from the one dangerous accuser who could have risen against the traitors to the fatherland.[1975]

That is, according to Hitler, Ludendorff was just another of the innumerable scapegoats of the Jewish narrative for the disaster of World War I in order to avoid properly laying the blame at the feet of Jews.

There was, in fact, a good deal of truth to Ludendorff's charge of a stab in the back. He had been unable to get the kaiser and the political class to silence the Jewish-led antiwar agitators. The various strikes, the propaganda directed at the troops, the upheavals and demoralization on the home front, and more, all contributed to the weakening of Germany's war effort, and all of these efforts were led by prominent Jews. Indeed, as Britain's Lloyd George told Hitler during a visit to Berchtesgaden, "Your [1918] revolution came to our aid at the last minute."[1976]

At the very least, even with U.S. entry into the war, Germany might have won a better peace had it not been for the internal collapse that was orchestrated by the Bolshevistic Jews of the time. The actions of radical leftists gave comfort to Germany's enemies and encouraged them to hold out for total, unconditional surrender.

With the signing of the Treaty of Versailles came still more suffering for the German people, and Hitler saw that treaty as the work of Jews who had been so very prominent in its creation and subsequently called so stridently for Germany's complete compliance with its provisions. It is safe to presume that the brutality of France's prime minister Georges Clemenceau toward Germany, and his close connection with Jews due to his strident support of Alfred Dreyfus, was seen by Hitler as still another Jewish perfidy in the torture of Germany after World War I. This was particularly so since so many prominent German Jews were veritable Francophiles.

Shortly after the war, Hitler returned to his beloved Munich only to find that it and the rest of Bavaria had been taken over by Marxist Jews who were then going about destroying the economy and adding further misery to a people already beset by starvation, cold, and pandemic disease (influenza). By April of 1919, the Jewish-led government in Bavaria was executing leading citizens of the city. He was also acutely aware of the atrocities being committed in Russia under Jewish stewardship as well as the utter brutality of the Kun regime in Hungary, a regime that was comprised entirely of Jews.

In 1921, due to internal bickering within Marxist ranks, it became widely known that the disastrous March Action in Germany's central region was launched by a conspiracy of Jewish members of the Comintern in the Soviet Union and by the Jewish leaders of Germany's KPD, which seemingly "proved" that Jews, both at home and abroad, were the leading culprits of Germany's grief.

Hitler's observations of profiteering during the war and during the hyperinflationary period of 1921–1923 abetted his hate. And the exceptional role played by Jews in the culture of Germany during the Weimar period, in conjunction with the foregoing, set him on a course of action to remove Jews from Germany, to follow the lead of over 100 predecessor nations, to expel all Jews.

With the end of World War I, Jews increasingly occupied positions of authority and leadership throughout Germany. They were roughly twenty times more numerous in such positions as they had been prior to the war. Worse, many of these people were Marxists of one srtipe or another and therefore took on the special hate of Hitler toward them.

SUCCESS OF HITLER—ASCENSION TO POWER

Throughout the 1920s, Hitler observed the vast decline in German culture. Music, literature, painting, architecture, and more were all debased, and to Hitler's lights it all happened under the auspices of Jewish leaders in politics, the press, and the arts.

He was also attuned to the various criminal scandals of the period by the likes of such Jewish personalities as the Barmat brothers, the Sklarz brothers, along with Bosel, Castiglioni, and others. He observed cities such as Berlin turned into sinkholes of vice. Prostitution, white slavery, and illegal drugs became commonplace in places where staid, honorable Germanism had previously prevailed. And he concluded that it was Jews who had reduced that city to its sorry condition.

As he gained traction in the polling booths, Jewish press moguls viciously attacked him and his Nazis, and did so with little to no regard for the truth. As Jews fled Germany some of them took up residence in places like Prague, Paris, and London. From those safe havens they continued to propagandize against Hitler, his Nazis, and more broadly, the German people. They also pressured the governments in those capitals and in the U.S. to do battle with Hitler and his Nazis.

Throughout the 1930s, the worldwide Jewish press attacked Germany at every turn, and organized Jewry employed a boycott on German goods that had the potential to devastate the German economy. Press outlets openly called for economic, social, and actual war with the German state. The boycott and the international press reports provided still more reasons for Hitler's hate.

As relations between Jews and the Nazi regime deteriorated still further, it became evident that Jews would represent a fifth column in Germany's populace during war. Hitler then, in accord with the common practice of the time, took action to confine Jews and other perceived enemies of the state in concentration camps. The initial target of this effort was the Marxists. That so many Jews were arrested by the Nazis was initially only because so many of them were also Marxists. Given the expressions of worldwide Jewish cohesion against Hitler, his Nazis, and the whole of Germany at that time, Hitler was far more justified in placing Jews in concentration camps than was the U.S. in confining its hapless Japanese population in similar camps. In 1900, during the Second Boer War, the British, too, had made use of concentration camps to confine civilians, and during that war some 30,000 of those prisoners died while in captivity. After September 1939, Germans were imprisoned in England. That is, initially, at least, Hitler's confinement of Jews was not particularly abhorrent or untoward for the times and circumstances. And we must, if we are to do justice, view his actions during that period in consonance with his times.

Demonstrating substantial moral courage, University of Berlin history professor Ernst Nolte gave a lecture in 1980 in which he justified as a defensive measure the German use of concentration camps to house Jews during the war. In his speech he cited remarks by Chaim Weizmann who had stated in September 1939 that "in this war the Jews of all the world would fight on England's side."[1977] Any number of similar statements by other prominent Jews and Jewish organizations could also have been cited in support of his thesis. At Nuremberg, German Admiral Karl Donitz justifiably claimed in one of his interviews that "If Hitler had not thrown the Communists into camps in 1933 there would have been civil war and bloodshed,"[1978] and too many of those Communists to count were Jewish.

The actions of Jews, such as the boycott of German goods, the earlier boycott of Russia, and the Balfour Declaration, all served as exemplars of Jewish power to act as an extranational body to the detriment of its enemies (and sometimes to the detriment of its friends as well).

Judaism was every bit as powerful an entity as any individual state, and its power was justifiably feared by the Nazis. Joachim von Ribbentrop, Hitler's foreign minister, once boldly told Hitler that it was mistake to incite world Jewry against Germany. "It was like having a fourth world power against us: England, France, Russia, and World Jewry,"[1979] he said. And so it was.

Upon experiencing reverses in his war with Russia and in the North Sea in the early 1940s and the possibility that Germany would lose the war, Hitler unleashed the full measure of his hate— his attempt at extermination, his death camps, the Holocaust.

In subsummary, it can be said quite simply that Hitler hated Jews because of the things that Jews had done in and to his beloved Germany.

Or maybe it was, instead, because he was denied a seat in the Vienna Academy of Art.

APPENDIX

POLITICAL PARTIES

Of the more than thirty German political parties that existed during the Weimar period, the main ones were as follows:

- The Social Democratic Party (SPD—*Sozialdemokratische Partei Deutschlands*). The SPD was a Marxist party that was nevertheless relatively moderate compared to its kindred Independent Social Democratic Party of Germany (USPD) and the Communist Party of Germany (KPD), both of which were spawned from SPD ranks. Labor unions were its focus and constituency. Its political playing field was limited to the big city.
- The Independent (minority) Social Democratic Party (USPD—*Unabhängige Sozialdemokratische Partei Deutschlands*). The USPD was a breakaway element of the SPD. Its membership was at one point in excess of 740,000. In 1922, the party was split due to its decision to join the Comintern. Those members who were unwilling to commit to the Bolshevistic KPD returned to their roots in the SPD. The USPD was radically leftist. It opposed both the *Kaiserrich* and the republic, preferring various shades of Communism to both. Like the SPD, the USPD focused on city dwellers, and particularly the unionists therein. Essentially, it was a radicalized version of the SPD.
- The Communist Party of Germany (KPD—*Kommunistische Partei Deutschlands*). This was essentially the Spartacus League, renamed, but also consisted of a large contingent of former members of the USPD. It was even more radically leftist than the USPD. It, too, focused on the cities and unionists. It was a puppet of the Moscow-based Comintern and was financially sponsored by the Soviet Union.

- The German Democratic Party (DDP—*Deutsche Demokratische Partei*). This was a liberal party with a large Jewish constituency that supported the republic. Its constituency was primarily business concerns. Its prominent leaders included Walther Rathenau, Friedrich Naumann, Hugo Pruess, and Theodor Wolff, all of whom were Jewish. The party played a dominant role in the creation of the Weimar constitution and stood steadfastly for the separation of church and state. It pushed for a uniform, national, secular school system. The party also undermined efforts by the Center Party and the Bavarian People's Party to win state funding for parochial schools. It sought to create a "United States of Europe."
- The Catholic Center Party (Center—*Zentrumspartei*). As the name implies, the Center Party was centrist in its political views but had both a progressive and a conservative wing. It took its name from its place in the seating of the Reichstag, not its political philosophy. Due to its Catholic core, it contained elements of the far Left and the far Right but was centrist in its politics. It was intransigent in confessional, educational, and cultural matters but willing to compromise with either the Left or Right with respect to economic and social affairs. It often sided with the SPD. Fatefully, it ultimately sided with Hitler in the early days of his regime.
- German Peoples Party (DVP). This was a party with a liberal-moderate, pro-Republican, free-trader, anti-Christian, and anti-Marxist constituency. It supported the Weimar constitution. The party chairman was the noble Gustav Stresemann.
- The German National People's Party (DNVP—*Deutschnationale Volkspartei*). This, like Hitler's party, was a rightist one. Its constituency was the upper and middle class and large landowners. Its platform was rightist, but it was not anti-Semitic. In 1922, it had expelled its anti-Semitic members.

- National Socialist German Workers Party (NSDAP, Nazi Party). Throughout most of the 1920s, the Nazis, like most others, centered their attention on the cities and its workers. After their disastrous showing in the elections of 1928, the Nazis reoriented their focus to rural areas of the country where most of the population still resided, but they simultaneously continued to seek support within the cities. Unlike the other parties, the Nazis did not focus their attention on a particular economic or social class. The party was the only one that sought a truly mass following from all sectors, classes, and confessions of society.

Michael Fitzgerald is the author of the book, *Adolf Hitler: a Portrait*. In my judgment, the book has a number of serious flaws (ill-supported speculations and misstatements of fact), but it also contains passages of praiseworthy summation and lucidity. One such passage correctly summarizes the tendencies of the various political parties of the Weimar era vis-à-vis the Nazis. Fitzgerald describes them as follows:

> The very fact that the Nazis genuinely were a party which included, and in a sense represented, almost every class within the country made them quite unique in Germany at that time. The Democrats represented the middle-class "liberal intellectuals", the Nationalists the upper and upper-middle classes, the Centre Party the Catholics, the Social Democrats and Communists the working classes, and the National Democrats the enlightened middle-class conservatives. Only the Nazis had no specific interest group with which they could be in any meaningful way identified. As such, Hitler's claim that he was the savior of the whole nation, not simply a section of it, was both new and extremely appealing to the electorate.[1980]

Of the foregoing parties, several deserve special mention and elaboration.

APPENDIX

Sozialdemokratische Partei Deutschlands, SPD. The SPD (*Sozialdemokratische Partei Deutschlands*) was the largest party, followed by the Center, the DNVP, and the USPD/KPD. SPD-Center coalitions reigned throughout the early 1920s in conjunction with a host of smaller parties needed to form a majority. The parties most distinctive as Marxist were the SPD and the USPD/KPD. According to historian Sarah Gordon, when Hitler came to power, the

> Political leaders of the SPD and KPD [the USPD was defunct by 1922] were more ruthlessly suppressed than were those of other parties, not just because they were numerous and influential, but also because they had historically been represented by prominent Jewish politicians and generally had had closer ties to Jews than had other political leaders. . . . The same logic applied to the trade unions, which had close political ties to the "Jewish" SPD.[1981]

The official position of the SPD, which at the time was the most successful Socialist party in the world, was that it was the legitimate heir of Marx, Engels, and Lassalle, and it declared itself as such by way of its Gotha and Erfurt programs. The implementation of Marxism (Communism) was its official objective. The party was approximately ten times as large as the second-place French Socialists movement.[1982]

As a Marxist party, the SPD saw itself as internationalistic. Thus, it was that on occasions when Hitler railed against internationalists, he was usually directing himself to the SPD. A large number of Jewish theoreticians, journalists, propagandists, and other intellectuals had risen to leading positions in the party. So many, in fact, it was the case that the SPD replaced the National Liberal Party as the purported "party of the Jews"[1983] (as were the Spartacists, the USPD, the KPD, and the DDP). Support for the party amongst Jewish politicians and intellectuals was not a Nazi myth; it was real enough. In addition to the SPD's large number of Jewish Reichstag delegates (in 1914, 67 percent of the Jewish Reichstag members were from the SPD—thirty-nine out of fifty-eight). Such notables as Eduard Bernstein and Rosa Luxemburg (who got her start in the SPD before joining in the founding of the Spartacist League and KPD) were very active in the party. They were only two among many Jewish theorists and propagandists for the party. Jews in general provided both overt and covert financial support.[1984] Moreover, the SPD established and retained a close relationship with Jewish defense organizations, such as the CV, outside the party.[1985]

In its hugely successful election campaign of 1912, the SPD was led by the Jews Eduard Bernstein and Karl Kautsky, August Bebel and the non-Jew Freidrich Ebert. In general, the Jewish Reichstag delegates were far more left wing than Jewish voters as a whole,* which led to anti-Semitic attitudes that associated all Jews with the radical leftist positions of the Jewish Reichstag leaders.[1986] With the enormous success of the party in 1912, the SPD became the largest party in Germany, and therefore became associated with all that occurred in the country, for good or for ill.

The 1912 election cycle also illustrates another important point: of the 300 candidates favored by Jews and their organizations, a total of eighty-eight were elected.[1987] Clearly, then, the German people at that time felt no widespread animosity toward Jews; they, instead, widely embraced them as leaders of the Reich. In actual fact, the 1912 election marked the utter demise of the few anti-Semitic parties; the whole of it was a significant setback for radical rightist forces.

The political rightists ascribed the victory of the left to the activities of "Jewish fellow-citizens."[1988] "The liberals," it was said, "have managed to make the party of subversion the numerically strongest faction in the whole Reichstag."[1989] The claim was not an exaggeration.

---

*But this fact should not be taken to mean that Jews on the whole strenuously objected to their SPD contingent. By way of example, contemporary writers frequently highlight Jewish opposition to the apartheid, ethnic cleansing, and subjugation practiced by the Israeli government with respect to the Palestinians, yet hard-core proponents of such policies keep getting elected in Israel (Begin, Shamir, Sharon, Netanyahu, et al.).

Importantly, the SPD's constituency existed wholly within the cities. It had little regard or use for the rural voter. Wanting to keep food prices low for its urban constituency, the SPD expended considerable effort to block moves to introduce higher tariffs on agricultural imports, a move that drove many a rural resident into the arms of the Nazis.

Referring to his days in Vienna, Hitler said in *Mein Kampf*, "When I discerned the Jews as leaders of the Social Democrats, the scales fell from my eyes. The long struggle of the soul thereupon concluded." Hitler would maintain his obsession with Jews and Social Democrats, saying that "Only knowledge of Jewry offers the key to grasping the inner and therefore actual intentions of the Social Democrats."[1990]

Shortly before the war, the German *Bund der Landwirte* complained about the "uncanny power of this alien people," the "kings of our time."[1991] They said that "Not the Junker but the Jews rule our people. This we must make clear to our people, and we should not be afraid to mention the Jews in this connection, even if each time the liberal and Social Democratic press will fall upon us."[1992] After the war, and especially in Bavaria, the fight against Jews was, on a broader scale, a fight against the SPD and its tendencies.

The party was not without ideological factionalism. There was, for example, a loud and lengthy debate between the Revisionists, led by Eduard Bernstein; the orthodox center represented by Karl Kautsky; and the radicals around Rosa Luxemburg and Rudolf Hilferding.[1993] Factional or not, the various leftist parties (Social Democrats, German Democrats, Communists, etc.) all had Marxism at their core. The debates among the disputing parties and factions centered on whether they would achieve their Marxist goals by way of peaceful evolution or by violent revolution: Bernstein, for example, favored evolution in opposition to Rosa Luxemburg's armed revolution.

The party's connection to the labor movement led to the venerated Jewish party leader August Bebel being called the "Worker's Kaiser." Indeed, together with the trade unions, the SPD formed a state within the state. In an organizational structure that would be mimicked by Adolf Hitler in the 1930s, the SPD built the trade unions and simultaneously built an extensive bureaucracy that constituted an alternative cultural and social network: Socialist clubs, sports teams, choirs, poetry groups, child care centers, even funeral homes. Workers were informed by the party's newspaper. When Hitler sought inroads to the workers he created the National Socialist Factory Cell Organization (NSBO) which was modeled after the shop-floor organizations of the KPD.[1994] So it was, then, that the Jewish-led SPD and its affiliate organizations served as prototypes for the infamous Hitler Youth organization and countless other Nazi entities.

A measure of Jewish involvement in Socialist politics was provided by Eduard Bernstein, who estimated in 1921 that 10 percent of the participants in party conferences were Jews. Throughout the Weimar years, Jews made up a similar percentage of the Social Democratic Reichstag deputies.[1995] Their numbers in the Reichstag understates their actual influence in party affairs, however, because "Jews avoided the top positions in the German Social Democratic Party despite 'a large Jewish presence in leadership positions of the second rank.'"[1996] The intellect of their membership, the finances of their political sponsors, and the sympathetic national and world press that they enjoyed provided an enormous multiplier for Jewish power both within the party and society as a whole. The conspicuous position of Jewish intellectuals in the SPD's leadership (e.g., starting with Lassalle, then on to Bernstein, Luxemburg, Liebknecht, and many others) made Jewish support for Socialism look somewhat bigger than it actually was. Still, from among the various Socialist parties, Jews managed to hold some 22 percent of the Reichstag seats by 1924; this, from a subset of the entire population comprising less than 1 percent. Rank-and-file workers remained loyal to the many Jewish leaders of the SPD[1997] and its various splinter parties throughout the Weimar years. Adolf Hitler understandably saw social democracy as indissolubly linked with Jewry.[1998] Adding still more to Jewish power were the many and varied Jewish organizations that played a political role, a traditional role played by Jews from the time of court Jews on down to their modern equivalents.

The SPD remained the largest party in Germany throughout the Weimar years. Importantly, for all of the party's popularity and strength, it was forever a party of the metropolis. It never really sought to gain the support of Catholic and rural areas, and it therefore remained underrepresented in these areas.

The SPD was staunchly opposed to anti-Semitism, but its position with respect to the Jewish community as a whole was ambiguous. It was hostile to organized religion of any kind, including Judaism, and was therefore looked upon with concern by some Jewish interests; but the thrust of its behavior with respect to religion centered on opposition to Christianity,[1999] making Jews, on the whole, comfortable within its ranks.

Unabhängige Socialdemokratische Partei (USPD) and the Kommunistische Partei Deutschlands (KPD). Spawned from the SPD, the *Unabhängige Socialdemokratische Partei* (Independent SPD—USPD) was founded in April 1917, by SPD members who opposed the war. "Many prominent USPD leaders were Jewish, and in some of the postwar people's councils over 30 percent of their delegates were Jews. . . ." By mid-1919 and in Scheidemann's cabinet about 14 percent of the USPD delegates were Jewish.[2000] According to Hitler, "*The Independent Party and the Spartacus League were the storm battalions of revolutionary Marxism.*"[2001] (Italics are in the original.)

The party's founding membership had been active as a political entity opposed to the war as early as 1915. Members of the USPD would later (1919) join with the Spartacists in creating the Communist Party of Germany (KPD). By late 1922, the USPD had split apart due to a decision to have it join the Comintern and thereby become a puppet of Moscow. When the split took place, roughly 400,000 USPD members merged with the KPD in support of the Comintern decision and the other 340,000 returned to the fold of the SPD. By 1930, KPD subservience to Moscow was so complete that its leaders were appointed from the Kremlin.[2002]

Each of these political entities was more radically leftist than its predecessor. Jews played a significant role in all three factions (SPD, USPD, and Spartacists/KPD). As Sarah Gordon points out, "Spartacists, the USPD, the KPD, and the revolutionary councils had extremely high percentages of Jews in their memberships...."²⁰⁰³ Most authors also identify the SPD as among the parties with a high number of Jews in its base; though the Jewish percentage in the SPD was a lower one due to its very large overall membership. Of the leftist parties, it is also the case that the SPD was the more moderate faction. Jewish presence and power in the various leftist parties, then, was inversely proportional to the party's numerical strength and directly proportional to its radicalism. The smallest party, the KPD (essentially the Spartacists with a new name), had the highest ratio of Jews to Gentiles and was the most radical of the three, then came the USPD, and finally, the very large SPD.

The KPD was founded and led by Rosa Luxemburg and Karl Liebknecht on January 1, 1919. As mentioned, its early membership was composed of Spartacists and breakaway elements of the USPD. After the deaths of Liebknecht and Luxemburg, which occurred only a few weeks after the founding of the party, it was headed in sequence by Leo Jogiches, Paul Levi, and Ruth Fischer, all of whom, like Luxemburg and Liebknecht before them, were Jews. Paul Levi was the one who had initiated movement of the party into a position of subservience to Moscow (and he later rebelled against that very subservience). Ruth Fischer's demise in the party was in part due to her opposition to following the lead of Moscow.* In 1925, leadership of the party was assumed by Ernst Thälmann, a non-Jewish philosemite who led the party under strict direction from Moscow from thence until well after Hitler came to power.

By the late 1920s, under Thälmann, the party was a veritable marionette of Moscow. Due to squabbles within the party, still another Communist party was born from the ranks of the KPD—this was the Communist Workers Party of Germany (KAPD). A fundamental distinction of the KAPD versus the KPD was that the KAPD refused to take its orders from Moscow. The very existence

---

* In 1933, Fischer fled Germany for the U.S. She thereafter lived, taught, and wrote in Cambridge, Massachusetts.

of the SPD, the USPD, the KPD, KAPD, and the DDP (discussed below) illustrates the schisms that existed within leftist-Jewish ranks and the internal bickering among strong personalities for dominance. It was comparable to schisms within the Zionist movement. All of these entities, however, schisms or no, were radically dedicated to Marxism in one or another of its various forms.

The idea of totally re-creating society according to their views appealed to large numbers of leftist intellectuals, artists, writers, and musicians. Such people were attracted to the KPD and helped its propaganda and avant-gardist cultural initiatives. In particular, they created plays, films, and concerts, the singular purpose of which was to spread the gospel of radical Socialism.

As previously emphasized, the SPD, USPD, and KPD were closely connected to labor unions within the country. When Walter Rathenau, then the Jewish foreign minister, was murdered on June 24, 1922, the KPD joined with others in a united front with the main workers' parties and union federations, and it was at this point that it began to seek its ends on a mass basis rather than through conspiratorial means.[2004] These parties demanded sweeping reforms. The government, they demanded, must purge both the police and judiciary, proceed against right-wing newspapers, and bar nationalists from both the civil service and the army.[2005]

The Left was unsuccessful in its demands, but Hitler, when he implemented identical actions against these parties, would be. The Hitler purges are, of course, emphasized by historians, while they simultaneously downplay the purges implemented by the Jewish-led Left. For those who care to represent the assassination of Rathenau as being rooted in his Jewishness (and to an extent, it certainly was), it is worth noting that others, non-Jews, were also targets. Between 1919 and 1922, there were 356 political murders in Germany.[2006] Rathenau's assassination was only one among many and was all the more prominent precisely because he was Jewish. Still, it has to be known that that there had been an unsuccessful assassination attempt on SPD leader Scheidemann only three weeks prior to Rathenau's death.[2007] Would Rathenau have been assassinated, Jew or not, had he not supported German liabilities related to the Treaty of Versailles? What if he had rejected both the Treaty of Versailles and had not negotiated the Treaty of Rappalo? The answer, I think, is that he would have lived to a ripe old age. It was not so much his Jewishness as his prominence as the main author of the fulfillment policy toward the Treaty of Versailles that so enraged his enemies.[2008] In addition to the foregoing, the disastrous March Action* of 1921, as well as its early failure in gaining power by force of arms also significantly contributed to the party's revised focus.

In conjunction with its union supporters, the KPD appealed to the working class to purge monarchists from the army, the police, and the courts. It called for the dissolution of all anti-republican armed groups (this, let us be reminded, was the party that tried to overthrow the republican government by violent means) and called for political amnesty for its own supporters. The appeal successfully energized the working class, culminating in massive demonstrations and clashes with police in July 1922.

Throughout the 1920s, the KPD managed to garner only about 10 to 15 percent of the vote, but it nevertheless managed to represent about one-third of the labor unionists. Moreover, in a country with over thirty political parties and resultant total dependency of the government on coalition governments, a voting block of 10–15 percent was significant indeed. Thus it was that the KPD was a major force in Weimar politics.

The KPD's radicalism, loyalty to Moscow, and size made it a fearful competitor to the larger SPD. Throughout the 1920s, the KPD was far and away more powerful than Hitler's NSDAP. As late as 1928, for example, the KPD had fifty-four seats in the Reichstag while the Nazis had but a pitiful twelve.[2009] Fatefully,

---

* March Action, 1921. A disastrous uprising in central Germany that was ordered by the Moscow-based Comintern. The Communists fabricated attacks on themselves in an attempt to incite workers. Perfidy, sabotage, arson, and murder were highlights of the Action. Hundreds of people were killed and thousands were imprisoned. The KPD lost upward of 100,000 members as a direct result of this ill-timed and poorly executed insurrection.

the KPD focus on doing battle with the SPD instead of Nazism (in accordance with direction from Moscow, the KPD denounced the SPD as "social fascists" and any suggestion of cooperating with them was utterly rejected)[2010] diluted the forces that might otherwise have focused on defeating Hitler. The political warfare between the SPD and KPD continued on, right up to the very moment of ultimate success of the Nazis. The KPD's choice to do battle with the SPD, rather than Hitler's Nazis was illustrated by its frequent resort to anti-Semitic appeals to the radical right wing in order to attract workers who resented the influence of Jews in the SPD. According to author Sarah Gordon, "The KPD . . . used anti-Semitism to placate nationalist sentiment and to compete with the [Nazis] after 1928."[2011]—this, from a party that was founded by Jews and continued to have Jews in its positions of leadership, though by this time not at the party's head.

Deutsche Demokratische Partei (DDP). The German Democratic Party (*Deutsche Demokratische Partei*—DDP) was founded in the early days of the Weimar Republic by the Jews Walther Rathenau, Eugen Schiffer, Otto Preuss, and two non-Jews, Otto Gessler and Erich Koch-Weser. Albert Einstein was one of the original signers of a manifesto announcing the creation of the party.[2012] The party was attacked by the right wing for being the party of Jews, and Jews did indeed constitute its leadership and its most loyal constituency.[2013] Jewish membership in the party included some twenty Jews in the provisional executive. Of its seventy-five deputies in the Reichstag, ten were of Jewish descent, the others being sycophants of the Jewish leadership. The party also had a strong Jewish representation in the Prussian Constituent Assembly, including six Jews. The half-Jew SPD politico Albert Grzesinski (born Albert Lehmann) served as the under-secretary of state in the Prussian War Ministry from 1919 to 1922 and thereafter served as the president of the Prussian police, and from 1925 to 1926 as the president of the Berlin police. Under Grzesinski was the Jewish DDP member Bernhard Weiss who served as the vice president of the Berlin police and there earned the unstinting hatred of Hitler's propaganda minister, Joseph Goebbels (among other things, Weiss was accused of promoting illegal gambling and pornography while in office).[2014] The party, being Jewish, of course had leftist sympathies. Second only to the SPD, the DDP was most committed to maintaining the viability of the Weimar Republic, the government so hated by Hitler and other members of the right wing.

The party's constituency was comprised of middle-class entrepreneurs, civil servants, teachers, scientists, and craftsmen. It was financed by a relatively small clique of wealthy Jews, including Carl Fürstenberg, Walther Rathenau, the Arnhold brothers, and the Tietz family, as well as some lesser-known Jewish industrialists—"in so far as Jewish money flowed in any direction," says Peter Pulzer, "it was towards the DDP."[2015]

The DDP did well in the first Reichstag election after World War I and participated in the first government of the Weimar Republic. One of the DDP's founding members, Rathenau, became the republic's minister for reconstruction in 1921 and its foreign minister in 1922. There were a total of twenty-four Jewish deputies elected to the new Reichstag. As Pulzer informs us, numerous DDP politicians combined their party activities with offices in Jewish organizations,[2016] and thereby added, no doubt, to right-wing complaints about Jewish agendas in public life.

Besides its dependence on financial support from a small cadre of wealthy Jews, the DDP also enjoyed the staunch support of the three leading publishing houses: those owned by the Jews Mosse, Ullstein, and Simons-Sonnermann. The information assets owned by these publishers were put to the service of the party. They "supported the DDP editorially and many of their employees, led by Theodor Wolff, editor in chief of the *Berliner Tageblatt*, were prominent party members,"[2017] says historian Peter Pulzer. It is little wonder, then, that the DDP was widely known as the Jew Party (*Judenpartei*). Throughout most of the 1920s, the DDP was a more powerful force in German politics than were the Nazis. By the end of the decade, however, the DDP had decayed into virtual nothingness. Its decline was in part due to its staunch support for the republic, which it viewed as advantageous to Jews.

Central Union of German Citizens of Jewish Faith (CV or C.V.). The Central Union of German Citizens of Jewish Faith

(*Centralverein deutscher Staatsbürger jüdischen Glaubens*; or more simply, the "*Centralverein*" or CV) was not a political party per se. Its primary focus was on defeating anti-Semitism and its membership, on the whole, followed its lead in voting for candidates who were most inclined toward Jewish interests—it was to Germany of the 1920s what AIPAC is to American politics today. The CV did, however, like AIPAC, wield substantial political power. Many Jews belonging to the CV could not conceive of a political home other than the DDP.[2018] The CV also maintained close ties with the SPD, secretly giving it aid in the form of money and propaganda material.[2019] Thus, says Pulzer, it was that the right wing viewed the CV as "a coherent, homogeneous group, with common interests and aims, anomalous in and harmful to the German Christian nation."[2020] That is, with respect to Christianity, the DDP was but another supporter of the SPD's anti-Christian stance. Moreover, the CV's connection to Jewish titans of the Weimar press was emphasized by the fact that Rudolf Mosse printed the CV's public journal.

Jewish voting patterns were such that 80 percent of German Jews voted for one or another of the liberal parties.[2021] Along with their voting patterns we can assume that the mass of Jews also provided their financial support in similar percentages, and given that the Jews of Germany of that era were exceedingly wealthy, that 80 percent of German Jews can be seen in much the same light as rich American Jews today—they sponsored the parties, policies, and politicians that were deemed to be in the best interest of Jewish objectives.

Other quasi-political organizations operating on behalf of Jewish particularism included the League of National German Jews (*Verband nationaldeutscher Juden*), and the Zionists. The League of National German Jews favored abandonment of the Jewish identity in favor of total assimilation. The Zionists, conversely, wanted to abandon Germany entirely and reestablish themselves in a Jewish state in Palestine. Clearly, the Zionists won that argument.

Center Party. The [Catholic] Center Party (*Deutsche Zentrumspartei or Zenturm*) was founded in 1870 in response to

Bismarck's attack on Catholicism, the *Kulturkampf*. One of the accusations against Catholics of the time was that they were more loyal to Rome than to Germany. Still, when the party was established, it managed to act independently of the Holy See in several important respects.

The name Center came from the fact that the party's predecessor organizations sat in the center of the legislative chamber, between the Liberals (who sat to the left), and the Conservatives (who sat to the right). The party's politics were, like both its name and its seating arrangement, Centrist. While it was essentially a Catholic party, it was not exclusively so. Many Protestants also belonged to the party due to its centrist leanings. The party represented a mainstay of the republican form of government throughout the Weimar era. It participated in nearly every coalition government formed during the Weimar period. Because of its support for the government, it also understandably shared in the blame for the dismal performance of the various coalitions. A certain odium was attached to the party due to its support for the many failures that the government experienced. Matthias Erzberger, a Center Party leader, was among those who signed the armistice ending World War I; he was assassinated by elements of the right wing in 1920, largely due to his contribution to the Stab in the Back.

German National People's Party (DNVP). The German National People's Party (DNVP—*Deutschnationale Volkspartei*) was formed in 1918 through a merger of several small conservative parties: the German Conservative Party, the Free Conservative Party, and breakaway elements of the rightist faction of the National Liberal Party. The DNVP was essentially a party of the monarchists and other bourgeoisie. The DNVP, like Hitler's NSDAP (Nazi) party, was a rightist one, though for a time (1925–1928) it cooperated with and participated in the Weimar government. Experiencing serious setbacks in the voting booths in 1928, the party modified its previous stance of cooperation with the government, and, under the leadership of Alfred Hugenberg, took on a more hard-line nationalist position. In 1931, the DNVP formed a brief coalition with Hitler's NSDAP that worked far more to the advantage of the Nazis than the DNVP. The Nazi coalition with the DNVP gave the Nazis access to funding and an air of respectability that had previously been denied them. In 1933, the party supported Hitler's Enabling Act that endowed the Hitler government with essentially dictatorial legislative powers. By mid-1933, the DNVP, along with all other parties, was dissolved.

INDEX

Adler, Victor, 153, 155, 250
AIPAC, 170, 469, 627
AJCommittee, 262
Alexander II, 139, 156, 228
All Quiet on the Western Front, 554, 555
Amann, Max, 2
architecture, xxvi, 15, 35, 37, 41, 72, 79, 93, 96, 97, 98, 101, 105, 128, 129, 133, 137, 150, 340, 382, 413, 426, 432, 434, 437, 439, 444, 454, 492, 493, 494, 495, 497, 498, 499, 500, 502, 503, 507, 532, 611
Arlosoroff, Dr. Chaim, 600, 602
Austria, xxv, 12, 14, 42, 49, 53, 54, 79, 81, 84, 89, 92, 108, 111, 123, 127, 128, 130, 131, 132, 138, 139, 143, 145, 147, 151, 156, 157, 160, 161, 162, 163, 165, 166, 167, 177, 181, 185, 188, 190, 193, 199, 200, 201, 202, 203, 204, 205, 206, 207, 227, 239, 271, 272, 293, 294, 297, 299, 301, 308, 312, 323, 325, 326, 327, 338, 361, 371, 390, 401, 416, 482, 506, 516, 538, 539, 549, 568, 569, 596, 602, 605, 606, 638
Austro-German Customs Union, 539
Austro-Hungarian Empire, 292
Autobahn, 440
Balfour Declaration, 88, 259, 260, 261, 262, 264, 265, 266, 275, 318, 319, 608, 612
Balkans, 307
Ballin, Albert, 194, 239, 241
Bambi, 478
Barmat (three brothers), 404, 550, 551, 552, 611
Barth, Emil, 279, 282

Baruch, Bernard, 264, 316
Battle of Jutland, 266
Bauhaus, 493, 494, 497, 498, 499, 500, 502, 503, 533, 534
Bavarian Revolution, xiv, 125, 253, 331, 362, 363, 367, 373, 388, 389, 391, 395, 396
Bayerische Volkszeitung, 366, 391
Beckmann, Max, 235
Beer Hall Putsch, 43, 48, 159, 192, 219, 329, 331, 338, 442
Ben-Gurion, David, 600, 602, 603
Berber, Anita, 487, 507, 508, 509, 510
Berlin Press Union, 484
Bernstein, Eduard, 86, 126, 213, 245, 246, 249, 282, 283, 469, 513, 531, 618, 619, 620
Blackshirt, 602
Blockade of the North Sea, 205, 266, 268, 269, 297, 298, 330, 344, 353, 595
Bolsheviks, 56, 119, 122, 123, 124, 125, 254, 269, 270, 336, 352, 367, 371, 380, 401, 494, 558
Bolshevistic
  Bolshevism, xiv, 119, 121, 222, 241, 277, 321, 331, 336, 340, 347, 383, 390, 449, 451, 503, 544, 557, 558, 609, 614
Börne, Ludwig, 125, 159, 457, 460
Bosel, Siegmund, 402, 405, 406, 611
Boycott, 53, 59, 118, 170, 180, 287, 444, 573, 590, 591, 592, 593, 594, 595, 598, 601, 602, 603, 611, 612
Brandeis, Louis, Supreme Court Justice, xxiii, xxiv, 263, 264, 315, 318
Brecht, Bertolt, 22, 238, 468, 485

Brest-Litovsk, 270, 314, 324, 511
Bund, 170, 230, 384, 596, 619
Burgfrieden, 244, 245
Cabaret, 99, 167, 486
Cassirer, Paul and Bruno, 132, 470, 473, 488
Castiglioni, Camillo, 402, 405, 406, 611
Center Party (Mostly Catholic), 338, 343, 353, 543, 568, 581, 589, 615, 627, 628
Centralverein CV, 232, 550, 627
Cesspool Republic, 417
Christmas Crisis, 328, 331, 347, 350
Clemenceau, Georges, 168, 177, 179, 294, 316, 610
Cohen, Sam, 82, 257, 593, 598, 599, 600, 602
Cohn, Oskar, 282, 348, 527, 608
Comintern (Moscow-based Communist International), 123, 124, 397, 398, 400, 610, 614, 621, 624
Compiegne, 310
culture, xxvi
Dada, 236, 415, 451, 452, 483
Davidson, Paul, 470
Dawes Plan, 325, 567
Dawidowicz, 107, 112, 185, 187, 216, 232
Dawidowicz, Lucy, 412
DDP, German Democratic Party, 49, 250, 320, 343, 353, 358, 368, 540, 568, 615, 617, 623, 625, 626, 627
Degenerate Art Exhibition, 452
Der Stürmer, xxvii
Dershowitz, Alan, xxix, 71
Die Aktion, 237, 416
Die rote Fahne, 336, 348
DNVP, German Nationalist Party, 326, 338, 354, 408, 552, 577, 581, 590, 615, 617, 628, 629
Donitz, Admiral Karl, 39, 612

Dreyfus, Alfred, 168, 169, 175, 176, 177, 178, 179, 213, 521, 610
Ebert, Friedrich, 253, 277, 279, 281, 282, 284, 290, 293, 336, 337, 341, 342, 345, 346, 347, 348, 349, 350, 351, 353, 354, 371, 396, 514, 618
Eckart, Dietrich, iii, 2, 48
Eichhorn, Emil, 350, 351, 395
Einstein Tower, 497
Einstein, Albert, 222, 235, 456, 513, 520, 526, 532, 533, 544, 625
Eisner, Kurt, 125, 213, 246, 253, 257, 282, 290, 327, 328, 337, 339, 345, 364, 365, 366, 367, 368, 369, 370, 371, 372, 373, 374, 375, 376, 381, 382, 383, 384, 390, 391, 407, 429, 445, 531, 608
Enabling Act, 575, 590, 629
Enlightenment, xviii, 25, 62, 78, 89, 135, 461, 587
Expressionism, 131, 132, 153, 154, 414, 442, 446, 449, 471, 474, 488
Expressionist Decade, 414
Feuchtwanger, Lion, 237, 470, 518
Fischer, Ruth, 125, 398, 399, 473, 482, 561, 622
Foch, General Ferdinand, 291, 294, 321
Fourteen Points, 299, 300, 301, 302, 303, 307, 312
Frank, Leonard, 248
Frankfurter Seating, 324
Frankfurter Zeitung, 143, 172, 253, 484
Freikorps, 278, 329, 347, 348, 349, 350, 352, 353, 364, 376, 385, 386, 387, 388, 397
Friedrich the Great, 5
George, David Lloyd, 35, 36, 93, 259, 263, 291, 294, 298, 316, 321, 609
German Press Association, 484
German Writer's Protection Association, 484
Goddess of Reason, 385

Goebbels, Dr. Joseph, xxvii, 2, 38, 40, 49, 50, 52, 96, 97, 429, 430, 436, 447, 448, 495, 496, 504, 506, 514, 528, 533, 547, 605, 625
Goering, Hermann
Göring, xxvii, 2
Goldhagen, Daniel, vii, viii, ix, x, xiv, xv, xxi, 60, 116, 229, 368, 403
Gothein, Georg, 608
Great Hall, 439, 495
Greece, 7, 61, 93, 96, 202, 294, 295, 299, 605
Grelling, Richard, 213, 253, 513
Groener, General Wilhelm, 346, 347, 348, 349, 352
Grosz, George, 112, 238, 330, 450, 468
Grzesinski, Albert, 576, 625
Gumbel, Emil, 235, 283, 462, 511, 512, 513, 514, 515, 529
Ha'avara, 599
Haas, Ludwig, 225, 339
Haase, Hugo, 125, 126, 195, 213, 245, 246, 252, 253, 257, 273, 279, 281, 282, 290, 337, 339, 342, 346
Hanfstaengl, Ernst, 2, 27, 28, 43, 44, 52, 547, 578
Harden, Maximilian, 143, 254, 418, 470
Hasidic
Hasidim, xx, 141
Heartfield, Helmut (Herzfelde), 236, 237, 450, 483, 577
Heine, Heinrich, 125, 159, 223, 339, 457, 460, 522
Herzberg Front, 326
Herzfelde, Wieland, 236, 237, 483
Herzl, Theodor, xxiii, xxiv, 88, 90, 139, 167, 181, 191, 198, 315, 525, 596
Hiller, Kurt, 470, 517, 518, 524, 530
Himmler, Heinrich, xxvii, 47, 50, 51, 80, 107, 429, 447
Hindenburg, Paul von, 21, 52, 275, 280, 342, 346, 348, 356, 357, 457,
512, 514, 536, 544, 564, 588, 589, 590, 608, 609
Hirsch, Paul, 253, 339, 353, 454, 490
Hirschfeld, Magnus, 475, 476, 507, 513, 524, 530, 563
House of Lords, 518
Hugenberg, Alfred, 326, 485, 577, 628
Hyperinflation, xxvi, 287, 329, 401, 402, 403, 404, 405, 588
Independent Social Democratic Party (USPD), 246
Influenza, 268, 298, 610
Institution for Sexual Science, 475
Iron Cross, 215
Jabotinsky, 296, 593, 598
Jacobsohn, Siegfried, 236, 418, 470, 490, 518, 524
Jessner, Leopold, 416, 479, 481, 482
Jew Count, 223, 234, 241
Jewish Autonomous Oblast, 597
Jewish World League, 595
Joffe, Adolf Abramovich, 90, 120, 126, 270, 271, 272, 348, 349, 360, 378, 462, 608
Jogiches, Leo, 243, 249, 251, 343, 348, 351, 352, 369, 378, 407, 622
Josef Thorak, 441, 495
Josefine Mutzenbacher, 478
Kafka, Franz, xxiii, 427, 456, 473, 540
Kaganovich, Lazar, xvi, 566
Kahr, Gustav von, 368, 395
Kapp Putsch, 329, 331, 338, 342, 396, 397, 399
Kautsky, Karl, 126, 245, 249, 618, 619
Kessler,Count Harry, 462, 463
Kessler,Count Harry, 237, 238, 329
Keynes, John Maynard, 55, 291, 321, 582, 588
Kiel, 240, 253, 273, 276, 277, 278, 285, 293, 327, 334, 339, 367, 389
Kiel Mutiny, 276, 278, 327, 334
Kisch, Egon Erwin, 237, 462, 468
Klimt, Gustav, 112, 473

Kokoschka, Oskar, 89, 236, 474
KPD (Communist Party of Germany), 119, 124, 126, 236, 244, 258, 335, 337, 338, 342, 351, 352, 354, 358, 384, 393, 394, 396, 397, 398, 399, 400, 402, 407, 454, 492, 514, 520, 524, 540, 542, 543, 544, 545, 547, 552, 555, 556, 557, 558, 559, 561, 570, 581, 588, 589, 610, 614, 617, 618, 620,鸭621, 622, 623, 624, 625
Kubizek, August, 1, 2, 15, 16, 17, 18, 19, 20, 23, 29, 30, 34, 37, 39, 145, 152, 166, 212, 436, 495
Kun (Kohn), Belá, 376, 399, 407, 462
Kutisker, Ivan, 404
Labor Procurement law, 603
Landsberg, Otto, 33, 251, 282, 342, 354, 366
Lang, Fritz, 236, 468
Lansdowne Letter, 267
Latsis, Latvian M., 558
League of Human Rights, 513
League of Nations, 301, 306, 307, 309, 312, 314, 323, 539, 567
Lecache, Bernard, 592
Lenin, Vladimir, 63, 90, 122, 197, 236, 240, 244, 249, 254, 268, 336, 348, 352, 359, 360, 362, 367, 373, 375, 378, 379, 380, 383, 384, 385, 388, 395, 398, 566
Lessing, Theodor, xi, 457, 511, 512, 527
Levi, Paul, 125, 236, 243, 246, 251, 336, 343, 352, 384, 398, 400, 622
Levien, Max, 125, 236, 328, 376, 382, 384, 386, 462
Levine, Eugen, 125, 243, 328, 329, 363, 364, 376, 385
Leviné, Eugen, 364, 370, 376, 378, 382, 383, 384, 385, 386, 387, 388, 390, 407, 462
Liebermann, Max, 460, 472, 473

Liebknecht, Karl, 110, 125, 126, 213, 237, 243, 244, 245, 246, 247, 248, 250, 252, 254, 257, 274, 275, 277, 280, 283, 290, 333, 334, 335, 336, 337, 341, 342, 343, 348, 349, 350, 351, 352, 360, 369, 396, 404, 407, 425, 531, 608, 620, 622
Lotte Lenya, 487
Lubitsch, Ernest, 236, 470, 472, 486
Ludendorff, General Erich, 242, 243, 253, 257, 266, 272, 275, 280, 338, 346, 348, 408, 608, 609
Lukács, Georg, 236, 377, 462
Mack, Julian, 315, 316, 487, 507
Mahagonny, 485
Mahler, Gustav, 50, 131, 144, 149, 150, 433
March Action, xiv, 127, 329, 331, 380, 398, 400, 544, 610, 624
Marshall, Louis, 316, 512
Marxists, iii, xiv, 5, 47, 64, 76, 90, 91, 125, 174, 183, 197, 213, 217, 222, 230, 243, 244, 247, 249, 250, 251, 259, 270, 271, 272, 276, 281, 289, 319, 320, 324, 330, 331, 335, 337, 338, 345, 346, 347, 362, 365, 372, 387, 392, 393, 394, 396, 407, 409, 410, 420, 442, 534, 544, 545, 547, 559, 567, 607, 610, 611
Maurice, Emil, 2, 47, 48, 171, 267
Max, Prince von Baden, 279, 280, 281, 341
May Day, 558
Mehring, Franz, 243, 456, 470, 563
Meidner, Ludwig, 236, 473
Mein Kampf, 14, 80, 82, 85, 92, 101, 108, 128, 129, 130, 140, 160, 172, 189, 191, 205, 221, 274, 285, 287, 288, 368, 393, 418, 441, 445, 446, 481, 619
Mendelssohn, Moses, xxiii, 62, 194, 228, 460
Michael Holzmann, 404, 552

Michael, Jakob, 404, 553
Mommsenm, Theodor, ii, 638
Mosse, Rudolf, 176, 361, 455, 469, 473, 483, 484, 626, 627
Muehsam, Erich, 125, 236, 277, 364, 370, 382
Muesham, Eric, 235
Mussolini, 49, 91, 97, 598
Naked Dance, 486, 509
nation within the nation, xii, xiii, 596
Naturalism, 466, 486
Neue Freie Presse, 143, 185, 482
New Secession, 415
Nordau, Max, 74, 315, 463, 464, 596
Noske, Gustav, 329, 352, 353, 387, 397
November Criminals, 212, 325, 569
Novembergruppe, 497
NSDAP (Nazi Party), 48, 358, 393, 394, 573, 574, 575, 577, 616, 624, 628
Olympic Games, 605
Oppenheimer, Franz, 231, 232, 473, 474
Ossietzky, Carl von, 320, 418, 458, 462, 483, 511, 515, 517, 518, 519, 520, 521, 522
Ostjuden, 140, 141, 232, 243, 252, 368, 388, 403, 419, 551, 607
Otto Brahm, xi, 418, 472, 486
Ottoman Empire, 202, 205, 301, 307
Palace of the Republic, 500
Papen, Franz von, 34, 323, 386, 429, 560, 568
Paris, 7, 8, 96, 162, 166, 167, 169, 177, 196, 286, 289, 291, 292, 298, 305, 309, 310, 414, 466, 493, 498, 505, 516, 544, 611
Paris Peace Talks, 291
Parvus, Alexander, 126, 254, 404, 552
Pechstein, Max, 415, 497
pilpul
    pilpulism, xix, xx, 114, 268
Piscator, Erwin, 386, 486, 506, 563

Polish Corridor, 165, 302, 323, 537, 568
Preuss, Hugo, 126, 282, 354, 355, 366, 625
Profiteers, 231, 241, 242, 267, 272, 298, 404, 406, 407
Radek, Karl, 120, 125, 236, 257, 336, 348, 349, 351, 352, 378, 388, 398, 401, 407, 462
Rathenau, Walter, 126, 194, 241, 242, 275, 283, 326, 337, 345, 407, 525, 615, 623, 625, 626
Red Front, 393, 394, 395, 399, 400, 559, 562
Red Guard, 237, 347
Red Terror, xi, 380, 559, 566
Redl, Redl, 239, 608
Reichstag fire, 444, 556, 557, 575, 590
Reinhardt, Max, 50, 152, 456, 462, 470, 472, 486, 487
Remarque, 554, 555
Rhineland, 53, 60, 312, 323, 326, 537, 553, 579, 605
Ribbentrop, Joachim von, 34, 35, 36, 44, 359, 612
Richard Wagner, 15, 21, 24, 39, 80, 93, 98, 160, 430, 437
Rome, 7, 21, 23, 91, 93, 96, 182, 436, 493, 505, 628, 638
Rosenberg, Alfred, xxi, xxvii, 52, 100, 119, 448
Rosenfeld, Kurt, 213, 246, 283, 339, 381, 454, 487, 527, 529
Rote Fahne, 230, 347, 399, 483
Roth, Alfred, 231
Rothschild, 120, 139, 145, 182, 194, 261, 263, 316, 463, 503
Russia, iii, xvi, xxii, 8, 24, 46, 81, 82, 84, 88, 90, 94, 118, 119, 121, 122, 123, 125, 139, 140, 157, 166, 169, 170, 171, 173, 180, 193, 194, 195, 197, 198, 199, 200, 201, 202, 203, 204, 207, 208, 223, 227, 228, 229,

232, 233, 236, 239, 245, 248, 250,
253, 259, 260, 261, 262, 268, 269,
270, 271, 272, 275, 277, 279, 293,
294, 295, 299, 325, 326, 327, 334,
336, 338, 339, 340, 344, 349, 352,
359, 360, 361, 367, 374, 375, 376,
378, 379, 380, 384, 388, 390, 404,
407, 409, 441, 459, 482, 495, 496,
556, 558, 565, 566, 596, 610, 612
Russian Revolution, 120, 121, 139,
170, 180, 199, 227, 250, 252, 262,
268, 271, 276, 278, 293, 334, 335,
338, 359, 367, 385
SA, 34, 48, 51, 157, 377, 392, 393,
394, 395, 559, 560, 573, 579, 580,
See Sturmabteilung
SA (*Sturmabteilung*), 392, 393
Salten, Felix, 451, 478, 479
Scheidemann, Philipp, 282, 321, 341,
342, 345, 354, 621, 623
Schleicher, General Kurt von, 356, 522,
568, 587
Schoenberg, Arnold, 131, 137, 152,
433, 533
Schönberg, Arnold, 89, 414, 432, 433,
456
Secessionists, 496
Segall, Jakob, 231, 232
Shiller, Friedrich, 479, 480, 481
Shopenhauer, Arthur, 217
Sinzheimerk, Hugo, 608
Sklarek, brothers Leo and Willy, 462,
552
Small kindnesses, 30, 32, 33, 36, 436
Social Democratic Party
SPD, 8, 82, 93, 139, 146, 155, 195,
240, 243, 246, 362, 380, 607,
614, 620
Sokolow, Nahum, 263
Soviets, 276, 277, 278, 333
Spartacus
Spartacist(s), xiv, 121, 213, 237,
244, 246, 247, 254, 255, 271,
331, 332, 333, 334, 349, 352,
353, 373, 391, 608, 614, 621
Spartacus Letters, 247, 255
Spartacus Uprising, xiv, 237, 331, 349,
353, 391
SPD
Social Democratic Party, 8, 292
Speer, Albert, xxvii, 2, 21, 40, 42, 49,
58, 81, 96, 97, 102, 165, 258, 429,
430, 436, 439, 440, 441, 492, 494,
495, 500
Spring Offensive, 257
Stab in the back, 212, 230, 255, 257,
266, 330, 410, 553, 609
Stauffenberg, Colonel Claus von, 219
Strasser, Gregor, xxvii, 49, 122, 123,
425, 429, 547
Streicher, Julius, xxvii, 529
Stresemann, Gustav, 253, 567, 568,
581, 615
Strikes, 250
Sudetenland, 45, 165, 312, 322, 323,
605
Szamuelly, Tibor, 377
Tandy, Henry, 219
Taut, Bruno, 416, 494
Tel Aviv, 503, 533, 599, 600, 601
Teutonic art, 439
Threepenny Opera, The, 468, 487
Toller, Ernst, 125, 235, 282, 290, 328,
363, 364, 370, 372, 376, 381, 382,
383, 384, 385, 388, 390, 391, 407,
445, 486, 520, 544, 608
Transfer Agreement, 598, 599, 600,
601, 602, 603
Treaty of Brest-Litovsk, 269, 270
Treaty of Rapallo, 326
Treaty of Versailles, v, xxvi, 46, 117,
165, 179, 208, 254, 283, 287, 291,
292, 293, 295, 309, 319, 320, 322,
323, 324, 325, 326, 329, 330, 371,
396, 401, 406, 408, 410, 511, 513,

539, 546, 551, 567, 569, 570, 585, 609, 624
Tretschke, Heinrich von, 411
Trotsky, Leon, 90, 120, 121, 122, 234, 268, 359, 367, 391, 407, 511
Tucholsky, Kurt, 115, 234, 235, 238, 320, 418, 424, 458, 459, 462, 470, 511, 515, 518, 522, 523, 524, 525, 542, 543, 564
Turnip Winter, 267, 268
Ullstein, Leopold, 473, 483, 484, 626
Untermyer, Samuel, 592
USPD, 119, 126, 199, 213, 222, 240, 246, 247, 248, 252, 253, 254, 255, 258, 269, 271, 275, 277, 278, 280, 281, 282, 292, 293, 319, 320, 324, 327, 332, 333, 334, 335, 337, 338, 342, 348, 349, 350, 351, 353, 354, 358, 369, 374, 396, 397, 402, 454, 490, 514, 515, 鴨524, 540, 543, 569, 614, 617, 621, 622, 623
Vienna, v, xi, xxiv, xxv, 2, 4, 14, 15, 18, 19, 20, 25, 30, 31, 33, 55, 79, 80, 82, 91, 95, 96, 101, 103, 106, 108, 110, 111, 115, 116, 117, 119, 127, 128, 129, 130, 131, 134, 135, 136, 137, 138, 139, 140, 141, 142, 143, 144, 145, 146, 147, 148, 149, 152, 153, 154, 155, 156, 158, 161, 162, 165, 166, 167, 180, 181, 182, 184, 185, 186, 187, 188, 189, 190, 191, 192, 207, 211, 212, 216, 222, 239, 243, 257, 268, 287, 345, 365, 368, 371, 380, 390, 411, 413, 415, 418, 429, 432, 436, 437, 442, 462, 470, 473, 477, 478, 479, 490, 495, 496, 604, 606, 619
Völkischer Beobachter, 562
Volksgeist, 60, 62, 543
Vorwaerts, 78, 274
Vorwärts, 274, 369, 483, *See Vorwarts*
Vossische Zeitung, 320, 553

Wagener, Otto, 11, 124, 281, 392, 557, 583
Walden, Herwarth, 471
Walter, Bruno, 65, 67, 95, 126, 198, 235, 237, 241, 275, 326, 367, 399, 407, 414, 421, 456, 470, 473, 486, 487, 488, 494, 499, 514, 520, 522, 525, 534, 563, 623
Warburg, Max, 223, 241, 253, 317
Weber, Max, 250, 277, 355, 368, 382
Weill, Kurt, 432, 434, 485
Weimar Republic, xxvi, 22, 117, 234, 253, 327, 331, 343, 344, 345, 353, 355, 388, 421, 427, 442, 443, 447, 450, 475, 487, 492, 504, 536, 538, 586, 587, 588, 625, 626
Weizmann, Chaim, 119, 229, 263, 296, 297, 298, 304, 593, 596, 600, 602, 612
Weltanschauung
Worldview, xxv, 91, 129, 455
Weltbühne, 115, 230, 231, 234, 236, 319, 321, 326, 483, 515, 516, 517, 518, 519, 522, 544, 582
William II, Kaiser, 90, 93, 194, 195, 196, 197, 198, 199, 201, 204, 280, 281, 289, 313, 331, 340, 346
William Tell, 81, 479, 480, 481
Wilson, Woodrow, 54, 254, 262, 263, 264, 279, 280, 294, 299, 300, 301, 302, 303, 305, 307, 308, 309, 310, 312, 314, 316, 318, 319, 322, 370
Wise, Rabbi Stephen, 172, 264, 315, 591
Wolf, Lucien, 262, 317
Wolff, Kurt, 237, 253, 473, 482, 484, 615, 626
Women'sLliberation Movement, 187, 490
Workers' and Soldiers' Councils, 282, *See* Soviets
World League for Sexual Reform, 476

World War One, v, xxv, 116, 117, 120, 193, 325, 327, 328, 329, 337, 343, 361, 364, 453, 497, 536, 607
WWI, xxv
WWI, xiii, xxvi, 3, 8, 9, 16, 22, 33, 35, 46, 51, 55, 61, 84, 93, 116, 119, 126, 153, 156, 157, 162, 165, 170, 172, 173, 175, 179, 195, 196, 197, 202, 204, 209, 211, 220, 227, 229, 230, 231, 233, 234, 235, 236, 237, 238, 239, 240, 253, 256, 259, 262, 264, 268, 287, 289, 291, 298, 310, 311, 327, 330, 331, 338, 340, 358, 359, 365, 366, 369, 405, 408, 409, 413, 417, 418, 423, 436, 454, 489, 491, 513, 515, 519, 520, 537, 551, 570, 587, 598, 607, 608, 609, 610, 626, 628
WZO, World Zionist Organization, 595, 596, 597, 603
Young Plan, 325, 539, 576
Zinoviev, Grigory, xvi, 120, 122, 123, 391, 398, 401, 407

ENDNOTES

[1] http://www.faem.com/books/yhik00.htm 06/16/14
[2] Lindemann, Albert S., *Esau's Tears: Modern Anti-Semitism and the Rise of the Jews* (Cambridge University Press, Cambridge, U.K., 2000), 103. Lindemann is quoting Theodor Mommsen from the *History of Rome* (Glencoe, 1957), 5:417–19.
[3] Ibid., 28.
[4] Fest, Joachim. *Hitler* (San Diego: Harcourt, 2002), 211.
[5] Lindemann, Albert S., *Esau's Tears: Modern Anti-Semitism and the Rise of the Jews* (Cambridge University Press, Cambridge, U.K., 2000), 29.
[6] MacDonald, Kevin. *Separation and Its Discontents: Toward an Evolutionary Theory of Anti-Semitism* (S. L.: 1stBooks Library, 2003), 71.
[7] Ibid., 38.
[8] Encarta Dictionary: English (North America).
[9] MacDonald, Kevin. *A People That Shall Dwell Alone: Judaism as a Group Evolutionary Strategy, with Diaspora Peoples* (San Jose: Writers Club Press, 2002), 18.
[10] Kauders, Anthony. *German Politics and the Jews: Düsseldorf and Nuremberg, 1910–1933* (Oxford: Clarendon Press, 1996), 11. The subquote refers to Peter Pulzer's *The Rise of Political Anti-Semitism in Germany and Austria* (London, 1988), 14.
[11] Lindemann, Albert S., *Esau's Tears: Modern Anti-Semitism and the Rise of the Jews* (Cambridge University Press, Cambridge, U.K., 2000), xvii.
[12] Ibid., 6.
[13] Stolfi, R. H. S. *Hitler: Beyond Evil and Tyranny* (Prometheus Books, Amherst, New York, 2011), 272.
[14] Lindemann, Albert. *Anti-Semitism before the Holocaust* (New York: Longman, 2000), 35.
[15] Bullock, Alan. *Hitler, A Study in Tyranny* (New York and Evanston: Harper & Row, 1964), 16.
[16] Bilski, Emily D. *Berlin metropolis: Jews and the new culture, 1890–1918* (University of California Press, 1999), 26.
[17] Avvineri, Shlomo. Mar 3, 2010. "Haaetz," *Where Hannah Arendt went wrong.* http://www.haaretz.com/hasen/spages/1153098.html 07/16/14
[18] Book review by John Abbott, University of Illinois at Chicago: Albert Lindermann's "Anti-Semitism before the Holocaust."
[19] http://www.mythsandfacts.com/Conflict/9/childrendyingtokill1.htm 10/31/10

[20] http://www.haaretz.com/blogs/strenger-than-fiction/strenger-than-fiction-in-order-to-change-its-image-israel-must-change-its-policy-1.291260 05/23/10
[21] Goldhagen, Daniel. *Hitler's Willing Executioners* (New York: Knopf, 1996), 42.
[22] Ibid., 49.
[23] Ibid., 141.
[24] Ibid., 146.
[25] Ibid., 147.
[26] Ibid., 6.
[27] Bilski, Emily D. *Berlin metropolis: Jews and the new culture, 1890–1918* (University of California Press, 1999), 221–22.
[28] Willett, John, *Art & Politics in the Weimar Period: The New Sobriety 1917–1933* (Da Capo Press, New York, 1996), 48.
[29] Elon, Amos. *The Pity of It All: A Portrait of the German-Jewish Epoch, 1743–1933* (New York: Holt, 2003), 23.
[30] http://www.kevinmacdonald.net/SlezkineRev.pdf. Dr. Kevin MacDonald's Review of Slezkine's "The Jewish Century," 06/18/08
[31] Shahak, Israel. *Jewish History, Jewish Religion: the Weight of Three Thousand Years* (Sydney: Pluto Press, 1994), 100.
[32] Fest, Joachim. *Hitler* (San Diego: Harcourt, 2002), 101.
[33] http://www.counterpunch.org/2008/06/21/why-israel-won-t-accept-a-two-state-solution 0531114. "Why Israel Won't Accept a Two-State Solution" by Bernard Chazelle. July 10, 2008, posted by Leonard Fein.
[34] Roderich-Stoltheim, F. *The Riddle of the Jew's Success* (RePortersNoteBook.com, NY, 2005.) Translated from the German by Capel Pownall. Originally published by Hammer-Verlag, Leipzig, 1927, 171.
[35] Ibid., 170–71.
[36] Kershaw, Ian. *Hitler, 1889–1936* (New York: W. W. Norton, 1999), 125.
[37] Goldhagen, Daniel. *Hitler's Willing Executioners* (New York: Knopf, 1996), 84.
[38] Williams, John. *Corporal Hitler and the Great War 1914–1918* (London: Frank Cass, 2005), 20.
[39] Stolfi, R. H. S. *Hitler: Beyond Evil and Tyranny* (Prometheus Books, Amherst, New York, 2011), 81.
[40] MacDonald, Kevin. *Separation and Its Discontents: Toward an Evolutionary Theory of Anti-Semitism* (S. L.: 1stBooks Library, 2003), 71.
[41] Finkelstein, Norman. *The Holocaust Industry* (London: Verso, 2003), 70.
[42] Ibid., 77.
[43] http://www.haaretz.com/hasen/spages/1130497.html 11/25/09
[44] Finkelstein, Norman. *The Holocaust Industry* (London: Verso, 2003), 78.
[45] Berkowitz, Michael. *The Crime of My Very Existence*. (Berkeley: University of California Press, 2007), 5.

[46] Finkelstein, Norman. *The Holocaust Industry* (London: Verso, 2003), 37.
[47] Shahak, Israel. *Jewish History, Jewish Religion: the Weight of Three Thousand Years* (Sydney: Pluto Press, 1994), ix.
[48] The quotation is attributed to Zukerman, William. *Voices of Dissent, Jewish Problems, 1948–1961* (Bookman Associates, NY, 1964), 68.
[49] The original of the quotation is at Kristol Irving, *Reflections of a Neoconservative. Looking Back, Looking Ahead* (Basic Books, New York, 1983), 278.
[50] http://www.jewishencyclopedia.com/view.jsp?artid=318&letter=P.
[51] Haumann, Heiko. *A History of East European Jews* (Budapest: Central European University Press, 2002), 23.
[52] Ibid., 47.
[53] http://en.wikipedia.org/wiki/Jacob_Frank 05/31/14
[54] Reed, Douglas. *The Controversy of Zion* (Western Australia: Veritas Publishing Company Pty., Ltd, 1985), 102.
[55] http://en.wikipedia.org/wiki/Pilpul 05/31/14.
[56] Brenner, Lenni. *51 Documents, Zionist Collaboration with the Nazis* (Fort Lee, Barricade Books, 2002), 333.
[57] Hornbeck, Stanley. The Heretical Press. Date of pub. unk. *The Culture of Critique* (review). Retrieved from URL: http://www.heretical.com/miscellx/culturec.html 5/9/15
[58] Finkelstein, Norman. *The Holocaust Industry* (London: Verso, 2003), 15.
[59] Friedlander, S. 1997. "Redemptive Anti-Semitism." Retrieved from URL: http://www.yarok.biz/icons-multimedia/ClientsArea/HoH/LIBARC/LIBRARY/Themes/Policy/Friedl2A.html
[60] Haumann, Heiko. *A History of East European Jews* (Budapest: Central European University Press, 2002), 202.
[61] Berkowitz, Michael. *The Crime of My Very Existence* (Berkeley: University of California Press, 2007), 5.
[62] Ibid., 5–10.
[63] Haumann, Heiko. *A History of East European Jews* (Budapest: Central European University Press, 2002), 7.
[64] Berkowitz, Michael. *The Crime of My Very Existence* (Berkeley: University of California Press, 2007), 8.
[65] Ibid., 12.
London, England © 2007 by The Regents of the University of California, 12.
[66]
http://students.washington.edu/njp/papers/undergraduate/german351_hitlerinvienna.htm 10/15/05. This site has apparently been changed or removed. The document I cite is "The Influence of Fin De Siecle Viennese Culture on Adolf

Hitler," Nathan Patterson, German, 351; Professor Heidi Tilghman, December 17, 2003.
[67] Fitzgerald, Michael. *Adolf Hitler: a Portrait* (Staplehurst: Spellmount, 2007), 1.
[68] Kershaw, Ian. *Hitler, 1889–1936* (New York: W. W. Norton, 1999), 29.
[69] Goldensohn, Leon, and Robert Gellately. *The Nuremberg Interviews* (New York: Knopf, 2004), 198.
[70] MacDonald, Kevin. *Separation and Its Discontents toward an Evolutionary Theory of Anti-Semitism* (S. L.: 1stBooks Library, 2003), 297.
[71] Tedor, Richard. *Hitler's Revolution: Ideology Social Programs Foreign Affairs* (Chicago, 2013), 6.
[72] Kauders, Anthony. *German Politics and the Jews: Düsseldorf and Nuremberg, 1910–1933* (Oxford: Clarendon Press, 1966), 4.
[73] Fest, Joachim. *Hitler* (San Diego: Harcourt, 2002), 129.
[74] Stolfi, R. H. S. *Hitler: Beyond Evil and Tyranny* (Prometheus Books, Amherst, New York, 2011), 63.
[75] Fest, Joachim. *Hitler* (San Diego: Harcourt, 2002), 69.
[76] Kershaw, Ian. *Hitler, 1889–1936* (New York: W. W. Norton, 1999), 63.
[77] Fest, Joachim. *Hitler* (San Diego: Harcourt, 2002), 142.
[78] Stolfi, R. H. S. *Hitler: Beyond Evil and Tyranny* (Prometheus Books, Amherst, New York, 2011), 267.
[79] Fest, Joachim. *Hitler* (San Diego: Harcourt, 2002), 69.
[80] Ibid., 135.
[81] Stolfi, R. H. S. *Hitler: Beyond Evil and Tyranny* (Prometheus Books, Amherst, New York, 2011), 267.
[82] Spotts, Frederic. *Hitler and the Power of Aesthetics* (New York: Overlook Press, 2003), 401.
[83] Fest, Joachim. *Hitler* (San Diego: Harcourt, 2002), 60.
[84] Kubizek, August. *The Young Hitler I Knew* (London: Greenhill Books, 2006). Abridged edition first published in English, 1954, by Allan Wingate Publishers Ltd., 221.
[85] Spotts, Frederic. *Hitler and the Power of Aesthetics* (New York: Overlook Press, 2003), 400.
[86] Tedor, Richard. *Hitler's Revolution: Ideology Social Programs Foreign Affairs* (Chicago, 2013), 61.
[87] Ibid., 69.
[88] Toland, John. *Adolf Hitler* (Garden City: Anchor Books, 1992), xiv.
[89] Spotts, Frederic. *Hitler and the Power of Aesthetics* (New York: Overlook Press, 2003), 29.
[90] Ibid., 118.
[91] Trevor-Roper, Hugh. *Hitler's Table Talk, 1941–1944* (New York, Enigma Books, 2000), 71.

[92] "Bombing of Rome in World War II." 8 March 2014. http://en.wikipedia.org/wiki/Bombing_of_Rome_in_World_War_II 07/06/14
[93] Toland, John. *Adolf Hitler* (Garden City: Anchor Books, 1992), xiii.
[94] Lindemann, Albert. *Anti-Semitism before the Holocaust* (New York: Longman, 2000), 58.
[95] Ibid., 64.
[96] Williams, John. *Corporal Hitler and the Great War 1914–1918* (London: Frank Cass, 2005), 201.
[97] Kershaw, Ian. *The "Hitler Myth"* (Oxford University Press, Inc., Oxford, New York, 2001), 32.
[98] Ibid., 6–7.
[99] Bradberry, Benton L. *The Myth of German Villainy* (Bloomington, IN, AuthorHouse), 6.
[100] Fest, Joachim. *Hitler* (San Diego: Harcourt, 2002), 374–75.
[101] Fischer, Conan. *The Rise of the Nazis*, 2nd ed. (Manchester University Press. Manchester and New York, 2002), 37.
[102] Lindemann, Albert. *Anti-Semitism before the Holocaust* (New York: Longman, 2000), 73.
[103] http://schikelgruber.net/artistic.html 01/30/09
[104] Ibid.
[105] Goldensohn, Leon, and Robert Gellately. *The Nuremberg Interviews* (New York: Knopf, 2004), 126.
[106] Fest, Joachim. *Hitler* (San Diego: Harcourt, 2002), 151.
[107] Turner, Henry, and Ruth Hein. *Hitler—Memoirs of a Confidant* (New Haven: Yale University Press, 1987), 33.
[108] Bullock, Alan. *Hitler, A Study in Tyranny* (New York and Evanston: Harper & Row, 1964), 41.
[109] Fest, Joachim. *Hitler* (San Diego: Harcourt, 2002), 25–26.
[110] Bullock, Alan. *Hitler, A Study in Tyranny* (New York and Evanston: Harper & Row, 1964), 42.
[111] Fest, Joachim. *Hitler* (San Diego: Harcourt, 2002), 26.
[112] Hitler, Adolf.. *Mein Kampf*. Trans. Ralph Manheim (Boston/NY, Houghton Mifflin Company, First Mariner Books edition, 1999), 7.
[113] Hamann, Brigitte, *Hitler's Vienna: A Dictator's Apprenticeship*. Trans. Thomas Thornton (Oxford, NY, 2000), 8.
[114] Kubizek, August. *The Young Hitler I Knew* (London: Greenhill Books, 2006). Abridged edition first published in English, 1954, by Allan Wingate Publishers Ltd. 90.
[115] Hitler, Adolf. *Mein Kampf*, Trans. Ralph Manheim. (Boston/NY, Houghton Mifflin Company, First Mariner Books edition, 1999), 14.

[116] Giblin, James, and Robert Payne. *The Life and Death of Adolf Hitler* (New York: Praeger, 1973).
[117] Kubizek, August. *The Young Hitler I Knew* (London: Greenhill Books, 2006). Abridged edition first published in English, 1954, by Allan Wingate Publishers Ltd., 78.
[118] Ibid., 245.
[119] Ibid., 14.
[120] http://en.wikipedia.org/wiki/Franz_Jetzinger 12/06/09
[121] Kubizek, August. *The Young Hitler I Knew* (London: Greenhill Books, 2006). Abridged edition first published in English, 1954, by Allan Wingate Publishers Ltd. 13–14.
[122] Giblin, James, and Robert Payne. *The Life and Death of Adolf Hitler* (New York: Praeger, 1973), 10.
[123] Kubizek, August. *The Young Hitler I Knew* (London: Greenhill Books, 2006). Abridged edition first published in English, 1954, by Allan Wingate Publishers Ltd., 132.
[124] Ibid., 136.
[125] Ibid., 135.
[126] Ibid., 56.
[127] Kershaw, Ian. *Hitler, 1889–1936* (New York: W. W. Norton, 1999), xxviii.
[128] Kubizek, August. *The Young Hitler I Knew* (London: Greenhill Books, 2006). Abridged edition first published in English, 1954, by Allan Wingate Publishers Ltd., 106.
[129] Ibid., 106.
[130] Ibid., 87.
[131] Ibid., 168.
[132] Ibid., 164.
[133] Ibid., 49.
[134] Ibid., 49.
[135] Ibid., 87.
[136] Ibid., 32.
[137] Ibid., 41.
[138] Ibid., 43.
[139] Ibid., 66.
[140] Ibid., 34, 38, 75.
[141] Williams, John. *Corporal Hitler and the Great War 1914–1918* (London: Frank Cass, 2005), 180.
[142] Fest, Joachim. *Hitler* (San Diego: Harcourt, 2002), 382.
[143] Spotts, Frederic. *Hitler and the Power of Aesthetics* (New York: Overlook Press, 2003), 321.

[144] Ibid., 244.
[145] Ibid., 57.
[146] Ibid., 49.
[147] Kubizek, August. *The Young Hitler I Knew* (London: Greenhill Books, 2006). Abridged edition first published in English, 1954, by Allan Wingate Publishers Ltd. 245.
[148] Fest, Joachim. *Hitler* (San Diego: Harcourt, 2002), 18.
[149] Ibid., 49–50.
[150] Tedor, Richard. *Hitler's Revolution: Ideology Social Programs Foreign Affairs* (Chicago, 2013), 53.
[151] Kubizek, August. *The Young Hitler I Knew* (London: Greenhill Books, 2006). Abridged edition first published in English, 1954, by Allan Wingate Publishers Ltd., 85.
[152] Shirer, William L. *The Rise and Fall of the Third Reich: A History of Nazi Germnay* (Touchstone, NY, 1998), 102.
[153] Hamann, Brigitte. *Hitler's Vienna: A Dictator's Apprenticeship*. Trans. Thomas Thornton (Oxford, NY, 2000), 250.
[154] Lindemann, Albert. *The Jew Accused* (Cambridge: Cambridge University Press, 1991), 25.
[155] Schroeder, Christa, and Roger Moorehouse. *He Was My Chief* (City: Frontline Books, 2009), xviii–xix.
[156] Ibid., 45.
[157] Fitzgerald, Michael. *Adolf Hitler: a Portrait* (Staplehurst: Spellmount, 2007), 41.
[158] Spotts, Frederic. *Hitler and the Power of Aesthetics* (New York: Overlook Press, 2003), xiii.
[159] Kershaw, Ian. *Hitler, 1889–1936* (New York: W. W. Norton, 1999), xxii.
[160] Spotts, Frederic. *Hitler and the Power of Aesthetics* (New York: Overlook Press, 2003), xv–xvi.
[161] Fest, Joachim. *Hitler* (San Diego: Harcourt, 2002), 324.
[162] Ibid., 324.
[163] Trevor-Roper, Hugh. *Hitler's Table Talk, 1941–1944* (New York, Enigma Books, 2000), xii.
[164] Rosenbaum, Ron. *Explaining Hitler* (NY: Harper Perennial edition, 1999), 230.
[165] Sereny, Gitta. *Albert Speer, His Battle with Truth* (New York: Vintage Books Edition, 1996), 103.
[166] Hamann, Brigitte. *Hitler's Vienna: A Dictator's Apprenticeship*. Trans. Thomas Thornton. (Oxford, NY, 2000), Paperback Edition, 23.

[167] Kubizek, August. *The Young Hitler I Knew* (London: Greenhill Books, 2006). Abridged edition first published in English, 1954, by Allan Wingate Publishers Ltd. 30.
[168] Fest, Joachim. *Hitler* (San Diego: Harcourt, 2002), 31.
[169] Spotts, Frederic. *Hitler and the Power of Aestetics* (New York: Overlook Press, 2003), 5.
[170] Stolfi, R. H. S. *Hitler: Beyond Evil and Tyranny* (Prometheus Books, Amherst, New York, 2011), 100.
[171] Toland, John. *Adolf Hitler* (Garden City: Anchor Books, 1992), 48.
[172] Giblin, James, and Robert Payne. *The Life and Death of Adolf Hitler* (New York: Praeger, 1973), 13.
[173] Linge, Heinz, and Roger Moorehouse. *With Hitler to the End* (City: Skyhorse Publishing, 2009), 28.
[174] Bullock, Alan. *Hitler and Stalin* (New York: Vintage Books, 1993), 169.
[175] Linge, Heinz, and Roger Moorehouse. *With Hitler to the End* (City: Skyhorse Publishing, 2009), 21.
[176] Sony Picture Classics. "Blind Spot: Hitler's Secretary" (Documentarians: Andre Heller and Othmar Schmiderer).
[177] Junge, Traudl. *Until the Final Hour* (City: Arcade Publishing, 2004), 5.
[178] Ibid., 37.
[179] Linge, Heinz, and Roger Moorehouse. *With Hitler to the End* (City: Skyhorse Publishing, 2009), 43.
[180] Ibid., 47.
[181] Fest, Joachim. *Hitler* (San Diego: Harcourt, 2002), 218.
[182] Ryback, Timothy. *Hitler's Private Library: the Books That Shaped His Life* (London: Vintage, 2010), 13.
[183] Toland, John. *Adolf Hitler* (Garden City: Anchor Books, 1992), 54.
[184] Williams, John. *Corporal Hitler and the Great War 1914–1918* (London: Frank Cass, 2005), 20.
[185] Toland, John. *Adolf Hitler* (Garden City: Anchor Books, 1992), 39.
[186] Fitzgerald, Michael. *Adolf Hitler: a Portrait* (Staplehurst: Spellmount, 2007), 86.
[187] Kubizek, August. *The Young Hitler I Knew* (London: Greenhill Books, 2006). Abridged edition first published in English, 1954, by Allan Wingate Publishers Ltd. 217.
[188] Ibid., 214.
[189] Ibid., 183.
[190] Ibid., 173.
[191] Goldensohn, Leon, and Robert Gellately. *The Nuremberg Interviews* (New York: Knopf, 2004), 166.
[192] Ibid., 185.
[193] Ibid., 191.

[194] http://www.biblebelievers.org.au/witness1.htm 05/19/06
[195] http://www.biblebelievers.org.au/witness1.htm 12/30/07
[196] http://www.biblebelievers.org.au/witness1.htm 05/19/06 (Winston Churchill. Fancis Nielson. *Makers of War*), 101.
[197] Rosenbaum, Ron. *Explaining Hitler* (NY: Harper Perennial edition, 1999), 67.
[198] Stolfi, R. H. S. *Hitler: Beyond Evil and Tyranny* (Prometheus Books, Amherst, New York, 2011), 317.
[199] Toland, John. *Adolf Hitler* (Garden City: Anchor Books, 1992), 129.
[200] Gilbert, G. *Nuremberg Diary* (New York: Da Capo Press, 1995), 68.
[201] Williams, John. *Corporal Hitler and the Great War 1914–1918* (London: Frank Cass, 2005), 205.
[202] http://euromanuk.blogspot.com/2008/07/requiem-for-adolf-hitler.html. Quoting from *Warnings and Predictions*, 180–83, 01/31/09
[203] Turner, Henry, and Ruth Hein. *Hitler—Memoirs of a Confidant* (New Haven: Yale University Press, 1987). Translator's Note, 127, 129.
[204] Fest, Joachim. *Hitler* (San Diego: Harcourt, 2002), 251.
[205] Kubizek, August. *The Young Hitler I Knew* (London: Greenhill Books, 2006). Abridged edition first published in English, 1954, by Allan Wingate Publishers Ltd., 39.
[206] Ibid., 39.
[207] Linge, Heinz, and Roger Moorehouse. *With Hitler to the End* (City: Skyhorse Publishing, 2009), 42.
[208] Ibid., 59.
[209] Kershaw, Ian. *The "Hitler Myth"* (Oxford University Press, Inc., Oxford, New York, 2001), 59.
[210] Ibid., 280–81.
[211] Ibid., 535.
[212] Linge, Heinz, and Roger Moorehouse. *With Hitler to the End* (City: Skyhorse Publishing, 2009).
[213] Fest, Joachim. *Hitler* (San Diego: Harcourt, 2002), 206.
[214] Toland, John. *Adolf Hitler* (Garden City: Anchor Books, 1992), 133.
[215] Kubizek, August. *The Young Hitler I Knew* (London: Greenhill Books, 2006). Abridged edition first published in English, 1954, by Allan Wingate Publishers Ltd., 179.
[216] Ibid., 180.
[217] Goldensohn, Leon, and Robert Gellately. *The Nuremberg Interviews* (New York: Knopf, 2004), 15.
[218] Stolfi, R. H. S. *Hitler: Beyond Evil and Tyranny* (Prometheus Books, Amherst, New York, 2011), 28.

[219] Spotts, Frederic. *Hitler and the Power of Aesthetics* (New York: Overlook Press, 2003), 94.
[220] Fest, Joachim. *Hitler* (San Diego: Harcourt, 2002), 206.
[221] Spotts, Frederic. *Hitler and the Power of Aesthetics* (New York: Overlook Press, 2003), 93.
[222] Ibid., 334.
[223] Ibid., 334–35.
[224] Toland, John. *Adolf Hitler* (Garden City: Anchor Books, 1992), 264.
[225] Gilber, G. M. *Nuremberg Diary* (Da Capo Press, 1995), 351–52.
[226] Toland, John. *Adolf Hitler* (Garden City: Anchor Books, 1992), 199.
[227] Giblin, James, and Robert Payne. *The Life and Death of Adolf Hitler* (New York: Praeger, 1973), 35.
[228] Toland, John. *Adolf Hitler* (Garden City: Anchor Books, 1992), 130.
[229] Fest, Joachim. *Hitler* (San Diego: Harcourt, 2002), 166.
[230] Goldensohn, Leon, and Robert Gellately. *The Nuremberg Interviews* (New York: Knopf, 2004), 26.
[231] Toland, John. *Adolf Hitler* (Garden City: Anchor Books, 1992), 192.
[232] Spotts, Frederic. *Hitler and the Power of Aesthetics* (New York: Overlook Press, 2003), 49.
[233] Stolfi, R. H. S. *Hitler: Beyond Evil and Tyranny* (Prometheus Books, Amherst, New York, 2011), 247.
[234] Spotts, Frederic. *Hitler and the Power of Aesthetics* (New York: Overlook Press, 2003), 44–47.
[235] Toland, John. *Adolf Hitler* (Garden City: Anchor Books, 1992), 285.
[236] Ibid., 129.
[237] Ibid., 129.
[238] Ibid., 129.
[239] Fest, Joachim. *Hitler* (San Diego: Harcourt, 2002), 74.
[240] Ibid., 74.
[241] Toland, John. *Adolf Hitler* (Garden City: Anchor Books, 1992), 242.
[242] Speer, Albert. *Inside the Third Reich: Memoirs* (New York: Simon & Schuster, 1997), 66.
[243] Toland, John. *Adolf Hitler* (Garden City: Anchor Books, 1992), 252.
[244] http://en.wikipedia.org/wiki/Emil_Maurice 02/03/09
[245] Giblin, James, and Robert Payne. *The Life and Death of Adolf Hitler* (New York: Praeger, 1973), 155.
[246] Turner, Henry, and Ruth Hein. *Hitler—Memoirs of a Confidant* (New Haven: Yale University Press, 1987), 125–26.
[247] Bullock, Alan. *Hitler and Stalin* (New York: Vintage Books, 1993), 152.
[248] Fitzgerald, Michael. *Adolf Hitler: a Portrait* (Staplehurst: Spellmount, 2007), 76.
[249] Ibid., 102.

[250] Spotts, Frederic. *Hitler and the Power of Aesthetics* (New York: Overlook Press, 2003), 84–85.
[251] Ibid., 274.
[252] Linge, Heinz, and Roger Moorehouse. *With Hitler to the End* (City: Skyhorse Publishing, 2009), 18.
[253] Smoter, Walter Frank. *Adolf Hitler, The Making of a Fuhrer*, Chapter 9, "Spark a Little Humor." URL: http://smoter.com/revoluti.htm 06/25/14
[254] Smoter, Walter Frank. *Adolf Hitler, The Making of a Fuhrer*, Chapter 9, "Cannes." URL: http://smoter.com/revoluti.htm 06/25/14
[255] Smoter, Walter Frank. *Adolf Hitler, The Making of a Fuhrer*, Chapter 9, "Jaunty." URL: http://smoter.com/revoluti.htm 06/25/14
[256] Toland, John. *Adolf Hitler* (Garden City: Anchor Books, 1992), 138.
[257] Trevor-Roper, Hugh. *Hitler's Table Talk, 1941–1944* (New York, Enigma Books, 2000), 227.
[258] Toland, John. *Adolf Hitler* (Garden City: Anchor Books, 1992), 261.
[259] http://reason.com/blog/show/127427.html. 05/31/14
[260] Irving, David. *Goebbels, Mastermind of the Third Reich*. (Parforce (UK) Ltd., 1996).
Online Version Downloaded from:
http://www.fpp.co.uk/books/Goebbels/index.html. 56. 05/31/14
[261] http://www.sweetliberty.org/issues/wars/witness2history/6.html. 05/31/14
[262] Tedor, Richard. *Hitler's Revolution: Ideology Social Programs Foreign Affairs* (Chicago, 2013), 47.
[263] Giblin, James, and Robert Payne. *The Life and Death of Adolf Hitler* (New York: Praeger, 1973), 110.
[264] Nicholls, Anthony. *Weimar and the Rise of Hitler* (London: Macmillan Press, 2000), 56.
[265] Giblin, James, and Robert Payne. *The Life and Death of Adolf Hitler* (New York: Praeger, 1973), 114.
[266] http://www.humanevents.com/article.php?id=30214. 05/31/14
[267] Brustein, William. *The Logic of Evil* (New Haven: Yale University Press, 1996), 55.
[268] http://www.sweetliberty.org/issues/wars/witness2history/6.html. 05/31/14
[269] Etlin, Richard A. (Editor) *Art, Culture, and Media under the Third Reich* (Chicago: University of Chicago Press, 2002), 162–63.
[270] Friedrich, Otto. *Before the Deluge* (New York: HarperPerennial, 1995), 390.
[271] Friedrich, Otto. *Before the Deluge* (New York: HarperPerennial, 1995), 390.
[272] Nicholls, Anthony. *Weimar and the Rise of Hitler* (London: Macmillan Press, 2000), 93–94.
[273] Gilbert, G. *Nuremberg Diary* (New York: Da Capo Press, 1995), 23.
[274] Fest, Joachim. *Hitler* (San Diego: Harcourt, 2002), 9.

[275] Speer, Albert. *Inside the Third Reich: Memoirs* (New York: Simon & Schuster, 1997), 65.
[276] Ibid., 65–66.
[277] Ibid., 65.
[278] http://www.biblebelievers.org.au/witness1.htm. 05/31/14
[279] Bilski, Emily D. *Berlin metropolis: Jews and the new culture, 1890–1918* (University of California Press, 1999), 45.
[280] Ibid., 45.
[281] Ibid., 44.
[282] Kauders, Anthony. *German Politics and the Jews: Düsseldorf and Nuremberg, 1910–1933* (Oxford: Clarendon Press, 1996), 190.
[283] Lindemann, Albert S. *Esau's Tears: Modern Anti-Semitism and the Rise of the Jews* (Cambridge University Press, Cambridge, U.K., 2000), 84.
[284] Ibid., 85.
[285] Peukert, Detlev. *The Weimar Republic*. (New York: Hill and Wang, 1993), 178.
[286] http://www.humanevents.com/article.php?id=32510.
[287] Jones, E. *Degenerate Moderns* (San Francisco: Ignatius, 1993), 98.
[288] MacDonald, Kevin. *The Culture of Critique: An Evolutionary Analysis of Jewish Involvement in Twentieth-Century Intellectual and Political Movements* (2002), 152.
[289] Elon, Amos. *The Pity of It All: A Portrait of the German-Jewish Epoch, 1743–1933* (New York: Holt, 2003), 263.
[290] Stibbe, Matthew. *Germany, 1914–1933* (Pearson Education Limited, 2010), 135.
[291] MacDonald, Kevin, *The Culture of Critique: An Evolutionary Analysis of Jewish Involvement in Twentieth-Century Intellectual and Political Movements* (2002), 152.
[292] Gidal, Nachum T. *Jews in Germany From Roman Times to the Weimar Republic* (Konemann, 1994 [First English Language Edition, 1998], Kohn, Germany, p. 354).
[293] MacDonald, Kevin. *The Culture of Critique: An Evolutionary Analysis of Jewish Involvement in Twentieth-Century Intellectual and Political Movements* (Kevin MacDonald), 2002), 229.
[294] http://www.heretical.com/miscellx/culturec.html. 05/31/14
[295] Jones, E. *Degenerate Modern*.(San Francisco: Ignatius, 1993), 164.
[296] MacDonald, Kevin. *The Culture of Critique: An Evolutionary Analysis of Jewish Involvement in Twentieth-Century Intellectual and Political Movements* (City: Authorhouse, 2002), 159.
[297] http://ualberta.ca/~cjscopy/articles/mclaughlin.html. 05/31/14
[298] http://www.heretical.com/miscellx/culturec.html. 05/31/14

299 http://ualberta.ca/~cjscopy/articles/mclaughlin.html. 05/31/14
300 http://www.marxists.org/subject/frankfurt-school. 05/31/14
301 Kimball, Linda. "Cultural Marxism." *American Thinker*. 15 Feb. 2007. http://www.americanthinker.com/2007/02/cultural_marxism.html. 06//05/14
302 MacDonald, Kevin. *The Culture of Critique: An Evolutionary Analysis of Jewish Involvement in Twentieth-Century Intellectual and Political Movements* (City: Authorhouse, 2002), 147.
303 Salmi, Hannu. *Nineteenth-Century Europe* (Cambridge: Polity, 2008), 70–73.
304 http://shankradioworldwide.typepad.com/shankradio_world_wide/2007/09/pay-no-attent-1.html. 05/31/14
305 http://en.wikipedia.org/wiki/Critical_theory. 05/31/14
306 Origin Myths in the Social Sciences: Fromm, the Frankfurt School and the Emergence of Critical Theory, Neil McLaughlin, Department of Sociology, McMaster University, *Canadian Journal of Sociology* 24, 1 (1999): 109–39. http://www.ualberta.ca/~cjscopy/articles/mclaughlin.html. 05/31/14
307 Origin Myths in the Social Sciences: Fromm, the Frankfurt School and the Emergence of Critical Theory, Neil McLaughlin, Department of Sociology, McMaster University, *Canadian Journal of Sociology* 24, 1 (1999): 109–39.
308 Origin Myths in the Social Sciences: Fromm, the Frankfurt School and the Emergence of Critical Theory, Neil McLaughlin, Department of Sociology, McMaster University, *Canadian Journal of Sociology* 24, 1 (1999): 109–39.
309 Jones, E. *Degenerate Moderns* (San Francisco: Ignatius, 1993), 172.
310 http://en.wikipedia.org/wiki/Authoritarian_personality. 05/31/14
311 MacDonald, Kevin. *The Culture of Critique: An Evolutionary Analysis of Jewish Involvement in Twentieth-Century Intellectual and Political Movements* (City: Authorhouse, 2002), 184.
312 MacDonald, Kevin. *The Culture of Critique: An Evolutionary Analysis of Jewish Involvement in Twentieth-Century Intellectual and Political Movements* (City: Authorhouse, 2002), 162.
313 http://en.wikipedia.org/wiki/Eros_and_Civilization. 05/31/14
314 MacDonald, Kevin. *The Culture of Critique: An Evolutionary Analysis of Jewish Involvement in Twentieth-Century Intellectual and Political Movements* (Kevin MacDonald, 2002), 106.
315 Salmi, Hannu. *Nineteenth-Century Europe* (Cambridge: Polity, 2008), 58.
316 Gordon, Sarah. *Hitler, Germans, and the "Jewish Question"* (Princeton University Press, New Jersey, 1984), 91.
317 Finkelstein, Norman. *Beyond Chutzpah* (Berkeley: University of California Press, 2008), xxvii.
318 http://en.wikipedia.org/wiki/Enhanced_interrogation_techniques. 05/31/14

[319] Finkelstein, Norman. *Beyond Chutzpah* (Berkeley: University of California Press, 2008), 273.
[320] Hitler's Speech, Munich, 27 April 1923.
[321] Peukert, Detlev. *The Weimar Republic* (New York: Hill and Wang, 1993), 241–42.
[322] Etlin, Richard A. (Editor) *Art, Culture, and Media under the Third Reich* (Chicago: University of Chicago Press, 2002), 8–9.
[323] Sereny, Gitta. *Albert Speer, His Battle with Truth* (New York: Vintage Books Edition, 1996), 266.
[324] Shirer, William L., *The Rise and Fall of the Third Reich: A History of Nazi Germany* (Touchstone, NY, 1998), 100.
[325] Trevor-Roper, Hugh. *Hitler's Table Talk, 1941–1944* (New York, Enigma Books, 2000), xxxiii.
[326] Hitler's Speech, Essen Party Convention, 23 November 1926.
[327] Fest, Joachim. *Hitler* (San Diego: Harcourt, 2002), 7.
[328] Ibid.
[329] Traverso, Enzo, and Janet Lloyd. *The Origins of Nazi Violence* (New York: New Press, 2003), 60.
[330] Ibid., 61.
[331] Fest, Joachim. *Hitler* (San Diego: Harcourt, 2002), 54.
[332] Ibid., 54.
[333] Traverso, Enzo, and Janet Lloyd. *The Origins of Nazi Violence* (New York: New Press, 2003), 59.
[334] Lindemann, Albert S. *Esau's Tears: Modern Anti-Semitism and the Rise of the Jews* (Cambridge University Press, Cambridge, U.K., 2000), 90.
[335] Ibid.
[336] MacDonald, Kevin. *The Culture of Critique: An Evolutionary Analysis of Jewish Involvement in Twentieth-Century Intellectual and Political Movements* (City: Authorhouse, 2002), 109.
[337] Lindemann, Albert S. *Esau's Tears: Modern Anti-Semitism and the Rise of the Jews* (Cambridge University Press, Cambridge, U.K., 2000), 87.
[338] Traverso, Enzo, and Janet Lloyd. *The Origins of Nazi Violence* (New York: New Press, 2003), 53–54.
[339] Fest, Joachim. *Hitler* (San Diego: Harcourt, 2002), 6.
[340] Ibid.
[341] Ibid., 64.
[342] Kershaw, Ian. *Hitler, 1889–1936* (New York: W. W. Norton, 1999), xxix.
[343] Tedor, Richard. *Hitler's Revolution: Ideology Social Programs Foreign Affairs* (Chicago, 2013), p. 5.
[344] http://www.jewishworldreview.com/cols/will100508.php3. 05/31/14
[345] http://www.jewishworldreview.com/cols/will100508.php3. 05/31/14

[346] Finkelstein, Norman. *The Holocaust Industry* (London: Verso, 2003), 12, fn 4.
[347] Peukert, Detlev. *The Weimar Republic* (New York: Hill and Wang, 1993), 139.
[348] Pulzer, Peter. *The Rise of Political Anti-Semitism in Germany & Austria* (Cambridge: Harvard University Press, 1988), 22.
[349] Ibid., xxiii.
[350] Kershaw, Ian. *Hitler, 1889–1936* (New York: W. W. Norton, 1999), 45.
[351] Spotts, Frederic. *Hitler and the Power of Aesthetics* (New York: Overlook Press, 2003), xiii.
[352] Hitler, Adolf. (1999). *Mein Kampf*. Trans. Ralph Manheim. (Boston/NY, Houghton Mifflin Company, First Mariner Books edition), 16–17.
[353] Speer, Albert. *Inside the Third Reich: Memoirs* (New York: Simon & Schuster, 1997), 63.
[354] http://en.wikipedia.org/wiki/Joseph_II,_Holy_Roman_Emperor. 05/31/14
[355] Toland, John. *Adolf Hitler* (Garden City: Anchor Books, 1992), 41.
[356] Hitler, Adolf. *Mein Kampf*. Trans. Ralph Manheim (Boston/NY, Houghton Mifflin Company, First Mariner Books edition, 1999), 6.
[357] Hamann, Brigitte. *Hitler's Vienna: A Dictator's Apprenticeship*. Trans. Thomas Thornton. (Oxford, NY, 2000). Paperback Edition, 393.
[358] Ibid., 12.
[359] Ibid., 167.
[360] Author not given. n.d. *Why Hitler Came to Power: One Rabbi's Explanation*. Retrieved from URL http://www.thephora.net/forum/archive/index.php/t-41837.html.
[361] Reed, Douglas. "The Controversy of Zion." *The Jewish Soul*. Retrieved from URL. http://www.controversyofzion.info/Controversybook/Controversybook_eng_45.htm. 01/01/14. Note: Reed and his publication are taken to be anti-Semitic.
[362] Gordon, Sarah. *Hitler, Germans, and the "Jewish Question"* (Princeton University Press, New Jersey, 1984), 48.
[363] http://en.wikipedia.org/wiki/Jewish_World_Conspiracy. 05/31/14
[364] MacDonald, Kevin. *Separation and Its Discontents toward an Evolutionary Theory of Anti-Semitism* (S. L.: 1stBooks Library, 2003), 42.
[365] Hitler, Adolf. *Mein Kampf* (Boston: Houghton Mifflin, 2001), 150.
[366] Wertheimer, Jack. *Unwelcome Strangers* (Oxford University Press, New York, 1987), 38.
[367] http://site.www.umb.edu/faculty/salzman_g/Strate/Discus/2002-12-05CraigOnElon.htm. 05/31/14
[368] Mearsheimer, John. and Stephen Walt. *The Israel Lobby and U.S. Foreign Policy* (New York: Farrar, Straus and Giroux, 2007), 18.

[369] Wertheimer, Jack. *Unwelcome Strangers* (Oxford University Press, New York, 1987), 40.
[370] http://en.wikipedia.org/wiki/Robert_Clive. 05/31/14
[371] http://en.wikipedia.org/wiki/Francisco_Pizarro. 04/20/08
[372] Trevor-Roper, Hugh. *Hitler's Table Talk, 1941–1944* (New York, Enigma Books, 2000), 116.
[373] http://www.kevinmacdonald.net/blog-Emperor.htm. 05/31/14
[374] Toland, John. *Adolf Hitler* (Garden City: Anchor Books, 1992), p. 34.
[375] Jones, E. *Degenerate Moderns* (San Francisco: Ignatius, 1993), 164.
[376] http://partners.nytimes.com/books/first/b/burleigh-reich.html. 05/31/14
[377] Brenner, Lenni. *Zionism in the Age of the Dictators* (London: Croom Helm, 1983), 5.
[378] http://shankradioworldwide.typepad.com/shankradio_world_wide/2007/09/pay-no-attent-1.html. 05/31/14
[379] Schorske, Carle E. *Fin-De-Siècle-Vienna: Politics and Culture* (Vintage Books Edition, New York, January 1981).
[380] Spotts, Frederic. *Hitler and the Power of Asthetics* (New York: Overlook Press, 2003), 20.
[381] Fest, Joachim. *Hitler* (San Diego: Harcourt, 2002), 274.
[382] Ascherson, Neal. 1998, May 10. *How Could They?* Retrieved from URL. http://articles.latimes.com/1998/may/10/books/bk-48194
[383] Fest, Joachim. *Hitler* (San Diego: Harcourt, 2002), 206.
[384] Ibid., 283.
[385] *Hitler's Table Talk, 1940–1944, His Private Conversations*. Trans. by Norman Cameron and R. H. Stevens. (Enigma Books, New York City, 2000.)
[386] Fest, Joachim. *Hitler* (San Diego: Harcourt, 2002), 240.
[387] Bullock, Alan. *Hitler, A Study in Tyranny* (New York and Evanston: Harper & Row, 1964), 44.
[388] Fest, Joachim. *Hitler* (San Diego: Harcourt, 2002), 274.
[389] Spotts, Frederic. *Hitler and the Power of Aesthetics* (New York: Overlook Press, 2003), 50.
[390] Fitzgerald, Michael. *Adolf Hitler: a Portrait* (Staplehurst: Spellmount, 2007), 10.
[391] Spotts, Frederic. *Hitler and the Power of Aesthetics* (New York: Overlook Press, 2003), 44.
[392] Stolfi, R. H. S. *Hitler: Beyond Evil and Tyranny* (Prometheus Books, Amherst, New York, 2011), 31.
[393] Trevor-Roper, Hugh. *Hitler's Table Talk, 1941–1944* (New York, Enigma Books, 2000), 24.
[394] Finkelstein, Norman. *The Holocaust Industry* (London: Verso, 2003), 145.

[395] Traverso, Enzo, and Janet Lloyd. *The Origins of Nazi Violence* (New York: New Press, 2003), 51.
[396] Fest, Joachim. *Hitler* (San Diego: Harcourt, 2002), 126.
[397] Spotts, Frederic. *Hitler and the Power of Aesthetics* (New York: Overlook Press, 2003), 15.
[398] Fest, Joachim. *Hitler* (San Diego: Harcourt, 2002), 382.
[399] Ibid.
[400] Spotts, Frederic. *Hitler and the Power of Aesthetics* (New York: Overlook Press, 2003), 10.
[401] Ibid., 23.
[402] Ibid.
[403] Ibid., 5.
[404] Ibid., 21.
[405] Fest, Joachim. *Hitler* (San Diego: Harcourt, 2002), 382.
[406] Spotts, Frederic. *Hitler and the Power of Aesthetics* (New York: Overlook Press, 2003), 322.
[407] Salmi, Hannu. *Nineteenth-Century Europe* (Cambridge: Polity, 2008), 1.
[408] Spotts, Frederic. *Hitler and the Power of Aesthetics* (New York: Overlook Press, 2003), xi.
[409] Ibid., 3.
[410] Ibid., 14.
[411] Ibid., xi.
[412] Ibid., 3.
[413] Ibid., 8.
[414] Speer, Albert, *Spandau: The Secret Diaries*. Translated from German by Richard and Clara Winston. (Pocket Books, New York,1976), 444–45.
[415] Fitzgerald, Michael. *Adolf Hitler: a Portrait* (Staplehurst: Spellmount, 2007). 36.
[416] Ibid., 101.
[417] Ibid., 102.
[418] Speer, Albert. *Spandau: The Secret Diaries*. Translated from German by Richard and Clara Winston. (New York: Pocket Books, 1976), 115.
[419] Rosenbaum, Ron. *Explaining Hitler* (NY: Harper Perennial edition, 1999). [Requires page number] http://www.irondale.org/newsletters/SPRING98.PDF#search='A%20History%20of%20Art%20Censorship%20in%20Nazi%20Germany' Irondale News: Ensemble Project, Spring 1988, Special "Nazi" Edition, Volume 1 No. 3. 05/31/14
[420] Fest, Joachim. *Hitler* (San Diego: Harcourt, 2002), 101.
[421] Speer, Albert. *Spandau: The Secret Diaries*. Translated from German by Richard and Clara Winston. (Pocket Books, New York,1976), 112.

[422] Speer, Albert. *Spandau: The Secret Diaries*. Translated from German by Richard and Clara Winston. (Pocket Books, New York, 1976), 112.
[423] Spotts, Frederic. *Hitler and the Power of Aesthetics* (New York: Overlook Press, 2003), 79.
[424] Ibid., 86–87.
[425] Ibid., 139.
[426] Ibid., 143.
[427] Hamann, Brigitte. *Hitler's Vienna: A Dictator's Apprenticeship*. Trans. Thomas Thornton. (Oxford, NY, 2000) Paperback Edition), 162.
[428] Fest, Joachim. *Hitler* (San Diego: Harcourt, 2002), 59–60.
[429] Spotts, Frederic. *Hitler and the Power of Aesthetics* (New York: Overlook Press, 2003), 134.
[430] Toland, John. *Adolf Hitler* (Garden City: Anchor Books, 1992), 49.
[431] https://www.google.com/search?q=Adolf+Hitler+Old+Water+Gate&rlz=1T4GZAB_enUS449US538&tbm=isch&tbo=u&source=univ&sa=X&ei=fdbcU92WLYfJsQSv6YGYDw&ved=0CCAQsAQ&biw=1008&bih=506 8/2/14
[432] https://www.google.com/search?rlz=1T4GZAB_enUS449US538&tbm=isch&imgil=fTlPZRaT_k_bgM%253A%253Byg1cL--_H4lnFM%253Bhttp%25253A%25252F%25252Fwww.snyderstreasures.com%25252Fpages%25252Fhartworks.htm&source=iu&usg=__DHNfjSkxFURnKo_ZoJ4yaayVCkc%3D&sa=X&ei=JtPcU__SDYeoyASglIKwCA&ved=0CCEQ9QEwAA&biw=1008&bih=506&q=Painting%20Boat%20at%20Sunset%20by%20Adolf%20Hitler#facrc=_&imgdii=_&imgrc=fTlPZRaT_k_bgM%253A%3Byg1cL--_H4lnFM%3Bhttp%253A%252F%252Fsnyderstreasures.com%252Fimages%252Fartworks%252Fbatsunset.jpg%3Bhttp%253A%252F%252Fwww.snyderstreasures.com%252Fpages%252Fhartworks.htm%3B215%3B332 8/2/14
[433] https://www.google.com/search?q=Sketch+Witch+on+a+Weathervane+by+Adolf+Hitler&rlz=1T4GZAB_enUS449US538&tbm=isch&tbo=u&source=univ&sa=X&ei=jtvcU7vbFpOryATV-oGADw&ved=0CB4QsAQ&biw=1008&bih=506#facrc=_&imgdii=_&imgrc=TmwtuYumRaWs1M%253A%3Byg1cL--_H4lnFM%3Bhttp%253A%252F%252Fsnyderstreasures.com%252Fimages%252Fthumbnails%252Fartworks%252FAHWitchWeathervane_small.jpg%3Bhttp%253A%252F%252Fwww.snyderstreasures.com%252Fpages%252Fhartworks.htm%3B195%3B300 8/2//14
[434] https://www.google.com/search?q=Adolf+Hitler+Red+Pencil+Sketch+of+Germania&rlz=1T4GZAB_enUS449US538&tbm=isch&tbo=u&source=univ&sa=X

&ei=FdzcU4GIFoiUyASSpoGQDw&ved=0CB4QsAQ&biw=1008&bih=506#f
acrc=_&imgdii=_&imgrc=_YiaMQC9Id5H2M%253A%3BmDcUKjBUy_J2u
M%3Bhttp%253A%252F%252F2.bp.blogspot.com%252F-
r9TI7uLzKN4%252FUUuHlhih9pI%252FAAAAAAAAALc%252F59tEH1zlqs
g%252Fs1600%252FGermania_hitler.jpg%3Bhttp%253A%252F%252Ftmwaya
rts.blogspot.com%252F%3B762%3B1196 8/2/14

[435] Trevor-Roper, Hugh. *Hitler's Table Talk, 1941–1944* (New York, Enigma Books, 2000), 338.

[436] Spotts, Frederic. *Hitler and the Power of Aesthetics* (New York: Overlook Press, 2003), 391.

[437] Trevor-Roper, Hugh. *Hitler's Table Talk, 1941–1944* (New York, Enigma Books, 2000), 74–75.

[438] Spotts, Frederic. *Hitler and the Power of Aesthetics* (New York: Overlook Press, 2003), 319.

[439] Rosenbaum, Ron. *Explaining Hitler* (Harper Perennial edition, 1999), xii.

[440] Kershaw, Ian. *Hitler, 1889–1936* (New York: W. W. Norton, 1999), 60.

[441] Ibid., 66.

[442] Ibid., 66.

[443] Dawidowicz, Lucy. *The War against the Jews, 1933–45* (Harmondsworth Eng.: Penguin, 1977), 104.

[444] Fitzgerald, Michael. *Adolf Hitler: a Portrait* (Staplehurst: Spellmount, 2007), 26.

[445] Fest, Joachim. *Hitler* (San Diego: Harcourt, 2002), 61.

[446] http://en.wikipedia.org/wiki/Emil_Fackenheim#_note-0. 05/31/14

[447] Rosenbaum, Ron. *Explaining Hitler* (NY: Harper Perennial edition, 1999), xv.

[448] Ibid.

[449] Fest, Joachim. *Hitler* (San Diego: Harcourt, 2002), 158.

[450] Author not given. n.d. The Accusation of Anti-Semitism. Retrieved from http://holywar.org/jewishtr/19antis1.htm

[451] Niewyk, Donald L., *The Jews in Weimar Germany* (Transaction Publishers, New Brunswick, 2001), 52.

[452] Stolfi, R. H. S. *Hitler: Beyond Evil and Tyranny* (Prometheus Books, Amherst, New York, 2011), 80.

[453] Spotts, Frederic. *Hitler and the Power of Aesthetics* (New York: Overlook Press, 2003), 124.

[454] Ibid.

[455] Hamann, Brigitte. *Hitler's Vienna: A Dictator's Apprenticeship*. Trans. Thomas Thornton. (Oxford, NY, 2000), Paperback Edition, 33.

[456] Bullock, Alan. *Hitler and Stalin* (New York: Vintage Books, 1993), 9.

[457] Finkelstein, Norman. *The Holocaust Industry* (London: Verso, 2003), 22.

[458] Dawidowicz, Lucy. *The War against the Jews, 1933–45* (Harmondsworth Eng.: Penguin, 1977), 21.
[459] Ibid., 17.
[460] Ibid., 22–23.
[461] Finkelstein, Norman. *The Holocaust Industy* (London: Verso, 2003), 53.
[462] http://www.ualberta.ca/~cjscopy/articles/mclaughlin.html. 05/31/14
[463] Speer, Albert. *Inside the Third Reich: Memoirs* (New York: Simon & Schuster, 1997), 97.
[464] Rosenbaum, Ron. *Explaining Hitler* (Harper Perennial edition, 1999), 81.
[465] Ibid., xxx.
[466] Fest, Joachim. *Hitler* (San Diego: Harcourt, 2002), 39–40.
[467] Bullock, Alan. *Hitler and Stalin* (New York: Vintage Books, 1993), 11.
[468] Rosenbaum, Ron. *Explaining Hitler* (Harper Perennial edition, 1999), xxx.
[469] http://www.slate.com/id/3073. 05/31/14
[470] *The New York Times*, Sunday World Herald. April 17, 2005, 7A. The referenced article was built around "The first psychological profile of Hitler" (1943), commissioned by the U.S. Office of Strategic Services.
[471] Toland, John. *Adolf Hitler* (Garden City: Anchor Books, 1992), 14.
[472] Ibid.
[473] Shirer, William L. *The Rise and Fall of the Third Reich: A History of Nazi Germany* (Touchstone, NY, 1998), 26.
[474] Fest, Joachim. *Hitler* (San Diego: Harcourt, 2002), 40.
[475] Hamann, Brigitte. *Hitler's Vienna: A Dictator's Apprenticeship*. Trans. Thomas Thornton (Oxford, NY, 2000), Paperback Edition, 193–94.
[476] http://www.webster.edu/~corbetre/personal/reading/hamann-hitler.html. 05/31/14
[477] Spotts, Frederic. *Hitler and the Power of Aesthetics* (New York: Overlook Press, 2003), 131.
[478] Rosenbaum, Ron. *Explaining Hitler* (NY: Harper Perennial edition, 1999), 322.
[479] Toland, John. *Adolf Hitler* (Garden City: Anchor Books, 1992), 255.
[480] Kershaw, Ian. *Hitler, 1889–1936* (New York: W. W. Norton, 1999), 152.
[481] Fest, Joachim. *Hitler* (San Diego, Harcourt, 2002), 137.
[482] Weizmann, Chaim. *Trial and Error* (Hmish Hamilton, London, 1949), 273.
[483] Aschheim, Steven. *Brothers and Strangers* (Madison: The University of Wisconsin Press, 1999), 197.
[484] Ibid., 231–33.
[485] Haumann, Heiko. *A History of East European Jews* (Budapest: Central European University Press, 2002), 210.

[486] Author Unknown. n.d. *Jews And Their Zionist Views*. Retrieved from http://cdn.preterhuman.net/texts/unsorted/Jews%20And%20Their%20Zionist%20Views.htm
[487] Ravage's biography of the Rothschilds is titled *Five Men of Frankfurt: The story of the Rothschilds*, Marcus Eli Ravage and Karl S. Woerner (Dial Press, 1934).
[488] http://www.faem.com/david/commu-5.htm. 05/31/14
[489] Toland, John. *Adolf Hitler* (Garden City: Anchor Books, 1992), 71.
[490] *The Jeruselem Post*. June 2013. Retrieved from URL: http://www.jpost.com/Jewish-World/Jewish-News/Putin-First-Soviet-government-was-mostly-Jewish-317150
[491] http://en.wikipedia.org/wiki/Bakunin. 05/31/14
[492] http://www.fpp.co.uk/bookchapters/WSC/WSCwrote1920.html>. 05/31/14
[493] MacDonald, Kevin. *The Culture of Critique: An Evolutionary Analysis of Jewish Involvement in Twentieth-Century Intellectual and Political Movements* (City: Authorhouse, 2002), 98.
[494] Slezkine, Yuri. *The Jewish Century* (Princeton University Press, Princeton NJ, 2004), 180.
[495] Shirer, William L. *The Rise and Fall of the Third Reich: A History of Nazi Germany* (Touchstone, NY, 1998), 84.
[496] Toland, John. *Adolf Hitler* (Garden City: Anchor Books, 1992), 106.
[497] Turner, Henry, and Ruth Hein. *Hitler—Memoirs of a Confidant* (New Haven: Yale University Press, 1987), 169.
[498] http://en.wikipedia.org/wiki/Comintern. 05/31/14
[499] Ehart, Adolf. *Communism in Germany* (The Noontide Press, Costa Mesa, CA., 1990, Reprint Edition). Original 1933 Edition published by General League of Anti-Communist Associations, Copyright 1933, by Eckart-Verlag, Berlin, 59.
[500] Turner, Henry, and Ruth Hein. *Hitler—Memoirs of a Confidant* (New Haven: Yale University Press, 1987), 58.
[501] http://www.vho.org/tr/2004/3/Strauss342-351.html. 05/31/14
[502] Fest, Joachim. *Hitler* (San Diego: Harcourt, 2002), 109.
[503] Stibbe, Matthew. *Germany, 1914–1933* (Pearson Education Limited, 2010), 53–54.
[504] Hamann, Brigitte. *Hitler's Vienna: A Dictator's Apprenticeship*. Trans. Thomas Thornton. (Oxford, NY, 2000), 26.
[505] Ibid., 69.
[506] Fest, Joachim. *Hitler* (San Diego: Harcourt, 2002), 53.
[507] https://www.google.com/search?q=Images+Vienna+Parliament+Building&rlz=1T4GZAB_enUS449US538&tbm=isch&tbo=u&source=univ&sa=X&ei=2-

3cU6HLIMScyATMnILgDQ&ved=0CB4QsAQ&biw=1008&bih=506#facrc=_
&imgdii=_&imgrc=A8gglMvs1Jg9KM%253A%3BpzxHkY005VqJwM%3Bhtt
p%253A%252F%252Fwww.casayego.com%252Feuropeancities%252Fvienna
%252Fvien-
c.jpg%3Bhttp%253A%252F%252Fwww.casayego.com%252Feuropeancities%
252Fvienna%252Fvienna.htm%3B1500%3B1023 8/2/14
[508]

https://www.google.com/search?q=Images+Vienna+buildings&rlz=1T4GZAB_
enUS449US538&tbm=isch&tbo=u&source=univ&sa=X&ei=eO7cU4W2Bpeky
AS4tIKoBw&ved=0CB4QsAQ&biw=1008&bih=506 8/2/14
[509]

https://www.google.com/search?q=Images+Vienna+Ringstrasse&rlz=1T4GZA
B_enUS449US538&tbm=isch&tbo=u&source=univ&sa=X&ei=Vu_cU4SABp
CWyATx_YLgBw&ved=0CB4QsAQ&biw=1008&bih=506#facrc=_&imgdii=_
&imgrc=zXJGLayyJvIAHM%253A%3B45ixFItZSceREM%3Bhttp%253A%25
2F%252Fblogs.getty.edu%252Firis%252Ffiles%252F2012%252F09%252Fvien
na_museumsquartier.jpg%3Bhttp%253A%252F%252Fblogs.getty.edu%252Firi
s%252Fbeing-jewish-in-austria-four-questions-for-writer-and-critic-ruth-
kluger%252F%3B615%3B408 8/2/14

[510] Ibid., 27.
[511] Hitler, Adolf. *Mein Kampf* (Boston: Houghton Mifflin, 2001), 53.
[512] Hamann, Brigitte. *Hitler's Vienna: A Dictator's Apprenticeship*. Trans. Thomas Thornton (Oxford, NY, 2000), 212.
[513] Ibid., 213.
[514] Fest, Joachim. *Hitler* (San Diego: Harcourt, 2002), 24.
[515] Hitler, Adolf. *Mein Kampf* (Boston: Houghton Mifflin, 2001), 59.
[516] Steed, Henry Wickham. *The Habsburg Monarchy* (London, 1914), 145. Quoted in Lindemann, Albert S., *Esau's Tears: Modern Anti-Semitism and the Rise of the Jews* (Cambridge University Press, Cambridge, U.K., 2000), Paperback Edition, 190.
[517] http://www.123helpme.com/view.asp?id=23550. 05/31/14
[518] Hamann, Brigitte. *Hitler's Vienna: A Dictator's Apprenticeship*. Trans. Thomas Thornton. (Oxford, NY, 2000), 81.
[519] Toland, John. *Adolf Hitler* (Garden City: Anchor Books, 1992), 46.
[520] Deak, Istvan, *Weimar Germany's Left-Wing Intellectuals: A Political History of the Weltbüne and Its Circle* (University of California Press, Berkeley and Los Angeles, 1968), 69–70.
[521] Kolb, Eberhard. *The Weimar Republic* (Routledge, New York, 1990), eBook, 106.
[522] http://www.trashface.com/germanexpressionism.html. 05/31/14
[523] http://www.trashface.com/germanexpressionism.html. 05/31/14

[524] Grange, William. *Cultural Chronicle of the Weimar Republic* (Metuchen: Scarecrow Press, 2008), 15.
[525] Pulzer, Peter. *The Rise of Political Anti-Semitism in Germany & Austria* (Cambridge: Harvard University Press, 1988), 3.
[526] Kaes, Martin; Jay, Martin; Dimendberg (Eds.). *The Weimar Republic SourceBook*, (California: University of California Press, 1995), 479.
[527] http://www.answers.com/topic/neo-expressionism?cat=entertainment&nr=1. 05/31/14
[528] http ://www.answers.com/topic/neo-expressionism?cat=entertainment&nr=1. 05/31/14
vent.org/cathen/09417a.htm. 05/31/14
[530] Hitler, Adolf. *Mein Kampf* (Boston: Houghton Mifflin, 2001), 351.
[531] Hitler's Speech, Berlin: Proclamation to the German Nation, 1 February 1933.
[532] Fest, Joachim. *Hitler* (San Diego: Harcourt, 2002), 27.
[533] Lindemann, Albert S. *Esau's Tears: Modern Anti-Semitism and the Rise of the Jews* (Cambridge University Press, Cambridge, U.K., 2000), 189.
[534] Ibid., 189.
[535] http://www.webster.edu/~corbetre/personal/reading/hamann-hitler.html. 05/31/14
[536] (or in the case of African art, continental culture), 6.
[537] Fest, Joachim. *Hitler* (San Diego: Harcourt, 2002), 25.
[538] Jones, Peter. *The 1848 Revolutions* (New York: Longman, 1991), 40.
[539] Wolff, Tom. *From Bauhaus to Our House* (Bantam Books, New York, 1999), 14.
[540] Salmi, Hannu. *Nineteenth-Century Europe* (Cambridge: Polity, 2008), 43.
[541] http://architecture.about.com/library/weekly/aa030199.htm. 05/31/14
[542]

https://www.google.com/search?q=Goldman+and+Salatsch+Building&rlz=1T4GZAB_enUS449US538&tbm=isch&tbo=u&source=univ&sa=X&ei=e_PcU5P9KMO0yATIi4C4BQ&ved=0CB4QsAQ&biw=1008&bih=506#facrc=_&imgdii=_&imgrc=koq81XZ7AUZYYM%253A%3BaaukiGHNw45uYM%3Bhttp%253A%252F%252Fclassconnection.s3.amazonaws.com%252F741%252Fflashcards%252F486741%252Fjpg%252Flecture_08_img_41.jpg%3Bhttp%253A%252F%252Fwww.studyblue.com%252Fnotes%252Fnote%252Fn%252Flecture-8%252Fdeck%252F872684%3B1204%3B827. 8/2/14
[543] Lindemann, Albert S. *Esau's Tears: Modern Anti-Semitism and the Rise of the Jews* (Cambridge University Press, Cambridge, U.K., 2000), Paperback Edition, 339.
[544] Bullock, Alan. *Hitler and Stalin* (New York: Vintage Books, 1993), 20.

[545] Lindemann, Albert S. *Esau's Tears: Modern Anti-Semitism and the Rise of the Jews* (Cambridge University Press, Cambridge, U.K., 2000), Paperback Edition, 189.
[546] Shirer, William L. *The Rise and Fall of the Third Reich: A History of Nazi Germany,* 21.
[547] Brenner, Lenni. *Zionism in the Age of the Dictators* (London: Croom Helm, 1983), 3.
[548] Ibid.
[549] Kershaw, Ian. *Hitler, 1889–1936* (New York: W. W. Norton, 1999), 36.
[550] Hamann, Brigitte. *Hitler's Vienna: A Dictator's Apprenticeship.* Trans. Thomas Thornton. (Oxford, NY, 2000), 343.
[551] Paperback Edition. 183.
[552] Schorske, Carle E. *Fin-De-Siècle-Vienna: Politics and Culture* (Vintage Books Edition, New York, January 1981), 168.
[553] MacDonald, Kevin. *A People That Shall Dwell Alone* (San Jose: Writers Club Press, 2002), 206–07. Quoted material is from Peter Gay, *Freud: A Life For Our Time* (New York: W. W. Norton, 1988), 21.
[554] MacDonald, Kevin. *Separation and Its Discontents toward an Evolutionary Theory of Anti-Semitism.* (S. L.: 1stBooks Library, 2003), 65.
[555] Pulzer, Peter. *The Rise of Political Anti-Semitism in Germany & Austria* (Cambridge: Harvard University Press, 1988), 13.
[556] Ibid., 13.
[557] Petropoulos, Jonathan. *Art as Politics in the Third Reich* (The University of North Carolina Press, Chapel Hill & London, 1996), 53–54.
[558] Lindemann, Albert S., *Esau's Tears: Modern Anti-Semitism and the Rise of the Jews* (Cambridge University Press, Cambridge, U.K., 2000), 194.
[559] Ibid., 25.
[560] Kubizek, August. *The Young Hitler I Knew* (London: Greenhill Books, 2006). Abridged edition first published in English, 1954, by Allan Wingate Publishers Ltd., 230.
[561] Hamann, Brigitte, *Hitler's Vienna: A Dictator's Apprenticeship.* Trans. Thomas Thornton (Oxford, NY, 2000), Paperback Edition, 328.
[562] Ibid., 135.
[563] Slezkine, Yuri. *The Jewish Century* (Princeton University Press, Princeton, NJ, 2004), 67.
[564] The Jewish Encyclopedia: The unedited full text of the 1906 Jewish Encyclopedia. n.d. http://www.jewishencyclopedia.com/articles/14699-vienna. 07/06/14
[565] Shahak, Israel. *Jewish History, Jewish Religion: the Weight of Three Thousand Years* (Sydney: Pluto Press, 1994), 53.

[566] Makow, Henry, Ph.D. 2003, October. *There Is only One Conspiracy, The Real Cause of Anti-Semitism*, quoting from Israel Shahak's book, *The Weight of History*. Retrieved from URL http://www.savethemales.ca/000258.html.
[567] Gordon, Sarah. *Hitler, Germans, and the "Jewish Question"* (Princeton University Press, New Jersey, 1984), 229.
[568] Jones, Michael. *Living Machines* (San Francisco: Ignatius Press, 1995), 33.
[569] MacDonald, Kevin. *The Culture of Critique: An Evolutionary Analysis of Jewish Involvement in Twentieth-Century Intellectual and Political Movements* (City: Authorhouse, 2002), 120–21.
[570] Ibid., 106.
[571] Ibid., 106.
[572] MacDonald, Kevin. *Separation and Its Discontents toward an Evolutionary Theory of Anti-Semitism* (S. L.: 1stBooks Library, 2003), 105 (endnote).
[573] Hamann, Brigitte. *Hitler's Vienna: A Dictator's Apprenticeship*. Trans. Thomas Thornton (Oxford, NY, 2000), 76.
[574] http://www.commentarymagazine.com/viewarticle.cfm/Hitler-s-Accompanist-11028. 05/31/14
[575] http://www.commentarymagazine.com/viewarticle.cfm/Hitler-s-Accompanist-11028. 05/31/14
[576] Hamann, Brigitte. *Hitler's Vienna: A Dictator's Apprenticeship*. Trans. Thomas Thornton (Oxford, NY, 2000), 76.
[577] http://www.buy.com/prod/affairs-of-anatol/q/loc/322/40142056.html. 05/31/14
[578] Weitz, Eric. *Weimar Germany* (Princeton: Princeton University Press, 2009), 106.
[579] Ibid., 106.
[580] Ibid., 107.
[581] http://corndancer.com/vox/deutsch/lesesaal/weimar/weimar_whois/schonberg.html. 05/31/14
[582] http://corndancer.com/vox/deutsch/lesesaal/weimar/weimar_whois/schonberg.html. 05/31/14
[583] Hamann, Brigitte. *Hitler's Vienna: A Dictator's Apprenticeship*. Trans. Thomas Thornton (Oxford, NY, 2000), 75.
[584] http://www.icons-multimedia.com/ClientsArea/HoH/LIBARC/LIBRARY/Themes/Policy/Friedl2B.html. 05/31/14
[585] http://www.icons-multimedia.com/ClientsArea/HoH/LIBARC/LIBRARY/Themes/Policy/Friedl2B.html. 05/31/14
[586] Kershaw, Ian. *Hitler, 1889–1936* (New York: W. W. Norton, 1999), 46.

587 Hamann, Brigitte. *Hitler's Vienna: A Dictator's Apprenticeship*. Trans. Thomas Thornton (Oxford, NY, 2000), 74.
588 Ibid., 74.
589 Ibid., 81.
590 http://gangway.net/1/gangway1.2.html. 05/31/14
591 http://www.kevinmacdonald.net/SlezkineRev.pdf. 05/31/14
592 Broué, Pierre, et al. *The German Revolution 1917–1923* (Boston: Brill Academic Publishers, 2004), 21.
593 Lindemann, Albert S. *Esau's Tears: Modern Anti-Semitism and the Rise of the Jews* (Cambridge University Press, Cambridge, U.K., 2000), Paperback Edition, 194 (Quoting Boyer, *Political Radicalism*, 48–49).
594 Reed, Douglas. *The Controversy of Zion* (Western Australia: Veritas Publishing Company Pty., Ltd, 1985), 166.
595 Ibid.
596 Fest, Joachim. *Hitler* (San Diego: Harcourt, 2002), 326.
597 http://www.jewishencyclopedia.com/view.jsp?artid=2152&letter=A&search=austria. 05/31/14
598 http://en.wikipedia.org/wiki/Gabriel_Riesser. 05/31/14
599 http://en.wikipedia.org/wiki/Robert_Blum". 05/31/14
600 http://www.cats.ohiou.edu/~Chastain/ip/jewemanc.htm. 05/31/14
601 http://cscwww.cats.ohiou.edu/~Chastain/ip/jewemanc.htm. 05/31/14
602 MacDonald, Kevin. *Separation and Its Discontents toward an Evolutionary Theory of Anti-Semitism* (S. L.: 1stBooks Library, 2003), 82–83.
603 Hamann, Brigitte. *Hitler's Vienna: A Dictator's Apprenticeship*. Trans. Thomas Thornton (Oxford, NY, 2000), Paperback Edition, 111.
604 Lindemann, Albert S. *Esau's Tears: Modern Anti-Semitism and the Rise of the Jews* (Cambridge University Press, Cambridge, U.K., 2000), 199.
605 Ibid., 182.
606 Ibid., 199.
607 http://cscwww.cats.ohiou.edu/~Chastain/ip/jewemanc.htm. 05/31/14
608 http://www.loyno.edu/~1848.html. 05/31/14
609 http://www.jewishencyclopedia.com/view.jsp?artid=2152&letter=A&search=austria. 05/31/14
610 Hamann, Brigitte, *Hitler's Vienna: A Dictator's Apprenticeship*. Trans. Thomas Thornton (Oxford, NY, 2000), Paperback Edition, 304.
611 http://www.worldwar1.com/tlwarorg.htm. 05/31/14
612 Hitler, Adolf. *Mein Kampf* (Boston: Houghton Mifflin, 2001), 123.

[613] http://query.nytimes.com/gst/fullpage.html?res=9C0CE7DB1E39F937A25752C0A966958260. 05/31/14
[614] Hitler, Adolf. *Mein Kampf*. Trans. Ralph Manheim (Houghton Mifflin Company, Boston/NY), First Mariner Books edition, 1999, 15.
[615] Speer, Albert. *Inside the Third Reich: Memoirs* (New York: Simon & Schuster, 1997), 50.
[616] Speer, Albert. *Spandau: The Secret Diaries*. Translated from German by Richard and Clara Winston. (New York: Pocket Books, 1976), 100–01.
[617] Ibid.
[618] Hamann, Brigitte. *Hitler's Vienna: A Dictator's Apprenticeship*. Trans. Thomas Thornton (Oxford, NY, 2000), Paperback Edition, 360.
[619] http://www.jweekly.com/article/full/4142/jewish-cabaret-singer-brings-songs-of-berlin-to-berkeley/. 05/31/14
[620] Hitler, Adolf. *Mein Kampf* (Boston: Houghton Mifflin, 2001), 56.
[621] http://en.wikipedia.org/wiki/Paris_Commune. 05/31/14
[622] Lindemann, Albert S. *Esau's Tears: Modern Anti-Semitism and the Rise of the Jews* (Cambridge University Press, Cambridge, U.K., 2000), 214.
[623] Ibid.
[624] Lindemann, Albert. *The Jew Accused* (Cambridge: Cambridge University Press, 1991), 68.
[625] http://en.wikipedia.org/wiki/Panama_scandals. 05/31/14
[626] http://www.marxists.org/archive/jaures/1893/panama-scandal.htm. 05/31/14
[627] Lindemann, Albert. *Anti-Semitism before the Holocaust* (New York: Longman, 2000), 171.
[628] Haumann, Heiko. *A History of East European Jews* (Budapest: Central European University Press, 2002), 165.
[629] Black, Edwin. *The Transfer Agreement: The Dramatic Story of the Pact Between the Third Reich & Jewish Palestine*. (Brookline Books, 1999), 31.
[630] Lindemann, Albert. *Anti-Semitism before the Holocaust* (New York: Longman, 2000), 83.
[631] Ibid.
[632] http://en.wikipedia.org/wiki/The_Protocols_of_the_Elders_of_Zion. 05/31/14
[633] Reed, Douglas. *The Controversy of Zion* (Western Australia: Veritas Publishing Company Pty., Ltd., 1985), 213.
[634] Ibid., 212.
[635] Friedrich, Otto. *Before the Deluge* (New York: HarperPerennial, 1995), 95–96.
[636] Gilbert, G. M. *Nuremberg Diary* (Da Capo Press, 1995), 270.
[637] Ibid., 22–23.
[638] Hitler, Adolf. *Mein Kampf* (Boston: Houghton Mifflin, 2001), 307–08.
[639] Kershaw, Ian. *Hitler, 1889–1936* (New York: W. W. Norton, 1999), 131.

[640] Ibid., 146.
[641] Ford, Henry. 1920. *The International Jew, World's Foremost Problem.* Retrieved from URL http://www.biblebelievers.org.au/intern_jew.htm. The quote is taken from an interview with Ford that was reported in the *New York World*, February 17, 1921.
[642] Site author unknown. *Zio Nazi Quotes.* Quoting Henry Hamilton Beamish, 1937, October. Retrieved from URL http://antimatrix.org/Convert/Books/ZioNazi_Quotes/Protocols_of_Elders_of_Zion.html.
[643] Pulzer, Peter. *The Rise of Political Anti-Semitism in Germany & Austria* (Cambridge: Harvard University Press, 1988), 217.
[644] Rosenbaum, Ron. *Explaining Hitler* (Harper Perennial edition, 1999), 345.
[645] Lindemann, Albert S. *Esau's Tears: Modern Anti-Semitism and the Rise of the Jews* (Cambridge University Press, Cambridge, U.K., 2000), Paperback Edition, 229.
[646] Schorske, Carle E. *Fin-De-Siècle-Vienna: Politics and Culture* (Vintage Books Edition, New York, January 1981), 162.
[647] Lindemann, Albert S. *Esau's Tears: Modern Anti-Semitism and the Rise of the Jews* (Cambridge University Press, Cambridge, U.K., 2000), Paperback Edition, 232.
[648] Brenner, Lenni. *Zionism in the Age of the Dictators* (London: Croom Helm, 1983), 2.
[649] Lindemann, Albert. *The Jew Accused* (Cambridge: Cambridge University Press, 1991), 126.
[650] Lindemann, Albert S. *Esau's Tears: Modern Anti-Semitism and the Rise of the Jews* (Cambridge University Press, Cambridge, U.K., 2000), Paperback Edition, 236.
[651] MacDonald, Kevin. *Separation and Its Discontents* (2004), 228.
[652] http://holywar.org/txt/Brenner/chapter1.html. 05/31/14
[653] *Burdick v. United States.* 22 June 2014. http://en.wikipedia.org/wiki/Burdick_v._United_States. 07/06/14
[654] MacDonald, Kevin. *Separation and Its Discontents toward an Evolutionary Theory of Anti-Semitism* (S. L.: 1stBooks Library, 2003), 228.
[655] http://en.wikipedia.org/wiki/Georges_Clemenceau. 05/31/14
[656] Author not given. n.d. *The French Connection: Protocols of the Meetings of the Learned Elders of Zion.* The quotation is taken from Protocol #12. http://www.iamthewitness.com/Protocols-of-Zion.htm.
[657] Weinzierl, Erika, Emeritus Professor of History, University of Vienna, Working Paper 01–1 October 2003. "The Jewish Middle Class in Vienna in the Late Nineteenth and Early Twentieth Centuries." www.cas.umn.edu/assets/pdf/WP011.PDF. 05/31/14

[658] Lindemann, Albert. *The Jew Accused* (Cambridge: Cambridge University Press, 1991), 69.
[659] Ibid., 204.
[660] Hamann, Brigitte. *Hitler's Vienna: A Dictator's Apprenticeship*. Trans. Thomas Thornton (Oxford, NY, 2000), Paperback Edition, 31.
[661] Ibid., 242.
[662] Ibid., 249.
[663] Ibid., 243.
[664] Schorske, Carle E. *Fin-De-Siècle-Vienna Politics and Culture* (Vintage Books Edition, New York, January 1981), 120.
[665] http://www.webster.edu/~corbetre/personal/reading/hamann-hitler.html. 05/31/14
[666] http://www.newadvent.org/cathen/09417a.htm. 05/31/14
[667] Smoter, Walter Frank. *Adolf Hitler, The Making of a Fuhrer*, Lueger, "relented" URL: http://smoter.com/revoluti.htm. 06/25/14

[668] Dawidowicz, Lucy. *The War against the Jews, 1933-45* (Harmondsworth Eng.: Penguin, 1977), 35.
[669] Brenner, Lenni. *Zionism in the Age of the Dictators* (London: Croom Helm, 1983), 3.
[670] Smoter, Walter Frank. *Adolf Hitler, The Making of a Fuhrer*. "workers." URL: http://smoter.com/lueger.htm. 05/31/14
[671] Schorske, Carle E. *Fin-De-Siècle-Vienna: Politics and Culture* (Vintage Books Edition, New York, January 1981), 6.
[672] Lindemann, Albert S. *Esau's Tears: Modern Anti-Semitism and the Rise of the Jews* (Cambridge University Press, Cambridge, U.K., 2000), Paperback Edition, 339.
[673] Schorske, Carle E. *Fin-De-Siècle-Vienna: Politics and Culture* (Vintage Books Edition, New York, January 1981), 138.
[674] Hamann, Brigitte. *Hitler's Vienna: A Dictator's Apprenticeship*. Trans. Thomas Thornton. (Oxford, NY, 2000), Paperback Edition, 281.
[675] Lindemann, Albert. *The Jew Accused* (Cambridge: Cambridge University Press, 1991), 45.
[676] Josef Haslinger. *Jewish Vienna*, © 1991–1996, by Josef Haslinger and Gangan Books, Australia http://gangway.net/1/gangway1.2.html. 05/31/14
[677] http://www.newadvent.org/cathen/09417a.htm. 05/31/14
[678] Hamann, Brigitte. *Hitler's Vienna: A Dictator's Apprenticeship*. Trans. Thomas Thornton (Oxford, NY, 2000), Paperback Edition, 290.
[679] Ibid., 323.
[680] Ibid., 298.

[681] Ibid., 274.
[682] http://www.newadvent.org/cathen/09417a.htm. 05/31/14
[683] Hamann, Brigitte. *Hitler's Vienna: A Dictator's Apprenticeship*. Trans. Thomas Thornton (Oxford, NY, 2000), Paperback Edition, 298.
[684] http://www.newadvent.org/cathen/09417a.htm. 05/31/14
[685] Hamann, Brigitte. *Hitler's Vienna: A Dictator's Apprenticeship*. Trans. Thomas Thornton (Oxford, NY, 2000), Paperback Edition, 301.
[686] Ibid., 285.
[687] Ibid., 299.
[688] http://en.wikipedia.org/wiki/Karl_Lueger. 05/31/14
[689] Hamann, Brigitte. *Hitler's Vienna: A Dictator's Apprenticeship*. Trans. Thomas Thornton (Oxford, NY, 2000), Paperback Edition, 278.
[690] Fest, Joachim. *Hitler* (San Diego: Harcourt, 2002), 42.
[691] Lindemann, Albert. *The Jew Accused* (Cambridge: Cambridge University Press, 1991), 31.
[692] Wistrich, Robert S. Jan. 14, 1990. *Blooming While the Sun Went Down*. http://query.nytimes.com/gst/fullpage.html?res=9C0CE7DB1E39F937A25752C0A966958260. 07/20/14
[693] Hamann, Brigitte. *Hitler's Vienna: A Dictator's Apprenticeship*. Trans. Thomas Thornton (Oxford, NY, 2000), vii.
[694] Hitler, Adolf. *Mein Kampf* (Boston: Houghton Mifflin, 2001), 453.
[695] Ibid., 447.
[696] Hitler's testimony before the Munich Court, 26 February 1924.
[697] Tedor, Richard. *Hitler's Revolution: Ideology Social Programs Foreign Affairs* (Chicago, 2013), 35.
[698] Stolfi, R. H. S. *Hitler: Beyond Evil and Tyranny* (Prometheus Books, Amherst, New York, 2011), 126–27.
[699] Fest, Joachim. *Hitler* (San Diego: Harcourt, 2002), 26.
[700] Roderich-Stoltheim, F. *The Riddle of the Jew's Success* (RePortersNoteBook.com, NY, 2005.) Translated from the German by Capel Pownall. Originally published by Hammer-Verlag, Leipzig, 1927, 279.
[701] Stibbe, Matthew. *Germany, 1914–1933* (Pearson Education Limited, 2010), 23.
[702] http://histclo.com/royal/ger/royal-gerawh.htm. 05/31/14
[703] http://www.worldwar1.com/biokais.htm. 05/31/14
[704] Ryback, Timothy. *Hitler's Private Library: the Books That Shaped His Life* (London: Vintage, 2010), 22.
[705] Porter, Ian, et al. *Imperial Germany, 1890–1918* (New York: Longman, 1991), 11.
[706] Brenner, Lenni. *Zionism in the Age of the Dictators* (London: Croom Helm, 1983), 5.

[706] Weber, Mark. Date of pub. unknown. Institute for Historical Review. *The Jewish Role in the Bolshevik Revolution and Russia's Early Soviet Regime.* Retrieved from URL http://www.ihr.org/jhr/v14/v14n1p-4_Weber.html.

[708] "Biography," Vladimir Lenin: Voice of Revolution (1997), A&E Television Network.
[709] Stolfi, R. H. S. *Hitler: Beyond Evil and Tyranny* (Prometheus Books, Amherst, New York, 2011), 266.
[710] Fischer, Conan. *The Rise of the Nazis*, 2nd ed. (Manchester University Press. Manchester and New York. 2002), 6.
[711] Ibid.
[712] Laqueur, Walter. *Weimar, A Cultural History* (G. P. Putnam's Sons, New York, 1974), 3.
[713] Pulzer, Peter. *Jews and the German State: The Political History of a Minority, 1848–1933* (Wayne State University Press, 2003), 214.
[714] Wikipedia. Jun 27, 2014. *Wilhelm II, German Emperor.* http://en.wikipedia.org/wiki/William_II,_German_Emperor. 05/31/14
[715] Ibid.
[716] Smoter, Walter Frank. *Adolf Hitler, The Making of a Fuhrer.* "dagger." URL: http://smoter.com/hate&def.htm. 05/31/14
[717] Frölich, Paul. *Rosa Luxemburg: Her Life and Work.* Translated by Johanna Hoornweg (Monthly Review Press, New York, 1972), 168.
[718] http://en.wikipedia.org/wiki/Franco-Russian_Alliance. 05/31/14
[719] http://www.srpska-mreza.com/library/facts/BiH_1908.html. 05/31/14
[720] http://en.wikipedia.org/wiki/First_Moroccan_Crisis. 05/31/14
[721] Hitler's Speech, Munich, 13 April 1923. "[I]n France a passionate hatred against Germany ... All the Jewish papers throughout France agitated against Berlin. Here again to seek and to exploit grounds for a conflict is the clearly recognizable effort of world Jewry."
[722] Williams, John. *Corporal Hitler and the Great War 1914–1918* (London: Frank Cass, 2005), 25.
[723] Ibid., 27.
[724] Ibid., 24.
[725] Pulzer, Peter. *The Rise of Political Anti-Semitism in Germany & Austria* (Cambridge: Harvard University Press, 1988), 260.
[726] Hitler, Adolf. *Mein Kampf.* Trans. Ralph Manheim (Houghton Mifflin Company, Boston/NY), First Mariner Books edition, 1999, 15.
[727] http://www.firstworldwar.com/features/balkan_causes.htm. 05/31/14
[728] Williams, John. *Corporal Hitler and the Great War 1914–1918* (London: Frank Cass, 2005), 28.

[729] http://www.worldwar1.com/tlplot.htm. 05/31/14
[730] Kaes, Martin; Jay, Martin; Dimendberg (Eds.). *The Weimar Republic SourceBook* (California: University of California Press, 1995), 10.
[731] Porter, Ian, et al. *Imperial Germany, 1890–1918* (New York: Longman, 1991), 51.
[732] Evans, Richard. *The Coming of the Third Reich* (New York: Penguin Books, 2004), 20.
[733] Fest, Joachim. *Hitler* (San Diego: Harcourt, 2002), 95.
[734] Evans, Richard. *The Coming of the Third Reich* (New York: Penguin Books, 2004), 30.
[735] http://www.spartacus.schoolnet.co.uk/GERhitler.htm. 05/31/14
[736] Tedor, Richard. *Hitler's Revolution: Ideology Social Programs Foreign Affairs* (Chicago, 2013), 75.
[737] Williams, John. *Corporal Hitler and the Great War 1914–1918* (London: Frank Cass, 2005), 23.
[738] Ibid., 22.
[739] Stolfi, R. H. S. *Hitler: Beyond Evil and Tyranny* (Prometheus Books, Amherst, New York, 2011), 25.
[740] Williams, John. *Corporal Hitler and the Great War 1914–1918* (London: Frank Cass, 2005), 13, 15.
[741] Ibid., 59.
[742] Giblin, James, and Robert Payne. *The Life and Death of Adolf Hitler* (New York: Praeger, 1973), 19.
[743] Williams, John. *Corporal Hitler and the Great War 1914–1918* (London: Frank Cass, 2005), 14.
[744] Ibid., 1.
[745] Shirer, William L. *The Rise and Fall of the Third Reich: A History of Nazi Germany* (Touchstone, NY, 1998), 30.
[746] Stolfi, R. H. S. *Hitler: Beyond Evil and Tyranny* (Prometheus Books, Amherst, New York, 2011), 209.
[747] Kubizek, August. *The Young Hitler I Knew* (London: Greenhill Books, 2006). Abridged edition first published in English, 1954, by Allan Wingate Publishers Ltd., 169.
[748] Toland, John. *Adolf Hitler* (Garden City: Anchor Books, 1992), 68.
[749] Kershaw, Ian. *Hitler, 1889–1936* (New York: W. W. Norton, 1999), 94.
[750] Hitler, Adolf. *Mein Kampf* (Boston: Houghton Mifflin, 2001), 376.
[751] Smoter, Walter Frank. *Adolf Hitler, The Making of a Fuhrer*. "3754" URL: http://smoter.com/abornsol.htm. 05/31/14
[752] Williams, John. *Corporal Hitler and the Great War 1914–1918* (London: Frank Cass, 2005), 10.
[753] http://www.spartacus.schoolnet.co.uk/GERhitler.htm. 05/31/14

[754] Williams, John. *Corporal Hitler and the Great War 1914–1918* (London: Frank Cass, 2005), 203.
[755] Ibid., 11.
[756] http://www.greatwar.nl/frames/default-hitlere.html. 05/31/14
[757] Smoter, Walter Frank. *Adolf Hitler, The Making of a Fuhrer*. URL: http://smoter.com/hate&def.htm. 05/31/14
[758] Smoter, Walter Frank. *Adolf Hitler, The Making of a Fuhrer*. URL: http://smoter.com/hate&def.htm. 05/31/14
[759] Fest, Joachim. *Hitler* (San Diego: Harcourt, 2002), 68.
[760] Ibid., 69.
[761] Bullock, Alan. *Hitler, A Study in Tyranny* (New York and Evanston: Harper & Row, 1964), 53.
[762] Fest, Joachim. *Hitler* (San Diego: Harcourt, 2002), 70.
[763] Williams, John. *Corporal Hitler and the Great War 1914–1918* (London: Frank Cass, 2005), 20.
[764] Ibid., 39.
[765] Ibid., 107.
[766] Ibid., 117.
[767] Dawidowicz, Lucy. *The War against the Jews, 1933–45* (Harmondsworth Eng.: Penguin, 1977), 39.
[768] Williams, John. *Corporal Hitler and the Great War 1914–1918* (London: Frank Cass, 2005), 203.
[769] Smoter, Walter Frank. *Adolf Hitler, The Making of a Fuhrer*. URL: http://smoter.com/hate&def.htm. 05/31/14
[770] Smoter, Walter Frank. *Adolf Hitler, The Making of a Fuhrer*. URL: http://smoter.com/hate&def.htm. 05/31/14
[771] Smoter, Walter Frank. *Adolf Hitler, The Making of a Fuhrer*. URL: http://smoter.com/hate&def.htm. 05/31/14
[772] Smoter, Walter Frank. *Adolf Hitler, The Making of a Fuhrer*. URL: http://smoter.com/hate&def.htm. 05/31/14
[773] http://www.historyplace.com/worldwar2/riseofhitler/warone.htm. 05/31/14
[774] Fest, Joachim. *Hitler* (San Diego: Harcourt, 2002), 69.
[775] Bullock, Alan. *Hitler, A Study in Tyranny* (New York and Evanston: Harper & Row, 1964), 52.
[776] Kershaw, Ian. *Hitler, 1889–1936* (New York: W. W. Norton, 1999), 91.
[777] Ibid., 92.
[778] Ryback, Timothy. *Hitler's Private Library: the Books That Shaped His Life* (London: Vintage, 2010), 23.
[779] http://www.firstworldwar.com/features/aslowfuse.htm. 05/31/14
[780] Fest, Joachim. *Hitler* (San Diego: Harcourt, 2002), 356.
[781] Ibid., 369.

[782] Shirer, William L. *The Rise and Fall of the Third Reich: A History of Nazi Germany* (Touchstone, NY, 1998), 98.
[783] Toland, John. *Adolf Hitler* (Garden City: Anchor Books, 1992), 65.
[784] Fest, Joachim. *Hitler* (San Diego: Harcourt, 2002), 71.
[785] Bullock, Alan. *Hitler and Stalin* (New York: Vintage Books, 1993), 46.
[786] Fest, Joachim. *Hitler* (San Diego: Harcourt, 2002), 77.
[787] http://en.wikipedia.org/wiki/Sulfur_mustard. 05/31/14
[788] Williams, John. *Corporal Hitler and the Great War 1914–1918* (London: Frank Cass, 2005), 196.
[789] Shirer, William L. *The Rise and Fall of the Third Reich: A History of Nazi Germany* (Touchstone, NY, 1998), 31.
[790] Giblin, James, and Robert Payne. *The Life and Death of Adolf Hitler* (New York: Praeger, 1973), 20.
[791] Toland, John. *Adolf Hitler*. Garden City: Anchor Books, 1992), 66.
[792] Stolfi, R. H. S. *Hitler: Beyond Evil and Tyranny* (Prometheus Books, Amherst, New York, 2011), 91.
[793] http://www.historyplace.com/worldwar2/riseofhitler/warone.htm. 05/31/14
[794] Hitler's Speech, Munich, 13 April 1923.
[795] Lindemann, Albert S. *Esau's Tears: Modern Anti-Semitism and the Rise of the Jews* (Cambridge University Press, Cambridge, U.K., 2000), Paperback Edition, 389–90.
[796] Pulzer, Peter. *Jews and the German State: The Political History of a Minority, 1848–1933* (Wayne State University Press, 2003), 205.
[797] http://www.icons-multimedia.com/ClientsArea/HoH/LIBARC/LIBRARY/Themes/Policy/Friedl2A.html. 05/31/14 Quoting S. Friedlaender, Redemptive Anti-Semitism, Source: S. Friedlaender, Chapter 3 in: *Nazi Germany and the Jews, Vol. I, The Years of Persecution 1933–1939* (New York, 1997), 73–112.
[798] Lindemann, Albert S. *Esau's Tears: Modern Anti-Semitism and the Rise of the Jews* (Cambridge University Press, Cambridge, U.K., 2000), Paperback Edition, 399.
[799] Niewyk, Donald L., *The Jews in Weimar Germany* (Transaction Publishers, New Brunswick, 2001), 10.
[800] Ibid.
[801] Bilski, Emily D. *Berlin metropolis: Jews and the new culture, 1890–1918* (University of California Press, 1999), 12.
[802] Niewyk, Donald L., *The Jews in Weimar Germany* (Transaction Publishers, New Brunswick, 2001), 10.
[803] Elon, Amos. *The Pity of It All: A Portrait of the German-Jewish Epoch, 1743–1933* (New York: Holt, 2003).

[804] Niewyk, Donald L. *The Jews in Weimar Germany* (Transaction Publishers, New Brunswick, 2001), 143.
[805] Ibid., 142–43.
[806] Aschheim, Steven. *Brothers and Strangers* (Madison: The University of Wisconsin Press, 1999), 189–90.
[807] Elon, Amos. *The Pity of It All: A Portrait of the German-Jewish Epoch, 1743–1933* (New York: Holt, 2003), 340.
[808] http://www.israelnationalnews.com/News/News.aspx/123436. 05/31/14
[809] http://www.haaretz.com/news/diplomacy-defense/idf-uses-facebook-to-catch-women-lying-their-way-out-of-the-army-1.326151?localLinksEnabled=false. 05/31/14
[810] http://www.haaretz.com/print-edition/opinion/the-draft-dodging-state-of-tel-aviv-1.326666. 05/31/14
[811] http://www.jewishpost.com/news/The-Few-The-Proud-The-Jewish.html. 05/31/14
[812] Williams, John. *Corporal Hitler and the Great War* 1914–1918 (London: Frank Cass, 2005), 37.
[813] Ibid., 202.
[814] Haumann, Heiko. *A History of East European Jews* (Budapest: Central European University Press, 2002), 95.
[815] Ibid., 95–96.
[816] Williams, John. *Corporal Hitler and the Great War 1914–1918* (London: Frank Cass, 2005), 131.
[817] Ibid.
[818] Haumann, Heiko. *A History of East European Jews* (Budapest: Central European University Press, 2002), 86.
[819] Lindemann, Albert S. *Esau's Tears: Modern Anti-Semitism and the Rise of the Jews* (Cambridge University Press, Cambridge, U.K., 2000), 44.
[820] http://en.wikipedia.org/wiki/Deuteronomy. 05/31/14
[821] Pranaitis, I. B. *The Talmud Unmasked: The Secret Rabbinical Teachings Concerning Christians* (New York: E. N. Sanctuary, 1939), 62.
[822] Lindemann, Albert S. *Esau's Tears: Modern Anti-Semitism and the Rise of the Jews* (Cambridge University Press, Cambridge, U.K., 2000), 47.
[823] http://en.wikipedia.org/wiki/Kingdom_of_David. 05/31/14
[824] Lindemann, Albert S. *Esau's Tears: Modern Anti-Semitism and the Rise of the Jews* (Cambridge University Press, Cambridge, U.K., 2000), Paperback Edition, 50.
[825] Ibid., 62.
[826] Lindemann, Albert. *Anti-Semitism before the Holocaust* (New York: Longman, 2000), 79.

[827] Tedor, Richard. *Hitler's Revolution: Ideology Social Programs Foreign Affairs* (Chicago. 2013), 19.
[828] Weizmann, Chaim. *Trial and Error* (Hamish Hamilton, London, 1949), 185.
[829] Kaes, Martin; Jay, Martin; Dimendberg (Eds.). *The Weimar Republic SourceBook* (California: University of California Press, 1995), 17.
[830] Kaes, Martin; Jay, Martin; Dimendberg (Eds.). *The Weimar Republic SourceBook* (California: University of California Press, 1995), 37.
[831] Kyrka, Kreativistens. Internet Archive. "National Socialism as an Anti-Jewish Group Evolutionary Strategy." https://archive.org/details/NationalSocialismAsAnAnti-jewishGroupEvolutionaryStrategy. 8/25/14
[832] Niewyk, Donald L. *The Jews in Weimar Germany* (Transaction Publishers, New Brunswick, 2001), 44.
[833] Ibid., 47–48.
[834] Pulzer, Peter. *Jews and the German State: The Political History of a Minority, 1848–1933* (Wayne State University Press, 2003), 206.
[835] Deak, Istvan. *Weimar Germany's Left-Wing Intellectuals: A Political History of the Weltbüne and Its Circle* (University of California Press, Berkeley and Los Angeles, 1968), 25.
[836] Pulzer, Peter. *Jews and the German State: The Political History of a Minority, 1848–1933* (Wayne State University Press, 2003), 263.
[837] Lindemann, Albert S. *Esau's Tears: Modern Anti-Semitism and the Rise of the Jews* (Cambridge University Press, Cambridge, U.K., 2000), 167.
[838] Ibid., 400.
[839] Pulzer, Peter. *Jews and the German State: The Political History of a Minority, 1848-1933* (Wayne State University Press, 2003), 39.
[840] Ibid., 79.
[841] Ibid., 39.
[842] Niewyk, Donald L. *The Jews in Weimar Germany* (Transaction Publishers, New Brunswick, 2001), 125.
[843] Ibid.
[844] http://en.wikipedia.org/wiki/Kurt_Tucholsky. 05/31/14
[845] Niewyk, Donald L. *The Jews in Weimar Germany* (Transaction Publishers, New Brunswick, 2001), 47–48.
[846] Willett, John. *Art & Politics in the Weimar Period: The New Sobriety 1917–1933* (Da Capo Press, New York 1996), 20.
[847] Deak, Istvan. *Weimar Germany's Left-Wing Intellectuals: A Political History of the Weltbühne and Its Circle*, 37.
[848] Ibid., 35.

[849] Pulzer, Peter. *Jews and the German State: The Political History of a Minority, 1848–1933* (Wayne State University Press, 2003), 260.
[850] Deak, Istvan. *Weimar Germany's Left-Wing Intellectuals: A Political History of the Weltbüne and Its Circle* (University of California Press, Berkeley and Los Angeles, 1968), 232.
[851] http://www.firstworldwar.com/features/munich_five.htm. 05/31/14
[852] Willett, John. Art & Politics in the Weimar Period: The New Sobriety 1917–1933 (Da Capo Press, New York, 1996), 24.
[853] Jones, E. Michael. *Living Machines* (San Francisco: Ignatius Press, 1995), 61.
[854] Ibid.
[855] Ibid.
[856] Gordon, Sarah. *Hitler, Germans, and the "Jewish Question"* (Princeton University Press, New Jersey, 1984), 92.
[857] Friedrich, Otto. *Before the Deluge* (New York: HarperPerennial, 1995), 16.
[858] Ibid., 37.
[859] Metzger, Rainer, and Christian Brandstätter. Clara Costa, trans. *Berlin, the Twenties* (Harry N. Abrams Inc., New York, 2007), 103.
[860] http://en.wikipedia.org/wiki/Alfred_Redl. 05/31/14
[861] http://ellhn.e-e-e.gr/books/assets/founder_of_Israel.pdf. 05/31/14
[862] Author unknown. Date published (revised): 25 May 2014. Alfred Redl. Retrieved from URL http://en.wikipedia.org/wiki/Alfred_Red.
[863] Pulzer, Peter. *Jews and the German State: The Political History of a Minority, 1848–1933* (Wayne State University Press, 2003), 174.
[864] Watt, Richard, M. *The Kings Depart. The Tragedy of Germany: Versailles and the German Revolution* (Barnes & Noble Books, 2002, Barnes & Noble, Inc.), 114.
[865] Ibid., 117.
[866] Aschheim, Steven. *Brothers and Strangers* (Madison: The University of Wisconsin Press, 1999), 215–16.
[867] Elon, Amos. *The Pity of It All: A Portrait of the German-Jewish Epoch, 1743–1933* (New York: Holt, 2003), 363.
[868] Hitler, Adolf. *Mein Kampf* (Boston: Houghton Mifflin, 2001), 193.
[869] Lindemann, Albert. *Anti-Semitism before the Holocaust* (New York: Longman, 2000), 78.
[870] Ibid.
[871] MacDonald, Kevin. *Separation and Its Discontents*, 2004, 43.
[872] http://www.icons-multimedia.com/ClientsArea/HoH/LIBARC/LIBRARY/Themes/Policy/Friedl2A.html. 05/31/14

[873] Aschheim, Steven. *Brothers and Strangers* (Madison: The University of Wisconsin Press, 1999), 178.
[874] Lindemann, Albert. *Anti-Semitism before the Holocaust* (New York: Longman, 2000).
[875] Aschheim, Steven. *Brothers and Strangers* (Madison: The University of Wisconsin Press, 1999), 230–31.
[876] Watt, Richard, M. *The Kings Depart. The Tragedy of Germany: Versailles and the German Revolution* (Barnes & Noble Books, 2002, Barnes & Noble, Inc.), 126.
[877] Ibid., 119.
[878] James, Harold. *Europe Reborn* (London: Pearson/Longman, 2003), 52.
[879] Stibbe, Matthew. *Germany, 1914–1933* (Pearson Education Limited, 2010), 13.
[880] Watt, Richard, M. *The Kings Depart. The Tragedy of Germany: Versailles and the German Revolution* (Barnes & Noble Books, 2002, Barnes & Noble, Inc.), 125.
[881] Pulzer, Peter. *Jews and the German State: The Political History of a Minority, 1848–1933* (Wayne State University Press, 2003), 164.
[882] Kershaw, Ian. *Hitler, 1889–1936* (New York: W. W. Norton, 1999), 99.
[883] Watt, Richard, M. *The Kings Depart. The Tragedy of Germany: Versailles and the German Revolution* (Barnes & Noble Books, 2002, Barnes & Noble, Inc.), 122.
[884] Ibid., 128.
[885] Deak, Istvan. *Weimar Germany's Left-Wing Intellectuals: A Political History of the Weltbüne and Its Circle* (University of California Press, Berkeley and Los Angeles, 1968), 70–71.
[886] http://en.wikipedia.org/wiki/Karl_Liebknecht. 05/31/14
[887] Smoter, Walter Frank. *Adolf Hitler, The Making of a Fuhrer*. URL: http://smoter.com/hate&def.htm. 05/31/14
[888] http://en.wikipedia.org/wiki/Rosa_Luxemburg. 05/31/14
[889] Frölich, Paul. *Rosa Luxemburg: Her Life and Work*. Translated by Johanna Hoornweg. (Monthly Review Press, New York, 1972), xiv.
[890] http://www.spartacus.schoolnet.co.uk/RUSluxemburg.htm. 05/31/14
[891] http://www.h-net.org/~german/gtext/kaiserreich/lux.html. 05/31/14
[892] Lindemann, Albert S. *Esau's Tears: Modern Anti-Semitism and the Rise of the Jews* (Cambridge University Press, Cambridge, U.K., 2000), 179.
[893] Ibid.
[894] Frölich, Paul. *Rosa Luxemburg: Her Life and Work*. Translated by Johanna Hoornweg. (Monthly Review Press, New York, 1972), 181.
[895] Ibid., 74.

[896] Bronner, Stephan Eric. *Radical Politics for Conservative Times* (Routedge, New York, NY, 2002). Retrieved from URL: http://books.google.com/books?id=d6_gKpb9zlkC&pg=PA28&lpg=PA28&dq=the+syphilitic+Luxemburg+bacillus&source=bl&ots=Ai5-M0TqID&sig=wLdTzanhI7Aa09miAkt_E91ViGc&hl=en&sa=X&ei=Qk6MU-uHMuHisATAz4GwCw&ved=0CCgQ6AEwAA#v=onepage&q=the%20syphilitic%20Luxemburg%20bacillus&f=false
[897] http://jewcy.com/daily_shvitz/inside_max_webers_head. 05/31/14
[898] Stibbe, Matthew. *Germany, 1914–1933* (Pearson Education Limited, 2010), 51.
[899] Tedor, Richard. *Hitler's Revolution: Ideology Social Programs Foreign Affairs* (Chicago, 2013), 40.
[900] Frölich, Paul. *Rosa Luxemburg: Her Life and Work*. Translated by Johanna Hoornweg. (Monthly Review Press, New York, 1972), 228.
[901] MacDonald, Kevin. *The Culture of Critique: An Evolutionary Analysis of Jewish Involvement in Twentieth-Century Intellectual and Political Movements* (Kevin MacDonald, 2002), Paperback. *The Culture of Critique* was originally published in 1998 by Praeger Publishers, an imprint of Greenwood Publishing Group, Inc., 54.
[902] Lindemann, Albert S. *Esau's Tears: Modern Anti-Semitism and the Rise of the Jews* (Cambridge University Press, Cambridge, U.K., 2000), Paperback Edition, 180.
[903] MacDonald, Kevin. *The Culture of Critique: An Evolutionary Analysis of Jewish Involvement in Twentieth-Century Intellectual and Political Movements* (City: Authorhouse, 2002), 58.
[904] Frölich, Paul. *Rosa Luxemburg: Her Life and Work*. Translated by Johanna Hoornweg. (Monthly Review Press, New York, 1972), 225.
[905] Ibid., 226.
[906] Ibid., 225.
[907] Watt, Richard, M. *The Kings Depart. The Tragedy of Germany: Versailles and the German Revolution* (Barnes & Noble Books, 2002, Barnes & Noble, Inc.), 251.
[908] Pulzer, Peter. *Jews and the German State: The Political History of a Minority, 1848–1933* (Wayne State University Press, 2003), 165.
[909] Ibid., 117.
[910] Ibid., 204.
[911] Deak, Istvan. *Weimar Germany's Left-Wing Intellectuals: A Political History of the Weltbüne and Its Circle* (University of California Press, Berkeley and Los Angeles, 1968), 121.
[912] http://www.online-literature.com/gertrude-atherton/white-morning/9/. 05/31/14. Gertrude Franklin Horn Atherton, commenting on her book *The White*

Morning, in which she proposes a German revolution led by German women. No date.

[913] Frölich, Paul. *Rosa Luxemburg: Her Life and Work*. Translated by Johanna Hoornweg. (Monthly Review Press, New York, 1972), 217.

[914] Watt, Richard, M. *The Kings Depart. The Tragedy of Germany: Versailles and the German Revolution*, Barnes & Noble Books, 2002, Barnes & Noble, Inc.), 128.

[915] http://www.kevinmacdonald.net/SlezkineRev.pdf. 05/31/14

[916] Hitler's Speech, Munich, 12 September 1923.

[917] Williams, John. *Corporal Hitler and the Great War 1914–1918* (London: Frank Cass, 2005), 5.

[918] Giblin, James, and Robert Payne. *The Life and Death of Adolf Hitler* (New York: Praeger, 1973), 22.

[919] Toland, John. *Adolf Hitler* (Garden City: Anchor Books, 1992), 71.

[920] Smoter, Walter Frank. *Adolf Hitler, The Making of a Fuhrer*. "I often think of Munich." URL: http://smoter.com/earlymon.htm. 03/24/09

[921] http://www.marxists.org/archive/cliff/works/1959/rosalux/5-partyclass.htm. 05/31/14

[922] Flanne, K. Date of pub. unknown. *World War One: A Discussion of Fact and Fallacy*. Retrieved from URL: http://www.mourningtheancient.com/ww1.htm.

[923] Broué, Pierre, et al. *The German Revolution 1917–1923* (Boston: Brill Academic Publishers, 2004), 92.

[924] Speer, Albert. *Spandau: The Secret Diaries*. Translated from German by Richard and Clara Winston. (New York: Pocket Books, 1976), 235.

[925] Speer, Albert. *Inside the Third Reich: Memoirs* (New York: Simon & Schuster, 1997), 235.

[926] Speer, Albert. *Inside the Third Reich: Memoirs* (New York: Simon & Schuster, 1997), 235.

[927] Hitler, Adolf. *Mein Kampf* (Boston: Houghton Mifflin, 2001), 321.

[928] Ibid., 323.

[929] Hitler's Speech, Berlin, Congress fo the German Work Front, May 10, 1933.

[930] Herwig, Holger H. *Journal of Military and Strategic Studies*, Vol I, No 1 (1998). Retrieved from URL: http://www.jmss.org/jmss/index.php/jmss/article/view/19/18.

[931] Rober, Joh. Date of pub. unk. Institute for Historical Review. "Behind the Balfour Declaration: Britain's Great War Pledge to Lord Rothschild." Retrieved from URL: http://www.ihr.org/jhr/v06/v06p389_John.html.

[932] http://www.worldwar1.com/tlwarorg.htm. 05/31/14

[933] Brenner, Lenni. *Zionism in the Age of the Dictators* (London: Croom Helm, 1983), 9–10.

[934] http://www.mideastweb.org/mebalfour.htm. 05/31/14

[935] Author unknown. October, 2010. "Leonard Stein, Political Secretary, Zionist Organization." Retrieved from URL: http://www.zoominfo.com/p/Leonard-Stein/93099628.
[936] MacDonald, Kevin. *Separation and Its Discontents*, 2004, 74.
[937] http://www.heretical.com/miscellx/culturec.html. 05/31/14
[938] Frankel, Josef. 2007. "Patriot, Judge, and Zionist." Retrieved from URL: http://archive.today/NAQor.
[939] Haumann, Heiko. *A History of East European Jews* (Budapest: Central European University Press, 2002), 180.
[940] Stein, Leonard. *The Balfour Declaration* (London: Vallentine, Mitchell & Col, Ltd., 1961), 649.
[941] Ibid., 569.
[942] Aschheim, Steven. *Brothers and Strangers* (Madison: The University of Wisconsin Press, 1999), 178.
[943] Stibbe, Matthew. *Germany, 1914–1933* (Pearson Education Limited, 2010), 39.
[944] Lindemann, Albert S. *Esau's Tears: Modern Anti-Semitism and the Rise of the Jews* (Cambridge University Press, Cambridge, U.K., 2000), Paperback Edition, 405.
[945] Broué, Pierre, et al. *The German Revolution 1917–1923* (Boston: Brill Academic Publishers, 2004), 90.
[946] Stolfi, R. H. S. *Hitler: Beyond Evil and Tyranny* (Prometheus Books, Amherst, New York, 2011), 122.
[947] Watt, Richard, M. *The Kings Depart. The Tragedy of Germany: Versailles and the German Revolution* (Barnes & Noble Books, 2002, Barnes & Noble, Inc.), 150.
[948] Kershaw, Ian. *Hitler, 1889–1936* (New York: W. W. Norton, 1999), 97.
[949] Tedor, Richard. *Hitler's Revolution: Ideology Social Programs Foreign Affairs* (Chicago, 2013), 143.
[950] Toland, John. *Adolf Hitler* (Garden City: Anchor Books, 1992), xvii.
[951] Smoter, Walter Frank. *Adolf Hitler, The Making of a Fuhrer*. "At the very moment." URL: http://smoter.com/hate&def.htm. 05/31/14
[952] Smoter, Frank Walter. 2004. *Adolf Hitler*. Chapter 12, "Hate & Defeat." http://smoter.com/hate%26def.htm. 07/08/14
[953] Watt, Richard, M. *The Kings Depart. The Tragedy of Germany: Versailles and the German Revolution* (Barnes & Noble Books, 2002, Barnes & Noble, Inc.), 174–75.
[954] Frölich, Paul. *Rosa Luxemburg: Her Life and Work*. Translated by Johanna Hoornweg. (Monthly Review Press, New York, 1972), 97.
[955] Frölich, Paul. *Rosa Luxemburg: Her Life and Work*. Translated by Johanna Hoornweg. (Monthly Review Press, New York, 1972), 105.

[956] http://www.marxists.org/subject/germany-1918-23/chron.htm. 05/31/14
[957] MacMillan, Margaret. *Paris 1919: Six Months that Changed the World* (Random House Trade Paperbacks, NY, 2003), 19.
[958] Watt, Richard, M. *The Kings Depart. The Tragedy of Germany: Versailles and the German Revolution* (Barnes & Noble Books, 2002, Barnes & Noble, Inc.), 143.
[959] Ibid.
[960] Toland, John. *Adolf Hitler* (Garden City: Anchor Books, 1992), xvii–xviii.
[961] Hitler, Adolf. *Mein Kampf* (Boston: Houghton Mifflin, 2001), 200.
[962] Watt, Richard, M. *The Kings Depart. The Tragedy of Germany: Versailles and the German Revolution* (Barnes & Noble Books, 2002, Barnes & Noble, Inc.), 145.
[963] Ibid., 251.
[964] Wiehe, Friederich Karl, Ph.D. 1938. *Germany and the Jewish Question.* Retrieved from URL: http://www.controversyofzion.info/germany_jewish_question.htm. This was a Nazi publication.
[965] Hitler, Adolf. *Mein Kampf* (Boston: Houghton Mifflin, 2001), 228.
[966] Lee, Stephen. *The Weimar Republic* (New York: Routledge, 1998), 36.
[967] Watt, Richard, M. *The Kings Depart. The Tragedy of Germany: Versailles and the German Revolution* (Barnes & Noble Books, 2002, Barnes & Noble, Inc.), 528.
[968] Elon, Amos. *The Pity of It All: A Portrait of the German-Jewish Epoch, 1743–1933* (New York: Holt, 2003), 346.
[969] Stibbe, Matthew. *Germany, 1914–1933* (Pearson Education Limited, 2010), 57.
[970] Weitz, Eric. *Weimar Germany* (Princeton: Princeton University Press, 2009), 17–18.
[971] Ibid., 23.
[972] Ibid., 23.
[973] Watt, Richard, M. *The Kings Depart. The Tragedy of Germany: Versailles and the German Revolution* (Barnes & Noble Books, 2002, Barnes & Noble, Inc.), 185–86.
[974] Grange, William. *Cultural Chronicle of the Weimar Republic* (Metuchen: Scarecrow Press, 2008), 8.
[975] Henig, Ruth. *The Weimar Republic: 1919–1933* (Routledge, New York, 1998), 14.
[976] Watt, Richard, M. *The Kings Depart. The Tragedy of Germany: Versailles and the German Revolution* (Barnes & Noble Books, 2002, Barnes & Noble, Inc.), 150.

[977] Pulzer, Peter. *Jews and the German State: The Political History of a Minority, 1848–1933* (Wayne State University Press, 2003), 214.
[978] Shirer, William L. *The Rise and Fall of the Third Reich: A History of Nazi Germany* (Touchstone, NY, 1998), 97.
[979] Turner, Henry, and Ruth Hein. *Hitler—Memoirs of a Confidant* (New Haven: Yale University Press, 1987), 53.
[980] Hiden, John. *The Weimar Republic* (New York: Longman, 1996), 72.
[981] Kauders, Anthony. *German Politics and the Jews: Düsseldorf and Nuremberg, 1910–1933* (Clarendon Press, Oxford, 1996), 47.
[982] Ibid., 50.
[983] Ibid.
[984] Ibid.
[985] Pulzer, Peter. *Jews and the German State: The Political History of a Minority, 1848–1933* (Wayne State University Press, 2003), 207.
[986] Watt, Richard, M. *The Kings Depart. The Tragedy of Germany: Versailles and the German Revolution* (Barnes & Noble Books, 2002, Barnes & Noble, Inc.), 204–06.
[987] Watt, Richard, M. *The Kings Depart. The Tragedy of Germany: Versailles and the German Revolution* (Barnes & Noble Books, 2002, Barnes & Noble, Inc.), 211.
[988] Stolfi, R. H. S. *Hitler: Beyond Evil and Tyranny* (Prometheus Books, Amherst, New York, 2011), 112.
[989] http://www.historyplace.com/worldwar2/riseofhitler/warone.htm. 05/31/14
[990] Hitler, Adolf. *Mein Kampf* (Boston: Houghton Mifflin, 2001), 204–05.
[991] Fest, Joachim. *Hitler* (San Diego: Harcourt, 2002), 77.
[992] Hamann, Brigitte. *Hitler's Vienna: A Dictator's Apprenticeship*. Trans. Thomas Thornton. (Oxford, NY, 2000), 352.
[993] http://ihr.org/books/connors/dealinginhate.shtml. 05/31/14
[994] Fest, Joachim. *Hitler* (San Diego: Harcourt, 2002), 377.
[995] Hitler, Adolf. *Mein Kampf* (Boston: Houghton Mifflin, 2001), 193.
[996] Ibid., 189–90.
[997] http://ihr.org/books/connors/dealinginhate.shtml. 05/31/14
[998] Williams, John. *Corporal Hitler and the Great War 1914–1918* (London: Frank Cass, 2005), 42.
[999] Conners, Michael F., Dr. *Dealing in Hate: The Development of Anti-German Propaganda*: The Germanophobic Fallacy. http://ihr.org/books/connors/dealinginhate.shtml. 05/31/14.
[1000] Bradberry, Benton L. *The Myth of German Villainy* (Bloomington, IN, AuthorHouse), 12.
[1001] Hitler, Adolf. *Mein Kampf* (Boston: Houghton Mifflin, 2001), 197–98.
[1002] Ibid., 197–98.

[1003] Ibid., 187.
[1004] Williams, John. *Corporal Hitler and the Great War 1914–1918* (London: Frank Cass, 2005), 117.
[1005] http://en.wikipedia.org/wiki/Ferdinand_Foch. 05/31/14.
[1006] Weitz, Eric. *Weimar Germany* (Princeton: Princeton University Press, 2009), 16.
[1007] Hitler, Adolf. *Mein Kampf* (Boston: Houghton Mifflin, 2001), 519.
[1008] Ibid., 201.
[1009] Lee, Stephen. *The Weimar Republic* (New York: Routledge, 1998), 5.
[1010] http://members.tripod.com/dailytrh/0414.html. 05/31/14
[1011] Dillon, E. J., Dr. *The Inside Story of the Peace Conference* (Harper & Brothers, NY, and London, 1920), 376.
[1012] Ibid., 99.
[1013] Ibid., 102.
[1014] Ibid.
[1015] Ibid., 113.
[1016] Tedor, Richard. *Hitler's Revolution: Ideology Social Programs Foreign Affairs* (Chicago, 2013), 7.
[1017] Dillon, E. J., Dr. *The Inside Story of the Peace Conference* (Harper & Brothers, NY, and London, 1920), 12.
[1018] MacDonald, Kevin. *The Culture of Critique: An Evolutionary Analysis of Jewish Involvement in Twentieth-Century Intellectual and Political Movements* (City: Authorhouse, 2002), 247.
[1019] http://news.bbc.co.uk/2/hi/middle_east/6666495.stm. 05/31/14
[1020] Brenner, Lenni. *Zionism in the Age of the Dictators* (London: Croom Helm, 1983), 110.
[1021] Weizmann, Chaim. *Trial and Error* (Hamish Hamilton, London, 1949), 304.
[1022] MacMillan, Margaret. *Paris, 1919: Six Months that Changed the World*, 60.
[1023] Weizmann, Chaim. *Trial and Error* (Hamish Hamilton, London, 1949), 301.
[1024] Brenner, Lenni. *Zionism in the Age of the Dictators* (London: Croom Helm, 1983), 11.
[1025] Kaes, Martin; Jay, Martin; Dimendberg (Eds.). *The Weimar Republic SourceBook* (California: University of California Press, 1995), 10.
[1026] http://en.wikipedia.org/wiki/Aftermath_of_World_War_I. 05/31/14
[1027] James, Harold. *Europe Reborn* (London: Pearson/Longman, 2003), 54.
[1028] Watt, Richard, M. *The Kings Depart. The Tragedy of Germany: Versailles and the German Revolution* (Barnes & Noble Books, 2002, Barnes & Noble, Inc.), 90.
[1029] Ibid., 89–90.
[1030] https://www.google.com/search?q=Map+of+Germany+1920&rlz=1T4GZAB_e

nUS449US538&tbm=isch&imgil=WhQP8yZyVTQnoM%253A%253B2RlN1Q
RlusEraM%253Bhttp%25253A%25252F%25252Fwww.rootsweb.ancestry.com
%25252F~wggerman%25252Fmap%25252Fgermany1920.htm&source=iu&usg
=__hs5of8xWy1ULXImXaFK_tEnCtvc%3D&sa=X&ei=7TreU63vDsuyyATPy
oDwBQ&ved=0CCEQ9QEwAA&biw=1008&bih=506#facrc=_&imgdii=_WhQ
P8yZyVTQnoM%3A%3Bc94rKkcvJ4s5UM%3BWhQP8yZyVTQnoM%3A&i
mgrc=WhQP8yZyVTQnoM%253A%3B2RlN1QRlusEraM%3Bhttp%253A%25
2F%252Fwww.rootsweb.ancestry.com%252F~wggerman%252Fmap%252Fima
ges%252Fgermany1920.jpg%3Bhttp%253A%252F%252Fwww.rootsweb.ances
try.com%252F~wggerman%252Fmap%252Fgermany1920.htm%3B1000%3B6
67. 8//2/14 [1031]

https://www.google.com/search?q=Map+of+Polish+Corridor&rlz=1T4GZAB_e
nUS449US538&tbm=isch&imgil=jNdVG1nfkn8TbM%253A%253BqOmwzX-
triTIrM%253Bhttp%25253A%25252F%25252Fsubversify.com%25252F2012%
25252F02%25252F10%25252Fdid-hitler-deliberately-lose-the-
war%25252F&source=iu&usg=__PVzRa5ZOwyipwmamrSv7lBun9Sc%3D&sa
=X&ei=EjzeU63iOMm1yAS884HYCw&ved=0CCEQ9QEwAA&biw=1008&b
ih=506#facrc=_&imgdii=_&imgrc=jNdVG1nfkn8TbM%253A%3BLu1kECAsv
FnXiM%3Bhttp%253A%252F%252Fgo.hrw.com%252Fvenus_images%252F0
327MC22.gif%3Bhttp%253A%252F%252Fgo.hrw.com%252Fhrw.nd%252Fgo
hrw_rls1%252FpKeywordResults%253Fkeyword%253Dst9%252520polish%25
2520wwi%3B560%3B420. 8/2/14

[1032] http://www.eaec.org/newsletters/1999/NL1999may.htm. 05/31/14
[1033] Watt, Richard, M. *The Kings Depart. The Tragedy of Germany: Versailles and the German Revolution* (Barnes & Noble Books, 2002, Barnes & Noble, Inc.), 417.
[1034] Stolfi, R. H. S. *Hitler: Beyond Evil and Tyranny* (Prometheus Books, Amherst, New York, 2011), 120.
[1035] Watt, Richard, M. *The Kings Depart. The Tragedy of Germany: Versailles and the German Revolution* (Barnes & Noble Books, 2002, Barnes & Noble, Inc.), 89.
[1036] Dillon, E. J. *The Inside Story of the Peace Conference* (Harper & Brothers, New York and London, 1920), 479.
[1037] Watt, Richard, M. *The Kings Depart. The Tragedy of Germany: Versailles and the German Revolution* (Barnes & Noble Books, 2002, Barnes & Noble, Inc.), 30.
[1038] Henig, Ruth. *The Weimar Republic: 1919–1933* (Routledge, New York, 1998), 46.
[1039] Lee, Stephen. *The Weimar Republic* (New York: Routledge, 1998), 40.
[1040] MacMillan, Margaret. *Paris 1919: Six Months that Changed the World* (Random House Trade Paperbacks, NY, 2003), 59.

[1041] Dillon, E. J., Dr. *The Inside Story of the Peace Conference* (Harper & Brothers, NY and London, 1920), 498.
[1042] Ibid., 498–99.
[1043] Ibid., 497.
[1044] Stolfi, R. H. S. *Hitler: Beyond Evil and Tyranny* (Prometheus Books, Amherst, New York, 2011), 132.
[1045] Dillon, E. J., Dr. *The Inside Story of the Peace Conference* (Harper & Brothers, NY and London, 1920), 498-99.
[1046] Ibid., 499.
[1047] Ibid.
[1048] Ibid., 500.
[1049] Ibid., 499.
[1050] Watt, Richard, M. *The Kings Depart. The Tragedy of Germany: Versailles and the German Revolution* (Barnes & Noble Books, 2002, Barnes & Noble, Inc.), 40.
[1051] Hitler, Adolf. Munich Speech, August 1, 1923.
[1052] James, Harold. *Europe Reborn* (Harlow, Eng., New York, N.Y: Pearson/Longman, 2003),74.
[1053] Evans, Richard. *The Coming of the Third Reich* (New York: Penguin Books, 2004), 63.
[1054] Lee, Stephen. *The Weimar Republic* (New York: Routledge, 1998), 45.
[1055] Kolb, Eberhard. *The Weimar Republic* (Routledge, New York, 1990), eBook, 44.
[1056] MacMillan, Margaret. *Paris 1919: Six Months that Changed the World* (Random House Trade Paperbacks, NY, 2003), 6.
[1057] Watt, Richard, M. *The Kings Depart. The Tragedy of Germany: Versailles and the German Revolution* (Barnes & Noble Books, 2002, Barnes & Noble, Inc.), 40.
[1058] Ibid.
[1059] MacMillan, Margaret. *Paris 1919: Six Months that Changed the World* (Random House Trade Paperbacks, NY, 2003), 460.
[1060] Ibid., 477.
[1061] Watt, Richard, M. *The Kings Depart. The Tragedy of Germany: Versailles and the German Revolution* (Barnes & Noble Books, 2002, Barnes & Noble, Inc.), 408.
[1062] Most of data was taken from http://en.wikipedia.org/wiki/Treaty_of_Versailles. 05/31/14. Some information was provided by the author on the basis of general assessments of a variety of sources. See also, http://www.ethicsineducation.com/weg.pdf. 05/31/14
[1063] http://en.wikipedia.org/wiki/Treaty_of_Versailles. 05/31/14

[1064] http://ihr.org/books/connors/dealinginhate.shtml. 05/31/14
[1065] http://www.spartacus.schoolnet.co.uk/GERhitler.htm. 05/31/14
[1066] Kolb, Eberhard. *The Weimar Republic* (Routledge, New York, 1990), eBook, 40.
[1067] Reed, Douglas. *The Controversy of Zion* (Torrance: Noontide Press, 1987), 207.
[1068] Hitler, Adolf. *Mein Kampf.*(Boston: Houghton Mifflin, 2001), 309.
[1069] Dillon, E. J., Dr. *The Inside Story of the Peace Conference* (Harper & Brothers, NY, and London, 1920), 67.
[1070] MacMillan, Margaret. *Paris 1919: Six Months that Changed the World* (Random House Trade Paperbacks, NY, 2003), 418.
[1071] MacDonald, Kevin. *Separation and Its Discontents toward an Evolutionary Theory of Anti-Semitism* (S. L.: 1stBooks Library, 2003), 225.
[1072] Niewyk, Donald L. *The Jews in Weimar Germany* (Transaction Publishers, New Brunswick, 2001), 142.
[1073] http://www.vho.org/aaargh/fran/livres/LBzad.pdf. 09/27/07
[1074] Dillon, E. J., Dr. *The Inside Story of the Peace Conference* (Harper & Brothers, NY, and London, 1920), 503–04.
[1075] Pulzer, Peter. *Jews and the German State: The Political History of a Minority, 1848–1933* (Wayne State University Press, 2003), 278.
[1076] http://en.wikipedia.org/wiki/Felix_Frankfurter. 05/31/14
[1077] MacMillan, Margaret. *Paris 1919: Six Months that Changed the World* (Random House Trade Paperbacks, NY, 2003), 422.
[1078] Deak, Istvan. *Weimar Germany's Left-Wing Intellectuals: A Political History of the Weltbüne and Its Circle* (University of California Press, Berkeley and Los Angeles, 1968), 84.
[1079] Fest, Joachim. *Hitler* (San Diego: Harcourt, 2002), 381.
[1080] Finkelstein, Norman. *The Holocaust Industry* (London: Verso, 2003), 23.
[1081] Pulzer, Peter. *Jews and the German State: The Political History of a Minority, 1848–1933* (Wayne State University Press, 2003), 213. See also http://swiki.hfbk-hamburg.de:8888/Lebensreform/98. 05/31/14
[1082] Watt, Richard, M. *The Kings Depart. The Tragedy of Germany: Versailles and the German Revolution* (Barnes & Noble Books, 2002, Barnes & Noble, Inc.), 490–91.
[1083] Kaes, Martin; Jay, Martin; Dimendberg (Eds.). *The Weimar Republic SourceBook* (California: University of California Press, 1995), 11.
[1084] Henig, Ruth. *The Weimar Republic: 1919–1933* (Routledge, New York, 1998), 19.
[1085] http://www.spartacus.schoolnet.co.uk/FWWversailles.htm. 05/31/14
[1086] http://www.johndclare.net/peace_treaties1_Answer.htm. 05/31/14

[1087] Dillon, E. J., Dr. *The Inside Story of the Peace Conference* (Harper & Brothers, NY, and London, 1920), 418.
[1088] Kolb, Eberhard. *The Weimar Republic* (Routledge, New York, 1990), eBook, 45-46.
[1089] Stolfi, R. H. S. *Hitler: Beyond Evil and Tyranny* (Prometheus Books, Amherst, New York, 2011), 135.
[1090] Tedor, Richard. *Hitler's Revolution: Ideology Social Programs Foreign Affairs* (Chicago, 2013), 107.
[1091] Stolfi, R. H. S. *Hitler: Beyond Evil and Tyranny* (Prometheus Books, Amherst, New York, 2011), 133.
[1092] Ibid., 220.
[1093] Ibid., 235.
[1094] Watt, Richard, M. *The Kings Depart. The Tragedy of Germany: Versailles and the German Revolution* (Barnes & Noble Books, 2002, Barnes & Noble, Inc.), 504–05.
[1095] Hamann, Brigitte. *Hitler's Vienna: A Dictator's Apprenticeship*. Trans. Thomas Thornton. (Oxford, NY, 2000), 352.
[1096] http://www.spartacus.schoolnet.co.uk/GERhitler.htm. 05/31/14
[1097] Fest, Joachim. *Hitler* (San Diego: Harcourt, 2002), 260.
[1098] Ibid., 261.
[1099] Ibid., 262–64.
[1100] Gordon, Sarah. *Hitler, Germans, and the "Jewish Question"* (Princeton University Press, New Jersey, 1984), 52.
[1101] Deak, Istvan. *Weimar Germany's Left-Wing Intellectuals: A Political History of the Weltbüne and Its Circle* (University of California Press, Berkeley and Los Angeles, 1968), 96.
[1102] Friedrich, Otto. *Before the Deluge* (New York: HarperPerennial, 1995), 36–37.
[1103] Evans, Richard. *The Coming of the Third Reich* (New York: Penguin Books, 2004), 140–41.
[1104] Peukert, Detlev. *The Weimar Republic* (New York: Hill and Wang, 1993), 158–59.
[1105] Kauders, Anthony. *German Politics and the Jews: Düsseldorf and Nuremberg, 1910–1933* (Clarendon Press, Oxford, 1996), 88.
[1106] Elon, Amos. *The Pity of It All: A Portrait of the German-Jewish Epoch, 1743–1933* (New York: Holt, 2003), 9.
[1107] Watt, Richard, M. *The Kings Depart. The Tragedy of Germany: Versailles and the German Revolution* (Barnes & Noble Books, 2002, Barnes & Noble, Inc.), 186.
[1108] http://www.firstworldwar.com/source/germancollapse_liebknecht.htm. 05/31/14

[1109] Frölich, Paul. *Rosa Luxemburg: Her Life and Work*. Translated by Johanna Hoornweg. (Monthly Review Press, New York, 1972), 98.
[1110] Watt, Richard, M. *The Kings Depart. The Tragedy of Germany: Versailles and the German Revolution* (Barnes & Noble Books, 2002, Barnes & Noble, Inc.), 192.
[1111] Frölich, Paul. *Rosa Luxemburg: Her Life and Work*. Translated by Johanna Hoornweg. (Monthly Review Press, New York, 1972), 258.
[1112] Watt, Richard, M. *The Kings Depart. The Tragedy of Germany: Versailles and the German Revolution* (Barnes & Noble Books, 2002, Barnes & Noble, Inc.), 198.
[1113] Ibid., 218.
[1114] Ibid.
[1115] Ibid., 216.
[1116] Ibid.
[1117] Stibbe, Matthew. *Germany, 1914–1933* (Pearson Education Limited, 2010), 77.
[1118] http://en.wikipedia.org/wiki/Erich_Ludendorff. 05/31/14
[1119] http://www.marxists.org/archive/trotsky/germany/index.htm. 05/31/14
[1120] http://www.history-of-the-holocaust.org/LIBARC/LIBRARY/Themes/Policy/Friedl2A.html. 05/31/14. See fn 80.
[1121] http://www.jrbooksonline.com/Intl_Jew_full_version/ij02.htm. 05/31/14. Article that quotes from the *Dearborn Independent*, 29 May 1920. 08/17/07
[1122] Watt, Richard, M. *The Kings Depart. The Tragedy of Germany: Versailles and the German Revolution* (Barnes & Noble Books, 2002, Barnes & Noble, Inc.), 196.
[1123] Gordon, Sarah. *Hitler, Germans, and the "Jewish Question"* (Princeton University Press, New Jersey, 1984), 108.
[1124] Ibid., 108–09.
[1125] Kaes, Martin; Jay, Martin; Dimendberg (Eds.). *The Weimar Republic SourceBook* (California: University of California Press, 1995), 36.
[1126] Kolb, Eberhard. *The Weimar Republic* (Routledge, New York, 1990), eBook. 14.
[1127] Deak, Istvan. *Weimar Germany's Left-Wing Intellectuals: A Political History of the Weltbüne and Its Circle* (University of California Press, Berkeley and Los Angeles, 1968), 209.
[1128] Broué, Pierre, et al. *The German Revolution 1917–1923* (Boston: Brill Academic Publishers, 2004), 231.
[1129] Bullock, Alan. *Hitler and Stalin* (New York: Vintage Books, 1993), 49.
[1130] Frölich, Paul. *Rosa Luxemburg: Her Life and Work*, translated by Johanna Hoornweg. (Monthly Review Press, New York, 1972), 276.

[1131] Tedor, Richard. *Hitler's Revolution: Ideology Social Programs Foreign Affairs* (Chicago, 2013), 153.
[1132] Watt, Richard, M., *The Kings Depart. The Tragedy of Germany: Versailles and the German Revolution* (Barnes & Noble Books, 2002, Barnes & Noble, Inc.), 237.
[1133] http://www.history-of-the-holocaust.org/LIBARC/LIBRARY/Themes/Policy/Friedl2A.html. 05/31/14
[1134] http://www.fsmitha.com/h2/ch09-sparticists.htm. 04/01/07
[1135] Watt, Richard, M., *The Kings Depart. The Tragedy of Germany: Versailles and the German Revolution* (Barnes & Noble Books, 2002, Barnes & Noble, Inc.), 223.
[1136] Ibid., 218.
[1137] Smoter, Walter Frank. *Adolf Hitler, The Making of a Fuhrer*. URL: http://smoter.com/revoluti.htm. 05/31/14
[1138] Watt, Richard, M., *The Kings Depart. The Tragedy of Germany: Versailles and the German Revolution* (Barnes & Noble Books, 2002, Barnes & Noble, Inc.), 254–55.
[1139] Ibid., 264–67.
[1140] Grange, William. *Cultural Chronicle of the Weimar Republic* (Metuchen: Scarecrow Press, 2008), 38.
[1141] Gay, Peter, *Weimar Culture: The Outsider as Insider* (W. W. Norton & Company, New York, 2001), Paperback, 13.
[1142] Toland, John. *Adolf Hitler* (Garden City: Anchor Books, 1992), 76.
[1143] Niewyk, Donald L., *The Jews in Weimar Germany* (Transaction Publishers, New Brunswick, 2001), 26.
[1144] Friedrich, Otto. *Before the Deluge* (New York: HarperPerennial, 1995), 47.
[1145] Pulzer, Peter. *Jews and the German State: The Political History of a Minority, 1848–1933* (Wayne State University Press, 2003), 208–09.
[1146] Lee, Stephen. *The Weimar Republic* (New York: Routledge, 1998), 17.
[1147] Gay, Peter. *Weimar Culture, The Outsider as an Insider* (W. W. Norton & Company, New York), Paperback, 17.
[1148] Ibid.
[1149] Elon, Amos. *The Pity of It All: A Portrait of the German-Jewish Epoch, 1743–1933* (New York: Holt, 2003), 356.
[1150] Niewyk, Donald L. *The Jews in Weimar Germany* (Transaction Publishers, New Brunswick, 2001), 142.
[1151] Ibid., 142–43.
[1152] Pulzer, Peter. *Jews and the German State: The Political History of a Minority, 1848–1933* (Wayne State University Press, 2003), 20.
[1153] http://en.wikipedia.org/wiki/Paul_von_Hindenburg. 05/31/14
[1154] http://en.wikipedia.org/wiki/Weimar_Republic. 05/31/14

[1155] Henig, Ruth. *The Weimar Republic: 1919–1933* (Routledge, New York, 1998).
[1156] Evans, Richard. *The Coming of the Third Reich* (New York: Penguin Books, 2004), 83.
[1157] Stolfi, R. H. S. *Hitler: Beyond Evil and Tyranny* (Prometheus Books, Amherst, New York, 2011), 235.
[1158] http://www.biblebelievers.org.au/witness1.htm#3. 05/31/14. The claim was cited from the *The Daily Mail*, July 10th, 1933.
[1159] Hitler's Speech, Munich, 1 August 1923.
[1160] http://www.serbianna.com/columns/savich/062.shtml. 05/31/14
[1161] http://www.serbianna.com/columns/savich/062.shtml. 05/31/14
[1162] Watt, Richard, M. *The Kings Depart. The Tragedy of Germany: Versailles and the German Revolution* (Barnes & Noble Books, 2002, Barnes & Noble, Inc.), 174.
[1163] http://www.marxists.org/archive/lenin/works/1918/nov/06a.htm. 05/31/14
[1164] http://www.biblebelievers.org.au/witness1.htm. 05/31/14. Taken from Hitler's closing speech, Nuremberg Congress of Honor.
[1165] Smoter, Walter Frank. *Adolf Hitler, The Making of a Fuhrer*. "denied." URL: http://smoter.com/hate&def.htm. 05/31/14
[1166] http://en.wikipedia.org/wiki/George_Mosse. 05/31/14
[1167] http://www.cassiopaea.org/cass/hostility-jews_3.htm. 05/31/14
[1168] Gordon, Sarah. *Hitler, Germans, and the "Jewish Question"* (Princeton University Press, New Jersey, 1984), 52.
[1169] Weitz, Eric. *Weimar Germany* (Princeton: Princeton University Press, 2009), 98.
[1170] MacDonald, Kevin. *Separation and Its Discontents* (2004), 83.
[1171] Elon, Amos. *The Pity of It All: A Portrait of the German-Jewish Epoch, 1743–1933* (New York: Holt, 2003), 346.
[1172] Ibid., 351.
[1173] Kauders, Anthony. *German Politics and the Jews: Düsseldorf and Nuremberg, 1910–1933* (Clarendon Press, Oxford, 1996), 84.
[1174] Ibid., 67.
[1175] https://www.google.com/search?q=Eugene+Levine-Nissen&rlz=1T4GZAB_enUS449US538&tbm=isch&tbo=u&source=univ&sa=X&ei=kGPfU9j6MYWQyAT-mYG4BQ&ved=0CB4QsAQ&biw=1008&bih=506#facrc=_&imgdii=_&imgrc=MXankhe19jh2aM%253A%3BPfH3cRyN9jkhNM%3Bhttp%253A%252F%252Fwww.bibliotecapleyades.net%252Fsociopolitica%252Fsignscorpion%252Fsignsc27.gif%3Bhttp%253A%252F%252Fwww.bibliotecapleyades.net%252Fsociopolitica%252Fsignscorpion%252Fsignscorpion07.htm%3B263%3B297. 8/2/14

[1176] https://www.google.com/search?q=Max+Levien&rlz=1T4GZAB_enUS449US5 38&tbm=isch&imgil=fET2pbNIQdR5fM%253A%253BpoExLCU75LhXLM%253Bhttp%25253A%25252F%25252Fthirdreichocculthistory.blogspot.com%25252F2014%25252F04%25252Fnational-socialism-and-occult-part-iii.html&source=iu&usg=__sPOsy1mtiLfnOGnMofBs2AOU8mk%3D&sa=X&ei=yWjfU7vTC4-OyAS3m4CAAQ&ved=0CCMQ9QEwAQ&biw=1008&bih=506#facrc=_&imgdii=_&imgrc=fET2pbNIQdR5fM%253A%3BpoExLCU75LhXLM%3Bhttp%253A%252F%252F1.bp.blogspot.com%252F-krHJbW3Ag2s%252FU1MUrXakN5I%252FAAAAAAAATgQ%252FJHPJB5pvACA%252Fs200%252FMax%252BLevien%252B-%252BNational%252BSocialism%252Band%252Bthe%252BOccult%252B-%252BThird%252BReich.png%3Bhttp%253A%252F%252Fthirdreichocculthistory.blogspot.com%252F2014%252F04%252Fnational-socialism-and-occult-part-iii.html%3B162%3B200. 8/2/14

[1177] Smoter, Walter Frank. *Adolf Hitler, The Making of a Fuhrer*. "recoil." URL: http://smoter.com/hate&def.htm. 05/31/14

[1178] http://www.firstworldwar.com/features/munich_five.htm. 05/31/14

[1179] Smoter, Walter Frank. *Adolf Hitler, The Making of a Fuhrer*. "Jew-Republic." URL: http://smoter.com/hate&def.htm. 05/31/14

[1180] Hitler, Adolf. *Mein Kampf* (Boston: Houghton Mifflin, 2001), 127.

[1181] Ibid., 127.

[1182] Ibid., 127.

[1183] Hamann, Brigitte. *Hitler's Vienna: A Dictator's Apprenticeship*. Trans. Thomas Thornton. (Oxford, NY, 2000), 395.

[1184] http://ellhn.e-e-e.gr/books/assets/founder_of_Israel.pdf. 05/31/14

[1185] Stolfi, R. H. S. *Hitler: Beyond Evil and Tyranny* (Prometheus Books, Amherst, New York, 2011), 152.

[1186] Ibid., 154.

[1187] Hitler's Speech, Munich, 13 April 1923.

[1188] Hitler's Speech, Munich, 18 September 1922. "Eisner said in 1918 that we had no right to demand the return of our prisoner—he was only saying openly what all Jews were thinking."

[1189] http://www.icons-multimedia.com/ClientsArea/HoH/LIBARC/LIBRARY/Themes/Policy/Friedl2A.html. 05/31/14

[1190] Pulzer, Peter. *Jews and the German State: The Political History of a Minority, 1848–1933* (Wayne State University Press, 2003), 241.

[1191] Ibid., 240–41.

[1192] Rosenbaum, Ron. *Explaining Hitler* (Harper Perennial edition, 1999), xxxviii.
[1193] Ibid., xxxvii.
[1194] Watt, Richard, M. *The Kings Depart. The Tragedy of Germany: Versailles and the German Revolution* (Barnes & Noble Books, 2002, Barnes & Noble, Inc.), 283.
[1195] Ibid., 185.
[1196] Ibid., 186.
[1197] Kauders, Anthony. *German Politics and the Jews: Düsseldorf and Nuremberg, 1910–1933* (Clarendon Press, Oxford, 1996), 116.
[1198] Kaes, Martin; Jay, Martin; Dimendberg (Eds.). *The Weimar Republic SourceBook* (California: University of California Press, 1995), 52.
[1199] http://www.angelfire.com/az3/goyim/communism. 05/31/14
[1200] http://www.firstworldwar.com/features/munich_two.htm. 05/31/14
[1201] Watt, Richard, M. *The Kings Depart. The Tragedy of Germany: Versailles and the German Revolution* (Barnes & Noble Books, 2002, Barnes & Noble, Inc.), 284.
[1202] Ibid., 284–85.
[1203] Frölich, Paul. *Rosa Luxemburg: Her Life and Work*. Translated by Johanna Hoornweg. (Monthly Review Press, New York, 1972), 99.
[1204] Watt, Richard, M. *The Kings Depart. The Tragedy of Germany: Versailles and the German Revolution* (Barnes & Noble Books, 2002, Barnes & Noble, Inc.), 289.
[1205] Pulzer, Peter. *Jews and the German State: The Political History of a Minority, 1848–1933* (Wayne State University Press, 2003), 165.
[1206] Watt, Richard, M. *The Kings Depart. The Tragedy of Germany: Versailles and the German Revolution* (Barnes & Noble Books, 2002, Barnes & Noble, Inc.), 289.
[1207] Hitler, Adolf. *Mein Kampf* (Boston: Houghton Mifflin, 2001), 557.
[1208] Watt, Richard, M. *The Kings Depart. The Tragedy of Germany: Versailles and the German Revolution* (Barnes & Noble Books, 2002, Barnes & Noble, Inc.), 281.
[1209] Ibid., 289–90.
[1210] http://www.firstworldwar.com/features/munich_three.htm. 05/31/14
[1211] http://www.firstworldwar.com/features/munich_three.htm. 05/31/14
[1212] http://www.firstworldwar.com/features/munich_three.htm. 05/31/14
[1213] http://www.firstworldwar.com/features/munich_three.htm. 05/31/14
[1214] Smoter, Walter Frank. *Adolf Hitler, The Making of a Fuhrer*. "whole revolution." URL: http://smoter.com/revoluti.htm. 05/31/14
[1215] Fest, Joachim. *Hitler* (San Diego: Harcourt, 2002), 110.

[1216] Watt, Richard, M. *The Kings Depart. The Tragedy of Germany: Versailles and the German Revolution* (Barnes & Noble Books, 2002, Barnes & Noble, Inc.), 294.
[1217] Ibid.
[1218] http://firstworldwar.com/features/munich_five.htm. 05/31/14
[1219] Fitzgerald, Michael. *Adolf Hitler: a Portrait* (Staplehurst: Spellmount, 2007), 12.
[1220] http://www.icons-multimedia.com/ClientsArea/HoH/LIBARC/LIBRARY/Themes/Policy/Friedl2A.html. 05/31/14
[1221] MacDonald, Kevin. *The Culture of Critique: An Evolutionary Analysis of Jewish Involvement in Twentieth-Century Intellectual and Political Movements* (Kevin MacDonald, 2002), Paperback. *The Culture of Critique* was originally published in 1998 by Praeger Publishers, an imprint of Greenwood Publishing Group, Inc., 99.
[1222] Ibid., 101.
[1223] http://www.serbianna.com/columns/savich/062.shtml. 05/31/14
[1224] Laqueur, Walter. *Weimar, A Cultural History* (G. P. Putnam's Sons, New York, 1974), 56.
[1225] Ibid., 58.
[1226] Toland, John. *Adolf Hitler* (Garden City: Anchor Books, 1992), 79.
[1227] http://en.wikipedia.org/wiki/B%C3%A9la_Kun. 05/31/14
[1228] Turner, Henry, and Ruth Hein. *Hitler—Memoirs of a Confidant* (New Haven: Yale University Press, 1987), 7.
[1229] http://en.wikipedia.org/wiki/Bela_Kun. 05/31/14
[1230] MacMillan, Margaret. *Paris 1919: Six Months that Changed the World* (Random House Trade Paperbacks, NY, 2003), 265.
[1231] Dillon, E. J., Dr. *The Inside Story of the Peace Conference* (Harper & Brothers, NY and London, 1920), 389.
[1232] Ibid., 390.
[1233] http://www.angelfire.com/az3/goyim/communism. 05/31/14. The quote is from historian John Toland's biography, *Adolf Hitler: The Definitive Biography*, 84.
[1234] http://en.wikipedia.org/wiki/Bela_Kun. 05/31/14
[1235] Fest, Joachim. *Hitler* (San Diego: Harcourt, 2002), 110.
[1236] Smoter, Walter Frank. *Adolf Hitler, The Making of a Fuhre.* "Bavarian Soviet." URL: http://smoter.com/revoluti.htm. 05/31/14
[1237] Watt, Richard, M. *The Kings Depart. The Tragedy of Germany: Versailles and the German Revolution* (Barnes & Noble Books, 2002, Barnes & Noble, Inc.), 326.

[1238] Bronner, Stephen Eric. 1995. *Persistent Memories of the German Revolution: The Jewish Activists of 1919*. Retrieved from URL: http://nova.wpunj.edu/newpolitics/issue18/bronne18.htm.
[1239] Watt, Richard, M. *The Kings Depart. The Tragedy of Germany: Versailles and the German Revolution* (Barnes & Noble Books, 2002, Barnes & Noble, Inc.), 326.
[1240] Author unknown. 2004. *Landauer, Gustav, 1970–1919*. Retrieved from URL: https://libcom.org/history/landauer-gustav-1870-1919
[1241] Evans, Richard. *The Coming of the Third Reich* (New York: Penguin Books, 2004), 159.
[1242] Fest, Joachim. *Hitler* (San Diego: Harcourt, 2002), 110.
[1243] Watt, Richard, M. *The Kings Depart. The Tragedy of Germany: Versailles and the German Revolution* (Barnes & Noble Books, 2002, Barnes & Noble, Inc.), 330.
[1244] http://www.firstworldwar.com/features/munich_three.htm. 05/31/14
[1245] http://en.wikipedia.org/wiki/Bavarian_Soviet_Republic. 05/31/14
[1246] http://www.firstworldwar.com/features/munich_three.htm. 05/31/14
[1247] Watt, Richard, M. *The Kings Depart. The Tragedy of Germany: Versailles and the German Revolution* (Barnes & Noble Books, 2002, Barnes & Noble, Inc.), 327.
[1248] Ibid., 328.
[1249] Smoter, Walter Frank. *Adolf Hitler, The Making of a Fuhrer*. "brothers." URL: http://smoter.com/revoluti.htm. 05/31/14
[1250] Watt, Richard, M. *The Kings Depart. The Tragedy of Germany: Versailles and the German Revolution* (Barnes & Noble Books, 2002, Barnes & Noble, Inc.), 327.
[1251] Evans, Richard. *The Coming of the Third Reich* (New York: Penguin Books, 2004), 160.
[1252] Bullock, Alan. *Hitler, A Study in Tyranny* (New York and Evanston: Harper & Row, 1964), 61.
[1253] Ibid., 61.
[1254] Standish, Russel, and Colin. 2001. *Two Beasts, Three Deadly Wounds, and Fourteen Popes*. Chapter 42, Pius XII—Part 1. Retrieved from URL: http://www.sundaylaw.net/books/other/standish/twobeasts/tb42.htm.
[1255] Fest, Joachim. *Hitler* (San Diego: Harcourt, 2002), 110–11.
[1256] Toland, John. *Adolf Hitler* (Garden City: Anchor Books, 1992), 76.
[1257] Peukert, Detlev. *The Weimar Republic* (New York: Hill and Wang, 1993), 160.
[1258] Toland, John. *Adolf Hitler* (Garden City: Anchor Books, 1992), 79.
[1259] Kershaw, Ian. *Hitler, 1889–1936* (New York: W. W. Norton, 1999), 114.
[1260] Ibid., 115.

[1261] Ibid., 120.
[1262] Ibid., 125.
[1263] Watt, Richard, M. *The Kings Depart. The Tragedy of Germany: Versailles and the German Revolution* (Barnes & Noble Books, 2002, Barnes & Noble, Inc.), 340.
[1264] Smoter, Walter Frank. *Adolf Hitler, The Making of a Fuhrer*, Chapter 13, "Hitler's cooperation." URL: http://smoter.com/revoluti.htm. 06/25/14
[1265] Watt, Richard, M. *The Kings Depart. The Tragedy of Germany: Versailles and the German Revolution* (Barnes & Noble Books, 2002, Barnes & Noble, Inc.), 329–30.
[1266] Toland, John. *Adolf Hitler* (Garden City: Anchor Books, 1992), 83.
[1267] Kauders, Anthony. *German Politics and the Jews: Düsseldorf and Nuremberg, 1910–1933* (Clarendon Press, Oxford, 1996), 58.
[1268] Ibid., 67.
[1269] Watt, Richard, M. *The Kings Depart. The Tragedy of Germany: Versailles and the German Revolution* (Barnes & Noble Books, 2002, Barnes & Noble, Inc.), 308.
[1270] Fest, Joachim. *Hitler* (San Diego: Harcourt, 2002), 126.
[1271] Kolb, Eberhard. *The Weimar Republic* (Routledge, New York, 1990), eBook, 53.
[1272] Kershaw, Ian. *The "Hitler Myth"* (Oxford University Press, Inc., Oxford, New York, 2001), 171.
[1273] Turner, Henry, and Ruth Hein. *Hitler—Memoirs of a Confidant* (New Haven: Yale University Press, 1987), 5.
[1274] Kershaw, Ian. *The "Hitler Myth"* (Oxford University Press, Inc., Oxford, New York, 2001), 172–73.
[1275] Tedor, Richard. *Hitler's Revolution: Ideology Social Programs Foreign Affairs* (Chicago, 2013), 20.
[1276] Fest, Joachim. *Hitler* (San Diego: Harcourt, 2002), 143.
[1277] Hitler, Adolf. *Mein Kampf* (Boston: Houghton Mifflin, 2001), 486.
[1278] Ibid., 357.
[1279] Stolfi, R. H. S. *Hitler: Beyond Evil and Tyranny* (Prometheus Books, Amherst, New York, 2011), 180.
[1280] http://www.hitler.org/speeches/11-09-21.html. 05/31/14
[1281] Stolfi, R. H. S. *Hitler: Beyond Evil and Tyranny* (Prometheus Books, Amherst, New York, 2011), 264.
[1282] Fest, Joachim. *Hitler* (San Diego: Harcourt, 2002), 175.
[1283] Bullock, Alan. *Hitler, A Study in Tyranny* (New York and Evanston: Harper & Row, 1964), 63.
[1284] Fest, Joachim. *Hitler* (San Diego: Harcourt, 2002), 211.
[1285] http://www.marxist.com/germany/chapter4.html. 05/31/14

[1286] http://www.marxist.com/germany/chapter4.html. 05/31/14
[1287] http://www.marxist.com/germany/chapter4.html. 05/31/14
[1288] http://www.marxists.org/archive/held-walter/1942/12/germrev.htm. 05/31/14
[1289] http://www.marxists.org/archive/held-walter/1942/12/germrev.htm. 05/31/14
[1290] http://en.wikipedia.org/wiki/inflation_in_the_Weimar_Republic. 05/31/14
[1291] Fest, Joachim. *Hitler* (San Diego: Harcourt, 2002), 164.
[1292] Toland, John. *Adolf Hitler* (Garden City: Anchor Books, 1992), 131–32.
[1293] Evans, Richard. *The Coming of the Third Reich* (New York: Penguin Books, 2004), 105.
[1294] Ibid., 111.
[1295] Fest, Joachim. *Hitler* (San Diego: Harcourt, 2002), 148.
[1296] Niewyk, Donald L. *The Jews in Weimar Germany* (Transaction Publishers, New Brunswick, 2001), 170.
[1297] Ibid.
[1298] Evans, Richard. *The Coming of the Third Reich* (New York: Penguin Books, 2004), 111.
[1299] Ibid., 112.
[1300] Toland, John. *Adolf Hitler* (Garden City: Anchor Books, 1992), 148–49.
[1301] Evans, Richard. *The Coming of the Third Reich* (New York: Penguin Books, 2004), 111–12.
[1302] Giblin, James, and Robert Payne. *The Life and Death of Adolf Hitler* (New York: Praeger, 1973), 36.
[1303] Bullock, Alan. *Hitler, A Study in Tyranny* (New York and Evanston: Harper & Row, 1964), 91.
[1304] Pulzer, Peter. *Jews and the German State: The Political History of a Minority, 1848–1933* (Wayne State University Press, 2003), 211.
[1305] Smoter, Walter Frank. *Adolf Hitler, The Making of a Fuhrer*, Chapter 1, "millions." URL: http://smoter.com/revoluti.htm. 06/25/14
[1306] Fest, Joachim. *Hitler* (San Diego: Harcourt, 2002), 219.
[1307] http://www.spartacus.schoolnet.co.uk/GERunemployment.htm. 05/31/14
[1308] Klatzkin, Jacob. 1921. This quotation is cited at a number of online sites, including: http://comedieus.blogspot.com/2009/01/seen-on-internet-re-journalistic.html.
[1309] Niewyk, Donald L. *The Jews in Weimar Germany* (Transaction Publishers, New Brunswick, 2001), 99.
[1310] http://www.simpletoremember.com/vitals/quotes.htm. 05/31/14. Quoting Ernest van den Haag, *The Jewish Mystique* (New York: Dell Publishing Company, 1971), 13.
[1311] Bilski, Emily D. *Berlin metropolis: Jews and the new culture, 1890–1918* (University of California Press, 1999), 16.

[1312] Ibid., 156.
[1313] Ibid., 166.
[1314] Weitz, Eric. *Weimar Germany* (Princeton: Princeton University Press, 2009), 270.
[1315] Stibbe, Matthew. *Germany, 1914–1933* (Pearson Education Limited, 2010), 207.
[1316] Dawidowicz, Lucy. *The War against the Jews, 1933–45* (Harmondsworth Eng.: Penguin, 1977), 51.
[1317] Grange, William. *Cultural Chronicle of the Weimar Republic*.(Metuchen: Scarecrow Press, 2008), x.
[1318] Ibid.
[1319] Goldensohn, Leon, and Robert Gellately. *The Nuremberg Interviews* (New York: Knopf, 2004).
[1320] Bilski, Emily D. *Berlin metropolis: Jews and the new culture, 1890–1918* (University of California Press, 1999), 19.
[1321] Haumann, Heiko. *A History of East European Jews* (Budapest: Central European University Press, 2002), 21.
[1322] Bilski, Emily D. *Berlin metropolis: Jews and the new culture, 1890–1918* (University of California Press, 1999), 63.
[1323] Spotts, Frederic. *Hitler and the Power of Aesthetics* (New York: Overlook Press, 2003), 151.
[1324] Bilski, Emily D. *Berlin metropolis: Jews and the new culture, 1890–1918* (University of California Press, 1999), 184.
[1325] Ibid., 184.
[1326] Ibid.
[1327] Laqueur, Walter. *Weimar, A Cultural History* (G. P. Putnam's Sons, New York, 1974), 111.
[1328] Ibid., 115.
[1329] Spotts, Frederic. *Hitler and the Power of Aesthetics* (New York: Overlook Press, 2003), 151.
[1330] Lindemann, Albert S. *Esau's Tears: Modern Anti-Semitism and the Rise of the Jews* (Cambridge University Press, Cambridge, U.K., 2000), Paperback Edition, 131.
[1331] Fest, Joachim. *Hitler* (San Diego: Harcourt, 2002), 93.
[1332] Ibid.
[1333] Kaes, Martin; Jay, Martin; Dimendberg (Eds.). *The Weimar Republic SourceBook* (California: University of California Press, 1995), 222.
[1334] Grange, William. *Cultural Chronicle of the Weimar Republic* (Metuchen: Scarecrow Press, 2008), 4.
[1335] MacDonald, Kevin. *Separation and Its Discontents toward an Evolutionary Theory of Anti-Semitism* (S. L.: 1stBooks Library, 2003), 34.

[1336] Lindemann, Albert S. *Esau's Tears: Modern Anti-Semitism and the Rise of the Jews* (Cambridge University Press, Cambridge, U.K., 2000), 195.
[1337] Weitz, Eric. *Weimar Germany* (Princeton: Princeton University Press, 2009), 39.
[1338] Weitz, Eric. *Weimar Germany* (Princeton: Princeton University Press, 2009), 59. See also Kolb, Eberhard. *The Weimar Republic* (Routledge, New York, 1990), eBook, 113.
[1339] Fest, Joachim. *Hitler* (San Diego: Harcourt, 2002), 99.
[1340] Weitz, Eric. *Weimar Germany* (Princeton: Princeton University Press, 2009), 76.
[1341] Fest, Joachim. *Hitler* (San Diego: Harcourt, 2002), 101.
[1342] http://www.biblebelievers.org.au/witness1.htm. 05/31/14
[1343] Brenner, Lenni. *51 Documents, Zionist Collaboration with the Nazis* (Fort Lee, Barricade Books, 2002), 58.
[1344] http://en.wikipedia.org/wiki/Weimar_culture.
[1345] Deak, Istvan. *Weimar Germany's Left-Wing Intellectuals: A Political History of the Weltbüne and Its Circle* (University of California Press, Berkeley and Los Angeles, 1968), 28.
[1346] Hitler, Adolf. *Mein Kampf*. Trans. Ralph Manheim. (Houghton Mifflin Company, Boston/NY, 1999), First Mariner Books edition, 59.
[1347] Gordon, Sarah. *Hitler, Germans, and the "Jewish Question"* (Princeton University Press, New Jersey, 1984), 27.
[1348] John, Robert. *Behind the Balfour Declaration*. Torrance: Institute for Historical Review, 1988, 35. John is quoting from Hess's *Rome and Jerusalem* (1862).
[1349] http://swiki.hfbk-hamburg.de:8888/Lebensreform/98. 05/31/14
[1350] James, Harold. *Europe Reborn* (London: Pearson/Longman, 2003), 37.
[1351] Gordon, Sarah. *Hitler, Germans, and the "Jewish Question"* (Princeton University Press, New Jersey, 1984), 14.
[1352] http://swiki.hfbk-hamburg.de:8888/Lebensreform/98. 05/31/14
[1353] Gay, Peter. *Weimar Culture: The Outsider as Insider* (W. W. Norton & Company, New York, 2001), Paperback, 132.
[1354] Wiehe, Friederich Karl, Dr. *Germany and the Jewish Question*, Institute for Studies of the Jewish Question, Berlin (1938).
[1355] Gay, Peter. *Weimar Culture: The Outsider as Insider*, W. W. Norton & Company, New York, 2001), Paperback, vi.
[1356] Ibid.
[1357] Ibid., xiv.
[1358] Niewyk, Donald L. *The Jews in Weimar Germany* (Transaction Publishers, New Brunswick, 2001), 33.

[1359] Lindemann, Albert S. *Esau's Tears: Modern Anti-Semitism and the Rise of the Jews* (Cambridge University Press, Cambridge, U.K., 2000), Paperback Edition, 120.
[1360] Bilski, Emily D. *Berlin metropolis: Jews and the new culture, 1890–1918* (University of California Press, 1999), 234.
[1361] Deak, Istvan, *Weimar Germany's Left-Wing Intellectuals: A Political History of the Weltbüne and Its Circle* (University of California Press, Berkeley and Los Angeles, 1968), 28.
[1362] Ibid., 28.
[1363] Evans, Richard. *The Coming of the Third Reich* (New York: Penguin Books, 2004), 126.
[1364] MacDonald, Kevin. *The Culture of Critique: An Evolutionary Analysis of Jewish Involvement in Twentieth-Century Intellectual and Political Movements* (City: Authorhouse, 2002), 8.
[1365] MacDonald, Kevin. *Separation and Its Discontents toward an Evolutionary Theory of Anti-Semitism* (S. L.: 1stBooks Library, 2003), 83.
[1366] Pulzer, Peter. *Jews and the German State: The Political History of a Minority, 1848–1933* (Wayne State University Press, 2003), 343.
[1367] Spotts, Frederic. *Hitler and the Power of Aesthetics* (New York. Overlook Press, 2003), xxi.
[1368] Fischer, Conan. *The Rise of the Nazis*. 2nd ed. (Manchester University Press, Manchester and New York. 2002), 41–42.
[1369] Williams, John. *Corporal Hitler and the Great War 1914–1918* (London: Frank Cass, 2005), 76–77.
[1370] Goldensohn, Leon, and Robert Gellately. *The Nuremberg Interviews* (New York: Knopf, 2004), 132.
[1371] Deak, Istvan. *Weimar Germany's Left-Wing Intellectuals: A Political History of the Weltbüne and Its Circle* (University of California Press, Berkeley and Los Angeles, 1968), 44.
[1372] Hitler, Adolf. *Mein Kampf* (Boston: Houghton Mifflin, 2001), x.
[1373] Lindemann, Albert. *Anti-Semitism before the Holocaust* (New York: Longman, 2000), 57.
[1374] Fest, Joachim. *Hitler* (San Diego: Harcourt, 2002), 96.
[1375] Roderich-Stoltheim, F. *The Riddle of the Jew's Success* (RePortersNoteBook.com, NY, 2005.) Translated from the German by Capel Pownall. Originally published by Hammer-Verlag, Leipzig, 1927, 207.
[1376] Gay, Peter. *Weimar Culture: The Outsider as Insider*. (W. W. Norton & Company, New York, 2001), Paperback. Gay is quoting Friedrich Meinecke.
[1377] Trevor-Roper, Hugh. *Hitler's Table Talk, 1941–1944* (New York, Enigma Books, 2000), 82.

[1378] Spotts, Frederic. *Hitler and the Power of Aesthetics* (New York: Overlook Press, 2003), 28.
[1379] Pulzer, Peter. *The Rise of Political Anti-Semitism in Germany & Austria* (Cambridge: Harvard University Press, 1988), 291.
[1380] Jones, E. *Degenerate Moderns* (San Francisco: Ignatius, 1993), 53.
[1381] Pulzer, Peter. *The Rise of Political Anti-Semitism in Germany & Austria* (Cambridge: Harvard University Press, 1988), 315.
[1382] Lindemann, Albert S. *Esau's Tears: Modern Anti-Semitism and the Rise of the Jews* (Cambridge University Press, Cambridge, U.K., 2000), 118.
[1383] Fest, Joachim. *Hitler* (San Diego: Harcourt, 2002), 379.
[1384] Ibid., 382.
[1385] Ibid.
[1386] Trevor-Roper, Hugh. *Hitler's Table Talk, 1941–1944* (New York, Enigma Books, 2000), xxiii.
[1387] http://en.wikipedia.org/wiki/Culture_and_Anarchy. 05/31/14
[1388] Gay, Peter. *Weimar Culture: The Outsider as Insider* (W. W. Norton & Company, New York, 2001), 3.
[1389] Ibid.
[1390] Kershaw, Ian. *The "Hitler Myth"* (Oxford University Press, Inc., Oxford, New York, 2001), 270.
[1391] Goldensohn, Leon, and Robert Gellately. *The Nuremberg Interviews* (New York: Knopf, 2004), 122.
[1392] Petropoulos, Jonathan. *Art as Politics in the Third Reich* (The University of North Carolina Press, Chapel Hill & London, 1996), 289.
[1393] Gilbert, G. *Nuremberg Diary* (New York: Da Capo Press, 1995), 31.
[1394] Kershaw, Ian. *The "Hitler Myth"* (Oxford University Press, Inc., Oxford New York, 2001), 271.
[1395] Etlin, Richard A. (Editor) *Art, Culture, and Media under the Third Reich* (University of Chicago Press, Chicago, 2002).
[1396] Steinweis, Alan. *Art, Ideology, & Economics in Nazi Germany* (Chapel Hill: The University of North Carolina Press, 1993), 11.
[1397] Etlin, Richard A. (Editor) *Art, Culture, and Media Under the Third Reich* (University of Chicago Press, Chicago, 2002), 53.
[1398] http://www.commentarymagazine.com/viewarticle.cfm/Hitler-s-Accompanist-11028. 05/31/14
[1399] Goldensohn, Leon, and Robert Gellately. *The Nuremberg Interviews* (New York: Knopf, 2004), 108.
[1400] http://www.commentarymagazine.com/viewarticle.cfm/Hitler-s-Accompanist-11028. 05/31/14. S. Friedlaender "Redemptive Anti-Semitism." Source: S. Friedlaender, Chapter 3 in: *Nazi Germany and the Jews, Vol. I, The Years of Persecution 1933–1939* (New York, 1997), 73–112.

[1401] Hamann, Brigitte. *Hitler's Vienna: A Dictator's Apprenticeship*. Trans. Thomas Thornton. (Oxford, NY, 2000), Paperback Edition, 144.
[1402] Bullock, Alan. *Hitler and Stalin* (New York: Vintage Books, 1993), 10.
[1403] Hitler, Adolf. *Mein Kampf* (Boston: Houghton Mifflin, 2001), 303.
[1404] Sachs, D. 1992. p. 21. Retrieved from URL: http://jewise.wordpress.com/2009/02/06/jewish-tribal-review-2/. This is an anti-Semitic site.
[1405] Niewyk, Donald L. *The Jews in Weimar Germany* (Transaction Publishers, New Brunswick, 2001), 38.
[1406] http://corndancer.com/vox/deutsch/lesesaal/weimar/weimar_whois/weimarwho.html. 05/31/14
[1407] Evans, Richard. *The Coming of the Third Reich* (New York: Penguin Books, 2004), 124.
[1408] Etlin, Richard A. (Editor) *Art, Culture, and Media under the Third Reich* (University of Chicago Press, Chicago, 2002).
[1409] Roderich-Stoltheim, F. *The Riddle of the Jew's Success* (RePortersNoteBook.com, NY, 2005.) Translated from the German by Capel Pownall. Originally published by Hammer-Verlag, Leipzig, 1927, 141–42.
[1410] Ibid., 142.
[1411] Ibid., 10.
[1412] Spotts, Frederic. *Hitler and the Power of Aesthetics* (New York: Overlook Press, 2003), 267.
[1413] Ibid., 268.
[1414] Ibid., 270.
[1415] Ibid., 32.
[1416] Hamann, Brigitte. *Hitler's Vienna: A Dictator's Apprenticeship*. Trans. Thomas Thornton. (Oxford, NY, 2000), 62.
[1417] Ibid.
[1418] Petropoulos, Jonathan. *Art as Politics in the Third Reich* (The University of North Carolina Press, Chapel Hill & London, 1996), 267.
[1419] Ibid., 188.
[1420] Ibid., 181.
[1421] http://www.personal.psu.edu/faculty/j/x/jxz8/Student_Webquests/Farber/trailo.html. 05/31/14
[1422] Petropoulos, Jonathan. *Art as Politics in the Third Reich* (The University of North Carolina Press, Chapel Hill & London, 1996), 247.
[1423] Salmi, Hannu. *Nineteenth-Century Europe* (Cambridge: Polity, 2008), 66.
[1424] Ibid., 3.

[1425] Bilski, Emily D. *Berlin metropolis: Jews and the new culture, 1890–1918* (University of California Press, 1999), 179.
[1426] Spotts, Frederic. *Hitler and the Power of Aesthetics* (New York: Overlook Press, 2003), 176.
[1427] Fest, Joachim. *Hitler* (San Diego: Harcourt, 2002), 96.
[1428] Spotts, Frederic. *Hitler and the Power of Aesthetics* (New York: Overlook Press, 2003), 321.
[1429] Petropoulos, Jonathan. *Art as Politics in the Third Reich* (The University of North Carolina Press, Chapel Hill & London, 1996), 23.
[1430] Spotts, Frederic. *Hitler and the Power of Aesthetics* (New York: Overlook Press, 2003), 107–08.
[1431] Kershaw, Ian. *Hitler, 1889–1936* (New York: W. W. Norton, 1999), 52.
[1432] Speer, Albert. *Spandau: The Secret Diaries.* Translated from German by Richard and Clara Winston. (New York: Pocket Books, 1976), 444–45.
[1433] Etlin, Richard A. (Editor) *Art, Culture, and Media under the Third Reich* (University of Chicago Press, Chicago, 2002), 62.
[1434] http://thecensureofdemocracy.150m.com/art5.htm. 05/31/14
[1435] Spotts, Frederic. *Hitler and the Power of Aesthetics* (New York: Overlook Press, 2003), 88.
[1436] Fitzgerald, Michael. *Adolf Hitler: a Portrait* (Staplehurst: Spellmount, 2007), 36.
[1437] http://thecensureofdemocracy.150m.com/art5.htm. 05/31/14
[1438] http://thecensureofdemocracy.150m.com/art5.htm. 05/31/14
[1439] Hitler's Speech to the Court, Munich, 26 April 1924.
[1440] Spotts, Frederic. *Hitler and the Power of Aesthetics* (New York: Overlook Press, 2003), 400.
[1441] Fest, Joachim. *Hitler* (San Diego: Harcourt, 2002), 104.
[1442] Kaes, Martin; Jay, Martin; Dimendberg (Eds.). *The Weimar Republic SourceBook* (California: University of California Press, 1995), 222–23.
[1443] Pulzer, Peter. *The Rise of Political Anti-Semitism in Germany & Austria* (Cambridge: Harvard University Press, 1988), 54.
[1444] Hitler, Adolf. *Mein Kampf* (Boston: Houghton Mifflin, 2001), 326.
[1445] Turner, Henry, and Ruth Hein. *Hitler—Memoirs of a Confidant* (New Haven: Yale University Press, 1987), 142.
[1446] Spotts, Frederic. *Hitler and the Power of Aesthetics* (New York: Overlook Press, 2003), 17.
[1447] Fest, Joachim. *Hitler* (San Diego: Harcourt, 2002), 99.
[1448] Ibid., 94.
[1449] Metzger, Rainer, and Christian Brandstätter. Clara Costa, trans. *Berlin, the Twenties* (Harry N. Abrams, Inc., New York, 2007), 364.

[1450] Spotts, Frederic. *Hitler and the Power of Aesthetics* (New York: Overlook Press, 2003), 158.
[1451] Ibid., 152.
[1452] Ibid., 159.
[1453] Ibid., 159.
[1454] Hitler, Adolf. Reichstag Speech, Berlin, March 23, 1933.
[1455] http://www.icons-multimedia.com/ClientsArea/HoH/LIBARC/LIBRARY/Themes/Policy/Friedl2B.html. 05/31/14S. Friedlaender "Redemptive Anti-Semitism" Source: S. Friedlaender, Chapter 3 in: *Nazi Germany and the Jews , Vol. I, The Years of Persecution 1933–1939* (New York, 1997), 73–112.
[1456] Lindemann, Albert. *The Jew Accused* (Cambridge: Cambridge University Press, 1991), 207.
[1457] Petropoulos, Jonathan. *Art as Politics in the Third Reich* (The University of North Carolina Press, Chapel Hill & London, 1996), 53–54.
[1458] Salmi, Hannu. *Nineteenth-Century Europe* (Cambridge: Polity, 2008), 75.
[1459] Hitler, Adolf. *Mein Kampf.*(Boston: Houghton Mifflin, 2001), 58.
[1460] http://www.hitler.org/writings/first_writing. 05/31/14
[1461] Hamann, Brigitte. *Hitler's Vienna: A Dictator's Apprenticeship*. Trans. Thomas Thornton. (Oxford, NY, 2000), 84.
[1462] Spotts, Frederic. *Hitler and the Power of Aesthetics* (New York: Overlook Press, 2003), 159.
[1463] Kaes, Anton; Jay, Martin; Dimendberg, Edward (Eds.). *The Weimar Republic SourceBook* (California: University of California Press, 1995), 474.
[1464] Petropoulos, Jonathan. *Art as Politics in the Third Reich* (The University of North Carolina Press, Chapel Hill & London, 1996), 243.
[1465] Ibid., 47.
[1466] Ibid., 48.
[1467] Ibid., 45.
[1468] Kaes, Martin; Jay, Martin; Dimendberg (Eds.) *The Weimar Republic SourceBook* (California: University of California Press, 1995), 483.
[1469] Spotts, Frederic. *Hitler and the Power of Aesthetics* (New York: Overlook Press, 2003), 278.
[1470] Hitler, Adolf. *Mein Kampf* (Boston: Houghton Mifflin, 2001), 262–63.
[1471] Ibid., 262.
[1472] http://cla.calpoly.edu/~mriedlsp/History437/Art/Entartete%20Kunst.htm. 05/31/14
[1473] https://www.google.com/search?q=Painting,+%22All+Their+Worldly+Goods%22&sa=N&rlz=1T4GZAB_enUS449US538&tbm=isch&tbo=u&source=univ&ei=ftLfU6CEBceQyASluYGYCQ&ved=0CGoQsAQ4Cg&biw=1008&bih=506#

facrc=_&imgdii=_&imgrc=YQTNLO0NwLCAlM%253A%3B2O7mDi2k5gL0
RM%3Bhttp%253A%252F%252Fwww.thepaganfront.com%252Fbrangolf%25
2Fgallery%252FDeutschland%252Fizob%252FKunst%252FPainting%252FAd
olf%252520Reich%252FAdolf%252520Reich%252520-
%252520All%252520Their%252520Worldly%252520Goods%252C%2525201
940.jpg%3Bhttp%253A%252F%252Fwww.thepaganfront.com%252Fbrangolf
%252Fgallery%252Fgallgermpaintar.htm%3B489%3B538. 8/2/114
[1474]

https://www.google.com/search?q=German+painting+%22Farm+Girls+Returni
ng+from+the+Fields%22&rlz=1T4GZAB_enUS449US538&tbm=isch&imgil=
Dbrh7g_lYxKBoM%253A%253BIudPcnDh12XLEM%253Bhttp%25253A%25
252F%25252Ffranklin.davidson.edu%25252Facademic%25252Fgerman%2525
2Fbuhenke%25252Fart%25252Fdefault.html&source=iu&usg=__Tfi2EcSRXI9
gl3uJrlLbXswJ73g%3D&sa=X&ei=oNTfU4K9MseXyASeqoDwAQ&ved=0C
CEQ9QEwAA&biw=1008&bih=506#facrc=_&imgdii=_&imgrc=Dbrh7g_lYx
KBoM%253A%3BIudPcnDh12XLEM%3Bhttp%253A%252F%252Ffranklin.d
avidson.edu%252Facademic%252Fgerman%252Fbuhenke%252Fart%252Fima
ges%252Fpaint_schmutzler_arbeitsmaiden.jpg%3Bhttp%253A%252F%252Ffra
nklin.davidson.edu%252Facademic%252Fgerman%252Fbuhenke%252Fart%25
2Fdefault.html%3B801%3B618. 8/2/14

[1475] Kaes, Martin; Jay, Martin; Dimendberg (Eds.) *The Weimar Republic SourceBook* (California: University of California Press, 1995), 485.

[1476] https://www.google.com/search?q=Marzella,+1909,+by+Ernst+Ludwig+Kirchn
er&rlz=1T4GZAB_enUS449US538&tbm=isch&imgil=-
jGc1f9TlRINpM%253A%253BTx3jvneJfQCnKM%253Bhttp%25253A%25252
F%25252Fwww.pinterest.com%25252Fpin%25252F324751823101128940%25
252F&source=iu&usg=__EBco3l1zpGNGmGOkUAD5vBpir6E%3D&sa=X&ei
=vtbfU77JL8eeyAS87YH4Dg&ved=0CCMQ9QEwAA&biw=1008&bih=523#f
acrc=_&imgdii=_&imgrc=-
jGc1f9TlRINpM%253A%3BTx3jvneJfQCnKM%3Bhttp%253A%252F%252F
www.kingsacademy.com%252Fmhodges%252F11_Western-
Art%252F26_20th-Century-
Experimentalism%252FKirchner_1909_Marzella_PLZ-
162.jpg%3Bhttp%253A%252F%252Fwww.pinterest.com%252Fpin%252F3247
51823101128940%252F%3B1479%3B1894. 8/2/14

[1477] https://www.google.com/search?q=Actresses,+Max+Beckmann&rlz=1T4GZAB
_enUS449US538&tbm=isch&imgil=jAILkvLfPb5J8M%253A%253BN0NFwO
7T-
zFmYM%253Bhttp%25253A%25252F%25252Fwww.leninimports.com%2525

2Fmax_beckmann.html&source=iu&usg=__r5Gs6ci4A_r4tr8sO5oMDTMcGaY
%3D&sa=X&ei=FNffU6LYBseMyAT5j4HADA&ved=0CCEQ9QEwAA&biw
=1008&bih=523#facrc=_&imgdii=_&imgrc=jAILkvLfPb5J8M%253A%3BN0
NFwO7T-
zFmYM%3Bhttp%253A%252F%252Fwww.leninimports.com%252Fmax_beck
mann_actressess_art_print_medium.jpg%3Bhttp%253A%252F%252Fwww.leni
nimports.com%252Fmax_beckmann.html%3B178%3B244. 8/2/14

[1478] http://www.freerepublic.com/focus/news/769982/posts. 05/31/14
[1479] Hitler, Adolf. *Mein Kampf* (Boston: Houghton Mifflin, 2001), 258.
[1480] http://www.csulb.edu/~kmacd/newtimes.html. 05/31/14
[1481] Deak, Istvan. *Weimar Germany's Left-Wing Intellectuals: A Political History of the Weltbüne and Its Circle* (University of California Press, Berkeley and Los Angeles, 1968), 116.
[1482] Bilski, Emily D. *Berlin metropolis: Jews and the new culture, 1890–1918* (University of California Press, 1999), 228.
[1483] Pulzer, Peter. *Jews and the German State: The Political History of a Minority, 1848–1933* (Wayne State University Press, 2003), 209.
[1484] Grange, William. *Cultural Chronicle of the Weimar Republic* (Metuchen: Scarecrow Press, 2008), 57.
[1485] MacDonald, Kevin, Ph.D. 2004. *Separation and Its Discontents: Toward an Evolutionary Theory of Anti-Semitism*. Retrieved from URL: https://archive.org/stream/SeparationAndItsDiscontents/SeparationAndItsDiscontents_djvu.txt
[1486] http://majorityrights.com/index.php/weblog/comments/more_holocaust_coercion_and_a_word_of_advice/. 05/31/14
[1487] Friedrich, Otto. *Before the Deluge* (New York: HarperPerennial, 1995), 111.
[1488] http://en.wikipedia.org/wiki/Bruno_Walter. 05/31/14
[1489] Lindemann, Albert S. *Esau's Tears: Modern Anti-Semitism and the Rise of the Jews* (Cambridge University Press, Cambridge, U.K., 2000), 193.
[1490] Bilski, Emily D. *Berlin metropolis: Jews and the new culture, 1890–1918* (University of California Press, 1999), 15.
[1491] Ibid.
[1492] Niewyk, Donald L. *The Jews in Weimar Germany* (Transaction Publishers, New Brunswick, 2001), 43.
[1493] MacDonald, Kevin. *Separation and Its Discontents: Toward an Evolutionary Theory of Anti-Semitism* (S. L.: 1stBooks Library, 2003), 60.
[1494] http://www.aish.com/literacy/jewishhistory/Crash_Course_in_Jewish_History_Part_53_-_The_Enlightenment.asp. 05/31/14

[1495] MacDonald, Kevin. *Separation and Its Discontents: Toward an Evolutionary Theory of Anti-Semitism* (S. L.: 1stBooks Library, 2003), 61.
[1496] Ibid.
[1497] Lindemann, Albert S. *Esau's Tears: Modern Anti-Semitism and the Rise of the Jews* (Cambridge University Press, Cambridge, U.K., 2000), 132.
[1498] Ibid., 91.
[1499] MacDonald, Kevin. *Separation and Its Discontents: Toward an Evolutionary Theory of Anti-Semitism* (S. L.: 1stBooks Library, 2003), 61.
[1500] Ibid., 60–61.
[1501] MacDonald, Kevin. *The Culture of Critique: An Evolutionary Analysis of Jewish Involvement in Twentieth-Century Intellectual and Political Movements* (Kevin MacDonald, 2002), Paperback, 89.
[1502] Hitler Munich Speech of 18 September 1922.
[1503] Deak, Istvan. *Weimar Germany's Left-Wing Intellectuals: A Political History of the Weltbüne and Its Circle* (University of California Press, Berkeley and Los Angeles), 102.
[1504] MacDonald, Kevin. *The Culture of Critique: An Evolutionary Analysis of Jewish Involvement in Twentieth-Century Intellectual and Political Movements* (Kevin MacDonald, 2002), Paperback, 90.
[1505] Bilski, Emily D. *Berlin metropolis: Jews and the new culture, 1890–1918* (University of California Press, 1999), 181. The essay is by Inka Bertz.
[1506] Bilski, Emily D. *Berlin metropolis: Jews and the new culture, 1890–1918* (University of California Press, 1999), 157–58.
[1507] Ibid., 160.
[1508] Pulzer, Peter. *Jews and the German State: The Political History of a Minority, 1848–1933* (Wayne State University Press, 2003), 30.
[1509] MacDonald, Kevin. *The Culture of Critique: An Evolutionary Analysis of Jewish Involvement in Twentieth-Century Intellectual and Political Movements* (Kevin MacDonald, 2002), 106.
[1510] Pulzer, Peter. *Jews and the German State: The Political History of a Minority, 1848–1933* (Wayne State University Press, 2003), 65.
[1511] http://www.icons-multimedia.com/ClientsArea/HoH/LIBARC/LIBRARY/Themes/Policy/Friedl2A.html. 05/31/14
[1512] Deak, Istvan. *Weimar Germany's Left-Wing Intellectuals: A Political History of the Weltbüne and Its Circle* (University of California Press, Berkeley and Los Angeles, 1968), 15.
[1513] Lindemann, Albert S. *Esau's Tears: Modern Anti-Semitism and the Rise of the Jews* (Cambridge University Press, Cambridge, U.K., 2000), 118–19.
[1514] Gay, Peter. *Weimar Culture: The Outsider as Insider* (W. W. Norton & Company, New York, 2001), 16.

[1515] Metzger, Rainer, and Christian Brandstätter. Clara Costa, trans. *Berlin, the Twenties* (Harry N. Abrams, Inc., New York, 2007), 251.
[1516] Gay, Peter. *Weimar Culture: The Outsider as Insider* (W. W. Norton & Company, New York, 2001), 109.
[1517] Degenerate Art Exhibition. (2014, March 24). In *Wikipedia, The Free Encyclopedia*. Retrieved 14:30, June 2, 2014, from http://en.wikipedia.org/w/index.php?title=Degenerate_Art_Exhibition&oldid=601065614.
[1518] Spotts, Frederic. *Hitler and the Power of Aesthetics* (New York: Overlook Press, 2003), 165.
[1519] Cowley, Jason. "New Statesman." Date of pub. unk. A review of Brigitte Hamann's book, *Hitler's Vienna*. Retrieved from URL: http://www.newstatesman.com/node/134640.
[1520] Salsitz, Norman. 19912. *A Jewish Boyhood in Poland: Remembering Kolbuszowa*. Retrieved from URL: http://books.google.com/books?id=CrxSwLSkMBsC&pg=PA88&lpg=PA88&dq=%22all+across+Poland+the+peasant+was+held+in+almost+universal+contempt%22&source=bl&ots=kt80REqjGc&sig=IoumDpkWzt3CRNZTmZTFRxOU3nU&hl=en&sa=X&ei=frCNU9_3EoPmsATF9oGwBA&ved=0CCgQ6AEwAQ#v=onepage&q=%22all%20across%20Poland%20the%20peasant%20was%20held%20in%20almost%20universal%20contempt%22&f=false.
[1521] Roderich-Stoltheim, F. *The Riddle of the Jew's Success* (RePortersNoteBook.com, NY, 2005.) Translated from the German by Capel Pownall. Originally published by Hammer-Verlag, Leipzig, 1927. 150–51.
[1522] Bilski, Emily D. *Berlin metropolis: Jews and the new culture, 1890–1918* (University of California Press, 1999), 34.
[1523] Ibid., 4.
[1524] Ibid., 5.
[1525] Ibid., 29.
[1526] Ibid., 33.
[1527] Ibid., 61.
[1528] Ibid., 59.
[1529] Ibid., 82.
[1530] Kaes, Martin; Jay, Martin; Dimendberg (Eds.). *The Weimar Republic SourceBook* (California: University of California Press, 1995), 490–91.
[1531] Hitler's Speech, Munich, 12 September 1923.
[1532] http://en.wikipedia.org/wiki/Degenerate_art. 05/31/14
[1533] MacDonald, Kevin. *Separation and Its Discontents toward an Evolutionary Theory of Anti-Semitism* (S. L.: 1stBooks Library, 2003), 60.
[1534] Kaes, Martin; Jay, Martin; Dimendberg (Eds.). *The Weimar Republic SourceBook* (California: University of California Press, 1995), 507–08.

[1535] Stibbe, Matthew. *Germany, 1914–1933* (Pearson Education Limited, 2010), 150.
[1536] Evans, Richard. *The Coming of the Third Reich* (New York: Penguin Books, 2004), 133–34.
[1537] Elon, Amos. *The Pity of It All: A Portrait of the German-Jewish Epoch, 1743–1933* (New York: Holt, 2003), 7.
[1538] Deak, Istvan. *Weimar Germany's Left-Wing Intellectuals: A Political History of the Weltbüne and Its Circle* (University of California Press, Berkeley and Los Angeles, 1968), 129.
[1539] Hitler, Adolf. *Mein Kampf* (Boston: Houghton Mifflin, 2001), 242–43.
[1540] Bilski, Emily D. *Berlin metropolis: Jews and the new culture, 1890–1918* (University of California Press, 1999), 3.
[1541] http://en.wikipedia.org/wiki/Georg_Heym. 05/31/14
[1542] Bilski, Emily D. *Berlin metropolis: Jews and the new culture, 1890–1918* (University of California Press, 1999), 234.
[1543] Grange, William. *Cultural Chronicle of the Weimar Republic* (Metuchen: Scarecrow Press, 2008), 15.
[1544] Bilski, Emily D. *Berlin metropolis: Jews and the new culture, 1890–1918* (University of California Press, 1999), 66.
[1545] Ibid,. 30.
[1546] Ibid.
[1547] Ibid., 6.
[1548] Ibid., 132–33.
[1549] Ibid., 133.
[1550] Ibid., 134–35, 137.
[1551] Ibid., 153.
[1552] Ibid., 6.
[1553] Ibid., 121.
[1554] Ibid., 153.
[1555] Ibid., 10.
[1556] Ibid., 8.
[1557] Ibid., 28.
[1558] Ibid., 181.
[1559] Grange, William. *Cultural Chronicle of the Weimar Republic* (Metuchen: Scarecrow Press, 2008), 46.
[1560] http://en.wikipedia.org/wiki/Ludwig_Meidner. 05/31/14
[1561] http://www.answers.com/topic/max-oppenheimer-2. 05/31/14
[1562] Tedor, Richard. *Hitler's Revolution: Ideology Social Programs Foreign Affairs* (Chicago, 2013), 25–6.
[1563] Gordon, Mel. *Voluptuous Panic: The Erotic World of Weimar Berlin*, Expanded Edition (Feral House, Los Angeles, 2006), 193.

[1564] Ibid., 42.
[1565] Evans, Richard. *The Coming of the Third Reich* (New York: Penguin Books, 2004), 128.
[1566] Kaes, Martin; Jay, Martin; Dimendberg (Eds.). *The Weimar Republic SourceBook* (California: University of California Press, 1995), 694.
[1567] Evans, Richard. *The Coming of the Third Reich* (New York: Penguin Books, 2004), 128.
[1568] Gay, Peter. *Weimar Culture: The Outsider as Insider* (W. W. Norton & Company, New York, 2001), Paperback, 7.
[1569] MacDonald, Kevin. *Separation and Its Discontents toward an Evolutionary Theory of Anti-Semitism* (S. L.: 1stBooks Library, 2003), 238.
[1570] Gordon, Mel. *Voluptuous Panic: The Erotic World of Weimar Berlin*, Expanded Edition (Feral House, Los Angeles, 2006), 21.
[1571] http://www.recess.ufl.edu/transcripts/2007/0820.shtml. 05/31/14
[1572] http://en.wikipedia.org/wiki/Josefine_Mutzenbacher. 05/31/14
[1573] http://en.wikipedia.org/wiki/Josefine_Mutzenbacher. 05/31/14
[1574] http://en.wikipedia.org/wiki/Josefine_Mutzenbacher. 05/31/14
[1575] Metzger, Rainer, and Christian Brandstätter. Clara Costa, trans. *Berlin, the Twenties* (Harry N. Abrams, Inc., New York, 2007), 126.
[1576] Kaes, Martin; Jay, Martin; Dimendberg (Eds.). *The Weimar Republic SourceBook* (California: University of California Press, 1995), 530.
[1577] Grange, William. *Cultural Chronicle of the Weimar Republic* (Metuchen: Scarecrow Press, 2008), 326.
[1578] http://www.scrapbookpages.com/EasternGermany/Weimar. 05/31/14
[1579] Hamann, Brigitte. *Hitler's Vienna: A Dictator's Apprenticeship*. Trans. Thomas Thornton (Oxford, NY, 2000), 75.
[1580] Hitler, Adolf. *Mein Kampf* (Boston: Houghton Mifflin, 2001), 544.
[1581] Friedrich, Otto. *Before the Deluge* (New York: HarperPerennial, 1995), 248.
[1582] Hitler, Adolf. *Mein Kampf* (Boston: Houghton Mifflin, 2001), 57–58.
[1583] Lindemann, Albert S. *Esau's Tears: Modern Anti-Semitism and the Rise of the Jews* (Cambridge University Press, Cambridge, U.K., 2000), 193–94.
[1584] Ibid., 193–94.
[1585] Laqueur, Walter. *Weimar, A Cultural History* (G. P. Putnam's Sons, New York, 1974), 51.
[1586] Metzger, Rainer, and Christian Brandstätter. Clara Costa, trans. *Berlin, the Twenties* (Harry N. Abrams, Inc., New York, 2007), 317–18.
[1587] Gay, Peter. *Weimar Culture: The Outsider as Insider* (W. W. Norton & Company, New York, 2001), 135.
[1588] Ibid., 134.
[1589] Metzger, Rainer, and Christian Brandstätter. Clara Costa, trans. *Berlin, the Twenties* (Harry N. Abrams, Inc., New York, 2007), 365.

[1590] Pulzer, Peter. *Jews and the German State: The Political History of a Minority, 1848–1933* (Wayne State University Press, 2003), 171.
[1591] Fest, Joachim. *Hitler* (San Diego: Harcourt, 2002), 94.
[1592] Ibid.
[1593] http://en.wikipedia.org/wiki/Secular_Jewish_culture. 05/31/14
[1594] Gordon, Mel. *The Seven Addictions and Five Professions of Anita Berber* (Venice: Feral House, 2006), 41.
[1595] Bilski, Emily D. *Berlin metropolis: Jews and the new culture, 1890–1918* (University of California Press, 1999), 223.
[1596] Grange, William. *Cultural Chronicle of the Weimar Republic* (Metuchen: Scarecrow Press, 2008), 9.
[1597] http://www.threepennyopera.org/quotes.php. 05/31/14
[1598] Grange, William. *Cultural Chronicle of the Weimar Republic* (Metuchen: Scarecrow Press, 2008), 294.
[1599] Gordon, Mel. *The Seven Addictions and Five Professions of Anita Berber* (Venice: Feral House, 2006), 55.
[1600] Deak, Istvan. *Weimar Germany's Left-Wing Intellectuals: A Political History of the Weltbüne and Its Circle* (University of California Press, Berkeley and Los Angeles, 1968), 31–32.
[1601] Ibid., 33.
[1602] http://en.wikipedia.org/wiki/Alfred_Kerr. 05/31/14
[1603] Bilski, Emily D. *Berlin metropolis: Jews and the new culture, 1890–1918* (University of California Press, 1999), 82.
[1604] Hitler, Adolf. *Mein Kampf* (Boston: Houghton Mifflin, 2001), 254.
[1605] Fest, Joachim. *Hitler* (San Diego: Harcourt, 2002), 140.
[1606] Hitler, Adolf. *Mein Kampf* (Boston: Houghton Mifflin, 2001), 254.
[1607] Wiehe, Karl, Ph.D. *Germany and the Jewish Question. Berlin*, Section 7. (1938). Note: This is a Nazi publication.
[1608] Hamann, Brigitte. *Hitler's Vienna: A Dictator's Apprenticeship*. Trans. Thomas Thornton. (Oxford, NY, 2000), 369.
[1609] Ankum, Katharina. *Women in the Metropolis* (Berkeley: University of California Press, 1997), 4.
[1610] Hamann, Brigitte. *Hitler's Vienna: A Dictator's Apprenticeship*. Trans. Thomas Thornton. (Oxford, NY, 2000), 372.
[1611] Gordon, Mel. *The Seven Addictions and Five Professions of Anita Berber* (Venice: Feral House, 2006), 53–54.
[1612] http://www2.facinghistory.org/Campus/weimar.nsf/e3385d83e5b7492785256c6f004e878a/$FILE/Weimar_Rationale.PDF. 05/31/14
[1613] Ankum, Katharina. *Women in the Metropolis* (Berkeley: University of California Press, 1997), 1.
[1614] Ibid., 2.

[1615] Ibid., 3.
[1616] Kaes, Martin; Jay, Martin; Dimendberg (Eds.). *The Weimar Republic SourceBook* (California: University of California Press, 1995), 196.
[1617] Etlin, Richard A. (Editor) *Art, Culture, and Media Under the Third Reich* (University of Chicago Press, Chicago, 2002), 236.
[1618] Spotts, Frederic. *Hitler and the Power of Aesthetics* (New York: Overlook Press, 2003), 329.
[1619] Ibid., 2003.
[1620] Ibid., 340.
[1621] Kolb, Eberhard. *The Weimar Republic* (Routledge, New York, 1990), eBook, 110.
[1622] Kaes, Martin; Jay, Martin; Dimendberg (Eds.). *The Weimar Republic SourceBook* (California: University of California Press, 1995), 429.
[1623] Weitz, Eric. *Weimar Germany* (Princeton: Princeton University Press, 2009), 200.
[1624] Jones, Michael. *Living Machines* (San Francisco: Ignatius Press, 1995), 82.
[1625] Kaes, Martin; Jay, Martin; Dimendberg (Eds.). *The Weimar Republic SourceBook* (California: University of California Press, 1995), 432–34.
[1626] Lindemann, Albert S. *Esau's Tears: Modern Anti-Semitism and the Rise of the Jews* (Cambridge University Press, Cambridge, U.K., 2000), 117.
[1627] Fest, Joachim. *Hitler* (San Diego: Harcourt, 2002), 94.
[1628] Jones, Michael. *Living Machines* (San Francisco: Ignatius Press, 1995), 82.
[1629] Ibid., 67.
[1630] Ibid., 107.
[1631] Speer, Albert. *Spandau: The Secret Diaries*. Translated from German by Richard and Clara Winston. (Pocket Books, New York,1976), 122–23.
[1632] Kubizek, August. *The Young Hitler I Knew* (London: Greenhill Books, 2006). Abridged edition first published in English, 1954, by Allan Wingate Publishers Ltd., 178.
[1633] Etlin, Richard A. (Editor) *Art, Culture, and Media Under the Third Reich* (University of Chicago Press, Chicago, 2002), 209–10.
[1634] Spotts, Frederic. *Hitler and the Power of Aesthetics* (New York: Overlook Press, 2003), 12–13.
[1635] Hamann, Brigitte. *Hitler's Vienna: A Dictator's Apprenticeship*. Trans. Thomas Thornton. (Oxford, NY, 2000), 71–72.
[1636] Metzger, Rainer, and Christian Brandstätter. Clara Costa, trans. *Berlin, the Twenties* (Harry N. Abrams, Inc., New York, 2007), 68–69.
[1637] Ibid., 140–41.
[1638] Ibid., 214.
[1639] Jones, Michael. *Living Machines* (San Francisco: Ignatius Press, 1995), 85–86.

[1640] Speer, Albert. *Spandau: The Secret Diaries*. Translated from German by Richard and Clara Winston. (New York: Pocket Books, 1976), 301.
[1641] Kuspit, Donald. *A Critical History of 20th-Century Art*. Chapter 3, Part 3. Published in "*Artnet* Magazine." Retrieved from URL: http://www.artnet.com/magazineus/authors/kuspit1.asp.
[1642] Kaes, Martin; Jay, Martin; Dimendberg (Eds.). *The Weimar Republic SourceBook* (California: University of California Press, 1995), 468–69.
[1643] Kuspit, Donald. *A Critical History of 20th-Century Art*. Chapter 3, Part 3. Published in "*Artnet* Magazine." Retrieved from URL: http://www.artnet.com/magazineus/authors/kuspit1.asp.
[1644] Steinweis, Alan. *Art, Ideology, & Economics in Nazi Germany* (Chapel Hill: The University of North Carolina Press, 1993), 175.
[1645] Jones, Michael. *Living Machines* (San Francisco: Ignatius Press, 1995), 54–55.
[1646] Ibid., 56.
[1647] Ibid., 57.
[1648] Fest, Joachim. *Hitler* (San Diego: Harcourt, 2002), 94.
[1649] Bilski, Emily D. *Berlin metropolis: Jews and the new culture, 1890–1918* (University of California Press, 1999), 11.
[1650] MacDonald, Kevin. *The Culture of Critique: An Evolutionary Analysis of Jewish Involvement in Twentieth-Century Intellectual and Political Movements* (Kevin MacDonald, 2002), 163.
[1651] Kaes, Anton, et al. *The Weimar Republic Sourcebook* (Berkeley: University of California Press, 1995), 561.
[1652] Friedrich, Otto. *Before the Deluge* (New York: HarperPerennial, 1995), 129.
[1653] Fest, Joachim. *Hitler* (San Diego: Harcourt, 2002), 178.
[1654] Bilski, Emily D. *Berlin metropolis: Jews and the new culture, 1890–1918* (University of California Press, 1999), 226–27.
[1655] Kaes, Anton, et al. *The Weimar Republic Sourcebook* (Berkeley: University of California Press, 1995), 561.
[1656] Ibid., 561.
[1657] Gay, Peter. *Weimar Culture: The Outsider as Insider* (W. W. Norton & Company, New York, 2001), Paperback, 129–30.
[1658] Friedrich, Otto. *Before the Deluge* (New York: HarperPerennial, 1995), 120.
[1659] http://www.everything2.com/index.pl?node_id=1706168. 05/31/14
[1660] Gordon, Mel. *Voluptuous Panic: The Erotic World of Weimar Berlin*. Expanded Edition. (Feral House, Los Angeles, 2006) ix.
[1661] http://www.everything2.com/index.pl?node_id=1706168. 05/31/14
[1662] Evans, Richard. *The Coming of the Third Reich* (New York: Penguin Books, 2004), 125.

[1663] Gordon, Mel. *Voluptuous Panic: The Erotic World of Weimar Berlin.* Expanded Edition. (Feral House, Los Angeles, 2006), 30.
[1664] Ibid., x.
[1665] http://search.barnesandnoble.com/booksearch/isbnInquiry.asp?z=&EAN=9781932595123&itm. 05/31/14
[1666] http://search.barnesandnoble.com/booksearch/isbnInquiry.asp?z=y&EAN=9781932595123&itm=7. 05/31/14
[1667] Gordon, Mel. *Voluptuous Panic: The Erotic World of Weimar Berlin.* Expanded Edition. (Feral House, Los Angeles, 2006), 1–2.
[1668] Ibid., 1.
[1669] Niewyk, Donald L. *The Jews in Weimar Germany* (Transaction Publishers, New Brunswick, 2001), 67.
[1670] Ibid., 64.
[1671] Wiehe, Friederich Karl, Dr. *Germany and the Jewish Question*, Institute for Studies of the Jewish Question, Berlin (1938). See also, Niewyk, Donald L. *The Jews in Weimar Germany* (Transaction Publishers, New Brunswick, 2001), 64, 67.
[1672] Henig, Ruth. *The Weimar Republic: 1919–1933* (Routledge, New York, 1998), 43.
[1673] http://www.sheynin.de/download/humb.pdf. 05/31/14. Oscar Sheynin, "Gumbel, Einstein and Russia." Moscow. *Sputnik*, 2003.
[1674] http://www.sheynin.de/download/humb.pdf. 05/31/14
[1675] Wiehe, Friederich Karl, Dr. *Germany and the Jewish Question*, Institute for Studies of the Jewish Question, Berlin (1938).
[1676] Finkelstein, Norman. *Beyond Chutzpah* (Berkeley: University of California Press, 2008), 108.
[1677] Elon, Amos. *The Pity of It All: A Portrait of the German-Jewish Epoch, 1743–1933* (New York: Holt, 2003), 368.
[1678] Conot, Robert E. *Justice at Nuremberg* (Harper & Row, Publishers, Inc., New York, New York), 78.
[1679] Irving, David. *Goebbels: Mastermind of the Third Reich* (London: Focal Point, 1996), 94.
[1680] Steinweis, Alan. *Art, Ideology, & Economics in Nazi Germany* (Chapel Hill: The University of North Carolina Press, 1993), 30.
[1681] http://www.israelect.com/reference/WillieMartin/1111.htm. 05/31/14
[1682] Turner, Henry, and Ruth Hein. *Hitler—Memoirs of a Confidant* (New Haven: Yale University Press, 1987), 64.
[1683] Laqueur, Walter. *Weimar, A Cultural History* (G. P. Putnam's Sons, New York, 1974), 13.

[1684] Goldensohn, Leon, and Robert Gellately. *The Nuremberg Interviews* (New York: Knopf, 2004), 158.
[1685] Gordon, Sarah. *Hitler, Germans, and the "Jewish Question"* (Princeton University Press, New Jersey, 1984), 13.
[1686] Niewyk, Donald L. *The Jews in Weimar Germany* (Transaction Publishers, New Brunswick, 2001), 75.
[1687] http://www.sheynin.de/download/humb.pdf. 05/31/14
[1688] Deak, Istvan. *Weimar Germany's Left-Wing Intellectuals: A Political History of the Weltbüne and Its Circle* (University of California Press, Berkeley and Los Angeles, 1968), 15.
[1689] Ibid., 24–25.
[1690] MacDonald, Kevin. *The Culture of Critique: An Evolutionary Analysis of Jewish Involvement in Twentieth-Century Intellectual and Political Movements* (City: Authorhouse, 2002), 8.
[1691] Deak, Istvan. *Weimar Germany's Left-Wing Intellectuals: A Political History of the Weltbüne and Its Circle* (University of California Press, Berkeley and Los Angeles, 1968), 23.
[1692] Ibid., 86.
[1693] Ibid., 5.
[1694] Kaes, Martin; Jay, Martin; Dimendberg (Eds.). *The Weimar Republic SourceBook* (California: University of California Press, 1995), 193.
[1695] Deak, Istvan. *Weimar Germany's Left-Wing Intellectuals: A Political History of the Weltbüne and Its Circle* (University of California Press, Berkeley and Los Angeles, 1968), 7.
[1696] Ibid., 88.
[1697] http://en.wikipedia.org/wiki/Weltb%C3%BChne. 05/31/14
[1698] Deak, Istvan. *Weimar Germany's Left-Wing Intellectuals: A Political History of the Weltbüne and Its Circle* (University of California Press, Berkeley and Los Angeles, 1968), 77–78.
[1699] Ibid., 71–72.
[1700] Ibid., 75.
[1701] Ibid., 90.
[1702] Ibid., 111.
[1703] Ibid., 53.
[1704] Ibid., 54.
[1705] Ibid., 59.
[1706] Metzger, Rainer, and Christian Brandstätter. Clara Costa, trans. *Berlin, the Twenties* (Harry N. Abrams, Inc., New York, 2007), 67.
[1707] Deak, Istvan. *Weimar Germany's Left-Wing Intellectuals: A Political History of the Weltbüne and Its Circle* (University of California Press, Berkeley and Los Angeles, 1968), 52.

[1708] Ibid., 52–53.
[1709] Gay, Peter. *Weimar Culture: The Outsider as Insider* (W. W. Norton & Company, New York, 2001), Paperback, 88.
[1710] Deak, Istvan. *Weimar Germany's Left-Wing Intellectuals: A Political History of the Weltbüne and Its Circle* (University of California Press, Berkeley and Los Angeles, 1968), 192.
[1711] http://nobelprize.org/nobel_prizes/peace/laureates/1935/ossietzky-bio.html. 05/31/14
[1712] Deak, Istvan. *Weimar Germany's Left-Wing Intellectuals: A Political History of the Weltbüne and Its Circle* (University of California Press, Berkeley and Los Angeles, 1968), Fn, 199.
[1713] http://swiki.hfbk-hamburg.de:8888/Lebensreform/98. 05/31/14 "Weimar—The left wing intellectuals," from Walter Laqueur, "Weimar—a cultural history 1918–1933."
[1714] Deak, Istvan. *Weimar Germany's Left-Wing Intellectuals: A Political History of the Weltbüne and Its Circle* (University of California Press, Berkeley and Los Angeles, 1968), 45.
[1715] MacDonald, Kevin. *The Culture of Critique: An Evolutionary Analysis of Jewish Involvement in Twentieth-Century Intellectual and Political Movements* (City: Authorhouse, 2002), 8.
[1716] Niewyk, Donald L. *The Jews in Weimar Germany* (Transaction Publishers, New Brunswick, 2001), 169–70.
[1717] Deak, Istvan. *Weimar Germany's Left-Wing Intellectuals: A Political History of the Weltbüne and Its Circle* (University of California Press, Berkeley and Los Angeles, 1968), 46.
[1718] Ibid., 43.
[1719] Ibid., 43.
[1720] Ibid., 41.
[1721] Kaes, Anton, et al. *The Weimar Republic Sourcebook* (Berkeley: University of California Press, 1995), 96.
[1722] Deak, Istvan. *Weimar Germany's Left-Wing Intellectuals: A Political History of the Weltbüne and Its Circle* (University of California Press, Berkeley and Los Angeles, 1968), 42.
[1723] Ibid., 37.
[1724] Ibid., 43.
[1725] Niewyk, Donald L. *The Jews in Weimar Germany* (Transaction Publishers, New Brunswick, 2001), 37.
[1726] Deak, Istvan. *Weimar Germany's Left-Wing Intellectuals: A Political History of the Weltbüne and Its Circle* (University of California Press, Berkeley and Los Angeles, 1968), 35.
[1727] http://en.wikipedia.org/wiki/Kurt_Hiller. 05/31/14

[1728] http://swiki.hfbk-hamburg.de:8888/Lebensreform/98.05/31/14
[1729] hhttp://swiki.hfbk-hamburg.de:8888/Lebensreform/98. 05/31/14
[1730] Bookbinder, Paul (Professor). Date of pub. unk. "Why Study Weimar Germany?" Retrieved from URL: https://www.facinghistory.org/weimar-republic-fragility-democracy/why-study-weimar-germany.
[1731] Deak, Istvan. *Weimar Germany's Left-Wing Intellectuals: A Political History of the Weltbüne and Its Circle* (University of California Press, Berkeley and Los Angeles, 1968), 13.
[1732] Brenner, Lenni. *Zionism in the Age of the Dictators* (London: Croom Helm, 1983), 7–8.
[1733] Hitler's Speech, Munich, 13 April 1923.
[1734] Pulzer, Peter. *Jews and the German State: The Political History of a Minority, 1848–1933* (Wayne State University Press, 2003), 113.
[1735] Ibid., 113.
[1736] Hamann, Brigitte. *Hitler's Vienna: A Dictator's Apprenticeship*. Trans. Thomas Thornton (Oxford, NY, 2000), 336.
[1737] Bilski, Emily D. *Berlin metropolis: Jews and the new culture, 1890–1918* (University of California Press, 1999), 15.
[1738] Ibid.
[1739] Pulzer, Peter. *Jews and the German State: The Political History of a Minority, 1848–1933* (Wayne State University Press, 2003), xix.
[1740] Gay, Peter. *Weimar Culture: The Outsider as Insider* (W. W. Norton & Company, New York, 2001), Paperback, 122.
[1741] Niewyk, Donald L. *The Jews in Weimar Germany* (Transaction Publishers, New Brunswick, 2001), 34.
[1742] Evans, Richard. *The Coming of the Third Reich* (New York: Penguin Books, 2004), 127.
[1743] http://www.calvin.edu/academic/cas/gpa/arier.htm#anchor2149693. 05/31/14
[1744] http://www.kevinmacdonald.net/SlezkineRev.pdf. (MacDonald's review of Slezkine's *The Jewish Century*. 04/26/07
[1745] http://www.calvin.edu/academic/cas/gpa/angrif02.htm. 05/31/14
[1746] http://stormfront.org/truth_at_last/archives/julius.htm. 05/31/14
[1747] http://www.solargeneral.com/library/TheJewAsCriminal.pdf. 12/12/08
[1748] Pulzer, Peter. *Jews and the German State: The Political History of a Minority, 1848–1933* (Wayne State University Press, 2003), 18.
[1749] Ibid., 21.
[1750] Niewyk, Donald L. *The Jews in Weimar Germany* (Transaction Publishers, New Brunswick, 2001), 41.
[1751] Ibid., 41.
[1752] http://www.aip.org/history/einstein/public1.htm. 05/31/14

[1753] Hamann, Brigitte. *Hitler's Vienna: A Dictator's Apprenticeship*. Trans. Thomas Thornton. (Oxford, NY, 2000), Paperback Edition, 81.
[1754] Gordon, Mel. *Voluptuous Panic: The Erotic World of Weimar Berlin*. Expanded Edition. (Feral House, Los Angeles, 2006), 253.
[1755] Petropoulos, Jonathan. *Art as Politics in the Third Reich* (The University of North Carolina Press, Chapel Hill & London, 1996), 243.
[1756] Ibid., 244.
[1757] Spotts, Frederic. *Hitler and the Power of Aesthetics* (New York: Overlook Press, 2003), 307.
[1758] Gordon, Sarah. *Hitler, Germans, and the "Jewish Question"* (Princeton University Press, New Jersey, 1984), 253.
[1759] Spotts, Frederic. *Hitler and the Power of Aesthetics* (New York: Overlook Press, 2003), 340.
[1760] http://www.conservapedia.com/Hitler. 05/31/14
[1761] http://www.conservapedia.com/Hitler. 05/31/14
[1762] Fest, Joachim. *Hitler* (San Diego: Harcourt, 2002), 262.
[1763] Giblin, James, and Robert Payne. *The Life and Death of Adolf Hitler* (New York: Praeger, 1973), 87–88.
[1764] Fest, Joachim. *Hitler* (San Diego: Harcourt, 2002), 367.
[1765] Williams, John. *Corporal Hitler and the Great War 1914–1918* (London: Frank Cass, 2005), 7.
[1766] Tedor, Richard. *Hitler's Revolution: Ideology Social Programs Foreign Affairs* (Chicago, 2013), 42.
[1767] Bullock, Alan. *Hitler, A Study in Tyranny* (New York and Evanston: Harper & Row, 1964), 178.
[1768] Weitz, Eric. *Weimar Germany* (Princeton: Princeton University Press, 2009), 274.
[1769] Nicholls, Anthony. *Weimar and the Rise of Hitler* (London: Macmillan Press, 2000), 120.
[1770] Bullock, Alan. *Hitler and Stalin* (New York: Vintage Books, 1993), 159.
[1771] Brustein, William. *The Logic of Evil* (New Haven: Yale University Press, 1996), 65–66.
[1772] Lee, Stephen. *The Weimar Republic* (New York: Routledge, 1998), 65.
[1773] Laqueur, Walter. *Weimar, A Cultural History* (G. P. Putnam's Sons, New York, 1974), 25.
[1774] Ibid., 27.
[1775] Brenner, Lenni. *Zionism in the Age of the Dictators* (London: Croom Helm, 1983), 27.
[1776] Bullock, Alan. *Hitler and Stalin* (New York: Vintage Books, 1993), 217.
[1777] Nicholls, Anthony. *Weimar and the Rise of Hitler* (London: Macmillan Press, 2000), 175.

[1778] Henig, Ruth. *The Weimar Republic: 1919–1933* (Routledge, New York, 1998), 64.
[1779] Peukert, Detlev. *The Weimar Republic* (New York: Hill and Wang, 1993), 233–34.
[1780] Kaes, Martin; Jay, Martin; Dimendberg (Eds.). *The Weimar Republic SourceBook* (California: University of California Press, 1995), 418–420.
[1781] Peukert, Detlev. *The Weimar Republic* (New York: Hill and Wang, 1993), 189.
[1782] Fischer, Conan. *The Rise of the Nazis*, 2nd ed. (Manchester University Press, Manchester and New York, 2002), 8.
[1783] Elon, Amos. *The Pity of It All: A Portrait of the German-Jewish Epoch, 1743–1933* (New York: Holt, 2003), 355.
[1784] Kauders, Anthony. *German Politics and the Jews: Düsseldorf and Nuremberg, 1910–1933* (Clarendon Press, Oxford, 1996), 182.
[1785] Peukert, Detlev. *The Weimar Republic* (New York: Hill and Wang, 1993), 268.
[1786] Deak, Istvan. *Weimar Germany's Left-Wing Intellectuals: A Political History of the Weltbüne and Its Circle* (University of California Press, Berkeley and Los Angeles, 1968), 137.
[1787] Lee, Stephen. *The Weimar Republic* (New York: Routledge, 1998), 102.
[1788] http://www.marxists.org/archive/trotsky/germany/index.htm. 05/31/14
[1789] Deak, Istvan. *Weimar Germany's Left-Wing Intellectuals: A Political History of the Weltbüne and Its Circle* (University of California Press, Berkeley and Los Angeles, 1968), 183.
[1790] http://www.spartacus.schoolnet.co.uk/GERunemployment.htm. 05/31/14
[1791] Bullock, Alan. *Hitler and Stalin* (New York: Vintage Books, 1993), 219.
[1792] Fest, Joachim. *Hitler* (San Diego: Harcourt, 2002), 151.
[1793] Ibid., 269.
[1794] Ibid., 314.
[1795] Bullock, Alan. *Hitler and Stalin* (New York: Vintage Books, 1993), 167.
[1796] Fest, Joachim. *Hitler* (San Diego: Harcourt, 2002), 104.
[1797] Bullock, Alan. *Hitler and Stalin* (New York: Vintage Books, 1993), 77.
[1798] Fest, Joachim. *Hitler* (San Diego: Harcourt, 2002), 292.
[1799] Fitzgerald, Michael. *Adolf Hitler: a Portrait* (Staplehurst: Spellmount, 2007), 93.
[1800] Ibid., 84.
[1801] Fest, Joachim. *Hitler* (San Diego: Harcourt, 2002), 311.
[1802] Giblin, James, and Robert Payne. *The Life and Death of Adolf Hitler*. New York: Praeger, 1973. p. 64.
[1803] Brustein, William. *The Logic of Evil* (New Haven: Yale University Press, 1996), 96.

[1804] Roderich-Stoltheim, F. *The Riddle of the Jew's Success* (RePortersNoteBook.com, NY, 2005.) Translated from the German by Capel Pownall. Originally published by Hammer-Verlag, Leipzig, 1927, 175.
[1805] Berkowitz, Michael. *The Crime of My Very Existence* (Berkeley: University of California Press, 2007), 5.
[1806] Ibid., 10.
[1807] Lindemann, Albert. *The Jew Accused* (Cambridge: Cambridge University Press, 1991), 69–70.
[1808] Ibid., 67.
[1809] Niewyk, Donald L. *The Jews in Weimar Germany* (Transaction Publishers, New Brunswick, 2001), 115.
[1810] Ibid.
[1811] Ibid.
[1812] Kauders, Anthony. *German Politics and the Jews: Düsseldorf and Nuremberg, 1910–1933* (Clarendon Press, Oxford, 1996), 151.
[1813] Lindemann, Albert. *The Jew Accused* (Cambridge: Cambridge University Press, 1991), 150.
[1814] http://en.wikipedia.org/wiki/Barmat_Scandal. 05/31/14
[1815] Kauders, Anthony. *German Politics and the Jews: Düsseldorf and Nuremberg, 1910–1933* (Clarendon Press, Oxford, 1996), 126.
[1816] Ibid., 151.
[1817] Ibid., 126.
[1818] http://en.wikipedia.org/wiki/Barmat_Scandal. 05/31/14
[1819] Niewyk, Donald L. *The Jews in Weimar Germany* (Transaction Publishers, New Brunswick, 2001), 77.
[1820] Peukert, Detlev. *The Weimar Republic* (New York: Hill and Wang, 1993), 173.
[1821] http://bookrags.com/biography/erich-maria-remarque. 05/31/14
[1822] http://www.kevinmacdonald.net/SlezkineRev.pdf. 05/31/14
[1823] Fest, Joachim. *Hitler* (San Diego: Harcourt, 2002), 357.
[1824] Fitzgerald, Michael. *Adolf Hitler: a Portrait* (Staplehurst: Spellmount, 2007), 93.
[1825] Ehrt, Adolf. *Communism in Germany* (The Noontide Press, Costa Mesa, CA, 1990 Reprint Edition), 29–30.
[1826] Ibid., 167–68.
[1827] Ibid., 101.
[1828] Ibid., 164–65.
[1829] Tedor, Richard. *Hitler's Revolution: Ideology Social Programs Foreign Affairs* (Chicago, 2013), 188.
[1830] Stolfi, R. H. S. *Hitler: Beyond Evil and Tyranny* (Prometheus Books, Amherst, New York, 2011), 121.

[1831] Stibbe, Matthew. *Germany, 1914–1933* (Pearson Education Limited, 2010), 75–76.
[1832] Kershaw, Ian. *The "Hitler Myth"* (Oxford University Press, Inc., Oxford, New York, 2001), 52.
[1833] Giblin, James, and Robert Payne. *The Life and Death of Adolf Hitler* (New York: Praeger, 1973), 73.
[1834] Ibid., 73.
[1835] Turner, Henry, and Ruth Hein. *Hitler—Memoirs of a Confidant* (New Haven: Yale University Press, 1987), 71.
[1836] Niewyk, Donald L. *The Jews in Weimar Germany* (Transaction Publishers, New Brunswick, 2001), 130.
[1837] Fest, Joachim. *Hitler* (San Diego: Harcourt, 2002), 92.
[1838] Ibid., 91.
[1839] Bullock, Alan. *Hitler, A Study in Tyranny* (New York and Evanston: Harper & Row, 1964), 88.
[1840] Fest, Joachim. *Hitler* (San Diego: Harcourt, 2002), 143.
[1841] Toland, John. *Adolf Hitler* (Garden City: Anchor Books, 1992), 251.
[1842] Bullock, Alan. *Hitler and Stalin* (New York: Vintage Books, 1993), 242.
[1843] Fest, Joachim. *Hitler* (San Diego: Harcourt, 2002), 339.
[1844] Evans, Richard. *The Coming of the Third Reich* (New York: Penguin Books, 2004), 296.
[1845] Tedor, Richard. *Hitler's Revolution: Ideology Social Programs Foreign Affairs* (Chicago, 2013), 90.
[1846] Evans, Richard. *The Coming of the Third Reich* (New York: Penguin Books, 2004), 265.
[1847] Gordon, Mel. *Voluptuous Panic: The Erotic World of Weimar Berlin.* Expanded Edition. (Feral House, Los Angeles, 2006), 253–54.
[1848] http://www.authorityresearch.com/2006-04%20Deductive-Inductive%20Reasoning%20Part%20II.htm. 05/31/14
[1849] Lindemann, Albert S. *Esau's Tears: Modern Anti-Semitism and the Rise of the Jews* (Cambridge University Press, Cambridge, U.K., 2000), Paperback Edition, 156.
[1850] Pulzer, Peter. *Jews and the German State: The Political History of a Minority, 1848–1933* (Wayne State University Press, 2003), 266.
[1851] Niewyk, Donald L. *The Jews in Weimar Germany* (Transaction Publishers, New Brunswick, 2001).
[1852] Weitz, Eric. *Weimar Germany* (Princeton: Princeton University Press, 2009), 85.
[1853] Stibbe, Matthew. *Germany, 1914–1933* (Pearson Education Limited, 2010), 175.

[1854] Evans, Richard. *The Coming of the Third Reich* (New York: Penguin Books, 2004), 289.
[1855] Petropoulos, Jonathan. *Art as Politics in the Third Reich* (The University of North Carolina Press, Chapel Hill & London, 1996), 30.
[1856] Pulzer, Peter. *Jews and the German State: The Political History of a Minority, 1848–1933* (Wayne State University Press, 2003), 241.
[1857] http://www.webster.edu/~corbetre/philosophy/vienna/reigen-schnitzler.html. 05/31/14
[1858] Wiehe, Karl Friederich, Ph.D. 1938. Published for the "Institute for Studies of the Jewish Question." This is a Nazi publication. Retrieved from URL: http://www.controversyofzion.info/germany_jewish_question.htm.
[1859] Deak, Istvan. *Weimar Germany's Left-Wing Intellectuals: A Political History of the Weltbüne and Its Circle* (University of California Press, Berkeley and Los Angeles, 1968), 117.
[1860] Niewyk, Donald L. *The Jews in Weimar Germany* (Transaction Publishers, New Brunswick, 2001), 130.
[1860] Pulzer, Peter. *Jews and the German State: The Political History of a Minority, 1848–1933* (Wayne State University Press, 2003), 164.
[1861] MacDonald, Kevin. *Separation and Its Discontents: Toward an Evolutionary Theory of Anti-Semitism* (S. L.: 1stBooks Library, 2003), 187.
[1862] Ibid.
[1863] http://www.kevinmacdonald.net/SlezkineRev.pdf. 05/31/14
[1864] http://www.kevinmacdonald.net/SlezkineRev.pdf. 05/31/14
[1865] http://www.kevinmacdonald.net/SlezkineRev.pdf. 05/31/14
[1866] Fest, Joachim. *Hitler* (San Diego: Harcourt, 2002), 288.
[1867] Fitzgerald, Michael. *Adolf Hitler: a Portrait* (Staplehurst: Spellmount, 2007), 58.
[1868] Toland, John. *Adolf Hitler* (Garden City: Anchor Books, 1992), 150.
[1869] Lee, Stephen. *The Weimar Republic* (New York: Routledge, 1998), 87.
[1870] Evans, Richard. *The Coming of the Third Reich* (New York: Penguin Books, 2004), 247.
[1871] Kolb, Eberhard. *The Weimar Republic* (Routledge, New York, 1990), eBook, 221.
[1872] http://www.spartacus.schoolnet.co.uk/GERhitler.htm. 05/31/14
[1873] Fest, Joachim. *Hitler* (San Diego: Harcourt, 2002), 268.
[1874] Brustein, William. *The Logic of Evil* (New Haven: Yale University Press, 1996), 1.
[1875] Fest, Joachim. *Hitler* (San Diego: Harcourt, 2002), 147.
[1876] Bullock, Alan. *Hitler and Stalin* (New York: Vintage Books, 1993), 83.
[1877] Brustein, William. *The Logic of Evil* (New Haven: Yale University Press, 1996), xiii.

[1878] Tedor, Richard. *Hitler's Revolution: Ideology Social Programs Foreign Affairs* (Chicago, 2013), 75.
[1879] Brustein, William. *The Logic of Evil* (New Haven: Yale University Press, 1996), 167.
[1880] Ibid., 171.
[1881] Ibid., 181.
[1882] Stolfi, R. H. S. *Hitler: Beyond Evil and Tyranny* (Prometheus Books, Amherst, New York, 2011), 286–87.
[1883] Henig, Ruth. *The Weimar Republic: 1919–1933* (Routledge, New York, 1998), 61–62.
[1884] Elon, Amos. *The Pity of It All: A Portrait of the German-Jewish Epoch, 1743–1933* (New York: Holt, 2003), 373.
[1885] Lee, Stephen. *The Weimar Republic* (New York: Routledge, 1998), 109.
[1886] Bullock, Alan. *Hitler and Stalin* (New York: Vintage Books, 1993), 83.
[1887] Kolb, Eberhard. *The Weimar Republic* (Routledge, New York, 1990), eBook, 234–35.
[1888] Fitzgerald, Michael. *Adolf Hitler: a Portrait* (Staplehurst: Spellmount, 2007), 91.
[1889] Bullock, Alan. *Hitler, A Study in Tyranny* (New York and Evanston: Harper & Row, 1964), 242.
[1890] Stolfi, R. H. S. *Hitler: Beyond Evil and Tyranny* (Prometheus Books, Amherst, New York, 2011), 240.
[1891] Stolfi, R. H. S. *Hitler: Beyond Evil and Tyranny* (Prometheus Books, Amherst, New York, 2011), 307.
[1892] Evans, Richard. *The Coming of the Third Reich* (New York: Penguin Books, 2004), 294.
[1893] Brustein, William. *The Logic of Evil* (New Haven: Yale University Press, 1996), 162.
[1894] Bullock, Alan. *Hitler, A Study in Tyranny* (New York and Evanston: Harper & Row, 1964), 173.
[1895] Ibid., 170.
[1896] Bullock, Alan. *Hitler and Stalin* (New York: Vintage Books, 1993), 155.
[1897] Fest, Joachim. *Hitler* (San Diego: Harcourt, 2002), 168.
[1898] Evans, Richard. *The Coming of the Third Reich* (New York: Penguin Books, 2004), 218.
[1899] Niewyk, Donald L. *The Jews in Weimar Germany* (Transaction Publishers, New Brunswick, 2001), 38.
[1900] Niewyk, Donald L. *The Jews in Weimar Germany* (Transaction Publishers, New Brunswick, 2001), 80.
[1901] Brustein, William. *The Logic of Evil* (New Haven: Yale University Press, 1996), 52.

[1902] Bullock, Alan. *Hitler and Stalin* (New York: Vintage Books, 1993), 219.
[1903] Fest, Joachim. *Hitler* (San Diego: Harcourt, 2002), 271.
[1904] Ibid., 149.
[1905] Bullock, Alan. *Hitler and Stalin* (New York: Vintage Books, 1993), 218–20.
[1906] Gordon, Sarah. *Hitler, Germans, and the "Jewish Question"* (Princeton University Press, New Jersey, 1984), 79.
[1907] Kershaw, Ian. *The "Hitler Myth"* (Oxford University Press, Inc., Oxford New York, 2001), 19.
[1908] Gordon, Sarah. *Hitler, Germans, and the "Jewish Question"* (Princeton University Press, New Jersey, 1984), 89.
[1909] Peukert, Detlev. *The Weimar Republic* (New York: Hill and Wang, 1993), 188.
[1910] Ibid., 188.
[1911] Evans, Richard. *The Coming of the Third Reich* (New York: Penguin Books, 2004), 224.
[1912] MacDonald, Kevin. *Separation and Its Discontents toward an Evolutionary Theory of Anti-Semitism* (S. L.: 1stBooks Library, 2003), 187.
[1913] Giblin, James, and Robert Payne. *The Life and Death of Adolf Hitler* (New York: Praeger, 1973), 105.
[1914] http://wikipedia.org/wiki/Weimar_Republic. 05/31/14
[1915] Henig, Ruth. *The Weimar Republic: 1919–1933* (Routledge, New York, 1998), 72, 74.
[1916] Fest, Joachim. *Hitler* (San Diego: Harcourt, 2002), 222.
[1917] Stolfi, R. H. S. *Hitler: Beyond Evil and Tyranny* (Prometheus Books, Amherst, New York, 2011), 238.
[1918] Fest, Joachim. *Hitler* (San Diego: Harcourt, 2002), 273.
[1919] Stolfi, R. H. S. *Hitler: Beyond Evil and Tyranny* (Prometheus Books, Amherst, New York, 2011), 285.
[1920] Black, Edwin. *The Transfer Agreement: The Dramatic Story of the Pact Between the Third Reich & Jewish Palestine* (Brookline Books, 1999), 173.
[1921] Black, Edwin. *The Transfer Agreement: The Dramatic Story of the Pact Between the Third Reich & Jewish Palestine* (Brookline Books, 1999), 51.
[1922] Giblin, James, and Robert Payne. *The Life and Death of Adolf Hitler* (New York: Praeger, 1973), 76.
[1923] http://www.wintersonnenwende.com/scriptorium/english/archives/articles/jdecwar.html. 05/31/14
[1924] http://www.heretical.com/mkilliam/wwii.html. 05/31/14
[1925] http://www.heretical.com/mkilliam/wwii.html. 05/31/14
[1926] http://www.sweetliberty.org/issues/wars/witness2history/10.html. 05/31/14
[1927] Black, Edwin. *The Transfer Agreement: The Dramatic Story of the Pact Between the Third Reich & Jewish Palestine* (Brookline Books, 1999), 301.

[1928] Brenner, Lenni. *51 Documents, Zionist Collaboration with the Nazis* (Fort Lee, Barricade Books, 2002), 10.
[1929] Brenner, Lenni. *Zionism in the Age of the Dictators* (London: Croom Helm, 1983), 10–11.
[1930] Ibid., 16.
[1931] http://www.heretical.com/mkilliam/wwii.html. 05/31/14
[1932] http://www.heretical.com/mkilliam/wwii.html. 05/31/14
[1933] http://www.heretical.com/mkilliam/wwii.html. 05/31/14
[1934] Tedor, Richard. *Hitler's Revolution* (Chicago, 2013), 176.
[1935] http://www.wintersonnenwende.com/scriptorium/english/archives/articles/jdecwar.html. 05/31/14
[1936] Black, Edwin. *The Transfer Agreement: The Dramatic Story of the Pact Between the Third Reich & Jewish Palestine* (Brookline Books, 1999), 201.
[1937] http://www.heretical.com/mkilliam/wwii.html. 05/31/14
[1938] http://www.heretical.com/mkilliam/wwii.html. 05/31/14
[1939] http://www.codoh.com/zionweb/zizad/zizad6.html. 05/31/14
[1940] Brenner, Lenni. *Zionism in the Age of the Dictators* (London: Croom Helm, 1983), 18.
[1941] Weizmann, Chaim. *Trial and Error* (Hamish Hamilton, London, 1949), 58.
[1942] Brenner, Lenni. *Zionism in the Age of the Dictators* (London: Croom Helm, 1983), 25.
[1943] Ibid., 142.
[1944] http://en.wikipedia.org/wiki/Jewish_Bund. 05/31/14
[1945] http://en.wikipedia.org/wiki/Jewish_Autonomous_Republic. 05/31/14
[1946] Hamann, Brigitte. *Hitler's Vienna: A Dictator's Apprenticeship*. Trans. Thomas Thornton. (Oxford, NY, 2000), Paperback Edition, 340.
[1947] Brenner, Lenni. *Zionism in the Age of the Dictators* (London: Croom Helm, 1983), 145.
[1948] Ibid., 149.
[1949] Ibid., 150.
[1950] Ibid., 1.
[1951] Ibid., 118.
[1952] Ibid., 120.
[1953] Ibid., 140.
[1954] Ibid., 125–26.
[1955] Shahak, Israel. *Jewish History, Jewish Religion: the Weight of Three Thousand Years* (Sydney: Pluto Press, 1994), 71.
[1956] Ibid., 71.
[1957] Black, Edwin. *The Transfer Agreement: The Dramatic Story of the Pact Between the Third Reich & Jewish Palestine* (Brookline Books, 1999), 85.

[1958] Ibid., 149.
[1959] Ibid., 84.
[1960] Brenner, Lenni. *Zionism in the Age of the Dictators* (London: Croom Helm, 1983), 61.
[1961] Black, Edwin. *The Transfer Agreement: The Dramatic Story of the Pact Between the Third Reich & Jewish Palestine* (Brookline Books, 1999), 166.
[1962] Ibid., 137.
[1963] Ibid., 137.
[1964] http://www.sweetliberty.org/issues/wars/witness2history/4.html. 05/31/14. Quote is from *Witness to History*, Michael Walsh, Chapter 3, "The Jews in Germany."
[1965] http://linguafranca.mirror.theinfo.org/9708/mahler.9708.html. 05/31/14
[1966] Black, Edwin. *The Transfer Agreement: The Dramatic Story of the Pact Between the Third Reich & Jewish Palestine* (Brookline Books, 1999), 253.
[1967] Brenner, Lenni. 1983. *Zionism in the Age of Dictators*. Chapter 6. Retrieved from URL: http://www.vho.org/aaargh/engl/zad/zad6a.html.
[1968] http://linguafranca.mirror.theinfo.org/9708/mahler.9708.html. 05/31/14
[1969] Black, Edwin. *The Transfer Agreement: The Dramatic Story of the Pact Between the Third Reich & Jewish Palestine* (Brookline Books, 1999).
[1970] Tedor, Richard. *Hitler's Revolution: Ideology Social Programs Foreign Affairs* (Chicago, 2013), 42.
[1971] Ibid.
[1972] Friedrich, Otto. *Before the Deluge* (New York: HarperPerennial, 1995), 390.
[1973] Fitzgerald, Michael. *Adolf Hitler: a Portrait* (Staplehurst: Spellmount, 2007), 103.
[1974] http://www.history-of-the-holocaust.org/LIBARC/LIBRARY/Themes/Policy/Friedl2A.html. Footnote 82. 05/31/14
[1975] Hitler, Adolf. *Mein Kampf* (Boston: Houghton Mifflin, 2001), 231.
[1976] Tedor, Richard. *Hitler's Revolution: Ideology Social Programs Foreign Affairs* (Chicago, 2013), 50.
[1977] http://louisproyect.wordpress.com/2005/02. 05/31/14
[1978] Goldensohn, Leon, and Robert Gellately. *The Nuremberg Interviews* (New York: Knopf, 2004), 11.
[1979] Gilbert, G. *Nuremberg Diary* (New York: Da Capo Press, 1995), 323.
[1980] Fitzgerald, Michael. *Adolf Hitler: a Portrait* (Staplehurst: Spellmount, 2007), 83.
[1981] Gordon, Sarah. *Hitler, Germans, and the "Jewish Question"* (Princeton University Press, New Jersey, 1984), 108–09.

[1982] Lindemann, Albert S. *Esau's Tears: Modern Anti-Semitism and the Rise of the Jews* (Cambridge University Press, Cambridge, U.K., 2000), Paperback Edition, 169.
[1983] Gordon, Sarah. *Hitler, Germans, and the "Jewish Question"* (Princeton University Press, New Jersey, 1984), 81. See also pages 38–39.
[1984] Gordon, Sarah. *Hitler, Germans, and the "Jewish Question"* (Princeton University Press, New Jersey, 1984), 23–24.
[1985] Ibid., 39.
[1986] Ibid., 42–43.
[1987] http://www.cdojerusalem.org/icons-multimedia/ClientsArea/HoH/LIBARC/LIBRARY/Themes/Policy/Friedl2A.html. 05/31/14
[1988] Pulzer, Peter. *Jews and the German State: The Political History of a Minority, 1848–1933* (Wayne State University Press, 2003), 21.
[1989] Kauders, Anthony. *German Politics and the Jews: Düsseldorf and Nuremberg, 1910–1933* (Clarendon Press, Oxford, 1996), 51.
[1990] http://www.h-net.org/~german/gtext/kaiserreich/hitler1#point1. 05/31/14
[1991] Kauders, Anthony. *German Politics and the Jews: Düsseldorf and Nuremberg, 1910–1933* (Clarendon Press, Oxford, 1996), 39.
[1992] Ibid.
[1993] Pulzer, Peter. *Jews and the German State: The Political History of a Minority, 1848–1933* (Wayne State University Press, 2003), 156.
[1994] Kolb, Eberhard. *The Weimar Republic* (Routledge, New York, 1990), eBook, 124.
[1995] Niewyk, Donald L. *The Jews in Weimar Germany* (Transaction Publishers, New Brunswick, 2001), 25–26.
[1996] MacDonald, Kevin. *Separation and Its Discontents* (2004), 235.
[1997] Lindemann, Albert S. *Esau's Tears: Modern Anti-Semitism and the Rise of the Jews* (Cambridge University Press, Cambridge, U.K., 2000), Paperback Edition, 169.

[1998] Smoter, Walter Frank. *Adolf Hitler, The Making of a Fuhrer*, Chapter 14, "indissolubly." URL: http://smoter.com/revoluti.htm. 06/25/14
[1999] Pulzer, Peter. *Jews and the German State: The Political History of a Minority, 1848–1933* (Wayne State University Press, 2003), 263.
[2000] Gordon, Sarah. *Hitler, Germans, and the "Jewish Question"* (Princeton University Press, New Jersey, 1984), 40.
[2001] Hitler, Adolf. *Mein Kampf* (Boston: Houghton Mifflin, 2001), 527.
[2002] http://www.marxists.org/archive/trotsky/germany/index.htm. 05/31/14
[2003] Gordon, Sarah. *Hitler, Germans, and the "Jewish Question"* (Princeton University Press, New Jersey, 1984), 52.

[2004] http://www.marxists.org/history/etol/document/germany/german02.htm. 05/31/14
[2005] Kauders, Anthony. *German Politics and the Jews: Düsseldorf and Nuremberg, 1910–1933* (Clarendon Press, Oxford, 1996), 119.
[2006] http://wikipedia.org/wiki/Ruhr_Red_Army. 05/31/14
[2007] Henig, Ruth. *The Weimar Republic: 1919–1933* (Routledge, New York, 1998), 34.
[2008] Kershaw, Ian. *The "Hitler Myth"* (Oxford University Press, Inc., Oxford, New York, 2001), 174.
[2009] http://www.spartacus.schoolnet.co.uk/GERkpd.htm. 05/31/14
[2010] http://en.wikipedia.org/wiki/Communist_Party_of_Germany. 05/31/14
[2011] Gordon, Sarah. *Hitler, Germans, and the "Jewish Question"* (Princeton University Press, New Jersey, 1984), 40.
[2012] http://www.aip.org/history/einstein/public1.htm. 05/31/14
[2013] http://en.wikipedia.org/wiki/German_Democratic_Party>. 05/31/14
[2014] Berkowitz, Michael. *The Crime of My Very Existence* (Berkeley: University of California Press, 2007), 21.
[2015] Pulzer, Peter. *Jews and the German State: The Political History of a Minority, 1848–1933* (Wayne State University Press, 2003), 220.
[2016] Ibid., 218.
[2017] Ibid., 220.
[2018] Ibid., 139.
[2019] Niewyk, Donald L. *The Jews in Weimar Germany* (Transaction Publishers, New Brunswick, 2001), 70.
[2020] Pulzer, Peter. *Jews and the German State: The Political History of a Minority, 1848–1933* (Wayne State University Press, 2003), 1–2.
[2021] http://www.icons-multimedia.com/ClientsArea/HoH/LIBARC/LIBRARY/Themes/Policy/Friedl2A.html Footnote 87. 05/31/14.

www.ingramcontent.com/pod-product-compliance
Lightning Source LLC
Chambersburg PA
CBHW020117240426
43673CB00038B/510